American Literary Scholarship 1990

In memory of J. Albert Robbins

American Literary Scholarship
An Annual 1990

Edited by Louis Owens

Essays by David M. Robinson, Frederick Newberry,
Benjamin Franklin Fisher IV, John Wenke, John Carlos
Rowe, Robert Sattelmeyer, Richard A. Hocks, George Kearns,
Cleo McNelly Kearns, M. Thomas Inge, Susan F. Beegel,
William J. Scheick, Gary Scharnhorst, Jo Ann Middleton,
Charlotte Hadella, Jerome Klinkowitz, Lee Bartlett, Richard
J. Calhoun, Peter A. Davis, Michael Fischer, Michel Gresset,
Massimo Bacigalupo, Hiroko Sato, Jan Nordby Gretlund,
Elisabeth Herion-Sarafidis, and Hans Skei

Duke University Press   Durham and London 1992

LC 65-19450   ISBN 0-8223-1234-4
Printed in the United States of America
on acid-free paper ∞

Contents

Foreword

The 1990 volume of *American Literary Scholarship* marks my initiation as coeditor with David Nordloh of this series. To say that I have been and continue to be daunted by this undertaking would be a significant understatement. The fact that I follow in the incomparable footsteps of James Woodress and J. Albert Robbins and that I have undoubtedly committed the kinds of grievous errors to which novitiates are prone has given me plentiful opportunities to contemplate human imperfectability.

As David Nordloh pointed out in last year's Foreword, like American literature *ALS* is in a state of transition, with even the very modifier "American" subject to question in both northern and southern hemispheres of the American continent. Expansion of the canon, newly intensified emphasis on multiculturalism, and growing interest in what has been termed "marginalized" literatures, as well as a broadening application of current critical theory, are changing the face of literary studies in the United States and abroad. It is an exciting period for those of us watching this evolution and will quickly require the alterations in *ALS* that David Nordloh promised last year.

Less global changes have also occurred in this year's volume. Our contributors for the German and East European selections, both in regions of rapidly changing geopolitical realities, have been unable to complete their reviews this year, leaving unfortunate lacunae in our "Foreign Scholarship" chapter. Nor have we succeeded in renewing our fledgling review of Spanish scholarship for 1990. New contributors have, as always, made appearances. As promised last year, Jo Ann Middleton has heroically covered two years in one for 1990 to make up for the "Fiction 1900 to 1930s" chapter missing from *ALS 1989*. Brian Higgins has relinquished the "Melville" chapter to John Wenke. Gary Scharnhorst has moved from "Fiction: The 1930s to the 1960s" to his first love, "19th-Century Literature," allowing a new contributor, Charlotte Hadella, to assume responsibility for chapter 14. Lee Bartlett, editor of *American Poetry,* kindly agreed to prepare "Poetry: 1900 to the 1940s" for this one year, while Michael Fischer has assumed "Themes, Topics and Criticism" for 1990. Hiroko Sato, Tokyo Woman's Christian University, has accepted from Keiko Beppu the responsibility for 1990 Japanese scholarship. Also new this year are Cleo McNelly Kearns and George Kearns, who very graciously agreed to prepare the "Pound and Eliot" chapter very late in the game when Bruce Fogelman found it necessary to withdraw from this year's volume. How did we survive without the fax?

Retiring from *ALS* this year are M. Thomas Inge, whose splendid coverage of Faulkner scholarship will be missed, and Michel Gresset, who has provided three years of excellent reviews of French scholarship. As we all know, *ALS* chapters can only be labors of love, and we are grateful. We also wish to express our deep sorrow for the death, in July 1991, of Professor Hans Galinsky, who contributed so much to *ALS* and to all who knew him.

We are grateful to the administrations of the University of California, Santa Cruz, and Indiana University for the continued support necessary to produce this great black book, and to the indefatigable and (relatively) unflappable editorial staff of Duke University Press, with particular gratitude to Pam Morrison and Bob Mirandon for patience with a neophyte editor. Finally, special thanks to my research assistant at UCSC, Marie Clary, for her invaluable assistance.

Professor David Nordloh will edit *ALS 1991.* Materials for review may be forwarded to him in care of the Department of English, Indiana University, Bloomington, IN 47405.

Louis Owens
University of California, Santa Cruz

Key to Abbreviations

Festchriften, Essay Collections, and Books Discussed in More Than One Chapter

Aesthetic Individualism / Olaf Hansen, *Aesthetic Individualism and Practical Intellect: American Allegory in Emerson, Thoreau, Adams, and James* (Princeton)

After the Fall / Josephine Donovan, *After the Fall: The Demeter-Persephone Myth in Wharton, Cather, and Glasgow* (Penn. State, 1989)

America the Scrivener / Gregory S. Jay, *America the Scrivener: Deconstruction and the Subject of Literary History* (Cornell)

American Declarations of Love / Ann Massa, ed., *American Declarations of Love* (Macmillan)

American Horror Fiction / Brian Docherty, ed., *American Horror Fiction: From Brockden Brown to Stephen King* (Macmillan)

American Literature, Culture, and Ideology / Beverly R. Voloshin, ed., *American Literature, Culture, and Ideology: Essays in Memory of Henry Nash Smith* (Peter Lang)

American Renaissance / Jeanetta Boswell, *The American Renaissance and the Critics: The Best of a Century in Criticism* (Longwood)

Bearing the Bad News / Sanford Pinsker, *Bearing the Bad News: Contemporary American Literature and Culture* (Iowa)

Chaos Bound / N. Katherine Hayles, *Chaos Bound: Orderly Disorder in Contemporary Literature and Science* (Cornell)

Chicano Narrative / Ramón Saldívar, *Chicano Narrative: The Dialectics of Difference* (Wisconsin)

CLHUS / Emory Elliott, gen. ed., *Columbia Literary History of the United States* (Columbia)

Conditions Handsome and Unhandsome / Stanley Cavell, *Conditions Handsome and Unhandsome: The Constitution of Emersonian Perfectionism* (Chicago)

Conflicting Readings / Paul B. Armstrong, *Conflicting Readings: Variety and Validity in Interpretation* (No. Car.)

Confluences américaines / Yves Carlet and Michel Granger, eds. *Confluences américaines: Mélange en*

l'honneur de Maurice Gonnaud
(PUN)

The Consolations of Space / Pamela
Schirmeister, *The Consolations of
Space: The Place of Romance in
Hawthorne, Melville, and James*
(Stanford)

Contingent Meanings / Jerry A. Varsava, *Contingent Meanings: Postmodern Fiction, Mimesis, and the
Reader* (Florida State)

Conversant Essays / James McCorkle,
ed., *Conversant Essays: Contemporary Poets on Poetry* (Wayne State)

The Crime Novel / Tony Hilfer, *The
Crime Novel: A Deviant Genre*
(Texas)

The Cunning Craft / Ronald G.
Walker and June M. Frazer, eds.,
*The Cunning Craft: Original Essays
on Detective Fiction and Contemporary Literary Theory* (Western Illinois)

Dark Eden / David C. Miller, *Dark
Eden: The Swamp in Nineteenth-
Century American Culture*
(Cambridge, 1989)

The Daybreak Boys / Gregory Stephenson, *The Daybreak Boys: Essays
on the Literature of the Beat Generation* (So. Ill.)

Democratic Eloquence / Kenneth
Cmiel, *Democratic Eloquence: The
Fight Over Popular Speech in
Nineteenth-Century America* (Mor-
row)

Designs of Darkness / Arthur M. Saltzman, *Designs of Darkness in Contemporary American Fiction* (Penn.)

Desire and the Political Unconscious /
Sam B. Girgus, *Desire and the Political Unconscious in American Lit-*

erature: Eros and Ideology (St. Mar-
tins)

Determined Fictions / Lee Clark
Mitchell, *Determined Fictions:
American Literary Naturalism* (Co-
lumbia, 1989)

Doing Literary Business / Susan
Coultrap-McQuin, *Doing Literary
Business: American Women Writers
in the Nineteenth Century* (No.
Car.)

Domestic Individualism / Gillian
Brown, *Domestic Individualism:
Imagining Self in Nineteenth-
Century America* (Calif.)

*Do the Americas Have a Common Lit-
erature?* / Gustavo Pérez Firmat,
ed., *Do the Americas Have a Common Literature?* (Duke)

Enabling Humility / Jeredith Merrin,
*An Enabling Humility: Marianne
Moore, Elizabeth Bishop, and the
Uses of Tradition* (Rutgers)

(Ex) Tensions / Elizabeth A. Meese,
*(Ex) Tensions: Re-Figuring Feminist
Criticism* (Illinois)

Fallen from the Symboled World /
Wyatt Prunty, *"Fallen from the
Symboled World": Precedents for the
New Formalism* (Oxford)

Fantasy Literature / Neil Barron, ed.,
Fantasy Literature: A Reader's Guide
(Garland)

Faulkner and Popular Culture / Dor-
reen Fowler and Ann J. Abadie,
eds., *Faulkner and Popular Culture:
Faulkner and Yoknapatawpha*
(Miss., 1988)

Feminism, Utopia, and Narrative /
Libby Falk Jones and Sarah Webster Goodwin, eds., *Feminism, Utopia, and Narrative* (Tennessee)

Fictions of Capital / Richard Godden, *Fictions of Capital: The American Novel from James to Mailer* (Cambridge)

The Gender of Modernism / Bonnie Kime Scott, *The Gender of Modernism: A Critical Anthology* (Indiana)

History and Post-War Writing / Theo D'haen and Hans Bertens, eds., *History and Post-War Writing* (Rodopi)

Horror Literature / Neil Barron, ed., *Horror Literature: A Reader's Guide* (Garland)

A House Undivided / Douglas Anderson, *A House Undivided: Domesticity and Community in American Literature* (Cambridge)

The Idea of Authorship / Kenneth Dauber, *The Idea of Authorship in America: Democratic Poetics from Franklin to Melville* (Wisconsin)

The Importance of Place / Robert Glen Deamer, *The Importance of Place in the American Literature of Hawthorne, Thoreau, Crane, Adams, and Faulkner: American Writers, American Culture, and the American Dream* (Mellen)

Inter/View / Mickey Pearlman and Katherine Usher Henderson, *Inter/View: Talks with America's Writing Women* (Kentucky)

The Irish Voice in America / Charles Fanning, *The Irish Voice in America: Irish-American Fiction from the 1760s to the 1980s* (Kentucky)

Literary Journalism / Norma Sims, ed., *Literary Journalism in the Twentieth Century* (Oxford)

Literature as Discourse / Robert Hodge, *Literature as Discourse: Tex-*

tual Strategies in English and History (Hopkins)

Located Lives / J. Bill Berry, ed., *Located Lives: Place and Idea in Southern Autobiography* (Georgia)

Making American Tradition / Cushing Strout, *Making American Tradition: Visions and Revisions from Ben Franklin to Alice Walker* (Rutgers)

Modern American Drama / June Schlueter, ed., *Modern American Drama: The Female Canon* (Fairleigh Dickinson)

The Modern American Novel / Linda Wagner-Martin, *The Modern American Novel, 1914–1945: A Critical History* (Twayne)

Out of Bounds / Laura Claridge and Elizabeth Langland, eds., *Out of Bounds: Male Writers and Gender(ed) Criticism* (Mass.)

Painterly Abstractions / Charles Altieri, *Painterly Abstractions in Modernist American Poetry: The Contemporaneity of Modernism* (Cambridge)

Performing Feminisms / Sue-Ellen Case, ed., *Performing Feminisms: Feminist Critical Theory and Theatre* (Hopkins)

Perspectives on Perception / Mary Ann Caws, ed., *Perspectives on Perception: Philosophy, Art, and Literature* (Peter Lang)

Pious Impostures / Steven C. Scheer, *Pious Impostures and Unproven Words: The Romance of Deconstruction in Nineteenth-Century America* (Univ. Press)

Psychoanalysis and— / Richard Feldstein and Henry Sussman, eds., *Psychoanalysis and—* (Routledge)

Reading and Writing Nature / Guy

Rotella, *Reading and Writing Nature: The Poetry of Robert Frost,
Wallace Stevens, Marianne Moore,
and Elizabeth Bishop* (Northeastern)

Reading and Writing Women's Lives /
Bege K. Bowers and Barbara Brothers, eds., *Reading and Writing
Women's Lives: A Study of the Novel
of Manners* (UMI Research)

Reconstructing Desire / Jean Wyatt, *Reconstructing Desire: The Role of the
Unconscious in Women's Reading
and Writing* (No. Car.)

Redefining American Literary History /
A. Lavonne Brown Ruoff and
Jerry W. Ward, Jr., eds., *Redefining
American Literary History* (MLA)

The Rhetoric of the "Other" / W. Ross
Winterowd, *The Rhetoric of the
"Other" in Literature* (So. Ill.)

Satire in Narrative / Frank Palmeri,
*Satire in Narrative: Petronius, Swift,
Gibbon, Melville, and Pynchon*
(Texas)

Seeking the Perfect Game / Cordelia
Candelaria, *Seeking the Perfect
Game: Baseball in American Litera-
ture* (Greenwood, 1989)

Sexual Personae / Camille Paglia, *Sexual Personae: Art and Decadence
from Nefertiti to Emily Dickinson*
(Yale)

*Southern Literature and Literary
Theory* / Jefferson Humphries, ed.,
*Southern Literature and Literary
Theory* (Georgia)

Spirit of Place / Frederick Turner,
*Spirit of Place: The Making of an
American Literary Landscape* (Sierra
Club)

Strategies of Reticence / Janice P. Stout,

*Strategies of Reticence: Silence and
Meaning in the Works of Jane Aus-
ten, Willa Cather, Katherine Anne
Porter, and Joan Didion* (Virginia)

The Stylistics of Fiction / Michael J.
Toolan, *The Stylistics of Fiction: A
Literary-Linguistic Approach* (Rout-
ledge)

This Is About Vision / William Bal-
lassi, John F. Crawford, and
Annie O. Eysturoy, eds., *This Is
About Vision: Interviews with
Southwestern Writers* (New Mexico)

Truth in American Fiction / Janet
Gabler-Hover, *Truth in American
Fiction: The Legacy of Rhetorical
Idealism* (Georgia)

The Voice of the Child / Mary Jane
Hurst, *The Voice of the Child in
American Literature: Linguistic Approaches to Fictional Child Language* (Kentucky)

*William Faulkner: The Yoknapataw-
pha Fiction* / A. Robert Lee, ed.,
*William Faulkner: The Yoknapa-
tawpha Fiction* (St. Martin's)

Winged Words / Laura Coltelli,
*Winged Words: American Indian
Writers Speak* (Nebraska)

Women and Violence in Literature /
Katherine Anne Ackley, ed.,
*Women and Violence in Literature:
An Essay Collection* (Garland)

Woman and War / Maria Diedrich
and Dorothea Fischer Hornung,
eds., *Woman and War: The Changing Status of American Women from
the 1930s to the 1950s* (Berg)

Writing the American Classics / James
Barbour and Thomas Quirk, eds.,
Writing the American Classics (No.
Car.)

Women's Re-Visions of Shakespeare /
Marianne Novy, *Women's Re-Visions of Shakespeare: On the Responses of Dickinson, Woolf, Rich, H. D., George Elliot, and Others* (Illinois)

Periodicals, Annuals, and Series

AI / *American Imago*
AIQ / *American Indian Quarterly*
AJS / *American Journal of Semiotics*
AL / *American Literature*
ALR / *American Literary Realism, 1870–1910*
AmBR / *American Book Review*
Americana (Univ. de Paris IV)
American Art Journal
American Jewish Archives
AmerP / *American Poetry*
AmerR / *American Review*
AmerSS / *American Studies in Scandinavia*
AmLH / *American Literary History*
Amst / *Amerikastudien*
Anais: An International Journal
AN&Q / *American Notes and Queries*
AnHuss / *Analacta Husserliana*
Annales du CRAA / Centre de Recherches sur l'Amérique Anglophone (Univ. de Bordeaux III)
APR / *American Poetry Review*
AQ / *American Quarterly*
AR / *Antioch Review*
Arete / *Arete, Tidskrift for litterature, konst och musik* (Stockholm)
ArielE / *Ariel: A Review of International English Literature*
ArmD / *Armchair Detective: A Quarterly Journal Devoted to the Appreciation of Mystery, Detective, and Suspense Fiction*

ArQ / *Arizona Quarterly*
ASch / *American Scholar*
ATQ / *American Transcendental Quarterly*
BALF / *Black American Literature Forum*
BB / *Bulletin of Bibliography*
Biography / *Biography: An Interdisciplinary Quarterly*
Black Ice (Boulder, Col.)
Boundary / *Boundary 2*
BSWWS / Boise State University Western Writers Series
BuR / *Bucknell Review: A Scholarly Journal of Letters, Arts and Sciences*
BWACET / *Bulletin of the West Virginia Association of College English Teachers*
CARA / *Centre Aixois de recherches anglaises*
C&L / *Christianity and Literature*
Caliban (Toulouse Le Mirail)
California History
Callaloo / *Callaloo: A Black South Journal of Arts and Letters*
CanL / *Canadian Literature*
Cather Studies
CCTES / *Conference of College Teachers of English Studies*
CE / *College English*
CEA / *CEA Critic*
CEDRIC / *Centre d'Etudes et de Recherches Interdisciplinaires* (Univ. de Paris IV)
CentR / *Centennial Review*
ChiR / *Chicago Review*
CIEFLB / *Central Institute of English and Foreign Languages Bulletin*
CIRNA / *Centre Interdisciplinaire de Recherches Nord-Américaines* (Univ. de Paris VII)
CL / *Comparative Literature*

CLAJ / College Language Assn. Journal

CLAQ / Children's Literature Association Quarterly

ClioI / CLIO: A Journal of Literature, History, and the Philosophy of History

CLQ / Colby Library Quarterly

Clues: A Journal of Detection

CML / Classical and Modern Literature

CollL / College Literature

Comparatistica

Il Confronto Letterario

ConL / Contemporary Literature

Connecticut Review

Contesti

CQ / Cambridge Quarterly

Cresset (Valparaiso, Indiana)

CRevAS / Canadian Review of American Studies

Crit / Critique: Studies in Modern Fiction

CritI / Critical Inquiry

Critica Hispanica

Criticism / Criticism: A Quarterly for Literature and the Arts

CSLL / Cardozo Studies in Law and Literature

Culture

DAI / Dissertation Abstracts International

DeltaES / Delta: Review du Centre d'Etudes et de Recherche sur les Ecrivains du Sud aux Etats-Unis (Montpellier)

Dickensian

DicS / Dickinson Studies: Emily Dickinson (1830–86), U.S. Poet

DLB / Dictionary of Literary Biography

DQ / Denver Quarterly

DQR / Dutch Quarterly Review of Anglo-American Letters

DrS / Dreiser Studies

EA / Etudes Anglaises

EAL / Early American Literature

EAS / Essays in Arts and Sciences

ECS / Eighteenth-Century Studies

Edda: Nordisk Tidsskrift for Literaturforskning / Scandinavian Journal of Literary Research

EdWR / Edith Wharton Review [formerly Edith Wharton Newsletter]

EigoS / Eigo Seinen (Tokyo)

EIHC / Essex Institute Historical Collections

EiT / Essays in Theatre

EJ / English Journal

ELH / [formerly Journal of English Literary History]

ELN / English Language Notes

ELWIU / Essays in Literature (Western Ill. Univ.)

EONR / Eugene O'Neill Review

ERNAS / European Review of Native American Studies

ES / English Studies

ESC / English Studies in Canada

ESQ: A Journal of the American Renaissance

EuWN / Eudora Welty Newsletter

Expl / Explicator

FictI / Fiction International

FJ / Faulkner Journal

FNS / Frank Norris Studies

FSt / Feminist Studies

Galleria

GaR / Georgia Review

Genders

Genre

GettR / Gettysburg Review

GPQ / Great Plains Quarterly

GRAAT / Groupes de Recherches Anglo-Américaines de l'Université François-Rabelais de Tours

GrandS / Grand Street
Granta
GRENA / Groupe de Recherches et
   d'Etudes Nord-Américaines (Aix:
   Univ. de Provence)
Hayden's Ferry Review
HDB / Harvard Divinity Bulletin
HDN / H. D. Newsletter
HEI / History of European Ideas
HJR / Henry James Review
HLB / Harvard Library Bulletin
HN / Hemingway Review
Horisont (Malmoe, Sweden)
HSL / Hartford Studies in Literature
HudR / Hudson Review
L'Indice
Interspace (Nice)
IowaR / Iowa Review
JAC / Journal of American Culture
JADT / Journal of American Drama
   and Theatre
JAmS / Journal of American Studies
JASAT / Journal of the American Stud-
   ies Assn. of Texas
JDN / James Dickey Newsletter
JEP / Journal of Evolutionary Psychol-
   ogy
JER / Journal of the Early Republic
JEthS / Journal of Ethnic Studies
JHI / Journal of the History of Ideas
JML / Journal of Modern Literature
JNT / Journal of Narrative Technique
Journal of Religion
JPC / Journal of Popular Culture
JQ / Journalism Quarterly
JSSE / Journal of the Short Story in En-
   glish [formerly Cahiers de la
   Nouvelle] (Angers, France)
JSw / Journal of the Southwest
KAL / Kyushu American Literature
KR / Kenyon Review
KRev / Kentucky Review

LAmer / Letteratura d'America: Rivista
   Trimestale
LangQ / The Language Quarterly
L&B / Literature and Belief
L&H / Literature and History
L&M / Literature and Medicine
L&P / Literature and Psychology
L&T / Literature and Theology: An In-
   terdisciplinary Journal of Theory and
   Criticism
LCUT / Literary Chronicle of the Uni-
   versity of Texas at Austin
Legacy / Legacy: A Journal of
   Nineteenth-Century American
   Women Writers
LFQ / Literature/Film Quarterly
LGJ / Lost Generation Journal
Lingue e letteratura
LitR / Literary Review: An Interna-
   tional Journal Devoted to English
   Studies
LJHum / Lamar Journal of Humanities
MagL / Magazine Littéraire
Malavoglia
MarkhamR / Markham Review
MD / Modern Drama
Mediterranean Historical Review
MELUS: The Journal of the Society for
   the Study of Multi-Ethnic Literature
   of the United States
Menckeniana: A Quarterly Review
Merope
MFS / Modern Fiction Studies
MHM / Maryland Historical Maga-
   zine
Midamerica: The Yearbook of the So-
   ciety for the Study of Midwestern Lit-
   erature
Mid-AmerR / Mid-American Review
MissQ / Mississippi Quarterly
MissR / Missouri Review
MLN / Modern Language Notes

MLQ / *Modern Language Quarterly*
MLS / *Modern Language Studies*
ModA / *Modern Age: A Quarterly Review*
Modern Austrian Literature
Mosaic / *Mosaic: A Journal for the Interdisciplinary Study of Literature*
MP / *Modern Philology*
MQ / *Midwest Quarterly: A Journal of Contemporary Thought* (Pittsburg, Kans.)
MQR / *Michigan Quarterly Review*
MR / *Massachusetts Review*
MSEx / *Melville Society Extracts*
MTJ / *Mark Twain Journal*
NAS / *Norwegian-American Studies*
NCC / *Nineteenth-Century Contexts*
NCF / *Nineteenth-Century Fiction*
NCL / *Nineteenth-Century Literature*
NConL / *Notes on Contemporary Literature*
NCS / *Nineteenth-Century Studies*
Nebraska Humanist
Neophil / *Neophilologus* (Groningen, Netherlands)
NEQ / *New England Quarterly*
NewC / *New Criterion*
New York State Journal of Medicine
NHCJ / *New Hampshire College Journal*
NHR / *Nathaniel Hawthorne Review*
NJH / *New Jersey History*
NLH / *New Literary History: A Journal of Theory and Interpretation*
NMW / *Notes on Mississippi Writers*
NOQ / *Northwest Ohio Quarterly*
NOR / *New Orleans Review*
Novel: A Forum on Fiction
N&Q / *Notes and Queries*
Nuova Corrente
NWR / *Northwest Review*
NWSA *Journal: A Publication of the*

National Women's Studies Association
NYRB / *New York Review of Books*
NYTBR / *New York Times Book Review*
Obsidian / *Obsidian II: Black Literature in Review*
ON / *The Old Northwest: A Journal of Regional Life and Letters*
Over Here
PA / *Profils Américains* (Univ. de Paul Valéry, Montpellier)
PAAS / *Proceedings of the American Antiquarian Society*
Paideuma: A Journal Devoted to Ezra Pound Scholarship
Palimpsest
PAPA / *Publications of the Arkansas Philological Society*
Paragone
Paragraph / *Paragraph: A Journal of Modern Critical Theory*
ParisR / *Paris Review*
PennH / *Pennsylvania History*
Phylon: The Atlanta University Review of Race and Culture
P&L / *Philosophy and Literature*
PLL / *Papers on Language and Literature*
PMHB / *Pennsylvania Magazine of History and Biography*
PMLA: *Publications of the Modern Language Assn.*
PNotes / *Pynchon Notes*
PoeS / *Poe Studies*
Poesia
Poetry Review
Political Theory
Polysemes (Univ. de Paris III)
POMPA / *Publications of the Mississippi Philological Association*
PQ / *Philological Quarterly*

P&R / *Philosophy and Rhetoric*

Prospects / *Prospects: An Annual Journal of American Cultural Studies*

Proteus: A Journal of Ideas

PULC / *Princeton University Library Chronicle*

QDLLSM / *Quaderni del Dipartimento di Lingue e Letterature Straniere Moderne* (Univ. di Genova)

QJS / *Quarterly Journal of Speech*

QQ / *Queen's Quarterly*

RALS / *Resources for American Literature*

RANAM / *Recherches Anglaises et Américaines*

Raritan, A Quarterly Review

RCF / *Review of Contemporary Fiction*

REAL / *RE Arts & Letters: A Liberal Arts Forum*

RFEA / *Revue Française d'Etudes Americaines*

Ritmica

RLA / *Romance Languages Annual*

RSAJ / *RSA Journal: Rivista de Studi Nord-Americani*

RSQ / *Rhetoric Society Quarterly*

SAD / *Studies in American Drama, 1945–Present*

SAF / *Studies in American Fiction*

Sagetrieb: A Journal Devoted to Poets in the Imagist/Objectivist Tradition

SAJL / *Studies in American Jewish Literature*

SALit / *Chu-Shikoku Studies in American Literature*

Salmagundi / *Salmagundi: A Quarterly of the Humanities and Social Sciences*

SAQ / *South Atlantic Quarterly*

SAR / *Studies in the American Renaissance*

SB / *Studies in Bibliography*

SBN / *Saul Bellow Journal*

SCR / *South Carolina Review*

SCRev / *South Central Review: The Journal of the South Central Modern Language Assn.*

Scripsi

SDR / *South Dakota Review*

SEEJ / *Slavic and East European Journal*

SELit / *Studies in English Literature* (Tokyo)

SFolk / *Southern Folklore*

Shenandoah

SHR / *Southern Humanities Review*

Signs / *Signs: A Journal of Women in Culture and Society*

SIR / *Studies in Romanticism*

SJS / *San Jose Studies*

SLitI / *Studies in the Literary Imagination*

SLJ / *Southern Literary Journal*

Smithsonian

SN / *Studies Neophilologica*

SNNTS / *Studies in the Novel* (North Texas State Univ.)

SoAR / *South Atlantic Review*

SoQ / *Southern Quarterly*

SoR / *Southern Review*

SoSt / *Southern Studies*

SPAS / *Studies in Puritan American Spirituality*

SPELL / *Swiss Papers in English Language and Literature*

SR / *Sewanee Review*

SSF / *Studies in Short Fiction*

StAH / *Studies in American Humor*

StQ / *Steinbeck Quarterly*

StTCL / *Studies in Twentieth-Century Literature*

Style

SWR / *Southwest Review*

Publishers

Calif. / Berkeley: Univ. of California Press

Cambridge / New York: Cambridge Univ. Press

Capra / Santa Barbara, Calif.: Capra Press

Carucci (Rome)

Chelsea / New York: Chelsea House Publishers (div. of Main Line Book Co.)

Chicago / Chicago: Univ. of Chicago Press

Christopher Helm (London)

Chronicle Books / San Francisco: Chronicle Books (div. of Chronicle Publishing)

Columbia / New York: Columbia Univ. Press

Confluence Press (Lewis and Clark State College)

Continuum / New York: Continuum Publishing Co. (dist. by Harper & Row Pubs., Inc.)

Cornell / Ithaca, N.Y.: Cornell Univ. Press

Council Oak Books (Tulsa, OK)

Crossing Press (Freedom, Calif.)

Delaware / Newark: Univ. of Delaware Press (dist. by Associated Univ. Presses)

Doubleday / New York: Doubleday & Co., Inc. (div. of Bantam Doubleday Dell Publishing Group, Inc.)

Duke / Durham, N.C.: Duke Univ. Press

Dutton / New York: E. P. Dutton

Facts on File / New York: Facts on File, Inc.

Fairleigh Dickinson / Teaneck, N.J.: Fairleigh Dickinson Univ. Press (dist. by Associated Univ. Presses)

Falcon Hill / Sparks, Nev.: Falcon Hill Press

Farrar / New York: Farrar, Straus & Giroux, Inc.

Feminist Press / Feminist Press at the City University of New York

Florida State / Tallahassee: Florida State Univ. Press

Freundlich Books (New York)

Gale / Detroit: Gale Research, Inc. (subs. of International Thompson Publishing, Inc.)

Garland / New York: Garland Publishing, Inc.

Georgia / Athens: Univ. of Georgia Press

Greenwood / Westport, Conn.: Greenwood Press, Inc.

Hall / Boston: G. K. Hall & Co. (div. of Macmillan Publishing Co.)

Harcourt / San Diego, Calif.: Harcourt Brace Jovanovich, Inc.

Harper / New York: Harper & Row Publishers, Inc.

Harvard / Cambridge: Harvard Univ. Press

Hill & Wang / New York: Hill & Wang, Inc. (div. of Farrar, Straus & Giroux, Inc.)

Hopkins / Baltimore: Johns Hopkins Univ. Press

Illinois / Champaign: Univ. of Illinois Press

Indiana / Bloomington: Indiana Univ. Press

Iowa / Iowa City: Univ. of Iowa Press

Iowa State / Ames: Iowa State Univ. Press

Kaibun-sha / Tokyo: Kaibun-sha Shuppan

Kent State / Kent, Ohio: Kent State Univ. Press

Kentucky / Lexington: Univ. Press of
Kentucky

Knopf / New York: Alfred A. Knopf,
Inc. (subs. of Random House, Inc.)

Kukusho-kankokai (Tokyo)

Lalo Press / La Jolla, Calif.

Lehigh / Bethlehem, Pa.: Lehigh
Univ. Press (dist. by Associated
Univ. Presses)

Liber / Tokyo: Liber Press

Library of America / New York: Library of America (dist. by Viking
Penguin, Inc.)

Library Association (London)

Little, Brown / Boston: Little, Brown
& Co. (div. of Time, Inc.)

Longwood / Wakefield, N.H.: Longwood Press

Loyola / Chicago: Loyola Univ. Press

LSU / Baton Rouge: Louisiana State
Univ. Press

McFarland / Jefferson, No. Car.:
McFarland & Co., Inc.

McGill-Queens: Toronto: McGill-
Queens Univ. Press (imprint of
Univ. of Toronto Press)

Macmillan / London: Macmillan
Publishers, Ltd.

Manchester / Manchester: Manches-
ter Univ. Press (dist. by St. Martin's
Press, Inc., subs. of Macmillan
Publishing Co.)

Mass. / Amherst: Univ. of Massachusetts Press

Mellen / Lewiston, N.Y.: Edwin
Mellen Press

Meridian / Utica, N.Y.: Meridian
Publications

Methuen / New York: Routledge,
Chapman & Hall, Inc.

Michigan / Ann Arbor: Univ. of
Michigan Press

Mich. State / East Lansing: Michigan
State Univ. Press

Minnesota / Minneapolis: Univ. of
Minnesota Press

Miss. / Jackson: Univ. Press of Mississippi

Missouri / Columbia: Univ. of Missouri Press

MLA / New York: Modern Language
Assn. of America

Morrow / New York: William Morrow & Co., Inc. (subs. of Hearst
Corp.)

National Poetry Foundation / Orono:
University of Maine

NCTE / Urbana, Ill.: National Council of Teachers of English

NCUP / Formerly New College &
University Press

Nebraska / Lincoln: Univ. of Nebraska Press

Nevada / Reno: Univ. of Nevada Press

New Directions / New York: New Directions Publishing Corp. (dist. by
W. W. Norton & Co., Inc.)

New England / Hanover, N.H.: University Press of New England

New Mexico / Albuquerque: Univ. of
New Mexico Press

No. Car. / Chapel Hill: Univ. of
North Carolina Press

No. Ill. / DeKalb: Northern Illinois
Univ. Press

Norske Samlaget (Oslo)

Northeastern / Boston: Northeastern
Univ. Press

Northwestern / Evanston, Ill.: Northwestern Univ. Press

Norton / New York: W. W. Norton &
Co., Inc.

NYU / New York: New York Univ.
Press

Odense / Odense Univ. Press

Ohio / Athens: Ohio Univ. Press

Ohio State / Columbus: Ohio State Univ. Press

Okla. / Norman: Univ. of Oklahoma Press

Omnigraphics (Detroit, Mich.)

Oxford / New York: Oxford Univ. Press, Inc.

Oxmoor / Birmingham, Ala.: Oxmoor House

Pantheon / New York: Pantheon Books (div. of Random House, Inc.)

Paragon / New York: Paragon House Publishers

Penguin / New York: Penguin Books

Penn. / Philadelphia: Univ. of Pennsylvania Press

Penn. State / University Park: Pennsylvania State Univ. Press

Peter Lang / New York: Peter Lang Publishing, Inc. (subs. of Verlag Peter Lang AG [Switzerland])

Pinter / Dover, N.H.: Frances Pinter Publishers, Ltd.

Pittsburgh / Pittsburgh: Univ. of Pittsburgh Press

Plenum / New York: Plenum Publishing Corp.

Pluto / London: Pluto Press

Praeger / New York: Praeger Publishers

Princeton / Princeton, N.J.: Princeton Univ. Press

Provence / Aix: Univ. de Provence

PUL / Presses universitaires de Lyon

PUN / Presses universitaires de Nancy

Purdue / West Lafayette, Ind.: Purdue Univ. Press

Putnam / New York: G. P. Putnam's Sons

Random House / New York: Random House, Inc.

Rodopi / Amsterdam: Editions Rodopi BV

Routledge / New York: Routledge, Chapman & Hall, Inc.

Rutgers / New Brunswick, N.J.: Rutgers Univ. Press

Rutledge Hill / Nashville, Tenn.: Rutledge Hill Press

St. James / Chicago: St. James Press

St. Martin's / New York: St. Martin's Press, Inc. (subs. of Macmillan Publishing Co.)

Salem Press / Pasadena, Calif.

Scarecrow / Metuchen, N.J.: Scarecrow Press, Inc. (subs. of Grolier Educational Corp.)

Scribner's / New York: Charles Scribner's Sons

Sierra Club / San Francisco: Sierra Club Books (dist. by Random House, Inc.)

Simon & Schuster / New York: Simon & Schuster, Inc. (div. of Paramount Communications, Inc.)

SMU / Southern Methodist Univ. Press

So. Car. / Columbia: Univ. of South Carolina Press

So. Ill. / Carbondale: Southern Illinois Univ. Press

Stanford / Stanford, Calif.: Stanford Univ. Press

Steinbeck Society / Muncie, Ind.: Steinbeck Research Institute, Dept. of English, Ball State Univ.

SUNY / Albany: State Univ. of New York Press

Susquehanna / Selinsgrove, Pa.: Susquehanna Univ. Press (dist. by Associated Univ. Presses)

Syracuse / Syracuse, N.Y.: Syracuse Univ. Press

TCG / New York: Theatre Communications Group, Inc.

Temple / Philadelphia: Temple Univ. Press

Tennessee / Knoxville: Univ. of Tennessee Press

Texas / Austin: Univ. of Texas Press

Texas A & M / College Station: Texas A & M Univ. Press

Twayne / Boston: Twayne Publishers (imprint of G. K. Hall & Co., div. of Macmillan Publishing Co.)

UMI / Ann Arbor, Mich.: University Microfilms International (div. of Bell & Howell)

UMI Research Press / Ann Arbor, Mich.: UMI Research Press (affil. of UMI)

Univ. Press / Lanham, Md.: University Press of America

Unwin Hyman / London and Boston: Unwin Hyman

Utah / Salt Lake City: Univ. of Utah Press

Vanderbilt / Nashville, Tenn.: Vanderbilt Univ. Press

Viking / New York: Viking Penguin, Inc.

Vintage / Healdsburg, Calif.: Vintage Publications

Virginia / Charlottesville: Univ. Press of Virginia

Washington / Seattle: Univ. of Washington Press

Wayne State / Detroit: Wayne State Univ. Press

Wesleyan / Middletown, Conn.: Wesleyan Univ. Press

Western Ill. / Western Illinois University

Whitston / Troy, N.Y.: Whitston Publishing Co.

Wisconsin / Madison: Univ. of Wisconsin Press

Yale / New Haven, Conn.: Yale Univ. Press

York / Fredericton, N.B., Can.: York Press

Part I

1 Emerson, Thoreau, and Transcendentalism

David M. Robinson

Three major new books on Thoreau, focusing on *Walden* and the Journal, three new editions of Emerson source material, and several important studies of Emerson's politics made 1990 a diverse and lively year, as interest in Transcendentalist historiography and interpretation continues apace.

i Emerson

a. Source Materials Eleanor Tilton's edition of volume seven of *The Letters of Ralph Waldo Emerson* (Columbia), containing letters from 1807 through 1844, extends Ralph L. Rusk's monumental work with a care and thoroughness worthy of Rusk. Tilton's volume includes newly discovered letters and gathers and restores letters published previously in the now superseded edition of the *Journals* and other scattered memoirs and biographies that unfortunately were not included in Rusk's edition. Of particular note is Emerson's letter of proposal to Lydian ("In the gravest acts of my life I more willingly trust my pen than my tongue") and new letters in the early 1840s to Caroline Sturgis, an important member of the circle that included Emerson and Fuller. All scholars working in this field will be grateful for the comprehensiveness and order that Tilton has brought to Emerson's massive correspondence. Teresa Toulouse and Andrew Delbanco's edition of volume 2 of *The Complete Sermons of Ralph Waldo Emerson* (Missouri) includes 47 sermons first preached from July 1829 to October 1830, an important phase encompassing Emerson's assumption of the pastorate of the Second Church from Henry Ware, Jr., his courtship of and marriage to Ellen Tucker, and his deepening exploration of the basis of his religious assumptions. These sermons evince a rapidly growing intellectual confidence and include

Emerson's retrospective analysis of his first year as minister of Second Church (Sermon LXIX) and early formulations of his doctrine of self-culture (Sermons LVI and LXVII). Susan Sutton Smith's edition of volume one of *The Topical Notebooks of Ralph Waldo Emerson* (Missouri) inaugurates an edition of working notebooks that will be of particular interest for the study of Emerson's later work. Emerson's procedure of compiling topical and lecture notebooks from earlier journal material began in the 1850s, and the notebooks represent an important bridge in the creative process, as Emerson reorganized, rethought, and reworked his philosophy in the 1850s, one of the most productive phases in his career. These notebooks give us some hint of the mosaic process of composition that he evolved and will be useful tools in fostering a long overdue reappraisal of late Emerson. Ronald A. Bosco's edition of "Note-book ABA" (" 'Blessed Are They Who Have No Talent': Emerson's Unwritten Life of Amos Bronson Alcott," *ESQ* 36:1–36) brings to our attention Emerson's compilation of biographical material on Alcott, "an intermediate step between the raw biographical materials [Emerson] had accumulated in his journals and what he envisioned as his finished biographical product." Bosco's introduction is informative about Emerson's relation with Alcott, his fascination with the genre of biography, and his devotion to biographical projects on his friends. In "1838: Ellis Gray Loring and a Journal for the Times" (*SAR*, pp. 33–47), Len Gougeon edits the 1838 journal of abolitionist and reformer Loring, who influenced Emerson's developing antislavery stance. The journal is of particular importance for its record of Loring's conversation with Emerson on the question of the personality of the deity the day after Emerson had delivered "Holiness," the lecture from which the Divinity School Address evolved. Kenneth W. Carpenter's "Ralph Waldo Emerson's Report on the Harvard College Library" (*HLB* n.s. 1.1:6–12) contains the text of a report Emerson prepared while a Harvard Overseer in 1868 calling for the establishment of a "Professor of Books."

b. Emerson and Politics   Len Gougeon's thorough analysis of Emerson's commitment to antislavery, *Virtue's Hero: Emerson, Antislavery, and Reform* (Georgia), is the most important contribution to our understanding of Emerson's politics for some years and promises to reorient Emerson studies toward the lesser-known later phase of his career. Gougeon's thesis that Emerson "was a committed social reformer all of his life" is based on an impressive accumulation of evidence that details Emerson's acceleration to prominence among the abolitionists in the 1850s and his close association with Wendell Phillips, Charles Sumner, and Franklin B. Sanborn in antislavery work. This Emerson is not well-known among modern readers, and Gougeon's astute account of the suppression of Emerson's reputation as a reformer (Oliver Wendell Holmes is the chief culprit) is an important contribution to our sense of the development of his modern reputation. Gougeon does not minimize Emerson's hesitancy or inner conflict about reform work, but he establishes that "the only serious doubts [Emerson] ever felt in the matter concerned how *he* might best make his contribution to the cause." Of particular importance are Gougeon's accounts of Emerson's various antislavery addresses of the 1850s, which will now have to be read as an integral, not peripheral, part of the Emerson canon.

Several other significant essays explore the political dimension of Emerson's work. In "Emerson, Individualism, and the Ambiguities of Dissent" (*SAQ* 89:623–62), Sacvan Bercovitch analyzes Emerson's political philosophy in the context of the emerging European socialist challenge to liberalism. Bercovitch notes the distinction made by Alexandre de Saint-Chéron and other European socialists between "individualism" ("mean egoism, lonely and disunited") and "individuality" ("the holy exaltation of man"), and aligns Emerson's early theory of the self with individuality. Bercovitch argues that the strains in Emerson's position came to a crisis in late 1842 in his search for a connective between radical individuality and liberal society. Although he came "*to the edge* of class analysis" and "to the verge of a sweeping repudiation of his society," Emerson "proceeded to situate individuality within culture, as individualism." Bercovitch places Emerson's philosophy of the self in a new and important frame of reference, but his resultant treatment of "the conservative 'later Emerson'" is overly dismissive, especially when read in the light of Gougeon's work on the antislavery background. The political implication of Emerson's philosophy of the self is also central to Stanley Cavell's *Conditions Handsome and Unhandsome,* which stresses the "aversive" (or "oppositional," "critical") quality of the perfectionist thinking of Emerson and Nietzsche. Cavell responds to John Rawls's critique of the elitism of perfectionism by arguing that "the project of Emersonian Perfectionism demands no privileged share of liberty and of the basic goods." For Cavell, "Emerson's version of perfectionism" is "essential to the criticism of democracy from within," and he finds "the particular disdain for official culture taken in Emerson and in Nietzsche . . . an expression of democracy" and "a dimension of any moral thinking." Of related importance is George Kateb's exposition of "Walt Whitman and the Culture of Democracy" (*Political Theory* 18:545–71), and the four commentaries that follow in the same issue: David Bromwich, "Whitman and Memory: A Response to Kateb" (pp. 572–76); Nancy L. Rosenblum, "Strange Attractors: How Individualists Connect to Form Democratic Unity" (pp. 576–85); Michael Mosher, "Walt Whitman: Jacobin Poet of American Democracy" (pp. 587–95); and Leo Marx, "George Kateb's Ahistorical Emersonianism" (pp. 595–99). As Mosher remarks, Kateb's conception of "the high culture of American democracy" would "include Emerson, Thoreau, and Whitman," and this dialogue conducted principally by political scientists bears in important ways on Bercovitch's analysis of Emersonian individuality and on Cavell's exposition of Emerson as both a philosopher of perfectionism and a cultural critic. Kateb emphasizes the concept of "democratic individuality" and its basis in the assumption that "all of us are always indefinitely more than we actually are," a realization that "intensifies the mutuality between strangers that is intrinsic to the idea of rights-based individualism in a democracy." An additional and more detailed response to Kateb's position in this issue is Judith N. Shklar's "Emerson and the Inhibitions of Democracy" (pp. 601–14), which perceptively explores the sometimes restrictive but finally redeeming quality of Emerson's commitment to fundamental democratic assumptions: the wide availability of the important human qualities, government founded on consent, and "an intuitive respect for one's fellow citizens." Shklar argues that Emerson's commitment to his townsmen saved him from the disturbing political outlook of Carlyle or Nietzsche and helped him focus his skepticism in the political sphere, where he excoriated the "social pettiness and competitiveness . . . and mental torpor" of his fellow citizens, but did not allow the reformers "to deflect him from his will to act only on his own grounds." Shklar's essay reminded me of how closely Emerson can be aligned with Jefferson as a political thinker, and it should be read along with Frank Shuffelton's essay on Jefferson and Thoreau (see below).

c. Biography, Criticism, and Influence   John McCormick refutes the view of a passionless and unemotional Emerson with reference to the differing qualities of his marriages in " 'The Heyday of the Blood': Ralph Waldo Emerson," pp. 35–45 in *American Declarations of Love,* ed. Ann

Massa. In "Emerson and the Wasting of Beauty: 'The Rhodora'" (*ATQ* n.s. 4:5–11), Richard Tuerk reads the poem as "a radical statement of revolt" against narrow utilitarianism, indicative of Emerson's developing theory of "beauty as an aspect of divinity." Robert E. Burkholder's "Emerson and the West: Concord, the *Historical Discourse,* and Beyond" (*NCS* 4:93–103) describes Emerson's 1835 move to Concord as an act of "beginning over, redefining himself," connected in part of his sense of Concord's past as a frontier settlement. In a brilliant analysis of "Emersonian Transparency" (*Raritan* 9:127–44), Lee Rust Brown finds the concept of the "transparent" at the heart of Emerson's epistemology and a significant indicator of his sense of the psychic economy of the self. Brown observes that transparency inevitably implies presence, even while denying it, and this inevitable presence indicates "the necessary 'space' between ourselves and our provisional objects." This dynamic of seeing, "an allegory of the mental life as a whole," expresses the mind's continual replacement of meaning, the achievement of a "new prospect" at the cost of an old perception. Brown notes the difficulties that this entails for self-perception, which can only be achieved "historically, in terms of causality and generation." Brown's essay should be read with David L. Smith's "The Open Secret of Ralph Waldo Emerson" (*Journal of Religion* 70:19–35), the premise of which is that "contemporary critical theories" have given us "an Emerson whose game is far deeper than we suspect." Smith argues that previous assumptions of Emerson's commitment to doctrines of compensation and the moral sense have overlooked his "subversive strategy" in revealing the contradictions of these doctrines. It might be argued that Smith overstates Emerson's ambivalence about these concepts, especially the moral sense, but the issue can quickly become semantic—as Smith points out, Emerson saw that the moral law was "not a code, but an energy or power." The value of Smith's essay is its conviction that in Emerson's "very predicaments, we may find the starting point for a genuinely postmodern spirituality." AnnLouise Keating's "Renaming the Dark: Emerson's Optimism and the Abyss" (*ATQ* n.s. 4:305–25) counters the recent scholarly tendency to emphasize the more skeptical Emerson by noting how paradoxically "the abyss is an essential component of Emerson's optimism." Keating compares Emerson's sense of the abyss with Rudolf Otto's concept of the religious as the "wholly other," and he equates the "abyssal unknown with the divine." In "Emerson's Compromised Optimism in the 'American Scholar': A Source in the Poetry"

(*ELN* 27, iii:40–43), Robert D. Habich connects "Philosopher," a poem Emerson composed in the late 1830s, with "The American Scholar," noting how both reinforce a larger pattern of skepticism. Wai-chee Dimock's "Scarcity, Subjectivity, and Emerson" (*Boundary 2* 17, i:83–99) focuses insightfully on "indigence," "scarcity," "sufficiency," and "superfluity" as important aspects of Emerson's metaphoric construction of mental process in "Experience," aligning "scarcity" with "subjectivity." Dimock's attempt to place this discourse in a larger framework is less persuasive—she argues that "Experience" constituted "Emerson's 'reply' to Malthus."

In *Emerson's Modernity and the Example of Goethe* (Missouri), Gustaaf Van Cromphout offers a thorough case for the "pervasive" influence of Goethe in Emerson's work, an influence centered in Emerson's perception of Goethe's "modernity." Van Cromphout attributes that modernity to Goethe's "self-consciousness," his sense of the ambivalent relation of the individual to culture, and his emphasis on process, all of which were key issues for Emerson. Van Cromphout establishes Goethe's authority for Emerson as a theorist of nature, art, and history, and makes an especially persuasive case for the influence of Goethe's idea (through Herder) of the concept of "representativeness" in history. He also demonstrates how Goethe's *Gedankenlyrik* influenced the development of Emerson's epigrammatic poetic style. Van Cromphout argues that "too much has been made of Emerson's hostile remarks about Goethe," and although the case for strong influence is undeniable, Van Cromphout's tendency to downplay the tension involved in Emerson's appropriation of Goethe is to me a weakness of the book, since that resistance was important to the course of Emerson's development and is revealing of New England culture. James W. Mathews traces "the disappearance of Edward Everett from the New England intellectual pantheon" in "Fallen Angel: Emerson and the Apostasy of Edward Everett" (*SAR*, pp. 23–32), noting how Everett's enormous influence on Emerson and others in the early 1820s waned steadily after his entry into politics. By the time Everett was elected governor in 1835, "Emerson's disenchantment had turned into near contempt," an opinion that was repaid by Everett's skepticism of Emerson's Transcendentalism. In "Medievalism and the Mind of Emerson," pp. 129–50 in Bernard Rosenthal and Paul E. Szarmach, eds., *Medievalism and American Culture* (Binghamton, N.Y.: Center for Medieval and Early Renaissance Studies, 1989), Kathleen Verduin notes that Emerson's 1835 discovery of Sharon Turner's *History of the Anglo-Saxons* was determinative in his validation of medieval culture, giving him "an exhilarating source of color and primitive energy" and contributing to his "existential triumph over the cosmic anxieties of his youth." Russell B. Goodman's "East-West Philosophy in Nineteenth-Century America: Emerson and Hinduism" (*JHI* 51:625–45) details Emerson's early discovery of the parallel between Berkeleyan idealism and Hinduism, noting however that Emerson differed from Hinduism in his emphasis on process. Goodman also describes the strong influence of the *Viṣṇu Purāṇa* in the 1840s, particularly on Emerson's portrait of Plato in *Representative Men.* Yoshinobu Hakutani finds several analogues between Zen and Transcendentalism in "Emerson, Whitman, and Zen Buddhism" (*MQ* 31:433–48), but notes that in Zen, "self-reliance would preclude our attainment of *satori,*" which implies an elimination of self-consciousness.

Cushing Strout's examination of Emerson's influence on William James, pp. 72–87 in *Making American Tradition: Visions and Revisions from Ben Franklin to Alice Walker* (Rutgers), focuses on James's reinvigoration while rereading Emerson for his address at the Emerson centenary. Strout argues that "Emersonian self-reliance (without Emerson's optimistic monism) . . . helps to animate *Pragmatism.*" In "Stein and Emerson" (*Raritan* 10:87–119), Steven J. Meyer characterizes Gertrude Stein as "a central figure in the main Emersonian line of American writing" and argues that the "fragmented" nature of their respective styles arose from a shared belief in "abandonment" as a law of composition. Each had an "autobiographical project" founded in a similar understanding of "a particular relation of the life to the work." In "Emerson's Image in Turn-of-the-Century Austria: The Cases of Kassner, Friedell, and Musil" (*Modern Austrian Literature* 22[1989]:227–40), Geoffrey C. Howes traces Emerson's reception in three Austrian thinkers, Rudolf Kassner, Egon Friedell, and Robert Musil, who contributed to an "Emerson boom" in the early 20th century in the German-speaking world. Musil, the most profound interpreter of the three, saw that *The Conduct of Life,* with its ethical emphasis, "represented a fresh confident alternative to the jaded end of the century." The best of the year's studies of Emerson's influence was Douglas Crase's explanation of "How Emerson Avails," pp. 48–58 in James McCorkle, ed., *Conversant Essays: Contemporary Poets on Poetry* (Wayne State), which captures the poetics of Emerson's prose and his compelling example to writers: "Emerson's so-called optimism is a strategy for writing: self-help for poets."

ii Thoreau

a. _Walden_ and the Journal   H. Daniel Peck's _Thoreau's Morning Work: Memory and Perception in_ A Week on the Concord and Merrimack Rivers, _the Journal, and_ Walden (Yale) is an exceptionally illuminating consideration of temporality, and ultimately of perception, in Thoreau. Peck argues that Thoreau conceived the purpose of his Journal as "the preservation of experience endangered by loss," but this tool of memory inevitably became a tool of perception as well: "journal-writing became (literally) Thoreau's 'morning work,'" a device through which he was "awakened" and kept "systematically alert." The Journal was the medium of Thoreau's spatial or "horizontal" perception of the world: "to acquire meaning . . . every natural object must be seen in relation to another, and then still another" in an endlessly extending process of relation and refinement. This mode of thinking, in some sense inimical to absolutism, put Thoreau at odds with the idealist inheritance of Transcendentalism, and Peck argues quite effectively that Thoreau attempted "to reconcile the power of the creative eye with the independent status of the world" through the term "phenomenon," a striking anticipation of Whitehead's theory of the "event" as constitutive of reality. Peck also devotes attention to relatively neglected chapters of _Walden_ such as "Brute Neighbors" (a "pivotal" chapter between "The Ponds" and "Spring") and "Former Inhabitants" ("all of Walden's former inhabitants are versions of the Thoreauvian self"). Peck's readings are consistently fresh, and his conceptual framework coherently grounds our sense of Thoreau's modernity.

In _Thoreau's Wild Rhetoric_ (New York University), Henry Golemba offers a decidedly contemporary Thoreau whose "language of desire . . . creates vacuums and erases statements as soon as they are made," impelling readers to pursue a deeper encounter with both the text and its author. Golemba astutely describes the "war between language and meaning" in the Journal, and its roots in Thoreau's "modern concept of the self as effervescent, as perpetually virtual, self-contradictory, and self-dissolving." One might almost conclude that Thoreau had studied in an English graduate program in the 1980s. I am somewhat resistant to the extent to which Golemba stresses Thoreau's captivation by the indeterminacy of language; at one point Golemba argues that for Thoreau "language had become life's most compelling activity." This claim slights the attention Thoreau gave to many other interests, most notably nature observation, which was arguably the most compelling element in his later life. Golemba's work on the Journal is accompanied by very insightful readings of *Walden;* his account of the "self-censorship and textual domestication" behind the framing of the authorial persona of *Walden,* based on a careful sifting of the manuscript evidence of the stages of composition, is an impressive rethinking of Thoreau's authorial strategy.

Gordon V. Boudreau's *The Roots of Walden and the Tree of Life* (Vanderbilt) centers on the sand foliage passages of *Walden's* "Spring" as fundamental to Thoreau's imaginative achievement. Recognizing that the thawing bank is contested critical ground, Boudreau works hard to free it from what he considers reductionistic psychological readings, arguing instead that "the mystery of the genesis of *Walden* is profoundly religious." That mystery is encoded in the sand foliage phenomenon, whose laws of "currents" and "vegetation" are guides to both physical and spiritual development. Boudreau organizes his study around a series of interrelated metaphors which were determinative for Thoreau. These natural phenomena, which include thawing frost, the lapse of currents, the growth of roots, and the tree of life, articulate the stages of Thoreau's artistic and spiritual development, culminating in crucial revisions of the *Walden* manuscript in 1851. In contrast to recent studies by Richardson (see *ALS 1986,* pp. 15–16) and Sattelmeyer (see *ALS 1988,* pp. 11–12), Boudreau downplays the intellectual influences of Thoreau's reading, arguing that Thoreau's outlook was molded through close observation of nature. Boudreau's book arrives at its thesis at the cost of a sometimes cumbersome organizational structure, and the peripheries of his argument seem at points less than compelling; but its centerpiece, a chapter on the metaphor of spring in *Walden's* sand foliage passages, succeeds beautifully. Everyone who teaches *Walden* will want to consult Boudreau's reading, and send his or her best students to it. The centrality of the Journal to all three of the above studies confirms its increasing importance to Thoreau studies, one which will be augmented as the new Princeton edition continues.

Leonard Neufeldt's *"Praetextus* as Text: Editor-Critic Responses to Thoreau's Journal" (*ArQ* 46, iv:27–72) makes plain the difficulties of editing and interpreting the Journal, activities which Neufeldt argues are closely connected: editors must involve themselves in criticism and theory as they edit, and any "reading" of the Journal implies a prior act of selection and editing. Neufeldt identifies the concept of authorial "intention" as the conceptual place at which questions of editing and of criticism and theory meet, and he surveys the shortcomings of previous editorial assumptions and critical approaches to the Journal with an eye toward the pragmatics of a new version.

The analysis of *Walden* in the three books discussed above was extended in several articles, the most significant of which was Robert Sattelmeyer's "The Remaking of *Walden*," pp. 53–78 in James Barbour and Tom Quirk, eds., *Writing the American Classics,* a thorough account of the two phases of *Walden's* composition (drafts 1–3, 1846–49; and drafts 4–7, 1852–54), which Sattelmeyer intertwines with Thoreau's profound metamorphosis in the early 1850s. The resulting text, "at once both retrospective and dramatic," was a blending of different purposes in which we find "an earlier self subsumed but still present, as it were, within the latter." Sattelmeyer's discussion of how Thoreau tied the seasonal cycle to an advancing self-knowledge tallies well with Boudreau's reading (see above). Douglas Anderson includes Emerson and Thoreau, pp. 71–96 in *A House Undivided,* in the tradition of domestic and communal discourse originating in John Winthrop's "A Modell of Christian Charity," a perspective that challenges the assumption of American literature's impoverished individualism. In reassessing the seeming archindividualist Thoreau, Anderson counters the common perception of his aggressive, stridently critical tone by noting the "curiously adversarial contentment" that marks *Walden,* and the strands of "compensatory admiration [that] mitigate many of Thoreau's most sharply expressed views." While Anderson's treatment of Emerson is less effective, he finds that domestic and familial traditions are advanced in Emerson's metaphoric use of the body and marriage. Joseph Adamson's excellent essay on "The Trials of Thoreau" (*ESQ* 36:137–72) examines the "spirit of trial and testing, of experiment and experience" which permeates *Walden,* characterizing Thoreau's stay at Walden as an experiment, and the resulting text as a test of its audience. Adamson's discussion of Thoreau's strategy of rhetorical provocation is a useful complement to Golemba's discussion of Thoreau's rhetoric of desire. Peter A. Fritzell (*Nature Writing and America: Essays Upon a Cultural Type* [Iowa State]) locates *Walden* as a "paradigm text for nature writing," describing how the book's competing elements of objective description and "personalist" or subjective rhetoric yield the dialectic position of the "self-conscious ecologist." Fritzell's thoughtful account of the genre of nature writing should be read in conjunction with Thomas J. Lyon's taxonomy of nature writing (see *ALS 1989,* p. 15). In "Feminism, Deconstruction, and the Universal: A Case Study on *Walden*," pp. 120–31, in Charles Moran and Elizabeth F. Penfield, eds., *Conversations: Contemporary Critical Theory and the Teaching of Literature* (Urbana, Ill.: NCTE), Irene C. Goldman argues that "the woman reader especially has no place to locate herself" in *Walden* and calls for teaching a "resisting reading of the text" as proposed in the work of Judith Fetterley. Diana J. Swanson's "'Born Too Far into Life': The Metaphor of the Bee in *Walden*" (*ATQ* n.s. 4:123–34) explores Thoreau's "analogies between the lives of social insects, including bees, and those of his human neighbors." In *"Walden* and Wordsworth's Guide to the English Lake District" (*SAR*, pp. 261–92), Joseph J. Moldenhauer notes that Thoreau's edition of Wordsworth, previously identified by Walter Harding, included *A Guide Through the District of the Lakes in the North of England,* an essay that exerted a "subtle shaping power" on Thoreau. Moldenhauer also records Thoreau's eventual disillusionment with Wordsworth, after his exposure in the late 1840s and early 1850s to accounts of the poet's personality. In an interesting analysis of "Thoreau's Diet at Walden" (*SAR*, pp. 243–60), Stephen Adams and Barbara Adams assemble the available information about Thoreau's eating habits, noting the influence of both diet reform theories and his mother's pies. They conclude that the high-carbohydrate, low-fat diet that he outlines in *Walden* could have been harmful to his tubercular condition, but that his dinners with the Emersons, and care packages from home, helped as a counterbalance.

These readings of *Walden* were supplemented by a significant reassessment of "The Contemporary Reception of *Walden*" (*SAR*, pp. 293–328), in which Bradley P. Dean and Gary Scharnhorst dispel the impression that *"Walden* was for the most part neglected or slighted by contemporary reviewers." Dean and Scharnhorst offer a chronological inventory of 93 "reviews, excerpts, and other notices of *Walden* published before Thoreau's death," 56 of which were "new to Thoreau scholarship." They include the texts of comments and reviews and indicate which passages from *Walden* were excerpted. Their work makes it clear that *"Walden* was more widely and favorably received by Thoreau's contemporaries than hitherto suspected," partly because of James T. Fields's aggressive promotion of the book. The comments, favorable though they generally were, "had the effect of cementing Thoreau's reputation as a 'quaint' and 'eccentric' author." Dean and Scharnhorst's work will be a crucial resource for future studies of Thoreau's reputation and cultural significance. Marc Chénetier explores Annie Dillard's "revisiting" of *Walden* in

"Tinkering, Extravagance: Thoreau, Melville, and Annie Dillard" (*Crit* 31:157–72), noting the "techniques of defamiliarization" and use of "literary 'bricolage' " in each text.

b. Other Works   Thoreau's early development is considered in Elizabeth Hall Witherell's "Thoreau's Watershed Season as a Poet: The Hidden Fruits of the Summer and Fall of 1841" (*SAR*, pp. 49–106), focusing on a cluster of six poems in 20 versions which reveal his growing desire to be a poet, but eventually mark "a shift away from poetry as a primary medium of expression." Thoreau's habit of composition by accretion, nurtured by the Journal, Witherell notes, was inimical to the conciseness required by poetry. In "True Pulpit Power: 'Natural History of Massachusetts' and the Problem of Cultural Identity" (*SAR*, pp. 119–48), Kevin P. Van Anglen argues that Thoreau made use of the form of the Puritan sermon and ironically aligned himself with the "clerical model of literary authority" in "pleading the case for a more Transcendentalist kind of nature writing than that of the Massachusetts reports" which he reviewed. I found both Witherell and Van Anglen perceptive in seeing these early works as part of Thoreau's struggle to establish a vocational identity. Van Anglen's discussion of Thoreau's struggle against "narrowly empiricist assumptions" accords well with William Rossi's recent assessment of Thoreau and contemporary science (see *ALS 1989*, p. 13). In "Another Look at the Text and Title of Thoreau's 'Civil Disobedience' " (*ESQ* 36:239–54), Fritz Oehlschlaeger reassesses the editing of "Resistance to Civil Government" in the Princeton edition, arguing that the 1866 edition of the text reveals a "pattern of substantive revision by Thoreau himself" that should have been incorporated into the 1849 copy-text. Such a change would result in a restoration of the more familiar title "Civil Disobedience." J. L. Campbell (" 'It is as if a green bough were laid across the page': Thoreau on Eloquence," *RSQ* 20:61–70) argues that "Thoreau presents a theoretical version of eloquence distinct from Emerson's," based on "an iconic re-creation of experience," the end of which is "the demonstration of an earnest and purified living." Working from theories of satire propounded by Frye and Bakhtin, Joseph Adamson ("The Scattered Body: Thoreau's Satiric Vision," *ESC* 16:75–90) argues that Thoreau's political writing is grounded in a "myth of a universal god-man who is torn apart and scattered," a satiric vision that Adamson compares with Blake and Nietzsche. In "Seeing New Englandly: Anthropology, Ecology, and Theology in Thoreau's *A Week on the Concord and Merrimack Rivers*" (*CentR* 34:81–94), Marvin Fisher notes Thoreau's use of early Puritan accounts of the settlement of New England, but his rejection of the values implicit in them: for Thoreau the early settlers "proceeded to violate, corrupt, and pollute" the "New Earth" they found. In "Henry Thoreau and Frederic Church: Confronting the Monumental Sublimity of the Maine Wilderness" (*Yearbook of Interdisciplinary Studies in the Fine Arts* 1:267–85), Kevin Radaker describes the similarities of Thoreau's response to the Maine wilderness with that of the luminist painter Church. Considering Thoreau's interest in the American Indian, Jarold Ramsey offers some perceptive comments on the lost opportunities to ground American literary history in American Indian culture, but also notes "the makings of a genuine literary engagement with the first literatures of the country" ("Thoreau's Last Words—and America's First Literatures," pp. 52–61 in A. LaVonne Brown Ruoff and Jerry W. Ward, Jr., eds., *Redefining American Literary History*). In a stimulating revision of the contours of American literary history ("From Jefferson to Thoreau: The Possibilities of Discourse," *ArQ* 46, i:1–16), Frank Shuffelton works to displace Perry Miller's line from Edwards to Emerson by showing how Jefferson and Thoreau can be thought of as "agents of an American pragmatics." Their varied interests, their "dialogic" forms of discourse, and their creative skepticism about received opinion are among the traits that Shuffelton feels can "center an open, non-exclusive literary history." Shuffelton finds that they were "continually reinventing their own human possibilities," a point crucial to their continuing relevance.

iii Fuller and the Transcendentalist Movement

a. Fuller In *Delicate Subjects: Romanticism, Gender, and the Ethics of Understanding* (Cornell), Julie Ellison offers a significant reassessment of Fuller in the larger context of European Romanticism. Ellison argues that Romanticism is conditioned by a conflict between "masculine," rational reading as mastery and a "feminine," intuitive reading as sympathetic understanding, and she traces in the movement a struggle toward a new "ethic of understanding" in the work of Schleiermacher, Coleridge, and Fuller. Ellison's book constitutes a major revision of the basis of Fuller's political significance, which Ellison locates in her reconfiguration of Romantic texts and assumptions. In this sense, Fuller's work in Italy is less an abandonment or growth beyond Transcendentalism, as Bell Gale

Chevigny has argued influentially (see *ALS 1973*, p. 13), than its translation into new social experience. Ellison's analysis of Fuller's contribution to the Romantic ethic of reading was consonant with Christina Zwarg's "Feminism in Translation: Margaret Fuller's *Tasso*" (*SIR* 29:463–90), a description of the "revisionary model of reading" that informed Fuller's early translations and the "linguistic complexity" that "grounded" her feminism. Zwarg finds Fuller's relation with Emerson inscribed in her work of translation, arguing that Fuller resisted Emerson's "agonistic" model of literary influence in favor of one emphasizing "dialogue and conversation." Susan J. Rosowski's "Margaret Fuller, an Engendered West, and *Summer on the Lakes*" (*WAL* 25:125–44) traces "the engendering of the narrative" of Fuller's Western journey, observing that "as Fuller advances into the West, she focuses increasingly upon women's roles." Fuller's sense of being an "outsider" in the West leads her to defer hope to a younger generation of Western women, an important step, Rosowski finds, in the formulation of *Woman in the Nineteenth Century*. In "Margaret Fuller, the Eternal Feminine, and the 'Liberties of the Republic,'" pp. 39–57 in *Women's Studies and Literature: Neun Beitrage aus der Erlanger Amerikanistic,* ed. Fritz Fleischmann and Deborah Lucas Schneider (Palm & Enke, [1987]), Fritz Fleischmann offers a persuasive account of Fuller's effort to "deconstruct the metaphor of gender" through her inclusion of lengthy discussions of "history, literature, mythology and religion" in *Woman in the Nineteenth Century,* an aspect of the text that has drawn negative critical comment. While these additions have made *Woman* a problematic text, they represent Fuller's attempt to reconceptualize gender in terms of "recognition and emancipation" rather than "power and domination." In "Positional Historiography and Margaret Fuller's Public Discourse of Mutual Interpretation" (*RSQ* 20:233–39), Joy Rouse discusses Fuller's "positioning of individuals within communities" in her work for the *Tribune,* a strategy that allowed her to use "her writing for social action." Louise D. Cary ("Margaret Fuller as Hawthorne's Zenobia: The Problem of Moral Accountability in Fictional Biography," *ATQ* n.s. 4:31–48) details the troubling procedure by which Hawthorne used Zenobia to turn Fuller into a "negative *exemplum* for the aspiring soul," raising the ethical implications of using "Fuller to testify against herself" in Zenobia's actions. The attention that Peter Conn devotes to Fuller as one of the three key members of the Transcendentalist movement (with Emerson and Thoreau) is indicative of her rising stature in American literary history (pp. 171–73 in *Literature in America: An Illustrated History* [Cambridge, 1989]). Readers of Fuller should also be aware of Laurie James's efforts to bring her to the attention of a wider audience in *Men, Women, and Margaret Fuller* (Golden Heritage).

b. The Transcendentalist Movement Catherine Albanese's important contextualization of Transcendentalism in American popular religion (pp. 80–116 in *Nature Religion in America: From the Algonkian Indians to the New Age* [Chicago]) identifies "wilderness preservation" and "mind cure" as the two influential tenets of American "nature religion" originating in the unresolved mind-matter dualism of Emerson's *Nature*. Albanese effectively demonstrates that Emerson's ambivalence over whether nature was "really real" found its cultural equivalent in America's parallel impulses to embrace the material world as it was manifested in nature and to assert the priority of spirit over matter through popular health theories stressing versions of mind cure and spiritual healing. Albanese's work is a fresh reminder of how the seemingly rarefied philosophy of Transcendentalism became central to American culture, a reinforcement of Lawrence Buell's recent exploration of the cultural impact of Thoreau's *Walden* (see *ALS 1989*, p. 14). In *Aesthetic Individualism and Practical Intellect: American Allegory in Emerson, Thoreau, Adams, and James* (Princeton), Olaf Hansen presents Transcendentalism as part of a larger "allegorical tradition" in American intellectual history, initiated by Emerson's split with William Ellery Channing to formulate a concept of selfhood that "included not only the possibility but the necessity of self-contradiction." Emerson initiated a work of "allegory" which Hansen understands not as "a simple trope but the expression of a specific view of the world," a form of consciousness whose elements of facticity and transcendence underlay both Emersonian Transcendentalism and Jamesian pragmatism. Hansen's case for Emerson's philosophical importance is obscured at points by a labored prose and structure, but it is nevertheless notable for its recognition of Emerson's sense of the "philosophical dignity of everyday events" and its explanation of how Transcendentalism was energized by "the inherent 'otherness' which the finite object represents, namely the simultaneous mute and telling concreteness of nature." In these respects, Hansen advances the case for what Lawrence Buell has termed a "de-transcendentalized" Emerson and joins several recent commentators (see Strout above) who see Emerson as William James's essential precursor. Gary Scharnhorst's *A Literary Biog-*

raphy of William Rounseville Alger (1822–1905) (Mellen) traces the complex, tragic life of Alger, a disciple of Emerson and Hedge, popularizer of Oriental poetry, and one of Boston's most prominent Unitarian ministers at mid-century. Scharnhorst transforms what might have been a perfunctory scholarly assignment by narrating not only Alger's life, but his own detective-like process of reconstructing it, labeling his project a "missing-person case over a century old." Working from Alger's puzzling turn away from Emerson in the 1860s, Scharnhorst uncovers the nervous collapse that Alger underwent after the death of two children in those years. Alger never wholly recovered from this blow, though his struggle to do so is rendered by Scharnhorst with sympathy and narrative effectiveness. Francis B. Dedmond's installment of "The Selected Letters of William Ellery Channing the Younger (Part Two)" (*SAR*, pp. 159–241) contains some extraordinary letters from the 1845–58 period, including his familiar advice to Thoreau in 1845 to "build yourself a hut, & there begin the grand process of devouring yourself alive," and a letter of aggressive intimacy to Elizabeth Hoar in 1848 that still has me puzzled. Dedmond's annotations are, as in the first installment, thorough and helpful. In "The 'Signs and Wonders' of Divinity: The Miracles Controversy in New England, 1836–1841" (*ATQ* 4:287–303), Elisabeth Hurth demonstrates how the miracles controversy fell into two key stages. The first, dominated by George Ripley and William Henry Furness and culminating in Emerson's Divinity School Address, emphasized the epistemological issue of the relation of historical evidence to religious truth, while the second, keyed by Theodore Parker, questioned the historical authenticity of biblical narrative. Hurth's astute research makes important distinctions among texts too-little-visited by scholars of Transcendentalism and is a fresh reminder of Ripley's importance to Transcendentalism. Readers of Gougeon's account of Emerson's antislavery involvement (see above) will also find Franklin A. Dorman's "Antislavery on the Banks of the Charles" (*HDB* 20, i:12–14, 23–24) of interest. Dorman recounts Henry Ware, Jr.'s leadership in the 1834 formation of the short-lived Cambridge Antislavery Society as a moderate alternative to Garrisonianism, and he argues that Ware's public witness was an important influence on a later generation, including Parker, who went far beyond Ware's moderate views. Jean Fagin Yellin has also contributed an informative survey of Lydia Maria Child as an antislavery feminist, pp. 53–76 in *Women and Sisters: The Antislavery Feminists in American Culture* (Yale), detailing her antislavery and feminist writing, her editing of the *National Antislavery Standard*, and her contribution in fiction of the figure of the "Tragic Mulatto" to "antislavery feminist iconography."

Scholars of Transcendentalism should also be aware of the recent launching of three new periodicals publishing specialized articles and notes in the field: Kenneth W. Cameron's *American Renaissance Literary Report*, Bradley P. Dean's *Thoreau Research Newsletter*, and the *Emerson Society Papers*, the newsletter of the newly formed Ralph Waldo Emerson Society. These supplement the long-serviceable *Thoreau Society Bulletin* to provide scholars of Transcendentalism a forum for news, discoveries, and opinions.

Oregon State University

2 Hawthorne

Frederick Newberry

"Our Hawthorne" continues to invite the interpretive diversity largely responsible for making him ours. Among the highlights in 1990 were Monika M. Elbert's historicist-feminist book on several canonized tales and *The Scarlet Letter,* Kenneth Dauber's tribute to Hawthorne's recognition of personal responsibility as the necessary origin of representation, Cathy N. Davidson's culturist study of *The House of the Seven Gables* within the context of daguerreotypy, Richard H. Millington's excellent revisionist study of *Gables,* and John Gatta's theological analysis of chapter 23 of *The Scarlet Letter,* together with Elbert's and Jean Fagan Yellin's feminist readings of that novel. After a hiatus of several years, *The Scarlet Letter* reclaimed its primacy; but the work of Wendy Steiner and Robert S. Levine on *The Marble Faun* must be added to the breakthrough studies of John Michael, Judy Schaaf Anhorn, and John Dryden (*ALS 1988*) in challenging the typically low opinion of that novel's gravity and achievement.

Because the following notices include a fair number of oversights from 1988 and 1989, limited space prevents coverage of several paperback editions that appeared in 1990. I shall at least try to mention them in the 1991 chapter. In accord with my practice over the past three years, I have generally disregarded notes and marginalia that might prove important to some readers. In addition to long essays, *The Nathaniel Hawthorne Review* contains most of these materials and an extensive bibliography.

i Books

The best book of the year, Monika M. Elbert's *Encoding the Letter "A": Gender and Authority in Hawthorne's Early Fiction* (Haag & Herchen), supports a growing minority of women critics: "I am always astounded by feminist criticism which would have Hawthorne a misogynist, and part of my maternal nature compels me to defend a much maligned Nathaniel." In four chapters Elbert details Hawthorne's habit of subverting theological and scientific "truths" of patriarchal authority, replacing them with a feminine mode of thinking amenable to the unanswerable questions to which time-bound and linear-minded men have detrimentally posed solutions. Hawthorne's repudiation of traditional masculine forms of self-definition and his sensitivity to feminine intuition, subjectivity, and open-endedness define an androgynous nature comfortable in "the magical realm of alchemy (to the medieval mind) and of quantum physics (to the modern mind)." Among early tales, questers Robin Molineux and Reuben Bourne fail precisely because they rely on phallocentric thought and exclude women. Fates of men in scientific tales are scarcely better, as Elbert contributes the importance of Francis Bacon to Hawthorne's accommodating but not unifying the scientific and spiritual (mental) worlds. Aylmer, Giovanni Guasconti, and Owen Warland struggle against and succumb to self-consuming scientific notions of power, a denial of their feminine potential for love and integration with community. "Ethan Brand" looks forward to *The Scarlet Letter,* which "validates and negates one last time the systems of authority" in earlier tales, but in which Hawthorne "allows various truths to co-exist as feminine/maternal thinking triumphs." Salient issues in the chapter on *The Scarlet Letter* appear in separate essays by Elbert below. Overall, though the first two chapters are unduly protracted, Elbert's study deserves recognition for redefining Hawthorne's scientific and feminist outlooks, explaining Hawthorne's ambiguity in sanguine feminine terms, and demonstrating impeccable scholarship.

In *Hawthorne's Early Narrative Art* (Mellen), Melinda M. Ponder undertakes the most extensive examination yet of 18th-century Anglo-Scottish theorists' influence on works eventually included in *Twice-Told Tales.* Separate chapters appear on the influences of Addison's *Spectator* essays (especially the use of imagery for moral and psychological ideas, as well as of a framing principle to integrate discrete stories), of Edmund Burke's and Hugh Blair's theories of the sublime (with the example of James Thomson's *The Seasons*), of Lord Kames's theories of pictorialism and ideal presence (particularly in making the past seem like the present), and of Archibald Alison's associationist psychology. The final chapter winnows these influences, applying them to the tales in the 1837 volume. This text constitutes a "group of narrative exemplifications of ideas concerned with the broad question of how the imagination functions and the sources of power and creativity of the literary artist." Hawthorne's arrangement of the tales "both demonstrates the virtuosity of the narrator's imagination and dramatizes the dangers and limitations of its creation of a fictive reality." Often demanding a generous editorial eye over matters of style, syntax, and repetition, Ponder's study does not pretend to offer new readings of tales but endorses previous interpretations that confirm, fortuitously or not, extrapolations from 18th-century commentators.

Alfred Weber, Beth L. Lueck, and Dennis Berthold write separately on Hawthorne's 1832 Northern tour in *Hawthorne's American Travel Sketches,* ed. Weber, Lueck, and Berthold (New England, 1989). Weber submits an edition of the original magazine publications of the sketches, along with helpful reproductions of paintings and engravings of the Northern tour. Despite excellent research, his reconstruction (pp. 1–23) contains too much guesswork. In "A Literary and Pictorial Iconography of Hawthorne's Tour," Berthold smartly correlates Hawthorne's description of sites with those in tour guides and the visual arts, concluding that "Hawthorne's traveler on the northern tour came prepared for sublimity; but as the iconographic record shows, he seldom found it." Instead, like a minority of perceivers on record, he saw depressing evidence of settlement, commerce, and spoilation of the landscape. Thus, "by admitting icons of commercial, social, and technological progress into his descriptions, [Hawthorne] almost entirely eliminated the nostalgia and sentimentality associated with the sketches of . . . Washington Irving," thereby anticipating the example of Mark Twain. Berthold's second essay, "History and Nationalism in 'Old Ticonderoga' and Other Travel Sketches" (pp. 131–52) correctly argues that Hawthorne eschews "patriotic moralizing" when addressing romantic ruins of American history. In the final essay, "Hawthorne's Ironic Traveler and the Picturesque Tour" (pp. 153–80), Lueck confirms and broadens Berthold's view, arguing that Hawthorne typically satirizes talismanic signs of American progress and undermines moral certainties commonly perceived in technological advances like the Erie Canal. Unfortunately, Lueck's piece suffers an editorial misadventure—repeating information provided by Weber and Berthold. More seriously, Weber's claim for the tour's pivotal influence on Hawthorne, about which Berthold clearly disagrees, is exaggerated.

No scholarly purpose is served by Edwin H. Cady and Louis J. Budd's edition, *On Hawthorne: The Best from* American Literature (Duke), a quasi-golden-oldies grab bag of essays originally published between 1941 and 1989. Other hit parade collections of its kind are in store for unsuspecting readers and acquisitions librarians.

ii General Essays

Hawthorne's literary and personal relationship to readers, culture, history, language, allegory, and craft reaches a new high in Kenneth Dauber's "Hawthorne and the Responsibility of Outsidedness," in *The Idea of Authorship*, pp. 154–91. Almost simple in vocabulary though not in style or content, the chapter insists on Hawthorne's autobiographical presence in tales and prefaces within a series of self-conscious linguistic evasions and veils that, despite confirming his and others' alienation, seek to bridge the distance between other(s) and self. It is in the difficulties that Hawthorne raises about the existence of self, the differences between reality and dream or self and other, "that Hawthorne exists. It is as responsible for how he appears that he would be read. Or better, if he appears to conceal himself in the face he puts on, then as one declaring his concealment exactly, he takes responsibility for himself all the more." Unlike other writers, Hawthorne accepts his obscurity, "acknowledging his alienation and so recovering himself as one for whom acknowledgment is the beginning of such speech as he can engage after all." By joining the ideal and real or the interior and exterior with the letter A, "in a representation whose standing as a resolution is established only by hearts committing themselves to it in the first place, [Hawthorne] thus establishes commitment as representation's very ground. . . . [T]he self, neither a self nor an other, becomes itself by committing *to* the other. Cognition . . . becomes a matter not of epistemology but of ethics. Or . . . representation becomes a rhetoric, and the establishment of rhetoricity as more real than the very alienation which would replace it with cognition becomes Hawthorne's greatest achievement." The rewards are many and rich in this brooding inquiry, which conveys the deepest-felt homage to Hawthorne that I have sensed in a long while.

Not as profound as Dauber in plumbing the relation of language and meaning, Janice Milner Lasseter in "Hawthorne's Stylistic Practice: A Crisis of Voice" (*ATQ* n.s. 4:105–22) demonstrates better than anybody else Hawthorne's stylistic indebtedness to 18th-century writers in "Young Goodman Brown," "My Kinsman, Major Molineux," "Ethan Brand," and "The Devil in Manuscript"; and she analyzes how rhetorical devices accentuate the breakdown in characters' "reason and faith and/or reason and imagination." Hawthorne's rationalist voice "functions as a discourse of containment," a mediation of horrific visions and cacophonous voices that would deny any truth about reason or imagination other than a language of confusion.

The most damning feminist charge against Hawthorne is challenged, complicated, and partly reconfirmed in James D. Wallace's "Hawthorne and the Scribbling Women Reconsidered" (*AL* 62:201–22). Wallace places the unfairly infamous, negative characterization in the proper context of a request made of Hawthorne to recommend distinctive American authors more or less unknown to a British readership. He finds that "the rhetoric of Hawthorne's comments on women writers is the rhetoric of his own self-critiques, that the indecorous exposures of the personal, the familial, and the bodily that he condemned in them were preoccupations of his own art, and that the woman writer came to represent for him the bodily, the mutable, the mortal that he sought both to purge from and to embrace in his own work." This revisionary analysis is persuasive if one accepts Hawthorne's self-deprecations as literal articles of faith.

In "Hawthorne: Re-placing Romance," in *Consolations of Space,* pp. 17–89, Pamela Schirmeister demonstrates how, through a process of metalepsis and eliding, Hawthorne transumes (re-places) Old World romancers (especially Spenser) and their conventions in creating, as in *The Wonder Book,* a landscape the inverse of Irving's, one "quite capable of sustaining its own homegrown mythology." A tale like "Feathertop" more obviously draws from romance models, but what seem like "naive representations" actually "transcend themselves as Hawthorne locates them in respect to a powerful tradition" from which he gains authority. Yet the story also marks a kind of "failure to re-place its pieces in the world of everyday reality," a failure looking forward to *The Marble Faun,* which "does not make compensation for what has been lost, but constitutes itself as a fable of lost correspondences, even as it shows them to be necessary." Shirmeister's contributions are slightly offset by her own admitted elidings, particularly her refusal to confront the quarrelsome issue of romance.

Sam B. Girgus's "The Law of the Fathers: Hawthorne," in *Desire and the Political Unconscious* (pp. 49–78), adopts Freud, Lacan, Jameson, and Bercovitch to argue the relation of individual psychological states to American culture and society. Girgus finds Hawthorne inscribing pre-

Freudian Oedipal conflicts whose "meaning" lies beyond Freudian patterns. Indeed, "in Hawthorne the psychological and social processes that are designed to direct love and organize cultural identity leave the individual unfulfilled and alienated." The journeys of Robin Molineux and Goodman Brown reveal a "chaos at the center of existence." As for *The Scarlet Letter,* "the search for psychic unity and community will remain frustrated. However, the novel also suggests that women may in fact be better prepared to deal with such frustration, partly because of their history of alienation and otherness."

The disunity and indeterminacy seen by Girgus is intelligently countered by Douglas Anderson, "Hawthorne's Marriages," in *A House Undivided,* pp. 97–120, who views Winthrop's "Model of Christian Charity" as a pretext for the binding ligaments of love and forgiveness in several stories and *The Scarlet Letter.* But Anderson provides no evidence for Hawthorne's having read the 1838 volume of the *Massachusetts Historical Society Collections* in which Winthrop's work first appeared. Moreover, he seems unaware of Michael Colacurcio's pertinent essay, " 'The Woman's Own Choice': Sex, Metaphor, and the Puritan 'Sources' of *The Scarlet Letter,*" in *New Essays on the Scarlet Letter* (Cambridge, 1985). Still, he forcefully argues for Hawthorne's typical effort to wed the disharmonious forces of life and death. To the challenge posed by "Ethan Brand" to such a wedding, Anderson contributes typological applications from Exodus and Deuteronomy to which "the reader is free to appeal" in opposing the gloom of the tale.

From a questionable reliance on Hawthorne's premarital habit of dividing Sophia into "dove" and "Sophie Hawthorne," Jennifer Fleischner, "Female Eroticism, Confession, and Interpretation in Nathaniel Hawthorne" (*NCL* 44:514–33), finds biographical warrant to connect Hawthorne's ambiguous fear of female sexuality with that of Goodman Brown, Dimmesdale, Coverdale, and Kenyon. Their "betrayals of eroticism coincide with the endings of all four works. The splitting off of the erotic female severs the link between writer and reader. Cut off from the erotic female, experience ends. And the end of experience signals the end of interpretation, which entails the end of the male artist's capacity for production." Within Fleischner's logic, however, one has to ask why the end of Hawthorne's production was delayed until the completion of *The Marble Faun.* The interpsychic relation of biographer and biographical subject is explored by Gloria C. Erlich, "Interpreting Hawthorne: Subjectivity in Biography" (*Biography* 12, 2 [1989]: 127–41), who relates the importance of events in her own life to her 1984 psychological study, *Family Themes and Hawthorne's Fiction: The Tenacious Web* (Rutgers).

Synthesizing the wilderness/society theme in several tales and *The Scarlet Letter,* Robert Glen Deamer's "Hawthorne's Dream in the Forest," in *The Importance of Place,* pp. 39–53, was already outdated in 1979 when it was first printed. Different in kind but also outdated is J. Bakker's "Nathaniel Hawthorne and the West" (*Neophil* 74:130–47). Critically naive and simplistic, Marco Portales's "Hawthorne and Aging," in *Youth and Age in American Literature* (Peter Lang), pp. 59–84, evidently considers women excluded from the categories of "contented" or "restless" that apply to old men in numerous works. Attempting to recast the influence of Common Sense psychology on Hawthorne in a positive light, Joseph Alkana, "Hawthorne's Drama of the Imagination and the Family" (*PQ* 69:217–31), eschews 18th-century practitioners in favor of Thomas C. Upham, Hawthorne's college professor. But all of Upham's works were published long after Hawthorne left Bowdoin; and with no effort to demonstrate Hawthorne's knowledge of them, Alkana would appear on shaky ground in arguing for their influence on "The Haunted Mind," "Egotism; or, the Bosom Serpent," and "Young Goodman Brown." Allan Gardner Lloyd-Smith, "Hawthorne's Family Romances," in *Uncanny American Fiction* (St. Martin's, 1989), pp. 53–63, cursorily surveys tales and novels for "derangements of the familiar in the direction of the supernatural" and for patterns of repetition (often involving incest) viewed from a Freudian understanding of *unheimlich.*

iii Essays on Novels

a. *The Scarlet Letter* With a cogency and clarity remarkable in these times, John Gatta, "The Apocalyptic End of *The Scarlet Letter*" (*TSLL* 32:506–21), illuminates the final chapters as a "soteriological drama of discernment," which shows us more about "the shifting boundaries of language and experience than it does about the psychology of sin." Gatta demonstrates how Hester and Dimmesdale's "consecrated" love resonates with an "intuitive Catholic proclivity toward mythic naturalism, iconism, and sacramentalism that survives vestigially" in Puritan culture. Most brilliantly, however, Gatta untangles the vexing theological and epistemological questions surrounding the letter's revelation in chapter 23, concluding that, while the novel's "convoluted texture of deception and skeptical evasion appeals to contemporary tastes, it would be anachronistic to suppose that its signifiers cannot possibly hold a transcendent signification. For even the book's indirections and ambiguities are so situated within an implied telos of Revelation that they draw the imagination more toward religious mystery than toward a wholly unresolved chaos of secular indeterminacy."

Deserving the attention of everyone interested in the novel, Monika M. Elbert's "Hester on the Scaffold, Dimmesdale in the Closet: Hawthorne's Seven-Year Itch" (*ELWIU* 16[1989]:234–55) conducts a splendid biographical and historical analysis of parallels between Hawthorne's idealized, pre-legal marriage to Sophia and Hester's self-consecrated marriage to Dimmesale, and between Puritan laws favoring divorce after seven years of desertion and Hawthorne's beginning to write the novel after seven years of legal marriage. Undismissable and strained (though intriguing) insights abound. Elbert defines the scaffold scenes as "tantamount to a divorce proceeding": first, Hester from Chillingworth; second, Dimmesdale from Chillingworth; and last, Hester from Dimmesdale. The main transgression is not Hester's adultery but Dimmesdale's deserting Hester. Indeed, Dimmesdale may be the real adulterer in his illicit union with Chillingworth. Elbert even wonders if Chillingworth, rather than Hester, is buried beside Dimmesdale. It does seem farfetched, however, to see Hester liberating herself and then to construe that freedom interrogatively as Hawthorne's desire to escape from a marriage no longer ideal. Classroom use of this essay will be wonderful.

Even more rewarding is Elbert's companion piece, "Hester's Maternity: Stigma or Weapon?" (*ESQ* 36:175–207). Like Dauber (above), Elbert views Hester as an outsider, but an outsider who acquires stature within a host of contemporary feminist contexts that Hawthorne more or less anticipates and that Elbert admirably documents. Through the gift of Pearl, Hester relies on her reproductive and emotional motherhood as a source of strength, in contrast to the negatively cast women in the marketplace who, reflecting the reigning patriarchy, fear and despise maternity. Opposing David Leverenz and Leland Person (*ALS 1989*), Elbert does not see Hester's enabling strength within male constructs of power or revenge. Instead, Hester's mothering, which collapses male distinctions between the spiritual and physical, allows her to become "the Great Mother (of life and death) to the community and is akin to 'the sympathy of Nature—that wild, heathen Nature of the forest, never subjugated by human law.'" Hester's silence is not manipulative but rather "a refusal to participate in male discourse" and thus "a sign of triumph over the male reality." Along with acute observations on Hester's relation to Mistress Hibbins, Elbert presents a strong case for Dimmesdale's unreconciled feminine qualities and for Hawthorne's own longing for mother. The "A" might now symbolize "Amazon," Hester's life being "a glorification of 'la différence,' of the language of the (m)other."

Proclaiming Hester as an unremitting romantic heroine posed against society, Sarah I. Davis, "Self in the Marketplace, or, *A* for Alienation" (*SoAR* 54, ii:75–92), agrees with Elbert that Hester's individualism has a "consecration of its own"; but beyond this instance, parallels between the two readings cease, to the disadvantage of Davis, who is obviously far more versed in romantic theory than in Hawthorne or Puritan scholarship, who consistently misspells the name of Nina Baym, and who analyzes the novel in the past tense.

Specifics on the novel's echoes of St. John the Divine appear in Evans Lansing Smith, "Re-Figuring Revelations: Nathaniel Hawthorne's *The Scarlet Letter*" (*ATQ* n.s. 4:91–104). Like Gatta (above), Smith defines Hawthorne's use of apocalypse as an uncovering; but he also limns four other biblical themes derived from Revelation. Drawing from Douglas Robinson's work, Smith concludes that "the uncovering of the scarlet letter . . . is tantalizingly partial, exactly that revelation within history which transforms its witnesses but does not finally, ultimately annihilate or illuminate them." Although providing new and valuable connections, Smith writes in a critical vacuum: some of his chief readings have been anticipated by unacknowledged others.

Jon B. Reed's " 'A Letter,——the Letter A': A Portrait of the Artist as Hester Prynne" (*ESQ* 36:78–107) presents the ambiguity of the letter as "the major empowering force of the novel" through which Hawthorne identifies himself with Hester and then endows her with "a mystical sanctity that gives her a special authority to make art." Reed extracts a "self-justifying sociopolitical allegory" that enables artistic privilege "to critique the social, political, and moral climate of nineteenth-century America." Initially echoing my own view, Reed finds the evocation of Chaucer and Burns in "The Custom-House" central to Hawthorne's enterprise, but he recasts my claim for Hawthorne's literary primacy by seeing Chaucer's gentility and Burns's democratic spirit as "validating authorities" for Hawthorne's establishing himself as a founder of a literature defined by distinctive cultural experience. Reed's compelling thesis produces several fresh insights, including applications of Kenneth

Burke's definition of *sacer* to the untouchable and holy state of artists Hawthorne and Hester. Moreover, Reed opposes (correctly, I think) Bercovitch's consensus thesis on Hawthorne's art. Given Puritan repression of art, "the American writer must not forget that every line is potentially an exercise in idolatry"; and with only "the wilderness, woman's heart, Antinomianism, and Satan" to counterbalance repression, "the true American artist has nothing or no one but the self to rely on against forces that say writing is a sinful act. Contemporary American writers who ignore this moral problem are ignoring the very factors that have created the distinctive vision American literature can offer, and they are thus not in a position to claim the moral high ground that Hawthorne has gained through his suffering."

Janet Gabler-Hover's " 'I Take the Shame Upon Myself': Ethical Veracity in *The Scarlet Letter*," in *Truth in American Fiction*, pp. 85–120, somewhat confuses rather than clarifies the mid-19th-century rhetorical ethos from which ethical judgments can be made on Hester and Dimmesdale. Hawthorne's knowledge of the Quintilian principle (ethical veracity based on and issuing from eloquence) is plausibly established, from which Gabler-Hover's analyses vie with deconstructionist efforts to render language and meaning indeterminate. Though narrative indeterminacy exists, "Hawthorne offers unambiguous ethical judgments on Hester's relationship to her passion, on the selfishness implicit within it, and on its potential to wound" Pearl, Dimmesdale, and Chillingworth. Both in her art and behavior, Hester "works artfully in complicity with the law so that she will *not* be transformed, so that she can entomb her passion within a stasis resistant to change and to redemption." Not surprisingly, Gabler-Hover concludes that, "in her need to keep her passion alive, Hester actually suppresses a potentially transformative type of art that would mediate it." Antipathetic to the view of Hester as victim or incipient revolutionary, Gabler-Hover presents a bewildering case for the romantic individual, at odds with a static society incapable of determining ethical truth, who is thrown back upon self-regulation to conform to a transcendent truth that the very static society believes it believes.

Jean Fagan Yellin's "Nathaniel Hawthorne's *The Scarlet Letter*," in *Women & Sisters*, pp. 125–50, adjusts our focus to imagery drawn from antislavery protest literature of mid-19th-century feminists and from such resonant emblematic sculptures as Hiram Powers's *The Greek Slave*. Relying on persuasive historical and biographical evidence for Hawthorne's knowledge of, though disagreement with, the feminist antislavery movement, Yellin discovers encoded images of enslaved females that record Hester's shifting allegiance to a sisterhood of enslaved women. She also presents a new and formidable case for Hawthorne's ultimately denying the womanhood of Hester until she becomes the Angel in the House. The final scaffold scene amounts to a marriage, albeit a reversal of the traditional elm and vine typology distinguishing male strength and feminine dependence. This is a far cry from the divorce scene advocated by Elbert (above), but such are the antipodes evidently permitted by this inexhaustibly discoverable and vulnerable novel.

Margaret Olofson Thickstun's "Adultery Versus Idolatry: The Hierarchy of Sin in *The Scarlet Letter*," in *Fictions of the Feminine: Puritan Doctrine and the Representation of Women* (Cornell, 1988), pp. 132–56, submits the key to the novel as the Puritan tension, inherited by Hawthorne, "between love of this world and devotion to God, and its salient locus is the female sexual body." A hierarchy of sin involves elevating "the crime of the spirit over the crime of the flesh by appropriating sexuality as a metaphor for spiritual truth. Hester's adultery, instead of being a literalization of the Puritan discomfort with the physical world, becomes an earthly shadow of a greater spiritual sin. Dimmesdale, the bride of Christ whose spiritual chastity is threatened, becomes the heroine of *The Scarlet Letter*." Chillingworth, disinterested in Hester's sexuality, avenges himself on Dimmesdale through a disguised 18th-century seduction plot, tempting the minister to an "idolatrous adultery of thought" far more serious than the offstage sin. Yet Dimmesdale triumphs in the closing scaffold scene, and his posture is spiritually correct, a denial of the body he has heretofore unsuccessfully flagellated. Hester also scourges her sexuality, but she cannot escape her sexual identity because of Pearl. Versed in Puritan theology and insightfully equating Milton's Adam and Eve to Dimmesdale and Hester, Thickstun argues well until suddenly concluding that, although Dimmesdale can claim preeminence for the dramatic death scene, "Hester remains; Pearl marries; the female line, at once representative of and accepting of the body, moves forward in history." Stripped of her intellectual side (and at least of Hawthorne's gestures toward taking her feminist protest seriously), Hester in this reading acquires a stature wholly at odds with the diminished figure seen by Yellin.

Steven C. Scheer's "Errors of Truth: Deconstruction in *The Scarlet Letter*," in *Pious Impostures and Unproven Words*, pp. 32–49, mostly offers predictable Derridian reinscriptions of the novel as an always already rewritten text, but in this case one that contains rereadings of deconstruction and self-deconstruction. Of note, however, is Scheer's treatment of art and artifice (Hester's, Dimmesdale's, and the Puritans') as a repression of sin. For example, "it is this denial of the sin of art, of the error of truth, which is responsible for imprinting the scarlet letter on Dimmesdale's bosom. Hawthorne's deconstructive point should not be overlooked here: whether it is there or not is not important here, for nothing that is 'merely' imprinted is *really* there at all, even though it *is*." Erecting a complicated tropological model on extracts from Derrida, Ricoeur, and rhetorical/linguistic theorists, Gerald Doherty, "Uncovering Plots: Secret Agents in *The Scarlet Letter*" (*ArQ* 46, ii:13–32), winds through metaphorical detours and displacements to claim that "the novel may be read as an allegory of the intimate co-implications of the 'knot' of the letter and the plot of the narrative, one which displays the method by which the original threads of the 'knot' . . . are unravelled and rewoven into the complex plot of the story." Emphasis here is strictly on method, not meaning.

Mary Jane Hurst, "Hawthorne's Pearl," in *The Voice of the Child in American Literature,* pp. 66–75, sees Pearl as a believable child, analyzes types of speech that Pearl utters and that adults address to her, and declares that "the success or failure of parent-child communication is vital for *The Scarlet Letter* in both its literal and symbolic contexts." Pearl is also crucial in Elizabeth Aycock Hoffman's "Political Power in *The Scarlet Letter*" (*ATQ* n.s. 4:13–29), which, through Foucault and penal theory, argues that "by making her mother constantly aware of the lawless, passionate self, Pearl enables Hester to recognize a higher than human law that authenticates the necessity of discipline." But inasmuch as Pearl's intervention is necessary in transforming "the original political-legal meaning of the letter's semiotic into the personal, transcendent 'truth' for Hester," Hawthorne's "literary model subverts his critical observations about the expediencies of political mechanisms of social control." Douglas Powers, a child psychiatrist, also analyzes Pearl as a real child in "Pearl's Discovery of Herself in *The Scarlet Letter*" (*NHR* 16, i:12–15).

b. *The House of the Seven Gables* One of the better essays on Hawthorne this year, Cathy N. Davidson's "Photographs of the Dead: Sherman, Daguerre, Hawthorne" (*SAQ* 89:667–701), contextualizes the postmodernist concerns with representation through the etiology of photocentrism in Cindy Sherman's work, and then, within an excellent historical survey of the development of and critical responses to the daguerreotype, analyzes the authorial and patronymic anxieties over representation in Hawthorne and Holgrave. Among a wealth of insights, Davidson exposes Hawthorne's clever metonymic connections between romance art and photography. And she finds the unsatisfactory "happy ending" of *Gables* entangled with Hawthorne's stalled composition, resulting from unresolved conflicts over reproduction, politics, and authorship itself. Overall, *Gables* reflects a lack of will and can best be seen "as a daguerreotype. The taint of death remains at the conclusion of this romance, like the negative death's-head flickering behind every daguerreotype. An unstable contradictory representation, simultaneously positive and negative, and always mirroring back the image of the reflecting and reflexive viewer, Hawthorne's daguerrean romance represents but cannot resolve midcentury anxieties over the technology of reproduction, the eugenics of the representational act."

Virtually incognizant of previous criticism on the novel and on the relevance of Andrew Jackson Downing to Hawthorne, Gillian Brown's "Women's Work and Bodies in *The House of the Seven Gables*," in *Domestic Individualism,* pp. 63–95, presents the novel as a tenacious effort to retain an aristocratic myth through the paradoxical means of a cottage commerce already outmoded in the midcentury marketplace. Hepzibah's dreams of class privilege and leisure are fulfilled through Phoebe, the Angel in the House whose body magically erases all evidence of the kind of labor once performed by mesmerized, exploited Pyncheon women (an erroneous plural outlook on Gillian's part). "This all too visible subjection of women is superseded by the elevation of the healthful housekeeper, whose work is imagined as unseen and incorporeal, and hence immune from any somatic impressions of social disorders. The replacement of the hysterical lady by the true woman represents domesticity as a welcome change that relieves the effects of other changes." Finally, the romance "consists in convertibility—the capacity to convert change itself into a tradition."

A reliable corrective to Brown's feminist agenda (and one of the finest essays ever written on *Gables*), Richard H. Millington's "Reading *The House of the Seven Gables:* Narrative as a Cultural System" (*Prospects* 15:39–90) distinguishes at least three narrative voices through whom Hawthorne interrogates, defends himself against, and seeks to reform the marketplace values of his time. Millington's Hawthorne is a far cry from the narrow-visioned, hypocritical escapist of Michael Gilmore and Walter Benn Michaels, a mere pawn relinquishing to capitalist forces. Limited space forbids reducing Millington's argument for Hawthorne's sophisticated analysis of and revisionary proposals for middle-class culture; but the essay convincingly validates the summary ideas on Hawthorne's achievement in the following extract. "The book identifies a marriage between—rather than a bifurcation of—domestic values and action in the world at large as the key both to resisting the authoritarian and constructing a community that can sustain its inevitable encounter with the economic and social forces that will unmoor it. Sentimental ideology, that is, must use the resources of the marginal perspective to see the world that it faces and to grasp itself as a form of power within that world rather than a refuge from it. In the same way, a rigorously thought-out art must give up the *éclat* of its marginality or the prestige of its ethereality and understand the culture that it addresses as contested ground, where different representations of value and meaning compete for the authority that only an audience can confer. By distinguishing between escape and action, between diagnosis and cure, between refuge and risk, *The House of the Seven Gables* is all along illustrating and enacting a theory of the cultural centrality of fiction." From such vantages, Millington does not find the happy conclusion to the novel a weakness or betrayal.

c. *The Blithedale Romance*   The most cogent finding in Steven C. Scheer's revisionist "Riddles of Truth: Subversion(s) at Blithedale," in *Pious Impostures,* pp. 49–66, is that Coverdale is not a failure as an artist or a man. Indeed, "Coverdale's lack of commitment turns out to be a virtue"; and his "ambivalence toward Zenobia/Priscilla is the inadvertently vicious side of his virtue." Without the benefit of Luther Luedtke's book (*ALS 1989*), Phillip N. Edmondson, "Hawthorne Turns to the East: Persian Influences in *The Blithedale Romance*" (*ELN* 28:25–38), unconvincingly submits Sufi mystical poets as sources for Coverdale as poet and Priscilla as creative force.

Suspect in its logic and use of criticism as courtly precedent, Louise D. Cary's "Margaret Fuller as Hawthorne's Zenobia: The Problem of Moral Accountability in Fictional Biography" (*ATQ* n.s. 4:31–48) derides Hawthorne's "insidious" portrait of "Queen Margaret" through her supposed fictional counterpart. Richard H. Millington would evidently agree with

Cary in "American Anxiousness: Selfhood and Culture in Hawthorne's *The Blithedale Romance*" (*NEQ* 63:558–83), though he gives only passing attention to Fuller/Zenobia within a larger frame of reference: the problematic nature of Hawthorne's cultural power to afford Coverdale the opportunity "to recognize and revise the self" and thus break the debilitating grip of anxiety and guilt. Especially challenging in Millington's reading is how the reader and Hawthorne become allies in their anger with Coverdale and the evasive tactics of the society he represents. "We feel Coverdale's narration . . . as alienating both us and the Hawthorne he has displaced." Coverdale's emptiness may finally suggest Hawthorne's intuition that the romance form is empty. Millington erroneously puts Hawthorne at Brook Farm in 1837 (rather than 1841), and he cites too few studies of *Blithedale;* but he can profitably be read with Gordon Hutner (*ALS 1988*) and Jonathan Auerbach (*ALS 1989*).

Somewhat better acquainted with criticism on *Blithedale* than on *Gables,* Gillian Brown's "The Mesmerized Spectator," in *Domestic Individualism,* pp. 96–132, scurries through several topics ("Looking, Leisure, and Labor"; "Work Ethics: Spiritualizing Labor, Erasing Desire"; "Leisure Ethics and Erotics"; "Voyeurism and Fetishism"; and "Mesmerism, Voyeurism, and Romance"), arriving at two notable points: (1) "Women's work and women's bodies move so far out of sight by the end of Hawthorne's Gothic Revival romances that their absence appears the very condition of individuality"; (2) "In the consumerist pleasures and anxieties of looking that Hawthorne explores, homophobia and misogyny proscribe not specific sexes and sexualities, but the visibility of specificity: they prohibit the possibility of the spectator being static enough to be seen."

d. *The Marble Faun* Wendy Steiner's "Virgins, Copyists, and the Gentle Reader: Hawthorne," in *Pictures of Romance: Form Against Context in Painting and Literature* (Chicago, 1988), pp. 91–120, should be read with John Michael's essay on *The Marble Faun* (*ALS 1988*), for together they catapult the critical significance of the romance beyond the allegorical fortifications within which it has for several decades often been attacked. Steiner sees the romance as a precursor of reader-response criticism in its sustained, sophisticated exploration of interpretive negotiations between subjects and objects that invariably exchange places with one another in the process of the soul's growth—much like the layers of history in Rome itself. She also finds Hawthorne confirming the

aesthetics of E. G. Lessing in his explorations of historical, epistemological, and moral implications that separate visual arts and narrative. Accordingly, she convincingly argues for Hawthorne's indebtedness to
Keats: "his whole book is, in a sense, an exploration of ekphrasis as a
symbol of human time-consciousness." Incomplete works of visual art
are valuable because they mirror the incomplete observer who must
interpret and thus create narrative. Hence the centrality of Hilda, who
shifts from a static copyist to an interpretive narrator of experience.

Extending his study of anti-Catholic movements in *Conspiracy and
Romance* (*ALS 1989*), Robert S. Levine, " 'Antebellum Rome' in *The Marble Faun*" (*ALH* 2:19–38), persuasively locates the romance in Hawthorne's deflected though "culturally specific representation of Rome's
body politic during a time in which the Roman Catholic authorities had
overcome one revolutionary challenge to their governing power and were
attempting to contain future subversive threats." Against this Franco-
papal effort, Miriam's "political plotting suggests that, despite her alleged
ties to the Cenci family and the larger papal power structure," she may be
seen "as an anti-Catholic revolutionary, perhaps even an assassin, of
1848." Levine's inferential evidence for this startling view is compelling.
Also persuasive is Levine's sociopolitical reading of the carnival, a revolutionary reenactment safely contained within a courtesy that nevertheless
allegorizes the political tensions in both Rome and America. In the statue
of Pope Julius, Hawthorne discovers the need for a grand presence that
might fill "the spiritual void resulting from the passing of America's
heroic Revolutionary fathers and their founding ideals"—harbinger of
"the fatherly, redemptive, unifying, but finally nonnegotiable force of
Abraham Lincoln."

Complementing Levine's study from anthropological and political
perspectives is Nancy Bentley's "Slaves and Fauns: Hawthorne and the
Uses of Primitivism" (*ELH* 57:901–37), which locates the romance in a
context of antebellum America's fascination with racial and national
types. Often failing to acknowledge Hawthornean and semiological
criticism upon which she depends, Bentley does break new ground:
primitivism "in part serves to supplant doubts about a middle-class
Protestant model of progress, a master narrative that all versions of
American destiny finally had in common. The novel's contradictory
doubling of mythic innocence and modern savagery supplies an evolutionary history for the rise of American civilization. What is really at
stake in the novel's mixed dictions (as in the mixed picture of Italy which

Hawthorne echoes) is a powerful story of social evolution." Adopting a Bercovitchean paradigm of Hawthorne's liberal compromise, Bentley sees dangerous primitives Donatello and Miriam as safely distanced icons at the end, while the threatening carnival finally "does not risk creating heretical sympathies but rather a release of ridicule and laughter that might mock the orthodoxy of progress."

Lucid and far more rewarding than the title might suggest, Eugenia C. DeLamotte's " 'Deadly Iteration': Hawthorne's Gothic Vision," in *Perils of the Night,* pp. 93–117, puts forth the psychological phenomena of repetition as the center of Hawthorne's Gothic. "Again and again, his work explores the way consciousness altered by guilt creates the self-iterative world of a 'haunted mind,' distorting that mind's ability to perceive the world outside it." Focusing on *Faun* but glancing at Hawthorne's other novels, DeLamotte observes how characters are entrapped within repetitive, mirror-imaged experiences of sin and death; how, paradoxically, "certain kinds of distorted perception are a form of insight"; and how Hawthorne generally allows an escape from romantic solipsism to the world of the not-me. While "knowledge of evil distorts the communications between the world of matter and of spirit," it also "intensifies them, because for Hawthorne the psychology of guilt is the psychology of imagination, of the 'sympathetic imagination' both in moral and aesthetic terms."

Deadly iteration also figures in Stacey Vallas's "The Embodiment of the Daughter's Secret in *The Marble Faun*" (*ArQ* 46, iv:73–94), which intends to unveil the novel's unvoiced mysteries: the unspeakable—because censored and silenced—origins of Donatello and Miriam, and the relation of Miriam and Hilda to Beatrice Cenci. The narrator's silence on Miriam's origins is "continuous with paternal [Cenci] abuse in that it serves to protect and perpetuate a patriarchal order which enables such transgressions." Incest is the abuse and, together with Hawthorne's "deep ambivalence towards the feminine," the key to the mystery and silence. Yet Vallas reserves the most cogent biographical connections for the endnotes, where she endorses Evan Carton's incest reading (*ALS 1989*) but, contra Carton, claims that "the daughter's sacrifice *generates* male art." In the essay itself, daughters Miriam and Hilda represent alternative traits expressed in the Beatrice Cenci portrait, Miriam overtly representing how "a woman's self-assertion or self-expression is simultaneously self-defeat." But Hilda's subservience to the masters suggests her own vulnerability to incestuous abuse. The two women finally enact a form of incest: "the drama of Miriam's victimization which has occurred off the novel's stage is displaced onto Hilda (as the innocent, wronged Beatrice) while Miriam (as Beatrice implicated in and contaminated by sin) assumes the position of Francesco Cenci." As a result, "Hawthorne's attention to characters making art and becoming art is inseparable from relations of power which inform the novel's moral conundrums, linking, in the multiple meanings of 'representation,' speech, art, and politics." Vallas carefully evades addressing the implication that in such a reading as hers Hawthorne, consciously or not, extends the enfranchised power of cultural (male) abuse.

In opposition to Fleischner (above), Judy Smith, "Fall into Human Light: Hawthorne's Vision of Love," in *American Declarations of Love,* pp. 17–34, maintains that Hawthorne "allows himself the freedom to combine the angelic and wayward parts of himself and his beloved [Sophia] into an inseparable whole." This practice appears in *Faun,* where he deconstructs convenient dualisms by subverting Kenyon's sterile and destructive Puritanic vision. "Hawthorne insists on a vision of love which needs neither angel nor demon but which affirms that we are midway between them, partaking of both but being neither." No surprises surface in Kristin P. McColgan's " 'By Long Perusal and Deep Love': Miltonic Parallels in Hawthorne's *The Marble Faun*" (*TPB* 26:20–29), which proposes that, in discovering their bond with humanity, Kenyon and Hilda become prepared to fight the good fight.

iv **Essays on Tales and Sketches**

A good piece of historical scholarship, Robert C. Grayson's "Curdled Milk for Babes: The Role of the Catechism in 'Young Goodman Brown' " (*NHR* 16, i:1–6) presents John Cotton's *Milk for Babes, Drawn from the Breasts of Both Testaments* as the source of youthful delusions during the witchcraft mania and of Brown's soured vision of total depravity. Dwelling on a husband's failure to protect his wife from demonic possession, Barbara Fass Leavy, "Faith's Incubus: The Influence of Sir Walter Scott's Folklore on 'Young Goodman Brown' " (*DAS* 18:277–308), draws both problematic and virtually certain connections between Hawthorne's tale and Scott's "Fairies of Popular Superstition," *Letters on Witchcraft and Demonology,* and the Auchinleck version of the medieval poem *Sir Orfeo.* Two further links should be noted: Hawthorne's debt to Scott in transmuting a traditional folklore realm of benign supernatural wonders into a dreaded world of Calvinistic demons; and the bearing of the Orpheus/Eurydice myth on Brown's failure with Faith.

Shifra Hochberg, "Etymology and the Significance of Names in 'Roger Malvin's Burial' " (*SSF* 26:317–21), trenchantly suggests that "etymological derivations and meanings of the given names 'Rueben,' 'Dorcas,' 'Cyrus,' and 'Roger' serve as plot pointers or echoes, as well as vehicles of both simple and proleptic irony." Robert Glen Deamer's "Hawthorne's Parricidal Vision of the American Revolution: 'My Kinsman, Major Molineux,' " in *The Importance of Place,* pp. 55–62, says nothing new and ignores almost all of the scholarship on the tale relevant to his purpose.

Barbara Eckstein's "Hawthorne's 'The Birthmark': Science and Romance as Belief" (*SSF* 26 [1989]: 511–19) cogently relates (1) Aylmer to a male scientist tradition of expropriating female creation in seeking immortality, (2) Georgianna to a romance tradition in which women's lives end or their imperfections become revealed after marriage, and (3) Aminadab to an industrial management ethos within which the laborers perform as obedient servants. More cogently yet, Nicholas K. Bromell, " 'The Bloody Hand' of Labor: Work, Class, and Gender in Three Stories by Hawthorne" (*AQ* 42:542–64), establishes antebellum distinctions between mental and physical labor in order to examine how "The Birth-mark," "Drowne's Wooden Image," and "The Artist of the Beautiful" reveal a kind of labor theory of art, culminating in Hawthorne's uneasiness over the power of woman's body to (pro)create through labor, which challenges a "masculine aesthetics that would fabricate enduring artifacts to outlast the body."

From a tissue of assumptions, shifting use of evidence, and contradictions in argument, Charles Chappell, "Pietro Baglioni's Motives for Murder in 'Rappaccini's Daughter' " (*SAF* 18:55–63), plays yet another sleuth in demystifying Baglioni's revenge plot, this time with Giovanni as the doctor's planted agent.

John N. Miller, " 'The Maypole [*sic*] of Merry Mount': Hawthorne's Festive Irony" (*SSF* 26 [1989]:111–23), tries to swerve around the tale's historical ironies advanced by Michael Colacurcio in order to present Edith and Edgar as nonrealistic Maypole celebrants who arrive at an antifestive Puritan outlook before Endicott enters the scene. Unaware of my own work, Miller also reverts to Joseph Strutt's *Sports and Pastimes* to show the disjunction between traditional forms of English merriment and Puritan opposition to them. Readers should be cautioned that

Francis J. Bremer's "Endecott and the Red Cross: Puritan Iconoclasm in the New World" (*JAmS* 24, i:5–22) does not address Hawthorne's story; but it magnificently documents the historical issues compassing Endicott's deed.

An important new discovery appears in Julie Hall's "A Source for 'Drowne's Wooden Image' and Hawthorne's Dark Ladies" (*NHR* 16, ii:10–12): a passage from Sophia's *Cuba Journal* describing a Spanish lady that Hawthorne copied into his 1838 notebook and virtually reproduced in the description of Drowne's image. For Hall, this source—not the treatment of Beatrice in "Rappaccini's Daughter"—is the origin of Hawthorne's notorious dark ladies. Far less reliable, because of tricky logic, stale critical views, and an unkept promise to provide a Puritan historical context, is Michael Wutz's "Hawthorne's Drowne: *Felix Culpa* Exculpated" (*SSF* 18:99–109). Wutz casts the hypothetical lady from Fayal as the evil agent in what begins as Drowne's fortunate but ends in his unfortunate fall, coordinated by a demonic Captain Hunnewell. Without citing Nina Baym, he finds passion at the root of artistic creation.

Linda Furgerson Selzer, "Beyond Anxiety and Wishfulfillment: 'The Haunted Mind' as Public Meditation" (*NHR* 16, ii:1–6), says the tale "is best understood not as a failed effort in psychoanalysis, but rather as a successful sketch that guides *readers* through a public meditation on human mutability." Hawthorne's second-person address permits our identifying with the narrator's temporal process, which "suggests that although human transcience is inescapable, the mind's mysterious motions *through time* may provide readers with an 'original' for conceiving of eternity."

v Miscellaneous

In "Sophia Peabody Hawthorne: A Study of Artistic Influence" (*SAR*, pp. 1–21), Patricia Dunlavy Valenti recounts the high estimation held by artists Chester Harding, Washington Allston, and Thomas Doughty for the paintings of Sophia, a rare instance of 19th-century American women having the necessary male mentors to pave the way into the professional art world. Valenti declares that Sophia's artwork and her comments on art in the *Cuba Journal* helped to draw Hawthorne and Sophia together. Thereafter, Sophia influenced the pictorial elements in his works. An appendix lists the surviving art of Sophia and their repositories.

With excellent investigative skill, William Peirce Randel, "Hawthorne and Sir William Pepperrell" (*EIHC* 126:37–51), traces Hawthorne's accurate and erroneous information on Pepperrell that appears in two works and, over a period of many years, in *The American Notebooks.* The essay belongs with other recent studies that explore Hawthorne's Maine connections. John Gatta's *"The Scarlet Letter* as Pre-text for Flannery O'Connor's 'Good Country People' " (*NHR* 16, ii:6–9) extends beyond the title to include connections between O'Connor and Rose Hawthorne (Mother Alphonsa) by way of *Our Old Home* and *The English Notebooks.* Gary Scharnhorst, "Hawthorne's Reception in England 1845–1849" (*NHR* 16, ii:13–15) tries to demonstrate that Hawthorne's exaggeration of his obscurity as a man of letters before the publication of *The Scarlet Letter* applies to England as well as to America. What is not clear is Hawthorne's knowledge of the notices Scharnhorst has uncovered.

Duquesne University

3 Poe

Benjamin Franklin Fisher IV

Diversity characterizes this year's work, as it has over the previous several years. Once again, brief studies far outnumber books. A move toward major revaluation of Poe as poet seems to be afoot, although the Dupin tales, "Usher," and other tales that give prominence to women, *Pym*, and *Eureka* continue to hold warhorse positions within the canon.

i Textual, Bibliographical Works

Stuart and Susan Levine's *The Short Fiction of Edgar Allan Poe: An Annotated Edition* (Illinois), originally published in 1976, is available again, with interesting notes. Jean Cash's "Edgar Allan Poe and Daniel Bryan: A Brief Correspondence" (*SAR*, pp. 107–18) supplements *The Poe Log* information on Poe/Griswold by publishing five letters from Bryan, postmaster in Alexandria, Virginia, and would-be poet, to Poe. Bryan's intentional courting of Poe's good offices, along with his reluctance to run afoul of Griswold—in case either might further his own poetic ambitions—is clear.

ii General Studies

David Ketterer's *Edgar Allan Poe: Life, Work, and Criticism* (York, [1989]), for the series "Authoritative Studies in World Literature" supplies a sensible biography, a chronology of Poe's works (citations to his criticism are selected), a selection of editions, chapters on the "Major Works" and "Critical Issues," and a selective "Annotated Bibliography" of books and special periodical numbers about Poe—all in 51 pages. In the "Major Works" chapter, Ketterer centers on "The Assignation," *Pym*, "Usher," the detective tales, "The Philosophy of Composition," "The Bells,"

"The Raven," and *Eureka.* Given the mandated brevity, Ketterer manages to zero in on crucial interpretative matters, although his focus on "The Assignation," for him a key to much of the Poesque, might be sharper if he employed additional critical opinion concerning that tale. Noël Carroll's *The Philosophy of Horror* (Routledge) includes analyses of Poe, whom she designates a writer of "terror" rather than "horror" fiction (that is, fiction which does not feature monsters, p. 15), among other 19th-century authors, although the mention of Le Fanu, in relation to Marshall Tymn's book, *Horror Literature* (1981), necessitates a reminder that Le Fanu was placed in a different chapter of the book than that of central focus in *The Philosophy of Horror.* If brief, Carroll is suggestive about locating Poe within provinces of Gothic and science fiction.

Several items treat Poe and other arts. A book that ranges widely in showing influences and adaptations (and to be used in conjunction with some of Burton Pollin's publications) is Ronald L. Smith's *Poe in the Media: Screen, Songs, and Spoken Word Recordings* (Garland). Glen A. Omans's "Poe and Washington Allston: Visionary Kin," in *Poe and His Times,* ed. Benjamin Franklin Fisher IV (Edgar Allan Poe Society, pp. 1–29), from the other end of the critical spectrum (i.e., what came before Poe) addresses aesthetic affinities between this pair in using German idealism as a springboard for their own concepts of Beauty, Truth, and Good. Companion reading appears in David C. Miller's *Dark Eden* (Cambridge, [1989]), an illuminating critique of swamp motifs in 19th-century American culture. Here we find remarks about Poe's swamp symbols tightening the psychology in his tales and poems, especially "Usher" and "Ulalume." The visual arts contexts that Miller examines supplement studies by Omans, Kent Ljungquist, and Burton R. Pollin—and Brennan, mentioned below. Along with general critical trends during recent years, Miller's book reveals a Poe much more within mainstreams of American culture than a fringe oddity. Camille Paglia's lively *Sexual Personae* contains scattered perceptions worthwhile to Poe enthusiasts. Her linkings of Poe to European Romantics, particularly Coleridge, should find receptive readers. A more controversial topic may be her idea that the shrouded white figure in the conclusion to *Pym* represents "the nature mother," into whom Pym is reabsorbed. "She" is shrouded because she's hermaphroditic.

Interrelationships between Poe and his audiences are addressed in portions of two recent books. Kenneth Dauber's probings of authors' authority, as applied to Poe, makes for interesting interpretations of a

variety of the works, from *Eureka* and the poems, on through many of
the humorous tales (*The Idea of Authorship*, pp. 118–53). More so than
several others included in the book, Poe "makes his very inauthority
authoritative" (p. 120). In attempting to penetrate the layered implications of "otherness" and alienation in Poe's writings, Dauber demolishes
much nonsense promoted by the biographical approaches of Bonaparte
and Krutch. Going over more familiar ground, Joseph R. Kronick
informs us that "to read Poe . . . is to confound the familiar with the
hidden" and that "Poe's tales are filled with clues both upon himself as
writer and on the reader as well" (p. 210). *Pym,* "Murders," and "The
Purloined Letter" revolve around situations of misreadings, writes Kronick, employing deconstructionism to buttress "Edgar Allan Poe: The
Error of Reading and the Reading of Error," in *Southern Literature and
Literary Theory,* ed. Jefferson Humphries, (pp. 206–25). Sighting in on
"The Purloined Letter," Kronick admits that his is "hardly the first
reading to suggest the tale as an allegory of reading" (p. 216), but his essay
sensibly, if not exhaustively, combines recent theory with preceding
work. Another, farther-reaching survey, Steven E. Kagle's "The Corpse
Within Us" (*Poe and His Times,* pp. 103–12), notes how Poe grafted
premature burial themes popular in his day onto his own preoccupations
with suppressed secrets and guilt to create subtle art in "Ligeia," "Usher,"
"Masque," "The Raven," "Ulalume," and—by implication—in several
critical essays. Likenesses to Bryant, Emerson, Melville, Hawthorne,
and Whitman are pointed out. Another kind of view, which draws on
kindred subject matter and Foucault, appears in John C. Long, "The
Scene at the Sickbed: Poe, Hawthorne, and Whitman: The Clinic as
Discourse in Tales and Poems of Morbid Physic" (*HSL* 21 [1989]:21–37).

iii Poems, *Politian*

Joan Dayan's "From Romance to Modernity: Poe and the Work of
Poetry" (*SIR* 29:413–37) provides penetrating critiques of Poe's poetics
seen in light of *Eureka,* "his final attempt to confound his earlier theoretical categories (Truth, Romance, and Poetry)," as well as the practices in
modern poetic sequences. Here is essential reading for anyone engaged
with Poe the poet and his descendants. Eye-opening reading also en-
livens "Poe's 'The City in the Sea'" (*Expl.* 48, iii:185–88), a challenge by
Joseph M. Garrison, Jr., to long-held opinions. Likening Poe's piece to
Wallace Stevens's "Anecdote of the Jar," Garrison reads the poem as an

exhortation to poets to dwell in reality instead of visionariness—a moral
also conveyed in "Sonnet—To Science," "Ligeia," and "Masque." Perennial fascination with "The Raven" informs three essays in *Poe and His
Times*. E. Kate Stewart turns up yet another source in a *Blackwood's* tale
by Samuel Warren—" 'The Raven' and 'The Bracelets' " (pp. 189–93). In
"The Raven and the Nightingale" (pp. 194–208), David H. Hirsch
brings Poe's poem into high relief against a background of Keatsian
aesthetics, such that "The Raven" sounds if not a death knell for "poetic
imagination as a source of cognition [an anticipation of] its eclipse by
the scientific mode of inquiry" (p. 206). Dennis W. Eddings convincingly probes hoax elements integrated with depiction of pitfalls in the
unbridled Romantic imagination—"Theme and Parody in 'The Raven' "
(pp. 209–17)—to illuminate interconnections of comic with grave foundations for Poe's art. Spellbinding readings of Poe's renowned poem
by James Edward Murdoch, an American actor, on through the 1880s
are charted in William Norris's "The Further Career of 'The Raven' "
(*NHCJ* 7:74–81). Bondings between the poem and "The Philosophy of
Composition" occupy Leland S. Person, Jr., in "Poe's Composition of
Philosophy: Reading and Writing 'The Raven' " (*ArQ* 46, iii:1–16). The
idea that anti-Romanticism in the poem counters Dupin's showing
limits to mathematical reasoning is engaging, as is Person's pointing out
structural similarities between "The Raven" and the essay devolving
from it. Those likenesses, I would think, should intensify our sense of
Poe's hoaxing, as it is expounded by Eddings. Person's treatment of the
speaker's subjectivity is, of course, no new topic.

A refreshing piece by that veteran Poe scholar, David K. Jackson,
"Prose Run Mad: An Early Criticism of Poe's *Politian*" (*Poe and His
Times*, pp. 88–93), supplements *The Poe Log* and increases our knowledge of a minor critical skirmish in contemporaneous periodicals, as we
read both sides' potshots consequent upon negative evaluation in the
Newbern [N.C.] *Spectator* of Poe's play. One of the editors and publishers, Robert G. Moore, was especially hostile to Poe's writings.

iv Tales

a. Tales of the Folio Club, Humor Poe's aims and achievements in
comedy, notably in "Epimanes," "MS. Found," and "Loss of Breath,"
along with others, as authoritatively investigated by the late Claude
Richard, will be more accessible in Mark L. Mitchell's translation, "The

Tales of the Folio Club and the Vocation of Edgar Allan Poe as Humorist" (*UMSE* n.s. 8:185–99). Poe's comic devil tales and his commonalities with frontier humorists, a topic approached from different angles by Harry M. Bayne and Fred Madden (*ALS 1989*, p. 44), are cited pertinently in my "Devils and Devilishness in Comic Yarns of the Old Southwest" (*ESQ* 36:39–60). In an overview that runs contrary to much on record, "Poe's Humor: A Psychological Analysis" (*SSF* 26 [1989]:531–46), Paul Lewis urges that by seeking in-jokes, critics overlook more obvious comic features. Thus we need a middle approach between old psychoanalytic and recent concepts of Poe "as detached, intellectual artist." Repeatedly, Poe's works show limits of humor, how it moves toward terror—natural from a writer whose own life was troubled by so much grimness.

b. Philosophic Background for the Tales One might suppose (but see Stewart, above) that little remained to say about Bruce I. Weiner's topic, "Poe and the *Blackwood's* Tale of Sensation" (*Poe and His Times*, pp. 45–65). Nevertheless, Weiner forcibly marshals evidence (with ample documentation) to reveal how Poe employed comic and sober strategies of Gothic fiction in wrestling his own ambivalences regarding Common Sense thought as juxtaposed to Romantic Imagination. In more general terms, Robert Giddings in "Poe: Rituals of Life and Death" (*American Horror Fiction*, pp. 33–58) analyzes Poe's modifications of Gothic tradition—in which death is central, and from which he switched emphasis to rituals of death—and its cognate, insanity (fascinating to the Romantic mind because it stood opposite to Classical order and reason). Giddings's panorama of Gothic fiction, Graveyard verse, and Orientalism is well handled within limited space, and his remarks about insanity are especially exciting (see Gruesser, and Thompson on *Pym*, below).

c. Tales About Women My own " 'Eleonora': Poe and Madness" (*Poe and His Times*, pp. 178–88), which takes account of Poe's revisions as they contributed to subtle ambiguities infusing the narrator's state of mind, may well be read in conjunction with Giddings's piece, and with David E. E. Sloane's "Usher's Nervous Fever: The Meaning of Medicine in Poe's 'The Fall of the House of Usher' " (*Poe and His Times*, pp. 146–53). Sloane shows how Poe used 19th-century medical publications as bases for the Usher twins' psychophysical troubles. Long neglected as inferior, or secondary, work, "The Sphinx" has recently attracted increased attention, most recently in connection with "Usher." Responding to Judith Saunders's critique (*ALS 1986*, p. 52), Edward E. Eller, in "Disruption and Control in and Out of Poe's Texts" (*PAPA* 16:41–49), suggests how, instead of reading Poe's texts reductively, we might better consider how the narrator in "The Sphinx," like Roderick Usher, his narrator-friend, and Eller himself, becomes "feminized and childized" (p. 42). To be used along with critiques of "Usher" by G. R. Thompson, Patrick Quinn, James W. Gargano, Kent Ljungquist, Craig Howes, and myself, is Matthew C. Brennan's explanatorily titled "Poe's Gothic Sublimity: Prose Style, Painting, and Mental Boundaries in 'The Fall of the House of Usher'" (*JEP* 11:353–59). A response to Beverly R. Voloshin (*ALS 1986*, p. 49) informs G. R. Thompson's "Locke, Kant, and Gothic Fiction: A Further Word on the Indeterminism of Poe's 'Usher'" (*SSF* 26 [1989]: 547–50). To Voloshin's idea that "much of the best of [Gothic fiction] is epistemologically indeterminate," Thompson counters that Voloshin takes too narrow a view of the Lockean drift in "Usher," thus overlooking Kantian possibilities.

In "'Visionary Wings': Art and Metaphysics in Edgar Allan Poe's 'Hans Pfaal'" (*Poe and His Times*, pp. 76–87), Maurice J. Bennett offers a reading of another early tale, often cited as pioneer science fiction or a hoax, stressing its covert urging of "transcendence of common reality," notably American in "its use of science and technology in the projects of idealism" (p. 86). Using representative early and late tales, Liliane Weissberg exemplifies Poe's narrators' searches after knowledge, truth, and beauty ("In Search of Truth and Beauty: Allegory in 'Berenice' and 'The Domain of Arnheim,'" pp. 66–75)—to demonstrate, paradoxically, that Poe establishes allegory by rejecting it. In another exploration of foundations for Poe's outlook, Joan Dayan cites "Morella," "Berenice," and "Usher" as representative of his testing Lockean assumptions while keeping a weather eye on the cant of "those misusers of language," the New England Transcendentalists, in "Poe, Locke, and Kant" (*Poe and His Times*, pp. 30–44, quoting p. 43). Keen insights, on topics that range beyond what the title may initially imply, enrich John C. Gruesser's "'Ligeia' and Orientalism" (*SSF* 26 [1989]:145–49). Orientalism reinforces Poe's portraying the imaginative process at work.

In addition to Dayan's, several other studies in *Poe and His Times* deal with Poe and Transcendentalism. April Selley, in "Poe and the Will" (pp. 94–102), demonstrates how Poe found Emerson's "confidence in the self-reliant, imaginative man . . . too simplistic" (p. 94), without sufficient attention to effects of the will on life in his era. Selley's survey

of tales establishes how Poe's tales implied that through art alone humanity comes close to infinity, although, ironically, that same creativity
proved our limitations. Jerry A. Herndon convincingly brings into play
Irving's "Adventure of the German Student" and Emerson's *Nature* to
argue that Poe consciously alluded to the former in honing his satire of
Emersonian Transcendentalism: "Poe's 'Ligeia': Debts to Irving and
Emerson" (pp. 113–29). Poe's satiric shafts were not loosed on Transcendentalism alone, as is evident in David A. Long's "Poe's Political Identity:
The Mummy Unswathed" (*PoeS* 23:1–22), which places "Some Words
with a Mummy" as expressive of Poe's Whiggish leanings and of his
personal scorn of mob thought.

d. Crime Tales   Another implicit transition is effected in turning to
"Emerson, Thoreau, and Poe's 'Double Dupin'" (*Poe and His Times,*
pp. 130–45), Stanton Garner's exciting suggestion that in "Murders" and
"The Purloined Letter" Poe was taking a long view of Emersonian and
Thoreauvian notions of idealism and the poet. Dupin, as Poe fashioned
him, never gives over his mathematical, or pragmatic, abilities, else he
would go mad. Garner's hypothesis, like Herndon's, will assuredly elicit
rejoinders. Poe's paternity of modern detective fiction appears to be
another inexhaustible interest. For example, allusions to Poe in Tony
Hilfer's *The Crime Novel* are noteworthy, as are those in several essays in
The Cunning Craft, ed. Ronald G. Walker and June M. Frazer. The
paradigm created in "Murders" has many progeny in self-reflexive detective stories, which bracket detection and the reading process, says S. E.
Sweeney in the first essay in *Cunning Craft*, "Locked Rooms: Detective
Fiction, Narrative Theory, and Self-Reflexivity" (pp. 1–14). The detective as an isolato from the community also originates in Dupin, according to Robin Woods, "'His Appearance Is Against Him': The Emergence
of the Detective" (pp. 15–24), whose idea is reinforced by George N.
Dove's perception that the convention of the "Trapped Detective" came
into being with Dupin—who entered the Rue Morgue affair out of
gratitude—"The Detection Formula and the Act of Reading" (pp. 25–37;
see Irwin, below). Catherine J. Cresswell's "Poe's Philosophy of Aesthetics and Ratiocination: Compositions of Death in 'The Murders in
the Rue Morgue'" (pp. 38–54), a reading that emphasizes the atypicality
of that tale, is unlikely to meet with great admiration. Much of what she
suggests (e.g., that "Murders" resides "at the borders of philosophy and
farce, reason and mystification," or as to matters of doubling or of

mingling criminal and good-guy traits, pp. 38, 39) is not new, and the wrenching of Henry James's comments about Poe and Baudelaire to fit a thesis about "Murders" proper is questionable. Counter-thinking occurs, of course, in Sweeney's essay, as well as in Otto Penzler's "Collecting Mystery Fiction: Rex Stout" (*ArmD* 23:314–17)—where Dupin and friend are seen as forerunners to Holmes and Watson or Nero Wolfe and Archie—and, in the same periodical, Norman E. Stafford's "Partners in Crime" (pp. 349–53), which reasonably charts the descent and, in certain cases, the expansion of Poe's character types and methods into hard-boiled detective fiction. Moreover, the Poesque descends through crime fiction into such other offspring as Richard Hallas's 1938 novel, *You Play the Black and the Red Comes Up*, which Brendan D. Strasser terms "a literary hoax, like Poe's short stories in the 1840s"—"Sugared Cain: Hard-boiled Parody in *You Play the Black and the Red Comes Up*" (*Clues* 11:113–27). Finally, and moving far beyond a "mere" source study, John T. Irwin thoughtfully examines the impact of Poe's Dupin tales upon a great 20th-century writer's crime fiction, in *"Knight's Gambit:* Poe, Faulkner, and the Tradition of the Detective Story" (*ArQ* 46, iv:96–116). Not restricting himself to the fiction in *Knight's Gambit,* Irwin convincingly demonstrates Faulkner's adaptations of locked-room motifs and expansions in traits of personal motives within the detective and other features of characterization.

It would not be a year of Poe scholarship were there no critique of "The Purloined Letter." Appropriately, Peter A. Muckley's "The Radical-ness of Those Differences: Reading 'The Purloined Letter' " (*UMSE* n.s. 8:226–42) provides (a) an overview of readings, which evaluates their excellences and weaknesses in contributing to our recognition of richness in that tale, (b) Muckley's own reading, which submits that disguise and duplicity are used to combat power—with inevitable side-glances toward money—and (c) ideas about the tale in Poe's canon and the literary community at large. Shorter, but as essential to fans of Poe's sleuth, is Hal Blythe and Charlie Sweet's "The Reader as Poe's Ultimate Dupe in 'The Purloined Letter' " (*SSF* 26 [1989]:311–15). Supplementing work by G. R. Thompson, Liahana K. Babener, Dennis Eddings, and myself, they argue that for Poe the "detective story was a game and the reader his opponent" (p. 312). No actual Minister D—— exists, they write; he is an imaginative creation of Dupin, the con man, one that permits the detective to play a role. Dupin's monetary concerns and his seeming extraordinary vision are two signal giveaways to Poe's comic intent.

Patrick White in " 'The Cask of Amontillado': A Case for the Defense" (*SSF* 26 [1989]: 550–55) argues against seeing Montresor as extraordinary, perhaps satanic. Instead, he is very ordinary in his devotion to feudal notions of family, which include taking revenge against intruders upon its sanctities, as emphasized in his motto.

v Pym

A thoroughly researched, carefully considered, and eminently engaging critique is G. R. Thompson's monograph, "Romantic Arabesque, Contemporary Theory, and Postmodernism: The Example of Poe's *Narrative*" (*ESQ* 35 [1989]:163–271). From Oriental carpets to Borges and Barth, from Schlegelian conceptions of the arabesque to quincunxial motifs, Thompson draws on a wealth of materials and figures relevant to perspectives on Poe's book. Within five large divisions (another quincunx?), Thompson offers sensible evaluations of many interpretations of *Pym*. Thompson's own idea is that human awareness of the void, more so than the void itself, "haunts" Poe's characters as they display their creator's vision of paradoxical human existence (mirrored in indeterminate meanings in his arabesque fiction). These Poesque elements are admirably depicted in *Pym,* which may ultimately leave us with a sense of Maya, of illusion, of "expanding and collapsing cycles of *nothingness*" (pp. 265–66). That Poe's novel, and his work overall, aim at suggesting instead of defining is well-known, but Thompson's thoughts on these matters are presented with considerably more persuasive verve and creativity than has often been put into print.

vi Critical Writings, Eureka

Cynthia Mieczmikowski's "End(ing)s and Mean(ing)s in *Pym* and *Eureka*" (*SSF* 27:55–64) makes for another deft transition because, as we read there, *Eureka* may be viewed as a kind of "apologia" for *Pym* in attempting to explain the workings of language. Both show that there are "no speakable ultimate truths in these texts." Arguing against perceptions of too much hoaxical substance in both works, Mieczmikowski concludes that *Eureka* "may be Poe's sincerest piece of plotting" in that it "goads" the writer himself to believe in the "truth of the universe which his works . . . could only struggle and ever fail to express" (p. 64). J. Lasley Dameron in "Poe's Concept of Truth" (*MissQ* 43:11–21) cites the essays and *Eureka* in positing that Poe's theory of unity in the short story devolves from his ideas about truth in content and form. Aligned with British formal criticism, found mainly in periodicals, regarding the tale, Poe first systematized such thought in America. (Won't it be wonderful to have the complete concordance to Poe, being prepared by Elizabeth S. Wiley, at hand to expedite this variety of study?) Another demonstration of Poe's conscious integration of form with content is Barbara Cantalupo's "'Of or Pertaining to a Higher Power': Involution in *Eureka*" (*ATQ* n.s. 4:81–90). Far less persuasive is Dennis A. Foster's "Re-Poe Man: A Problem of Pleasure" (*ArQ* 46, iv:1–26), where the dipping among *Eureka* and the tales for examples of perversity abounds in references so inclined toward recent critical theorists that the uninitiate might think nobody else ever published anything substantial about terror/pleasure in Poe's writings.

vii   Attributions, Sources, Influences, Affinities

A controversy that made for lively reading in the 19th century should be settled once for all by Adam Roberts's "A Tennyson Letter" (*N&Q* 235:425–26). Addressing the editor of the *Spectator,* Tennyson, in a hitherto unpublished letter, endorsed Poe's and denied his own authorship of "To One in Paradise," which had been ascribed to him, and plagiarism to Poe, by "G. D. B." Charles Swann finds a likely source for the inscription on the rocks in *Pym* in *Melmoth the Wanderer,* which Poe knew: "Poe and Maturin—A Possible Debt" (*N&Q* 235:424–25). Roberta Sharp's findings in "Poe's Chapters on 'Natural Magic'" (*Poe and His Times,* pp. 154–66) adds to what Burton Pollin and Selma Brody (*ALS 1989,* p. 46) have given us on Poe's use of Sir David Brewster's information on visual phenomena, ventriloquism, and minerals, in *Letters on Natural Magic.*

Turning to Poe's impacts, we meet, first, with his recurrent method of reworking his own materials in Richard Kopley's "Poe's *Pym*-esque 'A Tale of the Ragged Mountains'" (*Poe and His Times,* pp. 167–77). Theme and form in these fictions hint at Poe's attempts to recover his own lost family, which may only occur providentially. Two studies of a familiar, but constantly revaluated, relationship, are Jonathan Culler's "Baudelaire and Poe" (*ZFSL* 100:61–73) and Gary Wayne Harner's "Edgar Allan Poe in France: Baudelaire's Labor of Love" (*Poe and His Times,* pp. 219–25). Culler sets forth qualities in Poe's writings—*Lucidité,*

Etrangeté, and *Perversité*—that appealed to revolutionary Baudelaire, and from which he derived his own techniques in creating prose poems and handling allegory. With critical acumen, Harner examines pluses and minuses in the Frenchman's translation of "The Tell-Tale Heart."

The influence of Poe and the Poesque ramifies in other directions. A topic touched on by John E. Reilly in *The Image of Poe in American Poetry* (*ALS 1976,* p. 35) receives expansive treatment by J. Gerald Kennedy in "Elegy for a 'Rebel Soul': Henry Clay Preuss and the Poe Debate" (*Poe and His Times,* pp. 226–34). Kennedy reprints entire the Washington *National Intelligencer* (May 19, 1853) version of Preuss's elegy in verse, which defends Poe's "rebellious despair" (p. 232) against negative presentations by Griswold and R. H. Stoddard. Preuss's own career, one of a would-be poet, is set forth in detail. Another champion of Poe figures in Kent Ljungquist and Cameron Nickels's "Elizabeth Oakes Smith on Poe: A Chapter in the Recovery of His Nineteenth-Century Reputation" (*Poe and His Times,* pp. 235–46). Not only are Smith's periodical publications in defense of Poe against Griswold (which began earlier than Sarah Helen Whitman's 1860 appreciation) analyzed, but the activity of John Henry Ingram as Poe's apparently objective biographer is called into question. One more detractor is scrutinized by James W. Gargano, whose "Henry James and the Question of Poe's Maturity" (*Poe and His Times,* pp. 247–55)—wherein James's misunderstandings of Poe's intents and achievements, as well as the influence of Poe on James, are re-marked—should cause many to change their own opinions of Poe. Another round of championing and its counters informs Robert J. Scholnick's "In Defense of Beauty: Stedman and the Recognition of Poe in America, 1880–1910" (*Poe and His Times,* pp. 256–76), where we learn much about E. C. Stedman's exhortations in the periodical milieu on Poe's behalf.

Conversations with Richard Wilbur, ed. William Butts (Miss.), gathers into handy form opinions from one of Poe's outstanding critics. Wilbur's renowned "quarrel" with Poe's aesthetics is, of course, of central interest. So is his view that Poe's fiction, not his verse, stands as his greatest art. Wilbur's engagement with Poe, time and again, will also interest many who seek affinities between the pair of writers. Altogether, an indispensable book for Poe devotees. Arno Schmidt, a German enthusiast for Poe's work, is attracting increased attention (*ALS 1988,* p. 49). Thomas Ringmayr's translation of and commentary to Schmidt's "The Ascher Case" (*SHR* 24:323–36) adds to our knowledge of Schmidt's views of Poe, their

similar uses of submerged humor and wordplay, and, in this instance, a
special emphasis on "Usher," for which Schmidt submits yet another
source, Heinrich Clauren's tale of the 1820s, "Das Raubschloss," translated here by Dan Latimer as "The Robber's Castle: A Literally True
Story" (pp. 337–57). Some of Schmidt's parallels seem tenuous, not
nearly so convincing, for example, as many of the late T. O. Mabbott's
findings, or those of Stewart, Irwin, and Swann, mentioned above.

University of Mississippi

4 Melville

John Wenke

Highlighting Melville studies this year were three books by Peter J. Bellis, Paul McCarthy, and Hershel Parker; a resurgence in documentary and source studies; and a profusion of approaches to *Moby-Dick*. The year was marked by a noticeable decline in theoretical and ideological forays; Melville was minimally deconstructed, though occasionally New Historicized. It was a year in between acts for the Northwestern-Newberry edition.

i General

Peter J. Bellis in *No Mysteries Out of Ourselves: Identity and Textual Form in the Novels of Herman Melville* (Penn.) offers a probing analysis of Melville's representations of the self. Combining theoretical sophistication and close-reading, Bellis shows how three versions of selfhood—"bodily identity, genealogical identity, and textual identity"—underlie Melville's attempts to express the self in literary form. In his treatment of bodily identity, Bellis considers physicality, concentrating on disfigurement and its attending burden of self-alienation. Given the difficulties of establishing bodily identity as a continuous, cohesive, ordered entity, Melville examines genealogical identity: Melville's multiple attitudes toward "paternal authority"—"desire for a union with," "inevitable distance from," and rebellion against—suffuse *Redburn, Moby-Dick,* and *Pierre.* Especially illuminating is Bellis's discussion of Pierre and Isabel's obsessions with the absent father. What replaces bodily and genealogical identities is *"textual* identity . . . the integrity of the self becomes a function of the integrity and continuity of an autobiographical text." Bellis forcefully demonstrates the effects of "temporal gaps" between actor and narrator, which result in the narrator's inevitable failure to inscribe a unified self. The long chapter on "Textual Identity" includes a close-reading of Ishmael's narrative performance. Bellis's book is a major contribution.

In *"The Twisted Mind": Madness in Herman Melville's Fiction* (Iowa), Paul McCarthy pursues a narrower focus. He examines the "effects of [Melville's] personal experiences on his understanding and portrayal of madness or mental abnormality." Blessedly free of clever gibberish, McCarthy's book engages biographical contexts and mid-19th-century psychological theories to elucidate how madness figures in Melville's personal and fictive worlds: "The fear of the twisted mind or of inherited insanity might lie behind the writer's compelling interest in insanity, his apparent compulsion to learn about the disease, to observe its effects on the individual and on others, to write about it repeatedly in his fiction, and to dread its appearance in himself." Proceeding chronologically, McCarthy considers Melville's major fictions. Some readers may have trouble with McCarthy's too-easy identification between Melville's putative periods of stress or calm and the incidence or lack thereof of madness in his fiction. It is an overstatement, for example, to argue that the world of *Typee* is "essentially sane and stable." McCarthy deftly discusses a gallery of central and peripheral figures, though curiously absent is *Mardi*'s Donjalolo, Melville's most fully dramatized early portrait of psychological imbalance. McCarthy overworks such rubrics as "normal" and "abnormal" and the "thin red line" separating the two. At times, he levels distinctions to force a point. Regarding Ishmael's elaborately expressed worries that the universe may be meaningless, McCarthy responds, "That is to say, the universe may be without reason, or 'mad.'" His discussions of the unconscious forces impelling Ahab's monomania and Pierre's idealistic compulsions are acute. This valuable book extends the examinations of Henry A. Murray, among others, and illuminates how complexes in Melville's life inform the work.

Douglas Anderson in "Melville, Whitman, and the Predicament of Intimacy" (*A House Undivided,* pp. 121–47) explores Melville's "intimate fusion" of such apparent discontinuities as "madness and truth, love and the blackness of darkness" as a way to link Melville with a tradition initiated by John Winthrop wherein the realm of domesticity provides an arena for engaging choices between "life" and "death." Anderson connects "Melville's own scrutiny of the war with the self and his own celebration of the human household." With more on the home front, Laurie Robertson-Lorant's "Melville's Embrace of the Invisible Woman"

(*CentR* 34:401–11) examines the "sexual politics" of 19th-century America. She uses "The Grand Armada" chapter of *Moby-Dick* to introduce the "stark conflict between the masculine and the feminine principles of Nature." At times, the essay suffers from glib attempts to read the life through the work: "Queequeg implicitly whispers 'Home' and 'Mother' to the orphaned Ishmael in ways that the imperious Maria Melville never could." Robertson-Lorant finds in androgyny the antidote to brute masculinity. Late in life, Melville "achieved a harmonious marriage between the male and female sides of his own nature."

Sam B. Girgus in "Family Crisis: 'The Love Past All Understanding' " (*Desire and the Political Unconscious,* pp. 79–103) devotes his material on Melville to a consideration of family and power relationships. Unlike Bellis, Girgus connects "the search for the father" with the "search for America." He examines the interaction between consciousness and ideology, millenialism and power. His discussion of Pierre as "American Oedipus or Hamlet" shows how "his predicament and his condition prefigure a state of permanent immaturity and incompleteness for American culture and character." Unconscious desires explode his attempts to forge new structures of identity and value. "Melville's Silence," in Kenneth Dauber's *The Idea of Authorship,* pp. 192–228, sees Melville as summarizing Dauber's preceding chapters on Franklin, Brockden Brown, Cooper, Poe, and Hawthorne: "Melville writes *Moby-Dick* as an epic recuperation of the story of authorship's alienation—his own and his nation's both." According to Dauber, Melville's "dilemma" of authorship includes the incomprehension of his contemporary audience and his intense alienation as expressed through his narrative "wandering"—that is, through the composition of his works. At times, Dauber's indulgence in rhetorical nonsense undermines his predominantly trenchant readings. Commenting on the Bunker Hill inscription in *Israel Potter,* Dauber states, "The self, denied, cannot through writing be made more than self as compensation. In effect, Melville's writing has become a kind of marker. It is the writing on a tombstone which can say but here am I, a tombstone only."

The most general of the general studies is Kathleen E. Kier's *A Melville Encyclopedia: The Novels* (Whitston). Kier states her purpose: "I have attempted to identify specific things (people, places, events, ideas) mentioned in the novels—not from our modern perspective but from that of Melville and his contemporaries—in order to give a frame of reference." This valuable two-volume reference set runs almost 1,200 pages. It includes a chronology of Melville's life, an alphabet of items, and three appendixes—the sources of "Extracts," a glossary of nautical terms, a compilation of quotations. The *Encyclopedia* offers all the pleasures of serendipitous browsing as well as a useful and practical resource for finding basic information. The items range from the mundane (Baltimore, casks, soft-tack) to the arcane (Casuarinas, Gog and Magog, Sesostris). Cross-referenced items are marked by asterisks. The work will serve specialist, student, and enthusiast. Part four of Jeanetta Boswell's *The American Renaissance and the Critics* (Longwood) treats Melville. Her alphabetically arranged annotated bibliography offers 171 items from the past century of criticism.

ii Documentary, Source, and Comparative Studies

Melville scholars will soon have easy access to a host of new treasures. In *"The 'New Melville Log'*—A Progress Report and an Appeal" (*MLS* 20:53–66), Hershel Parker provides a narrative of his frustrating and fruitful labors in correcting and augmenting the two-volume 1969 *Log* and Supplement, a process that was initiated with the aging, and now deceased, Jay Leyda. The *New Log* will expand to three (or four) volumes and have all post-1951 additions situated in proper chronological order: "Many documents that were in the 1951 *Log* and the Supplement will make fuller sense in the third edition because we know better what the overt and covert messages were and can point up the significances by slight alterations in the italic lead-ins." Parker asks that any materials, information, or corrections be sent his way. Continuing his indefatigable pursuits, Merton M. Sealts, Jr., in "A Supplementary Note to *Melville's Reading* (1988)" (*MSEx* 80:5–10) reports on new findings and changes in the holdings of Melville and his family, and he notes corrections to the 1988 volume. Of special interest are Melville's annotations in Hazlitt on Ossian. The title of Mark Heidmann's "The Markings in Herman Melville's Bibles" (*SAR* 341–98) might seem to promise a dry-as-dust "poor devil of a Sub-Sub" excavation. Instead, Heidmann's essay is engaging, meticulous, and informed. Given the obvious difficulties of dating Melville's marginalia, the study is thematically organized with four sections focusing on "literary issues, wisdom/skepticism and natural theology, the conflict between divine and human values, and God's judgment and God's love." Of special note is his exploration of Melville's knowledge of the "Higher Criticism"—the examination of the Bible in relation to its authorial, literary, textual, and historical exigencies.

MSEx devoted Number 81 to matters relating to Melville's letters. Lynn Horth's "Letters Lost Letters Found: A Progress Report on Melville's *Correspondence*" (1–8) discusses 39 new letters, transcribing six. Hershel Parker (9) and David Jaffee (10–11) reprint letters between Melville and Evert Duyckinck and Elizabeth Melville and Elihu Vedder, respectively. Kevin J. Hayes in "Two Melville Reviews in the London *Economist* (*MSEx* 80:12–13) reports on and reprints newly discovered reviews—the first an April 10, 1847, review of *Omoo*, the other a May 5, 1855, notice of *Israel Potter.*

Thomas Farel Heffernan's *Stove By a Whale: Owen Chase and the Essex* (New England), reissued in a beautifully illustrated quality paperback edition, contains the definitive account of the nautical catastrophe. Along with reprinting Chase's *Narrative,* Heffernan offers a compelling narrative of the *Narrative,* a detailed examination of the circumstances attending the shipwreck and its victims. Of special interest is Heffernan's consideration of Melville's uses of the *Essex* materials. *Stove By a Whale* remains a model of lucid and engaging documentary scholarship. Stuart M. Frank's "Melville in the South Seas and *The Friend*" (*MSEx* 82:1, 4–6) examines Melville's relationship to this South Seas periodical. In " 'Bound to the Marquesas': Tommo Runs Away" (*MSEx* 82:2–3), Mary Malloy considers whaleman William H. Macy's journal and presents "new information about American and French activity in the Marquesan harbor of Nukaheva."

Back in New York, Melville became an inveterate museumgoer. According to John M. J. Gretchko in "Melville at the New-York Gallery of the Fine Arts" (*MSEx* 82:7–8), Melville signed on as a lifetime member of the museum on May 4, 1847—his "first recorded attendance of an art gallery anywhere." Gretchko sketches the gallery's history and holdings—a matter of importance to scholars interested in Melville's relation to the fine arts. Gretchko's *Melvillean Ambiguities* (Falk and Bright) is a recondite collection of three notes and one essay. "Herman Melville, the Knights Templars, and the Temple Church" (pp. 7–39) reports on Melville's knowledge of the Knights Templars and, in particular, on the influence of Charles Addison's writings on *Israel Potter,* "The Two Temples," and *Pierre.*

This year saw a number of source and comparative studies. John M. J.

Gretchko in "A Pre-Raphaelite Marianna and a Question of Liberty" (*MSEx* 82:9–11) conjectures that Melville may have drawn the Marianna of "The Piazza" from *Mariana,* a painting by John Everett Millais. Gretchko seeks to amend the generally held belief that Melville's lonely woman derived from Tennyson's "Mariana" and "Mariana in the South." In "The Dramatis Personae of Robert Browning and Herman Melville" (*Criticism: A Quarterly for Literature and the Arts* 32:221–40), James Duban and William J. Scheick fashion a three-part stylistic paradigm to show how the narrative voices of Browning and Melville are intentionally unreliable and no reflection of the author's (hidden) point of view. Duban and Scheick explain how "asymmetry, hesitation and verbal traces" operate in Browning's "Pictor Ignotis" and Melville's *Billy Budd, Sailor.* The success of this provocative argument will depend on a reader's willingness to accept the applicability of the interpretive model. While their discussions of "asymmetry" and "hesitation" address the textual complexities of *Billy Budd,* "verbal traces" strikes me as more of a critical fiction. They define the "belying verbal trace [as] the author's careful placement of a very particular word or phrase in the mouth of the narrator, an expression which will vex the author's ideal audience's reliance upon the narrator." We are asked to accept that Duban and Scheick, presumably members of the "ideal" audience, know the absent author's intentions. So much of the critical quagmire associated with *Billy Budd* emanates from attempts to establish interpretive authority *either* by ascribing it to the narrator *or* to an ironic author.

Three books respectively engage Melville's relation to a predecessor, contemporary, and successor; each book is disappointing. Carol Moses's *Melville's Use of Spenser* (Peter Lang) deftly treats specific cases of Melville's many Spenserian allusions; but her book is seriously flawed in its claim that Spenser's poetry is "integral" to Melville's art, a kind of key to it all. Media, Moses contends, "seems to be derived from Prince Arthur, Guyon's companion in Alma's castle." Pierre's failures are said to derive from his "misunderstanding of Spenser." The Spenserian lens becomes repeatedly distorting, especially when it reveals that Hunilla of "The Encantadas" "may be a trickster, whose pieties only foreshadow the confidence game of Melville's last novel." Melville's markings in his volume of Spenser, made in 1861, allow Moses to read backward, while at the same time making developmental arguments about Melville's changing use of Spenser. This study lacks a balanced and refined appreciation for Melville's complex assimilation of his sources. All quests are Spenserian; metaphysical contexts oscillate between such dualities as optimism and pessimism. Melville's greatness owes all to his wise use of Spenser: "In the short fiction—as in the earlier work—Spenser is an integral part of Melville's writing. Without the allusions to the poet, the stories would lose much of their meaning." A less accomplished work is F. D. Reeve's *The White Monk: An Essay on Dostoevsky and Melville* (Tennessee). This glib, facile book offers an impressionistic cultural assay that skitters between broad-based thematics and diffuse topical organization. Reeve positions his subjects against a background of 18th-century Enlightenment, Romantic individualism, colonial expansion, and industrial development. He informs the reader that the 19th century was a period of "raging social contrasts and intolerable injustices. Each [Melville and Dostoevsky] posited an order to define man's elusive nature." Reeve's egregious factual errors undercut his authority of statement. Consider for starters, "Even utopist ideas, such as Melville's concept of Brook Farm . . . are tempered by social exigency," or his reference to "Melville's forty years of nonwriting." The "specialist reader" must have been asleep. In *Songs of American Experience: The Vision of O'Neill and Melville* (Peter Lang), Marc Maufort examines O'Neill's thematic affinities with Melville and tries thereby to illuminate the playwright's debt to American literary tradition. Where possible, Maufort reports on cases of direct influence. Most of the study, however, elaborates upon the broadest topics: Melville's "pessimistic viewpoint"; his creation of "cosmologies"; both writers' "romantic visions," "metaphysical consideration," "Existential themes." Maufort's blunt assertions about Melville's works are frequently problematic: "Ahab's demise is ordained in a large measure by a Calvinist deity," or "Ahab, as a true follower of Emerson, is unable to accept that the world is void." While Melville was a minor influence on O'Neill, there is much to question, doubt, and repudiate in this (seemingly) exhaustive treatment. Marc Chénetier in "Tinkering, Extravagance: Thoreau, Melville, and Annie Dillard" (*Crit* 31:157–72) engages "the dialogue" of "meta-intertextual" resonances among *Walden*, "The Encantadas," and *Pilgrim at Tinker Creek.*" Along with a skein of post-structuralist truisms about the inadequacies of language, the reader will puzzle to find that a work entitled *"Billy Budd and the Piazza Tales"* [*sic*] was published in 1856. Linda Wagner-Martin in *"Billy Bathgate* and *Billy Budd:* Some Recognitions" (*NConL* 20, i:4–7) proposes some tenuous connections between the devious Billy Bathgate and the innocent Billy Budd.

iii Early Works

John Bryant works with the *Typee* manuscript fragment in "Melville's
L-Word: First Intentions and Final Readings in *Typee*" (*NEQ* 63:120–31).
He compellingly examines a curious crux, what he calls the L-word: Did
Melville intend "liberally interpreted" as in Northwestern-Newberry or
"literally interpreted" as in the copy-text and the first American edition?
In making like Ishmael before the painting in The Spouter Inn, Bryant
reveals how elementally exciting textual studies can be. In "Cultural
Relativism and Melville's *Typee:* Man in the State of Culture" (*ESQ*
36:329–47), John Alberti engages more expansive vistas when arguing
that Melville's "cultural relativism . . . also introduces the problem of
moral relativism." Identity, therefore, has no transcendent referent but is
contingent upon culturally imposed forms. This extremely well-written,
and successful, essay seems at times to impose ontological contexts that
the text does not warrant, especially the contention that Tommo desires
to "escape the soul/body dualism of his own culture while preserving the
essential spiritual identity that dualism exists to define and protect." The
year's lone article on *Mardi* claims to decipher the hidden riddle that
organizes the text. Brett Zimmerman's "The Cosmic Drama of Melville's
Mardi" (*ESC* 16:417–32) proposes that the work is a "grand cosmic
allegory" with the questers turned into "space-travellers voyaging within
the Milky Way galaxy through a plurality of worlds."

iv Moby-Dick

Moby-Dick attracted considerable attention this year. In " 'All My Books
Are Botches': Melville's Struggles with *The Whale*" (*Writing the American
Classics,* pp. 25–52), James Barbour lucidly discusses the novel's genesis
and composition. He argues that the cetological chapters, written in late
1850, "sank Melville's book"; that is, Melville undermined his book's potential popularity in favor of pursuing a "mighty theme." Melville's discovery of his theological intensities made Ahab a fit protagonist. Barbour
sees *Pierre* as "an extended allegory of Melville's year-and-a-half struggle
with his 'Whale,' " and he concludes with a discussion of "three distinct
periods of composition." His charts schematize dated and undated
materials, late additions, and revisions. Sheila Post-Lauria in " 'Philosophy in Whales . . . Poetry in Blubber': Mixed Form in *Moby-Dick*"
(*NCL* 45:300–316) dismisses genetic accounts in favor of the notion that

"Melville's debt to the popular literary forms of his day is central to understanding the narrative form of *Moby-Dick*." In arguing that Melville derived *Moby-Dick*'s formal discontinuities from the contemporary "mixed form narrative," Post-Lauria evinces the reductive cause-effect tendencies of New Historicism. She asserts that Melville shares a "consensus of aesthetics" and a "collective practice" with such English mixed-form novels as *Bleak House* and *Wuthering Heights*. The terms of comparison are, at times, so broad—"Other writers mixed science with fiction"—as to be overly inclusive. What can it mean to think of Melville and Dickens as working within the same framework of metaphysical fiction? Still, the essay is provocative and worthy of serious attention. Jonathan Arac in "A Romantic Book: *Moby-Dick* and Novel Agency" (*Boundary 2* 17, ii:40–59) also engages the issue of genre. He reports that *Moby-Dick* encompasses four kinds of narrative: "national," "local," "personal," and "literary." Arac offers a useful description of the narrative's generic multiplicity, making intercultural connections that reflect a considered understanding of Melville's reading.

Among this year's most accomplished essays is Mark Bauerlein's "Grammar and Etymology in *Moby-Dick*" (*ArQ* 46, iii:17–32). According to Bauerlein, "Etymology" and "Extracts" "unveil a philological background, a lexical history, a retrospective index of meaning and usage from which the ensuing whaling narrative will draw." Bauerlein sees the etymologist as analogous to Ahab as each penetrates the "masks" of surface representation and embarks on a quest for origin and elemental meaning. Melville's absorption and transformation of his reading materials focuses Paul Lyons's "Melville and His Precursors: Styles as Metastyle and Allusion" (*AL* 62:445–63). Lyons argues for the existence of "a true method at work behind the surface disorderliness of Ishmael's languages." Demonstrating "how technique becomes statement," Lyons discusses how allusions come into play as "dialogic" expressions of interactive styles. These "invocations through style" incorporate a precursor's personality and materials into Melville's text. In *Moby-Dick* Melville's use of multiple styles constitutes "different epistemological approaches."

A number of articles consider specific cases of Melville's adaptation. Matthew Mancini in "Melville's 'Descartian Vortices'" (*ESQ* 36:315–27) examines the important question of Melville's understanding of Descartes as it impinges on the philosophical concerns of *Moby-Dick*. Though valuable in his elucidation of Cartesian thought, Mancini tends to overstate the case, especially the contention that *"Moby-Dick* in part narrates a journey parallel to that of philosophy from Descartes to Kant." Goethe is Martin Bidney's focus in "Character Creation as Intensive 'Reading': Ahab and the Sea in *Faust* and *Moby-Dick*" (*ESQ* 36:295–313). Bidney offers "a reading of Ahab's sea-madness that relates it for the first time to the sea-madness of the Ahabian Faust." While there is no documentary evidence that indicates Melville owned, borrowed, or read *Faust,* Bidney marshals an impressive array of textual resonances to make plausible the claim that Melville reformed the biblical Ahab in relation to Faust's mad combat with the sea. Melville's American sources were not slighted. In "Drunk with the Chase: The Influence of Francis Parkman's *The California and Oregon Trail* upon Herman Melville's *Moby-Dick, or The Whale*" (*JASAT* 21:1–14), Thomas L. Altherr examines Melville's review of Parkman's book and goes on to propose general and specific resemblances between the two hunting expeditions. Two essays consider the impress of nonliterary materials on *Moby-Dick.* Robert K. Wallace's "Melville, Turner, and J. E. Grey's Cetology" (*NCC* 13:151–76) argues that Melville affirms and emulates the "exploratory aesthetic" of painter J. M. W. Turner. Conversely, Melville repudiates and satirizes the obsessive cetological classification of J. E. Gray. In "The Theme of Blindness in Herman Melville's 'Symphony'" (*EAS* 19:109–14), John M. J. Gretchko makes the tenuous suggestion that "a real musical composition . . . the oratorio *Samson* by George Frederick Handel" informs Melville's chapter. Gretchko proposes that blindness thematically links a number of potential sources in painting, sculpture, and music.

Three works suffer from tunnel vision. In *Ishmael Alone Survived* (Bucknell), Janet Reno treats *Moby-Dick* as Ishmael's "survivor narrative." His tale expresses his ongoing attempt "to heal himself, to recover psychic and emotional wholeness." Reno attempts to apply such concepts as "survival guilt," "bearing witness," and "mourning the dead" as aspects of the survivor's passage from "victimhood" to "survivorship"— the jargon word for "adjustment to survival." Reno rides the thesis hard. "Extracts" presents "Ishmael's library searchings," his attempts to find "what may have been written about his disaster." The novel's narrative discontinuities, we are told, are symptoms of avoidance: "The *Pequod*'s disaster negatively affected Ishmael's ability to tell a story conventionally from beginning to end." Reno insistently presents Ishmael as "shattered," "devastated," a victim of "the hideous past," a man "wracked by the torments of the experiences he has endured." Reno's profile takes little account of Ishmael's "genial, desperado" voice and waggish sense of humor. Clayton Knight Marsh in "Sabbath Whaling in *Moby-Dick*" (*ESQ* 36:267–93) imposes a specious explanatory paradigm: "The inherent conflict between nature's 'Sabbath' and the whaler's calling contributes significantly to the tragic momentum of Ahab's unholy quest for Moby Dick." The absence of "Sabbatarian piety," Marsh avers, causes the crew's degradation, just as the "desecration of the Sabbath" brings on "the destruction of the *Pequod*." Ishmael survives—you guessed it— because he achieves "a Sabbatarian state of consciousness." Marsh's argument overloads a minor, if not inconsequential, point and enmeshes Melville in a suffocating net of pious intentions. Ishmael's dismissive response to all this might well be, "Ex officio professors of Sabbath-breaking are all whalemen." Not only do officers and crew violate the Sabbath, but Ahab is a Nazi prototype. So claims Christopher S. Durer in *"Moby-Dick* and Nazi Propagandistic Techniques" (*MQ* 31:449–68). Durer sees John C. Calhoun and Andrew Jackson as prefiguring the dictatorial Ahab. The essay propounds a series of shrill analogical distortions as Ahab is recast as Hitler: "In many respects the *Pequod* resembles the Nazi state." Missing is any attempt to balance the totality of Ahab's control with both his "humanities" and his lofty metaphysical apprehension and purpose. Philip Young brings us much closer to Ahab's gnarled and grand complexities. In " 'These Be Thy Gods, O Ahab!' " (*SAR:* 329–40), he presents a close reading of Ahab's "layered," God-defiant speech in "The Candles" chapter. Young views the soliloquy as offering both "the story's spiritual climax" and a clue to Melville's relation to his own father.

In "Whaling Voyage Round the World: Russell and Purrington's Moving Panorama and Herman Melville's 'Mighty Book' " (*American Art Journal* 22:50–78), Kevin J. Avery provides an informative study of the 19th-century genre of the moving panorama. He makes plausible conjectures as to whether Melville, while completing his masterpiece, might have seen a panorama of "a global whaling adventure." Lois M. Case in "Ishmael, Ahab, and the Leviathanic Text" (*MSEx* 83:6–9) considers "the interpretation of texts" within *Moby-Dick* as a central epistemic activity. In "Traditions and Functions of the Songs in 'Midnight, Forecastle' " (*MSEx* 83:1–5), Joan Tyler Mead convincingly argues that the suggestive content of the song fragments in chapter 40 illuminate the crew members' motivations in supporting Ahab's quest. Thomas Farel Heffernan's "Eonism on the *Town-Ho;* or, What Did

Steelkilt Say?" (*MSEx* 83:10–12) discusses an interesting find, a pamphlet account that parallels incidents relating to Steelkilt's flogging. John Seelye in "Moby-Kong" (*CollL* 17:33–40) considers the film *King Kong* and its self-conscious allusions to Melville's *Moby-Dick*. Seelye views these intersections between film and book as offering "a very complex referentiality." In "Melville: Inland Voyages" (*The Consolations of Space*, pp. 93–136), Pamela Schirmeister examines the sea in *Moby-Dick* as a reflection of "transitional strength." She presents readings of Ishmael and Ahab and their activities of seeing in relation to specific places. Catherine Zuckert's "Melville's Meditations" (*Natural Right and the American Imagination*, pp. 99–129) is a muddled consideration of the relationship between "nature and convention." On one page, "Melville suggested that human nature is fundamentally innocent—and hence good," while two pages later, "All are cannibals who destroy and are destroyed." When not downright puzzling, Zuckert sanitizes Melville's politics into feel-good truisms that simplify, without illuminating, Melville's complexity: "As Ishmael's narrative reveals, the preservation of individual freedom and liberal political institutions depends not only on reason, but also on a continuing sense of the value, the beauty, and the dignity of humanity."

v   Pierre to *The Confidence-Man*

Kris Lackey's "The Despotic Victim: Gender and Imagination in *Pierre*" (*ATQ* n.s. 4:67–76) provocatively relates *Pierre*'s "destabilizing" aspects of genre and characterization to an "overriding fiction"—the notion that the reader is contained in a "skepticism" that outstrips Pierre's own. Lackey explores the novel's sexual politics, especially as reflected in Pierre's alliance with society's victimized women. In " 'The Gulf of the Soul': Melville's *Pierre* and the Representation of Aesthetic Failure" (*An Huss* 28:351–67), Giuseppe Nori discusses the novel "as a controlled representation of the failure of aesthetics as such, through a deliberate authorial annihilation of the hero and his experiences." Nori deftly links Melville's aesthetic preoccupations to the novel's informing philosophical problems: "The binary logic of the metaphysical quest, the development and the distortion of the concept of being as idea, the relation between religion and metaphysics, the concept of nothing and the transvaluation of values, the instability of the self and its identity."

Within an otherwise brilliant essay, Nori evokes turgid explanatory paradigms from Nietzsche, Husserl, and Heidegger and winds up complicating the already sufficiently complicated.

James D. Wallace in "Pierre *en regarde:* Apocalyptic Unity in Melville's *Pierre*" (*ATQ* n.s. 4:49–65) unconvincingly argues that a "unity" does animate, and stand as functional counterpart ("systole and diastole") to, Melville's multilayered ambiguities. The unity of *Pierre,* according to Wallace, is "apocalyptic" insofar as surfaces give way to a "monstrous" implosion of all separate entities into nihilistic emptiness. Wallace argues for the influence of Poe's *Eureka.* Lacan provides Priscilla Wald's psychological contexts in "Hearing Narrative Voices in Melville's *Pierre*" (*Boundary* 2 17, i:100–32). Wald sees in the novel "a compilation of unravelings that frustrate narrative expectations as it explores the impulse to narrativize." "To narrativize" must mean "to tell stories." Pierre's various failures of authorship derive from his lack of autonomy. David Heddendorf in "Pragmatists and Plots: *Pierre* and *The Damnation of Theron Ware* (*SNNTS* 22:271–81) reassesses Plinlimmon's pamphlet as reflecting "the therapeutic message of pragmatism."

Hershel Parker in "Herman Melville's *The Isle of the Cross:* A Survey and a Chronology" (*AL* 62:1–16) mounts a convincing case for believing that following *Pierre* Melville completed a book called *The Isle of the Cross* and "that its subject (almost surely) was what we have long known as 'the story of Agatha.'" Drawing upon the Augusta Melville papers, Parker summarizes the history of the "Agatha" materials. The most fetching proof that there was a manuscript with at least the working title appears in letters from cousin Priscilla Melvill to Augusta Melville. Though the manuscript was presented to Harpers, Melville did not write as though they had rejected it: "It is perhaps significant that Melville specified that he had been prevented from publishing the work 'at that time': the implication is that he still regarded the work as a piece of literary property." Parker concludes that "we have to discard our old notions of what Melville was doing through the first three quarters of 1853." *The Isle of the Cross,* in the absence of a stupendous manuscript find, will share the teasing fate of Shakespeare's putative lost play *Cardenio.*

It should be no surprise that Bartleby went back on the couch, though he and his condition remain as intractable and elusive as ever. Fred A. Whitehead, Bruce S. Liese, and Michael L. O'Dell in "Melville's 'Bartleby the Scrivener': A Case Study (*New York State Journal of Medicine* 90:17–22) attempt "to see if current diagnostic criteria can be of any help in comprehending the scrivener and his plight." They might be, but few will be satisfied. Dismissing the so-called standard diagnosis of schizophrenia as inadequate, the authors make the new old-sounding diagnosis that Bartleby suffers from "major depression." Several spirited letters (422–24) dispute the findings. In "Experimental Melville: Cockeye-Doodle-Dee!" (*ATQ* n.s. 4:343–51), Philip Young wonders how critics "avoid the sexual emphasis in 'Cock-A-Doodle-Doo!'" Young briefly summarizes how "the cock . . . figures in symbol, folklore, and myth" and then gives his own spin to the story's "smuggled [sexual] symbolism." After reading this enjoyable piece, one sees how Melville meant to tweak Victorian cheeks. In *The Consolations of Space,* pp. 113–26, Pamela Schirmeister discusses the relationship between "The Encantadas" and Spenser. She argues that "The Piazza" constitutes a schematic reduction of the spatial qualities of "The Encantadas." Charles Berryman in "'Benito Cereno' and the Black Friars" (*SAF* 18:159–70) convincingly argues that "on the eve of the Civil War . . . Melville's description of slaves as 'Black Friars' is neither a simple gothic image nor a common appeal to the prejudice, racial or religious, of his audience." Rather, Melville creates a "double perception" with his "addition of religious imagery to the historical account of the slave revolt." Berryman illuminates the relationship between "religious asceticism and slavery" with emphasis on the ideology of Captain Cereno and the Dominican Order.

In "*Israel Potter:* Autobiography as History as Fiction" (*AmLH* 2:607–26), Peter Bellis sees *Israel Potter* as "a meditation on two parallel issues: the difference in status between first- and third-person texts . . . and the gap between individual self-consciousness (autobiography) and the wider perspective of history as a whole." Bellis focuses on the theoretical implications of Melville's fictionalizing a putative autobiography. Bellis's belabored reading tends to reduce historical narrative to ironic deflations and ideological posturing; his rhetoric descends, at times, into New Historicist involution: "For every demystification is itself ideologically conditioned, itself an involuntary remystification." Michael S. Kearns's "How to Read *The Confidence-Man*" (*ESQ* 36:209–37) constructs theoretical portraits of Melville's various readers. Melville, according to Kearns, "did want to educate one type of reader, the thought-diver, and . . . part of his method involved the implication of another type, the worldly skeptic." Not everyone will agree that the text affirms Melville's "humanistic values" and that these values reside at the center of what Kearns intrepidly offers as "the new standard interpretation." James Duban and William J. Scheick in "The Commodious 'Life-Preserver' in Melville's *The Confidence-Man*" (*AL* 62:306–09) reprint a newspaper piece that suggests "there actually was a life preserver similar in appearance to the stool held by the Cosmopolitan." The factuality of such a device unsettles the much beleaguered reader and "reinforces . . . the epistemological gap between appearance and reality."

vi Late Works

Harrison Hayford's monograph, *Melville's "Monody"; Really for Hawthorne?* (Northwestern), considers "the history and rationale of this legend. . . . The notion that the poem is about Hawthorne can so far neither be proved nor disproved. But the assumptions and logic behind the identification are brought into the open." In sketching how the legend took shape, Hayford concentrates on "three lively decades" between 1921 and 1951. Hayford's fine, open, and genially skeptical mind weighs evidence, particularly the potential hazards of "arguing identity from images." The monograph is a model of judicious reasoning in which facts, however disputable or ambiguous in themselves, are required to ground the more heady reaches of interpretive fancy.

An essential first stop for anyone interested in avoiding New Critical pratfalls or deconstructionist vaporization is Hershel Parker's *Reading "Billy Budd"* (Northwestern). Parker explores the biographical and historical exigencies that culminate in the publication and canonization of various versions of Melville's last fiction. Parker insists that *Billy Budd* is a "flawed text"—unfinished and therefore finally unrealized. Parker's book stands "not only as a guide to Melville's last story but also as a guide to the Hayford-Sealts edition, especially the 'Genetic Text,' the great treasure-house of information about Melville's artistry." Parker gives an especially sensitive reading of Melville's last years. The *Billy Budd* manuscript "needs to be seen in relation to many other pieces of 'unfinished' literary work . . . and perhaps in relation to a certain number of new undertakings—not as the single obsessive labor of Melville's last lustrum." Parker flogs critics for failing to base their arguments on the Genetic Text. In part three, Parker offers "A Chapter-by-Chapter Reading" which seeks "to make a start at acknowledging and assimilating the implications of the Hayford-Sealts Genetic Text of the Chicago edition." His reading offers a formidable challenge to future critics of the book.

Discussions of *Billy Budd* continue to recast the narrative's irresolvable centers of tumult. Steven Mailloux in "Judging the Judge: *Billy Budd* and 'Proof to All Sophistries'" (*CSLL* 1, i [1989]:83–88) provides a dissenting response to Richard Weisberg's "theory of considerate communication" as a basis for interpreting Vere's behavior. Working with the Genetic Text, Mailloux establishes that "the word 'considerate' and its variants do not just refer to covertness and deception in Melville's text. Rather, the terms refer more broadly to *taking into account*." Ultimately, *Billy Budd* "enacts the conflict between the dangers of sophistry and the security of foundation: that perennial conflict, if you will, between rhetoric and philosophy." In "Melville's Dansker: The Absent Daniel in *Billy Budd*" (*The Uses of Adversity: Failure and Accommodation in Reader Response,* ed. Ellen Spolsky [Bucknell], pp. 153–73), Sharon Baris offers a discerning treatment of how the narrative contains a series of signs "full of significance that other characters do try to unravel. Responses, reactions, reports are prevailing activities for the other sailors." According to Baris, Billy is both sign, "a kind of hieroglyphic device," and a human being, "a young man with volition, fears, and secrets of his own." Baris lucidly draws on language theories of Stanley Fish, among others, to show how Melville anticipates current considerations of the problematic relationship between texts and readers.

Cary Goodwyn's "How to Read Republican: An Analysis of Herman Melville's *Billy Budd, Sailor (An Inside Narrative)* (*ATQ* n.s. 4:239–55) is a tired reconsideration of the novel's ideological conflict. The schism between "'the ancient and the modern' . . . forced Melville to speak in a language of politics that was progressive, diversified, and modern to deliver a message that was republican, virtuous, and ancient." William Bartley in "'Measured Forms' and Orphic Eloquence: The Style of Herman Melville's 'Billy Budd, Sailor'" (*UTQ* 59:516–34) essentially mounts a pro-Vere argument. Closely reading the "measured forms" and "symmetry of form" passages, Bartley proposes that "'measured form' [*sic*] precisely characterizes both Vere's actions and Melville's creative apprehension of them in his style." To make his case, he contends that Melville's Orpheus derives not from the "syncretic and Neoplatonic traditions, but from "the Orpheus who represents the ideal of eloquence in the service of civil order." Susan Mizruchi's "Cataloging the Creatures of the Deep: 'Billy Budd, Sailor' and the Rise of Sociology" (*Boundary 2* 17, i:272–304) presents *Billy Budd* "as a work of realism which theorizes the problem of social sight and visibility that so concerned sociologists in this era." Finally, in an essay providing appropriate closure for this year's chapter, Geraldine Murphy in "The Politics of Reading *Billy Budd*" (*AmLH* 1 [1989]:361–82) considers the novel as a battleground for the "struggle between old and new liberalism."

Salisbury State University

5   Whitman and Dickinson

John Carlos Rowe

i   Walt Whitman

a. Bibliography, Editing   As always, Ed Folsom's "Whitman: A Current Bibliography" (*WWR* 7:150–54, 198–99; 8:56–58, 115–21) provides valuable annotations and bibliographical information on many items otherwise likely to be missed by scholars.

Jeanetta Boswell's *The American Renaissance and the Critics* (Longwood) includes a section on Whitman and annotations of 131 essays, chapters in books, and other criticism that Boswell judges the "best" of work on Whitman with "a broad-based interest." Boswell excludes brief explications, "purely biographical character profiles or related narratives," and "the Doctoral dissertation and the Master's thesis." The figures covered in Boswell's volume—Emerson, Thoreau, Hawthorne, Melville, and Whitman—were selected on the basis of Matthiessen's *American Renaissance,* a strange procedure given the date of publication of a study now half a century old and, although venerable, subject to considerable criticism since then for its exclusions. Boswell turns out to be quite wide-ranging in her summaries and annotations of the items she selects, but her criteria for selecting such items are never justified more than by her claim for "variety and representation over a good spread of time" and "excellence."

Judith Bassat's *"With Walt Whitman in Camden:* A Progress Report and a Supplement" (*WWR* 7:163–79) reports on the work of Jeanne Chapman, Robert McIsaac, and Bassat to edit "the last two years" of Whitman's conversations with Horace Traubel, "from July 7, 1890, to March 26, 1892," and includes a "sampling of several days of conversa-

---

Krista Walter assisted me in the research for this essay.—JCR

tions" and an appeal for help in finding a publisher for such important work.

Technically, Geoffrey Sill's "Whitman on 'The Black Question: A New Manuscript'" (*WWR* 8:69–75) belongs in this category of Bibliography and Editing, but it also has significance for a number of the contributions to Whitman's political views discussed below. Sill's new manuscript is "Of the Black Question," a Whitman manuscript owned by William F. Kurry and dealing "with the same subject as that of 'The Problem of the Blacks'" published and discussed by Kenneth Price [*RALS* (1985) 15:205–08]. This postbellum manuscript of a brief prose note (Sill dates it between 1867 and 1876) suggests to him that Whitman "saw racial assimilation as the key to 'the black question,' and that he also saw it was impossible for him to propose this solution in print. . . . To avoid this explicit statement of his beliefs . . . Whitman enlisted the aid of an impersonal, irresistible historical force—natural selection—and its human descriptive apparatus, ethnological science." Far from recent critical and scholarly efforts to situate Whitman within the politics of his age smacking of "political correctness," as some have argued, these approaches have led to the recovery of Whitman's (among other American Renaissance writers') conflicting views on questions of race, reminding us once again that even "genius" rarely transcends its time and place.

b. Biography Edwin Haviland Miller's *Selected Letters of Walt Whitman* (Iowa) draws on the six-volume *Correspondence of Walt Whitman* (1961–77), selecting 250 of the 2,800 letters included in the latter and approximately following its periodization of Whitman's life. Miller has added to the selection Whitman's letters of 1840–41 to Abraham Paul Leech, which "surfaced only a few years ago" when they were sold at auction to the Library of Congress (and published in 1986 by Alfred Golden in *American Literature*). In addition to a brief preface and general introduction, Miller offers a commentary preceding each of the seven chronologically arranged sections. He has succeeded in editing an extremely readable and useful selection; the commentaries are full of useful information, despite their intended brevity.

c. General Criticism I have previously criticized the MLA's "Approaches to Teaching" series because the idea for the series strikes me as a well-intentioned but misguided rejoinder to those critical of higher education's "overspecialization." Teaching and research should be viewed as indispensably dialectical parts of the educational process, and my first response to this series was that it tried to "condense" the research and substitute lesson plans for class preparation. I confess it—that was a reductive judgment that has been challenged by several fine volumes in the MLA's series. *Approaches to Teaching Whitman's "Leaves of Grass,"* ed. Donald D. Kummings, shows what a good volume in this series can do—in short, how it can be useful to the *relation* between research and classroom teaching at several levels. In addition to the usual bibliographical tools, this volume includes a guide to pedagogical studies and aids to teaching that include a wide range of multimedia materials (facsimile editions, collections of photographs, audiocassettes, and videocassettes). The sections on teaching "Song of Myself" and "Other Major Works" represent a good cross section of theoretical and historical approaches to Whitman. The selections in these two sections are most effective when they are miniessays. Thus Betsy Erkkila's " 'Song of Myself' and the Politics of the Body Erotic" (pp. 56–63) sketches out the "activist poetics" in Whitman that she develops at length in *Whitman, the Political Poet* [Oxford, 1989]. More adventurous, but I fear less usable by teachers, are contributions that describe the author's plan for teaching. M. Jimmie Killingsworth's "Whitman's I: Person, Persona, Self, Sign" (pp. 28–40), for example, is a fascinating effort to introduce students to critical theory, "Song of Myself," and general strategies of self-consciousness by means of different approaches (rhetorical, ideological, semiotic) to the subject that is at the center of many undergraduate classrooms: "Who is 'myself'?" But just what makes Killingsworth's classes undoubtedly exciting experiences for everyone involved is what makes these suggestions virtually unusable by others. The very complexity of Killingsworth's program probably serves to provide varied contexts for the students and Killingsworth in the moment of educational transaction. I can admire that, but I can only emulate it by developing my own flexible program. There are, in this volume, some fine efforts to use Whitman to critique and thus change the conventional teaching situation: schoolmaster droning to alphabetized desks. Ed Folsom in " 'Scattering it freely forever': Whitman in a Seminar on Nineteenth-Century American Culture" (pp. 139–45) reminds us that "Whitman's reading and learning anticipated the more individualized, broadly based curricula offered today" to encourage teachers to tap "into the diversity of student interests represented in any one class" (pp. 139, 141). In a similar manner, Sherry Ceniza in "Whitman and Democratic Women" (pp. 153–58) begins by encouraging students to discuss the "cultural space" of the classroom. Self-consciousness about the activity of education seems to me very much in the spirit of Whitman's own sense of how poetry ought to "teach," and it can be used, as Ceniza does, to explore other ideas of "authority," including discussion of gender roles and the ways sexual and human relations are constituted. The volume also identifies new areas of emphasis for teachers and scholars more familiar with the traditions of American literature as a nationalist discipline. Doris Sommer's "The Bard of Both Americas" (pp. 159–67) sketches out some of the comparatist approaches that would encourage debate of the literatures produced in the several Americas and especially focus on the role of a major "American" poet in the different conceptions of Spanish America. This is an emphasis in this year's Whitman criticism (see Grünzweig and Santí, below) that is likely to receive fuller attention from cultural critics in the coming years, and it is good this volume indicates these directions. My only suggestion is that such volumes take *students'* responses more directly into account. Why not ask students from the several different levels represented in these volumes (lower-division, upper-division majors, and graduate students) to contribute to these volumes, either directly or at least as respondents to the surveys?

James E. Miller, Jr.'s updated edition of his TUSAS *Walt Whitman* is a carefully revised version of the 1962 edition. Miller's Whitman is the originator of an American poetry that establishes the foundation for the now-canonical moderns—Pound, Eliot, Williams, Hart Crane—and their heirs—John Berryman, Allen Ginsberg. The major "issues" of the 19th century for Miller are still "science" and "democracy," much in the manner that the conflict between materialist and "spiritual" America once figured as the defining conflict for the century introducing modern America. Much as this remains a book from another literary age—the late 1950s and early 1960s—Miller's updated *Walt Whitman* does include revisions attentive to changing critical views of Whitman. In general, Miller historicizes Whitman in his revisions, and that is probably the best procedure for an introductory text of this sort. Commenting on Whitman's "poet of the woman the same as the man," Miller now qualifies Whitman's apparent egalitarianism by noting that "some readers today will see Whitman . . . celebrating women's unique biological role, while others will see his reference as one-dimensional and patronizing" (p. 64). Admittedly, Miller locates the "conflicts" in our contemporary criticism rather than in Whitman's times, but Miller's attentiveness to these critical changes justifies the claim of an "updated" edition of an otherwise 30-year-old book.

Thomas B. Byers's *What I Cannot Say: Self, Word, and World in Whitman, Stevens, and Merwin* [Illinois, 1989] is another contribution to the interpretation of the American poetic tradition as fundamentally Emersonian—that is, poetry as the modern version of theology. Thus visionary, Orphic, heroic Whitman is stressed in this study, identifying him with the romantic Emerson and offering both as poetic origins for an American modernity represented in subsequent chapters by Stevens and Merwin. Byers claims to be an "eclectic" theorist, and he does draw on a wide range of other critical theories. On the other hand, his real interest is in the poets themselves, whom he rightly considers theorists in their own rights, but whose poetry is finally for Byers the principal object of interest. Byers's focus in chapter 1 on Whitman is "Song of Myself," but the poem is a synecdoche for Whitman as the American Poet. As it turns out, Whitman's Americanness is also his capacity to connect English Romanticism and modern European phenomenology, a combination Byers finds well-suited to reading Emerson and Whitman. Byers is right, of course, but what makes this combination uniquely *American?*

Douglas Anderson's *A House Undivided* looks for its literary tradition and continuity in the Puritan Origins thesis. Beginning with John Winthrop's "A Modell of Christian Charity" (1630), Anderson details how Puritan ideas of community are figuratively represented in the family, thus cojoining domesticity and political community. Like other revisers of Perry Miller, Anderson turns to the great tradition of 19th-century American writing to find warrant for the complex but nevertheless persistent influence of Puritanism in American experience. Whitman is treated primarily in chapter 5 as the complement of Melville, both of whom confront the "predicament of intimacy" in their writings. For Whitman, poetry enacts "a marriage that fails because of Whitman's inability to locate a lover, outside himself," who might be adequate to the prophetic and redemptive purposes of the poetic ego. In effect, Anderson finds this "marriage" in the persistent figuration of the poet as Christ, so that the poetry itself can become an incarnation of both poet and reader. A typological reading of Whitman is certainly justifiable, but Anderson overdetermines the Puritanism in Whitman (and thus the usual "line" from Winthrop through Franklin and Emerson to Whitman) and thus neglects Whitman's significant rebellion against the religious ethos of the 19th century.

Some critical and rhetorical approaches developed in the 1970s and early 1980s show that they continue to have relevance to the study of particular authors and literary issues, in part because they have attempted to address challenges from New Historicists, cultural critics, and others who use recent approaches. James Perrin Warren, *Walt Whitman's Language Experiment* (Penn. State), locates Whitman within 19th-century efforts to legitimate an "American English." Warren accomplishes this by showing how Whitman's specific writings on language adapt the linguistic theories of such European romantics as Humboldt and Hegel to the "evolution" of an American English out of its Anglo-European sources. He relates his scholarship on Whitman's linguistic theories to Whitman's poetic practices by arguing that his poetry articulates the unconscious communal bond of a national language. Warren shows clearly that for Whitman poetry played a key role relating "an evolutionary account of language" with "an evolutionary account of the national spirit." He characterizes his study as "rhetorical or formalist" and the argument "deconstructive," but the latter refers primarily to Warren's Whitman, whose "language experiment" is clearly a late Romantic anticipation of "language-based" theories of knowledge. In fact, Warren's rhetorical method is quite historical.

Ezra Greenspan's *Walt Whitman and the American Reader* (Cambridge) reflects the interests of reader-response criticism as it has developed from a text-specific practice of interpretation to a method of understanding the historical concreteness of the culture of letters in the 19th century. The "professionalization of writing" from the late 18th century to the Civil War remains a subject of great importance for all literary scholars and critics since it is part of our professional history. Because the subject must be addressed in a dialectical manner that takes in both the author's self-conception and "implied reader" as well as the audience's conception of "authorship" (thus "implied author") and its own standards of taste, this is extraordinarily difficult for periods in which there is little empirical information about readers' tastes. Greenspan solves this problem by focusing his study on the technological and commercial changes occurring in printing, publishing, bookselling, writing, and reading, locating "Whitman" as a figure constituted by all of these practices. Greenspan's second chapter, "The Evolution of American

Literary Culture, 1820–1850," is a marvelous account of the shift of "authorship" from a dilettantish avocation to a commercial enterprise, figurally if not literally central to the emergent economy of urban industrialism. He shows that Whitman's "barbaric yawp" was calculated—sometimes by Whitman, sometimes simply by the changing times—to provide the sort of mediation between the private and public spheres that urban industrialism had increasingly separated. Greenspan is consistently attentive to the conflicts in Whitman as well as in his 19th-century readers, and it is just this attentiveness to historical complexities that allows him to conclude with some authority that Whitman was able to achieve the nearly impossible task of turning a book of poetry—*Leaves of Grass*—into "an American institution." What it "instituted" was the possibility of a liberal consensus in a society subject to conflicts likely to have torn any other new nation apart.

Kenneth Price's *Whitman and Tradition: The Poet in His Century* (Yale) is also an important contribution to our understanding of Whitman's role in 19th-century literary tastes. Ostensibly an influence study of both the romantic influences on Whitman and Whitman's influence on 19th-century American writers, the book is attentive to the cultural contexts for such influences not only in the 19th century but also in our own critical 20th century. The book is written in the spirit of a comparative approach to "American" literature that will carry us beyond narrow nationalism and help us understand our writers in wider cultural contexts, although Price's contexts in this book are admittedly those of the English Romantic heritage that he argues had a formative influence on Whitman's poetic practice. Nevertheless, Price can be read profitably in conjunction with Santí (below), Sommers (below), and others interested in Whitman's influence in the "other" Americas, even if Price's gesture toward "world literature" risks some of the dangers of an older comparatist model often criticized by Latin Americanists. For Price, the English Romantic "influence" (Wordsworth, Tennyson, Browning) is by no means simple or literal, since Whitman was deliberately misreading that heritage to legitimate a progressive "American" tradition. The theoretical model for such poetic misprision is, of course, Harold Bloom, but Price revises Bloom's model significantly by substituting Whitman for Emerson as the American "origin" and doing so in a manner that challenges a long tradition of criticism that situates Whitman as the Emersonian ephebe. Reading Whitman "otherwise" means for Price to stress the sexual metaphors and physicality in the poetry in reaction to "Emerson's discomfort with intimacy, his distrust of the body," and thus his defensive idealism. Perhaps most interesting of the book's several innovations is the discussion of Whitman's influence on the novel, not in terms of the usual relation between the genres of poetic and prose narratives but by way of his sexual politics. In readings of Garland's *Rose of Dutcher's Coolly,* Forster's *A Room with a View,* and Chopin's *The Awakening,* Price shows how Whitman's emancipatory sexual politics helps relax some of the inherent constraints of the novel form with its traditional emphasis on problems of marriage ("a theme Whitman downplays," according to Price).

New Historicist, gay, and feminist approaches and cultural criticism of various sorts continue to enrich Whitman studies, often by challenging his genius, or at the very least *historicizing* his indubitable poetic powers. Timothy Sweet's *Traces of War: Poetry, Photography, and the Crisis of the Union* (Hopkins) uses Whitman's *Drum-Taps* and *Memoranda during the War* (1875) to open the argument of a far-reaching study of how American culture romanticized the Civil War. Sweet's account of how Civil War photography by Brady, Gardner, and Barnard draws on the conventions of literary and pictorial pastoralism and the picturesque to normalize and rationalize the carnage and political ambiguities of the war is among the best of recent interdisciplinary interpretations of photography's place in 19th-century American culture. In his reading of *Drum-Taps,* Sweet shows Whitman working out patriotic propaganda in the subtleties of such poetic figurations as the "body politic" or the will of the Union subsuming the interests of the individual soldier. Sweet then shows how Whitman addresses the very problem of representing war (and its suffering and destruction) in *Memoranda during the War* but can offer no rational solution to the problem. Instead, the representative experience, the poetic substitute, and thus the propaganda of pastoral (well-represented for Sweet in poems like "When Lilacs Last in the Dooryard Bloom'd") must take the places of the terrible knowledge and very real pain experienced by bodies and minds in war.

Richard Dellamora's *Masculine Desire: The Sexual Politics of Victorian Aestheticism* (No. Car.) is an important contribution to post-Foucauldian studies of the modern history of sexuality. Dellamora revises Foucault and others by showing how many different modes of male-male relations are operative in Victorian society prior to the end of the century when the "homosexual subject" became a specific and demonized object of culture. In effect, Dellamora (along with Eve Sedgwick and others) shows the uneven development of the ideology of homophobia in the culture of the Victorians. Dellamora's chapter dealing with Whitman focuses on Hopkins's and Swinburne's letters and their references to "Whitman" as a name that is coded with "the American poet's expansive notions of sexuality." This section is very brief (a mere "Excursus"), but the book has considerable significance for those interested in developing similar subjects in the history of modern *American* sexuality.

Robert Scholnick's " 'This Terrible, Irrepressible Yearning': Whitman's Poetics of Love," in *American Declarations of Love,* pp. 46–67, treats Whitman's sexuality as an unresolved issue for the man that is only worked out in the poetry. For Scholnick, the daring, happy celebration of the body prior to the "Calamus" poems is figured primarily in onanistic terms; the lover-poet's "yearning" is simply for himself. In "Calamus," Whitman expresses the crisis of a truly yearning and abandoned or spurned lover, who finds only a partial reconciliation in the poetic appeal to "his 'yet unborn reader' " ("Full of Life Now"). In a similar manner, Carmine Sarracino's "Dyspeptic Amours, Petty Adhesiveness, and Whitman's Ideal of Personal Relations" (*WWR* 8:76–91) focuses on such key words in Whitman as "amorous," "amative," and "adhesiveness," to argue the larger thesis that Whitman's poetic argument against sexual shame is "not necessarily to endorse sexual looseness." What for Sarracino turns out to be "precise" is Whitman's poetic diction, and the mystical discovery of a sort of phenomenological energy that is a substitute for more material physical contacts.

Karen Oakes's " 'I stop somewhere waiting for you': Whitman's Femininity and the Reader of *Leaves of Grass,*" in *Out of Bounds: Male Writers and Gender(ed) Criticism,* ed. Laura Claridge and Elizabeth Langland (Mass.), tests Scholnick's conclusion (that Whitman's poetic love is realized in the reader) from the perspective of a feminist reader. Oakes demonstrates well how the conflicts regarding Whitman's own sexuality, which he turned into poetic resources, are the poet's own means of rebelling against a patriarchy that is not identical with "men" or "maleness" but rather with the strict binaries of "masculine" and "feminine" that feminist criticism, like other modes of cultural criticism, seeks to deconstruct. The conflicts are still there in Whitman, but Oakes's poet manages to "embrace feminine otherness" in a voice that, "though it speaks in whispers, speaks loudest to his feminine readers."

Jay Grossman's " 'The Evangel-Poem of Comrades and Love': Revising Whitman's Republicanism" (*ATQ* 4:201–18) treats the issues of sexuality in Whitman's poetry and life in a far more historical fashion, attempting to demonstrate (via Smith-Rosenberg and Foucault) that we have imposed on Whitman and his century our own anxieties about sexual preferences. Grossman's point is, I think, apt criticism of a wide range of well-intentioned commentary in the past few years on Whitman's sexuality. What Grossman attempts to do is to resituate the sexuality and eroticism of the "Calamus" poems "within the framework of reform, communitarianism, and more fluid definitions about the family" in the 19th century, thus giving back to Whitman's "sexual rebellion" its appropriate rebellious spirit for its own times.

George Hutchinson's "Whitman's Confidence Game: The 'Good Gray Poet' and the Civil War" (*SCRev* 7:20–35) is an interesting attempt to develop a social psychology out of Whitman's post-Civil War enactment of the myth of the "good gray poet." Criticizing other treatments of Whitman's postwar work as lacking the tension and vital anxiety of the poetry up to "Lilacs," Hutchinson argues that Whitman underwent a crisis of "self-representation" following the war that adds tension and interest to his poetry (see Sweet, above). Hutchinson speculates that the poet's crisis, insofar as it focuses on the death of Lincoln (both in "Lilacs" and in his address, "The Death of Lincoln"), may provide insight into the general crisis of representation in postbellum U.S. culture.

John Schwiebert's "A Delicate Balance: Whitman's Stanzaic Poems" (*WWR* 7:116–30) "examines Whitman's use of stanzaic forms and of accentual-syllabic meters in several poems written during and after the Civil War, with the aim of showing how . . . he [used] poetic structures that are novel and yet suggestive of traditional forms and rhythms." In his "Passage to More than Imagism: Whitman's Imagistic Poems" (*WWR* 8:16–28), Schwiebert treats the pictorial techniques and themes throughout *Leaves of Grass* to suggest Whitman's anticipation of the modern Imagists.

d. Criticism: Individual Works   Edward Wheat's "Walt Whitman's Political Poetics: The Therapeutic Function of 'Children of Adam' and 'Calamus'" (*MQ* 31:236–52) finds Whitman's politics primarily in the self-consciousness most reader-response theories find characteristic of literary reading. Arguing that "Children of Adam" and "Calamus" have been dealt with customarily as of interest to students of Whitman's psychobiography, Wheat treats them in terms of their purposes for liberating 19th-century readers "from repressive and distorted notions of sex and physicality inherited from the Old World." Wheat wants to reconcile the sexual politics with the larger, albeit related, social politics of Whitman's writing, which is a direction that subsequent critics should certainly follow.

Mark Edmundson's " 'Lilacs': Walt Whitman's American Elegy" (*NCL* 44:465–91) offers a comprehensive reading of "the greatest American elegy" through Freud's "Mourning and Melancholia" (1917). The reading is in effect an interpretation of "America" as the object of mourning in the poem, and the problematic of representation Edmundson identifies as the poet's is also modern America's. For Edmundson, this modernity is fundamentally divided between the lure of the past and the desire to live "with no precedents," echoing Bloom's adaptation of Freudian psycho-analysis to the culture of America (Freud's ideal case study). Read together with Sweet, Hutchinson, and Grossman (above), Edmundson adds to the debate concerning Whitman's contributions to the post-Civil War cultural dilemma: what are the hermeneutics of this new "Union"?

e. Affinities and Influences Bernard Schmidt's "Whitman and American Personalistic Philosophy" (*WWR* 7:180–90) argues that Whitman's close identification with American Transcendentalism has caused us to neglect his significance as a founding figure of American Personalism, a philosophy best represented by late 19th- and early 20th-century phi-losophers like Border Parker Bowne and Ralph Tyler Flewelling.

Martin Bidney's "Leviathan, Yggdrasil, Earth-Titan, Eagle: Bal'mont's Reimagining of Walt Whitman" (*SEEJ* 34:176–91) surveys Konstantin Bal'mont's ("the father of Russian Symbolism") interest in Whitman, including Bal'mont's publication of a volume of selections from *Leaves of Grass* (*Pobegi travy*) and four essays on Whitman.

Ernest Fontana's "Working Speakers in Whitman and Hopkins" (*WWR* 7:105–15) is "not primarily arguing influence" of Whitman on Gerard Manley Hopkins, but the essay puts forward the more interesting thesis that both poets "are among the first English language poets to represent and dramatize a first person lyric voice . . . as someone who is . . . engaged in ordinary labor." The workers are "wound-dresser or nurse in Whitman" and "working priest in Hopkins." Fontana argues that one purpose of the working persona or voice is to free the poet from the abstractions of poetry.

Richard Pascal's "Walt Whitman and Woodie Guthrie: American Prophet-Singers and Their People" (*JAmS* 24:41–59) is an interesting account of Woody Guthrie's interest in Whitman and his work. Pascal attempts to show the key themes in Whitman's poetry—sensuality, communal personality, poetic prophecy, the open road, and populist democracy, among others—at work in Guthrie's songs. Pascal reads Whitman in the well-established leftist political tradition. In that vein, he makes some good points about how both Whitman and Guthrie attempted to adapt popular media of their different periods to their own purposes, even as each was critical of the mass media.

As critics and scholars continue to situate Whitman within the turbulent politics of his times, they should remember how Whitman was *read* in his times. William Moss's "Walt Whitman in Dixie" (*SLJ* 22:98–118) shows how Whitman infuriated pro-Confederacy Southern writers (John Reuben Thompson and Paul Hamilton Hayne) during the Civil War, not only because he had received more literary attention but also because he flew so flagrantly "in the face of standards of literature, morality, and social order, and championed by the combined forces of abolition and of absolute license. . . . had achieved a notoriety, if not genuine fame, far beyond that accorded any Southern poet." In short, we must remember that Whitman did have a powerful political impact in his own times, infuriating just those groups most in need of challenge.

Walter Grünzweig's "Noble Ethics and Loving Aggressiveness: The Imperialist Walt Whitman," in *An American Empire: Expansionist Cultures and Policies, 1881–1917,* ed. Serge Ricard (Publications de l'université de Provence), argues that the liberal-progressive and leftist endorsement of Whitman in the 20th century has distracted us from the compatibility of Whitman's cosmopolitanism and internationalism with U.S. expansionist policies. Grünzweig's conclusion that "Whitman *was* an imperialist poet" is too extreme, even according to Grünzweig's own argument, but the essay reminds us that one important aspect of work on Whitman ought to be his reception in those countries and cultures in which U.S. expansionist policies had immediate impact—in particular, Latin America, the Philippines, and Asia at the turn of the century.

Enrico Mario Santí's "The Accidental Tourist: Walt Whitman in Latin America" in *Do the Americas Have a Common Literature?* addresses more carefully the issues raised in Grünzweig's essay. Santí offers an interesting institutional and intellectual history of the role Whitman's poetry played in "the Pan-Americanist ideology of the Roosevelt era." Whitman, the "Poet of Democracy," also played a part in the developing discipline of comparative literature, with its own "Good Neighbor Policy" in its "world literature" curriculum during this period. For Santí, this "pious Pan-American chorus" is typified by Fernando Alegría's *Walt Whitman en Hispanoamérica* (1954). For Santí, "the Whitman reception in Latin America" is not a simple story of cultural colonialism, but "a discourse that remains polemical and thus open to further transformation and change," in short identifying ways in which "foreign influences" can exceed ideological overdetermination and play a credible part in the "working through" of the history of, in this case, the long project of decolonization in Latin America.

ii Emily Dickinson

a. Bibliography and Editing Barbara Kelly's "Bibliography (1987–88 Mainly)" (*DicS* 73:7–22) keeps scholars up-to-date, although I wonder if we cannot begin to coordinate some of these different (and time-consuming) bibliographical endeavors now that we have the computer technologies to do more efficient searches.

b. Biography Polly Longsworth's *The World of Emily Dickinson* (Norton) is a pictorial history of Dickinson associations, focusing primarily on family portraits and photographs and locales in Amherst and its environs. It is a fine teaching aid, which may help students better visualize the time and place, if only obliquely the life, of Emily Dickinson.

c. Criticism: General Benjamin Lease's *Emily Dickinson's Readings of Men and Books: Sacred Soundings* (St. Martin's) deals primarily with two contemporaries, Charles Wadsworth and Thomas Wentworth Higginson, and such religious and literary influences as the Bible, Shakespeare, Watts's hymns, and 17th-century devotional prose and poetry. In a sense, this sort of literary and psychological biography is one way to supplement the poverty of biographical information. Lease's careful account of the fragments of correspondence (such as the "Master Letters"), biographical anecdotes regarding Dickinson's relations with Wadsworth and Higginson, and literary influences are organized around his thesis that Christian Spiritualism of the 1850s had a profound impact on Dickinson's work. This, then, is an effort to provide a history for Dickinson as inheritor of the metaphysical literary traditions and contemporary of numerous challenges to faith. But as the title all too obviously suggests,

Lease's Dickinson belongs primarily to the patriarchal times represented by the men and books she knew.

A very different history is written by the second-wave feminists who are rediscovering Dickinson's poetic power and trying thereby to reconstruct her relations to other 19th-century women writers, both in America and abroad. Paula Bennett's *Emily Dickinson: Woman Poet* (Iowa) challenges the view that Dickinson was a conflicted, middle-class poet difficult to align with 19th-century women's rights movements and changing attitudes toward gender. Instead, Bennett views Dickinson as a strong woman poet, whose poetry celebrates homoeroticism and franker treatment of sexuality in general. For Bennett, Dickinson criticizes phallocentrism in favor of a "cliterocentrism that . . . is fundamental to her work." Bennett acknowledges that there can be little biographical and historical data to support arguments that depend primarily on Dickinson's poetry, but it is an interesting thesis that lends Dickinson a power and authority commensurate to what many readers (I include myself among them) sense is a poetic authority somehow different from the usual masculine definitions of literary "mastery." Although Joanne Dobson's *Dickinson and the Strategies of Reticence* [*ALS 1989*] appeared too late for Bennett to take its arguments fully into account, Bennett's study may be interestingly read in dialogue with Dobson. Whereas Dobson views Dickinson's poetic "reticence" as characteristic of the pose of "middle-class femininity," Bennett reads this posture—Dickinson, the "poetess"—as far less determining and finally subordinate to an assertive poetic voice that anticipates the New Woman.

Bennett offers a reflection on the feminist issues in her book in "The Pea That Duty Locks: Lesbian and Feminist-Heterosexual Readings of Emily Dickinson's Poetry," in *Lesbian Texts and Contexts: Radical Revisions,* ed. Karla Jay and Joanne Glasgow (NYU): "Because of her ambiguity, . . . Dickinson has become a preeminent example of the splitting of feminist criticism along sexual orientation lines." Bennett does identify a crucial issue for feminist approaches to Dickinson (as well as other writers) in her claim that "feminist-heterosexual" approaches stress the poet's relation to patriarchy, whereas lesbian approaches, such as her own, emphasize a more confident homoeroticism in which men are "irrelevant." I think, however, that this is a reductive treatment of "feminist-heterosexual" theories. The feminist rereading of Dickinson is still very much under way and can benefit from complementary approaches, rather than adversarial positions. Without recognizing Dickinson's criticism of and often anxiety before the power of patriarchy, we are likely to modernize her excessively, thus repeating the errors of various formalisms that found her poetry's lack of historical specificity so appealing.

Bennett's lesbian reading of Dickinson certainly radicalizes the "Belle of Amherst," but in a way that other revisionary approaches to the old Dickinson—divided between Transcendentalist and modernist—must take into account. Camille Paglia's strained effort to "radicalize" Dickinson as "Amherst's Madame de Sade" in her 700-page *Sexual Personae: Art and Decadence from Nefertiti to Emily Dickinson* (Yale) is finally less essential. For one thing, Paglia subordinates the important feminist issues to her overarching concerns with the survival of Dionysian, pagan, chthonic energies in what she feels to be the excessively Apolline, Protestant worlds of "western civilization." But behind the tour-de-force performances on androgyny, theater of cruelty, barrier-bashing and crashing in the most "literary" works of that history, Paglia ends up simply defending a romantic decadence once imagined by Bloom and de Man to be the essence of Art. Paglia is rather good on "sex and violence" in Dickinson, because Dickinson *does* anticipate Artaud. De Sade may not be a "traceable" influence, but his critique of Enlightenment rationality anticipates a "romantic irony" or "extremism" with which critics have long associated Dickinson. And the high moderns long ago understood Dickinson as symbolist poet in the manner of Baudelaire, even though Paglia taunts her readers by claiming: "When she is rescued from American Studies departments and juxtaposed with Dante and Baudelaire, her barbarities and diabolical acts of will become glaringly apparent." But Paglia traces this poetic "willfulness" to Blake and Spenser, reinscribing the rather tedious patriarchal bias of such "romantic avant-gardes" as *Symbolisme* and Decadence. In sum, Paglia's own version of "romantic rebellion" in her reading of Dickinson is far too conventional, despite the stylistic pyrotechnics. Even so, Paglia's insistence on the dualism in Dickinson ("the Sadean" vs. "the Wordsworthian") does remind us that "without her struggle with God and father, there would have been no poetry." Bennett would disagree with this conclusion, but there is some justification in reconsidering the purposes of conflict and anxiety for the writer (man or woman), albeit not within the narrow confines of the Bloomian universe of macho struggles.

Judy Jo Small's *Positive as Sound: Emily Dickinson's Rhyme* (Georgia) is nominally a technical study of Dickinson's unusual rhymes and general experiments with sound. It is an especially interesting study for its treatment of music in the poetry, but also because Small adopts a reasonable approach to the feminist issues in Dickinson's poetry. Small criticizes feminist critics, such as Wendy Martin in the "Dickinson" chapter of *CLHUS,* who exaggerate the political subversion involved in Dickinson's "revolution in poetic language." As Small points out, Dickinson suffered from and addressed the patriarchal domination of women in her time, but this does not mean that all her poetic innovations constitute feminist political acts. Indeed, many politically reactionary writers throughout literary history have been able to work "innovatively" with the techniques of poetry. Although this book promises to be a formalist study of an important subject, it revises the basic assumptions of previous formalists regarding rhyme and sound—that this affective dimension allows a certain "alogical" semantic dimension to be played out in poetry otherwise committed to its own "poetic logic." Small argues that the "musical aspect" of Dickinson's poetry is far more central to her poetic arguments and that she had none of our more modern contempt for excessive melopoeia. Of special value is Small's chapter on Dickinson's use of *rime riche* (identical rhyme), "which had been for nearly three centuries unconventional and even unacceptable in English poetry." Small helps explain just why those identical rhymes in Dickinson ("sew" and "so"; "sea" and "see") produce such uncanny effects.

Gary Lee Stonum's *The Dickinson Sublime* (Wisconsin) treats the uncanniness in Dickinson's poetry in a far more comprehensive manner, arguing that she adapts the romantic aesthetics of the sublime for the sake of provoking and ultimately empowering her readers. In her special concern for the reader, Stonum's Dickinson "parts company with at least some romantic values" and heralds modernism. Stonum's method is frankly "idealist," following as it does the romantic model of self-consciousness in the Hegelian dialectic of master and servant. Yet the "advantage of the Hegelian model" for Stonum is that it offers a "far more general" theory of mastery than "Harold Bloom's theory of the anxiety of influence and any feminism that considers mastery a derivative of patriarchy rather than the other way around." Unfortunately, Hegel's own role in such patriarchy cannot be forgotten, and thus there is a sense in which the post-structuralist "romantic sublime" that Stonum adapts from Thomas Weiskell needs to be interpreted differently from the fantastic poetic sublimation we associate with Bloom's reading of Wordsworth reading Milton, for example. Stonum argues that Dickinson provides us with a model for post-romantic "mastery" that belongs to the *empowered reader*, rather than to the authoritative romantic (and patriarchal) poet-genius. Why, then, bury an argument that is complementary to the feminist readings of Dickinson in the rhetoric of a neo-Hegelianism we associate with triumphant romanticism? The answer to that is subtle, perhaps too subtle for the kinds of criticism this book will attract (unfairly, I think): Dickinson deconstructs the essential romantic paradigm for the sake not simply of empowering her gender (a "woman's poet") but also for the sake of empowering those readers that romanticism has traditionally *feminized*. Beyond the mere "emulation of mastery" called for by the romantic sublime, Dickinson offers an "affirmation of difference" that "escapes the snares of identificatory appropriation." The feminist models here would be Irigaray and Cixous, among others, who have constituted "feminine identity" in the "difference" that phallogocentrism must repress. Stonum does not draw on these Continental feminists, but he shows how Dickinson anticipates them (in a manner different from the strictly lesbian-feminist criticism of Bennett). Rather than repeating the "war" between the genders, Stonum tries to develop a theory of Dickinson's "rhetorical humanization of mastery" that is available not only to women but men as well within a "rhetoric" that is no longer simply "poetic" but communicative. If post-structuralist romanticism can adapt its terms to the debates of the 1990s, then Stonum's book shows one of the ways to do it.

On Dickinson: The Best from "American Literature", ed. Edwin Cady and Louis Budd (Duke), is a useful volume to have on the shelf, including as it does what the editors "modestly" claim to be the "best" on Dickinson from the pages of the journal from 1929 to 1988. A number of the best recent critics of Dickinson are represented—Ed Folsom, Vivian Pollak, Betsy Erkkila, Joan Burbick—but the volume is probably more valuable as a quick reference to good essays on Dickinson for classroom teachers than as a scholarly tool.

Thomas Foster's "Homelessness at Home: Placing Emily Dickinson in (Women's) History," in *Engendering Men: The Question of Male Feminist Criticism,* ed. Joseph Boone and Michael Cadden (Routledge), takes up the feminist issues in Bennett and Paglia from the theoretical perspective of reception, arguing that the status of Dickinson as either instance of the cult of domesticity or political feminist rests in large part on our "habits of reading rather than the author's individual eccentricities or any external historical determination of her life's choices."

Foster views Dickinson as a conflicted poet, who nonetheless discovers in the "contradictions" between her assigned femininity and "her capacity as a woman to resist" such a role the resource for her own poetic creativity. Most important, Dickinson must be read by male readers in terms of the contradictory position in which they are generally placed by her poetry. While the masculine gaze is thematized in the poetry, it is negated by the "privacy" Dickinson makes available to herself and other women. With its echo of Freud's " 'The Uncanny,' " Foster's title suggests how Dickinson transforms her contradictions into the *différance* of a thoroughly postmodern Emily.

The traditionally Christian Dickinson survives, although proponents of the approach make little effort to defend its positions against revisionary critics. Unlike Stonum and Foster, Suzy Holstein's "Lightning on the Landscape" (*DicS* 76:3–13) understands rhetorical sublimity in Dickinson as an allusion to "the apocalyptic vision of Revelation." In a similar manner, Kim Colton's "Sovereign Anguish: Emily Dickinson's Expanse of Pain" (*DicS* 76:30–40) treats Dickinson's poetic pain and suffering as fundamentally Christian: "Images of cross and crucifixion dominate the poems on grief." Thus the transcendental impulse in the poetry is profoundly Christian, rejecting, I presume, even the contemporary liberalism of secular transcendentalists. Both critics interpret Dickinson as if romanticism had no impact on her and as if her anticipation of modernism is of little moment. Terry Telfer's "A Religious Context for Emily Dickinson's Poetry" (*DicS* 73:37–52) also tries to address Dickinson's apparently "inconsistent religious beliefs" by claiming that her orthodox Puritan upbringing involved a skepticism that made it necessary for her to establish "a personal relationship with God," which also turns out to be Puritan orthodoxy.

If some feminist approaches to Dickinson risk dehistoricizing her work by rendering the poetry far more contemporary to our own concerns than we might like, then it is fair to conclude that previous literary histories have dehistoricized Dickinson by locating her so relentlessly within the prepackaged "Emersonianism" (and its Puritan subtext) that has caricatured the complex literature of the 19th century. Such is Margaret Dickie's argument in "Reperiodization: The Example of Emily Dickinson" (*CE* 52:397–409), which turns on her substitution of Dickinson as proto-pragmatist for Dickinson as the heiress of Transcendentalism. It is an interesting argument, albeit still very much in the context of the modernist Dickinson celebrated for her anticipation of existentialism, since Dickie's "pragmatism" (adapted from Rorty) is just that: the "philosophical counterpart of literary Modernism that denies a pre-existent or essential human truth that can be represented, takes language as part of the behavior of human beings and not as referring adequately to some world, and accepts 'the contingent character of starting-points.'"

Dickinson continues to play a part in contemporary theories of literature and art, often in terms of her anticipation of those theories (thus, the "modern" Dickinson). In "Kristeva and Poetry as Shattered Signification" (*CritI* 16:807–29), Calvin Bedient uses Dickinson's "The Malay—took the Pearl—" and "A still—Volcano—Life—" to revise Julia Kristeva's theories of desire and poetic *jouissance;* Lynn Shakinovsky's "Hidden Listeners: Dialogism in the Poetry of Emily Dickinson" (*Discourse Social/Social Discourse* 3:199–215) uses both Bakhtin and Kristeva to apply contemporary theories of "dialogism," "emphasising the double aspects of language, indeterminacy of reference" to Dickinson's obviously apt poetic examples of the same.

c. Criticism: Individual Works   The fact that Dickinson's poetry still receives attention from close readers is evident in the six items appearing throughout the year in *Expl,* which I will merely list for the sake of reference: Bernhard Frank, "Dickinson's 'I saw no way—The Heavens were stitched'" (48:28–29), who also published "Dickinson's 'I started early . . . ' [P. 520]: An Anatomy: or, Whatever Happened to Emily's Dog" (*DicS* 76:14–20); Jonnie Guerra, "Dickinson's 'The Soul has Bandaged Moments'" (48:30–32); Jesse Bier, "Dickinson's 'A Visitor in the Marl'" (48:191–93); George Monteiro, "Dickinson's 'We thirst at first'" (48:193–94) and "Dickinson's 'I'm Nobody! Who are you?'" (48:261–62); Lynn Shakinovsky, "Dickinson's 'I got so I could hear his name'" (48:258–61).

d. Affinities and Influences   Paula Bennett's "'The Orient is in the West': Emily Dickinson's Reading of *Antony and Cleopatra*," in *Women's Revisions of Shakespeare,* develops Bennett's lesbian-feminist reading of Dickinson (see above, General Criticism) by way of Dickinson's reading of Shakespeare's tragedies, especially *Antony and Cleopatra.* Although Shakespeare's Orientalized Cleopatra clearly belongs to the history of Eurocolonialism that culminates in a certain romantic thinking about that imaginary place, "The Orient" (as Edward Said has shown us), Bennett argues that Dickinson identifies with this Orientalized Cleopatra in a manner that fills the poet "with visions she could not otherwise possess." The exoticism of a feminine, pagan "Egypt" is convincingly shown by Bennett as a frequent theme in the poetry, but Bennett does not reflect on the extent to which Dickinson, in emulating this romantic cliché about the "feminine" Orient, has contributed to the ideology of her own century regarding such an imaginary "East." As John Irwin has demonstrated, such an Orient was a familiar Transcendentalist topos.

In his chapter on Dickinson in *A House Undivided,* Douglas Anderson more conventionally argues that Dickinson's conflicts typify those of the mid-century romantic struggling to translate Puritan spiritual community into terms appropriate to her times. Treating Dickinson as a more traditional heiress of Puritan typology, Anderson may thus resolve her inner conflicts, including those regarding gender, by way of the conventions of Puritan spirituality. For Anderson, the key figures are Winthrop (for his own thesis) and Milton, whom he shows Dickinson "reading" in a wide range of poems for the sake of her revisionary, but still Miltonic, *Eve:* "Rather than slip into a despair from which Adam's measured advice finally frees her, as she does in *Paradise Lost,* Dickinson's Eve is the one who explains the basis for hope, invoking the 'peace' that Eve had pleaded for."

The proto-modernist Dickinson is discussed in Eileen Gregory's "H.D.'s Volume of Dickinson's Poems; and, a Note on Candor and Iniquity" (*HDN* 3:44–46), which comments on H.D.'s copy of *The Complete Poems of Emily Dickinson* (1924 Martha Dickinson Bianchi edition) in the Beinecke Rare Book and Manuscript Library at Yale. John Felstiner also discusses the influence of Dickinson on another modernist, Paul Celan, in "So You Are Turned" (*The Threepenny Review* 43:14).

Harriet Bermann's " 'A Piercing Virtue': Emily Dickinson in Margaret Drabble's *The Waterfall"* (*MFS* 36:181–94) argues that *The Waterfall* is "a novel in which Dickinson seems almost as much incarnation as she is influence" and that the heroine, Jane Gray, "is Emily Dickinson's poetic persona reimagined by Margaret Drabble." This is, of course, another way to constitute Dickinson within the growing tradition of "herstory," insofar as the historical Dickinson "only listened in on this conversation among the women authors of her century" but now may be said to have taken an influential role in the literary conversation of modern women authors.

University of California, Irvine

6 Mark Twain

Robert Sattelmeyer

The discovery of the original manuscript of the first half of *Adventures of Huckleberry Finn* in early 1991 overshadowed the previous year's (or any year's, for that matter) scholarly work. As this essay was about to be published, the ownership of the manuscript was in dispute, and hence it was not available to scholars. Assuming that it will eventually become accessible, the Mark Twain Project hopes to revise its recently completed scholarly edition to incorporate information from the manuscript. Otherwise, a number of interesting studies made 1990 a good year for *Huck Finn* anyway, and *Pudd'nhead Wilson* continued to attract the attentions of cultural critics in ever-increasing numbers.

i Biography

Two trade press biographies appeared, neither intended primarily for a scholarly audience. John Lauber's *The Inventions of Mark Twain* (Hill & Wang) treats the entire life but in bell curve fashion: the early years and the last two decades are covered briefly, with about three-fourths of the text devoted to the period of Twain's greatest activity and success as writer/entrepreneur, from *Innocents Abroad* in 1869 to *Huck Finn* and the Grant *Memoirs* in 1885. As the title implies, the notion of Twain as inventor underlies the story, a rubric flexible enough to cover his writing, his involvement in business and technology, and his complex domestic life. Neither thesis-ridden nor psychologically adventurous, *The Inventions of Mark Twain* rests firmly though not uncritically on primary doc-

*Thanks to Leigh Kirkland and Pearl McHaney for research assistance in preparing this essay.

uments and can be trusted as a reliable guide to the more smiling aspects of Twain's major phase. Less reliable is Margaret Sanborn's *Mark Twain: The Bachelor Years* (Doubleday), a popular study that does tend to rely uncritically on Mark Twain's fictional and autobiographical accounts of his early years for most of its information. It thus adds little to what has been known and perpetuates many myths and misconceptions about Twain's early years. Characteristic of its technique of biographical back-formation is an observation about Twain's experience on the Quarles farm: "He also learned to tell time with his nose—whether it 'smelt late' or early" (p. 26).

There were a smattering of biographical articles, the most significant of which was Gary Scharnhorst, "Mark Twain's Imbroglio with the San Francisco Police: Three Lost Texts" (*AL* 62:686–91), which prints a part of Twain's hitherto lost "San Francisco Letter" (attacking police chief Martin Burke) from the Virginia City *Territorial Enterprise* of January 23, 1866. Scharnhorst discovered that it was partially reprinted in the San Francisco *Daily Examiner,* along with two sequels. Comparing the chief to a dog and implying that he kept a mistress, the letters help explain why Twain was persona non grata with the police during the months before his departure for the East. Carl Dolmetsch's "Mark Twain Abroad: How the American Humorist Explored the Musical Life of *Fin-de-Siècle* Vienna" (*Musical America: The Journal of Classical Music* 110, March: 53–56) usefully surveys Twain's involvement in Viennese musical circles from 1897 to 1899 while Clara was studying piano with Theodor Lesche-tizky. During this period Twain had more significant contacts with music and musicians than at any other time in his life, hearing or meeting the likes of Johann Strauss, Gustav Mahler, Artur Schnabel, and Fritz Kreisler. Dennis Welland's "Mark Twain in Scotland" (*Scots Maga-zine* 133:600–607) is less about its titular subject than about Twain's friendship with Dr. John Brown, Scottish physician and essayist (best known as the author of "Rab and His Friends"), who treated Livy for an illness during the Clemenses' visit to Britain in 1873. Finally, three brief articles in *MTJ* 26, ii (Fall 1988, but actually mailed in early 1991) provide details from local newspapers relating to Twain's 1895 lecture tour around the world: David Zmijewski, "Hawaii Awaits a Legend" (pp. 21–27), Miriam J. Shillingsburg, "Additional Antipodean Anecdotes, Apocry-phal Adventures" (pp. 28–29), and Philip V. Allingham, "Mark Twain in Victoria, British Columbia, August, 1895" (pp. 30–31).

ii Editions

Anyone seriously (or humorously) interested in Mark Twain will want to own as well as read Michael J. Kiskis's edition of *Mark Twain's Own Autobiography: The Chapters from The North American Review* (Wisconsin). It reprints for the first time the selections Twain made from his autobiographical writings and dictations for the *North American Review* in 1906 and 1907. The text is quite different from the editions compiled by Paine, De Voto, and Neider, and *Mark Twain's Own Autobiography* will have a critical as well as a documentary significance as examination of the complex issues raised by Twain's published and unpublished autobiographical works continues. Kiskis's introduction summarizes the history and distinguishing features of the posthumous editions, and the appendix lists the varying contents and arrangement of episodes in the different published autobiographical texts.

iii General Interpretations

Maria Ornella Marotti's *The Duplicating Imagination: Twain and the Twain Papers* (Penn State) takes as its nominal subject the mass of material gradually coming out in the Mark Twain Papers series, but focuses mainly on the late, fragmentary fiction. The originality and usefulness of her study lie in its "text-centered" approach. Instead of the customary interpretation of these late works in biographical or cultural contexts, she selectively applies a smorgasbord of contemporary, mostly European, theoretical and critical perspectives to various works, especially quasi-science fiction pieces like "The Enchanted Sea-Wilderness" and the *Mysterious Stranger* manuscripts. Her study is suggestive in establishing links between these late works and patterns that emerged in Twain's earliest burlesques and satires, and in examining from a structuralist angle the functions of myth in the late works. She sees Twain as simultaneously enacting the three relations toward myth proposed by Roland Barthes: mythmaker, mythologist (critic of myth), and reader of myth. Twain is customarily associated with the mythologist's role, as critic of the myths of his culture, but Marotti stresses the importance of his mythmaking role in the late fiction, as he strives to revitalize genuine myth in his adaptations of archetypes like the child/trickster figure of "No. 44" in the *Mysterious Stranger* manuscripts. (See, in this context,

Tuckey's "Mark Twain, the Youth Who Lived on in the Sage," below.)
Conceptually, this study is compromised by the heteroglossia (to use one
of Marotti's favorite Bakhtinian terms) of its multiple theoretical perspectives, as well as by its premise that the Mark Twain Papers themselves
are a discrete body of works that can usefully be studied together, when
the title represents a necessarily arbitrary editorial designation.

There were only a few articles treating general aspects of Twain's
career. A posthumously published essay by Henry Nash Smith, "Mark
Twain, Ritual Clown," pp. 235–54 in Beverly R. Voloshin, ed., *American
Literature, Culture, and Ideology,* sees Twain's celebrity and the anxiety it
caused some guardians of high culture as stemming from his status as
Ritual Clown, a subspecies of the Trickster figure observed by anthropol-
ogists in some preliterate cultures. The Ritual Clown violates taboos and
challenges conventions, and in so doing incurs the guilt of society as a
whole. Smith posits that Twain served this function in his culture "as
part of an underground stream of folklore, of which neither he nor his
audience was aware" (p. 240). Following up a 1989 article, Marlene Boyd
Vallin's " 'Manner is Everything': The Secret to Mark Twain's Performing
Success" (*JPC* 24:81–90) suggests that Twain's success as a lecturer was a
result of his lifelong fascination with the speech process. She treats the
somewhat neglected aspect of Twain's career as a public performer in a
general way; more attention needs to be paid to the actual records—
reading texts, newspaper accounts, etc.—of Twain's public performances.

Mainly theoretical pieces that cite Mark Twain include Robert Weimann, "Realism, Ideology, and the Novel in America (1886–1896):
Changing Perspectives in the Works of Mark Twain, W. D. Howells, and
Henry James" (*Boundary 2* 17, i:189–210). Like most studies of this
nature, it paints with a broad brush. Weimann says that Twain was ill-
equipped to adjust to the "impersonal realities of economic centraliza-
tion, political corruption, imperialist expansion and exploitation, and
the changing social and cultural norms of city-centered life" that characterized his age, and consequently his late works exhibit "either the cynical
use or the rejection of current ideological concepts of morality" (p. 196).
Forrest G. Robinson's "The New Historicism and the Old West" (*WAL*
25:103–23) mentions a number of "westerns," among them *Roughing It,
Tom Sawyer,* and *Huckleberry Finn,* in considering how the New Historicism approaches the history and myths of the West. Robinson also
attempts to define the New Historicism (no easy task) and to differentiate
it from what he terms the New Americanism of Sacvan Bercovitch.

iv **Individual Works Through 1885**

Americanists of most persuasions are likely to find Eyal Naveh's "A Spellbound Civilization: The Mediterranean Basin and the Holy Land According to Mark Twain's Travel Book *Innocents Abroad*" (*Mediterranean Historical Review* 5:44–61) old news rather than new history. He argues that the book's perennial popularity in the 19th century stemmed from its dramatization of American ideology: the moribund Old World (especially the Near East and the Holy Land) leaves the way clear for the renewal of civilization in the New World. Like the owl who visited the knothole, though, he does not find anything funny about it. Neither does James L. Busskohl in " 'The Story of the Old Ram' and the Tenderfoot Writer" (*SAF* 18:183–92) find much amusing about Jim Blaine's story. Instead, it is a cautionary tale that dramatizes the problems faced by a young writer when the chaos of facts encounters the failure of romantic expectations. He links the tale to its context in *Roughing It*, where Twain is about to set out for San Francisco to become a writer. The solemnity of this article may be gauged by Busskohl's reference to the episode of Miss Wagner and her glass eye as "a version of the disassembled woman motif" (p. 185). Truly a deadpan performance.

Edgar M. Branch provides a characteristically meticulous and insightful study of " 'Old Times on the Mississippi': Biography and Craftsmanship" (*NCL* 45:73–87), documenting the considerable gulf between Twain's actual experiences as a steersman and pilot and his imaginative re-creation of them in "Old Times." These disparities serve as a springboard for Branch to examine not only the personal reasons underlying Twain's shadings of truth but also his careful artistic shaping of the series. Stephen Cooper's " 'Good Rotten Material for Burial': The Overdetermined Death of Romance in *Life on the Mississippi*" (*L&P* 36:78–89) is a psychoanalytic study that correlates the pattern of violent and gory death in *Life on the Mississippi* with its critique of romanticism, and sees both as a delayed reaction to Twain's guilt over his brother Henry's death, a process Cooper terms "the displaced hostility of defensive overcompensation" (p. 82). It is a study that could profit by a consideration of the evidence about Twain's reaction to Henry's death collected and analyzed in Edgar M. Branch's *Men Call Me Lucky* (1985).

A thoroughly modern Mark Twain can be found in William H. Andrews, "Mark Twain, William Wells Brown, and the Problem of Authority in New South Writing," pp. 1–21 in Jefferson Humphries, ed.,

Southern Literature and Literary Theory. Andrews claims that *Life on the Mississippi* and Brown's *My Southern Home* (1880) are the first avatars of a new kind of post-Reconstruction Southern writing concerned with establishing a new, more provisional and contingent basis for literature because old sources of authority had been de-authorized by the Civil War. *Life on the Mississippi,* then, "authorizes itself by de-authorizing its narrator, southern life and history, even its reader's expectations, as priorities to which it must bind itself and appeal in order to assume an 'author-function' in the new literary scheme of things" (p. 10). In many ways the opposite is argued—but with equal density—in Howard Horwitz's " 'Ours by the Law of Nature': Romance and Independents on Mark Twain's River" (*Boundary 2* 17, i:243–71). Here the economic constraints of capitalist culture rather than the freedoms of the text are foregrounded. Horwitz argues that the fabled independence of the Mississippi pilot as described by Mark Twain has been too narrowly conceived; it is only a contractual freedom which, like all freedoms in a market economy, is constrained, and thus "the more-than-regal independence Twain imagines for the pilot is impossible" (p. 271). Horwitz does not distinguish between the portraits of piloting in "Old Times" and *Life on the Mississippi*—citing only the latter, and in the Signet paperback edition to boot.

Finally, Lawrence I. Berkove follows up a recent piece with "New Information on Dan De Quille and 'Old Times on the Mississippi' " (*MTJ* 26, ii:15–20). He shows that a sketch De Quille wrote on "Pilot Wylie," which probably influenced Twain's portrait of "Stephen W.," was reprinted in the Hartford *Courant* while Twain was working on the final section of "Old Times." Berkove also locates an additional source for "Old Times" in an 1861 newspaper piece by De Quille.

Not surprisingly, there were more than a dozen substantial articles on *Adventures of Huckleberry Finn.* More surprisingly, many of them were good. The only book-length work was edited by Harold Bloom, a collection of previously published essays and extracts, *Huck Finn,* in his Major Literary Characters series (Chelsea). The volume has a brief introduction and a note on "The Analysis of Character" by Bloom (whose proliferating editorial projects threaten to make him the Earl Scheib of American criticism), 21 "critical extracts" on Huck, and a dozen essays reprinted in their entirety. It is a useful sampler of commentary on Huck (though printed in one of the most spidery typefaces ever inflicted on a reader), collecting most of the old chestnuts (Howells,

Hemingway, Faulkner, Trilling, Marx, Fiedler, etc.) in the "extracts" section, and focusing on more recent, often revisionist opinion by such critics as Harold Beaver, Forrest G. Robinson, and Susan K. Harris in its choice of essays.

Among new essays, general revaluations were offered by Tom Quirk and Wayne Fields. Quirk's "Nobility Out of Tatters: The Writing of *Huckleberry Finn,*" pp. 79–105 in James Barbour and Tom Quirk, eds., *Writing the American Classics,* is a genetic interpretation based mainly on Walter Blair's scholarship and Wright Morris's perceptive comments about the nature of fiction. Quirk's account of the novel's composition stresses its affirmations pressing irresistibly against Twain's stated pessimism and determinism. He finds that the possibilities of fiction allowed Twain, through his identification with Huck, to imagine "himself more completely human than he probably was himself, and in so doing he provided his readers with the same opportunity" (p. 80). Also written for the general reader, Wayne Fields's "When the Fences Are Down; Language and Order in *The Adventures of Tom Sawyer* and *Huckleberry Finn*" (*JAmS* 24:369–86) takes a leisurely excursion through the worlds of Twain's boy books, finding that the walls and fences in *Tom Sawyer* mark St. Petersburg as a place of strict moral, civil, and linguistic order. In *Huckleberry Finn* the fences are down, especially the linguistic ones, and Huck's language establishes a positive alternative to the stifling, life-denying atmosphere of the small town.

The most original and provocative essay was Gerry Brenner's "More than a Reader's Response: A Letter to 'De Ole True Huck'" (*JNT* 20:221–34), which purports to be a letter from Jim's son Johnny to Huck, recounting his father's reactions to hearing Huck's account of their adventures read to him. If you can get past the improbable "plot" and the awkward dialect in which Jim's version of events is cast, it is a fascinating premise, played out cleverly, that interrogates the racial issues from a new angle. Jim claims to have been "signifying" Huck right along to protect his life and safety. For his part, Huck, without the protective coloration of his own narrative voice, reveals a "mean streak," playing dangerous tricks on Jim in response to having been bested by him in debates. James Phelan responds to Brenner's article in "On the Nature and Status of Covert Texts: A Reply to Gerry Brenner's 'Letter to 'De Ole True Huck'" (*JNT* 20:235–44), using it as an occasion to explore the intricacies of "covert texts" and the grounds for their interpretation. Phelan argues that the nature of naive, first-person narration makes Brenner's critique of Huck less than convincing, but finds that his reading opens up possibilities for seeing Jim's complexity and sophistication. Another sympathetic look at Jim is Aileen Chris Shafer's "Jim's Discourses in *Huckleberry Finn*" (*SoSt* 1:149–63), a Bakhtinian analysis of his language, focusing on his shifting discourses and his "signifying" to further his aims and overcome his status as an object within racial discourse.

The literal portrayal of Jim is the subject of Earl F. Briden, "Kemble's 'Specialty' and the Pictorial Countertext of *Huckleberry Finn*" (*MTJ* 26, ii:2–14). Kemble's specialty (which would have been known to Twain when he was chosen to illustrate *Huck Finn*) was the depiction of black characters in demeaning and grotesque comic stereotypes. His portrayals of Jim generally conform to these stereotypes and are part of a "pictorial countertext" designed to lead a reader's response away from the novel's serious or controversial aspects. For choosing Kemble and failing to object to the portrayal of Jim (he did object to Kemble's depictions of other characters in the novel), Twain himself is partly to blame. This is one of the rare treatments of race in the novel that really dramatizes—all distressingly—the cultural climate in which *Huck Finn* appeared.

A monograph published by *MTJ*, Dennis J. Spininger's *Tom Sawyer's "Whoopjamboreehoo": The Mixed-Up and Splendid Ending of "Huckleberry Finn,"* adds to recent attempts to rehabilitate Tom Sawyer. Spininger finds the "mixed-up and splendid" concluding episodes are entirely appropriate, since according to the conventions of its genre—tragicomedy—all tragic implications must finally be overcome. No positive resolution is possible through Huck's vernacular values, which point toward realism and hence the impossibility of Jim's freedom. Tom Sawyer's "Evasion," besides its function as satire of romantic literature, also serves to elevate Jim into a truly "noble prisoner" and to suggest both the heroic dimension of his suffering and the significance of his freedom. Another, less compelling defense of the ending is Ronald J. Black's "The Psychological Necessity of the Evasion Sequence in *Huckleberry Finn*" (*CEA* 52:35–43), which diagnoses Huck as suffering "severe depression, paranoia, and an overriding wish to escape from his mental torment through death" (p. 37), brought on by unexpiated guilt incurred from his defiance of society. The Evasion "fulfills Huck's unconscious desire for expiation" by prolonging his and Jim's suffering.

Two very nice essays appeared in the same issue of *TSLL*. John Bird's "The Chains of Time: Temporality in *Huckleberry Finn*" (32:262–76) examines the flow of time, both literal and psychological, and argues that the novel as a whole can be read as Huck's failed attempt to escape "the confinement of time's pervasiveness," since it begins with Huck being called by the Widow's bell and concludes with his looking at Tom Sawyer's watch. One of the essay's more notable achievements is its careful compilation of references to the passage of time, dating the events of the narrative quite convincingly. Keith Opdahl's " 'The Rest Is Just Cheating': When Good Feelings Go Bad in *Adventures of Huckleberry Finn*" (32:277–93) seems at first as though it might be another impressionistic derogation of the conclusion, but turns out instead to be a very sensitive and sensible analysis of the precise changes in style and narrative technique that might cause a reader's good feeling to go bad. Opdahl argues that Huck, after his moving description of the Sunday stillness at the Phelps plantation, ceases for the most part to describe his own sensations, with the result that "the novel . . . ceases to be a first-person narration. Huck remains the technical narrator, of course, but the story moves outside of him, where Huck describes not his private sensations but external events" (p. 281).

Ed Kleiman's "Mark Twain's 'Rhapsody': Printing and the Oral Tradition in *Huckleberry Finn*" (*UTQ* 59:535–48) gives an Ongian spin to the familiar idea that the rendering of vernacular speech gives a special significance to the novel. He argues that the book denigrates the written word and that not merely vernacular speech but the oral tradition itself provides the basis for just about everything of value in the novel. This privileging of the oral over the written may be the current version of the golden age scam. It seems naive to suppose that life was more authentic and people more virtuous because nobody could make a shopping list, and Kleiman's enterprise has the marks of a Sunday school about it besides. Here is his description of the (written) prefatory matter of *Huck Finn*: "Together, both 'Notice' and 'Explanatory' insist that we open our ears to the authentic tones of all the voices that sound through this work, the living 'word' speaking in familiar tongues from the surface of the Mississippi waters" (p. 542).

In what must have been a labor of considerable love, Erik Löfroth compared 15 Swedish translations of *Huckleberry Finn* going back to 1885 in "Huck for Short; or One Hundred Years of Solicitude" (*SN* 62:61–77). Aside from a tendency to make Jim sound moronic by rendering his dialect in a form of pidgin Swedish, the most persistent trend over time was that the translations got shorter, omitting more and more of the moral complexity of the book, especially of Huck's conflict over freeing

Jim, and turning it increasingly into a simple adventure story. In "Satire and the Evolution of Perspective in Children's Literature: Mark Twain, E. B. White, and Louise Fitzhugh" (*CLAQ* 15:119–22), J. D. Stahl discusses Huck's naive reading of his society as a stage in the emergence of satire in literature for children. The only new source offered for the novel was Peter G. Beidler's "Christian Schultz's *Travels:* A New Source for *Huckleberry Finn?*" (*ELN* 28, ii:51–61), which suggests the influence on the basis of similarities of description and incident, but without direct verbal parallels or evidence that Twain actually read Schultz's travel book. An *Expl* item by William Thierfelder, "Twain's *Huckleberry Finn*" (48:194–95), proposes that Huck's account of his faked murder alludes to the biblical stories of Joseph's feigned death (in which his coat was sprinkled with blood) and the Passover story of lambs' blood smeared on doorposts. Finally, a fascinating article by Steven Mailloux, "The Rhetorical Use and Abuse of Fiction: Eating Books in Late Nineteenth-Century America" (*Boundary 2* 17, i:133–57), touches briefly but intriguingly on *Huckleberry Finn* in the context of a wave of anxiety over juvenile delinquency during the mid-1880s—what one newspaper called the "Bad-Boy Boom."

v Individual Works After 1885

In an apparent instance of the duplicating imagination at work, Wayne R. Kime published the same article twice, as "Huck Finn Out West: Mark Twain's Use of Richard Irving Dodge's *The Plains of the Great West and Their Inhabitants*" (*BWVACET* [1989] 11:1–11), and as "Huck Among the Indians: Mark Twain and Richard Irving Dodge's *The Plains of the Great West and Their Inhabitants*" (*WAL* 24:321–33). He thus doubly elaborates what Walter Blair and others have noted about Twain's extensive use of Dodge's negative portrayals of Native Americans, and suggests that both the rape/violation plot and the unfamiliar setting caused him to abandon the sequel.

Connecticut Yankee continued to generate interest in the year following its centennial. The most substantial essay was Horst H. Kruse, "Mark Twain's *A Connecticut Yankee:* Reconsiderations and Revisions" (*AL* 62:464–83), which greatly extends our knowledge of the public launching of the novel, showing how Twain manipulated both a charge of plagiarism (from Max Adeler's "The Fortunate Island") and current newspaper stories about aristocratic depravity and the founding of a republic in Brazil into favorable publicity and reviews for his book. Most fascinating in the unfolding of this story is Twain's reconceiving his book in the light of events which happened after he finished it.

In *"A Connecticut Yankee:* A Serious Hoax" (*EAS* 19:28–44), Lawrence I. Berkove takes a stand against Hank Morgan, arguing that his efforts to teach the villagers political economy in chapters 31–34 reveal the inconsistencies in both his character and his principles; the novel constitutes a "serious hoax" because its underlying message is that human beings are double damned in a Calvinistic sense—both by predestination and their inherently evil nature. Ronald M. Johnson's "Future as Past, Past as Future: Edward Bellamy, Mark Twain, and the Crisis of the 1880s" (*AmerSS* 22:73–80) is a fairly generalized comparison of *Connecticut Yankee* and *Looking Backward* as utopian novels responding to labor and economic troubles.

Continuing a trend of recent years, *Pudd'nhead Wilson* was subjected to intense scrutiny for its evocations of 19th-century American cultural maladies, particularly in a collection of 12 essays edited by Susan Gillman and Forrest G. Robinson, *Mark Twain's "Pudd'nhead Wilson": Race, Conflict, and Culture* (Duke). Nearly all the essays assume that the novel's celebrated flaws are really its most important features: "We read the incoherence in Twain's narrative not as aesthetic failure but as political symptom, the irruption into this narrative about mistaken racial identity of materials from the nineteenth-century political unconscious" (p. vii).

Two of the essays (Gillman's "Sure Identifiers: Race, Science, and the Law in *Pudd'nhead Wilson,*" and Eric J. Sundquist's "Mark Twain and Homer Plessy") are reprinted and have already been reviewed in *ALS,* but a formidable lineup remains. In *"Pudd'nhead Wilson* Revisited" (pp. 1–21), James M. Cox provides a typically canny meditation on the novel in relation both to Twain's earlier career and to the issues it dramatizes. He emphasizes the significance of *will*—both the legal instrument and volition—and notes what a number of critics have stressed recently, that the apparently deracinated figure of David Wilson is not only an exposer of the ills of American culture but also an example of them. Although he is "the very instrument for exposing the passage of sexual energy crossing racial lines," Wilson "comes not to destroy the society but to occupy, examine, and finally administer it"—colonial imperialism, antebellum Missouri-style.

Cox's concluding observation, that Mark Twain sought freedom rather than mastery in his art, surrendering to impulse and leaving the mastery to Henry James, is taken up by Forrest G. Robinson in "The Sense of Disorder in *Pudd'nhead Wilson*" (pp. 22–45). Robinson extends his conception of "bad faith" (developed in his earlier study *In Bad Faith: The Dynamics of Deception in Mark Twain's America* [1988]). He argues that the murder/mystery plot and the race/slavery plot are interdependent at the deepest level because Twain needed the former in order to suppress the latter; he needed a conclusion—Wilson's courtroom triumph—that would permit him to suppress the disturbing implications of the story of Roxy and Tom and thus complete the circuit of bad faith endemic in a culture in which slavery existed in a nominally Christian and democratic context. Michael Rogin's "Francis Galton and Mark Twain: The Natal Autograph in *Pudd'nhead Wilson*" (pp. 73–85) explores the race/slavery complex from the perspective opened up by Galton, who was the father both of fingerprinting as a device for determining identity and of eugenics. He argues, rather elliptically, that whereas Galton was disappointed in his efforts to link these markers of identity with racial characteristics, the fingerprints in *Pudd'nhead Wilson* become the sure identifiers of precisely the fixed and inescapable taint of "blackness" that characterizes Tom Driscoll, and that Twain's reversal of Galton reflects the increasing racial polarization of America in the 1890s.

Making perhaps the most extreme case for the "failure" of the novel as a reflection of the failures of American civilization, Myra Jehlen in "The Ties That Bind: Race and Sex in *Pudd'nhead Wilson*" (pp. 105–20) claims that the problems the novel raises "were made impossible to resolve by the history of racial and sexual thinking in America" (p. 105). In addition to noting, as many others have done, the absurd nature of racial identity in the novel, Jehlen argues for the importance of sexual identity as a powerful contributor to the representative confusion in the novel. She points out that there are deep-seated cultural reasons, having to do with the construction of black/white, male/female identities, for the fact that Twain "endorses a black woman's subversion of the white patriarchy, whereas in Tom, he rejects a black man's takeover" (p. 112). In a complementary vein, Carolyn Porter focuses on "Roxana's Plot" (pp. 121–36), in which—however temporarily—Roxana seizes the white male slaveowners' power of naming (or rather not naming) their progeny by her switching of the babies. The fact that "the condition of the mother" determined one's status as a slave opens a space for Roxy to act. If she and her plan are ultimately defeated, they nevertheless succeed in exposing the fallacies of the white patriarchy.

In contrast to most of the articles, which see the novel as reflecting the worsening racial climate of the 1890s, John Carlos Rowe's "Fatal Speculations: Murder, Money, and Manners in *Pudd'nhead Wilson*" (pp. 137–54) locates the roots of Gilded Age corruption and speculative excess in the antebellum slaveholding economy of places like Dawson's Landing, and it links the maze of speculations in *Pudd'nhead Wilson* to Twain's earlier critique in *The Gilded Age.* The argument rests somewhat tenuously on Rowe's attempt to establish Tom Driscoll as the son of Percy Driscoll rather than Cecil Burleigh Essex, but is on firmer ground in seeing David Wilson as the "appropriate heir" to the FFVs, the man who as mayor will lead the town from its rural to its urban phase—an accountant/lawyer who legitimizes the sins of the fathers on the scientific footing of fingerprints.

Two essays take up the issues of politics and government in the novel: Michael Cowan, " 'By Right of the White Election': Political Theology and Theological Politics in *Pudd'nhead Wilson*" (pp. 155–76), and Wilson Carey McWilliams, "*Pudd'nhead Wilson* on Democratic Governance" (pp. 177–89). Cowan argues that the narratives "offer in fragmentary, provisional form what we might call a politics of theological discourse, or a theological politics, one related complexly to the racial politics of *Pudd'nhead Wilson* and to the general political and legal processes and assumptions of *Those Extraordinary Twins*" (p. 156). The reader will be required to find a way through a thicket of slippery metaphoric analogies and allusions to find out if this is so. McWilliams takes a more direct approach, pointing out cogently that while the novel's preoccupations with who should rule, party politics, and principle provide an apparently "complete chapter in the democratization of political life" in Jacksonian America, the treatment of these issues also reveals the structural flaws and limits of the system.

Unlike most of the other essays, George E. Marcus's " 'What did he reckon would become of the other half if he killed his half?': Doubled, Divided, and Crossed Selves in *Pudd'nhead Wilson;* or, Mark Twain as Cultural Critic in His Own Times and Ours" (pp. 190–210) considers Mark Twain as an active and self-conscious cultural critic rather than an inadvertent one. He does not describe an "irruption . . . of materials from the nineteenth-century political unconscious" but a writer poised through his experimentation with doubled and divided selves on the brink of a modern and even postmodern insight into the breakdown of belief in the authority and the autonomy of the self.

The editors left the back door of the collection open, and a chill wind blows in from the last essay, John H. Schaar's "Some of the Ways of Freedom in *Pudd'nhead Wilson*" (pp. 211–27). Dissenting from the premises of the other contributors, Schaar questions the "marshaling of so much intellectual artillery upon so small a target" (p. 211), and he is certainly not the first to feel that such relentless analyses demonstrate that "the study of literature in universities is threatened by overtheorization and by the methodist passion that has wasted vast tracts of the social sciences" (p. 213). With respect to *Pudd'nhead Wilson,* he believes that the characters do not repay deep analysis because "they are collections of themes or traits rather than individual human beings. . . . There is no more there than meets the eye" (p. 215), a point which, if taken, would cast a kind of Emperor's New Clothes pall over much recent work on the novel. The novel's value, Schaar believes, is only that reading it might stimulate one's thinking about such troublesome and ill-defined concepts as "freedom" and "liberty," and the classifications according to which we designate human beings and thereby accord or deny them rights and liberties.

Shelley Fisher Fishkin's "Race and Culture at the Century's End: A Social Context for *Pudd'nhead Wilson"(EAS* 19:1–27), on the other hand, sees the novel as a beacon shining against the racism and repression of the 1880s and 90s, stressing Twain's many statements and actions on behalf of African Americans during a time when most white authors were silent. Still, Fishkin points out, Twain remained embedded in white culture, as a comparison of *Pudd'nhead Wilson* to works by W. E. B. DuBois and Paul Laurence Dunbar reveals. Less au courant approaches to the novel were taken by Patricia M. Mandia, "Children of Fate and Irony in *Pudd'nhead Wilson* (*LangQ* 28:29–40), who finds the novel to be a forerunner of contemporary black humor, and David Zmijewski's "The Design of Doom in Mark Twain's *Pudd'nhead Wilson*" (*Tokei University Junior College Life Science Research Center Journal,* 3:68–75), whose "design of doom" is the closed frontier community which enslaves the characters without their being aware of it.

"Villagers of 1840–3" had its severed ending reunited with the beginning of the sketch for the first time in last year's *Huck Finn and Tom Sawyer Among the Indians, and Other Unfinished Stories* (see *ALS* 1989). Additional details of that reunion are provided by Sam Howard, who first discovered the matching sections, in "The Ending to Mark Twain's 'Villagers of 1840–3'" (*ALR* 22, iii:87–90).

The late John S. Tuckey's "Mark Twain: The Youth Who Lived on in the Sage," the second in the *Quarry Farm Papers* series published by the Elmira College Center for Mark Twain Studies, briefly recapitulates the three versions of the Mysterious Stranger manuscripts, emphasizing "No. 44" as a figure who represents a late growth by Twain toward "psychic wholeness," given both his own creative powers and the fact that those powers latently reside in August, the human protagonist of this version.

Along with Michael Kiskis's edition of *Mark Twain's Own Autobiography* (discussed in the Editions section above), the autobiographical writings were examined in an illuminating essay by Robert Atwan, "The Territory Behind: Mark Twain and His Autobiographies," pp. 39–51 in J. Bill Berry, ed., *Located Lives*. After surveying the editorial principles of Paine, De Voto, and Neider, Atwan addresses the "compositional challenge" that Twain set for himself by abandoning chronological structure, and places his autobiographical writing in the Southern tradition by virtue of its oral qualities, its emphasis on place and family, and (here diverging most sharply from conventional American autobiography) the fact that it is neither successive (i.e., developmental, progressive) nor a success story.

Georgia State University

7 Henry James

Richard A. Hocks

Although James scholarship in 1990 stays high in quantity with more than a hundred items (plus 15 more dissertations!), some of its physiognomy is changing interestingly. Last year (1989) produced 15 books. For 1990 there are "only" seven critical studies (plus Bonney MacDonald's *Henry James's Italian Hours,* which I covered in advance last year); these include an annus mirabilis by Daniel Fogel, superb work by Philip Horne and Jonathan Freedman, excellent analyses by Peggy McCormack and Edwin Fussell, and a new study of the tales. There are two important collections of critical essays, one of which, ed. James Tuttleton and Agostino Lombardo, is a major achievement signaling two of those new "facial features" of James scholarship—Italy and James family relations. The reader will also find outstanding articles by William Veeder, Linda Raphael, Dana Ringuette, Myler Wilkinson, Henry McDonald, Mary Ventura, Gary Scharnhorst, Richard Lyons, and several others a grace note below. Moreover, Greg Zacharias and Ian F. A. Bell are 1990's most prolific article writers. Finally, we have for once "almost" a reprieve from *The Turn of the Screw.*

i Editions, Reference Works, Biographical Studies

Jamesian aficionados will be delighted by the republication of Leon Edel's edition of *The Complete Plays of Henry James* (Oxford) 41 years after its original appearance. James's well-known failure as playwright unfortunately has obscured Edel's magnificent editorial work with this volume, the high quality of which exceeds, to my mind, his *Complete Tales* and makes one think instead of his and Lyall Powers's recent *Complete Notebooks.* The edition was (and thus is) clearly a labor of love, with its separate generous prefaces for each of the 21 plays or fragments between 1869 and 1913, its extensive biographical chapter on James's dramatic years, and its new preface-retrospection which perceptively explores a double irony many Jamesians know: first, the fact that James "was in reality a dramatist who could not write plays," so that the late novels and tales somehow converted the playwright's inability into fictive gold; second, the fact that James's works have flourished, indeed "been metamorphosed into new media. Other less gifted hands have achieved the translation of James's subtle fiction into the audiovisual realm"— much of which Edel surveys (overlooking, however, the BBC *Spoils of Poynton* and the early 1960s "Playhouse 90" version of *Wings of the Dove*). The handsome volume even includes correspondence between James and Bernard Shaw. Bernice Grohskopf's " 'I'll be a Farmer': Boyhood Letters of William James" (*VQR* 66:585–600) examines William's letters expressing anxieties about his future vocation, but mentioning as well his feelings about his European travels and education, experiences he shared with Henry, whose illness with typhus fever he recounts. A brief note by Henry on this same subject is included.

Steven H. Jobe performs an enormous service for all Jamesians with his "A Calendar of the Published Letters of Henry James: Parts I & II" (*HJR* 11:1–29; 77–100), thereby beginning the arduous process of bringing some system to the long-standing confusion over the full corpus of James's prolific letter writing. This inclusive calendar contains 2,422 entries from what is now an estimated 15,000 extant letters by James. Edel's four-volume edition has 1,092; Lubbock's 1920 edition has but 403. Jobe's "labor intensive" project is obviously an ongoing one made possible by computer technology. All entries (which do not include fragments) provide the reader with all pertinent information regarding each letter in abbreviated form. Jobe's other 1990 contribution, "Henry James and the Philosophic Actor" (*AL* 62:32–43), argues that James's preference for self-controlled "philosophic" actors like William Charles Macready reflects his indebtedness to Emerson's vision of the "selfless self," an idea reminiscent of Keats's negative capability.

Novelists in Their Youth by John Halperin (St. Martin's) takes the position, contra deconstruction, that a "secret life" or "psychic wound" accessible to biography provides the link to an author's creativity. While applying this thesis to six novelists, Halperin's "Inside Henry James" (pp. 11–54) contends that his stressful youth resulted in an epiphany, at eighteen, when Lincoln called for troops, that he was not meant for "normal male activities"—like "fighting and sex." The celebrated obscure wound was thus "psychic," but it released him to create fiction wherein no "relationship between the sexes . . . is wholly satisfactory," and his *literary* pleasure at beloved Minny Temple's death was the source of his lifelong "vampire" theme. "It was always the extinction of vitality that was to move James, not its fulfillment or its triumph." James's "passional death," as Halperin also calls it, is too univocal a cause even for those fictions that fit the thesis; but what does one do with *The Golden Bowl*? "Henry James's Boston" (*IowaR* 20:158–65) by Alexander Theroux outlines James's Boston as holding for the artist ghostly memories of his youth, even though his former haunts were radically changed when he revisited them 20 years later. Finally, R. W. B. Lewis's "Henry James Senior: The Engendering Self" in *American Literature, Culture, and Ideology,* ed. Beverly R. Voloshin (pp. 133–68), and Lewis's "Homecomings" (*SAQ* 89:457–500) are verbatim excerpts from Lewis's new biography, *The Jameses: A Family Narrative* (Farrar, 1991), and should be read as part of the book, unless one wishes to study Lewis's graceful prose style.

ii Sources, Backgrounds, Influences, Parallels

Rosella Mamoli Zorzi in "Henry James In a 'Venetian' Diary," (*HJR* 11:101–14) explores the various references to James within the Venetian diary of "Ariana and Daniel Sargent Curtis," the "American owners of the Palazzo Barbaro," a palace which disappeared after 1914 yet still lives on in James's letters, his preface to *A London Life,* and in *Wings of the Dove.* "The Friendship of Fanny Kemble and Henry James" (*CQ* 19:230–42) by Tamara Follini outlines James's relationship with Kemble, an older admirer of the young James and perhaps a model for Juliana Bordereau, that "very old" and "formidable" woman who "gives up everything to the poet Aspern." And in "Michelangelo, Henry James's Artistic Hero in 'The Madonna of the Future'" (*AN&Q* 3:110–13), Lynne P. Shackelford thinks that the statues of David, Moses, and Lorenzo offer a portrait of courage, strength, and grandeur for James's "parable-like tale" of Theobald.

In her influence study, "Woolson's Response to James: The Vindication of the American Heroine" (*WS* 18:287–94), Joanne F. Vickers claims that although both *Daisy Miller* and Woolson's *The Street of the Hyacinth* (1881) are about the struggles for independence and identity of the American woman in the class-conscious structured society of Rome, Wolson's heroine pursues a career and has the self-confidence to survive as a breadwinner in the face of difficulty, while James's Daisy perishes in Roman high society. Ed Kleiman in "Henry James and the Haunted House of Fiction: Hawthorne's Influence in *The American*" (*CRevAS* 21, 1:31–48) suggests not surprisingly that James's early novel, even with certain reversals, is still haunted by Hawthorne's themes of an old aristocratic house tainted by a terrible past secret, isolated aristocrats cut off from the life around them, and by certain parallel structures. "Jamesian Gleanings" (*HJR* 11:42–57) by Arthur Sherbo records a letter by James to the Executive Committee of the American Copyright League not in Edel's edition of letters, together with several forgotten (not very favorable) reviews of James's works. He suggests that scholars can uncover such "gleanings" concerning English reaction to James's and other American writers' work if they more carefully scrutinize English periodicals.

Martin Price in "Heroines of Consciousness: James, Turgenev, and Flaubert" in *Dilemmes Du Roman: Essays in Honor of Georges May*, ed. Catherine LaFarge (Stanford, 1989; pp. 327–39), says unsurprisingly that James's respect for Turgenev and lack of respect for Flaubert was based on the degree of consciousness they rendered in their characters, especially their females. In "The Artistic Exchange: *Dorian Gray* at the *Sacred Fount*" (*TSLL* 32:522–35), Kathryn Humphreys deals with the problematic of mimesis in these two works, proposing that recognitions of selves often turn into shadows, bafflements, and "opacity," mainly because critics cannot locate the authenticity in either the character or the portrait. Edward J. Piacentino's "Henry James and *All the King's Men* (*MissQ* 43:521–28) points to a previously unnoticed reference in *All the King's Men* to "The Real Thing." The implication of Warren's allusion is presumably that Jack Burden, like James's painter-narrator-artist, needs to achieve aesthetic distance in order to draw on his "trove of experience" for the creation of his narrative. And in "Realism, Ideology, and the Novel in America (1886–96): Changing Perspectives in the Work of Mark Twain, W. D. Howells, and Henry James" (*Boundary 2* 17, i:189–210), Robert Weimann's heady survey makes the point that James's novelistic images of individuals with highly cultivated sensibilities, his "beautiful artists," at once reflected and tried to overcome "the crisis in the function of liberal ideology." Finally, Ross Posnock's too glib but still interesting "William and Henry James" (*Raritan* 8, iii [1989]:1–26) explores William's "dialectic of repression"—especially such "defensive dualisms" as his belief in an "insulated self" alongside doctrines that seemingly reconstruct reality—in contrast to Henry's more pliable subjectivity which converts "wayward curiosity" into experience and text by a "psychic economy." Posnock suggests an opposition between William's (and pragmatism's) hostility to curiosity and Henry's type of wise passiveness that makes for continual "interest." In proposing to "understand William [as] the best way to appreciate Henry's type of subjectivity," Posnock, while rejecting Edel's Freudianism, claims William to be a case of continual repression and Henry as Freud's "rare" and "perfect" sublimation.

iii Critical Books

For the last 12 years Daniel Mark Fogel has been copious and synonymous with excellence in James studies, but 1990 has to be a crowning year with the publication of *two* excellent books, *Covert Relations: James Joyce, Virginia Woolf, and Henry James* (Virginia) and *Daisy Miller: A Dark Comedy of Manners* (Twayne). *Covert Relations* is a marvelous piece of critical detective work on behalf of James's anxiety-laden influence on his two famous successors. In a sense, the very hardest kind of study to write successfully is one in which all the major players have long been "felt" informally to be somehow connected, yet nobody could show it. Fogel pulls it off by constructing a Bloom-based "psychodynamics of transmission" transpiring between James, a major founder of modernism, and both Joyce and Woolf. The Joyce argument is ingenious, involving a complex network of concealed allusions to James in *Ulysses,* mostly revolving around the figure of "Philip Beaufoy" but also incorporating "J. B. Pinker," James's own publisher, and extending to various connections between *The Portrait* and *Stephen Hero* as well as *The Better Sort* and *Dubliners,* particularly John Marcher and James Duffy. Most significantly, Joyce's "open references" to James cease after 1906, whereupon his concealed weaving of nothing less than a "Henry James trope" into his fiction begins to incubate. Virginia Woolf's quite enormous and oppressive anxiety of Jamesian influence is proved by Fogel through very careful examination of her almost bizarre "ambivalence"—indeed her "swerving" back and forth in evaluation, often within the same document—to James over many years of criticism. Such demonstrable feelings of identity/oppression/anxiety are decisively augmented by Fogel's new corroborating evidence drawn from several hitherto unpublished suppressed manuscript sources. Fogel argues powerfully that Woolf identified James with her father, Leslie Stephen (James's friend and publisher of *Daisy Miller*), and both with "the Victorian Patriarchy"; James is thus the "tyrant father/writer father." Yet if he was to be resisted, he was also the father of the modern psychological novel, a situation which elicited Woolf's veering alternation of uneasy high praise and equally uneasy *dis*praise. Fogel even shows meticulously that Woolf actually associated James with both "influence" and "influenza." He tactfully demurs from concluding that the differences between Joyce's and Woolf's anxiety of authorship are gender-specific; however, if I may suggest momentarily a post-Freudian model, I cannot help remarking that Joyce's deft concealment in contrast to Woolf's overt "fickle Jacobean" reactions (as she herself put it) bespeak Lacanian structures of obsession and hysteria, respectively.

Fogel's *Daisy Miller* study (like Terry Heller's on *Turn of the Screw* last year) is a distinguished addition to the fine Twayne Masterworks series. Obviously, there is not the "scholar's adventure" quality here found in *Covert Relations,* but it would be a mistake to minimize Fogel's accomplishment simply because he published *Covert Relations* the same year. For despite all the work over the years, there is no better overall guide to James's famous story than this slim volume. The hope that "some of [his] observations will open up *Daisy Miller* in new ways even for seasoned Jamesians" is realized, especially by the way he dissects the story's "fusion of literary realism and mythmaking" as well as his discussion of Victorian ideology and chaperonage. Fogel writes beautifully, which makes even familiar material seem fresh. My only caveat is with his choice and defense of the early unrevised text, though I dare say more scholars nowadays may be in his corner than in mine. Nonetheless, I would urge anyone with Fogel's preference to read the *Daisy Miller* chapter in Philip Horne's *Henry James and Revision* (Oxford).

Horne's volume is one of the fine studies this year and as deeply satisfying a treatment of this important issue of revision as I have ever read. First of all, it is a comprehensive study, incorporating a great fund of pertinent information and previous scholarship. Second, Horne exhibits exquisite critical acumen in his close reading of James's revisions, especially very subtle changes. Third, he incorporates an enlightening and refreshing allusiveness to the broader tradition of English literature when contextualizing James's revision processes. Finally, Horne, without being dogmatic, offers a persuasive counterbalance to the "hot" problematic-oriented views at present concerning James's revision epitomized by Michael Anesko's fine book a few years back or Dana Ringuette's strong essay reviewed below—that is, Horne neither retheoretizes revision per se nor translates James's artistic endeavors into commercial contingencies. The book's 10 chapters cover a good bit of territory. The first reasserts the case for James as perfectionist; the second explores the often neglected distinction between James's errors in revision vs. his successful revisions readers may not like; the third takes up James's "confidence" in revision during the period of *The American Scene*. The next seven chapters are exemplary analyses of specific works, though they also range widely through James's corpus as well as English and American literary history. The chapter on *Roderick Hudson* emphasizes Rowland's "eternal second thoughts" analogous to James's; *The American* shows the felicity of certain *kinds* of revisions, especially with dialogue, that most scholars do not see, since they do not like James's enhancing of Newman's conscious-ness; *The Portrait* chapter brilliantly explores the changes surrounding Countess Gemini's disclosures to Isabel to elaborate their critical im-plications. Remaining chapters on *Daisy Miller, The Aspern Papers,* and *The Lesson of the Master* all exceed anything hitherto done by anyone: Horne shows James's sharpening of Winterbourne's perceptual angle of confusion as well as the tale's increased "variety of tone"; next, he addresses the heightened "authorial inscrutability" in *Aspern*'s revisions; then, the enhanced ambiguity, mainly through "musical dialogue" and the refining of Paul's consciousness, in *Lesson of the Master*. Horne even provides a thick chronology of James during the period of the New York Edition. Finally, in contrast to, say, Alfred Habegger, Horne believes James's Prosperolike relation to his last texts impels him to revise Minny's letters out of "duty to them [rather] than a disservice or an imposition of self." This last is probably heresy to most academicians, but the heart of the book dealing with Jamesian revision of his *own* text is not to be easily dismissed. There are more things to say: *The Golden Bowl* preface, as one might expect, provides a continual reference point throughout the study. This book should be read by any number of American scholars who these days just assume that the unrevised texts are fresher and thus freer of the Master discourse. Horne's monition is worth pondering: "Literature is a process which demands deliberate striving for effects; and the intricacy of studying revisions should not tempt us into too impatient an assumption that the complexity of the final product is excessive."

The French Side of Henry James by Edwin Sill Fussell (Columbia) is a lively quasi-apologia intent on reminding conceptual critics of James's factual "depth" and "detail" of French topography, manners, morals, habits, customs, culture, politics, economics, "and more than anything else the French language" in his fiction. For us as "Tourist Reader," Fussell's Baedeker-like approach is especially good on *The American,* as one might expect, but there are informative segments on James's "Italianate fictions (with more French than Italian language), his "multilinguis[m]" in *The Princess Casamassima* (again, French predominates over German or Italian), and the overwhelming "French-English linguistic relations" in *The Tragic Muse. The Ambassadors,* James's "last sequential encounter with the French," is another obvious focal point. Fussell feels that we critics are much too provincial in assuming that "international" in James means "Americans" and Europe—witness *The Tragic Muse.* But Fussell himself overlooks the American vs. Europeanized American conflict so prominent in James. All the same, his emphasis on the "bilingual or multilingual nature of the Jamesian text" is a good reminder and corrective; his final "Add-A-Pearl" chapter, a quick look at six French-related tales from 1864 to 1909, suggests something of the study's methodology as a whole, and the claim that the princess in "The Velvet Glove" is James's own Christina Light, not Edith Wharton, almost out-Tintners Adeline Tintner!

Diametrically opposed is *Professions of Taste: Henry James, British Aestheticism, and Commodity Culture* (Stanford) by Jonathan Freedman, for not only is James's French side replaced by deep problematic ties with late 19th-century British aestheticism, but Fussell's reasonably simple study of French allusiveness gives way to a highly sophisticated, conceptually dense approach to a historical and aesthetic phenomenon. Freedman's long, complex analysis hinges on the point that James took the "uneasy instabilities" of British aestheticism and "reshaped the essential agendas" of that movement—including the "Artist with a capital A"— then transformed its "volatile and unstable" ingredients "into that more austere form of aestheticism we call modernism." In the selfsame process, James also "professionalized" the quintessential aesthete-artist with incredible cultural success yet with problematic response to that very success resulting in an ongoing aesthetic instability, still with us now a hundred years later and transposed into our postmodern academy. Freedman's conceptual complexity can only be hinted, but one can easily recommend this book on several levels: its newly complicated analysis of British aestheticism; its *very* fresh examination of how James in effect "re-aestheticizes" Pater, Ruskin, and Wilde; its fascinating foray into the transatlantic impact of aestheticism on American culture, including

Stickney and even Howells's *Hazard of New Fortunes;* its unexpected readings of *Roderick Hudson, Portrait, Wings,* and *The Golden Bowl;* and even its expected connections drawn with the Pound/Eliot school of modernism. As Freedman himself says, he has interwoven two books in one—the "crystallization of aestheticism" into "formalist dogma" and "the discontinuities, contradictions, and problematics of aesthetic theory and practice."

Together with Bonney MacDonald's *Henry James's Italian Hours,* UMI Research Press generates still another thoughtful and helpful study of James, *The Rule of Money: Gender, Class, and Exchange Economics in the Fiction of Henry James* by Peggy McCormack. McCormack focuses astutely on James's well-known use of economic language and imagery and extends the investigation to their larger contextual categories, especially the exchange economies attending marriage, the comparative impact and reaction by males and females so caught in the exchange, and the relationship of the foregoing to the salient phases of James's biography. She discerns a "developmental" pattern, in which (1) early James characters like Newman and Isabel are naive and equally victimized (though each victimization is rendered gender-specific by James's narrator); (2) middle-year characters like Nick Dormer and Nanda Brookenham, analogous to James's own "downward turn," recognize the terrible exchange market and resist it, yet at great personal cost; and, finally, (3) the resolution by late James through the inevitable figure of Maggie Verver, his "prime negotiator with the exchange system," who, during James's own resurgent period of life, competes successfully in the exchange economy without becoming corrupted by it or affirming its worst values. McCormack is open and engaging, often citing persuasively from the larger corpus of the fiction, modest in her claims, and seeing her work as part of a building process by other critics. Her various theoretical sources are also nicely backgrounded in the argument. Ultimately, her rationale for claiming that James is "both feminist and feminine in his writing"—a controversial topic these days—is both low-keyed and very convincing.

Lastly, the awkwardness of reviewing one's own critical book in *ALS* should be obvious, but my *Henry James: A Study of the Short Fiction* (Twayne) is the first critical overview of James's tales since Krishna Baldev Vaid in 1964, except for Wagenknecht's nice summaries and some partial study by Richard Gage, James Kraft, and a couple of others. My analysis first addresses the nature of James's art of short fiction, then traces his linear development from social international realist, through

psychological moralist and exponent of art-parable, to poetic expressionist and delineator of ghostly reality—these corresponding, of course, to
early, middle, and late James short fiction. The study has several new
features, but given the relation of this reviewer to his work, I shall
mention only an unusually long interpretation of James's last published
tale, "A Round of Visits," and a compact introduction to some back
matter which analyzes the relationship between Jamesian poetics and
Maupassant. Incidentally, "tale" or "short fiction" in my study includes
the Jamesian nouvelles as well as even longer pieces like "The Aspern
Papers" or, say, "In the Cage."

iv Collections of Critical Essays

James W. Tuttleton and Agostino Lombardo have edited a major international collection of 13 essays on the James Family and Italy, *The Sweet-
est Impression of Life* (NYU; Istituto della Enciclopedia Italiana). *ALS* is
never scaled to do justice to such collections, yet the importance and
freshness of this subject and the internationalism of the project deserve
applause and prominence—and at least some halting attempt by me to
cover the contents. So here goes. Leon Edel's "The Italian Journeys of
Henry James" (pp. 8–21) explores James's "passion" for Italy through a
maturing "archeology of feeling," reflected both in the travel essays and
the fiction of all three periods. " 'Dipped in the Sacred Stream': The
James Family in Italy" (pp. 22–47) by coeditor Tuttleton probes in detail
the family's various modes of attachment to Italy (even before traveling
there), then recounts Alice and Bob's tentative interest, Henry Sr. and
William's suspicion and alternating enchantment and disgust, respectively, and Henry Jr.'s deep sense of possession. Sergio Perosa's "Italy in
Henry James's International Theme" (pp. 48–65) efficiently shows how
in James's "scissorlike" international paradigm, Italy's beauty and en-
ticement "prove a double-edged" menace. Josephine Gattuso Hendin's
"The Uses of Italy in *Roderick Hudson* and *The Princess Casamassima*"
(pp. 66–88) examines the "Dionysian" complexities of James's Italianate-
American Christina Light and his conflation of art and politics. "Henry
James's American Girls in Darkest Rome: The Abuse and Disabuse of
Innocence" (pp. 89–106) by Daniel Mark Fogel provides an engaging
examination of James's Browningesque conventionalism in the abuse of
innocent Daisy and Isabel—and the latter's gradual succumbing to a
"mistress of shades." Adeline Tintner's "Rococo Venice, Pietro Longhi,

and Henry James" (pp. 107–27) is vintage Tintneresque illumination of James's appreciation and use of 18th-century Venetian art well in advance of its respectability. Bonney MacDonald's "The Force of Revelation: Receptive Vision in Henry James's Early Italian Travel Essays" (pp. 128–48) stresses early James's "unified perception" of Italy in line with father-of-phenomenology William's theory of perception. In "Alice James and Italy" (pp. 149–61), Maria Antonietta Saracino chronicles Alice's brief encounter with Italy, her vicarious response through Henry's letters, and her discourse on Italian politics during the latter segment of *The Diary*. "The Influence of William James's Pragmatism in Italy" (pp. 162–81) by Gerald E. Meyers is an important essay which explores how William, who found Italy's ambience of the past irksome, was then surprised to discover his influence and consanguinity with philosophers Giovanni Vailati and, especially, Giovanni Papini. Similarly, Claudio Gorlier's "Listening to the Master: William James and the 'Making of the New' in Italian Culture" (pp. 182–96) traces the legacy of pragmatism in the two avant-garde journals, *Leonardo* and later *La Voce*—with its fascist bent. "Henry James and the Literature of Italy" by Lyall H. Powers (pp. 197–209) isolates James's criticism of Matilde Serao and Gabriele D'Annunzio in order to clarify James's mature moral view that mere eroticism devoid of context and character robs the "human spectacle" of its significance. In *"William Wetmore Story and His Friends:* The Enclosing Fact of Rome" (pp. 210–27), Denis Donoghue elaborates James's creative faculty of Roman "remembrance" and the "precursive relation" of first-generation expatriates within his fictive biography of a subject he otherwise found trivial. Finally, coeditor Agostino Lombardo's "Italy and the Artist in Henry James" (pp. 228–39) proposes that Italy for James is the fundamental metaphor for art and life: hence, he exhibits it over and over again as the "land of sorrow"—a vision startlingly like that of Poe.

New Essays on The Portrait of a Lady, ed. Joel Porte (Cambridge), though admittedly addressed to a novel infinitely discussed in previous collections, contains psychoanalytic interest. It begins, however, with Porte's extended "Introduction" (pp. 1–31), which stresses James's fresh textual use of the *"topos* of Italy" and proposes the principle of "tangibility" through Isabel's suffering so consanguine with Virgil's elegiac vision. Donatello Izzo's *"The Portrait of a Lady* and Modern Narrative" (pp. 33–48) emphasizes the novel's "self-referential nature" and "enclosed structure" in fairly familiar formalist terms, including the point that James presents narrative development by levels of awareness rather than

transformation in events themselves. "The Fatherless Heroine and the
Filial Son: Deep Background for *The Portrait of a Lady*" (pp. 49–93) by
Alfred Habegger reargues his psychoanalytic, gender-based analysis of
James's novel, emphasizing its reformulation of orphan-heroine fiction
by popular women authors, and also James's "betrayal" of Minny Temple's actual feisty character to his filial endorsement of his father's antifeminism. William Veeder's "The Portrait of a Lack" (pp. 95–121) is the
most intricate reading in this collection. Essentially, Veeder claims that
The Portrait projects James's Freudian family romance, in which the
orphan self compensates for his lifelong lack by creating a fairy tale that
both reveals and substitutes for the death drive. Veeder's psychoanalytic
elaboration is far more complex than his basic thesis, as James is,
in effect, refracted through a number of the characters (see also Criticism: General Essays below). Another complex analysis of Isabel is Beth
Sharon Ash's "Frail Vessels and Vast Designs: A Psychoanalytic Portrait of
Isabel Archer" (pp. 123–62). Ash develops several original insights by
pursuing the implications of Isabel's maternal absence and its resulting
narcissistic/masochistic elements in her character. Especially interesting
is the analysis of Osmond as "bad mother" and Merle as "phallic
mother." This essay implies that Isabel's famous "independence" is a
mere tip of a huge psychic iceberg.

v Criticism: General Essays

In "The Self-Forming Subject: Henry James's Pragmatistic Revision"
(*Mosaic* 23, i:11–30), Dana J. Ringuette argues very persuasively that
Henry James's revision is the expression of a broader principle of unfore-
seen growth best articulated by Charles S. Peirce's triadic conception of
identity-consciousness-community. Ringuette holds that the Jamesian
"self" has the same contingent nature (despite centers of interest) that
obtain between character, author, and reader—an agency in the process
of continual revision. Of similar interest, Pamela Schirmeister's chapter
on James in her study *The Consolations of Space* (Stanford; pp. 137–66)
rereads James's Prefaces first as metaphorical adaptations of Hawthorne's
preface to *Mosses,* then as Keatsian responses to the aesthetics of possibility with "the world as imaged in the mind's desire." The Prefaces
constitute a "romance," not only as "reinterpretation by way of place,"
but as "immortality snatched before the fact." Obversely, Ruth Newton
and Naomi Lebowitz in *Dickens, Manzoni, Zola, and James: The Impossi-*

ble Romance (Missouri) discuss the "unmediated dialectic between history and heaven everywhere" in James's writing, together with his "structure of the salvational mode within the realistic novel." Most of Newton and Lebowitz's Jamesian allusions and discussions center on *Portrait* and *Wings*. A different critical world, however, is Eunice Merideth's "Gender Patterns in Henry James: A Stylistic Approach to Dialogue in *Daisy Miller, The Portrait of a Lady,* and *The Bostonians*," in *Literary Computing and Literary Criticism,* ed. Rosanne G. Potter (Penn., 1989; pp. 189–205), which compares by "computational stylistics" the language patterns of males and females to show that, while James may write with concern for his female characters, he still inadvertently empowers his males and undercuts his females through his creation of their speech characteristics. Merideth's method—Potter's COMP STYLE computer program—tends to focus on individual utterances.

Clare E. Goldfarb's "Female Friendship: An Alternative to Marriage and the Family in Henry James's Fiction?" (*CLQ* 26:205–12) states that, although James's female characters do not find success in their heterosexual unions to become "an angel in the house," James nevertheless resists the notion of female bonding—"the empowering support of a female friend." Also, Larry A. Gray's "Sibyls, Seekers, and Sacred Founts in the Tales of Henry James" (*HJR* 11:189–201) neatly evaluates the Jamesian configuration of frustrated male seeker of the mystery, or sacred fount, and the thwarted female sibyl, a pattern nicely reversed in certain fictions like *The Portrait* and *The Golden Bowl,* where the female becomes the seeker. However, in "Varieties of Love: Henry James's Treatment of the 'Great Relation,'" in *American Declarations of Love,* ed. Ann Massa (St. Martin's; pp. 68–87), Elsa Nettels declares that the animating force of James's fiction is for his characters to find a "mutually sustaining love" that often eludes them or else to live in the imagination of such a love. She analyzes the various manifestations of this theme in the fiction through structure, tone, and style. Another love variation is Stanley Cavell's "Postscript (1989): To Whom It May Concern" (*CritI* 16:248–89) which uses Eve Kosofsky Sedgwick's study on homosexual panic in James's "Beast in the Jungle" as the springboard to rethink various issues—ranging from Freud to Lacan to Plato—raised in his previous published work that connects to Sedgwick's topic.

In the "The Jamesian Balloon: Romancing the Marketplace" (*JAmS* 24:351–68), Ian F. A. Bell uses James's memorable quote about the "balloon of experience" and two quotes from Bakhtin about dialogical forms to show their relation to Jamesian syntax, but also to observe that James "advertises the advertisement of the history he lives through, the Romance of display, surface, and performance." "The Marine Metaphor, Henry James and the Moral Center of *The Awkward Age*" (*PQ* 69:91–105) by Greg W. Zacharias speculates that whereas James uses this metaphor in his letters "to advance his moral outlook," he uses it in his fiction to chart "his attitude toward living" and to help readers positively interpret the characters—like *Awkward Age*'s Longdon—to whom they are ascribed. In "Henry James and the Ethical Moment" (*HJR* 11:153–75), Myler Wilkinson seeks with eloquence to redeem deconstruction from the charge of ethical nihilism by applying Hillis Miller's *Ethics of Reading* (also de Man's concept "ethicity") to three touchstone works by James, which show that "the ethical is no longer grounded in the transcendent law (as in Kant) but within the difference of language with its perpetual call on us to read, reread, and read again, and in those acts to perform the error that is a necessity." Wilkinson gives exemplary readings as "necessary-failures" to *Daisy Miller* (an "allegory about the implied possibility of reading and its subsequent failure"), to *Turn of the Screw* (an "allegory of the impossibility of knowing"), and to *The Ambassadors* (in effect, an allegory of the Kantian "as if"). Were there only time, I would argue why the first analysis is unsatisfactory, the second quite well done, and the third very persuasive and important.

Finally, William Veeder's "Henry James and the Uses of the Feminine" in *Out of Bounds: Male Writers and Gender[ed] Criticism,* Laura Claridge and Elizabeth Langland, eds. (Mass.; pp. 219–51), makes fine complementary reading with Veeder's contribution to the *Portrait* collection earlier reviewed, for here he extends his complex psychoanalysis of James's enabling-female-orphan fantasy beyond *Portrait* to the whole curve of the later career, during his "therapeutic" nineties (with Morgan, Maisie, Fleda, Nanda) on to, and through, the three major-phase novels—a bit sketchy to convince me, admittedly, yet more than sufficiently provocative to make me want to learn more. Even more important, Veeder in this essay explains his basic psychoanalytic "archaic" perspective originating in James's childhood more successfully than in the Joel Porte collection; both essays, though, do a splendid job of showing how incredibly "diverse" is James's psychic "self-representation" in *Portrait.* Jamesians should definitely read *both* essays, despite some obvious overlapping, to catch on to Veeder's intricate psychoanalysis, one that gives rise to such fine formulations as this: "James thus subverts that basic opposition of the sexes upon which patriarchal hegemony is based, for he insists upon lack, 'castration,' at the very heart of commercial America."

vi Criticism: Individual Novels

"James's Morality in *Roderick Hudson*" (*HJR* 11:115–32) by Greg W. Zacharias develops a broad-based thesis that James constituted an "American [Matthew] Arnold," that is, a "tutor" or guardian of culture. The essay is simultaneously about James's profound understanding of "power relations" between individuals: thus there are good and bad "tutors" throughout his fiction. In *Roderick Hudson,* Rowland Mallet is the preeminent bad tutor/patron whose self-interest and lack of achievement prove destructive to Roderick. James provides a "constructive" alternative, however, by Gloriani's tutelage of Singleton. Ultimately, James's "career-long interest in the quality of human relations, thus the quality of culture itself, demonstrates [his] concern with the subject of moral responsibility."

Ian F. A. Bell in "Sincerity and Performance in *The Europeans*" (*MP* 88:126–46) sets this earlyish novel within the context of Emerson and Hawthorne by demonstrating the changing conception of self from inner- to other-directedness brought about principally by "the designs of consumption." The body thus becomes a "social construct," and, for James, "the great stylists of the self and the body" are female.

In addition to the *New Essays* collection cited earlier, there were three more *Portrait* essays. Mary K. Ventura's nifty updating of Richard Chase's classic formalist approach is *"The Portrait of a Lady:* The Romance/Novel Duality" (*ALR* 22, iii:36–50). In an essay saturated with citations from the text, Ventura shows that whereas Isabel is the author of her romance in the earlier segments of the work, James effectively surrenders the novel "to Isabel to rewrite her destiny in a realist framework," i.e., to rewrite her own "past through Pansy." As romancer she "recognizes few boundaries, as novelist few freedoms." Ventura is especially good at showing the various repetitions of elements—characters, setting, manipulation, etc.—in the novelistic "rewrite" of the romance. "Dualities" may not be critically fashionable right now, but Ventura indeed gets at "the heart of [James's] dialectic." Next, "The Delicate Organisms and Theoretic Tricks of Henry James" (*AL* 62:583–606) by Stephanie A. Smith argues sinuously that what fuels the tragedy and creates the sense of the gothic in *Portrait of a Lady* is the dialectic between "strict fantasy of proprietal possession of the mother and the post-Freudian fantasy of the pre-Oedipal mother's murder." It is James the Master, Smith further claims, "the (male) artist with a (female) consciousness" who can gestate and bring to birth the perfect *Portrait*. Finally, Kurt Hochenauer's "Sexual Realism in *The Portrait of a Lady*: The Divided Sexuality of Isabel Archer" (*SNNTS* 22:19–25) suggests that James refused to accept sexlessness as the only answer to women's independence, and that critics' inability to take this into account is one reason they cannot reconcile Isabel's divided sexuality—which is "the *point,* not the *problem*" with her.

Greg W. Zacharias's "Henry James' Style in *Washington Square*" (*SAF* 18:207–24) emphasizes the novel's important transitional status from social comedy toward individual characterization. What makes it a "decisive turning point" in James's career is the mature heroine's capacity to understand herself from another's perspective, even though James's "condensation" of the work (for *Cornhill* and *Harper's*) disallowed fuller treatment of such Isabel-like epiphanies from Catherine Sloper. Zacharias's interest in this work is in line with contemporary James criticism; his ultimate subordination of it to the later work probably is not.

Claire Kahane's *"The Bostonians* and the Figure of the Speaking Woman" in *Psychoanalysis and . . . ,* eds. Richard Feldstein and Henry Sussman (Routledge; pp. 163–74), argues that the novel examines the phenomenon of hysteria, which often causes women to lose their voices, and the woman's movement, which enables women to gain their voices; this dual theme of the speaking woman is both fascinating and repellent to James, and indeed a subject that aroused his own hysterical response. And in "The Personal, the Private, and the Public in *The Bostonians*" (*TSLL* 32:240–56), Ian F. A. Bell shows by both textual nuance and historical context how consistently the realm of the "personal" and "private"—as James understood such concepts from Emerson and Sainte-Beuve—are distorted by the cultural ethos of "publicity," thus promoting blinkered "schismatic" oppositions between Ransom, Chancellor, Pardon, and Verena herself.

Deborah Esch's deconstructive exercise, "Promissory Notes: The Prescription of the Future in *The Princess Casamassima*" (*AmLH* 1, 2 [1989]:317–38), uses an analogy between James's "The Future of the Novel" and Hyacinth's pivotal promise to terrorist Hoffendahl to explore the rhetorical status of prediction and its "obsession" as expounded by

J. L. Austin. Esch believes that Hyacinth's dilemma is the "intervention of time into the configuration of promise and redemption," that his mother "threatens to 'survive' Hyacinth in an act . . . commit[ted] in her memory," and that the "rhetorical predicament of James's protagonist is a thoroughly temporal one," in which his promissory note to kill the Duke is ultimately "blind." *"The Princess Casamassima Revisited"* (*VQR* 66:479–87) by Edwin M. Yoder proposes this work as a "post-political novel," which enables the reader to address its issues "in a rather different light, and with a fresh sense of virtues" that may have escaped earlier readers who sought a "documentary narrative." Yoder is seemingly unaware of the mountain of work done on *Princess* since Trilling and Howe.

Heath Moon in "Saving James from Modernism: How to Read *The Sacred Fount*" (*MLQ* 49 [1988]:120–41) claims that, "impenetrability being the hallmark of modernism," the novel's ambiguity is overstated, and therefore critics who read against the grain of the text—unreliable narrator and ironic comedy at his expense—are wrong. Moon is not the first to recommend a context for *Fount* by reading it along the lines of James's other vampire theme works written during the same period.

The late Dorothea Krook bequeaths us *"The Ambassadors: Two Types of Ambiguity"* (*Neophil* 74:148–55), a lovely little critical exercise which distinguishes ambiguous passages that are intrinsically mystifying from issues, such as the question of Chad's transformation, which (like the Ghosts in *Screw*) admit of but "two alternate and contradictory readings." More ambitiously, "The Incredible Floating Man: Henry James's Lambert Strether" (*HJR* 11:176–88) by Reginald Abbot employs close reading of the innumerable floating and air images to establish *The Ambassadors'* connection with fin-de-siècle art—except that James deploys a "reversal of gender and iconographical roles." Like Isabel, Strether is "weightless," yet what he finds in Europe "is not sexual activity or fulfillment but sexual (in the sense of gender) use at the hands of women in a society in which . . . male power [is] . . . a camouflage for real female power and control."

"Levels of Knowing: Development of Consciousness in *The Wings of the Dove*" (*HJR* 11:58–71) by Linda Raphael is an intricate narratological examination of the subtleties of "voice and vision" in Kate Croy, especially, as well as in Merton Densher. Raphael applies theory from Gerard Genette and others by close-reading numerous passages to show the sort of "double-voiced discourse" that allows a perceptive Jamesian reader access to the "discriminations between the voices of the narrator and characters" and to apprehend Kate's complex inability for growth and Merton's potential for it. Although Raphael takes issue with Nicola Bradbury's conclusions, her own subtle approach reminds me of Bradbury's. Rita Charon's "The Great Empty Cup of Attention: The Doctor and Illness in *The Wings of the Dove*" (*L&M* 9:105–24) explores James's projection of his own fears regarding health and death—including the deaths of Minny Temple and Constance F. Woolson—onto the character of Milly Theale. Both Milly in the novel and James in real life perform "self-diagnoses," whereby no physical illness seems conclusive, for the purpose of gaining the attention of others and, in James's case, to purge him of a morbid sense of responsibility and guilt for the deaths of Minny and Constance. Similarly, "Fierce Privacy in *The Wings of the Dove*" (*L&M* 9:125–33) by Joan Lescinski argues that the novel begins and ends in a prodigious state of "mystery" concerning Milly's illness, life, and death, causing "major problems of interpretation."

Three new essays appeared on *The Golden Bowl*. The first, "Knowledge and Silence: *The Golden Bowl* and Moral Philosophy" (*CritI* 16: 397–437) by Daniel Brudney, is a very long, often chatty soliloquy/analysis which investigates Maggie's crucial "lie" to Charlotte as well as her purposely *not* seeking knowledge (such as whether her father knows of the Charlotte/Amerigo adultery) as examples of genuine, philosophically defensible moral activity which prevents "disfiguring" other persons while at the same time furthering Maggie's own "heart's desire." Much of this essay is taken up with exploring presuppositions about the pertinence of an ambiguous text like James's to philosophical method and discourse per se. The second, Greg Zacharias's "The Language of Light and Dark and James's Moral Argument in *The Golden Bowl*" (*PLL* 26:249–70), cuts across much current analysis of the novel by holding that Adam Verver's "educational mission" and "covert tutelage" of daughter Maggie is unambiguously propitious. Zacharias contends that Adam's "growth of consciousness," no less than his apt pupil Maggie's, is formally signaled by a "vocabulary of light and dark," a Jamesian motif and moral reference likewise found outside the novel, especially in his letters. This essay clearly complements Zacharias's approach to *Roderick Hudson* earlier. In "Henry James's Gentle Heretics and the Old Persuasion: Roman Catholicity in *The Golden Bowl*" (*HJR* 11:30–41), Edwin Sill Fussel's different tack is that James's making the four main characters all

Catholic and three of them American in effect "cancel[s] Protestantism," that is, he underscores the point that the "best-behaving people—when they are at their best"—are Americans. "Literary patriotism" remains, and Maggie, says Fussell, is James "beskirted and Catholicized."

vii Criticism: Tales

Before we look at specific interpretations, we should mention how Bruce Bassoff in "Turning the Tables: The Stories of Henry James" (*EA* 43:284–93) perceives in numerous tales a turning-the-tables pattern of loss, renunciation, and recuperation, i.e., a means of regaining indirectly what was lost. Also, there is my own *Study of the Short Fiction* (see Critical Books).

Three pieces actually appeared on "The Author of *Beltraffio.*" The first, by Fred L. Gardaphe, "The Echoes of *Beltraffio:* Reading Italy in Henry James's 'The Author of *Beltraffio*'" (*RLA 1989* i:121–27), is an ingenious semiotic explication of all the various Italian "echoes" in the title and characters' names which collectively signify (pardon the pun) James's newer "modern" ambiguous treatment of Italy in his fiction, especially its cross-cultural exchange of "interculturality." Semiotically, the tale is an "open" work. The second piece, "James's 'The Author of *Beltraffio*'" (*Expl* 48, iii:188–90) by Craig E. Vickers and Robert T. Backus, argues that the color red or "crimson" associated with little Dolcino Ambient reinforces his status as a Christ figure and the tale as an allegory of the Fall and Redemption; this is not the first time the story has been proposed as biblical allegory. Finally, Lawrence R. Schehr in "'The Author of Beltraffio' as Theory" (*MLN* 105:992–1015) elaborates the thesis that the theory in this story is, in fact, James's rejection of all theories of representation, leaving only the unreadable and inaccessable text as the perfect text.

In "James, 'The Aspern Papers,' and the Ethics of Literary Biography" (*MFS* 36:211–17), Gary Scharnhorst argues with deftness and perspicacity that this tale is a kind of metacommentary on the ethics surrounding the publication of Hawthorne's biography, an invasion of privacy in James's opinion, that he himself avoided by burning many of his papers. "Writing and the Dispossession of Woman in *The Aspern Papers*" (*AI* 47:23–42) is Joseph Church's intricate Lacanian reading of "Aspern." He proposes, among other things, that the phallus, represented by the

letters, is in the wrong place—in the possession of a "phallic woman,"
Juliana—and that the narrator must dispossess her or else lose his own
identity.

"The *Atlantic Monthly's* Rejection of 'The Pupil': An Exchange of
Letters Between Henry James and Horace Scudder" (*ALR* 23, i:75–83) by
George Monteiro rereads this rejection through a reexamination of the
correspondence. Although Scudder's letter was destroyed at his request,
Monteiro suggests that James may have actually made the revisions
Scudder proposed before sending it off to another publisher; however,
Scudder never crossed or angered James again for fear of losing his work
from *Atlantic* publication. Kris Lackey in "Art and Class in 'The Real
Thing'" (*SSF* 26 [1989]:190–92) states that the tale serves as a parable of
power on two levels: that of aesthetic mastery and that of social mastery.

In "'The Altar of the Dead': James's Grammar of Grieving" (*ESC*
16:315–24), Karen Smythe claims that this story is a Jamesian allegory on
how to write an elegy—i.e., to allow the past to bring life to the present
and to let history and language "take on a 'present' life of their own."

Marcel Cornis-Pope's "Poststructuralist Narratology and Critical
Writing: A *Figure in the Carpet* Textshop" (*JNT* 20:245–65) describes in
some detail the findings from an experimental workshop on critical
reading and writing using this James tale, a piece obviously, indeed
extraordinarily, well suited to any narratological enterprise.

"Floundering About in Silence: What the Governess Couldn't Say"
(*SSF* 26 [1989]:135–43) by Bruce E. Fleming affirms at this late date in
scholarship that the "moral dualisms"—i.e., dividing the world into good
and evil—of the governess and the housekeeper and their firm belief in
the mythic powers of speech are what cause their various "muffling" and
"silence[s]" which in turn produce the ghosts at Bly.

Donald Callen's "Stories of Sublimely Good Character" (*P&L* 14:40–
52) analyzes "The Story in It" and the *Critical Prefaces* [*sic*] for the
purpose of locating James's notion of the sublimely good person and its
contrast to Aristotle's view of the tragic hero. Though James cautions
against the sublime and concentrates on reality, Callen argues that "the
sublime may be the mode in which ideals first and most powerfully
appear," as with Maud Blessingbourne.

Henry McDonald writes one of the best pieces in years on "The
Birthplace," "Nietzsche Contra Derrida: Two Views of Henry James's
'The Birthplace'" (*HJR* 11:133–48), by arguing that James's potential
deconstructionist parable is in fact a case of Morris Gedge's growth into

creative "self-division" when he lies to the tourists. Like Derrida, James "undercuts the notion of a centered essential self by pointing up its illusory basis," yet like Nietzsche, James "puts faith in the value of such illusions." This essay contains a fine analysis of the differences of Nietzsche from Derrida.

To conclude, one expects good work from Richard S. Lyons, and he comes through again in "Ironies of Loss in *The Finer Grain*" (*HJR* 11:202–12), a perceptive analysis of all five tales in James's last collection, emphasizing their "complexities of tone and attitude" in treating "the various forms of loss." Lyons dissects not only the "social satire" of these late pieces but their distinctive "mixture of comedy and pathos," even a Chekhovian "intermingling of tragedy and comedy, an evocation of moods of loss, of transience, of ironies just fending off despair." Lyons detects not so much a Jamesian fourth manner as a "shift of emphasis." His discussion of "The Bench of Desolation" is particularly fine.

University of Missouri

8 Pound and Eliot

George Kearns and Cleo McNelly Kearns

For 1989, Reed Way Dasenbrock noted a decline in the number of Pound studies; the decline continues in 1990, although the quality of the best items remains high. A decline in quantity may be accounted for in part by the passing of the heroic age of discovery, annotation, and basic decoding of the *Cantos,* in part by a declining involvement with literary modernism among younger scholars. Eliot studies in 1990 were somewhat overshadowed by the previous two years, which saw publication of the first volume of the letters and of Jeffrey Perl's *Skepticism and Modern Enmity* (1989), one of the most important books on Eliot in recent years. Many of the Eliot articles are roughly representative of more extended publications by their authors. The notes on Pound are by G.K., those on Eliot by C.M.K.

i Pound

a. Text, Biography, and Bibliography   The year saw publication of two outstanding contributions: a revised edition of the 1926 *Personae* (New Directions), ed. Lea Baechler and A. Walton Litz, and the second volume of J. J. Wilhelm's ongoing biography of Pound. The new *Personae,* now subtitled *The Shorter Poems of Ezra Pound,* corrects or eliminates various editorial accretions that have crept into New Directions printings since 1949. The "major editorial aim was to produce a volume that would provide, in conjunction with *Collected Early Poems,* a comprehensive record of Pound's published shorter poems through 1920." It is substantially the volume Pound prepared, the order of poems unchanged except for a chronological repositioning of the 1914 "Poems from *Blast.*" The notoriously confusing typography of the table of contents in older editions—especially in regard to the structure of *Mauberley*—has been clarified. The editors have adopted the text of *Mauberley* established by John Espey and the orthographical changes authorized by Pound for J. P. Sullivan's text of *Propertius*. A few uncollected poems are supplied in an appendix, which also includes the first printed version of "In a Station of the Metro," with its expressive spacing and punctuation. Another appendix provides the *Three Cantos* that appeared in *Poetry* in 1917 "since they are of great interest and are not easily available." I wish, although it might do little more than satisfy my curiosity, that Litz and Baechler had provided some notation of all textual changes from the familiar New Directions and Faber texts. This is a splendid edition and is surely now the copytext for the poems it includes. Unfortunately, a few serious errors crept into the first printing: the editors have provided corrections in a note in *Paideuma* 19, iii:157.

A few years ago I felt obliged to write that there was no really satisfactory biography of Pound. Now there is, or promises to be, when J. J. Wilhelm completes the project he began in *The American Roots of Ezra Pound* and continues in *Ezra Pound in London and Paris, 1908–1925* (Penn. State). Wilhelm sticks closely to Pound's "Contacts and Life" (as the subtitle of *Mauberley* becomes in the new *Personae*), leaving for other occasions analysis and commentary on Pound's writing. There is no gratuitous psychologizing, nor are there the touches of fiction writing that often embellish biography. Wilhelm's extensive, at times ingenious, research is the basis for an extremely readable account of the poet's activities and his milieus, and is able to correct various errors, especially in the dating of letters. He provides lively, sometimes gossipy sketches of the entire cast of characters who surrounded the poet in these incredibly busy years, including his many amours. The reader of the *Cantos* will profit from the contexts Wilhelm offers for the often oblique personal memories evoked throughout the poem (there is a useful index of references to the *Cantos*). The volume leaves Pound in his fortieth year, having published *A Draft of XVI Cantos,* settled at Rapallo, "essentially a happy man," but with darker clouds on the horizon. "Sometimes knowing the end of a story," Wilhelm writes, "impedes us from understanding the beginning." He has done well to re-create Pound's beginnings as they were perceived at the time—a time almost impossible to unstick from the mythology of modernism.

Wilhelm's research has surely left him with many outtakes. In "Nancy Cunard: A Sometime Flame, A Stalwart Friend" (*Paideuma* 19, i–ii:201–21), Wilhelm supplies a spirited review of Cunard's career, together with extensive paraphrase and quotation from the Pound-Cunard correspondence. In the briefer "Letters of William Brooke Smith to Ezra Pound" (*Paideuma* 19, i–ii:163–68), Wilhelm recounts what is known of Pound's early friend and mentor to whom *A Lume Spento* was dedicated in the year of Smith's death at 24.

A thoughtful meditation on Pound's later politics and anti-Semitism is provided by Leon Surette's "Ezra Pound's Fascism: Aberration or Essence? The Correspondence with William Bird" (*QQ* 96, 3 [1989]:601–24). The letters between Pound and Bird in the 1930s are in fact the least part of this substantial article, showing Pound at his most ignorant and stubborn. The vein has become, alas, too familiar. Surette certainly does not budge an inch in his opposition to Poundian errors and excesses, and he offers no excuses, yet he declares himself of that party—in which he includes Robert Casillo and Michael André Bernstein—that would "like somehow to save the poetry from the errors of the man." Surette's piece is best read together with his review-article on Casillo's *Genealogy of Demons* (*Paideuma* 19, i–ii:233–39).

Timothy Materer has carefully edited and annotated "Ezra Pound and *The Little Review:* Letters to John Quinn" (*Scripsi* 5, iv [1989]:1–26). The letters, from August 1915 to June 18, 1917, are of interest for dating Pound's activities as well as for many curious sidelights, such as an evening when he and G. B. Shaw jointly "commended" abstract art. Ann Saddlemeyer has provided meticulous background and annotation for letters to and from George Yeats and Ezra and Dorothy Pound in "George, Ezra, Dorothy and Friends: Twenty-Six Letters, 1918–59" (*YeA* 7:4–28).

b. General Studies Almost 25 years ago, K. K. Ruthven published probably the single most used book on Pound, *A Guide to Ezra Pound's Personae (1926).* Now Ruthven offers another distinguished contribution to the Pound shelf, an astonishingly thorough study of *Ezra Pound as Literary Critic* (Routledge). Ruthven wisely defines criticism in the broadest possible terms, considering not only Pound's more formal literary essays such as those on James, Dante, and Joyce, but his conversations and letters; his work as editor, reviewer, arranger, anthologizer, and propagandist for himself, others, and "Modernism"; his interaction with other artists; the relations among economics, politics, and literature; in short, every way this busiest of poets made his influence felt through rhetoric, industry, and charm. The spirit of Foucault hovers above the study, which is primarily interested in "constructions" of self and discourse as exercises in power. "Literary" becomes a word requiring quotation marks. In a brief preface, Ruthven frankly announces his position: he works within the hermeneutics of suspicion of our post-Pound era. He excuses himself for a foray into idealist metacriticism in one chapter, but trusts that most of his book is "more materialist in its emphasis on the discursive formations which shaped Pound's literary education, and the social and cultural conditions in which he practiced as a literary critic." Such a position will be immediately attractive to some, off-putting to others. Yet a reader who may be suspicious of such hermeneutics should not disregard Ruthven, who writes with a dry, often oblique wit, and who not only has chronicled Pound's work as critic, but has played across that work with inventive, intelligent analysis. Pound might secretly have taken some pride in such a book as a record of how well he had occupied "as much of the discursive space as possible." Yet, himself a vigorous analyst of discursive formations he did not like, he would probably have found Ruthven's study, for all its brilliance, inade-quate in resting with discourse analysis and setting aside questions of truth or value.

Peter Crisp, who teaches in Hong Kong and appears well-versed in Western and Chinese philosophy, provides in *Paideuma* a related pair of serious, technical studies in intellectual history, of interest in helping us "place" Pound within philosophical traditions. In "Ezra Pound and the Li Xue" (19, i–ii:37–49), Crisp sorts out for the amateur of classical Chinese thought conflicting strains in neo-Confucianism and claims Pound as a "follower" of Zhu xi, whom Pound knew (if not well) as Chu Hsi, the dominant figure in the Li Xue (School of Principle). Crisp finds Kenner's assertion, "accepted by many now as a truism," that Pound was "Taoist in his deepest impulses," to be misleading. Pound, he argues, was "perhaps as Confucian as a Westerner could be. And to say that is also to say that, despite the views of some revisionist historians of Modernism, he was not Romantic in his deepest impulses either." Crisp continues the discussion in "Pound, Leibnitz and China" (19, iii:33–46). Although Pound seemed unaware of the connection between Leibniz and China, Crisp claims an indirect influence or shared tradition. The articles are interesting in relation to Neoplatonism as an approach to Confucianism and as a careful attempt to define the "spiritualized Confucianism" through which Pound "fully realized his metaphysic."

In "Ezra Pound, Progressive" (*Paideuma* 19, i–ii:77–92), Keith Tuma considers Pound's early politics, largely through a reading of *Patria Mia,* and finds the young Pound firmly within traditions of the American Progressive movement.

The recent explosion of postmodernist studies will surely produce a good flurry in Pound criticism. If we can have a book on postmodern Yeats, surely Pound offers a wide-open field. In "Eliot, Pound and the Subject of Postmodernism" (*CIEFLB* 1, ii:1–10 [1989]), following, although he seems unaware of it, Marjorie Perloff's well-known sorting out of modernism (which includes Eliot) and postmodernism (where we find Pound), Antony Easthope puts Pound briskly through a rather mechanical exercise of measuring him by a series of tags: "No transcendental subject in the text; a failed or perhaps botched transcendence in the place of the grand narrative; the possibility of a metaphysical anchoring point not envisaged at all; the *Cantos* are grounded in a decentered immanence" which "radically affects the rendering of subjectivity and gender." Then postmodernism itself is put into some question as presuming a historical metanarrative *malgré lui.* There will be valuable postmodern revisions of Pound, but Easthope's is not. It is rather provincial, too, in referring mostly to trendy British critics.

c. Relation to Other Writers   The most ambitious project this year of placing Pound within a larger textuality is Dennis Brown's *Intertextual Dynamics Within the Literary Group: Joyce, Lewis, Pound and Eliot* (Macmillan). It should be useful—as an encyclopedic ingathering—to students of literary modernism. For the clarity of writing and organization, and for Brown's willingness to explain everything as he goes along, it would be an excellent source for graduate students and advanced undergraduates. They should be warned, however, not to take too literally some, but by no means all, of the more speculative and attenuated echoes Brown hears. Is *Four Quartets* really in dialogue with Virginia Woolf? By concentrating on the "groupography" (Joyce's word) of these four "Men of 1914," their support of each other (even when on the attack), and their propaganda for the kinds of modernist writing and ways of reading they favored, the book contributes, by means of its exclusions, to the very version of modernism that is the target of so much contemporary wrath and scorn. Yet if one can bracket for a while other perspectives from which Anglo-Irish-American modernism can be viewed, Brown's work is lively and instructive. Even when retracing familiar anecdotes, texts, and documents, he has a fresh way of putting things and of bringing scattered information into stimulating juxtaposition. His chief contribution, he believes, and I agree, is "to argue for the stylistic influence of the early Vorticist prose of Wyndham Lewis on key texts of Joyce, Pound and Eliot [one should add: on Beckett, as well], and to reaffirm Lewis's important role within the Modernist venture." Beyond that, Brown's book is perhaps of less interest for its larger theses—including gestures toward "group psychoanalytic literature"—than in hundreds of suggestive details. There is no bibliography, in the maddening British manner, and the extensive notes are not indexed, so I may have missed references I would expect to find in such a study, and from which Brown could have profited, such as Ian F. A. Bell's *Critic as Scientist: The Modernist Poetics of Ezra Pound* (Methuen, 1981) and Ronald Bush's *The Genesis of Ezra Pound's Cantos* (Princeton, 1976). Yet Brown's apparent unawareness of related studies and his concentration on primary texts allows him a certain freshness, a way of looking at his subject with innocent eyes.

In "Romantic Modernisms: Early Pound and Late Keats" (*Paideuma* 19, i–ii:93–105), Ian F. A. Bell and Patricia A. Agar contribute a particularly ingenious, well-wrought study of intertextual relations among Pound's "Silet," Whitman, Dorothy Shakespear, Pound's own early work, the Roman poet Flamininus, and especially the Keats of "When I have fears" and *Endymion*. This is not only fine criticism but superb detective work, for, as Pound wrote in an earlier poem, " 'Tis Art to *hide* our theft exquisitively." He can hide little from Bell and Agar, who know that "Silet" finds its three major resources "in the secrecy of Pythagorean doctrine, an *uncollected* poem of Whitman, and a rejected draft of Keats." The article is richer than its title suggests, with interesting comments on poetic "impersonality," and on Pound's poetics at the very brink of modernism ("Silet" is dated "Verona 1911" and introduced the *Ripostes* of 1912).

Scott Hamilton is another ingenious critic-detective, one who knows the literature of Symbolism well enough to see around Pound's famous rejections of Symbolism, too often taken at face value, to show how deeply familiar Pound was with an earlier generation of French poets. In "Serenely in the Crystal Jet: A Note on Pound's Symbolist Heritage" (*Paideuma* 19, iii:79–89), Hamilton convincingly recognizes an allusion to Verlaine in Canto 74 as not to "Clair de Lune" but to a poem about London, "Fountain Court," which Verlaine dedicated to Arthur Symons. He provides a much richer explication of Laforgue's "deeps" (in Canto III) than any I have seen. Here, Hamilton focuses primarily on the celebration of Symbolist poets in the Pisan Cantos, but ends with a call for "an extensive reassessment of the influence of French verse on Pound's early poetry." Hamilton's essay is clearly a sampler for a book he is completing on Pound's relations with Symbolism, in which he presumably will answer his own call. It promises to be of great interest.

David Roessel supplies an informative note on Sulpicia (Canto 25) in " 'Or Perhaps Sulpicia': Pound and a Roman Poetess" (*Paideuma* 19, i–ii:125–35). It matters little that the poems Pound quotes from may not be by Sulpicia; Pound thought so, and as a poignant female voice she takes her place in his poem. Yet it is interesting to hear what little there is to know about Sulpicia, and to read her poems, which Roessel supplies, with translations. In "A Periplum of Pound's Pronouncements on John Milton" (*Paideuma* 19, i–ii:147–661), Todd Sammons has printed out everything Pound is known to have said on the subject, little of it complimentary. Bell and Agar, incidentally, have some interesting remarks on Pound and Milton in their piece noted above.

d. The Shorter Poems and Translations   The quality of two essays on *Mauberley* more than compensates for the lack of entries in this category. In " 'It Draws One to Consider Time Wasted': *Hugh Selwyn Mauberley*" (*AmLH* 2, 1:56–78), Ronald Bush contributes a major study of a poem which is not for the young, as I discover whenever I attempt to teach it. It is something of a quandary that a poem can be so rich and moving to one who has lived with it a long time, yet can turn upon clues so subtle as to be almost self-erasing. There are times when one wishes Pound might have found it in him to be just a bit more readerly in his writing. He told Ford that the poem "has form, hell yes, structure," but left that form/structure something for generations to argue about. Bush's essay is a landmark in the critical reception of the poem. Bush offers a lucid summary of the principal disputes and interpretations it has gathered over the years, and he surrounds his reading with extensive quotation from well-known, obscure, and unpublished letters as well as essays and drafts of Cantos. He includes everything that Pound is known to have said about the poem, which is not much (and that to be taken with some suspicion). To one of the critical cruxes of the poem—who "wrote" the final "Medallion," Pound or Mauberley?—Bush offers what seems to me the best answer—both of them. "The product of Mauberley's 'constant elimination,' it embodies one of his 'series / Of curious heads in medallion,' but is mediated by Pound's sardonic controlling frame." I wish he had been as clear about how exactly we should read the full-throated "Envoi" of Part One—who is the "her" the lyric celebrates?—but Bush says little more than that it is a melancholy "lament, distanced by archaic diction and syntax." I cannot agree, for I find the self-consciously bravura gesture of writing within the context of *Mauberley* a lyric which evokes but which is not identical with any older form (technically, the "Envoi" can only be a modern poem) anything but distancing; and it is not particularly melancholy, either. That aside, anyone concerned with *Mauberley* will have to consider Bush's essay, to which this note has hardly done justice.

Another fine essay is William Doreski's *"Mauberley:* The Single Voice" (*Paideuma* 19, i–ii:111–23), which closely examines the relation between the poem and the ongoing *Cantos* project with which it overlapped in composition. Doreski argues for a presiding consciousness across the poem, one that "sees all" in somewhat the manner of Tiresias in *The Waste Land* without being limited by "dramatically identifiable characteristics." This consciousness is to be taken as a "consciously literary voice," critical, not dramatic, and separate from the split personae of Pound/Mauberley. Like Bush, Doreski gives a viable suggestion for reading "Medallion," but avoids a confrontation with "Envoi." Both writers move the discussion away from schematic answers to the question that has dominated readings of the poem: which sections are spoken or written by Pound (or E.P.), which by Mauberley?

Zhaoming Quian's "Translation or Invention: Three *Cathay* Poems Reconsidered" (*Paideuma* 19, i–ii:51–75) gives a close transcultural reading of "Taking Leave of a Friend," "Song of the Bowmen of Shu," and "The River-Merchant's Wife." He builds on the work of others, primarily that of Chinese and Japanese scholars (his "Works Cited" should be helpful to students of Chinese verse), without departing from the familiar judgment that for all of Pound's errors and Fenollosa's misdirections, the spirit of the originals is wonderfully re-created. The careful, almost word-for-word comment by one who seems equally at ease with classical Chinese and with English will be of interest to all students of these poems, especially for many asides on the cultural allusions that have been lost in translation. Included are two transcripts of Fenollosa's notes.

e. The Cantos   There are no major contributions to reading the *Cantos* this year. The articles and the single book noted below can be sorted out:

first, those in which informed writers display an active intelligence moving across the text, sparking ideas in the minds of readers familiar with the poem, sometimes offering new bits of information to the specialist; second, pieces that sound like seminar papers or dissertations that should count themselves lucky to have found publication.

In the first group, by far the most ambitious is Norman Wacker's "Constructive Traditions/Poetic Abstractionism: Discursive Politics in the *Cantos*" (*W & D* 6, i–ii:41–63). Unfortunately, Wacker writes in a rebarbative style that can be irritating. One must also read past the routine warming-up in which Wacker knocks down various straw persons who have not been serious participants in the discourse for a long time—that is, "formalists" and those who "privilege" the lyric. Foucault seems the presiding master here, along with Charles Altieri on "Modernist Abstraction," and Katherine Lindberg, with whose excellent, somewhat Derridean *Reading Pound Reading* Wacker's work is in harmony. Unlike many poststructuralist approaches to Pound, Wacker's is neither reductive nor dismissive; his theory allows for an openness, even a generosity, toward what he calls the poet's "double effort to dominate and yet resist discursive practices." Wacker is good on Pound's sense of tradition, but when he gets round to an attempt to find a viable politics in Pound's textual practice, I see more a leap of faith than anything I can follow—unless I read it as an unwitting poststructural rewriting of Trilling's liberal imagination.

Pound's references to the fourth dimension are part of the *Cantos* that has resisted convincing interpretation. Demetres P. Tryphonopoulos makes a useful (I think probable) suggestion about the source-discourse in "'The Fourth: the Dimension of Stillness': D. P. Ouspensky and Fourth Dimensionalism in Canto 49" (*Paideuma* 19, iii:117–21). He traces the notion through *The New Age* and its editor, Orage, a disciple of Ouspensky and Gurdjieff, and while the evidence remains circumstantial, it is hard to think of Pound walled off from Orage's interests. The article makes one wonder about an aspect of Pound that readers often shy from, in part because of Pound's fuzziness—namely, the fragments of occultism that haunt the poem's margins.

Peter Dale Scott is an alert reader of Pound, and his two contributions this year are well worth reading, less for overriding theses than for a proliferation of suggestive remarks. "Pound in *The Waste Land*, Eliot in *The Cantos*" (*Paideuma* 19, iii:99–114) studies Pound's work on Eliot's poem, and a lifetime's friendship, *agon* and intertextuality. I find it hard,

however, to accept the thesis that the "*Cantos* might have never evolved
from a Browningesque rag-bag towards a sense of order and gradations,
if Pound had not learned, through editing *The Waste Land,* to refine
and assimilate the architectonic referentiality of Eliot's 'true Dantescan
voice.'" But my cavil does not diminish the essay's wider interest. Scott's
"Anger in Paradise: The Poetic Voicing of Disorder in Pound's Later
Cantos" (*Paideuma* 19, iii:47–63) considers the poet's outbursts of anger,
when they are in control, when not, within larger contexts of epic
tradition. Anger and a progressive loss of control are a "great blemish," a
"flaw." Yet, paradoxically, loss of control can become a "redeeming
quality" if one can read through the overt programs of Pound's anger to
an "involuntary poetics" in which cultural and historical ironies are
displayed and exposed. This way of reading may remind one of Fredric
Jameson's reading of Wyndham Lewis. Scott's piece will interest students
of another angry and anti-Semitic figure in the *Cantos,* Sir Edward Coke,
and it touches on Pound's stupid references to right-wing contemporary
extremists such as Admiral John Crommelin and General Pedro del
Valle.

    In "Art and the Spirit of Capitalism: Iconography and History in the
Usura Canto" (*Paideuma* 19, iii:7–31), Jeffrey Twitchell offers a "teasing
out of the specific architectural and artistic references that Pound had in
mind when composing this Canto." Some of the works Twitchell decides
on are associated with Malatesta's Tempio. At times he is frankly speculative, while at other times he offers reasonable identifications. Included
are not-too-easy-to-read reproductions of Bellini, Piero della Francesca,
Botticelli's *Calumny of Apelles,* Fra Angelico, Ambrogio Praedis, and
Mantegna. For the most part, I do not find the extended contextuality
helpful in reading a Canto that speaks better when we are not asked, as
we are in so many other Cantos, to complicate it.

    Sounding like term papers and offering little for serious consideration
are Gregory Eiselein, "Jefferson in the Thirties: Pound's Use of Historical
Documents in *Eleven New Cantos*" (*Clio1* 19, i:32–40); Ellen Brinks,
"On Pound's Fourth Canto" (*Paideuma* 19, i–ii:137–44); Timothy H.
Schermann, "Towards a New Translation of Canto III" (*Paideuma* 19,
iii:123–27); and Barbara Will, "Pound's Feminine Other: A Reading of
Canto 29" (*Paideuma* 19, iii:139–42). The last is a clever-enough manipulation of gender studies discourse to find that Pound "must reveal his
own feminine 'essence' as the source of osmosis."

    Stephen Sicari's "The Epic Ambition: Reading Dante" (*Paideuma* 19, iii:65–78) is said to be an early version of a forthcoming book on Pound, Dante, and the epic. As if asked by a dissertation director to clear a space for himself, Sicari picks spiky arguments with other writers on the subject, such as J. J. Wilhelm and Michael André Bernstein; having cleared the space, he has little to fill it with other than the unstartling idea that we follow the adventures of a "composite wanderer" in a poem deploying and developing something called "the Ulysses theme."

Really, Garland Publishing should be more restrained in its publications aimed, apparently, at hapless libraries. Hilary Clark's *The Fictional Encyclopaedia: Joyce, Pound, Sollers* began as a 1986 doctoral dissertation in comparative literature. It displays its research and attempts to be up to date, but adds little to our sense of Pound or the encyclopedia. In an afterword dated 1990, Clark notes "that encyclopaedic works are largely written by men; a feminist critique of literary encyclopaedism, the project of mastering knowledge, like a political critique, remains to be undertaken." *O tempora, O mores.*

ii Eliot

a. Text, Biography, and Bibliography In the category of biography, Charles Monteith offers a pleasant recollection of his association with Eliot as a fellow junior editor at Faber and Faber in "Eliot in the Office" (*GrandS* 9, iii:90–100). The major attraction of this reminiscence is the inclusion of the text of an intriguing memo Eliot wrote reporting on a French treatise called, fatally, *Vers un Nouveau Prophetisme: essai sur le role du sacré et la situation de Lucifer dans le monde moderne.*

Somewhat less enticing is a four-volume anthology called *T. S. Eliot: Critical Assessments,* ed. Graham Clarke (Christopher Helm), which contains not only a chronology and bibliography of Eliot's major work and some published memoirs, but more than 250 reviews and critical essays up to 1988. Clarke's bibliography of Eliot's publications seems adequate as a checklist, but it does not indicate, even in general terms, the journals in which Eliot published occasional and sometimes very interesting reviews and articles, nor does it point to the existence of important unpublished manuscripts such as the Clark Lectures. (No mention is made of Gallup's bibliography.) The selection of memoirs, interviews, and critical assessments is useful as far as it goes, but it offers no notes on contributors to go with the chronology of entries by date of publication. There are, moreover, major problems with the *terminus ad quem* of the book, which is early 1988, the year of the Eliot centennial, a year which produced many new studies and threw others into new prominence. The resulting omissions might well have been anticipated and a delay in publication advised.

Clarke himself tells us that he has not attempted full coverage, even of all that might be considered major or indispensable, but has rather tried to give a sense of the different voices, viewpoints and kinds of critical writing Eliot's work has spawned. Among other omissions, however, there is not much indication of the continuing controversy over Eliot's putative anti-Semitism and his putative antifeminism. Of course, the easy assumptions that often pass for serious debate on these issues are hardly worth reprinting. (A good step toward setting the record straight is Robert Fleissner's "T. S. Eliot and Anti-Semitism One More Time" in this year's *Yeats Eliot Review* [10, iii:80–81].) But not to offer considered discussions or to reflect these debates in any way is a failure of responsibility to the historical facts of Eliot reception. On a lighter note, *Cats* is a part of Eliot's legacy he would himself by no means have disavowed. Could there not have been a sample review?

Much of the more recent criticism gathered in Clarke's four volumes is also often feeble and/or incidental, and it keeps uncertain company with the stronger entries from earlier times. Compare, for instance, Terry Eagleton's lurid caricature of Eliot (4:190–94)—which begins, incidentally, by mistaking the nature of Eliot's class position, no small error for a critic of Eagleton's persuasion—with Raymond Williams's acute, subtle, and important assessment, still one of the finest perspectives on Eliot we have (4:144–56). Or look at Maude Ellmann's "The Time of Tension" (4:205–10), which recycles the tired notion that Eliot attempted a suppression of personality in the name of some totalizing organic unity, an idea long recognized as inadequate to either Eliot's theory or his practice. Ellmann does better with a sprightly, if superficial quasi-Kristevan reading of *The Waste Land* (2:377–83), but one wants to ask why these and other recent very occasional pieces are *here,* when the issues they address have been addressed far better earlier and/or elsewhere.

Much more rewarding are Clarke's selections from sources contemporary with his subject, both in the form of reviews and memoirs. There you will find many of the major early responses to Eliot's work and person, together with some curious ephemera. Among the latter is a short, weird, and little-known 1945 interview with one J. P. Hodin called "T. S. Eliot on the Condition of Man Today" (1:67–71). Here, Eliot offers Mr. Hodin some uncanny prophecies—which must at the time have seemed almost incomprehensible to this earnest and somewhat portentous inquirer—on the future unification of Europe and its attendant problems, together with equally percipient remarks on communism, the Soviet Union, and its capitalist twin, the United States. Clarke's compendium offers an undoubted abundance of materials that allows for everything from a brilliant extended essay by Wyndham Lewis (which the absence of context has rendered obscure, but which will bear rereading in light of the Constable essay discussed below) to a touching reflection by the now rather obscure American writer Paul Goodman. Goodman's inclusion suggests that Clarke has an eye for the eccentric, even if, at least in approaching recent times, he loses sight of the main line of discussion.

Finally, as a species of "biographical" criticism, I should probably note James Miller's "*Four Quartets* and an 'Acute Personal Reminiscence'" (in Cowan, ed., *T. S. Eliot: Man and Poet,* see below). In an earlier book, Miller implied that Eliot was obsessed with some putative early homosexual encounter with Jean Verdenal and that *The Waste Land* might be read in terms of this obsession. Now, he further insinuates that Eliot had a similarly vexed relationship with John Hayward, which explains, one is amazed to discover, many of the difficulties of interpretation we associate with *Four Quartets.* The tone of these works is queasy, the argument rests on no sound evidence, and the whole does violence to sense and sensibility alike. The biographical issues are covered by Peter Ackroyd (*T. S. Eliot: A Life,* Simon and Schuster, 1984); and a far better critical discussion of Eliot and homoeroticism may be found in John Mayer's *T. S. Eliot's Silent Voices* (Oxford, 1989).

b. General Studies Apart from anthologies, usually the aftermath of conferences during the centennial, I saw no book-length general studies on Eliot of note for 1990. Among the most consistently interesting of these is Shyamal Bagchee's *T. S. Eliot, A Voice Descanting: Centenary Essays* (Macmillan), which contains reproductions of four paintings by David Finn together with thoughtful and lengthy studies by, among others, Charles Altieri, Richard Shusterman, G. Singh, Grover Smith, and the editor. Several of these on specific aspects of Eliot's work will be discussed under the appropriate categories. Shyamal Bagchee is adept at close reading, and the pleasures of his criticism involve watching a good critic employ an apparently incidental motif to tease out a whole pattern of meanings. To take up *unpleasant* as an especially revealing term in Eliot's criticism may seem to be to fabricate a conceit, but consider Bagchee's claim for it: "this matter," he calls it, "of avoidance of the bloody, the real and the contingent," avoidance of that "unnameable something" in the "hollow round of the skull" (p. 265). G. Singh discusses the relation between Leavis and Eliot in "T. S. Eliot and F. R. Leavis" (pp. 226–54) and makes the case that Leavis's was the superior conscience which Eliot had in mind when he wrote in the lines from "Little Gidding": "then fools' approval stings, and honor stains."

Also in anthology form comes the first volume of *T. S. Eliot: Man and Poet* (National Poetry Foundation), ed. Laura Cowan. Like the occasion from which they stem (the pleasant conference on Eliot at Orono, Maine, organized by the foundation in 1988), most of these essays have a relaxed, warm, and collegial tone, a pleasure to reexperience, though it means that some of the great names represented—and indeed some of the lesser ones as well—are not perhaps seen at their best here. Still, there are felicities. A. D. Moody, for instance, lends his poet's ear to the fine registration of tone in Eliot's work and allows us to see in several poems what Pound called "the rose in the steel dust / . . . the ordered dark petals of iron" (pp. 21–35). Moody's essay might be compared to Bruce Campbell's " 'The Word within a Word': The Poetics of T. S. Eliot" (*AmerP* 8, iii:37–45) and Peter Egri's "Reflections on T. S. Eliot's *Vers Libre*" (Bagchee, pp. 164–77). James Longenbach discusses the pervasive gothic shudder in Eliot's work (Cowan, pp. 47–71). Longenbach says acutely of *Sweeney Agonistes* that in reading it "we are victims of a conspiracy, each character having jumped to the degree of reality he showed no evidence of comprehending—now only we are left below" (p. 63). Longenbach is also the first critic to my knowledge to have noted in print how *scary The Waste Land* is. Bagchee, who also has an entry in this anthology, has picked up sharply on the potential offered by Eliot's use of the little qualifiers 'only' and 'all' to lead to deeper issues, including the interplay between determinate and indeterminate meanings in his work (Cowan, pp. 91–107).

In the category of general studies in article form, a solid discussion of Eliot's modernism with emphasis on the term as it pertains to issues of science and religion is James W. Tuttleton's "T. S. Eliot and the Crisis of the Modern" (*Modern Age:* 31, iii–iv [1987]:275–83), and an informative though not newsy overview of Eliot's identity as an American poet by Eloise Knapp Hay in "Conversion and Expatriation. T. S. Eliot's Dual Allegiance" (*Mosaic* 23, ii:89–104). An essay by C. A. Patrides, "T. S. Eliot: Alliances of Levity and Seriousness" (*Sewanee Review* 96, i [1988]:76–94), approaches a difficult issue with tact and trepidation: Eliot's tendency, when not fully in control, to seem to render detachment and impersonality as levity and even callousness.

c. Relation to Other Writers   The sole 1990 book in this category is *Intertextual Dynamics Within the Literary Group—Joyce, Lewis, Pound and Eliot: The Men of 1914,* discussed in the Pound section.

A good read among the articles is Harvey Gross's piece on T. S. Eliot and Thomas Mann, "Compound Ghost, Triple Devil, Terminal Books" (Cowan, pp. 107–23). A friend apparently sent Mann a copy of *Four Quartets* as he was beginning *Dr. Faustus.* Gross does not rest on remarking this connection, however, but explores the ensuing textual intersections with wisdom and understanding. I cherish the apt quotation of one of Mann's devil's best lines: "The situation is too critical to be dealt with without critique." In the same anthology, Joan Fillmore Hooker introduces the translations of Pierre Leyris, alerting us to surprising ranges of tone in the French and demonstrating the enormous gulf between good translation and bad. Also in Cowan's anthology, Mohammad Shaheen has provided a useful introduction to Eliot's influence on Arabic poetry, certainly an essay to consult should anyone wish to undertake a task for which Eliot studies cry out: an estimate of his influence outside Europe, which has been remarkable and, I suspect, unprecedented for any other English language poet except perhaps Whitman. Japan and India come instantly to mind, but Shaheen puts the Arabic-speaking cultures on the agenda as well.

Keith Alldritt finds allusions to "Burnt Norton" in Pound's *Cantos* and takes the occasion to compare the two poems in some detail (Cowan pp. 100–108). The allusions seem tangential, though at least one is striking, but the comparison is perhaps useful pedagogically. Far better, a model of influence studies at once meticulous and sensible, is Grover Smith's "Eliot and the Ghost of Poe" (Cowan, pp. 149–63), which not only makes its case but makes several lucid points about the way influence works in Eliot's poetry. Jonathan Monroe's "Idiom and Cliché in T. S. Eliot and John Ashbery" (*ConL* 31, i:17–36) compares Eliot and Ashbery, a comparison not new, but as the link between the two poets is profound, always worth reconsidering. Monroe does not quite manage to specify their differences clearly, and he spends too much time arguing

a tendentious case for three class divisions, not two, in the second section
of *The Waste Land,* but he raises important issues of diction in modernism and postmodernism.

d. The Poems and Plays A major publication this year is Joseph
Bentley and Jewel Spears Brooker's *Reading* The Waste Land: *Modernism
and the Limits of Interpretation* (Mass.), which elaborates a hermeneutical
approach to the text informed by wide reading from Foucault through
Piaget. The authors situate their work in terms of the epistemological
crisis of 20th-century thought, and they proceed to elaborate, via Bradley, a doubly coded approach to *The Waste Land* that allows them to
move in and out of Eliot's intentions with respect to the text without
trapping themselves inside either his horizon of meaning or the dizzying
wilderness of mirrors that has grown up around the poem. There are
many points at which the reader may wish to part company with these
critics, but it is always in the hope of rejoining them again at a later time,
for the book is well-written and generously conceived. The authors also
have an article on *The Waste Land* in the Cowan anthology, but it does
not do justice to their book.

One article that raises wider issues and offers fine readings as well is
Charles Altieri's "'Preludes' as Prelude: In Defence of Eliot as Sym-
boliste," in the Bagchee anthology. Altieri undertakes to analyze Eliot's
understanding and transformation of Symbolist techniques and offers a
fine critical appraisal of the import and effect of the resulting poetry.
This is one of the few essays I have read in a long time that struck me as
literary criticism in the fullest sense of the term, informed but not
constrained by critical theory and able to register very fine nuances of
aesthetic effect. Altieri manages to show why lyric self-reflexivity in the
hands of genius is capable of producing not only a certain frisson, but a
genuine mutation of consciousness, and his argument, offered both by
precept and example, on the limits of a merely literary historical approach to poetry is entirely convincing and deeply satisfying.

Shorter pieces on *The Waste Land* include Russell Murphy's attempt
to record the impact of the poem on the generation of the sixties (in
Cowan's anthology, pp. 83–91) and Murphy's corresponding argument
that the poem is essentially antiliterary and mimetic of the difficulties of
language (in Bagchee, pp. 51–68).

For "Ash-Wednesday," we have Lois Cuddy's "Circles of Progress in
T. S. Eliot's Poetry: 'Ash-Wednesday' as a Model" (Bagchee, pp. 68–

97) and Louis Martz's "'Ash-Wednesday': Voices for the Veiled Sister" (Cowan, pp. 189–97). Cuddy's essay represents a straightforward interpretive effort governed by Dante and by the poem's Christian background. Louis Martz's seminal work on poetry and meditation has long been vital to Eliot studies, and it is a pleasure to find here his brief and delicate essay, which begins by remarking on Eliot's deletion of the dedication to his (first) wife and ends by recommending its reinstatement on grounds that Martz's critical tact has led us to understand.

Four Quartets are, it seems, poems so elusive that they seem to defeat criticism even more fatally than Eliot's apparently more difficult early work. This year, they continue to elicit a very uneven response, much of it entailing lofty pieties, uncertain divigations into philosophy, stern pronouncements, and/or defensive counterattacks. Patrick Grant, "Knowing Reality: A Reading of *Four Quartets*" (Bagchee, pp. 109–22), understands this problem but does not solve it; Barbara Everett, "East Coker: The Village of the Heart" (Cowan, pp. 197–205), is folksy; my own "Doctrine and Wisdom in *Four Quartets*" (Cowan, pp. 205–19) does not represent my best; and Doris T. Wight, "Metaphysics Through Paradox in Eliot's *Four Quartets*" (*Philosophy and Rhetoric* 23, i:63–69), obscures more than she clarifies.

Here and there, however, a new note is heard, particularly with reference either to the Indic background of Eliot's work or to its possible relationship to deconstruction. (The two issues are perhaps related.) On the Indic influence, we have Siew-Yue Killingley's well-informed "Time, Action, Incarnation: Shades of the *Bhagavad Gita* in the Poetry of T. S. Eliot" in the relatively new, theoretically sophisticated, and sometimes interesting *Literature and Theology* (4, i:50–71). On deconstruction, there are two articles of very unequal quality, one on each side of the perhaps injudiciously posed question of whether "Burnt Norton" is or is not a deconstructive text. Scott R. Christianson, in his curiously titled and underinformed "Defoliating the Garden: Deconstructing 'Burnt Norton'" (*YER* 10, iii:74–79), argues that the poem *is* deconstructive, by which he appears simply to mean self-reflexive. Christianson rests his case too heavily on a binary distinction between "abstract" and "illustrative" levels of diction and on secondary sources for deconstruction to be effective. By contrast, R. V. Young's "'The Loud Lament of the Disconsolate Chimera': Speech and Presence in 'Burnt Norton'" (*C & L* 39, iii:261–80) is a professional job by one who knows Derrida's views on the sign and their relation to philosophical concepts of time and can summarize the Derridean argument on this matter with some degree of accuracy. Young traces the lineage of these articles from William Spanos's (rather torturous) "Hermeneutics and Memory: Destroying T. S. Eliot's *Four Quartets*" (*Genre* 11:523–73), through Gregory Jay's suggestive remarks in *T. S. Eliot and the Poetics of Literary History* (LSU, 1983), to Michael Beehler's *T. S. Eliot, Wallace Stevens, and the Discourses of Difference* (LSU, 1987). Young argues that "Burnt Norton" is, appearances to the contrary, *not* deconstructive, indeed is a kind of preemptive rejoinder to deconstruction and a defense of old-fashioned logocentrism of the most thoroughly Christian kind. Young's position is tenable, but his argument is undercut by its failure to deal with Eliot's own philosophical position, which, as many fine critics have argued, is hard to assimilate to classic logocentrism and indeed seems to anticipate deconstruction in remarkable ways. (See, inter alia, works by Jeffrey Perl, Richard Shusterman, William Skaff, Sanford Schwartz, and Cleo McNelly Kearns.) Young also makes a number of concessions that almost lead him into the deconstructive camp, and he demonizes Derrida by attributing to him views unwarranted by any textual source of which I am aware. We hear, for instance, of Derrida's "resolute atheism" and his "scornful dismissal of the least hint of God or divine influence in human thought or experience." This is certainly not the Derrida heard in "Denials: How to Avoid Speaking," a major statement on negative theology, or in *Of Spirit,* with its explicit dialogue with theology, its talk of *gift* and *grace* and *promise.* Neither of these works by Derrida is mentioned, and hence Young's attack both misses its target and mistakes the target's aim. Still, anyone would benefit from tracing his line of thought and trying to figure out where it goes astray.

The only book-length consideration of Eliot's plays this year is Virginia Phelan's *Two Ways of Life and Death:* Alcestis *and* The Cocktail Party (Garland), which is thoroughly grounded in a knowledge of the classics and demonstrates good interpretive skills, though it still carries a faint aura of its previous life as a thesis. In Badenhausen and Worthen's talks on the plays found in Cowan's *T. S. Eliot: Man and Poet,* we have another too pat antithesis. Phelan argues that the chorus in *Murder in the Cathedral* speaks not in a fully projected "third voice" of poetry, but in something far closer to the poet's first person, while Badenhausen and Worthen argue almost the opposite, that Eliot's attention to the role of the spectator anticipates the impersonal, communal rhetoric of political theater (" 'When the Poet Speaks Only for Himself': The Chorus as

'First Voice' in *Murder in the Cathedral*," in Cowan, pp. 237–52, and "*Murder in the Cathedral* and the Work of Acting," in Cowan, pp. 253–76). You can take your choice on these; each seems to depend on the way the play registers on the writer's own ear and sensibility.

e. Criticism   Understanding of Eliot's critical theory and practice has undergone a major revision in the last few years. For a long time the dominant view was that Eliot was primarily an unsystematic close reader of texts. His work in philosophy was dismissed as a youthful and passing interest, and his dissertation on the idealist philosopher F. H. Bradley regarded as incoherent and irrelevant to his later development. Even after publication of the dissertation itself, this view prevailed. Recently, however, it has been challenged by a number of critics, among them several whose works are reviewed here. These critics have argued that Eliot's critical position was systematic and theoretically informed, well-grounded in philosophy, and indeed anticipated a number of important thinkers, Derrida, Foucault, and Adorno among them. The dissertation in particular has been carefully reread, and presented as it should be, in the words of a member of Eliot's dissertation committee, as "the work of an expert."

The early misunderstanding is due in part to Eliot's own suave distancing of himself from philosophical discourse—a move based on his philosophical position—and his tendency to write about highly technical matters in low-key and deceptively ordinary terms. This stance has deceived many, not least I. A. Richards, who, as John Constable's article on their relationship inadvertently reveals, consistently misunderstood Eliot's objections to his theory of the pseudo-statement as the resistance of an amateur ("I. A. Richards, T. S. Eliot, and the Poetry of Belief," *EIC* 40:222–43). Constable shares this misperception, and his article suffers on that account, although its contribution to research is important. (Wyndham Lewis, however, was not so mystified, and his essay in the Clarke compendium, read in the context of Constable's discoveries, may usefully be reread as an attempt at clarifying the issues at stake between Eliot and Richards.)

Constable's article is complemented by G. Singh's lengthy, informed, and interesting discussion of the personal and critical relationship between Eliot and Leavis and also perhaps by John Needham's "Eliot's Significance as a Critic," both in the Bagchee anthology (pp. 226–54, 271–89, respectively). Needham is on to a number of good leads, draw-

ing Empson, Richards, Leavis, and Eliot together, suggesting the importance of Peirce (whose name is consistently misspelled). Still, his essay is
marred by yet another of a tendentious set of references to deconstruction described here as a "theory of meaning which has no place for
creative complexity; no place, for instance, for rhythm"—so much for the
author of *Tympan!*—and which founders on the familiar rock of asserting
that postmodern criticism is all a tremendous nonsense and that Eliot
was already arguing along those lines. Far better and very helpful on
Eliot's relation to romanticism is J. P. Riquelme's thoughtful "Aesthetic
Values and Processes in Eliot, Arnold and the Romantics" (Cowan,
pp. 277–302).

The reader who wants to chart a more secure path toward understanding Eliot's criticism might well begin with Jewel Spears Brooker's "T. S.
Eliot and the Revolt Against Dualism: His Dissertation on F. H. Bradley in Its Intellectual Context" (Cowan, pp. 303–21) and then proceed
through Sanford Schwartz's clear exposition of Eliot's concept of the objective correlative in terms of his philosophical views, "Beyond the 'Objective Correlative': Eliot and the Objectification of Emotion" (Cowan,
pp. 321–43), to Richard Shusterman's complementary critical appraisal
of that same concept, "Eliot and the Mutations of Objectivity" (Bagchee,
pp. 195–225). A greater sense of the scope of Shusterman's revisionary
views as developed in his important 1988 book, *T. S. Eliot and the
Philosophy of Criticism,* would be gained by reading his "Reactionary
Meets Radical Critique: Eliot and Contemporary Culture Criticism"
(Cowan, pp. 366–94), which has deep affiliations with the Raymond
Williams essay mentioned above. This series of readings might be
capped by Jeffrey Perl's dark consideration of the late, post-Holocaust
Eliot as the ironic dissenter from the chorus of sunny expectations of a
"new world order" ("A Post-War Consensus," in Cowan, pp. 343–66).
All of these essays are mere samplers of their authors' fine books, to
which the reader should at once repair, with Eliot's still vital poetry and
criticism in hand.

Rutgers University
Princeton Theological Seminary

9   Faulkner

M. Thomas Inge

Faulkner criticism continues to maintain its pace ahead of work on other major American writers, at least in quantity. The present essay surveys 17 book-length studies, 16 concordance volumes, two editions, and almost 90 single essays in journals and books, and much of the work is distinguished, representing all modes of theory and ideology. The feminists continue to dominate with no sign of letting up, Faulkner being a tough puzzle on that score, but another big topic this year was Faulkner and popular culture. This was true not so much because that was the topic of the proceedings of the annual conference at Mississippi but because many critics are beginning to understand the importance of viewing a major writer within the whole of the culture and not merely the elite aspects of it. This trend will continue, there being so much more to learn by looking at Faulkner in relation to film, romance, popular literature, and the media, for example. But others will chart its course as this is my final *ALS* essay.

i   Bibliography, Editions, and Manuscripts

While the annual checklists found in the MLA bibliography and the spring issue of *MissQ,* as well as the quarterly ones in *The Faulkner Newsletter,* provide a reasonable amount of information, research for this chapter suggests that a lot of scholarship never makes it onto one or the other. Since neither *The Faulkner Journal* (now three years behind in its publication schedule) nor the *Faulkner Society Newsletter* appear inclined to take up bibliography, we are effectively without comprehensive control of Faulkner research and criticism. One hopes that this will not continue to be the case very long for one of the most discussed writers in American literature.

A useful brief overview of recent criticism in France is found in Arthur Wilhelm's "An Assessment of Current Faulkner Scholarship in France: The Bibliographies of André Bleikasten, Michel Gresset, and François Pitavy" (*MissQ* 43:417–30), also a deserved tribute to three accomplished and influential critics and translators. Those interested in keeping up with the selling prices of first editions can do so through the loose-leaf updated checklists available in the *Author Price Guide* series from Quill & Brush, Box 5365, Rockville, Maryland 20851, compiled by Patricia and Allen Ahearn.

The second Faulkner volume in the Library of America series contains newly edited texts by Noel Polk of *Novels 1936–1940* including *Absalom, Absalom!; The Unvanquished; If I Forget Thee, Jerusalem,* originally published as *The Wild Palms;* and *The Hamlet.* Polk has returned to the typescripts for his texts to discover the author's intentions before the editorial process began at Random House, an approach which he is the first to admit raises more questions than it solves. Whether these typescript texts should entirely replace the texts as originally published remains a matter of debate, but Polk is to be complimented for the faithful fulfillment of his commitment to a textual ideal. Joseph Blotner has contributed an excellent chronology of Faulkner's life to the edition. Louis D. Brodsky and Robert W. Hamblin have once again expanded the published canon by editing a text of *Stallion Road* (Miss.), another screenplay that never made it onto film but which demonstrates Faulkner's clear skills as a screenwriter.

Noel Polk is also to be thanked for seeing through to completion with John D. Hart the Faulkner Concordances project from UMI Research Press with a final complement of 16 volumes covering seven titles (the largest number to appear in any one year): *Collected Stories* (including *These 13* and *Dr. Martino and Other Stories*) in 5 vols.; *The Hamlet* in 2 vols.; *The Unvanquished; Sanctuary: The Original Text; Sanctuary: Corrected First Edition Text; Uncollected Stories* in 5 vols.; and *The Reivers.* Except for the first three novels which are not included, scholars can now locate a remembered passage, trace Faulkner's allusions and symbolic patterns, or study his diction and word choices throughout the major works. A testing out of selected pages in these volumes, as proved true in the earlier ones, will demonstrate an unfailing accuracy.

Another valuable reference project, The Garland Faulkner Annotation Series (Garland), saw two titles published: *Soldiers' Pay* annotated by Margaret Yonce and *As I Lay Dying* annotated by Dianne C. Luce. These provide identifications for allusions, language, and events that may puzzle readers, and most of us need all the help we can get. Any effective Faulkner parody must include such vagueness, as the winners of the first annual Faulkner Write-Alike Contest found out, eight of whose efforts were published in "Faux Faulkner" (*American Way* 23, xv [August 1, 1990]:55–64).

ii Biography

Most of Louis D. Brodsky's *William Faulkner, Life Glimpses* (Texas) has previously appeared in several journals (see *ALS 1981*, p. 147; *1982*, p. 149; *1985*, pp. 149, 151; *1986*, p. 141; *1987*, pp. 132, 137; *1988*, pp. 140, 145), but it is useful to have his carefully researched and thoughtful pieces and interviews gathered together in a revised form. Drawing on his impressive collection of documents, the essays give us new glimpses of Faulkner the public figure, the poet, the screenwriter, and the family man. It would be good to have a full biography from Brodsky, a collector turned scholar. Casual in its approach and containing little that we do not already know about Faulkner, Herman E. Taylor's memoir *Faulkner's Oxford: Recollections and Reflections* (Rutledge Hill Press) is largely about growing up in Oxford where his family was prominent and well-known to the Falkners. It is a congenial book of primary interest to local historians.

Faulkner's Mississippi (Oxmoor) is a handsome oversized book with a lucid text by Willie Morris and evocative color photographs by William Eggleston. Morris has expanded his journalistic essay written for the March 1989 issue of *National Geographic* into an engaging personal disquisition on a man he never met but whose presence pervades the lives of all writers of his generation. While focusing on the present, Eggleston somehow captures in his photographs glimpses of the past that Faulkner knew and wrote about. Another famous writer, Richard Wright, praised Faulkner's artistic honesty and personal integrity in the face of racist forces in the United States in a 1950 essay now translated from the French as "A Man of the South" (*MissQ* 42:255–57). Jane Isbell Haynes locates actual events probably known to Faulkner that may have inspired "Afternoon of a Cow" in "A Note on Faulkner's Cows" (*MissQ* 43:413–16). William Boozer continues to publish useful biographical items in *The Faulkner Newsletter*.

iii Criticism: General

The Ink of Melancholy: Faulkner's Novels from The Sound and the Fury *to*
Light in August (Indiana) by André Bleikasten began as his doctoral
thesis from which he extracted two books published in English on *As I
Lay Dying* in 1973 (see *ALS 1973*, p. 143) and *The Sound and the Fury* in
1976 (see *ALS 1976*, pp. 131–32) as well as a number of essays (see *ALS
1969*, p. 116; *1970*, p. 123; *1983*, pp. 156, 164; *1985*, pp. 160–61, 459; *1986*,
pp. 150, 421; *1987*, p. 140). The thesis was revised for publication in
French as *Parcours de Faulkner* in 1982, and now the entire monumental
work is made available in English. Bleikasten adopts no single critical
strategy but employs them all as they fit the texts in one of the most
insightful and intelligent studies to appear in the last decade. He believes
"Faulkner's texts are not deposits of fixed and final meaning for us to
decipher; they are discharges of mental energy, fields of turbulence,
records of battles won and lost, and we never find them again in the same
state as we left them." His jargon-free prose and unexpected insights
make Bleikasten a pleasure to read, and his readings of the four major
works of Faulkner's best period have already had a considerable influence
on the critical community.

In *Faulkner's Fables of Creativity: The Non-Yoknapatawpha Novels*
(Georgia), Gary Harrington searches exhaustively for self-reflexivity in
the five novels outside the mainstream fiction and sees Faulkner's self-
conscious reflections on what it means to be an artist and a reader as
central concerns. The results are often ingenious readings of generally
neglected novels, and the individual chapters are insightful, but in
general the works appear to have been forced to yield a consistency
beyond Faulkner's intentions. A study of all Faulkner's works as metafiction would be a next logical step for Harrington and probably more
revealing.

While Faulkner expressed disdain for popular culture in general, just
how important it can be in understanding a writer of his generation is
amply displayed in *Faulkner and Popular Culture* (Miss.), Doreen Fowler
and Ann J. Abadie, eds., the proceedings of the fifteenth Faulkner
conference held at the University of Mississippi in 1988. In the first essay
(pp. 3–21), Joseph Blotner traces the ways popular culture touched the
writer's life and career, while my essay on "Faulknerian Folklore: Public
Fictions, Private Jokes, and Outright Lies" (pp. 22–33) argues that he

well understood how the mass media worked, and he consciously used that knowledge to create in the public eye the image of a shy, reclusive farmer (this essay oddly enough has been translated and published in Chinese in *Foreign Literature* 36 [1989]:13–23 and in Russian in *Inostrannia Literatura,* no. 7:197–210). Likewise, Louis Budd suggests correctly I believe in "Playing Hide and Seek with William Faulkner: The Publicly Private Artist" (pp. 34–58) why we should take lightly Faulkner's insistence on privacy given his own frequent excursions into the public spotlight. George Garrett's "What William Faulkner Got and Gave Us from Pop Culture" (pp. 59–74) wittily examines the pitfalls Faulkner faced in trying to write serious works that were also popular novels.

Judith L. Sensibar's "Pop Culture Invades Jefferson: Faulkner's Real and Imaginary Photos of Desire" (pp. 110–41) is an especially skillful analysis of how relations among gender issues, creativity, and desire are made manifest in Faulkner's own drawings, photographs, and fictional photographs (another version of the essay appears in *Out of Bounds,* pp. 290–315), and William Brevda finds unusual but engaging fare in discussing "Neon Light in August: Electric Signs in Faulkner's Fiction" (pp. 214–41). In a general essay unrelated to the conference topic, "The High Sheriff of Yoknapatawpha County: A Study in the Genius of Place" (pp. 242–64), Louis D. Rubin, Jr., deftly summarizes a lifetime of thinking and writing about the author. The other essays in this book dealing with specific novels are discussed in the appropriate sections below.

A. Robert Lee's fine collection of new essays, *William Faulkner: The Yoknapatawpha Fiction* (St. Martin's), contains three general pieces (the four specific ones will be discussed below also). James H. Justus intelligently discusses "Faulkner's Fortunate Geography" (pp. 19–41) as it relates to feeling, memory, and literal place, and Lee's "Modernist Faulkner? A Yoknapatawpha Trilogy" (pp. 42–63) examines the tensions between modernism and ancient writ in *The Sound and the Fury, As I Lay Dying,* and *Absalom, Absalom!* Eric Mottram takes up a fresh topic which elucidates the fiction in "Law, Justice and Justification in William Faulkner" (pp. 85–127).

Thomas Daniel Young carefully traces the changes in Narcissa Benbow through *Flags in the Dust, Sanctuary,* and "There Was a Queen" and how her understanding of love reflects her character in "Narcissa Benbow's Strange Love/s" (*American Declarations of Love,* pp. 88–103), and

Mark Frisch begins to make progress in a new and regretfully under-studied area of research in "Self-Definitions and Redefinition in New World Literature: William Faulkner and the Hispanic American Novel" (*Critica Hispanica* 12:115–31), with specific attention to Eduardo Mallea and Gabriel García Márquez. A most unusual topic is approached by Paul Carmignani in "Olfaction in Faulkner's Fiction" (*MissQ* 43:305–15), but to what purpose is unclear, except for the scent of satire (a longer version appears in French as "William Faulkner: à vue de nez [following one's nose]," *RFEA* 45:137–48).

"A Dialogic Hereafter: *The Sound and the Fury* and *Absalom, Absalom!*" by Olga Scherer (*Southern Literature and Literary Theory*, pp. 300–317) is, of course, a Bakhtinian analysis of the two novels, one of many the critic has been writing on Faulkner in French since 1968. The argument cannot be summarized in a sentence but must be carefully and patiently fol-lowed. Patience is also required but with less reward in the impene-trable psychoanalytic jargon of "Faulkner's Dispossession of Personae Non Gratae" by Richard Feldstein (*Psychoanalysis and . . .*, pp. 175–86). Linda Wagner-Martin's succinct survey, *The Modern American Novel 1914–1945*, in just a few pages strongly argues that "Faulkner's fiction serves as a showcase for his belief in organic form."

It is a concern for Faulkner's tendency to recycle and rewrite material, to engage in continual revision and repetition that attracts Richard C. Moreland's interest as a way of understanding the author's response to the social and psychological forces of modernism in *Faulkner and Mod-ernism: Rereading and Rewriting* (Wisconsin). Using structuralist, Marx-ist, and deconstructive theory with discretion, and paying attention to matters of race, gender, and class, as well as irony and humor, Moreland finds positive forces at work in Faulkner's artistic struggles. Most of the novels and some stories are treated, with fullest attention to *Absalom, Absalom!, The Hamlet, Requiem for a Nun,* and *Go Down, Moses.*

iv Criticism: Special Studies

Gender, race, and ethnicity may be the trinity of the day in critical circles, although the phrase itself has become almost a cliché. The latter two have been fairly well mined by Faulknerians; feminism, however, remains a significant preoccupation. The major book this year is *The Feminine and Faulkner: Reading (Beyond) Sexual Difference* (Tennessee) by Minrose Gwin, who finds that in Faulkner's "most problematic texts, woman is force—not force which derives simply from procreation, as many of Faulkner's critics have maintained, but one which extends procreatively beyond its obvious boundaries toward an intellectual velocity relating to subversion and modernity." Gwin adopts a bold strategy of speaking in a very personal voice and engaging in what she calls a "conversation" with the texts of *The Sound and the Fury*, *Absalom, Absalom!*, and *The Wild Palms*. The result is a disarming and astonishing piece of criticism that cleverly wends its way through the minefields of postmodern theory to challenging conclusions.

More problematic and reductive in its approach is *Faulkner's Marginal Couple: Invisible, Outlaw, and Unspeakable Communities* (Texas) by John N. Duvall, who finds it necessary to construct and oppose a straw man (not straw person) conspiracy at work in criticism by something called the "Southern Agrarian influence" led by Cleanth Brooks and Robert Penn Warren. Brooks has emerged lately as everyone's good old whipping boy in Faulkner studies. This is unnecessary because Duvall's point that Faulkner created "deviant" couples who formed alternative communities and violated "normal" gender roles is true enough and can be defended without oversimplifying Brooks's opinions, which are arguably more complex than Duvall allows. *Light in August*, *The Wild Palms*, *Sanctuary*, *Pylon*, and *Absalom, Absalom!* are the main novels treated here with what mainly is considerable insight on matters of gender.

Two essayists came out in strong support of Faulkner's fair treatment of women, "Faulkner, Women and Yoknapatawpha: From Symbol to Autonomy" by Faith Pullin (*William Faulkner: The Yoknapatawpha Fiction*, pp. 64–84) and "Victim Unvanquished: Temple Drake and Women Characters in Faulkner's Novels" by Abby H. P. Werlock (*Women and Violence in Literature*, pp. 3–49), but neither is as sophisticated as Gwin or Duvall in their perceptions.

Place remains a matter of concern for at least two critics. Frederick Turner includes a chapter on "Place Spirits: William Faulkner's *Absalom, Absalom!* and 'The Bear'" in his book *Spirit of Place* (pp. 203–45), and Robert Glen Deamer discusses "The Adamic Hero and the Southern Myth: Faulkner's Isaac McCaslin and Quentin Compson" in his study *The Importance of Place* (pp. 153–69). By combining biography, criticism, and interviews made during a visit to the Oxford countryside, Turner provides some engaging new views, but Deamer summarizes the traditional consensus.

Faulkner's debts to two writers are briefly discussed in Lance Lyday's "Faulkner's Miss Reba and Shakespeare's Drunken Porter" (*LJHum* 16:69–80) and Jeffrey Meyers's "Conrad's Influence on Modern Writers" (*TCL* 36:186–206, specifically pp. 190–91). Faulkner's influence on Styron is detailed by Christopher Metress in " 'a new father, a new home': Styron, Faulkner, and Southern Revisionism" (*SNNTS* 22:308–22).

v **Individual Works to 1929**

Among Faulkner's first four published novels, only *The Sound and the Fury* received significant attention this year. The Sound and the Fury: *Faulkner and the Lost Cause* by John T. Matthews (Twayne) is elucidating for specialists and students alike. While reflecting on the background, reception, and critical consensus about the meaning of the novel, Matthews advances his own view that the work is one that "wonders about how speech grows out of loss and longing, how language both desires and prevents true communion." Sally Wolff and David Minter provide a meticulous and informative account of the composition of the novel in "A 'Matchless Time': Faulkner and the Writing of *The Sound and the Fury*" (*Writing the American Classics,* pp. 156–76), and Philip Cohen and Doreen Fowler have edited and helpfully introduced yet another but remarkable text of "Faulkner's Introduction to *The Sound and the Fury*" (*AL* 62:262–83), which is more revealing of Faulkner's attitude toward his masterwork than anything we have seen so far. "Harrison Smith: The Man Who Took a Chance on *The Sound and the Fury*" (*Faulkner and Popular Culture,* pp. 163–78) by Tom Dardis is an engaging vignette of the publisher who saw the book into print.

"The Necessity of Signifying Something: Quentin Compson's Rejection of Despair" by Janet St. Clair (*MissQ* 43:317–34) takes a new and interesting approach by persuasively arguing that Quentin is more a success than a failure and "his heroic devotion to communal solidarity remains central to the novel's significance." Ineke Bockting puts Quentin on the couch and through an analysis of language finds him to be a psychotic in "The Impossible World of the 'Schizophrenic': William Faulkner and Quentin Compson" (*Style* 24:484–97).

Webb Salmon rightly comments on the oddity of "Quentin's Absence from Caddy's Tree-Climbing Scene" (*FJ* 3, ii [1988]:48–53) in the novel, particularly since he is the one most tragically affected by the sight. Whether this was an oversight on Faulkner's part remains a question, since his later comments indicate that he thought Quentin was there. Harold Bloom has given us another of his factory-made anthologies devoted to major literary characters, *Caddy Compson* (Chelsea). The selection of abstracts in this case is judicious and useful. The cover painting strangely depicts a child of about twelve in shorts standing in the branches of a tree rather than Caddy as a seven-year-old child with muddy drawers ascending the tree as in the novel. Leon Forrest's "Faulkner/Reforestation" (*Faulkner and Popular Culture*, pp. 207–13) is an appreciation of the Deacon and Dilsey who survive through reinvention, a major attribute of black culture.

vi   Individual Works, 1930–1939

Recalcitrance, Faulkner, and the Professors (Iowa) by Austin M. Wright is a piece of fiction, a critical tour de force, and a genuine pleasure to read amid so much scholarship that takes itself far too seriously. In an imaginary English department, two professors, one a formalist and the other a postmodernist, engage in a debate over the relative merits of theory using *As I Lay Dying* as the text and the daughter of the chair of the department as the prize. The novel is entertainingly examined from all variety of critical perspectives, and a good deal is revealed about the state of recent criticism, but the reader will have to finish the book to discover the outcome. Patrick Samway's position in the above debate would be clear in his essay on "Addie's Continued Presence in Faulkner's *As I Lay Dying*" (*Southern Literature and Literary Theory*, pp. 284–99). He thoroughly supports his view that "the narrative, structural, and semiotic techniques are so innovative and bold in terms of theories of art, film, language, communication, and even advances in recording technology . . . that the total imaginative effect reaches cosmic proportions." Except for an occasional lapse into specialized vocabulary, José Angel García Landa provides a straightforward accounting of "Reflexivity in the Narrative Technique of *As I Lay Dying*" (*ELN* 27, iv:63–72).

Donald M. Kartiganer sees the novel as situated "squarely in the center of the theoretical dualisms that have come to dominate the way we think about modern and postmodern writing" (as Wright makes clear) and brilliantly explores the modes of language in "The Farm and the Journey: Ways of Mourning and Meaning in *As I Lay Dying*" (*MissQ* 43:281–303). Georgiann Potts summarizes the use of African American cultural elements in "Black Images in Faulkner's *As I Lay Dying*" (*UMSE* n.s. 7 [1989]:2–26), based on much intriguing original research in the black community. The lore of Native Americans is brought to bear by Reuben J. Ellis in "Faulkner's Totemism: Vardaman's 'Fish Assertion' and the Language Issue in *As I Lay Dying*" (*JAmS* 24:408–13). Two intelligent and useful source notes are "The Bundrens on the Road to Armageddon: Faulkner's Use of St. John's Revelation in *As I Lay Dying*" (*POMPA*, pp. 192–95) by Deborah Wilson and "The Symbolic Significance of Dewey Dell Bundren's Name" (*AN&Q* n.s. 3:114–16) by Charles M. Chappell and John M. Churchill.

In admirably lucid prose, Laura E. Tanner well substantiates her disturbing thesis that Faulkner manipulates the reader into actually becoming the violator of Temple in "Reading Rape: *Sanctuary* and *The Women of Brewster Place*" (*AL* 62:559–82), and she provides interesting comparisons with the fiction of Gloria Naylor and the art of Marcel Duchamp. David Seed reads the novel as horror fiction in "The Evidence of Things Seen and Unseen: William Faulkner's *Sanctuary*" (*American Horror Fiction*, pp. 73–91) with interesting results, again suggesting Faulkner's awareness and uses of popular culture. Leslie Fiedler views the novel in the broader context of popular fiction of the time, especially romance, detective fiction, and pornography, and finds unexpected connections in "Pop Goes Faulkner: In Quest of *Sanctuary*" (*Faulkner and Popular Culture*, pp. 75–92), and David Madden establishes the use and meaning of photographic images in the novel in "Photographs in the 1929 Version of *Sanctuary*" (*Faulkner and Popular Culture*, pp. 93–109), an engaging personal essay. "'A Cheap Idea . . . Deliberately Conceived to Make Money': The Biographical Context of William Faulkner's Introduction to *Sanctuary*" by Philip Cohen (*FJ* 3, ii [1988]:54–66) is a meticulous reconstruction of why Faulkner wrote the notorious introduction which has served to tarnish the novel undeservedly.

Brian Richardson's "Death by Fiction in *Light in August*" (*FJ* 3, ii[1988]:24–33) argues that it "contains a subterranean though insistent metafictional drama which centers on the interpretation of signs and the generation of narratives" and well substantiates his view. Paul S. Nielsen examines the way the method of deliberately withholding meaning affects three main characters, as well as the importance of ritual in their lives, in "Secrets, Ritual and Inheritance in *Light in August*" (*SoR* 26:801–13), and Christopher Jowise takes a fresh look at the use of Christian symbols in "Living Fiction: Redefining the Symbol in Faulkner's

Light in August" (*MissQ* 43:367–76). David Timms reads the novel as Bakhtinian Carnival literature in "Carnival Yoknapatawpha: Faulkner's *Light in August"* (*William Faulkner: The Yoknapatawpha Fiction*, pp. 128–46), and David M. Toomey attempts to support the possibility that Faulkner knew the work of Carl Jung in "A Jungian Reading of *Light in August's* 'Christmas Sections'" (*SoQ* 28, ii:43–57). Joan Wylie Hall demonstrates the importance of separating two characters with the same name in "The Two Nathaniel Burringtons of *Light in August"* (*FJ* 3, ii[1988]:34–39). John T. Matthews also finds Bakhtin's theories of Carnival literature extremely useful in "The Autograph of Violence in Faulkner's *Pylon*" (*Southern Literature and Literary Theory*, pp. 247–69) and has new things to say about that generally neglected work.

Dirk Kuyk, Jr., author of *Threads Cable-strong: William Faulkner's* Go Down, Moses (see *ALS 1983*, p. 167), has given us another book-length study of a complex work in *Sutpen's Design: Interpreting Faulkner's* Absalom, Absalom! (Virginia). Kuyk believes that nearly all critics have misunderstood "both what Sutpen is trying to do and how the narration works." As in a detective novel, he works his way through all the possibilities to come with conviction to clear conclusions. Whether or not one agrees with him entirely, there is little doubt in my mind that his careful reading must be acknowledged or addressed by future critics. Relying as it does on theoretical vocabulary from Derrida and Lacan, a good deal more difficult and less rewarding is Alexandre Leupin's "*Absalom, Absalom!:* The Outrage of Writing" (*Southern Literature and Literary Theory*, pp. 226–46), the main concerns of which are narrative and voice. Leslie Heywood is also concerned with language and narrative voice in a finely tuned feminist reading, "The Shattered Glass: The Blank Space of Being in *Absalom, Absalom!*" (*FJ* 3, ii [1988]:12–23).

Perhaps the most original essay this year is "*Absalom, Absalom!:* The Movie" (*AL* 62:56–73) by Joseph Urgo, who brilliantly supports the seemingly unlikely thesis that the novel is about "movie-making" and the production of narrative and images under the collaborative conventions of Hollywood. The positive importance of Faulkner's screenwriting is once again underlined as well. Although Kuyk would argue that he has misunderstood Sutpen's "design," Bernhard Radloff finds "vengefulness, transcendence, and willful innocence" at the heart of Sutpen's intentions in a sensible reading of the novel, "The Fate of Demonism in William Faulkner" (*ArQ* 46, i:27–50). Richard Gay finds interesting things to say by placing the novel into the context of chivalric romance and *Le Morte d'Arthur* in "Arthurian Tragedy in Faulkner's *Absalom, Absalom!*" (*NMW* 22:29–40). George P. Landow suggests that Graham Swift's 1983 novel *Waterland* is a "postmodern rewriting" of *Absalom, Absalom!*, among other things, in "History, His Story, and Stories in Graham Swift's *Waterland*" (*SLitI* 23, ii:197–211).

Susan Donaldson has studied the revisions Faulkner made in the original *Post* stories incorporated in *The Unvanquished* in "Dismantling the *Saturday Evening Post* Reader: *The Unvanquished* and Changing 'Horizons of Expectations' " (*Faulkner and Popular Culture*, pp. 179–95) and concludes that he rebuked the circumscribed expectations of the average *Post* reader by addressing questions in the novel that would have unsettled the reader. Donaldson is an astute critic, but I doubt this reading of Faulkner's intentions as a writer who set out intentionally either to rebuke or educate his readers in book or magazine. He did know how to write, however, for different audiences. David Rogers considers the attitudes toward race found in the novel through an imaginative evaluation of hands and handshakes in "Shaking Hands: Gestures Toward Race in William Faulkner's *The Unvanquished*" (*MissQ* 43:335–48). Equally interesting are two articles whose titles reflect their content: "Moving Fast Sideways: A Look at Form and Image in *The Unvanquished*" (*FJ* 3, ii [1988]:40–47) by Robert Gibb and "Seasonal Imagery and the Pattern of Revenge in *The Unvanquished* (*NMW* 21:41–51) by Susan Garland Mann. *The Wild Palms* seems to have become a center for gender studies, and Anne Goodwyn Jones submits it to her practical critical intelligence in a feminist essay, " 'The Kotex Age': Women, Popular Culture, and *The Wild Palms*" (*Faulkner and Popular Culture*, pp. 142–62). Her insights are stimulating.

vii   Individual Works, 1940–1949

Arthur F. Kinney's excellent lengthy survey of the presence of the Mc-Caslin family in Faulkner's fiction, their historical backgrounds in life and lore, and the criticism of the works about them in what stands as the introduction to his edition of *Critical Essays on William Faulkner: The McCaslin Family* (Hall) is alone worth the price of admission. Add to that the rich collection of resources, documents, reprinted essays, and five brand-new essays by Mick Gidley, Albert J. Devlin, Elisabeth Muhlenfield, Bernard W. Bell, and Richard H. King, each a substantial contribution, and the book becomes indispensable to a study of *Go*

Down, Moses, Intruder in the Dust, The Reivers, and other works featuring the McCaslins. Michael Toolan's intent in *The Stylistics of Fiction* (Routledge) is to determine whether the study of style more properly belongs to the field of linguistics or literary criticism, using *Go Down, Moses* as his display text. The study is impressive and exhaustive, but only the diehard lover of language study will see him through to the end.

Also concerned with language, but for its symbolic functions and ability to evoke place, is Graham Clarke's "Marking Out and Digging In: Language as Ritual in *Go Down, Moses*" (*William Faulkner: The Yoknapatawpha Fiction*, pp. 147–64). William P. Dawson examines the themes of free will and fate in the book by placing it in the context of Greek thought and literature, and he finds interesting insights in "Fate and Freedom: The Classical Background of *Go Down, Moses*" (*MissQ* 43:387–412). Brief but noteworthy are "From Getting Married to Getting Buried: The Agenda of Women in *Go Down, Moses*" (*JASAT* 21:50–56) by David L. Vanderwerken, and "Sam Fathers' Identity—A Puzzle" (*NMW* 22:41–47) by Webb Salmon, who notes the confusion in the texts about Sam Fathers's ethnic heritage.

Patricia R. Schroeder has written a thorough account of Faulkner's shifting uses of Ratliff as comic narrator in "Ratliff's Descent from the Buckboard: Tall Tale Techniques in *The Hamlet*" (*FJ* 3, ii [1988]:2–11), and she shows how Faulkner improved on his Old Southwestern humor forebears. Jean E. Graham takes one more look at the seeming conflict between moralizing and dramatizing in *Intruder in the Dust* and discovers the rhetoric essential to the structure and meaning of the novel in "Gavin Stevens in Faulkner's *Intruder in the Dust*: Only Too Rhetorical Rhetoric?" (*SLJ* 22, ii:78–89). "Can only Southerners know what it is to be Southern?" is the philosophic question asked by David Millard in "What Is It Like to Be a Faulkner?" (*Perspectives on Perception*, pp. 139–56) using *Intruder in the Dust* as a basis for his discourse. He concludes: "I don't know, and can't know, what it is like to be a Faulkner, but I have his word for it that I have a significant capacity for some pretty good inferences." I suspect we knew that already. "Faulkner's Gambit" by William Schafer (*ArmD* 23:282–91) is an amiable survey of the mystery and detective elements in all of Faulkner's fiction, settling on *Knight's Gambit* for special attention; "*Knight's Gambit*: Poe, Faulkner, and the Tradition of the Detective Story" by John T. Irwin (*ArQ* 46, iv:95–116) is a more scholarly and richer appreciation. Both are worth reading, and both explore another popular culture connection.

viii Individual Works, 1950–1962

Andrew Hook surveys some of the virtues and failings of "The Snopes Trilogy" (*William Faulkner: The Yoknapatawpha Fiction,* pp. 165–79), that is, *The Town, The Hamlet,* and *The Mansion,* to determine why they have a lesser reputation than other works and finds worthy things but no reason to elevate them as great novels. George Anderson focuses on the second work in "Toward a Reading of *The Town* as a Chronicle: Respectability and Race in Three Episodes" (*MissQ* 43:377–85) and argues that the episodic structure is the very thing that gives it coherence. Except for the general discussions already mentioned, neither *Requiem for a Nun, A Fable,* nor *The Reivers* was the subject of an individual article this year.

ix The Stories

"Marking Space, Charting Time: Text and Territory in Faulkner's 'The Bear' and [Alejo] Carpentier's *Los pasos perdidos*" by Wendy B. Faris (*Do the Americas Have a Common Literature?,* pp. 243–65) is an important comparative study of the ways two experimental writers make effective use of time, space, and place. Kathy Cackett argues that *The Garden of Eden* by Hemingway was partly written to settle the rivalry between him and Faulkner and finds it "thematically similar" to "The Bear" in *"The Garden of Eden:* Challenging Faulkner's Family Romance" (*HN* 9, ii:155–68). Judson D. Watson III turns to two stories in " 'Hair,' 'Smoke,' and the Development of the Faulknerian Lawyer Character" (*MissQ* 43:349–66) to trace the character development of Gavin Stevens. Bruce Kawin uses "Golden Land" to expand in sensible ways on Faulkner's attitude toward Hollywood and the impact of screenwriting on his work and career in "Sharecropping in the Golden Land" (*Faulkner and Popular Culture,* pp. 196–206).

Three of the usual notes appeared this year. Joan Wylie Hall's "Faulkner's Barn Burners: Ab Snopes and the Duke of Marlborough" (*NMW* 21:65–68) explains a reference in "Barn Burning" to John Churchill, first duke of Marlborough. Paul Rogalus explicates one scene in "Faulkner's 'Dry September' " (*Expl* 48, iii:211–12) as an example of his "technical genius." Finally, there is the inevitable note on that most explicated of all short stories, Michael L. Burduck's "Another View of the Narrator in 'A Rose for Emily' " (*UMSE* n.s. 8:209–11), which takes the equally inevitable tack, all others being exhausted, that the narrator is a woman. The evidence is not convincing. Why not assume that the narrator collectively represents the community, male and female? But for Faulknerians, bless their complex hearts, why take a simple solution when a more complicated one is at hand? Sho now, what would Faulkner do?

Randolph-Macon College

10 Fitzgerald and Hemingway

Susan F. Beegel

This year I have reviewed 17 Fitzgerald and 78 Hemingway items. Some disparity in the publication record on these authors is normal, but if it were not for the triumphant appearance of *The F. Scott Fitzgerald Manuscripts,* 1990 would be a black year indeed for Fitzgerald studies, so scarce are books and articles. One hopes the F. Scott Fitzgerald Society, fledged this spring, will rejuvenate the field by providing forums for discussion and publication, as well as a running bibliography. An overview of Hemingway studies holds clues to continuing vigor—feminist approaches and attention to gender issues have entered the mainstream, and a wide variety of critical methods are tolerated. Scholars are just beginning to contemplate Hemingway's potentially controversial role in a multicultural classroom, while keeping sight of values in his work that might unite even the most diverse community. Finally, it is good to see Fitzgerald and Hemingway scholars doing their spadework, making a start at filling the need for facsimile reproductions, concordances, reference guides, and bibliographies.

i Textual Studies

Thanks to the efforts of Matthew J. Bruccoli, both Fitzgerald and Hemingway studies benefited this year from the publication in facsimile of important manuscripts. Nineteen ninety marks the appearance of the inaugural volumes in what is to be an 18-volume set of *The F. Scott Fitzgerald Manuscripts* (Garland), ed. Bruccoli, with associate editor Alan Margolies, and consulting editors Alexander P. Clark and Charles Scribner III. The project, surely the most ambitious undertaking in Fitzgerald scholarship for many years, aims to democratize textual studies of the author's work by making available in facsimile virtually the entire contents of the Fitzgerald archive at Princeton University, supplemented by materials held in other collections.

I have received two handsome, folio-sized volumes of material on *This Side of Paradise*, two on *The Beautiful and Damned*, one on *The Great Gatsby*, and three on *The Last Tycoon*. An introduction, inventory of extant materials, and chronology of composition is provided for each title in the series, followed by large, comfortably legible facsimiles of all known working notes, manuscripts, typescripts, corrected carbons, and galley proofs of the work, arranged in chronological order of their composition according to the editors' best judgment. There is little here to criticize, except perhaps the editors' decision not to include a facsimile of *The Great Gatsby* manuscripts. Yes, a facsimile was published in 1973, and so a repetition ought not to be necessary—but it is disconcerting to see Fitzgerald's best-known novel represented solely by a slender volume of revised and rewritten galley proofs in what could be a complete collection.

However, the project is executed with great care, and although Bruccoli wisely counsels that it is often necessary for textual scholars to examine paper and ink, there is no doubt that this set is almost as serviceable as a carrel at Princeton. College and university libraries nationwide should be urged to add *The F. Scott Fitzgerald Manuscripts* to their collections, and the set's widespread availability ought to spur a renaissance of interest in Fitzgerald's considerable craft. Volumes on *Tender is the Night, The Vegetable,* the short stories, and the articles are forthcoming in 1991.

Hemingway scholars, of course, would love to have a similar multi-volume set of *The Ernest Hemingway Manuscripts,* but given the Dickensian legal difficulties that continue to plague his estate, such a potentially mammoth project will not be possible for some time. However, editor Matthew Bruccoli, in conjunction with Richard Layman, has made a small beginning. Bruccoli and Layman's new Archive of Literary Documents series, published by Omnigraphics, includes *The Sun Also Rises*—a two-volume set including facsimile reproductions of the seven notebooks that constitute the original manuscript of this novel, together with line-by-line reading transcripts. I have not, perhaps understandably, received a review copy of this $250 work and so cannot comment on its quality, but textual scholars should make haste to investigate, and, if satisfied, encourage their libraries to purchase *The Sun* manuscripts.

Textual scholars at work on Hemingway's early short fiction have been given a different sort of tool by compiler Peter L. Hays. His *A Concordance to Hemingway's* In Our Time (Hall) is based on the Boni & Liveright first edition of *In Our Time* (1925) and divided into two sections. The first lists alphabetically all of the words used in the short story collection—including articles, prepositions, and conjunctions—and counts the number of times each word appears, both in the collection and in individual stories. The second section lists key words, excluding articles and most prepositions and conjunctions, and provides the page, line, and phrase in which the word appears. Appendixes provide frequency counts and key words for "On the Quai at Smyrna" and the revised "Mr. and Mrs. Elliot," both occurring in the second, 1930 edition of *In Our Time.* I could wish the introduction to the concordance said more about the technology used to compile it, and the addition of a table of contents and a list of abbreviations would make the volume more user-friendly. Still, Hays's work provides important new assistance for stylistic analyses.

No hitherto unpublished works by F. Scott Fitzgerald appeared this year, but textual events in Hemingway studies predictably include the appearance of more previously unpublished material from the seemingly limitless collection of the John F. Kennedy Library. Donald Junkins has arranged an untitled holograph text as a lightly edited short story, giving it the nonce title "Philip Haines Was a Writer" (*HN* 9, ii:2–9). His presentation encompasses remarks on the work's composition, "Hemingway's Paris Short Story: A Study in Revising" (pp. 10–21), and transcriptions of relevant manuscripts offered in the form of appendixes (pp. 22–47). "Philip Haines Was a Writer" has distinct artistic merit, and, because it treats a promising young writer blighted by divorce, biographical significance hinted at by Jeffrey Meyers in his 1985 *Hemingway: A Biography* (Harper & Row) and examined at greater length by Peter Griffin in his 1990 *Less Than a Treason: Hemingway in Paris* (Oxford). The editing of the "Philip Haines" material has caused a great deal of controversy in the Hemingway community. The dating of the manuscripts, the identification of the work as a short story, and the completeness and accuracy of its transcription have all been called into question. Interested scholars should consult the manuscripts at the John F. Kennedy Library and draw their own conclusions.

In the spring issue of *The Hemingway Review* (9, ii), I present an edition of an unfinished Hemingway short story, "A Lack of Passion" (pp. 57–68), a transcription of its several manuscript versions ("The Lack of Passion Papers," pp. 69–93), and a discussion of its creation (" 'A Lack of Passion': Its Background, Sources, and Composition History," pp. 50–56). Begun in 1924 as a companion piece to "The Undefeated," "A Lack of Passion" treats the initiation into homosexuality of a cowardly teenage bullfighter. The incomplete story's artistic merit is perhaps questionable (Hemingway himself declared that it "wasn't good enough"), but it should interest those studying the development of Hemingway's thematic preoccupation with impotence and androgyny.

Both Fitzgerald and Hemingway were the subjects of essays with a textual focus. Amy J. Elias's "The Composition and Revision of Fitzgerald's *The Beautiful and Damned*" (*PULC* 51, iii:245–66) tackles a complex problem—the relationship of the surviving holograph of Fitzgerald's second novel to the serialized version appearing in *Metropolitan Magazine* and to the Scribner's first edition. Elias shows how Fitzgerald revised narrative point of view, improved characterization, and developed a subtly ironic ending as the novel progressed, and she also deals with Fitzgerald's plagiarism of Zelda's diary, Edmund Wilson's editing of the manuscript, Carl Hovey's cutting of the magazine version for conservative readers, Fitzgerald's own changes in galleys that have not survived, and Maxwell Perkins's editing of Maury's potentially offensive observations on the Bible. It is a fascinating story, and Elias tells it well.

Writing the American Classics (No. Car.), an anthology ed. James Barbour and Tom Quirk, offers essays on the "genesis and composition of several major works in American literature," including Fitzgerald's *Tender is the Night* and Hemingway's *The Sun Also Rises*. This anthology's contents are admittedly "twice-told tales" intended more for the student than the specialist, but both Scott Donaldson's "A Short History of *Tender is the Night*" (pp. 177–208) and William Balassi's "Hemingway's Greatest Iceberg: The Composition of *The Sun Also Rises*" (pp. 125–55) are up-to-date, useful, and eminently readable overviews of their subjects.

Finally, in "The Characterization and the Dialogue Problem in Hemingway's 'A Clean, Well-Lighted Place' " (*HN* 9, ii:94–123), Warren Bennett uses textual methods to attack the recent assertion that the younger waiter's apparent knowledge of the old man's suicide is *not* the result of a misprint, but an example of antimetronomic dialogue. Critical controversy over which waiter speaks the disputed line has been raging for 40 years, and some contemporary anthologies print the 1933 version of this short story, while others choose the 1965 emendation. Students, therefore, are reading two different stories, while their professors feud. I find Bennett's argument wholly convincing, particularly as he compares the holograph manuscript with a newly available typescript, and his essay is certainly exhaustive. I hope it will be the last word on the subject, but somehow I rather doubt it.

ii Bibliography

Given the stale and disastrously incomplete bibliographies of Fitzgerald and Hemingway provided by the *1989 MLA Bibliography I* (MLA, 1990), persons continuing to rely on this and other similarly elephantine printed bibliographies should be warned that they are courting disaster. Hemingway studies are well-served by Al DeFazio, whose annotated bibliographies in *The Hemingway Review* (*HN* 9, ii:188–201; 10, i:83–92) are as encyclopedic and up-to-the-minute as any nonelectronic compendia can be. Megan Floyd Desnoyers and Lisa Middents's "News from the Hemingway Collection" (*HN* 9, ii:184–87; 10, i:67–69), a regular feature of *The Hemingway Review,* continues to keep scholars abreast of newly available unpublished materials at the John F. Kennedy Library.

The most exciting bibliographic event of the Hemingway year, however, may be the appearance of Kelli Larson's *Ernest Hemingway: A Reference Guide, 1974–1989* (Hall). I have not been able to review the volume, out of stock at the publisher as I write, but I understand that it updates Linda Welshimer Wagner's 1977 *Ernest Hemingway: A Reference Guide* (Hall), an easy-to-use annotated bibliography of books and articles on Hemingway. Surely a second printing is at hand. Equally exciting for short story aficionados is Jackson Benson's "A Comprehensive Checklist of Hemingway Short Fiction Criticism, Explication, and Commentary, 1975–1989" (pp. 395–458) in his collection *New Critical Approaches to the Short Stories of Ernest Hemingway* (Duke). Section III of Benson's checklist is phenomenally useful, allowing readers to locate references to individual stories in everything from specific articles to general books. Today's Fitzgerald scholarship quite simply lacks such tools. The newly formed Fitzgerald Society should address itself to the problem.

iii Biography

There were no books or articles on Fitzgerald's life this year, and the biographical front in Hemingway studies was quieter than usual. Peter

Griffin's *Less Than a Treason* focuses less on intellectual ferment in Paris during the 1920s and Hemingway's evolution as a writer than on the dissolution of his first marriage. Here Griffin takes the intriguing but, in my view, questionable position that Hemingway's posthumously published fictions "Philip Haines was a Writer" and *The Garden of Eden* are not fictions at all, but "historic" accounts of the marital breakup. In his preface, Griffin confesses that he has "told a story of Ernest's Paris years." An engrossing story it is, to be sure, but given Griffin's tendency to ignore the established chronology of events; to imagine what individuals said, thought, and felt; to accept memoirs as gospel truth and fictions as autobiography; *Less Than a Treason* must be regarded as a nonfiction novel, a literary entertainment. For scholars, Michael Reynolds's *Hemingway: The Paris Years* (Blackwell, 1989) remains the most comprehensive and reliable account of this period.

Martha Gellhorn, early feminist, distinguished war correspondent, novelist, travel writer, and political activist, is still best-known as Ernest Hemingway's third wife. Carl Rollyson endeavors to correct this injustice in *Nothing Ever Happens to the Brave: The Story of Martha Gellhorn* (St. Martin's), the first full-scale biography of this remarkable woman. Despite Gellhorn's lack of cooperation, Rollyson manages to provide a detailed, readable, and exciting portrait that is must reading not only for those interested in Hemingway's third marriage, but for those ready to investigate Gellhorn's life and work as absorbing subjects in their own right. *Nothing Ever Happens to the Brave* comes equipped with a detailed bibliography of writing by and about Gellhorn that should greatly enhance future study. If this biography has a flaw, it is a tendency to focus on Gellhorn's divorces, wars, and travel adventures to the exclusion of her literary achievements—the dust jacket touts "The Adventurous Life of America's Most Glamorous and Courageous War Correspondent." Scholars of Martha Gellhorn's second husband, however, already understand the problems a tempestuous life can pose for biographers, and should welcome Rollyson's important contribution regardless.

Three articles on various aspects of Hemingway's life appeared this year. William Braasch Watson's "Joris Ivens and the Communists: Bringing Hemingway into the Spanish Civil War" (*HN* 10, i:2–18) postulates that Hemingway was deliberately and successfully recruited by documentary filmmaker Joris Ivens to help fulfill the propaganda objectives of the Comintern. F. J. Bosha's "Hemingway and MacLeish on Pound: A

Consideration of Certain Unpublished Correspondence" (*Paideuma* 19, iii:133–38) explores a different type of literary relationship. According to Bosha, unpublished correspondence in the Library of Congress Archibald MacLeish Papers reveals that both authors were revolted by Pound's treasonous World War II broadcasts (Hemingway calls them "pathological business," MacLeish "insane, obscene drivel"), but jointly planned a public defense of Pound out of compassion for his illness and appreciation of his genius as a poet. In "Hemingway and Hemochromatosis" (*HN* 10, i:57–66), I examine evidence that Hemingway may have suffered from an inherited metabolic disorder and suggest that biographers explore the possible medical bases both of Hemingway's preoccupation with impotence and androgyny and of the depressive illness that culminated in his suicide.

iv Influences, Sources, Parallels

Source studies of Fitzgerald's work were scarce in 1990. Ironically, the most extended study, Alan Margolies's " 'Particular Rhythms' and Other Influences: Hemingway and *Tender is the Night,*" appeared in a book titled *Hemingway in Italy and Other Essays,* reviewed under the heading "Collections: Hemingway" below. Charles Swann in "A Fitzgerald Debt to Keats? From 'Isabella' into *Tender is the Night*" (*N&Q* 37:437–38) notes similarities between stanzas describing how Isabella's "ancestral merchandise" has been obtained by the sufferings of myriad exotic laborers and a passage in *Tender* detailing the heiress Nicole's indebtedness to harried workers ranging from men who mix mouthwash in copper vats to half-breed Brazilian Indians.

Two excellent studies establish the influence of women writers on the Hemingway style. In " 'Ninety Percent Rotarian': Gertrude Stein's Hemingway" (*AL* 62:668–82), Marjorie Perloff reexamines the mentor-pupil relationship between Stein and Hemingway and challenges the conventional view that "Hemingway, obviously Stein's superior, had found a way to turn her base metal into gold." Reading Hemingway's short story "Mr. and Mrs. Elliot" against Stein's "Miss Furr and Miss Skeene," Perloff finds Hemingway's style both less modern and less writerly than Stein's. Glen A. Love in *"The Professor's House:* Cather, Hemingway, and the Chastening of American Prose Style" (*WAL* 24:295–311) explores the "common stylistic inclinations" of these two writers and asserts that

Cather's essays "On the Art of Fiction" (1920) and "The Novel Démeublé" (1922) predict both the emerging Hemingway voice and the movement toward modernism in fiction.

Other source studies of Hemingway's work include *"The Garden of Eden:* Challenging Faulkner's Family Romance" (*HN* 9, ii:155–68), where Kathy Cackett argues that this posthumously published novel was written out of a sense of competition with Faulkner. Giving special attention to the interpolated story about killing an elephant, she details parallels between *The Garden of Eden* and "The Bear" and finds Hemingway's flawed and ambitious work indebted to the historical consciousness of Southern fiction, its tradition of exploring the past and "working through" the sins of the father. In "Hemingway and Chaplin: Monkey Business in 'The Undefeated'" (*SSF* 27:89–97), John M. Howell compares the grotesque pratfalls of the hapless matador Manuel Garcia with the antics of Charlie Chaplin in popular films of the day. Howell defies the critical consensus dictating that Garcia is dying at the work's conclusion to read "The Undefeated" as a comedy of unsuppressed illusions. I personally am not ready to go quite that far, but applaud Howell for an original interpretation that enriches appreciation of this easy-to-oversimplify story.

v Criticism

a. Full-Length Studies: Fitzgerald   There were no book-length studies of Fitzgerald's work.

b. Full-Length Studies: Hemingway   *Hemingway's Quarrel with Androgyny* (Nebraska, 1989) by Mark Spilka is the densest and most ambitious book on Hemingway this year. Spilka broadens the concept of androgyny to include not only the sexual confusion made celebrated by Kenneth Lynn's controversial biography of Hemingway, but also the feminist ideal, spawned in the mid-19th century, of a sociopolitical androgyny, a refusal to assign roles and values based on gender to either men or women. In "Victorian Keys to the Early Hemingway," part one of this treatise, Spilka looks at androgynous representations in Hemingway's boyhood reading, including works by Dinah Craik, Frances Hodgson Burnett, Emily Brontë, Captain Marryat, John Masefield, and Mark Twain. I found this portion of the book particularly valuable, deepening one's understanding of Hemingway's indebtedness to Victorian experiments with gender identity, and of his suffragist mother's contributions to his intellectual and literary growth. The second portion of *Hemingway's Quarrel with Androgyny*, titled "Return of the Repressed," treats Hemingway's own experiments with androgyny in works ranging across the canon, but with particular emphasis on the unfinished novels *The Last Good Country* and *The Garden of Eden*. If Spilka's book has a flaw, it is its somewhat episodic character. Half of the chapters have been previously published as essays, and, while they make up a fine collection, the sense of a developing argument one expects from a book-length analysis is missing. Still, Spilka is a formidable scholar and critic, and *Hemingway's Quarrel with Androgyny* enhances the study of gender issues in Hemingway's fiction.

Kathleen Morgan's *Tales Plainly Told: The Eyewitness Narratives of Hemingway and Homer* (Camden House) is the most astonishing book on Hemingway this year, and the most original study of the author's famous style in decades. Morgan is a welcome newcomer to the field of American literary scholarship; she is a professor of classics at CUNY, and her previous book was on Ovid's *Amores*. Taking as her credo that "nothing is incomparable," Morgan uncovers in *Tales Plainly Told* wonderfully resonant similarities between the narrative styles of Hemingway and Homer. In the process, aided by her classicist's command of grammar (how many of the rest of us are at home with aorist indicatives?), she achieves an unprecedented insight into the elements of Hemingway's style. Morgan has read widely and carefully in the Hemingway canon, but her poet's eye falls on material seldom if ever quoted (quick—where does Hemingway describe a sky full of locusts as "a pink dither of flickering"?). She has done more than the requisite amount of reading in Hemingway criticism, yet she has adroitly avoided parroting any of its innumerable clichés. Scholarly *and* enjoyable, Morgan's book is must reading. It will restore one's appreciation of long-familiar stylistic beauties and hold startling new beauties up to light.

Ronald Weber has given us *Hemingway's Art of Non-fiction* (St. Martin's), a workmanlike and worthwhile study of Hemingway's four nonfiction books and his posthumously serialized "African Journal," still awaiting publication in book form. Weber provides composition and publication histories for each of the five works, as well as solid critical interpretations. On *Death in the Afternoon* and *A Moveable Feast*, Hemingway's most-studied works of nonfiction, Weber provides valuable syntheses of existing information. On *Green Hills of Africa, The Dangerous Summer*, and the "African Journal," works that have received less attention, *Hemingway's Art of Non-fiction* is essential background reading. Weber's investigation may invigorate Hemingway studies with its insistence that the author's experience of journalism was "useful to him only in negative ways as a writer of fiction" and that his nonfiction is worthy of attention in and of itself.

Peter L. Hays's *Ernest Hemingway* (Continuum) is a brief (about 120 pages of text) critical biography, a book that would be most serviceable to beginning students requiring a "quick fix" on Hemingway's life and work. Hays provides an enormously compressed discussion of the highlights of the author's crowded life, and then canvasses his writing career from start to finish, focusing on the development of Hemingway's characteristic style and thematic preoccupations. Hays sometimes seems unduly opinionated (is "A Clean, Well-Lighted Place" really the only story in *Winner Take Nothing* worthy of consideration?), but his sturdy refusal to excuse the racism in *To Have and Have Not,* to admire the maudlin *Across the River and into the Trees,* and to be surprised by the sexual metamorphoses in *The Garden of Eden* is a relief, when so much Hemingway criticism is afflicted by hagiography. The book helpfully includes a detailed, year-by-year chronology of the author's life, but, sadly, its bibliography lists only five secondary sources, an oversight that significantly limits this volume's usefulness to the student audience it seems best-designed to serve.

Wolfgang E. H. Rudat's *A Rotten Way to Be Wounded: The Tragicomedy of* The Sun Also Rises (Peter Lang) conducts an imaginative quest for possible sources of the novel's alleged obsession with impotence and finds such sources in *The Odyssey,* in Shakespeare's Henriad, in *The Great Gatsby,* and, most persuasively, in *Tristram Shandy.* This study's method is psychoanalytic, with much ado about castration anxiety, *vagina dentata,* and the therapeutic nature of jokes. Rudat reads the novel as intensely gynecophobic—if Brett merely calls herself a "chap," that is a "castration-threatening arrogation of masculinity," and arrogations of masculinity are profoundly to be feared. Ignoring recent feminist rehabilitations of Hemingway and attacking Michael Reynolds's efforts to place *The Sun Also Rises* in its historical context of sexual experimentation, Rudat conducts a phallocentric analysis that uncritically uses terms such as "bitch-goddess" and unconsciously presents the novel as profoundly hostile to women. I would rank this book as the work most likely to bolster Hemingway's reputation as a chainsaw sexist since Judith

Fetterley's 1978 observations on *A Farewell to Arms* in *The Resisting Reader: A Feminist Approach to American Literature* (Indiana).

A. Carl Bredahl, Jr., and Susan Lynn Drake have produced the first-ever book-length study of *Green Hills of Africa*. In *Hemingway's* Green Hills of Africa *as Evolutionary Narrative: Helix and Scimitar* (Mellen), the authors set out to demonstrate, by means of close reading, "the richness and importance of this consistently overlooked work." There's little doubt that Hemingway's account of his 1934 safari is unjustly neglected. However, it seems to me that Bredahl and Drake's critical method more nearly resembles free association than close reading, and that much of the richness and importance they discover in *Green Hills of Africa* is of their own invention.

c. Collections: Fitzgerald There were no collections of essays on Fitzgerald's work this year.

d. Collections: Hemingway Three collections offer Hemingway scholars a cornucopia of interesting essays. Jackson Benson's anthology, *New Critical Approaches to the Short Stories of Ernest Hemingway* (Duke) is an eagerly awaited and extremely welcome addition to Hemingway studies, a book certain to enjoy a long and useful shelf life. A sequel to Benson's 1975 collection, *The Short Stories of Ernest Hemingway: Critical Essays,* the volume gathers 27 outstanding articles published on the short stories since 1975, with a strong emphasis on the most current approaches, including structuralism, narratology, semiotic analysis, reception theory, and historical-biographical analysis, among others. Benson's choices treat a diverse and unusual selection of short stories, presenting the contemporary reader with a refreshed Hemingway canon.

To such previously published materials, Benson adds six new essays written specifically for the collection. My personal favorite is Nina Baym's feminist analysis of "The Short Happy Life of Francis Macomber"—"Actually, I Felt Sorry for the Lion" (pp. 112–20). Baym, departing from previous criticism that gives undue weight to masculine points of view, enfranchises this story's feminine perspective, and thereby enhances our appreciation of its complex sexual politics. Another favorite, Gerry Brenner's "From 'Sepi Jingan' to 'The Mother of a Queen': Hemingway's Three Epistemologic Formulas for Short Fiction" (pp. 156–71), identifies three "problem(s) in knowledge" that characterize Hemingway's short stories. There are stories of "textual perplexity," posing paradoxes they do not resolve; stories pivoting on "lexical riddles," or the interpretation of unarticulated or ambiguous words (abortion, lesbian, corrupt); and stories characterized by "extratextual reversals," Hemingway's exploitations of his readers' "mental predispositions, cultural codes, and ideologies."

Other fine new essays in the Benson collection include Robert W. Lewis's " 'Long Time Ago Good, Now No Good': Hemingway's Indian Stories" (pp. 200–212). Lewis examines how Hemingway used Native Americans in his short fiction to develop a paradigm of primitivism, a version of "first nature" that civilized man both aspires to and destroys. In "Hemingway's 'After the Storm': A Lacanian Reading" (pp. 48–57), Ben Stoltzfus explores the latent value and metaphorical content of the story's images of impotence, death, and desire. William Adair in "Hemingway's 'Out of Season': The End of the Line" (pp. 341–46) uses both textual and extratextual evidence to develop a persuasive argument that the suicide of the "quite drunk and very desperate" Peduzzi is the real, though omitted conclusion of the story, as Hemingway claimed. Finally, we have Paul Smith's "A Partial Review: Critical Essays on the Short Stories, 1976–1989" (pp. 375–91). Here, Smith, whose comprehensive *A Reader's Guide to the Short Stories of Ernest Hemingway* (Hall, 1989), has made him our leading authority on the short fiction, offers a witty summary of criticism's successes and failures since 1975.

Hemingway in Italy and Other Essays (Praeger), ed. Robert W. Lewis, helps make 1990 a vintage year for Hemingway collections. The volume brings together 17 never-before-published commentaries selected from papers presented at the Second International Hemingway Conference, held in Lignano Sabbiadoro, Italy. A number of the essays are excellent, and together they constitute an influential contribution to Hemingway studies that should be much sought after. In his introduction (pp. ix–xiv), Lewis delineates the strengths and interconnections of the articles selected and explains that while some treat works and biographical events with Italian settings, in others the Italian connection is absent or nonexistent. The anthology is divided into four sections—"Hemingway's Women," "Hemingway's Relations to Other Writers," "Hemingway's Texts," and "Hemingway in Italy."

Linda Patterson Miller's "Hemingway's Women: A Reassessment" (pp. 3–9) leads off the opening section. Touching briefly on various women characters presented in *The Sun Also Rises, A Farewell to Arms,* and *For Whom the Bell Tolls,* Miller finds them on the whole "feminine, intuitive, realistic, direct, quiet, and principled" and attacks the "extreme feminist view" that Hemingway's fiction has little to say to women. In "Ministrant Barkley in *A Farewell to Arms*" (pp. 11–19), Peter L. Hays reads Catherine Barkley as "the code hero of this novel: the embodiment of admirable qualities and Henry's tutor in committing to life and love." Unfortunately, the essay repeats work already accomplished in Sandra Whipple Spanier's 1987 "Catherine Barkley and the Hemingway Code" (pp. 131–48, in *Ernest Hemingway's* A Farewell to Arms, ed. Harold Bloom [Chelsea House]). Fern Kory's "A Second Look at Helen Ferguson in *A Farewell to Arms*" (pp. 21–33) is actually the first extended examination of this minor character. Kory finds Ferguson "complex, interesting, and realistically portrayed," reflecting "the sensitivity towards women of the story's narrator and, finally, its author." E. Roger Stephenson in "Hemingway's Women: Cats Don't Live in the Mountains" (pp. 35–46) canvasses *The Sun Also Rises, A Farewell to Arms,* and *For Whom the Bell Tolls* to find that Hemingway's heroes consistently view women "as whores or at least whore-like," and that the men's "need to do so clearly shows their shortcomings and inadequacies."

James Brasch's article, " 'Christ, I Wish I Could Paint': The Correspondence between Ernest Hemingway and Bernard Berenson" (pp. 49–68), heads up the anthology's second section on Hemingway's relations to other writers. Brasch describes the extensive correspondence, largely unpublished, that took place from 1949 through 1957 between Hemingway and the renowned art critic and historian Bernard Berenson. Then in his fifties, Hemingway, according to Brasch, wrote to the far senior Berenson as to a respected father. If the quotations that appear in Brasch's essay are an indication, these letters contain rambling discussions on life, literature, art, friends, and spouses. This descriptive work whets one's appetite to see the Hemingway-Berenson correspondence published in full, and the article's appendixes, enumerating the relevant letters and their locations, should help make such a publication an eventual reality. In " 'Particular Rhythms' and Other Influences: Hemingway and *Tender is the Night*" (pp. 69–75), Alan Margolies supplies evidence that Fitzgerald's fear of having his style invaded by the Hemingway influence was real. Margolies scrutinizes those portions of the *Tender is the Night* manuscripts where Fitzgerald scribbled such notes to himself as "No Hemingway [sic]," "Beware Ernest in this scene," and "Now cheerful cafe scene but remember to avoid Hemingway," and made revisions accordingly. Each instance cited by Margolies provides an entertaining problem in literary influence. "Borges on Hemingway. Hemingway on Hemingway: Craft, Grief, and Sport," by Lawrence H. Martin, Jr. (pp. 77–84), refutes Jorge Luis Borges's self-revealing assertion in *La literatura norteamericana* that Hemingway's suicide was in part due to his regret at having devoted so many hours to "physical adventures" rather than the "pure and simple exercise of the intelligence." Drawing examples from *Green Hills of Africa* and "The Short Happy Life of Francis Macomber," Martin takes the somewhat conventional stand that for Hemingway "rightness and competitiveness" were the "shared ingredients of art and sport." The section's allusion-rich final essay, Eugene Kanjo's "Signs Are Taken for Nothing in *The Sun Also Rises*" (pp. 85–97), probes Jake Barnes's and Brett Ashley's encounters with various human value systems (hedonism, Catholicism, romanticism, anti-Semitism, and phallocentrism, to name a few). Each system is found wanting, and the protagonists struggle with a "morbid nihilism," finally abandoning it for a transcendent existentialism.

The third section of the Lewis anthology treats Hemingway's texts. Barry Gross's "Dealing with Robert Cohn" (pp. 123–30) explores unflinchingly and without apology the unpleasant depths of Hemingway's anti-Semitism and his handling of Robert Cohn's Jewishness in *The Sun Also Rises*. Particularly fascinating is Gross's account of a post-Holocaust Bantam edition of the novel that deleted its anti-Semitic slurs, and of a German publisher's trial by a court of denazification for translating intact the original Scribner's edition we read today. Gross, in an extremely evenhanded way, raises a number of vital questions about the moral purpose and cultural values of *The Sun Also Rises*. This standout essay provides an excellent catalyst for discussion of the novel in today's multicultural classroom. Other fine essays in section three include "Hemingway's 'My Old Man': Turf Days in Paris" (pp. 101–06). Here, Michael S. Reynolds places a very early short story in its historical context, describing—the better to gauge Hemingway's fictional achievement—the actual horses and jockeys whose careers are transformed in "My Old Man." Paul Smith's contribution, " 'Mons (Three)': An Unpublished *In Our Time* Chapter" (pp. 107–12), uncovers a compelling vignette about the disorderly retreat of the British Expeditionary Force from the 1914 battle of Mons. The piece was originally intended to follow the two published *In Our Time* vignettes on Mons (chapter III, about "potting" Germans climbing a garden wall, and chapter IV, concerning the "absolutely perfect barricade" at the bridge). Smith's argument about why this vignette should not have been left out of *In Our Time* is, to me, less impressive than his sharp assessment of Hemingway's probable reasons for omitting it. Donald Junkins's "The Poetry of the Twentieth Chapter of *Death in the Afternoon:* Relationships Between the Deleted and Published Halves" (pp. 113–21) takes prose material deleted from the final chapter of the bullfight book and relines it as poetry, a clever technique originating with Selden Rodman, who treated published portions of *Death in the Afternoon* as poetry in his 1949 anthology, *One Hundred Modern Poems* (Pellegrini & Cudahy). Oddly, this essay treats the deleted passages as unpublished and uncriticized, but they appeared, and were considered at length in my *Hemingway's Craft of Omission* (UMI, 1988). Nor does the article engage Allen Joseph's fine 1982 meditation on the material in *"Death in the Afternoon:* A Reconsideration" (*HN* 2, i:2–16).

The anthology's final section, "Hemingway in Italy," contains five essays. I found a pair of articles on the neglected Italian novel *Across the River and Into the Trees* particularly satisfying. Charles M. Oliver in "Hemingway's Study of Impending Death: *Across the River and Into the Trees*" (pp. 143–52) examines the novel's use of time-present narration and flashbacks to enhance appreciation of Colonel Cantwell's handling of death and to promote awareness of Alvarito's developing relationship with Renata. "To Die Is Not Enough: Hemingway's Venetian Novel" (pp. 153–80) by John Paul Russo, reads *Across the River and Into the Trees* as a "significant, late representation in the tradition of the European Venetian novel." Comparing Hemingway's work to that of Barres and D'Annunzio, among others, Russo shows how "myths of Venice . . . overlay the thematic complexity of the novel," giving it "organizational strength and complexity."

Robert E. Gajdusek's "The Ritualization of Death and Rebirth: The Reconstruction of Frederic Henry" (pp. 133–42) is another strong essay in this section. Concentrating on chapter nine of *A Farewell to Arms,* Gajdusek views Frederic's wounding as "a night journey to the other side," his rescue from the collapsed dugout as a cesarean rebirth attended by obstetrician fathers, the wounded soldier's blood dripping on his face as a baptism. I cannot quite see Frederic as a "sacrificed and resurrected god/child," but I very much like the way Gajdusek finds in the masculine theater of combat the properties of shared suffering and sacrifice, mutual salvation and nurture, that will prepare Frederic for love and for the rejection of war itself. Other articles in the final section include "Emotional Order and the Disorder of Things: Nick Adams in Italy," by

Erik Nakjavani (pp. 189–202). Taking chapter VI of *In Our Time* and the short stories "Now I Lay Me," "A Way You'll Never Be," and "In Another Country" as his texts, Nakjavani studies how Nick's "diverse modes of consciousness and their images operate as strategies against the threat of the loss of his consciousness." Nick's anxiety about losing consciousness is also the subject of Frank Scafella's "The Way It Never Was on the Piave" (pp. 181–88), an essay on "A Way You'll Never Be" that examines Nick's coming to terms with his war trauma.

Scott Donaldson has contributed a worthwhile volume—*New Essays on* A Farewell to Arms—to the Cambridge University Press series of anthologies on the American novel. Designed to provide students and contemporary investigators with an introductory critical guide to *A Farewell to Arms,* the collection succeeds admirably, beginning with an overview by Donaldson of the novel's composition, publication history, and critical reception (introduction, pp. 1–25). The volume continues with four commissioned essays. Paul Smith's "The Trying-Out of *A Farewell to Arms*" (pp. 27–52) is a must for textual scholars, recording the 10 years of experimentation (1919–29) with World War I vignettes, short stories, and unpublished materials that ultimately led to the novel's final realization. In "Distance, Voice, and Temporal Perspective in Frederic Henry's Narration: Success, Problems, and Paradox" (pp. 53–73), James Phelan provides a critically savvy look at the techniques, successes, and failures of *A Farewell to Arms*'s first-person narrative. "Hemingway's Unknown Soldier: Catherine Barkley, the Critics, and the Great War," by Sandra Whipple Spanier (pp. 75–108), reviews 60 years of conflicting critical interpretations of Catherine's character and of the cultural assumptions driving those interpretations. By reconstructing the novel's historical context, Spanier, who perceives Catherine as an exemplary Great War heroine, builds a case for judging this controversial character by the standards of her own rather than her critics' time. The final essay, Ben Stoltzfus's "A Sliding Discourse: The Language of *A Farewell to Arms*" (pp. 109–38), contributes a Lacanian reading of the novel, examining the complex interactions between the conscious and unconscious discourses of both narrator and author.

e. General Essays: Fitzgerald   Fitzgerald attracted only one general essay, "The Unfortunate Fate of Seventeen Fitzgerald 'Originals': Towards a Reading of *The Pat Hobby Stories* 'On Their Own Merits' Completely" (*JSSE* 14:87–110). There, Elizabeth M. Varet-Ali conducts a lengthy survey of "a few major misunderstandings concerning the Hobby stories, with the view of reconsidering their unfortunate reputation." She concludes that the stories speak in "inverted terms" of "the necessary conditions" for "professionalism and quality in Art."

f. General Essays: Hemingway J. Gerald Kennedy has given us an extremely important general essay—"Place, Self, and Writing" (*SoR* 26:496–516). In this essay, which briefly considers Hemingway's "The Snows of Kilimanjaro" along with works by Miller, Proust, Flaubert, Welty, and many others, Kennedy constructs a "theory of setting" to assist critics in exploring the relationships "between the authorial self and lived and located experience." Insisting that we take setting as seriously as we take narration, Kennedy offers a powerful program for improving our study of place in literature. "Place, Self, and Writing" will enhance appreciation of any author's work, but as Kennedy's theory particularly emphasizes expatriate writings, its relevance to the study of Hemingway, and not incidentally Fitzgerald, is obvious.

The anthology *American Declarations of Love* (St. Martin's), ed. Ann Massa, takes issue with Leslie Fiedler's assertion that "adult, heterosexual love" has been "embarrassing and even alien to the American literary consciousness." The volume contains a choice essay titled "Ernest Hemingway: Men With, or Without Women," by Brian Harding (pp. 104–21). Reviewing the entire Hemingway canon in brief, Harding argues that Hemingway has been unfairly branded a sexist because "sexist attitudes to gender roles" in his fiction are expressed in dialogue, while the silences of Nick Adams and other sympathetic characters imply authorial dissent. Harding's reading of the short story "Cross-Country Snow" is particularly refreshing.

A last general essay, "Hemingway's *In Our Time:* 'Pretty Good Unity' " (*HN* 9, ii:124–41) by Harbour Winn, reviews existing criticism on the problem of unity in the *In Our Time* collection. Winn explores interconnections between the stories' situations, motifs, and themes, and concludes, not surprisingly, that *In Our Time* is "too finely patterned to be described as a mere collection of stories and too dependent on individual components to be described as a novel."

g. Essays on Specific Works: Fitzgerald *Tender is the Night* garnered two articles this year. Most original is George Toles's "The Metaphysics of Style in *Tender is the Night*" (*AL* 62:423–44), an intriguing study of the impact of authorial self-consciousness on style. Investigating Fitzgerald's "recurring difficulty in this novel with events turning phantasmagorical at the approach of language," Toles finds that *Tender's* "images of paralysis" are presented defensively as "symptom(s) of authorial confusion and aesthetic defeat." Robert Wexelblatt's *"Tender is the Night* and History" (*ELWIU* 17:232–41) contains some fresh observations on an oft-canvassed subject, but the article disappointed me by quoting and then failing to confront a "shamefully racist" Fitzgerald letter and by contemplating the indebtedness of *Tender* to Spengler's *Decline of the West* without considering Nazism's indebtedness to the same vision of history.

Peter Messent has produced this year's sole essay on *The Great Gatsby.* Messent's "Speech Representation, Focalization, and Narration in *The Great Gatsby*" appears as the opening chapter in his book *New Readings of the American Novel: Narrative Theory and Its Application* (St. Martin's, pp. 8–43). Using theoretical models drawn from the work of Gerard Gennette, Boris Uspensky, and Shlomith Rimmon-Kenan, Messent focuses on discovering, describing, and explaining the mechanics of Nick Carraway's narration. The novel here is more a vehicle for elucidating critical theory than critical theory a vehicle for elucidating the novel—Messent refers to his methods, proudly, as "not necessarily . . . preclud[ing] the possibility of interpretation."

"Babylon Revisited" was the only Fitzgerald short story to receive individual attention. Joan Turner's note, "Fitzgerald's 'Babylon Revisited'" (*Expl* 48, iv:282–83), briefly explores how the author uses references to time to reinforce one of the story's main themes—"the past cannot be escaped."

h. Essays on Specific Works: Hemingway   *The Sun Also Rises* collected five essays exclusive of those appearing in books. Best are two articles on characterization. In "The Dialectic of Discourse in *The Sun Also Rises*" (*UMSE* 8:168–84), Louise K. Barnett examines the speech patterns of various characters and finds them, with the exception of Robert Cohn, hopelessly alienated from the romantic idea that "speech mean something, and that meaning be communicated." Her article should be read in conjunction with Peter Messent's "Slippery Stuff: The Construction of Character in *The Sun Also Rises.*" Appearing in Messent's *New Readings of the American Novel* (pp. 86–129), this challenging essay applies the theories of Rimmon-Kenan to characterization in the novel.

In "(Re) Teaching Hemingway: Anti-Semitism as a Thematic Device

in *The Sun Also Rises*" (*CE* 52:186–93), Gay Wilentz attributes Hemingway's anti-Semitism to mainstream America's apprehension about its
swelling population of immigrants and to the replacement of traditionally American frontier values with the alien values of a postindustrial, urban society. Wilentz's article is sound, but I found Barry
Gross's essay, described above, wider-ranging. Wolfgang Rudat's "Hemingway's *The Sun Also Rises:* Masculinity, Feminism, and Gender-Role
Reversal" (*AI* 47:43–68) reads Brett Ashley as an "androgynous bitch"
whose "inability to reach orgasm" leaves her suffering from "penis envy"
until Pedro Romero "makes her a woman, albeit only temporarily" by
gratifying her in bed. According to Rudat, Brett also suffers from a less
well-known ailment—"condom envy." Condoms, in Rudat's view, are
"sign(s) of male power" and symbolized by hats and newspaper wrap-
pers. "Superwoman Brett" is finally fixed, however, by Jake's famous
"Isn't it pretty to think so?," which Rudat describes as a "mythopoeic
clitorectomy." Ouch. The feminism mentioned in the essay's title is
never discussed in any recognizable form, leading me to suspect that
Rudat equates feminism with androgynous bitchery and penis envy.

A last-minute interlibrary loan snafu prevents me from reviewing
Ernest Lockridge's "Primitive Emotions: A Tragedy of Revenge Called
The Sun Also Rises" (*JNT* 20, i:42–55). Please, out of fairness to your-
selves and Professor Lockridge, seek this essay out if you are at work on
Hemingway's *Sun*.

A Farewell to Arms, well-covered in the Lewis and Donaldson anthologies, also attracted Mary Prescott's "*A Farewell to Arms:* Memory
and the Perpetual Now" (*CollL* 17, i:41–52). Prescott disputes the "opinion that *A Farewell to Arms*'s concern with so-called objective, empirical
experience overwhelms any serious attempt that Hemingway might have
made to trace the workings of consciousness." Instead, she finds the
novel rich with the "creative interplay of memory, association, and
perception," directed by a Jamesian "interpreting consciousness . . .
grappling with the intricacies of inwardness."

An issue of *The Hemingway Review* celebrating the fiftieth anniversary
of the publication of *For Whom the Bell Tolls* brought that novel a
modicum of attention. Best is "Pilar's Tale: The Myth and the Message"
by Robert E. Gajdusek (*HN* 10, i:19–33). Arguing that Pilar's story of the
massacre of fascists in Pablo's village is "an intellectual and psychological
tour de force," Gajdusek sees the slaying of the fascists by peasants as "a
destructive activity that is coevally creative . . . a fertility ritual," an

enriching of the barren earth with spilled blood. For Gajdusek, who finds a method in mythology, the massacre has "sexual dynamics," but also illustrates the "instantaneous way a revolution, even as it is being established, creates the same struggle for ascendancy and power . . . it tries to replace." James Seaton in "Was Hemingway an Intellectual?" (*HN* 10, i:52–56) challenges Paul Johnson's assertion that Hemingway was an intellectual in the pejorative sense, someone who believed he could "refashion the world by his own unaided intelligence," rejecting "the vast corpus of inherited wisdom." Seaton takes *For Whom the Bell Tolls* as proof for his thesis, and reads the novel as embracing traditional values such as "courage, honor, and loyalty," and rejecting the possibility of a revolutionary breakthrough. Wolfgang Rudat's "Hemingway's Rabbit: Slips of the Tongue and Other Linguistic Games in *For Whom the Bell Tolls*" (*HN* 10, i:34–51) finds Robert Jordan's custom of calling Maria "rabbit" (in Spanish, the word for rabbit, *conejo*, is also slang for the female pudendum), a "huge linguistic joke," a slip of the tongue committed by "the sexually aroused instructor of Spanish." More usefully, Rudat asks whether Maria is pregnant at the novel's conclusion and what prognostications about the future of fascist Spain can be drawn from her fecundity or lack thereof.

Two posthumously published novels also drew notice. John Raeburn's "Sex and Art in *The Garden of Eden*" (*MQR* 29:111–22) assumes a potentially controversial stance. Raeburn views *The Garden of Eden* as a "proto-feminist" novel and considers Catherine's madness as a "heroic and pathetic" attempt to circumvent the "cultural and biological restrictions" of her sex, as well as a response to her husband's treatment of her as a "specimen." The essay is somewhat flawed by its unquestioning acceptance of the ending selected for this posthumously published novel by Scribner's editor Tom Jenks, but otherwise contains much to engage the critic interested in Hemingway's depictions of human sexuality and its politics. G. R. Wilson, Jr.'s "Saints and Sinners in the Caribbean: The Case for *Islands in the Stream*" (*SAF* 18:27–40) is a valuable reading of an often overlooked work. By examining the novel's religious imagery and by drawing parallels with *The Old Man and the Sea*, Wilson finds hitherto unsuspected levels of structural and thematic coherence in it.

The short story "In Another Country" attracted two essays. Peter Halter's "Indeterminacy in Hemingway's 'In Another Country'" (*ES* 71:523–34) is particularly good. Departing from traditional tutor/tyro readings, Halter finds unresolved tensions between the separate stories of the major and the narrator, and suggests that in this story Hemingway uses "the underlying pattern of initiation not to fulfill its inherent expectations but, at least partly, to frustrate them." Al Soens's "Hemingway and Hawks: The Hierarchy of Heroism in 'In Another Country' " (*ELN* 28, ii:62–79) looks at the story's hawk imagery and considers that imagery's indebtedness to medieval falconry, ornithological tracts, and biblical passages.

Three other short stories each received an essay's worth of concern. Susan Schmidt's "Ecological Renewal Images in 'Big Two-Hearted River': Jack Pines and Fisher King" (*HN* 9, ii:169–73) explores how the fire ecology of the jack pine, in addition to interpretations of nature drawn from folklore and mythology, contributes to the story's resonances. In "Hemingway and the Thing Left In 'God Rest You Merry, Gentlemen' " (*HN* 9, ii:169–73), Rick Moss inquires into the narrator's motives for telling this story and discovers that he "challenges the doctors for their nonchalance and lack of professionalism while implicitly confessing his own failure to do more than witness the tragic event with a similar carelessness." "Ernest Hemingway's Message to Contemporary Man" by E. A. Lambaridou (*HN* 9, ii:146–54) finds in "Old Man at the Bridge" a collision between the brutal mechanism of the approaching fascist order and the values of an older agrarian world, where even the lives of animals have worth. Lambaridou reminds us, via Hemingway, that in the contemporary world, these values are as frail as an exhausted old man in the teeth of an advancing army.

One essay considered a work of nonfiction. Lawrence H. Martin, Jr.'s "Odd Exception or Mainstream Tradition: 'The Shot' in Context" (*WAL* 24:313–20) treats a seldom-read 1951 Hemingway article for *True* magazine. Martin concludes that "The Shot," a nonfiction account of a hunt for pronghorn antelope in Idaho, contains "many essential characteristics of Hemingway's best work," while "at the same time perpetuating a self-glorified personal image."

vi Miscellaneous

Last but not least, Hemingway devotees may want to be aware of three works of fiction published this year—*Hunting Hemingway's Trout: A Fiction* by Lauri Anderson (Atheneum), *Hemingway's Suitcase* by MacDonald Harris (Simon & Schuster), and *The Hemingway Hoax* by Joe Haldeman (Morrow)—all interesting examples of how Hemingway's

ghost continues to haunt the highways and byways of American literature. And finally, we have a travel guide, Noel Riley Fitch's *Walks in
Hemingway's Paris: A Guide for the Literary Traveler* (St. Martin's). Fitch,
who teaches at the American University in Paris and has given us a fine
literary history of the city in *Sylvia Beach and the Lost Generation*
(Norton, 1983), knows her subject thoroughly. Equipped with a bibliography, an index, and photographs as well as a readable text crammed
with scholarly detail, *Walks in Hemingway's Paris* can either serve as a
useful reference tool for Hemingway and Fitzgerald scholars alike, or
help them to arrange a rendezvous at the Dingo Bar.

Part II

11 Literature to 1800

William J. Scheick

As a new decade commences, perhaps a brief observation about colonial studies during the last decade is in order. During the 1980s several new directions emerged. Principally, colonial letters have been read in terms of more recent critical methods and their *American* identity has been questioned. Not only have the European features of colonial writings received more attention, but New World works written by people from countries other than Britain have generated more interest. The geographical boundaries of colonial studies have expanded beyond the Eastern coast to accommodate North America generally, including Native American cultures.

If these studies have expanded their definitional, geographical, and cultural concerns, they have also changed substantially concerning late 18th-century works. Prior to the 1980s, interest in Puritan literature predominated, as if literary colonialists found late 18th-century writings, in comparison, less appealing aesthetically, at least in formalist terms. These works appeared to be grounded less in art than in politics and society; and these works seemed to be an intellectual hodgepodge lacking the sort of tidy, overarching ideational structure that Puritan literature was thought to evidence (à la Perry Miller's persistent legacy). Even the chief exception to this general aversion, Franklin's autobiography, has undergone a major change.

During the 1980s, *as if* in reaction to Reaganocracy, scholars increasingly implied disapproval of Franklin's representation of his character, a critical development that paralleled scholarly exposures of certain myths about the origins and nature of the American republic. The *Autobiography* has been shown to be contradictory, or masked, or dialogic, which are precisely the characteristics of other late 18th-century writings that currently attract interest. The once lamented absence of formalist aesthetic features and of monolithic ideation in these writings—their heteroglossia, in short—now fascinates, rather than frustrates, scholars. Many critics prefer to hear the less-prominent voices, including women's; to witness the contestations submerged beneath the explicitly declared; and to celebrate the various dislocations of discourse—in short, to rediscover the wilderness that is late 18th-century American literature as if it were an unexplored new world to be described (ambivalently, to be sure) in the light of contemporary political and social experience.

i Native Americans and the Colonial Imagination

In "Indian Princess and Roman Goddess: The First Female Symbols of America" (*PAAS* 100:45–79), John Higham collects colonial illustrations that convert Native Americans into iconic representations of the New World. John Eliot's effort to convert these New World inhabitants to Christianity emerges in "A Reappraisal of the Praying Indians: Acculturation, Conversion, and Identity at Natick, Massachusetts, 1646–1730" (*NEQ* 63:396–428) by Harold W. Van Lonkhuyzen; Native American interest in Eliot's religion originated not from desperation but from a political strategy that appropriated Christianity as an alternative social structure—as leverage—in the struggle for power within tribal bands.

New World explorers were also undergoing a conversion, explains Rolena Adorno in "New Perspectives in Colonial Spanish American Literary Studies" (*JSw* 32:173–91) and Peggy Samuels in "Imagining Distance: Spanish Explorers in America" (*EAL* 25:233–52). Adorno lauds the shift of literary studies from a concern with aesthetics (e.g., form and genre) to an emphasis on cultural discourse (e.g., exchange and dialogue), which includes treating an author as a colonial subject. Samuels agrees, and notes that whereas Spanish colonists were acutely aware of their distance from their homeland, they often concealed from themselves the extent of their cultural transformation, particularly in their interactions with Native Americans; unable to accept distance from Europe or deviation from revered cultural codes, they adopted narrative strategies that insisted on their uninterrupted relationship with their former culture.

French colonists experienced a related gap, Paul Perron and Gilles

Thérien disclose in "Ethno-Historical Discourse: Jean Brébeuf's *Jesuit Relation* of 1636" (*AJS* 7:53–67); a lacuna emerges between Brébeuf's experience of an event as spatially seen and his edited textual reconstruction of it as temporally remembered. Another French clergyman's Calvinist encounter with the New World, and his inquiry into whether the apostle Thomas had already preached there, are recorded in Jean de Léry's *History of a Voyage to the Land of Brazil* (Calif.), excellently translated by Janet Whatley. Several serious mistranslations of a 17th-century Dutch narrative are corrected in Ada van Gastel's "Van der Donck's Description of the Indians: Additions and Corrections" (*WMQ* 47:411–21).

The colonial imagination made symbols of the Native Americans and, as well, of various features of their land. John Canup's *Out of the Wilderness: The Emergence of an American Identity in Colonial New England* (New England) associates the retardation of the Puritan's formation of a national identity with their fear of nature in the New World. In "The Feathered Scribe: The Discourses of American Ornithology before 1800" (*WMQ* 47:210–34), Kevin R. McNamara details the tendency of New World colonists to anthropomorphize their descriptions of birds so that they serve symbolic functions in religious, political, and social contexts. The colonial habit of reading landscape in a biblical context interests Jan Bakker, whose *Pastoral in Antebellum Southern Romance* (LSU, 1989) suggests that Robert Beverley's vision of Virginia as a new Eden was gainsaid by his sense of a second paradise lost to time and human inadequacy.

That a neighboring colony was likewise no paradise regained is observed in "George Alsop's Indentured Servant in *A Character of the Province of Maryland*" (*MHM* 85:221–35), in which Darin E. Fields concludes that Alsop self-consciously resorted to diction, puns, and innuendo to satirize and undermine his apparent explicit endorsement of colonization and indenture. And that 18th-century colonists, typified by Thomas Jefferson, failed to create prospects (literary devices of redemptive order and stability) out of their encounters with the New World, and, instead, recorded their anxiety over the potentially uncontrollable and overwhelming powers of nature form the thesis of Robert Clark's "The Absent Landscape of America's Eighteenth Century," in *Views of American Landscapes,* ed. Mick Gidley and Robert Lawson-Peebles (Cambridge, 1989), pp. 81–99.

ii Early Colonial Poetry

Puritans sometimes ordered their New World experience in their use of
the Psalms. One minister's habit of citing from more than one Psalter
and of making selections from the *Bay Psalm Book* that reinforced the
topic of his sermons is documented in David W. Music's "The Diary of
Samuel Sewall and Congregational Singing in Early New England" (*The
Hymn* 41:7–15). Willis Barnstone's "Misalliance of Theory and Practice
or Parable of the *Bay Psalm Book*" (*TRev* 32–33:22–26) focuses on the
disparity between the declared intention and the actual performance of
Puritan translators, who relied less on the Hebrew text than on earlier
English Psalters. Whereas in "The Sweet Defender of New England"
(*NEQ* 63:294–302) Rosemary Fithian Guruswamy notes that David
increasingly served Puritan authors as an ideal for the partaker of the
Lord's Supper, in "Singing with Grace: Allusive Strategies in Anne
Bradstreet's 'New Psalms' " (*SPAS* 1:148–69) Raymond A. Craig indicates
that Bradstreet follows John Cotton's articulation of tradition and at the
same time develops distinctive techniques to express her various conflicts, including her belief in gender equality within the orthodoxy of
dominant male discourse on the Psalms.

Interaction with male discourse also interests Douglas Anderson in *A
House Undivided* (pp. 8–39). For Anderson, Bradstreet's writings (suggesting at times that the deity is female) are rooted in John Winthrop's
social vision; Winthrop not only presented Eve as a model of redemption
but also analogized marriage and community in a way that made (as
Edward Taylor's verse also demonstrates) domestic and family values the
basis for one's exercise of choice and power. That certain male readers
sensed Bradstreet's interaction with the dominant discourse of her day
concerns Kathryn Zabelle Derounian-Stodola, whose " 'The excellency
of the inferior sex': The Commendatory Writings on Anne Bradstreet"
(*SPAS* 1:129–47) outlines the contemporary attitudes toward women
authors and notes both the identity and the ambivalence of the poets
who introduced the tenth muse; these male poets played off stereotypes
of women and resorted to pun, double entendre, irony, and metaphor as
subtle indicators of Bradstreet's inferiority as a poet. An annotated record
of 300 years of response to her work is provided in Raymond F. Dolle's
excellent *Anne Bradstreet: A Reference Guide* (Hall).

The influence of the themes and imagery of Canticles is explored by
Jeffrey A. Hammond, whose "Approaching the Garden: Edward Taylor's

Progress Toward the Song of Songs" (*SPAS* 1:65–87) detects the increasing centrality of this biblical site in the poet's meditations generally, not just at the end of his life when he no longer experienced an exclusion from scriptural types. In "Who Is Edward Taylor?: Voice and Reader in the *Preparatory Meditations*"(*AmerP* 7, iii:2–19), Hammond provides an insightful analysis of the poet's dichotomized voice, which simultaneously confesses the weakness of his art and suggests its possible remedy; the poet's double-voiced persona evades the traps of despair and presumption by properly imagining, rather than claiming, the elect's experience of evangelical confidence.

My "Unfolding the Serpent in Taylor's 'Meditation 1.19' " (*SPAS* 1:34–64) details the poet's effort to unfold (disclose) the serpentine bondage of the fallen world and to unfold (predict) the apocalyptic uncoiling of the great dragon; Taylor fashions an emblem, an inverted arch, to give coherence to his elaborate system of imagery pertaining to demons, serpents, graves, deeps, darkness, and Herculean labors. Rejecting the need for integration of parts, Lincoln Konkle's "Puritan Epic Theatre—A Brechtian Reading of Edward Taylor's *Gods Determinations*" (*IBSC* 19, ii:58–71) points to the late Renaissance masque as a form of epic theater that may have influenced the poet; Taylor might have appreciated the masque's paradigmatic representation of the macrocosm and its acknowledgment of the audience.

Donald E. Stanford, Norman S. Grabo, Thomas M. Davis, and Charles W. Mignon review (*SPAS* 1:3–33) the trials, tribulations, and shortcomings of their influential editions of Taylor's writings. The influence of commentaries on Petrus Ramus's work is reviewed by John C. Adams in "Alexander Richardson and the Ramist Poetics of Michael Wigglesworth" (*EAL* 25:271–88), which remarks Richardson's eclectic combination of many arguments, particularly concerning the management of eloquence to affect readers. And the subtle management of argument, designed to appeal to both English and colonial audiences, interests Gregory A. Carey; his useful "The Poem as Con Game: Dual Satire and the Three Levels of Narrative in Ebenezer Cooke's 'The Sot-Weed Factor' " (*SLJ* 23, ii:9–19) unmasks Cooke (the artist) as a dishonest dealer behind a "cheating" narrator who presents himself as the "cheated."

A major undertaking that is likely to become critically influential, in part because it presents a virtual encyclopaedic inventory of previously neglected writers, emerges in David S. Shields's *Oracles of Empire: Po-*

etry, Politics, and Commerce in British America, 1690–1750 (Chicago). Shields convincingly demonstrates a lack of consensus among these debating poets, who stress the function of mercantilism in transmitting civilization and wealth from the homeland to the colonies, and who generally prize an ethical empire based on provincialism and trade rather than on metropolitan privilege and conquest. Among many other concerns, these poets express (1) a commercial mythology that often restrains free trade, (2) a legal mystique that pits the gospel of contracts against the cult of liberty, (3) an autarkical politics that prioritizes virtuous monarchical authority, and (4) an imperial demonology that villainizes the Spanish and the French.

iii Early Colonial Prose

In *The Estrangement of the Past: A Study in the Origins of Modern Historical Consciousness* (Oxford), Anthony Kemp explores William Bradford's increasing awareness of the opposition between providential history and secular event; eventually Bradford grounded his faith in this gap, in the absence of the deity in history. In contrast, Kemp contends, Edward Johnson rhetorically translated history into metaphor; his use of the language of typology subsumed the world of contradictions and incompatible ideas into a comprehensive divine revelation. Two men who thought about and made history are the subject of "Humor and the Techniques of Humor in William Bradford's *Of Plymouth Plantation*" (*StAH* 5 [1986]:158–67), Ian Marshall's reading of incongruity and irony as deliberate strategies designed to reconcile or confront difficult social and environmental factors; and *John Winthrop* (TUSAS 556), Lee Schweninger's successful case for treating Winthrop's writings from a literary point of view and, especially, for the need to review Winthrop's manuscripts before interpreting his journals.

That Winthrop's authority, idea of order, and sense of self were challenged by the actions, mysticism, and claims to personal revelation of a disruptive female is the thesis of Marilyn J. Westerkamp's "Anne Hutchinson, Sectarian Mysticism, and the Puritan Order" (*EIHC* 125:482–96); for the sake of Winthrop and the clergy, whose male mediation she rejected, "Hutchinson had to be destroyed" and "women were disempowered." Lad Tobin, however, focuses on Hutchinson's challenge to the male belief in the capacity of language to represent reality objectively. In

"A Radically Different Voice: Gender and Language in the Trials of Anne Hutchinson" (*EAL* 25:253–70), Tobin notes that the charges against Hutchinson included her privileging of personal relationships over allegiance to the state; this charge stemmed in part from her belief that human comprehension of the divine word is necessarily limited and that the meanings of words are contextually determined, not absolute in the way her male peers were using them to impose order, control, and closure in their argument with her.

The writings of a minister deeply involved in the Hutchinson controversy are usefully reviewed in Everett Emerson's *John Cotton: Revised Edition* (TUSAS 80), and a good edition of one of these writings appears in Jesper Rosenmeier's "John Cotton on Usury" (*WMQ* 47:548–65). That a spiritual horoscope suggests the careful study of the occult by Cotton's grandson is noted in "Cotton Mather, Astrologer" (*NEQ* 63:308–14) by Michael P. Winship. Mather's exercises in editing and reediting, David Levin explains in "Cotton Mather's Misnamed Diary: Reserved Memorials as a Representative Christian" (*AmLH* 2:183–202), indicate a conflict between his persona as a typical pious voice and the immediate feelings of his passionate actual self.

Whereas John S. Erwin's *The Millennialism of Cotton Mather: An Historical and Theological Analysis* (Mellen) details Mather's notions concerning the biblical prophecies, witchcraft as apocalyptic sign, the Second Coming, the Last Judgment, salvation, and paradise, Reiner Smolinski's excellent "*Israel Redivivus:* The Eschatological Limits of Puritan Typology in New England" (*NEQ* 63:357–95) thoroughly explores the views of Mather and others concerning the restoration of the Jews, the millennial role of America, and the location of the New Jerusalem. Smolinski finds that Puritan ministers used typology in a way which did not abrogate divine prophecy, and they, accordingly, did not think of the New World as the site of the New Jerusalem, though in Mather's time it was thought that America would be included in the call of the Israelites. Similarly demystifying is "God's Chosen People: Anglican Views, 1607–1807" (*SPAS* 1:97–128), in which Pascal Covici, Jr., reports that Anglican ministers spoke of Britain as a new Israel and the British as the chosen people. Covici might have gone further, however, and observed that this Anglican and Puritan analogy had been fashioned by the early Christians.

In *American Puritanism and the Defense of Mourning: Religion, Grief, and Ethnology in Mary White Rowlandson's Captivity Narrative* (Cambridge), Mitchell Robert Breitwieser observes Rowlandson's resistance to the Matherian view that mourning, like all experiences in life, should be reduced to general moral types or exempla. In its reflection of authentic human and historical complexities that go against the grain of explicit moralizing intentions, Rowlandson's document records her desire to hold on to personal memories; these memories testify to her emotions, to her unhealed trauma, and to her renunciation of imposed sanctioned meanings and established modes of sublimation and representation. Fine editions of various accounts appear in *Journeys in New Worlds: Early American Women's Narratives*, ed. William L. Andrews et al. (Wisconsin), which includes introductory comments by Annette Kolodny on Elizabeth House Trist, Daniel B. Shea on Elizabeth Ashbridge, Sargent Bush, Jr., on Sarah Kimble Knight, and Amy Schrager Lang on Mary Rowlandson. Another edition of Rowlandson's narrative has been published as *The Captive* (American Eagle), and various dates concerning Rowlandson's family have been established by Kathryn Zabelle Derounian-Stodola and David L. Greene in "Additions and Corrections to 'A Note on Mary (White) Rowlandson's English Origins'" (*EAL* 25:305–06).

If, as Breitwieser argues, Rowlandson's account inherently expresses various types of resistance to established authority, it may have encouraged resistance to monarchical power during the Revolutionary period; the revival of interest in reports like Rowlandson's at that time, explains Greg Sieminski in "The Puritan Captivity Narrative and the Politics of the American Revolution" (*AQ* 42:35–56), shaped colonial antagonism toward controlling imperialistic forces. A related conflict is disclosed in Lianne Beukelman Smith's "'Strange Adventures and Signal Deliverances': Narrative Masks in John Barnard's *Ashton's Memorial*" (*NEQ* 63:60–79), which observes Barnard's pointed inversion of narrative conventions as a means of questioning the adequacy of providential theology: is Ashton's outcome the result of self-reliance or submission, and is his ordeal lamentable fate or admirable providence? In challenging the Massachusetts Bay structure of dominion (based on scriptural precedent), one radical colonist disassociated himself from the dominant religious linguistic system by demoting biblical typology and applying legal hermeneutics; he based this revision, Christopher D. Felker argues in "Roger Williams's Uses of Legal Discourse: Testing Authority in Early New England" (*NEQ* 63:624–48), on his study of Native Americans and on the linguistic assumptions of English common law concerning the function of language in evaluating alleged statements of truth.

The importation of ideas of another kind concerns Rick Kennedy in two essays: "The Alliance between Puritanism and Cartesian Logic at Harvard, 1687–1735" (*JHI* 51:549–72) stresses Brattle's use of René Descartes's thought in reinforcing the Puritan intellectual hegemony based on biblical authority, and "Thomas Brattle and the Scientific Provincialism of New England, 1680–1713" (*NEQ* 63:584–600) emphasizes Brattle's sense of colonial insularity in his decision to disseminate at Harvard the findings of Robert Boyle and John Flamsteed. An Anglophile who also found much of colonial life to be limited and who particularly wished for an intellectual climate receptive to prose is the subject of *The Comic Genius of Dr. Alexander Hamilton* (Tennessee). In this study, Robert Micklus features Hamilton's tendency to undercut the authority of his own texts, even the idea that luxury threatens society, because he thought of life as comic, as a medley of inflated trifles. In an admirable editorial feat, Micklus has produced a three-volume edition of Hamilton's *The History of the Ancient and Honorable Tuesday Club* (No. Car.), which he suggests might be read as essentially an anatomy and a comic novel that anticipates *Tristram Shandy.*

iv Edwards, the Great Awakening, and the New Divinity

Kenneth P. Minkema has produced a note more valuable than its size might suggest; his "The Authorship of 'The Soul'" (*YULG* 65:27–32) reveals that the document often considered as Jonathan Edwards's earliest writing was actually written by his oldest sister, Esther. The early Calvinistic themes of estrangement and exclusion are not merely atavistic in Edwards's work, argues Susan Manning in *The Puritan-Provincial Vision: Scottish and American Literature in the Nineteenth Century* (Cambridge, pp. 26–38); in trying to reconcile the structures of belief and the facts of experience, Edwards converted inhuman thought into beautiful vision.

Edwards stressed the approaching apocalypse, explains Joseph Dewey in *The Apocalyptic Temper in the American Novel of the Nuclear Age* (Purdue, pp. 17–24), as a way to revivify his contemporaries' sense of the present and to give them hope in a time of religious declension. Declension of Edwardsean thought concerns Allen C. Guelzo, whose sensitive *Edwards on the Will: A Century of American Theological Debate* (Wesleyan, 1989) presents a detailed intellectual history of the failure of the New Divinity to carry on the progenitor's heritage; especially noteworthy are Guelzo's comments on Timothy Dwight's confiscation of Edwards's authority.

v Franklin, Jefferson, and the Revolutionary Period

Paine's confiscation of an authoritative five-stage religious pattern, from providential gestation to an electionlike apotheosis, is detected by Charles J. Norman, who introduces a complete edition of *The Crisis Papers* (NCUP). Whereas religious echoes can be heard in *A Concordance to Thomas Paine's Common Sense and* The American Crisis (Garland, 1989), compiled by Manfred Pütz and Jon-K. Adams, political fervor characterizes Paine's peripheral and unsuccessful claim that commerce and republicanism are compatible, as reported by Gregory Claeys in "Republicanism versus Commercial Society: Paine, Burke, and the French Revolution Debate" (*HEI* 11 [1989]:313–24). The use of the established language of moral reformation to urge African Americans to achieve an autonomous identity within New World society is remarked in Phillip M. Richards's "Nationalist Themes in the Preaching of Jupiter Hammon" (*EAL* 25:123–38). And a Revolutionary male slave narrative, ed. Daniel B. Thorp, appears in "Chattel With A Soul: The Autobiography of a Moravian Slave" (*PMHB* 112 [1988]:433–51).

Writings at once autobiographical and representative of the 18th-century interest Carla Mulford in "Loyal Verses, Tory Curses of the American Revolution" (*NJH* 106:87–99), which considers Jonathan Odell's dialogic use of sources and his transformation of certain imitated texts into works with new effects and meanings. Mulford's "Representing Early American Drama and Theatre" (*RALS* 17:1–24) assails the myth of the Puritan effect on drama and specifically highlights the function of the theater in promoting American interests during and after the Revolution. And the use of drama specifically to promote the education of women and the emergence of a female era is vaguely sketched by Mary Anne Schofield in "The Happy Revolution: Colonial Women and the Eighteenth-Century Theater" (*Modern American Drama*, pp. 29–37). The role of pastoral as a rhetorical strategy interests Stephen H. Browne, whose "The Pastoral Voice in John Dickinson's First *Letter from a Farmer in Pennsylvania*" (*QJS* 76:46–57) notes the management of authorial voice, at once distant and present, situated in a middle space between contemplation and action against a background contrasting present confusion with ideal simplicity.

Rhetorical concerns likewise inform four studies in *American Rhetoric: Context and Criticism,* ed. Thomas W. Benson (So. Ill.). Stephen T. Olsen's "Patrick Henry's 'Liberty or Death' Speech: A Study in Disputed Authorship" (pp. 19–65) concludes, on the basis of an analysis of the encoding norms of its vocabulary, that the speech was written by St. George Tucker. In "Justifying America: The Declaration of Independence as a Rhetorical Document" (pp. 67–130), Stephen E. Lucas explores nuance, drama, and logic to argue that the Declaration is an almost perfect synthesis of style, form, and content. Exposing the various unsuccessful attempts of rhetoricians to invoke the authority of the people is the aim of Carroll C. Arnold's "Early Constitutional Rhetoric in Pennsylvania" (pp. 131–200). And in "The Rhetorical Birth of a Political Pamphleteer: William Cobbett's 'Observations on Priestley's Emigration'" (pp. 201–20), James R. Andrews scrutinizes one Tory's use of moral and political simplicities as a rhetorical reality designed to impugn all Revolutionary events.

A female fantasy of a revolutionary empowerment of subservience interests Janet Todd, whose *The Sign of Angelica: Women, Writings, and Fiction, 1660–1800* (Columbia, 1989, pp. 176–91) discloses in Frances Brooke's *The History of Emily Montague* how passive femininity sometimes becomes powerful through others' extreme reverence toward it. Various female voices resisting the sexual and racial politics of male-defined Revolutionary principles can be heard in *Women in the Age of the American Revolution,* ed. Ronald Hoffman and Peter J. Albert (Virginia, 1989); included is "Anglo-American Racism in Phillis Wheatley's 'Sable Veil,' 'Length'ned Chain,' and 'Knitted Heart'" (pp. 338–444) by David Grimsted, who discusses Wheatley's management of imagery pertaining to race and gender, and also reports that her verse became a pawn in arguments for or against the alleged inferiority of African Americans. That Mercy Otis Warren's moral concepts conflicted with those of John Adams is documented in Frank Shuffleton's "In Different Voices: Gender in the American Republic of Letters" (*EAL* 25:289–304); although their letters share a common language of Whig politics, their dissimilar inflections reveal the general problem of systematic mistranslation that results from differences between women and men.

The specific, and paradoxical, revision of the patriarchal figure into the affectionate pedagogue (in school, home, and government) concerns

Harold Hellenbrand, whose *The Unfinished Revolution: Education and Politics in the Thought of Thomas Jefferson* (Delaware) details Jefferson's readings and beliefs. Whereas the influence of Epicurus, the Stoics, and Tacitus is assessed in Carl J. Richard's "A Dialogue with the Ancients: Thomas Jefferson and Classical Philosophy and History" (*JER* 9 [1989]:431–55), the influence of the natural sciences, especially as an alternative to theological and historical tradition, is assayed in Charles A. Miller's *Jefferson and Nature: An Introduction* (Hopkins, 1988). In "The Discourse of Modernism in the Age of Jefferson" (*Prospects* 15:23–37), Frank Shuffleton discerns a polymorphous modernism concerned simultaneously with the American capacity for innovation and with life or historical cycles that undercut this capacity to break from the past; and in "From Jefferson to Thoreau: The Possibilities of Discourse" (*ArQ* 46, i:1–16), Shuffleton advances Jeffersonian skepticism as an alternative model for assessing American writing.

Benjamin Franklin's role as one of the two most prominent journalists who advocated Jeffersonian republicanism is featured in Jeffrey A. Smith's *Franklin and Bache: Envisioning the Enlightened Republic* (Oxford). Interest in Franklin's attitudes informs Edmond Wright's edition *Benjamin Franklin: His Life as He Wrote It* (Harvard) and J. A. Leo Lemay's lecture *Benjamin Franklin: Optimist or Pessimist* (University of Delaware); in spite of Franklin's dark view of human nature (particularly evident in his satires and personal expression), Lemay contends, his pragmatism urged optimism as a state of mind that enables one to enjoy and succeed in life. And that Franklin served as a symbolic type expressing the early-republic desire for a stabilizing mythology is documented in my edition of a manuscript dialogue in "Benjamin Franklin and Lord Bute: Legendary Eighteenth-Century Representations" (*LCUT* 20, iii:64–73).

Franklin's self-representation is the subject of *Making American Tradition* (pp. 9–12), in which Cushing Strout focuses on Franklin's autobiographical narrowing of his talents to create a cultural myth of the self-made man identified by the economic virtues of industry and frugality. But Joanne Cutting-Gray's "Franklin's *Autobiography*: Politics of the Public Self" (*Prospects* 14 [1989]:31–43) argues that commerce was not the defining feature of Franklin's thought; his sense of self was not shaped by private ego but by public service, and his sense of self grew in a communal space open to thought expressed as speech and action. This development of self strikes Ada Van Gastel as sinister. In "Franklin and Freud: Love in the *Autobiography*" (*EAL* 25:168–82), Van Gastel finds that the persona's intellectual labor sublimates the pursuit of personal pleasure; to gain control over his life, he transfers emotion (including sexual drive) from personal relationships, especially with women, to the realm of public affairs.

Franklin harmoniously merged this public realm of democratic society with the individual, Herbert Leibowitz reports in *Fabricating Lives: Explorations in American Autobiography* (Knopf, 1989); to maintain this coalescence, he sanctioned honorable dissembling as a utilitarian means to overcome occasions when tension develops between society and the self. Moreover, Kenneth Dauber insists in *The Idea of Authorship* (pp. 3–38), Franklin found specific authority for writing his life in the idea of democracy; this idea suggests that any life is as true as another and that one's life ought to be written by one's self. The resultant combination of looseness and coherence in the *Autobiography,* Dauber concludes, becomes a model for American writing. Coherence is stressed in J. A. Leo Lemay's "Lockean Realities and Olympian Perspectives: The Writing of Franklin's *Autobiography*" (*Writing the American Classics,* pp. 1–24); not only does Franklin's expansion of the opening of the *Autobiography* anticipate his themes and his two personae (sage and self-critic), but his first ending enlarges perspectives beyond Lockean temporal or spatial limits, and his second ending circularly returns the reader to the author's introduction.

In "Franklin's Purloined Letters" (*ArQ* 46, ii:1–12) Christopher Looby emphasizes Franklin's conversion of the precarious transmission of messages into a master metaphor that construes the Revolution as the purloining of the epistolary carriers of political legitimacy. Other studies of influences on Franklin's thought include I. Bernard Cohen's *Benjamin Franklin's Science* (Harvard), which argues that he was a true scientist; Jacquelyn C. Miller's "Franklin and Friends: Benjamin Franklin's Ties to Quakers and Quakerism" (*PennH* 57:318–36), which indicates that his repudiation of Quaker inflexibility did not erode his appreciation of Quaker agreement with some of his views; and Ralph Frasca's "From Apprentice to Journeyman to Partner: Benjamin Franklin's Workers and the Growth of the Early American Printing Trade" (*PMHB* 114:229–48), which observes that his business partners emphasized the importance of associational networks in distributing information.

vi The Early National Period

Concerning other 18th-century printed materials, Richard C. Fyffe offers 101 entries in "A Catalogue of Previously Unrecorded and Unlocated American Imprints, Printed before 1801, in the Essex Institute" (*EIHC* 125:288–328); and Sam G. Riley and Gary Selnow provide a statistical survey in "Southern Magazine Publishing, 1764–1984" (*JQ* 65 [1988]:899–901). Such print-centered activities as almanacs, explains David Jaffee in "The Village Enlightenment in New England, 1760–1820" (*WMQ* 47:327–46), not only transmitted knowledge in the popular marketplace but also intrinsically challenged the controlling authority of the clergy and the college-educated elite. Richard Brown arrives at the same conclusion; his *Knowledge Is Power: The Diffusion of Information in Early America, 1700–1865* (Oxford, 1989) studies the transition from oral (community-intensive) to written (individual-intensive) culture in the colonies and finds that the dissemination of information lessened communal cohesiveness and elite control over knowledge and society. In *The Letters of the Republic: Publication and the Public Sphere in Eighteenth-Century America* (Harvard), a part of which appeared as "The *Res Publica* of Letters" (*Boundary 2* 17:38–68), Michael Warner abstrusely discusses the reciprocal relationship between print and culture in creating a gap between the public and the private, and the state and society. An erasure of identity occurred, for Revolutionary authors and readers alike, that first severed the connection between personal authority and public leadership, and then led to a distinction between republican readers/voters and government. Early national novels, such as Charles Brockden Brown's, register this gap when they proffer virtue as a private experience that might not be publicly realized and, at the same time, claim to belong to a civic arena of imagined readers participating in public discourse rather than in private consumption.

In contrast, Maxwell Bloomfield's "Constitutional Values and the Literature of the Early Republic" (*JAC* 11, iv [1988]:53–58) claims that formal constitutions provided a unifying cultural symbol during this time of cultural diffusion and confusion. And that the formation of early national clubs indicates a popular desire to reconstruct a sense of social and political community, particularly through an emerging national literature, is argued by David S. Shields in "Dining Clubs and Literary Culture in Federal New York" (*Federal New York: A Symposium,* ed. Robert I. Goler [Fraunces Tavern Museum], pp. 35–40).

At the forefront of this effort to forge a national literature were the Connecticut Wits, seen as an anxious group by Robert E. Shalhope in *The Roots of Democracy: American Thought and Culture, 1760–1800* (Twayne). These authors, observes William C. Dowling in *Poetry and Ideology in Revolutionary Connecticut* (Georgia), pitted themselves against social corruption and decline by advocating a classical republican ideal; since they believed that ideas constitute individuals and societies, and that language could remake the world, they particularly used literary Augustanism and the Country ideal as strategies to unmask hidden, false ideologies. Dowling provides an insightful analysis of Joel Barlow's use of the same terms he found deficient in Timothy Dwight, resulting in an inadvertent implosion of his moral premises. Barlow's management of ambiguity, as a means of hiding from Dwight his developing allegiance to radical ideas, is disclosed in Dowling's "Joel Barlow and *The Anarchiad*" (*EAL* 25:18–33).

Dwight's own revelation and concealment of conflicted vocational and familial emotions interest Peter Kafer in "The Making of Timothy Dwight: A Connecticut Morality Tale" (*WMQ* 47:189–209). The use of natural setting, as a topographical mirror of the millennial destiny of the new nation, is the subject of " 'In These Contrasted Climes, How Chang'd the Scene': Progress, Declension, and Balance in the Landscapes of Timothy Dwight" (*NEQ* 63:80–108), in which Jane Kamensky ascertains Dwight's struggle to evaluate the uncertain changes he has witnessed. Like Dwight, William Bartram extracted a social moral from his journeys, including his observation of a correspondence between natural violence and human warfare; and in "Bartram's *Travels* and the Politics of Nature" (*EAL* 25:3–17), Douglas Anderson concludes that the naturalist urged the replacement of exuberant politics with a vision of life's limits and obligations.

However, in "New World" (*Granta* 30:235–51), Jonathan Raban discusses Crèvecoeur's belief that American character not only is influenced by the new environment but is, accordingly, venomous and predatory. Doubts concerning the young republic surface as well in *A House Undivided* (pp. 40–70), in which Douglas Anderson scrutinizes the highly idealized narrator in Crèvecoeur's *Letters;* this narrator alerts the reader to the discrepancy between the public reality (with slavery) and the private domestic potentiality, a discrepancy also evident in the digressive and episodic manner of Franklin's *Autobiography.* In "Community and Utopia in Crèvecoeur's *Sketches*" (*AL* 62:17–31), David M. Robinson inter-

prets Crèvecoeur's vision of an ideal egalitarianism as an implicit repudiation of American materialism that might be an opportunity for
revision but might also be an insurmountable obstruction to the attainment of genuine community. Pertinently, in "The 'Progressive Steps' of
the Narrator in Crèvecoeur's *Letters from an American Farmer*" (*SAF*
18:145–58), Stephen Carl Arch observes the persona's rejection of social
fictions about humanity and his inability, in disjointed sketches reflective
of a time of American cultural uncertainty, to resolve certain fears about
the dangers of revolution.

My "'An Allegorical Description of a Certain Island and Its Inhabitants': Eighteenth-Century Parable or Satire?" (*NEQ* 63:468–74) notes
the subversion of an ostensible religious message by political nuances
that raise questions about the intent of the author and the reliability of
the narrator, who might suggest that all beliefs are merely a matter of
perspective. That the satiric note of the earliest examples of Irish-
American literature set the tone for the next generation is argued by
Charles Fanning in *The Irish Voice in America* (pp. 6–18).

vii Brown and Contemporaries

A satiric challenge to conventional assumptions about truth, authority,
and identity interests Daniel E. Williams, whose "In Defense of Self:
Author and Authority in the *Memoirs of Stephen Burroughs*" (*EAL* 25:96–
122) reflects on Burroughs's various identities as an index to how unstable, unreliable, and manipulable are all external transactions of belief.
How another double-edged "revolutionary" satire at once conserves and
subverts the boundaries of a genre is disclosed in "The Parodic Mode and
the Patriarchal Imperative: Reading the Female Reader(s) in Tabitha
Tanny's *Female Quixotism*" (*EAL* 25:34–45), Cynthia J. Miecznikowski's
discussion of Tanny's assault on readers who privilege the aesthetic
norms of romance. Likewise, in Hannah Foster's *The Coquette* the norms
of domestic and social virtue, based on an ideal of economic security, are
vexed by early national concepts of female independence and individualism—the thesis of Carroll Smith-Rosenberg's "Domesticating 'Virtue':
Coquettes and Revolutionaries in Young America," in *Literature and the
Body: Essays on Populations and Persons,* ed. Elaine Scarry (Hopkins,
1988), pp. 160–84. Antagonism also surfaces in Sarah Emily Newton's
"Wise and Foolish Virgins: 'Usable Fiction' and the Early American
Conduct Tradition" (*EAL* 25:139–67); in conduct fiction the dramatiza-

tion of ideal female ethical behavior, as prescribed by conduct books, sometimes reveals that self-discipline and passivity can covertly evince the power of control, particularly in marital and familial relations.

The specific ethical responsibilities of speaker and audience alike emerge in *Truth in American Fiction* (pp. 59–84) by Janet Gabler-Hover, who convincingly demonstrates Brown's familiarity with the prevailing theories of his time about the proper study and use of rhetoric; *Wieland* implies that a naive trust in rhetorical eloquence and in the virtue of its user are characteristics of a solipsistic audience adopting flawed standards of judgment because (like Clara) it has failed to fulfill its moral role of assessing language in terms of both personal experience and concern for others. A pervasive rhetorical model in early national discourse also interests Shirley Samuels in *"Wieland:* Alien and Infidel" (*EAL* 25:46–66); just as the seductive inner desire for disorder is displaced by the official rhetorical advancement of familial and social order, the invasion of the Wieland household by an extrinsic alien force (Carwin) reveals the hidden intrinsic abnormalities of the self, family, and society that are displaced by official normalization. Although Clara seeks responsible agents for events, reports Toni O'Shaughnessy in " 'An Imperfect Tale': Interpretive Accountability in *Wieland"* (*SAF* 18:41–54), she fails to find any unmasking definitive interpretation and accordingly reveals that language itself serves as a transformative agency.

The inability of writing to affirm a Franklinesque sense of democratic self-authorship, Dauber argues in *The Idea of Authorship* (pp. 39–77), is evident in the confusions and inconsistencies of Brown's fiction; these features intimate the author's sense of lost autobiographical origins as well as alienation from the older authoritative role of the author, a role eroded by the formalities that came with the professionalization of writing. Brown's inconsistencies, observes G. St. John Stott in "Second Thoughts about *Ormond*" (*EA* 43, ii:157–68), are artistic flaws, the unintentional result of the author's revision of his original idea for the romance. In *The Place of Fiction in the Time of Science: A Disciplinary History of American Writing* (Cambridge, pp. 30–69), John Limon remarks Brown's struggle for a form of professional identity at a time when science was replacing religion; a doubleness emerges in Brown's work, at once allied with science in opposition to David Hume and allied with art in opposition to Baconian reductionism.

Brown also makes an appearance in two thinly argued works: Louis S. Gross's *Redefining the American Gothic: From* Wieland *to* Day of the

Dead (UMI, 1989), which claims that Gothic fiction provides an alternative history of the American experience because it includes women and African Americans as a marginalized Other; and Robert A. Lee's "A Darkness Visible: The Case of Charles Brockden Brown" (*American Horror Fiction*, pp. 13–32), which stresses the Gothic effect of darkness and illumination. That certain letters generally ascribed to Brown were really written by his friend Joseph Bringhurst, Jr., is revealed by John R. Holmes and Edwin J. Saeger in "Charles Brockden Brown and the 'Laura-Petrarch' Letters" (*EAL* 25:183–86). And several of Brown's contemporaries appear in Barbara A. White's *American Women's Fiction 1790–1870*.

At this point of my "deliverance," I shall conclude with a few pertinent words by the Huguenot explorer Jean de Léry: "I know . . . that having such a fine subject, I have not treated the various matters that I have mentioned in a style or a manner as grave as was required; I admit that . . . I have sometimes . . . touched too briefly on some matters that should have had a longer treatment. To compensate for these defects of language, I once again entreat the readers to consider how hard and troublesome for me was the experience of this history's content, and to receive my affection as payment."

University of Texas at Austin

12 19th-Century Literature

Gary Scharnhorst

In 1990, more so perhaps than in any previous year, the most interesting and provocative literary scholarship on the 19th-century was devoted to recovering once-forgotten or neglected women writers in the ongoing critical project of redefining the canon. The year was marked by the appearance of such works as Emily Toth's long-awaited biography of Kate Chopin, Ann J. Lane's biography of Charlotte Perkins Gilman, a veritable plethora of essays on Sarah Orne Jewett, and an issue of *ALR* guest-edited by Margaret O'Connor on women writers of the post-bellum period. Meanwhile, the lesser male writers covered by this chapter, especially the poets, but with such exceptions as Irving, Cooper, and Henry Adams, continue to suffer a slow eclipse.

i General Studies

Several volumes this year survey the work of women writers of the period, in effect building on an earlier generation of feminist scholarship which rehabilitated these writers individually. In *19th-Century American Women's Novels* (Cambridge), Susan K. Harris undertakes a remarkably ambitious project: to plot the subversive strategies encoded within a wide variety of women's texts, what Harris terms "exploratory novels," including Augusta Evans Wilson's *St. Elmo,* Susan B. Warner's *Queechy,* Fanny Fern's *Ruth Hall,* E. D. E. N. Southworth's *The Deserted Wife,* Elizabeth Drew Stoddard's *The Morgesons,* Elizabeth Stuart Phelps's *The Silent Partner* and *The Story of Avis,* Louisa May Alcott's *Work,* Jewett's *A Country Doctor,* and Chopin's *The Awakening.* All of these texts share, in Harris's view, a complex rhetorical code which permitted readers to configure them "differently than the cover story indicated" and which over time "effected a change in readers' horizons of expectations." Theoretically sophisticated, yet readable, the study is a model of its kind. It may not be convincing at every point—e.g., Harris tends to cite published reviews in lieu of private responses to argue her thesis—but on the whole the analysis of these novels is both ground-breaking and persuasive.

In *Doing Literary Business,* Susan Coultrap-McQuin stakes out an adjacent claim. Focusing on the careers of five typical if not representative women—Southworth, Stowe, Phelps, Mary Abigail Dodge, and Helen Hunt Jackson—Coultrap-McQuin situates their "literary activities within the histories of women, the literary marketplace, and literary professionalism" of the period. The product of prodigious research, the book is particularly good at describing these writers' star-crossed relations with their (male) publishers. Unfortunately, it also tends toward repetition, surprisingly so given the short circumference (on average, about 30 pages) of the biographical chapters. Of related interest is "Breaking the Silent Partnership: Businesswomen in Popular Fiction" (*AL* 62:238–61), in which Susan Albertine contends that Phelps's *The Silent Partner* both registered the change in the public spheres women were permitted to enter and encouraged "young middle-class women to work," and that Margaret Deland's *The Iron Horse* was written to warn readers of the consequences of admitting women into the industrial marketplace.

Patricia Marks makes much the same point about the changing roles of women in the 1880s and 1890s, albeit in much greater detail and from a different perspective, in *Bicycles, Bangs, and Bloomers: The New Women in the Popular Press* (Kentucky). As increasing numbers of women entered the economic mainstream, as Marks demonstrates, Anglo-American journalists responded to this domestic revolution by satirizing and caricaturing its various iterations. So too did such popular novelists as Robert Herrick and Henry Blake Fuller, according to Syril Weir in "A Bacchante Invades the American Home: The Disappearance of the Sentimental Heroine, 1890–1910," in *American Literature, Culture, and Ideology,* pp. 191–218. On the other hand, as Amy Kaplan notes in "Romancing the Empire: The Embodiment of American Masculinity in the Popular Historical Novel of the 1890s" (*AmLH* 2:659–90), the virile hero of the formulaic fin de siècle romance "uncannily parallels the popular narrative of the Spanish-American war as a chivalric rescue mission that in turn rejuvenates the liberator." The New Women depicted in such tales as Richard Harding Davis's *Soldiers of Fortune,* Charles Major's *When Knighthood Was in Flower,* George Barr McCutcheon's *Graustark,* and Mary Johnston's *To Have and to Hold* become "imperial subjects" by at once "freeing themselves from traditional hierarchies" and voluntarily submitting to "real men." Kaplan's thesis is bold and her analysis resourceful; still, the fiction formula she identifies is scarcely unique to the 1890s or to the era which witnessed the "chivalric liberation of Cuba and the Philippines." Its essential elements may be found as early as 1887, for example, in *The Crusade of the Excelsior,* Bret Harte's allegory of imperialism.

Barbara Bardes and Suzanne Gossett adopt a more traditional historical approach to a number of canonical and noncanonical texts in *Declarations of Independence: Women and Political Power in Nineteenth-Century American Fiction* (Rutgers). Bardes and Gossett avoid tortured and faddish rationalizations in favor of a refreshingly literal approach to these novels. Organized topically, their study focuses on three themes— the "intersection of the public and private spheres," the emerging "power of the female voice," and "the threat of the female body"—as they recur in such works as Sarah Hale's *Northwood,* Catharine Maria Sedgwick's *Hope Leslie* and *Redwood,* Stowe's *Uncle Tom's Cabin,* Southworth's *The Discarded Daughter,* Phelps's *Zay* and *The Silent Partner,* Gilman's *The Crux,* and Mary E. Wilkins Freeman's *The Portion of Labor,* as well as Cooper's *The Ways of the Hour,* Howells's *Dr. Breen's Practice,* Adams's *Democracy,* Bayard Taylor's *Hannah Thurston,* and Hamlin Garland's *A Spoil of Office* and *Rose of Dutcher's Cooley.* In all, *Declarations of Independence* is literary history at its best—the product of impeccable scholarship, written in concise prose, conclusive without becoming esoteric, pedantic, or thesis-ridden. Would but it were still in fashion.

Three essays in *Feminism, Utopia, and Narrative* (Tennessee), ed. Libby Falk Jones and Sarah Webster Goodwin, are also germane to this chapter. In "The Grand Marital Revolution" (pp. 69–84), Carol Farley Kessler ponders the critique of marriage in two feminist utopian romances, Marie Rowland's *Papa's Own Girl* and Martha Bruere's *Mildred Carver, U.S.A.* Dorothy Berkson predictably and rather tiresomely indicts "the abuses of patriarchal culture" in " 'So We All Became Mothers': Harriet Beecher Stowe, Charlotte Perkins Gilman, and the New World of Women's Culture" (pp. 100–115). While her readings of such works as *The Pearl of Orr's Island* and *Herland* are provocative, Berkson surely overstates the case for Stowe's and Gilman's radicalism. The "traditional utopian structure" of Gilman's *Herland* also becomes the baseline against which Libby Falk Jones measures the more implicitly rhetorical designs of recent utopian fiction in "Gilman, Bradley, Piercy, and the Evolving Rhetoric of Feminist Utopias" (pp. 116–29). The airy dreams of the utopians aside, Barbara A. White's *American Women's Fiction, 1790–1870: A Reference Guide* (Garland) fills a niche of more practical concern. White lists, cross-lists, and annotates nearly 400 books and articles about women writers of the period. Though the entries might have been more selective—White includes many items she excoriates for their perceived ideological shortcomings—this bibliography should prove to be a handy research tool.

In "The Indian Gallery: Antebellum Literature and the Containment of the American Indian" (*American Literature, Culture, and Ideology,* pp. 37–64), Eric J. Sundquist compares the official policy of Indian Removal with the marginalization of Native Americans and the "savagism" with which they were portrayed in such popular historical and literary texts of the period as Francis Parkman's *History of the Conspiracy of Pontiac,* Longfellow's *Hiawatha,* Cooper's *The Last of the Mohicans,* and Robert Montgomery Bird's *Nick of the Woods.* The nostalgic appeal of these works, Sundquist concludes, paradoxically contributed to "the double cultural process of Indian removal and preservation." A. La-Vonne Brown Ruoff makes much the same point about personal narratives written by Native Americans—particularly William Apes's *Son of the Forest,* George Copway's *Life, History, and Travels,* and Sarah Winnemucca's *Life among the Piutes*—in "Three Nineteenth-Century American Indian Autobiographers," pp. 251–69 in *Redefining American Literary History,* ed. Ruoff and Jerry W. Ward, Jr.

Two articles this year explore the sources of the distinctive African American narrative tradition. In "The Novelization of Voice in Early African American Narrative" (*PMLA* 105:23–34), William L. Andrews, the author of *To Tell a Free Story: The First Century of Afro-American Autobiography, 1760–1865,* focuses on the narratorial strategies of Frederick Douglass's *The Heroic Slave* and William Wells Brown's *Clotel,* two transitional works in the evolution of slave narrative to novel. As Andrews explains, these two fictive texts contain all the narrative acts and authenticating conventions "that have traditionally informed, structured, and given context to written African American storytelling." Less satisfactory, if more polemical, is Maryemma Graham's "The Origins of Afro-American Fiction" (*PAAS* 100:231–49), a welter of ethnographic information that never quite delivers what the title promises.

The American Civil War, or more precisely the literature it inspired, also continues to attract the interest of scholars. Conceding the force of Whitman's claim that "the real war will never get in the books"—and Daniel Aaron's thesis that the war is literally "unwritten"—these scholars weigh repeated literary attempts, as Timothy Sweet allows in *Traces of War: Poetry, Photography, and the Crisis of the Union* (Hopkins), "to envision the meaning of the war in terms of existing ideological schemata." Though primarily concerned with imaginative transformations of pastoral landscape in the verse of Whitman and Melville, Sweet refers at least incidentally to the war poetry of Whittier, the stories of Crane and Bierce, and the photography essays of Oliver Wendell Holmes, Sr. In "Where My Heart Is Turning Ever: Civil War Stories and National Stability from Fort Sumter to the Centennial" (*AmLH* 2:627–58), the latest installment in her Civil War fiction project, Kathleen Diffley analyzes the appeal of "domestic discourse" or Old Homestead narratives by such writers as Horatio Alger, Jr., and Louisa May Alcott which "tried to contain the war's disruption." By insisting the nation was but a form of extended family, as Diffley persuasively contends, these popular tales with their "promises of continuity, safety, and restoration were more in keeping with the ideals of the Revolution than the projects of Reconstruction." Also of interest is Henry M. W. Russell's "The *Memoirs* of Ulysses S. Grant: The Rhetoric of Judgment" (*VQR* 66:189–209), a dispassionate commentary on the varied styles and personae Grant adopted in his autobiography; and John E. Hallwas's "Civil War Accounts as Literature" (*WIRS* 13:46–60), an appeal for "the recovery and study" of personal nonfiction about the war.

Two other general studies merit at least brief mention: Steven Mailloux's "The Rhetorical Use and Abuse of Fiction: Eating Books in Late Nineteenth-Century America" (*Boundary 2* 17:133–57), an erudite investigation "of how cultural rhetoric enables and constrains the interpretation and use of fiction" in the late 1860s and mid-1880s, an essay no reception historian should henceforth overlook; and Everett F. Bleiler's monumental *Science Fiction: The Early Years* (Kent State), a 1,000-page, phonebook-sized encyclopedia of plot synopses and biographical sketches of science fiction writers before 1930, including such

19th-century stalwarts as Fitz-James O'Brien, Lillie Devereux Blake, Julian Hawthorne, and Edward Bellamy. An obvious labor of love to compile, it would no doubt be one to read.

ii Irving, Cooper, Simms, and Contemporaries

Nineteen ninety was something of a banner year for Irving, albeit not in his Diedrich Knickerbocker or even his Geoffrey Crayon incarnations, with a book, two major articles, and a collection of essays devoted mostly to his works about the American West. In *Tales of Adventurous Enterprise: Washington Irving and the Poetics of Western Expansion* (Columbia), the most significant of these contributions to Irving scholarship, Peter Antelyes proposes both to examine the tale of capitalist expansionism as an indigenous American literary form and to trace Irving's role in the development of the formula. By subscribing to the ideology of Manifest Destiny in *A Tour on the Prairies* and celebrating the entrepreneurial spirit in *Astoria* and *The Adventures of Captain Bonneville,* Antelyes explains, Irving shrewdly exploited popular fascination with the West as a literary topic and rationalized its exploitation for commercial purposes. Two articles in *CRevAS* supplement Antelyes's book. In "Washington Irving's Problems with History and Romance in *Astoria*" (21:1–13), I. S. MacLaren deftly tracks the literary difficulties Irving faced in writing his account of the fur trade (e.g., how to portray his hero-patron Astor). And in " 'Lords of the Ascendant': Mercantile Biography and Irving's *Astoria*" (21:15–30), Alan Leander MacGregor crudely echoes (or anticipates?) Antelyes by arguing that in the book Irving "created an accommodationist rhetorical strategy which legitimized the emergent capitalist mode of production and its class values, and sanctified this new order by conferring the values of the residual, aristocratic-heroic order on a man like Astor, rescripting commercial speculation and the accumulation of wealth through the genre of romance." Enough said?

In "The Author as Professional: Washington Irving's 'Rambling Anecdotes' of the West," one of two original articles, pp. 237–53 in Ralph M. Aderman, ed., *Critical Essays on Washington Irving* (Hall), Wayne Kime surveys the same territory from the perspective of a nonpartisan literary biographer. Eschewing the New Historicist and ideological predilections of Antelyes and MacGregor, Kime defends Irving from the charge he had become a mere hack by the mid-1830s. Rather, according to Kime, Irving was the consummate literary professional in these books, his treatment of the West "remarkably sure-handed." Aderman's volume reprints a sheaf of reviews and essays by such respected Irving scholars as Henry A. Pochmann, Lewis Leary, Donald A. Ringe, and Jeffrey Rubin-Dorsky. It also includes a second original essay, Jenifer S. Banks's "Washington Irving, the Nineteenth-Century American Bachelor" (pp. 253–65). In both his published writings such as "Rip Van Winkle" and his private correspondence, Banks opines, Irving was a "prototype of the American male struggling to reconcile the conflict between freedom and adult responsibility, independence and social obligation, fantasy and reality." The genial author of *The Sketch Book* and *Bracebridge Hall* is featured, too, in Christopher Mulvey's *Transatlantic Manners* (Cambridge), a fine study of the representation of social codes in 19th-century Anglo-American travel literature. Among the other writers of this period discussed in the book are N. P. Willis, William Austin, Stowe, Adams, and, of course, Cooper.

Two new MLA-approved volumes appear this year in the Cooper Edition (SUNY): the nautical romance *The Two Admirals* and the social satire *Satanstoe,* with excellent historical introductions by Donald A. Ringe and Kay Seymour House, respectively. Much as the publication of the new Irving edition has fueled the recent revival of interest in his work, these authoritative texts should help to bolster Cooper's critical reputation. Indeed, several major Cooper studies were issued in 1990. Robert Emmet Long's *James Fenimore Cooper* (Continuum) is a solid alternative to Ringe's TUSAS volume—a sprightly introduction to the author's life and complete works which revises the assessment of Leslie Fiedler and others, for example, that miscegenation is the "secret theme" of the Leatherstocking series. Long's comparisons of Cooper with Hawthorne and Melville in his last chapter are particularly insightful. Ringe also reexamines Cooper's defense of republican institutions in both America and Europe in "Go East, Young Man, and Discover Your Country" (*KRev* 10, i:3–20). In *"The Guardian of the Law": Authority and Identity in James Fenimore Cooper* (Penn. State), Charles Hansford Adams revises ever so slightly the thematic approach to Cooper's work taken a generation ago by James P. McWilliams in *Political Justice in a Republic.* Whereas McWilliams focused on the law "as an object of concern for Cooper the social critic," Adams purports to examine "the way the law in Cooper's novels determines identity, and the way identity conditions the law." Though his analysis is less detailed than McWilliams's, Adams builds a strong case for his view that Cooper felt an "imaginative parity" among "law, nation, and self" in his legal fiction, that his republicanism resists simple reduction to the dynamic of "head versus heart." Similarly, Paul Lukacs summarizes Cooper's critique of the social and political upheavals epitomized by Jacksonian democracy in "Lingering Beside His Father's Grave: James Fenimore Cooper's Novels of Country and Home" (*ESQ* 36:109–35). Lukacs traces the ebbs and flows in Cooper's ideals of domestic life by contrasting his ideas of home in three novels set on the shores of Lake Otsego: *The Pioneers, Home as Found,* and *The Deerslayer.* Robert Daly notes Cooper's recurring fascination with the frontier in American history in "Liminality and Fiction in Cooper, Hawthorne, Cather, and Fitzgerald," pp. 70–85 in *Victor Turner and the Construction of Cultural Criticism* (Indiana), ed. Kathleen M. Ashley; and Doris Sommer discusses the Argentine writer Domingo Faustino Sarmiento's appropriations from the Leatherstocking series in "Plagiarized Authenticity: Sarmiento's Cooper and Others," a piece (pp. 130–55) in *Do the Americas Have a Common Literature?* ed. Gustavo Pérez Firmat. Unfortunately, Sommer seems more familiar with Sarmiento's work than with Cooper's. In "The Mackenzie Court-Martial Trial: Cooper's Secret Correspondence with William H. Norris" (*SAR,* pp. 149–58), Hugh Egan fleshes out the context in which Cooper reviewed a celebrated lawsuit in 1844 after surreptitiously comparing notes with the judge advocate in the case. The third chapter of Kenneth Dauber's *The Idea of Authorship,* pp. 78–117, is of an altogether different species of criticism. Dauber deconstructs "Cooper's Myth," undermining his claim to be a "representative" American writer, indeed debunking any claim he was even a representational writer. Rather, according to Dauber, Cooper negotiated a difficult (ir)resolution to the problem of narrative authorization: he struggled "to repossess himself" or "recapture" what he wrote in the events of his life. The elegant simplicity of his title notwithstanding, Dauber is enraptured by theory and uses "other" as a verb. Most Cooper scholars will, I suspect, be troubled by his brash assertion that "Spiller and those in his tradition" have "misrepresented [Cooper's] significance" by attempting to relate his fiction to topical social and political issues.

The modest Simms revival of recent years shows no signs of flagging in 1990, with a new edition of his poems and four articles in print. Of the nearly 200 verses in *Selected Poems of William Gilmore Simms* (Georgia), ed. James E. Kibler, Jr., more than half are previously uncollected, and more than a third are printed under Simms's name for the first time. Still, the volume strikes me as overpriced at $50. Kibler also comments perceptively on the author's stories in "The Major Fiction of William Gilmore Simms" (*MissQ* 43:85–95), though he seems overly determined to plead the case for Simms's "position front-and-center among the very best writers of the day," as a figure "squarely in the grander company of the masters," capable "no less than Melville" of "deep diving" to the "great universal depths." The same tone of apology mars "William Gilmore Simms and Current Literary Criticism" (*MissQ* 43:105–08), David Aiken's review-essay of *"Long Years of Neglect"* (see *ALS 1988*, p. 206). According to Aiken, "Simms strides through nineteenth-century American literature like a colossus." Such hyperbole is usually reserved for defending a lost cause. In "The Ongoing Study of William Gilmore Simms: Literary Critics vs. Historians" (*SCR* 22, ii:7–15), a circumlocuted bibliographical essay, Charles S. Watson comes to the rather startling, because so modest, conclusion that both critics and historians might profit from an "interdisciplinary exchange" of views on the writer. Carol Steinhagen notes the "infantile nature" of the "fantasy of masculine power" in Simms's late novel *The Cub of the Panther* in "Stalking the Feline Female," pp. 207–20 in *Women and Violence in Literature,* ed. Katherine Anne Ackley. David C. Miller also devotes part of a chapter in *Dark Eden,* pp. 81–88 and passim, a book overlooked last year, to an analysis of Simms's ambiguous iconography of the swamp in his poem "The Edge of the Swamp" and such romances as *The Forayers* and *Woodcraft.*

Among the other figures of the antebellum period who receive critical attention this year is William J. Grayson, a South Carolinian best known, if at all, for his pastoral poem *The Hireling and the Slave,* a qualified defense of the peculiar institution. Grayson's autobiography, admirably edited by Richard J. Calhoun and with a foreword by Eugene D. Genovese, is published for the first time in an unabridged version under the title *Witness to Sorrow* (So. Car.). In "The Anti-secession Satires of William J. Grayson" (*SCR* 22, ii:50–57), Calhoun also resurrects the Swiftian prose of *Letters from "Curtius"* from that literary hell, the footnote. Daniel Aaron discusses a pair of Brahmin travel narratives, *Two Years Before the Mast* and *The Oregon Trail,* as "expressions or consequences of what might be called ancestral influences and vocational pressures" in "Two Boston Fugitives: Dana and Parkman," another essay in *American Literature, Culture, and Ideology* (pp. 115–29). Aaron brings to these books an extraliterary perspective grounded in biobibliography that will seem anachronistic only to, in Richard Poirier's memorable phrase, "the most benighted of Francophile theoreticians." William E. Lenz exhumes a similar travel record, in this case an epic poem, in "The Poetics of the Antarctic: James Croxall Palmer's *Thalia: A Tale of the Antarctic* (1843)" (*ATQ* n.s. 4:327–42). While Lenz sensibly refrains from claiming too much for Palmer—e.g., "he is no Byron, no Bryant, no Longfellow or Poe"—he may in fact err too far in the other direction by describing the poet as a "representative American" whose perceptions of his journey were neither "deformed" like the official record of the U.S. Exploring Expedition nor "left unformed in a personal journal." As a representative type, according to Lenz, Palmer somehow "contributed to the process of change in American attitudes" toward the Antarctic. Literary history need not be construed as a zero-sum game in which historical significance must be made a sort of trump card. Finally, three reprints from the period deserve brief notice: Joseph Holt Ingraham's first novel, *Lafitte* (NCUP), ed. Robert W. Weathersby II; Charles Fenno Hoffman's only novel, *Greyslaer* (NCUP), ed. Daniel A. Wells; and James E. Seaver's *A Narrative of the Life of Mrs. Mary Jemison* (Syracuse), with a foreword by George Abrams.

iii Popular Writers of Mid-Century

Harriet Beecher Stowe's critical stock continues to soar, though it might have been bought for pennies on the dollar only a few years ago. The opening section of Gillian Brown's *Domestic Individualism* (pp. 1–60) traces the alignment between individualism and the ethos of domesticity in *Uncle Tom's Cabin.* In the first chapter, originally published in *AQ* (see *ALS 1984,* p. 222), Brown demonstrates that Stowe's polemic was directed at "conventional domestic ideology" no less than at slavery and the marketplace. The previously unpublished second chapter complicates this point, however, for it seems Stowe also developed "an aesthetics of property relations" in the novel that was "characteristic of a certain racism." Thus, Brown refers darkly to "the troubling contradictions of *Uncle Tom's Cabin:* the novel's simultaneous advancement of domestic feminism, anti-slavery, and racism." Such a statement betrays, I fear, the ahistorical premises of Brown's cultural criticism. A proponent of colonization and never an abolitionist—though Brown repeatedly identifies her as one—Stowe simply resists reinvention as a radical reformer in the modern mold. Lisa Watt MacFarlane makes a point similar to Brown's but more succinctly in " 'If Ever I Get to Where I Can': The Competing

Rhetorics of Social Reform in *Uncle Tom's Cabin*" (*ATQ* n.s. 4:135–47). According to MacFarlane, Stowe's "domestic ideology, republicanism, and post-millennial evangelicalism each involved competing beliefs and assumptions" which destabilize the novel. Carl E. Krog's "Women, Slaves, and Family in *Uncle Tom's Cabin:* Symbolic Battleground in Antebellum America" (*MQ* 31:252–69) is a much more prosaic and rudimentary analysis of Stowe's domestic ideology and the contemporary Southern response it elicited. Similarly, Stephen J. DeCanio's *"Uncle Tom's Cabin:* A Reappraisal" (*CentR* 34:587–93) merely outlines the argument for canonizing Stowe's novel on the basis of its social significance. Nor has recent comment on Stowe been restricted exclusively to her first novel. In *Dark Eden,* his study of the swamp image in 19th-century American culture (pp. 90–104), David C. Miller relates "the great dismal swamp" which gives Stowe's *Dred* its subtitle to the "normally repressed darker side of the Northern white psyche."

The works of two other prominent antislavery writers at mid-century, Douglass and Harriet Jacobs, also warranted critical review in 1990. *Frederick Douglass: New Literary and Historical Essays* (Cambridge), ed. Eric J. Sundquist, contains an introduction and 13 original articles by such eminent scholars as Sterling Stuckey, Henry Louis Gates, Jr., Wilson J. Moses, and Richard Yarborough. Of special interest are "From Wheatley to Douglass: The Politics of Displacement" (pp. 47–65), in which Gates contends that Douglass's rise to prominence in the 19th-century abolitionist press was "marked by the simultaneous eclipse" of Phillis Wheatley; "Writing Freely? Frederick Douglass and the Constraints of Racialized Writing" (pp. 66–83), in which Moses traces Douglass's struggle "to free himself from the literary confinement of the slave narrative"; and "The Punishment of Esther: Frederick Douglass and the Construction of the Feminine" (pp. 141–65), in which Jenny Franchot considers the implications of Douglass's "shift from often impassioned descriptions of women in slavery to virtual silence about them in the comparative freedom of the North." Gregory S. Jay attributes Douglass's "new status as a canonical figure" to the "revisionary return to history" in literary studies in "American Literature and the New Historicism: The Example of Frederick Douglass" (*Boundary 2* 17:211–42). In "Up from 'Twoness': Frederick Douglass and the Meaning of W. E. B. Du Bois's Concept of Double Consciousness" (*CRevAS* 21:301–19), David W. Blight relates Douglass's "dual roles as black leader and national patriot" to Du Bois's observation that the African American incarnates "two warring ideals in one dark body." As Blight explains, Douglass in his public speeches and autobiographies "demonstrated his American nationalism, while at the same time exhibiting a strong commitment to an antebellum form of black cultural nationalism." Rather than joining it, Andrew Levy transcends this debate "over whether Douglass ironically or involuntarily consented to the forces of mainstream American culture" by juxtaposing his *Narrative* with the *Autobiography* of a Founding Father in "Frederick Douglass, Benjamin Franklin, and the Trickster Reader" (*CE* 52:743–55). However, Levy's glib conclusion—that in an age of critical dissensus readers "must be a dissensus-unto-themselves"—raises more questions than it answers.

Levy is less circuitous and more analytical in "Dialect and Convention: Harriet A. Jacobs's *Incidents in the Life of a Slave Girl*" (*NCL* 45:206–19). Jacobs's use of dialect, he argues, "must be read as a rhetorical strategy designed to manipulate set responses from her reader." More specifically, Jacobs produced "a text that mediated between deference and self-assertion." In "Culture, Gender, and the Slave Narrative" (*Proteus* 7, i:37–42), James L. Gray makes a number of superficial comparisons between Douglass's *Narrative* and Jacobs's *Incidents* (e.g., Douglass "establishes a relationship with and a perspective on mid-century American culture as a public person" whereas Jacobs "asserted the inability of the cultural and literary conventions to understand the private life of the slave"). P. Gabrielle Forman more perceptively compares the gaps of indeterminacy in Jacobs's text with those in Harriet E. Wilson's novel in "The Spoken and the Silenced in *Incidents in the Life of a Slave Girl* and *Our Nig*" (*Callaloo* 13:313–24). Similarly, Sarah Way Sherman considers Jacobs's conflicted or "troubled voice" in "Moral Experience in Harriet Jacobs's *Incidents in the Life of a Slave Girl*" (*NWSA Journal* 2:167–85). As Sherman explains, the narrator of *Incidents* must resist both "the brutal, exploitative bonds of slavery and the idealized, altruistic bonds of true womanhood."

Louisa May Alcott continues to attract attention this year, virtually all of it given to *Little Women*. Gloria T. Delamar's *Louisa May Alcott and Little Women* (McFarland) is, unfortunately, the stuff of fanzines. It contains a biographical sketch of the author and a reception history of the book but little documentation and precious little that is new. It is also written in an utterly banal style: e.g., Alcott "slipped peacefully into death from a deep, dreaming sleep." Now how could anyone possibly know that? In "Laughing with the Boys and Learning with the Girls:

Humor in Nineteenth-Century American Juvenile Fiction" (*CLAQ* 15:127–30), Lynne Vallone uses *Tom Sawyer* and *Little Women* as springboards to speculation about "differences in the function of humor which seem related to gender." More satisfactory than either of these studies are three major articles by feminist critics. Catharine R. Stimpson coins the concept of the *paracanon*, "a tenet that neither ranks cultural works nor travels a compromised *via media* among them," and she illustrates the notion by reference to *Little Women* in "Reading for Love: Canons, Paracanons, and Whistling Jo March" (*NLH* 21:957–76). In "The Borders of Ethical, Erotic, and Artistic Possibilities in *Little Women*" (*Signs* 15:562–85), Ann B. Murphy brilliantly interprets the novel according to Carol Gilligan's theories of female ethical development, concluding that its power "derives in large measure from the contradictions and tensions it exposes and from the pattern it establishes of subversive, feminist exploration colliding repeatedly against patriarchal repression." Similarly, Jean Wyatt's chapter on the novel in *Reconstructing Desire*, pp. 51–63, identifies its "two different stories": one that is "linear and developmental," governed by the demands of the absent father; the other "of circular stasis" that centers on "the space filled by the unity of mother and sisters" in the home.

No longer merely a cottage industry, Rebecca Harding Davis is the subject of four major articles in 1990. In "The 'Feminization' of Rebecca Harding Davis" (*AmLH* 2:203–19), the indefatigable Jean Fagan Yellin summarizes the composition history of *Margret Howth* in order to center Davis's realistic treatment in the novel of "issues of gender and race" and the essentially false, sentimentalized conclusion she appended to it at the insistence of her (white/male) editor James T. Fields. Yellin's essay also appears as the afterword to a new edition of the novel (Feminist). Maribel W. Molyneaux offers a class- and gender-based analysis of Davis's novella *Life in the Iron Mills,* her first work of fiction, in "Sculpture in the Iron Mills: Rebecca Harding Davis's Korl Woman" (*WS* 17:157–77). As Molyneaux argues, Davis's working-class protagonist Hugh Wolfe "functions as a thinly-disguised surrogate" for the woman artist, and in the image of the korl woman he sculpts, Davis "brings the special problems of the woman worker and the woman writer into focus in a space of labor that, like the iron mill, was once the exclusive province of male work and male artistry." *Life in the Iron Mills,* along with Gilman's "The Yellow Wall-paper," Jewett's *The Country of the Pointed Firs,* and Edith Wharton's "Souls Belated," is reprinted with a splendid introduction by Cynthia Griffin Wolff in an inexpensive paperback edition suitable for classroom adoption entitled *Four Stories by American Women* (Penguin). Jean Pfaelzer also profiles Davis's career for readers of *Legacy* (7, ii:39–45), and Jane Atteridge Rose compiles a list of some 500 of her works in "A Bibliography of Fiction and Non-Fiction by Rebecca Harding Davis" (*ALR* 22, iii:67–86).

A spate of articles on other popular mid-century women writers also appears this year, the most exemplary of them by Nina Baym. In "Reinventing Lydia Sigourney" (*AL* 62:385–404), Baym forcefully disputes Sigourney's skewed reputation—"based on only some fraction of what she wrote and published"—as a funerary poet, and she erects the scaffolding for constructing "several Sigourneys who are unknown to modern criticism," especially "Sigourney the history teacher and the historian." Baym undertakes a similar project of critical revisionism—the reclamation of the career of the editor of *Godey's Lady's Book* and author of the encyclopedic *Woman's Record*—in "Onward Christian Women: Sarah J. Hale's History of the World" (*NEQ* 63:249–70). Rather than, as the standard literary histories have it, simply a "retrograde force" who editorially "impeded the development of egalitarian feminism" by advocating "separate spheres" for the sexes, Hale attempted in *Woman's Record,* according to Baym, "to reconstitute world history *as* the history of women," particularly Christian women. Nicole Tonkovich Hoffman usefully silhouettes the salient events in Hale's life in a *Legacy* profile (7, ii:47–55). In "Widening the World: Susan Warner, Her Readers, and the Assumption of Authorship" (*AQ* 42:565–86), Susan S. Williams emphatically underscores a relatively minor point: that Warner chose to write in the sentimental mode in order to raise and satisfy her pious readers' expectations. The essay perfectly illustrates the danger, sounded by D. G. Myers (see *ALS 1988,* p. 208), of canonizing, not Warner's novel per se, but Jane Tompkins's reading of it. Cynthia Schoolar Williams compares Warner's second novel to the structure of male initiation stories in "Susan Warner's *Queechy* and the *Bildungsroman* Tradition" (*Legacy* 7, ii:3–16); however, the significant points of comparison are often lost in the forest of plot synopses. Sandra Zagarell contributes an admirable introduction to a new edition of Caroline Kirkland's satirical western novel *A New Home, Who'll Follow?* in the American Women Writers Series (Rutgers). Zagarell also writes a headnote to the first modern reprinting of Elizabeth Barstow Stoddard's story "The Chimneys" (*Legacy* 7, ii:27–28). Two other biographical notes warrant mention: Paul C. Helmreich's

"Lucy Larcom at Wheaton" (*NEQ* 63:109–20), a brief comment on Larcom's early career as a teacher with excerpts from the diary she kept between 1859 and 1862, at most a footnote to the Larcom biography Shirley Marchalonis published last year (*ALS 1989*, p. 206); and Gloria Oden's "The Black Putnams of Charlotte Forten's Journal" (*EIHC* 126:237–53), a genealogical history of the George Putnam family who figure in Forten's Civil War diary.

Popular men of letters at mid-century were mostly but not entirely ignored in 1990. The Fireside poets in particular seem to have slipped ineluctably into the black hole of critical neglect. The only significant exceptions to this generalization: John Paul Russo's *"Isle of the Dead:* Italy and the Uncanny in Arnold Böcklin, Sheridan Le Fanu, and James Russell Lowell" (*RLA 1989*, pp. 202–09), a comparativist treatment of the morbid imagery each of these artists associated with Italy; Arthur Sherbo's "John Greenleaf Whittier in *The Critic*, 1881–1892" (*SB* 43:222–38), a workmanlike review of references to and by the poet in the magazine; and chapter 4 of Alan Shucard's *American Poetry: The Puritans Through Walt Whitman* (Mass.), a serviceable introduction to both the Fireside and Knickerbocker schools. Jerome Meckier's "George Dolby to James T. Fields: Two New Letters Concerning Dickens's American Reading Tour" (*Dickensian* 86:171–83) takes as its subtext the promotional genius of Fields, the influential Boston publisher and editor. Incredibly, Horatio Alger, Jr., gets more ink this year than all the Fireside poets and their publishers together. Ralph D. Gardner's *Horatio Alger, or the American Hero Era*, first published in 1964 and long since discredited, is inexplicably reissued in 1990 by Amereon House. As I wrote in 1978, the last time a small press marketed a version of this claptrap, Gardner "caught a carp he pretends in the telling was a rainbow trout." Victor Berch and Edward T. LeBlanc compile a reliable and comprehensive list of nearly 700 items in their privately printed *The Short Stories, Articles and Poems of Horatio Alger, Jr.* Madonne M. Miner's "Horatio Alger's *Ragged Dick:* Projection, Denial and Double-Dealing" (*AI* 47:233–48) is symptomatic of the strain in contemporary criticism that invests every literary text with ambiguity and deception, no matter how simple and straightforward it may first seem. Alan Trachtenberg's graceful introduction to a new Signet reprint of *Ragged Dick*—the first modern edition to include Alger's original preface to the novel—is more satisfactory if only because it is grounded not in armchair psychoanalysis but in the historical and biographical record.

iv **Humorists**

Scholarship in this category slowed to a trickle in 1990. Despite the diminution, however, most of it was of consistently high quality. Two noteworthy anthologies of Southern humor literally resurrect material from newspaper morgues: *Old Southwest Humor from the* St. Louis *Reveille, 1844–1850* (Missouri), admirably edited and introduced by Fritz Oehlschlaeger, and *Ham Jones, Ante-Bellum Southern Humorist* (Nevada), no less admirably compiled and introduced by Willene Hendrick and George Hendrick. The subject of neither volume is particularly fashionable in the present climate of literary studies. To Oehlschlaeger's and the Hendricks' credit, however, each book proves the continuing worth of pioneering research on neglected 19th-century Anglo male writers. In "Joel Chandler Harris and the Ethnologists: The Folk's View of Early American Folkloristics" (*SFolk* 47:227–37), Eric L. Montenyohl chronicles Harris's conflicted relations with the scientific folklorists of his day; and in "Remus Redux, or French Classicism on the Old Plantation: La Fontaine and J. C. Harris," an essay in *Southern Literature and Literary Theory,* pp. 170–85, the volume editor Jefferson Humphries compares what would seem at first glance to be entirely different species of fiction—the Uncle Remus tales and the fables of the French writer Jean de la Fontaine—to underscore Harris's "paradoxical view of the black man" and his "complicated attitude toward literature." William L. Frank also edits and contributes a perfunctory introduction to *Dialect Tales and Other Stories* by Catherine McDowell (aka Sherwood Bonner) for the Masterworks of Literature series (NCUP). Frank concedes that Bonner was "a minor writer," but still he exaggerates the case for her artistry—e.g., "her women characterizations are very possibly the finest drawn in the nineteenth century." I stay my hand from heaping scorn.

As for non-Southern humorists: Largely through the herculean efforts of Lawrence I. Berkove, the works of the Westerner William Wright (aka Dan De Quille) are enjoying a critical revival. Berkove continues De Quille's rehabilitation in his most recent publications, most prominent among them his edition of *The Fighting Horse of the Stanislaus* (Iowa), a collection of stories and essays mined from the Comstock Lode. As Tony Hillerman remarks in his review of the volume for the *NYTBR* (September 23, 1990, pp. 33, 62), De Quille combined "the yarn-spinner's knack of using mundane details to set off his flights of fancy" with "the wordsmith's skill with language." Berkove also edits a second De Quille volume, the moral allegory *The Gnomes of the Dead Rivers* (Falcon Hill), and he contributes a headnote to a reprinting of De Quille's "Odd Sticks" (*NOQ* 62:54–64). Obviously, Berkove has struck a rich vein which shows no sign of petering out. Like '49ers attracted by the news of discovery, Richard A. Dwyer and Richard E. Lingenfelter establish a rival claim in *Dan De Quille the Washoe Giant* (Nevada), which includes a biographical sketch, 42 reprinted stories and essays, and a checklist of De Quille's writings.

A trio of solid essays in *StAH* (1986–87) round out this section. Edward J. Piacentino continues to champion the New York humorist Mortimer Neal Thomson (aka Q. K. Philander Doesticks) in "'Seeing the Elephant': Doesticks' Satires of Nineteenth-Century Gotham" (n.s. 5:134–44). John Rees dissects the dialect games and verbal slapstick of the Chicago pundit Finley Peter Dunne in "An Anatomy of Mr. Dooley's Brogue" (n.s. 5:145–57). And Elvin Holt predictably concludes that the author-illustrator E. W. Kemble exploited a "repulsive and degrading" racism by his stereotypical depiction of blacks in *"A Coon Alphabet* and the Comic Mask of Racial Prejudice" (n.s. 5:307–18).

v Post-Civil War Women Writers

The volume of scholarship on postbellum women continues to expand like air in a vacuum, though much of it still centers on such New Englanders as Jewett and Freeman. Jewett alone was the subject of 11 decidedly uneven articles in 1990. Melissa McFarland Pennell argues cogently for the significance of women's rituals in her stories in "A New Spiritual Biography: Domesticity and Sorority in the Fiction of Sarah Orne Jewett" (*SAF* 18:193–206). Through such tales as "Miss Tempy's Watchers" and "The Passing of Sister Barsett," Jewett attempts to prove, according to Pennell, that "the power of [women's] community, strengthened by an inner grace, is a force equal to the challenge of the decline wrought by economic failure." The narrative tradition of spiritual biography which Jewett taps in these early stories "later gives shape to *The Country of the Pointed Firs.*" In "Age and Life's 'Great Prospects' in Sarah Orne Jewett's *The Country of the Pointed Firs*" (*CLQ* 26:161–70), Helen Westra elaborates the point by noting that Jewett particularly celebrates the maturity of aging women in her masterwork. Marilyn M. Fisher compresses the notion of matriarchal community so that it fits into a nice theological box in "Community and Earthly Salvation: Christian

Intimations Within the Setting of Jewett's *Pointed Firs*" (*L&B* 10:67–77). According to Fisher, Almira Todd performs "salvific service" and "symbolizes Dunnet Landing's Christian way of life"—this despite Jewett's repeated satire of sterile religious orthodoxy. Jean Rohloff in "'A Quicker Signal': Women and Language in Sarah Orne Jewett's *The Country of the Pointed Firs*" (*SoAR* 55, ii:33–46) reads the novel as "a model of a female-centered psycholinguistic myth" with the middle-aged narrator "representing women's ambivalent position within that myth." Patricia Keefe Durso analyzes the work as a type of female bildungsroman, albeit with few new insights, in "Jewett's 'Pointed Firs': An 'Index Finger' to Character Development and Unity of Vision in *The Country of the Pointed Firs*" (*CLQ* 26:171–81). Karen Oakes opens her essay "'All That Lay Deepest in Her Heart': Reflections on Jewett, Gender, and Genre" (*CLQ* 26:152–60), a fairly pedestrian attempt to explain Jewett's relative neglect over the years despite the artistry of her novel, by gratuitously berating F. O. Matthiessen as a patriarchal canonizer—though Oakes nowhere acknowledges that Matthiessen was one of Jewett's earliest and staunchest defenders and the author of the first full-length critical study of her work. Each of three other Jewett stories occasions a single critical essay. The prolific Thomas A. Maik discusses the author's "most thorough examination" of gender roles in his rather discursive "Reclaiming Paradise: Role Reversal as Liberation in Sarah Orne Jewett's 'Tom's Husband'" (*Legacy* 7, i:23–29). Terry Heller attributes the success of Jewett's most anthologized tale largely to her subversion of a "masculine plot" (i.e., one that is linear and realistic) with "feminine rhetoric" (i.e., devices of "the fanciful and of fantasy") in "The Rhetoric of Communion in Jewett's 'The White Heron'" (*CLQ* 26:182–94). Joseph Church creatively interprets another of her tales according to Melanie Klein's theory of mourning in "Absent Mothers and Anxious Daughters: Facing Ambivalence in Jewett's 'The Foreigner'" (*ELWIU* 17:52–68). Finally, two essays trace literary influences on or by Jewett: Jules Zanger's "'Young Goodman Brown' and 'A White Heron': Correspondences and Illuminations" (*PLL* 26:346–57), which "suggests the possibility" that "Jewett's indebtedness to Hawthorne" in this particular story "extended well beyond the generalized relationships" critics often cite; and Ann Romines's "The Hermit's Parish: Jeanne Le Ber and Cather's Legacy from Jewett" (*Cather Studies* 1:147–58), which argues for the importance of Jewett's example of the solitary heroine for the author of *Shadows on the Rock*.

Meanwhile, Freeman scholarship receives a boost this year with five articles. Thomas Maik compares the stories "A New England Nun" and "Louisa" in "Dissent and Affirmation: Conflicting Voices of Female Roles in Selected Stories by Mary Wilkins Freeman" (*CLQ* 26:59–68), observing that while both protagonists are liberated, the narrators "are ambivalent as well as skeptical of their characters' behavior." Martha J. Cutter compares the same stories to far different purposes in "Mary E. Wilkins Freeman's Two New England Nuns" (*CLQ* 26:213–25). Reading the fiction in light of Carol Gilligan's theories on ethical development, Cutter contends that Louisa Ellis of "A New England Nun" is unable to "mediate the conflict between self and other," whereas Louisa Britton of "Louisa" both decides "where duty lies" and defies "the combined forces which [would] hold her back." Joseph Church disputes, with good reason, the critical tradition that has trivialized or marginalized one of the author's most popular stories in "Reconstructing Woman's Place in Freeman's 'The Revolt of "Mother"' " (*CLQ* 26:195–200): the tale "actually advances a serious analysis of the difficulties a woman confronts when attempting to realize her interests." In " 'Friend of My Heart': Women as Friends and Rivals in the Short Stories of Mary Wilkins Freeman" (*ALR* 22, ii:54–68), however, Mary R. Reichardt challenges the very assumption that Freeman was a type of protofeminist. To be sure, according to Reichardt, Freeman's women frequently "form an intricate social network" for purposes of "emotional interaction," but these bonds "more often than not take on a disturbingly threatening or ominous tone." In addition, Philip Eppard and Reichardt collaborate on one of the most substantial contributions to Freeman studies in years: "A Checklist of Uncollected Short Fiction by Mary Wilkins Freeman" (*ALR* 23, i:70–74), which identifies over 50 hitherto unknown stories from her pen.

The most important biography of any of the writers covered by this chapter to appear this year is doubtless Emily Toth's monumental *Kate Chopin* (Morrow). Toth does not so much rescue Chopin from a biographical blind spot—Per Seyersted deserves that credit (see *ALS 1969*, p. 171)—as she demythologizes the events of Chopin's life, particularly her relationship with the man on whom she modeled the roué Alcée Arobin in *The Awakening* and the circumstances surrounding the alleged banning of that novel. Toth's research is exhaustive, her finished work definitive. As a sidebar of sorts, she critiques the original inscription of the myths in "The Shadow of the First Biographer: The Case of Kate

Chopin" (*SoR* 26:285–92). For better or worse, most of the critical attention given to Chopin continues to focus on *The Awakening* to the neglect of her other fiction. Both Jean Wyatt in *Reconstructing Desire* (pp. 64–81) and Ivy Schweitzer in "Material Discourse and the Romance of Self-Possession in Kate Chopin's *The Awakening*" (*Boundary 2* 17:158–86) read the novel through the veil of feminist psychoanalytical theory and, predictably, reach comparable conclusions about it, particularly about the heroism of Edna's apparent suicide. Of the two, Wyatt's chapter is the more accessible. Sam B. Girgus also devotes part of a chapter (pp. 132–52) in *Desire and the Political Unconscious* to an avowedly Freudian analysis of the novel and reaches very different conclusions, specifically that Edna covets "false freedom," "acts out of unconscious need," lacks "power and direction," and dies "on a sea of emotions she never fully understands or controls." Pat Shaw ponders the relevance of shifts in point of view and Chopin's "management of two modes of reality" in "Putting Audience in Its Place: Psychosexuality and Perspective Shifts in *The Awakening*" (*ALR* 23, i:61–69). And in "Literature of Deliverance: Images of Nature in *The Awakening*" (*SoSt* 1:127–47), Douglas Radcliff-Umstead catalogs various types of natural metaphor Chopin ostensibly used "to illustrate the entrapment of women under patriarchy and their battle to achieve deliverance." Part of a book and two other articles buck the trend: Mary E. Papke's *Verging on the Abyss: The Social Fiction of Kate Chopin and Edith Wharton* (Greenwood), pp. 21–88 and passim, is a useful introduction to Chopin's stories, though Papke offers no new perspective and her sketch of Chopin's life contains some of the errors Toth corrects. Nor should the phrase "social fiction" in Papke's subtitle be taken too seriously. Ellen Peel's "Semiotic Subversion in 'Désirée's Baby'" (*AL* 62:223–37) is a commendable but overwritten and jargon-ridden exegesis of the story's racial and sexual implications. Heather Kirk Thomas also edits a newly discovered Chopin essay, "Development of the Literary West," for *ALR* (22, ii:69–75).

As in Chopin's case, Charlotte Perkins Gilman's career has become the raw material of a burgeoning critical industry, her increasing stature among academics suggested by the founding of a Gilman Society in 1990. Like Chopin, moreover, Gilman is best-known for a single text, the story "The Yellow Wall-paper," which normally dominates the critical discourse about her. This year is no exception. Greg Johnson scarcely extends the frontiers of this discourse, however, in "Gilman's Gothic Allegory: Rage and Redemption in 'The Yellow Wallpaper'" (*SSF* 26:521–

30). Johnson contends, simply enough, that the story is "an allegory of literary imagination unbinding the social, domestic, and psychological confinements" of the 19th-century woman writer. Two essays in *L&M*— Pamela White Hadas's "Madness and Medicine: The Graphomaniac's Cure" (9:181–93) and Stephen L. Post's "His and Hers: Mental Breakdown as Depicted in Evelyn Waugh and Charlotte Perkins Gilman" (9:172–80)—superficially compare the clinical etiologies portrayed in Gilman's tale and *The Ordeal of Gilbert Pinfold*. Elizabeth Boa's comparativist approach in "Creepy-crawlies: Gilman's *The Yellow Wallpaper* and Kafka's *The Metamorphosis*" (*Paragraph* 13:19–29) is largely remarkable for its insights on the Kafka story. Fortunately, Gilman scholarship this year is not limited to these studies. Ann J. Lane's *To "Herland" and Beyond: The Life and Work of Charlotte Perkins Gilman* (Pantheon) satisfactorily chronicles Gilman's first 40 years, then basically abandons its chronological organization and flounders through her remaining 35 years. The problem, I suspect, is that Gilman's later life, after the publication of *Women and Economics* in 1898, was essentially anticlimactic. Mary A. Hill has not, to date, published the second volume of her projected two-volume Gilman biography, though the first appeared more than a decade ago. In any event, neither Lane nor Hill writes primarily as a literary biographer. In his discussion of Gilman in *Desire and the Political Unconscious* (pp. 126–34), Girgus concedes her importance as "a true pioneer of social thought" but contends the ideas she expressed in *Women and Economics* "constitute a program for neurosis." In perhaps the most significant and compelling contribution to Gilman studies this year, "The Rape of the Text: Charlotte Gilman's Violation of *Herland*" (*TSWL* 9:291–308), Kathleen Margaret Lant sensibly revises the conventional interpretation of this utopian romance. Rather than a delicious satire of androcentrism, according to Lant, *Herland* "is permeated with aggressive, assaultive, and threatening sexuality." Gilman "cannot, it seems, satisfy her narrative requirements without violating her own ideologies." I heartily recommend Lant's essay to every teacher who assigns Gilman's text.

A number of other women writers earn more cursory notice in 1990. Celia Thaxter's life is sketched by Barbara A. White (*Legacy* 7, i:59–64), and her residence on Appledore Island is briefly reviewed by Stephen May (*Smithsonian* 21, ix:69–76). Annie Fields, Thaxter's and Jewett's friend and James T. Fields's wife, is the subject of Judith A. Roman's hagiographical *Annie Adams Fields: The Spirit of Charles Street* (Indiana).

Constance Fenimore Woolson inspires two essays this year: Joanne F. Vickers's "Woolson's Response to James: The Vindication of the American Heroine" (*WS* 18:287–94), which basically if inadvertently proves that Woolson misunderstood *Daisy Miller,* and Victoria Brehm's "Island Fortresses: The Landscape of the Imagination in the Great Lakes Fiction of Constance Fenimore Woolson" (*ALR* 22, iii:51–66), a turgid taxonomy that betrays its origins in the dissertation. Jane Atteridge Rose convincingly pleads the case for another forgotten late-century realist in "Recovering Lillie Buffum Chace Wyman and 'The Child of the State'" (*Legacy* 7, i:39–43). Similarly, Marilyn Elkins helps to repair the neglect of a pioneering African American writer in "Reading Beyond the Conventions: A Look at Frances E. W. Harper's *Iola Leroy, or Shadows Uplifted*" (*ALR* 22, ii:44–53). *Iola Leroy* is reissued, along with Brown's *Clotelle* and Charles Chesnutt's *The Marrow of Tradition,* in *Three Classic African-American Novels* (Vintage), ed. Henry Louis Gates, Jr. Excerpts from the novel, as well as all of Harper's verse and many of her letters, also appear in *A Brighter Coming Day: A Frances Ellen Watkins Harper Reader* (Feminist), ed. and with a first-rate introduction by Frances Smith Foster. Joan DeJean's "Critical Creolization: Grace King and Writing on French in the American South" (*Southern Literature and Literary Theory,* pp. 109–26) explores King's unique perspective on "the politics of Creoleness" in her Louisiana stories. And in *Helen Hunt Jackson and Her Indian Reform Legacy* (Texas), Valerie Sherer Mathes details events in the final six years of the life of the author of *Ramona* and *A Century of Dishonor.*

Finally, a pair of historical overviews reach print this year that, while not directly contradictory, in effect compose two halves of a study on gendered aesthetics that yet remains unwritten. In "Sentiment, Naturalism, and the Female Regionalist" (*Legacy* 7, i:3–22), Elaine Sargent Apthorp contends that the assumptions about human nature and narrative technique of the domestic sentimentalists were shared by the "women Local Colorists of Jewett's and Freeman's school" and fundamentally distinguish them from their contemporaries in the naturalist school, such as Crane, Norris, and Dreiser, who were more or less determinists and male. Apthorp "underscores the distinction" between the two schools by contrasting Freeman's "A Mistaken Charity" with Norris's *McTeague.* Elise Miller at once complicates Apthorp's tidy analysis and plugs its holes in "The Feminization of American Realist Theory" (*ALR* 23, i:20–41). According to Miller, the realists of the Howells and James stripe, not only the women regionalists, wrote "feminine" fiction in "a very self-conscious process": "complaints about the *feminization* of American literature shifted to a growing recognition of the *feminine* nature of realism." The sharp distinction Apthorp draws between the local-colorists and naturalists, and between Freeman and Norris in particular, is not simply a matter of socialization or sexual difference, it would seem, but of the gender codes inscribed in their respective literary strategies. Norris's quarrel was with "effeminate" realism, not female realists.

vi The Howells Generation: Realism and Utopianism

Howellsians nowadays seem to be gravitating toward the author's early years like farmers to fallow soil. The only book in this section to break new ground is Thomas Wortham's *The Early Prose Writings of William Dean Howells, 1853–1861* (Ohio), a surprisingly original study of Howells's literary apprenticeship with liberal selections from his work. As Wortham observes, "Viewed in terms of the context provided by these many pages, the emergence of Howells as a finished writer of prose with the publication of *Venetian Life* in 1866 is not so remarkable as it might otherwise seem." Howells had, after all, "published well in excess of a half-million words"—a career-full—before his first major book appeared. In "The Great Lakes Childhood: The Experience of William Dean Howells and Annie Dillard" (*ON* 14:311–29), Eugene H. Patterson compares—albeit to uncertain purpose and to tiresome effect—Howells's reminiscences of his boyhood, especially in *A Boy's Town,* and Dillard's memoirs. Ginette de B. Merrill marshals evidence in "Actualities into Reality and Complicity in Composition: Howells' *A Fearful Responsibility*" (*ALR* 23, i:42–60) that the novelist based elements of his story on the adventures of his sister-in-law Mary Mead, who lived with the Howellses in Venice in the mid-1860s. Despite its alluring title, Eric Savoy's "The Subverted Gaze: Hawthorne, Howells, James and the Discourse of Travel" (*CRevAS* 21:287–300) devotes eight pages to theoretical posturing and but two paragraphs to *Italian Journeys.* My own "Howells and W. R. Alger: An Overlooked Review" (*ANQ* n.s. 3:171–74) adds one more small item to the Howells bibliography: his 1867 notice for the *Atlantic* of Alger's *The Solitudes of Nature and of Man.* Two other essays discuss major novels of Howells's New York period. Wai-chee Dimock muses on the peculiar supply-side moral economics which govern relationships and transactions in *The Rise of Silas Lapham* in "The

Economy of Pain: The Case of Howells" (*Raritan* 9:99–119), and Robert Weimann, an accomplished scholar in the Germanic tradition, extrapolates an "ideological upheaval of considerable magnitude" from the precarious narrative and tentative form of both *Silas Lapham* and *A Hazard of New Fortunes* in "Realism, Ideology, and the Novel in America (1886–1896): Changing Perspectives in the Work of Mark Twain, W. D. Howells, and Henry James" (*Boundary 2* 17:189–210).

The African American writer Charles W. Chesnutt is the only significant exception to the relative neglect accorded other male realists this year. Chesnutt studies span the critical spectrum, moreover, from source criticism to deconstruction. In "The Literary Imagination and the Historic Event: Chesnutt's Use of History in *The Marrow of Tradition*" (*SoAR* 55, iv:37–48), Joyce Pettis examines in detail his appropriation of the circumstances surrounding the 1898 Wilmington, North Carolina, race riot in his second novel. Jean Smith Filetti speculates about another source—Jesus' parable of the vineyard—for Chesnutt's story "The Goophered Grapevine" (*Expl* 48, iii:201–03). The most intriguing scholarship on Chesnutt, however, focuses on questions of racial identity and the (un)veiling of narrative voice in his fiction. Much as the characters in his second collection of tales "define themselves through their negotiations" of the color line, the author's "experiments with the short story form mark his own process of creating a positive identity," as Lorne Fienberg remarks in "Charles W. Chesnutt's *The Wife of His Youth:* The Unveiling of the Black Storyteller" (*ATQ* n.s. 4:219–37). In "The Framing of Charles W. Chesnutt: Practical Deconstruction in the Afro-American Tradition" (*Southern Literature and Literary Theory*, pp. 339–65), Craig Werner takes a step beyond Fienberg, concluding that Chesnutt was "an exceptionally complex modernist/postmodernist ironist" whose stories in *The Conjure Woman* deliberately manipulate "the self-deconstructive form of *Uncle Remus*" and whose tale "Baxter's *Procrustes*" anticipates "both the Afro- and Euro-American understandings of literary signification."

Other minor male realists fare little better than the Fireside poets in 1990. In my edition of *Bret Harte's California* (New Mexico), I exhume 37 essays, most of them previously unknown, which Harte wrote as the San Francisco correspondent for two Massachusetts papers in 1866–67, three years before he hit paydirt with his *Overland* stories. These articles, as I suggest in the introduction, "are obviously not finished coin, though they display an abundance of 'color.'" Gerald Haslam surveys "Literary

California" in an essay by that title (*California History* 68:188–95) which features Harte, among others. Jon Christopher Hughes edits a collection of 51 articles Lafcadio Hearn wrote for Cincinnati newspapers in 1872–77 under the title *Period of the Gruesome* (Univ. Press); and Joseph B. McCullough edits and writes an exemplary introduction to a collection of 14 early Hamlin Garland stories entitled *Tales of the Middle Border* (NCUP). Leslie T. Whipp commends the work of yet another Westerner in "Owen Wister: Wyoming's Influential Realist and Craftsman" (*GPQ* 10:245–59), though the attempt to prove Wister's influence on Cather strikes me as strained. The late George C. Carrington, Jr., in "Robert Herrick, *Clark's Field,* and the Underlying Farce" (*ALR* 23, i:3–19) rescues yet another obscure novel from critical neglect. Similarly, Christopher Wilson in *"Unleavened Bread:* The Representation of Robert Grant" (*ALR* 22, iii:17–35) begins to correct Grant's modern reputation as a "shallow elitist" and self-anointed Mugwump laureate. As Wilson demonstrates, Grant's 1900 best-seller "stimulated two cultural enterprises—the growing legitimation of professional expertise and the reciprocal debunking of the 'average' middle American"—which were earmarks of modern liberalism. In "Phantom Limbs and 'Body Ego': S. Weir Mitchell's 'George Dedlow' " (*Mosaic* 23, i:87–99), a remarkably fresh commentary on a little-known story, Debra Journet suggests that Mitchell, the Philadelphia nerve specialist (and implied villain of Gilman's "The Yellow Wall-paper"), explored in fiction a phenomenon "he could not fully articulate within the scientific paradigms of his time." Two more essays illustrate the critical dissensus regarding Harold Frederic's best-known novel: Lionel Lackey's brief for the defense of the protagonist in "Redemption and *The Damnation of Theron Ware*" (*SoAR* 55, v:81–91), and David Heddendorf's argument in "Pragmatists and Plots: *Pierre* and *The Damnation of Theron Ware*" (*SNNTS* 22:271–81) that Ware's failure to heed Sister Soulsby's "therapeutic message of pragmatism" intensifies the "ironic light" in which he appears. Lewis Fried devotes a superb chapter of *Makers of the City* (Mass.), pp. 10–63, to Jacob Riis, whose journalistic exposé *How the Other Half Lives* profoundly influenced the urban fiction of Howells and Stephen Crane and the documentary style of the muckrakers. Finally, two reprints of works by late-century nature writers celebrated by the realists for their fidelity to detail deserve praise: Charles Dudley Warner's *In the Wilderness* (Syracuse), with an introduction by Alice Wolf Gilborn, and John Burroughs's *Deep Woods* (Gibbs Smith), ed. and introduced by Richard F. Fleck.

In a coda to the recent centennial of *Looking Backward,* Lawrence I. Berkove reviews the "contemporary context" of its publication (*CEA* 52:80–86). With the centennial now past, moreover, Bellamy's other works begin to receive at least passing notice. William J. Scheick edits a special section on "Reading Edward Bellamy Against the Grain" in the Summer 1990 issue of *TSLL.* "Bellamy's seemingly provincial and insular tales of small-town life and middle-class character disclose a radical system of ethics based on man's temporality," Janet Gabler-Hover contends in "Man's Fragile Tenure: Discontinuous Time and the Ethos of Temporality in Edward Bellamy's Short Fiction" (32:302–28). Gabler-Hover skillfully teases out the evidence for Bellamy's ontological skepticism from his early tales "The Old Folks Party," "Lost," and "A Summer Evening's Dream." And in " 'Swept Away by One Breath': Selfhood and *Kenosis* in Edward Bellamy's 'A Love Story Reversed' " (32:329–44), Jeffrey A. Hammond maintains that the short fiction collected in *The Blindman's World and Other Stories* speaks "directly to the processes" by which Bellamy's utopia will be inaugurated.

vii   Crane, Norris, Adams, and Fin de Siècle Writers

The most significant item of Crane scholarship this year is undoubtedly Stanley Wertheim and Paul Sorrentino's "Thomas Beer: The Clay Feet of Stephen Crane Biography" (*ALR* 22, iii:2–16), which presents incontrovertible evidence that Beer fabricated letters and other sources that he cites in his 1923 biography of the novelist. Much as the publication of the authoritative edition of Dickinson's poems in 1955 discredited a number of earlier studies of her versification, this discovery of tainted sources raises serious questions about the integrity of some past critical work on Crane and should reorient "our understanding of Crane's personality, his literary career, and the interrelationships between his life and art." As usual, Crane's war novel inspires several fine essays, among them Mary Neff Shaw's "Henry Fleming's Heroics in *The Red Badge of Courage:* A Satiric Search for a 'Kinder, Gentler' Heroism" (*SNNTS* 22:418–28), which situates the story within "the continuum of Crane's war fiction canon" in order to argue that in it the author meant to satirize "the absurdity of traditional notions of heroism." Donald Pizer's edition of *Critical Essays on Stephen Crane's* The Red Badge of Courage (Hall) contains a selection of contemporary notices by such reviewers as Howells and Frederic, critical commentary by such Crane scholars as R. W.

Stallman, Charles C. Walcutt, Edwin H. Cady, and James Nagel, and two original essays specifically commissioned for the volume. In "Fighting Words: The Talk of Men at War in *The Red Badge*" (pp. 229–38), Alfred Habegger mediates between the ironic and more traditional readings of the novel by analyzing Crane's representations of speech: Henry becomes "a man among men" in this tale of "an individual's moral and social *Bildung*" by "learning how important it is never to tell the truth about himself." James Colvert joins the critical debate over the text of the novel in defense of the published 1895 edition, largely elaborating Pizer's own reservations about the reconstructed manuscript version published a decade ago by Henry Binder, in "Crane, Hitchcock, and the Binder Edition of *The Red Badge of Courage*" (pp. 238–63). Kevin J. Hayes also joins the debate, albeit on behalf of the Binder edition, concluding from his comparison of an early fragmentary draft and the reconstructed "final" manuscript that the latter best preserves the author's designs for the story and that the changes he subsequently made in it "seem more and more like simple publishing house expurgations" in "How Stephen Crane Shaped Henry Fleming" (*SNNTS* 22:296–307). By far the most desultory of the essays on Crane this year is William E. Harkins's "Battle Scenes in the Writings of Tolstoy and Stephen Crane," in *Russianness* (Ardis), ed. Robert L. Belknap, pp. 173–84, a superficial comparison of *The Red Badge* with several Tolstories. Unfortunately, Crane's other work is slighted in 1990, with three exceptions. James Stanford Bradshaw reprints Robert Barr's recollections about completing Crane's last novel *The O'Ruddy* (*ANQ* n.s. 3:174–78). Robert Glen Deamer in *The Importance of Place* (pp. 103–52) insists that Crane's attitude toward the myth of the West, revealed in his Western writings, "was not parodic, not satiric—but serious, sympathetic, and even tragic." Lee Clark Mitchell, the author of last year's *Determined Fictions* (*ALS 1989*, p. 195), returns in "Face, Race, and Disfiguration in Stephen Crane's 'The Monster'" (*CritI* 17:174–92). Crane's story, according to Mitchell, reflects on its rhetorical surface "the disfigurement that generates its theme." Paradoxically, Henry Johnson becomes "most bodily present to blacks as well as to whites (and to the presumably white narrator as well) only when he loses his face." Mitchell explicitly contests Michael Fried's assertion in *Realism, Writing, Disfiguration* (see *ALS 1987*, p. 215) that the recurring trope of the upturned face in Crane's work represents the act of inscribing words on upturned sheets of paper. Fried defends his point about the materiality of writing, extending it to Frank

Norris's *A Man's Woman*, in "Almayer's Face: On 'Impressionism' in Conrad, Crane, and Norris" (*CritI* 17:193–236). The reader of Fried's essay should beware lest s/he sink up to the neck in jargonological quicksand.

Norris appears to better advantage this year in the pages of *FNS*, though the focus there is on the author's life rather than his fiction. In "Toward a Biography of Frank Norris" (9:2–5), Edwin Haviland Miller chides some earlier scholars for their skewed portrayal of "the boy-man" and opines that Norris's fiction is rich in biographical evidence. Barbara Hochman discusses several revealing episodes, as if in response to Miller's challenge, in "Self-Disclosure in the Fiction of Frank Norris" (9:5–7). Joseph R. McElrath, Jr., harvests a number of details about the author and his family from a San Francisco literary weekly in "Frank Norris: Biographical Data from *The Wave*, 1891–1901" (10:1–12). Thomas K. Dean also publishes two essays on the film adaptation of *McTeague:* "The Critical Reception of Erich von Stroheim's *Greed"* (*FNS* 9:7–11) and "The Flight of McTeague's Song-Bird: Thematic Differences Between Norris's *McTeague* and von Stroheim's *Greed"* (*LFQ* 18:96–102), which concludes that the filmmaker subtly altered the philosophical framework of the novel.

Scholarly interest in Henry Adams continues to abound and proliferate, as if to defy the second law of thermodynamics, more than 70 years after his death. William Merrill Decker's *The Literary Vocation of Henry Adams* (No. Car.), a comprehensive and absorbing literary biography, is the most significant new study. Opening the narrative in medias res with Adams's ostensible "retirement from authorship" in 1890, a vocational crisis compounded by Clover Adams's suicide in 1885, before "systematically addressing the rhetorical dimensions" of his literary, historical, and philosophical texts, Decker succeeds admirably in capturing the high drama of Adams's life of the mind. Olaf Hansen in *Aesthetic Individualism* (pp. 143–74) discusses the allegorical mode of Adams's major literary works, including *Democracy, The Education,* and *Mont-Saint-Michel and Chartres.* Similarly, Russell L. Hanson and W. Richard Merriman in "Henry Adams and the Decline of Republican Tradition" (*ATQ* n.s. 4:161–83) represent Adams as a republican historiographer whose treatises, especially his monumental *History of the United States During the Administrations of Jefferson and Madison,* were often akin to morality plays. More prosaically, David Partenheimer inspects Adams's glosses in his copies of works by three *Naturphilosophen* in "Henry Adams' Scientific History and German Scientists" (*ELN* 27, iii:44–52). Whereas most critics have regarded Adams's typical heroine as a Christian fertility goddess, Daniel L. Manheim contends in "Motives of His Own: Henry Adams and the Genealogy of the Virgin" (*NEQ* 63:601–23) that the "characteristic strain running through all of [his] female figures"—particularly Madeleine Lee of *Democracy,* Esther Dudley of *Esther,* and, of course, the Virgin of Chartres—is virginity. Adams's version of Mariolatry, according to Manheim, is a unifying force which he "saw as central to the ability to resist dissolution in modern cultural multiplicity." Each of the novels inspires a fine journal essay this year: Andrew Scheiber's "The Widow and the Dynamo: Gender and Power in Henry Adams' *Democracy*" (*ATQ* n.s. 4:353–69), which hypothesizes that the story contains a radical critique of the 19th-century notion of "separate spheres" for women and men, especially in politics; and Robert F. Sommer's "The Feminine Perspectives of Henry Adams' *Esther*" (*SAF* 18:131–44), which suggests that the "apparently unresolvable gender conflict" between the heroine and the trinity of men who would oppress her "represents a historical tension between anarchy and determinism, chaos and order." Peter Katopes also prepares a new edition of *Democracy* (NCUP) with an introduction that emphasizes its topical satire. Several studies confine their focus to *The Education.* In the third chapter of *Chaos Bound* (Cornell), pp. 61–90, N. Katherine Hayles notes the formal chaos of the narrative, which, as she concludes, "embodies the process it describes in the dynamic theory of history." Less ambitiously, Robert Glen Deamer suggests in *The Importance of Place* (pp. 63–77) that Adams deconstructs the American myth of success in his *Education.* And Daniel Aaron edits a critical notice of the book apparently suppressed in 1918 in " 'Strongly-Flavored Imitation Cynicism': Henry Adams's *Education* Reviewed by John Jay Chapman" (*NEQ* 63:288–93).

Quite by chance, I close this chapter with remarks on Ambrose Bierce and L. Frank Baum, the odd couple of the fin de siècle. S. T. Joshi's chapter on Bierce in *The Weird Tale* (Texas) is the stuff of informational footnotes. In "Writing the Civil War: Ambrose Bierce's 'Jupiter Doke, Brigadier-General' " (*SAF* 18:87–98), a more substantial critical essay, G. Thomas Couser explains how Bierce satirically conflated episodes in U. S. Grant's career in the tale. Edward W. Hudlin argues for the artistic unity of *The Wonderful Wizard of Oz* by comparing its structure to that of "heroic myth" in "The Mythology of *Oz:* An Interpretation" (*PLL* 25:443–62). Hudlin at one point compares Dorothy in the cyclone to

Jonah in the belly of the whale. One wonders what he would make of
Moby-Dick. Finally, Celia Catlett Anderson analyzes the elements of
humor in the Oz series in "The Comedians of Oz" (*StAH* 5 [1986]:229–
42), a solid piece of research that understandably overlooks the allusion
to leviathans in Kansas.

University of New Mexico

13   Fiction: 1900 to the 1930s

Jo Ann Middleton

i Willa Cather

The most newsworthy item in Cather scholarship this year is her appearance in the revised Great Books of the Western World (Encyclopaedia Britannica), the lone American woman to make it. Furthermore, the quantity of substantial scholarship is astounding: 15 books (including several major studies) and more than 50 articles appeared in the two years this chapter covers. I regret that I cannot include them all.

We begin with three new biographies. Hermione Lee's *Willa Cather: Double Lives* (Pantheon, 1989) is a major addition to Cather scholarship. Lee's highly readable study of the oppositions in Cather's life and work, based on solid research and offering perceptive interpretations that incorporate and balance history, biography, and literary traditions, is a fine complement to the Woodress and O'Brien biographies. Susie Thomas's *Willa Cather* (Barnes and Noble), a less ambitious study, argues that Cather's work "acts as a corrective to the aggressively masculine tendencies in American literature" and emphasizes Cather's response to European literature, music, and painting. Jamie Ambrose's *Willa Cather: Writing at the Frontier* (Berg Women's Series, 1989), a bare-bones, factually accurate life, includes no critical assessment and relies heavily on Lewis's *Willa Cather Living* and Sergeant's *Willa Cather: A Memoir.* In a biographical vein, "Willa Cather and the Southern Genteel Tradition" (*CCTES* 55:59–66) by Lady Falls Brown contends that not only did Cather absorb the Southern genteel tradition, but its manners and customs make up the ideology which shapes her life-style and her fiction.

Two discerning studies deal with Cather's intellectual life. In *After the World Broke in Two: The Later Novels of Willa Cather* (Virginia), an "intellectual history" rather than a psychobiography, Merrill Maguire

Skaggs convincingly proves Cather's thesis that we get to know a writer through her books. Responding to the "dominant riddle of Cather's life: Why did she say, 'The world broke in two in 1922 or thereabouts?'" Skaggs poses her own question: "What does such a one as Cather do *after* the world breaks in two?" In perceptive chapters that trace persistent themes and images, she identifies the sources of Cather's "newer, darker vision" after *One of Ours* and explicates that novel and the seven that followed, exploring Cather's intellectual struggles as she worked out a way to make the world whole. The epigraphs to each chapter underline the paradox in Cather: she often returned to the same starting point, then set off in another direction, ultimately reaching an opposite conclusion. Skaggs's brilliant explication of the intricate interrelations among the books establishes Cather as a complex and highly intelligent woman who is "neurotically controlling and self-conscious about her work" and a writer who "knows at all points what she is doing." In *Bergson and American Culture: The Worlds of Willa Cather and Wallace Stevens* (No. Car.), Tom Quirk traces the impact of Henri Bergson on America and Cather's response to his thought. One of several enabling circumstances for the "inner explosion" that produced *O Pioneers!* was Cather's reading of Bergson's *Creative Evolution* in 1912. Cather embraces Bergson's objections to the fallacies of the scientific method, his concept of *moi fundamentale,* his understanding of the backward and forward movement of consciousness, and his conviction that "we were artisans before we were artists." Differences between *Alexander's Bridge* and both *O Pioneers!* and *The Song of the Lark* reflect Cather's adoption of a Bergsonian worldview in place of her earlier Spencerian vision: *Alexander's Bridge* is an intellectual effort, but *O Pioneers!* and *Song of the Lark* are intuitive. Quirk locates Bergsonian thought throughout Cather's early work, pointing out that, though she acquired a "certain personal bitterness and regret" as she grew older, her aesthetic and philosophical stance remained rooted in a Bergsonian vitalism.

Conrad Ostwalt, Jr., pairs Cather with Theodore Dreiser in his study of the transformation of American religious identity at the turn of the century in *After Eden: The Secularization of American Space in the Fiction of Willa Cather and Theodore Dreiser* (Bucknell). Cather's fiction describes a changing attitude toward natural space and Dreiser's toward social space; both reflect the turn from the religious to the secular. Although his thesis is provocative and he offers some interesting insights into Cather's "redefinition of Darwin's worldview," Oswalt neglects recent Cather scholarship, which weakens his argument. Langdon Elsbree's contribution to *The Frontier Experience and the American Dream: Essays on American Literature,* ed. David Mogen et al. (Texas A&M, 1989), "Our Pursuit of Loneliness: An Alternative to This Paradigm" (pp. 31–49), puts Cather's fiction in a group of texts that embodies a "significantly different paradigm" from the archetypal pattern stressing movement, the primary tradition of American myth in the innocent hero as restless quester, and the flight from social and cultural traditions. *My Ántonia* and *Death Comes for the Archbishop* manifest another paradigm: the archetypal action that "enacts the making of the garden, the building of the home (town, city), the clearing of the land—the sustaining of the human community."

Several items question Cather's "backwardness." In *"The Professor's House:* Cather, Hemingway and the Chastening of American Prose Style" (*WAL* 24:295–311), Glen A. Love charges that Cather has been unjustly neglected in the development of American literary prose style and speculates that Hemingway must have read Cather's essays in which she set forth a theory of omission and simplification. In a brief companion piece, "Willa Cather's Commentary on Three Novels by Dorothy Canfield Fisher" (*AN&Q* 3, i:13–15), Mark J. Madigan paraphrases four Cather letters to Dorothy Canfield Fisher that "provide interesting evidence of her literary theories in practice." To support the case for Cather as modernist, I analyze style and technique in my *Willa Cather's Modernism: A Study of Style and Technique* (Fairleigh Dickinson), focusing on what Cather leaves out of the text as the key to her enduring art and borrowing a scientific term *vacuole* as a metaphor to explain how the omissions work on the reader. Marilyn Arnold draws on contemporary accounts of Cather's statements about writing in lectures and interviews of the 1920s and early 1930s to refute Cather's alleged traditionalism in "Willa Cather's Artistic 'Radicalism'" (*CEA* 51:2–10). Janis P. Stout's extensive chapter on Cather (pp. 66–111) in *Strategies of Reticence* also addresses the problem of the gaps and omissions in Cather's fiction, but Stout's interest is not so much in the technique of positioning and selectivity "as in the evasiveness and disguise that accompany and . . . determine the art and in the rhetorical use to which she is sometimes able to put her reticent and evasive art." Cather leads the reader, by her silences as well as by her words, to question the adequacy of both her male and female narrators.

A number of scholars explored recurrent themes and motifs. Marilyn

Berg Callander's *Willa Cather and the Fairy Tale* (UMI Research Press, 1989), the first study to focus on Cather's use of fairy-tale themes and plot elements, stresses the wholly intentional quality of these references. *The Song of the Lark* is a Cinderella story; *My Mortal Enemy* incorporates "The Sleeping Beauty" and "Snow White"; and in *Shadows on the Rock,* Cather creates her own fairy tale. A chronologically ordered appendix lists references to fairy tales, folktales, and legends. Callander opens the door for future work and, furthermore, gives Cather scholars a valuable tool to expedite their efforts. Erik Ingvar Thurin's *The Humanization of Willa Cather: Classicism in an American Classic* (Lund) is a significant contribution to Cather scholarship. Thurin argues that Cather, "never very religious in a traditional way," demonstrated an "affinity for the universalist aspect of classical humanism" throughout her life and became in her old age "a whole-hearted apologist for earthly life." He contends that she consciously and subconsciously used Greek and Latin myth to work out this process through her writing. Thurin finds and explicates classical references throughout Cather's entire canon, indicates her sources, and points out strains of Hellenic, Roman, and medieval thought. Most impressive is Thurin's ability to locate deeply embedded and implicit references which illuminate the "autobiographical impulse" in Cather's work. The intent of Mary Ruth Ryder's *Willa Cather and Classical Myth* (Mellen) is to explore Cather's use of Greco-Roman myth, but Ryder frequently refers to Cather's biblical allusions as well, which sometimes results in a foggy discussion. Ryder argues that Cather "moved away from classical myth as a primary pattern of imagery" toward a Christian mythos "focused on the Rock of the New Testament" in the later novels. However, Ryder provides only a brief reading of the novels which follow *My Mortal Enemy*. Cather's classical training also influenced her style, as Joseph S. Salemi demonstrates in "The Measure of the Music: Prose Rhythm in Willa Cather's *Paul's Case*" (*CML* 10:319–26). By scanning the text, we can see that her prose rhythm deliberately employs cadences echoing "stately Ciceronian periods." Joan Wylie Hall's "Nordic Mythology in Willa Cather's 'The Joy of Nelly Deane' " (*SSF* 26 [1989]:339–41) is convincing evidence that Cather source studies must look beyond the myths of Greece and Rome; in this story Cather alludes to the Scandinavian Norns, "spinners of fate, tenders of the water of life."

Josephine Donovan's *After the Fall* (1989), which continues Donovan's feminist and political exploration of American women's literary traditions, proposes that the Demeter-Persephone myth describes the changing mother-daughter relationship as 20th-century "new women" rebelled against their actual and literary 19th-century mothers. Cather, Wharton, and Glasgow came to maturity during a period of "male-supremacist ideology," but rejected that ideology, adopting instead a "healing, matriarchal vision." Although the underlying mythic patterns are the same, each writer focuses on different phases of the myth. Donovan defines the central issue of Cather's fiction as the reconciliation of the two realms of feminine experience (pp. 85–127). Defining the Jewett-Cather relationship as the mother-daughter connection that freed Cather to appreciate the feminine-maternal, Donovan offers readings of 16 short stories and six novels that explore Cather's pessimistic vision of the daughter's struggle, but she finds that Cather had still not resolved the issue when she wrote her final story, "The Best Years."

Susan Rosowski's important essay, "Writing Against Silences" (*SNNTS* 21 [1989]:60–77), maintains that Cather "provided as full and as complex an exploration of adolescence, and particularly of female development, as we have in American literature," particularly in *The Song of the Lark* and *Lucy Gayheart*. Males develop in linear, sequential stages, but Cather's females are transformed: "Her girls contain within themselves the women they will become, and her adult women remain in touch with the children they once were." Cather's treatment of Thea anticipates the current perception that success is particularly threatening to a woman; *Lucy Gayheart* and *Sapphira and the Slave Girl* both deal with girls who enter adolescence unprepared. Rosowski's astute reading of *Lucy Gayheart* as the "other side of the coin from *The Song of the Lark*" clearly establishes the differences between healthy female development and the "nightmare of adolescence" and confirms the importance Cather vested in the mother-daughter relationship. " 'Paul's Case': The Outsider" (*Youth Suicide Prevention: Lessons from Literature,* ed. Sara Munson Deats and Lagretta Tallent Lenker [Plenum, 1989], pp. 135–54) is an intriguing essay by Carlos A. Perez that explores Cather's understanding of the male adolescent. Perez, a practicing psychotherapist, performs a "psychological autopsy" to provide a close reading which demonstrates Cather's duality in sketching Paul's character and traces Paul's ultimate fate "to the lack of genuine interaction between himself and his worlds." It is refreshing to read this clear analysis of Cather's "careful profile of an insecure, frustrated, defensive, frightened and impotent youth"; Perez proves that one can be both clear *and* psychologically astute.

Of Cather's novels, *My Ántonia* continues to draw the most critical attention. John J. Murphy's *My Ántonia: The Road Home* (Twayne Masterwork Series, 1989) is the first book-length study of a Cather novel and the first to consider the impact of impressionism and luminism on Cather's style. Murphy's expert reading of the text clearly explains the complexity beneath the apparent simplicity of style; he also follows classical themes throughout the novel and offers substantial treatment of other critical approaches in this impressive study, which includes a previously unpublished letter by Annie Pavelka in an appendix and a definitive bibliography for the novel. Susan Rosowski does a fine job of editing *Approaches to Teaching Cather's* My Ántonia (MLA, 1989). The collection contains Rosowski's introductory materials section, a valuable compilation of suggestions from instructors and works that would be helpful for teaching the novel, and 25 essays by scholar-teachers. John L. Selzer asks why Jim abandoned Ántonia if he loved her so much in "Jim Burden and the Structure of *My Ántonia*" (*WAL* 24 [1989]:45–61), then shows that the question is answered quite clearly in the novel: Jim's failure to commit himself to Ántonia is "simply the final act in a consistent series of moral failures that typify Jim as a young man—and that Jim now understands and repudiates." Selzer considers Jim a far more reliable narrator than previously suspected and reads *My Ántonia* as "a comic novel recording its title character's triumph and its narrator's tardy but resolute enlightenment."

Cather's "war novel" occupied two critics. In "No Woman's Land: Gender in Willa Cather's *One of Ours*" (*SAF* 18:65–75), Maureen Ryan speculates that critics who were affronted by Cather's treatment of war objected to her reinterpretation of a male subject rather than to her presumptuousness. For Cather, war is fought not only by Claude and David Gerhardt, but also by women and children. Evelyn Haller's ingenious "Willa Cather and Woman's Art" (*Nebraska Humanist* 11 [1989]:59–66) suggests that Margie's log cabin, laurel leaf, and blazing star quilts provide modernist abstract patterns (log, leaf, and star) that structure *One of Ours*. Fritz Oehlschlaeger seeks to build on the critical analyses of feminist critics and the concrete phenomenology of Gabriel Marcel in *"Indisponibilité* and the Anxiety of Authorship in *The Professor's House*" (*AL* 62:74–86). Cather's Professor suffers *indisponibilité;* he is "self-preoccupied, self-encumbered, self-enclosed" and therefore experiences a split between body and mind, a disruption between past, present, and future. James Woodress contributes a graceful retelling of the events and techniques that produced *The Professor's House* in *Writing the American Classics,* pp. 106–24. He locates the seed of the novel in an early Pittsburgh story, "The Professor's Commencement," and indicates its ties to *Alexander's Bridge.* John J. Murphy compares *Alexander's Bridge* to *The Age of Innocence* "In Imitation and Anticipation of 'Mrs. Wharton'—Cather's *Alexander's Bridge*" (*Edith Wharton Review* 7:10–16) and finds that Cather's novel, published nine years earlier, resembles Wharton's fiction more than James's "in its visual crispness and in the clarity of its psychological probing."

Several articles this year examine Cather's work in its historical context. C. Susan Wiesenthal challenges the prevailing critical preoccupation with the "absent" and "unwritten" in an excellent essay, "Female Sexuality in Willa Cather's 'O Pioneers!' and the Era of Scientific Sexology: A Dialogue Between Frontiers" (*Ariel E* 21:41–63). Wiesenthal argues that *O Pioneers!* discloses Cather's challenge to the dominant contemporary medical and cultural assumptions about female sexuality with its courageous portrayal of "hermaphroditic, heterosexual and same-sex relationships." In "How Context Determines Fact: Historicism in Willa Cather's *A Lost Lady*" (*SAF* 17 [1989]:183–92), Joseph R. Urgo employs historical, narrative, and textual contexts to investigate the novel's coupling of historical representation and ideological positioning. Niel carries on the pioneer tradition of "transposing history into myth," failing to realize that "pleasant memories are nourished at the cost of historical suppression." Ivy Peters, like the Captain before him busy making history, carries on the pioneer tradition of land acquisition, dispossessing the Indians, and building a fortune.

Mike Fischer accuses Cather of rewriting Nebraska history and ignoring the conquest of the Plains Indians in "Pastoralism and Its Discontents: Willa Cather and the Burden of Imperialism" (*Mosaic* 23:31–44). Arguing that Cather's Nebraska was not a tabula rasa, as so many critics claim, Fischer uses *My Ántonia* and *Death Comes for the Archbishop* to explicate the Native American references embedded in Cather's narratives, reading these novels in the historical context of western expansion and the displacement of the Native American. An unusual political essay, Walter Benn Michaels's "The Vanishing American" (*AmLH* 2:220–41), treats *The Professor's House* as Cather's reaction to both the Indian Citizenship and Johnson Immigration acts of 1924. In its hostility to assimilation and its assertion of cultural identity, *The Professor's House* provides a "model of cultural Americanism . . . that has turned out to be—for better or worse—the great cultural contribution of the classic American literature of the twenties."

Finally, a wealth of scholarship is available in three collections of essays and the annual Special Literary Issue of the *Willa Cather Pioneer Memorial Newsletter*, which always has a number of first-rate essays. The first volume of *Cather Studies* (Nebraska), ed. Susan Rosowski, contains 12 essays on a variety of topics; distinguished Catherians Woodress, Stouck, Murphy, and Rosowski herself, each contribute one. A special issue of *Modern Fiction Studies* (36 [Spring 1990]) contains nine essays and a review article. *Willa Cather: Family, Community, and History (The BYU Symposium)* (Brigham Young University and Willa Cather Educational Foundation), ed. John J. Murphy et al., contains a selection from the presentations given at BYU's 1988 Willa Cather Symposium and 16 vintage photographs from the Nebraska State Historical Society. The 33 essays are organized into five groups: "Cather's Family and Home Place," "The Family Idealized and Explored," "Feminist Perspectives on Family and Community," "Issues of History and Fictional Communities," and "Communities of Art, Families of Faith." Murphy's summary introductions to each chapter are every bit as good as the essays themselves. This is a consistently excellent collection that rewards the reader with fresh insights in almost every essay.

ii Edith Wharton and Ellen Glasgow

Wharton scholars will applaud the publication of two new bibliographies. Stephen Garrison's *Edith Wharton: A Descriptive Bibliography* (Pittsburgh) is a valuable resource, impressive in its clear organization, that lists all known primary sources through 1986. Complementing this ambitious project is *Edith Wharton: An Annotated Secondary Bibliography* (Garland), prepared by Kristin O. Lauer and Margaret Murray. Containing over 1,200 annotated entries, this user-friendly volume begins with an introductory overview of Wharton criticism, followed by chapters that usefully annotate bibliographical studies, contemporary studies, biographical materials, book-length studies, essay collections, articles from 1938 to the present, dissertations, and literary surveys. In *Henry James and Edith Wharton: Letters, 1900–1915* (Scribner's), James scholar Lyall H. Powers collects the letters, postcards, and telegrams composing the Wharton-James correspondence. Of the 180 items, only 13 are by

Wharton; Powers adds three letters and four postcards that do not appear in *The Letters of Edith Wharton* (see *ALS 1988*, p. 233).

Edith Wharton's Women (New England) by Susan Goodman seeks to correct the image of Wharton as a "woman who did not really care for other women." She examines Wharton's friendships with women, concentrating on the writer's relationships with her mother, Lucretia Jones, and her longtime friend Sara Norton, models of competitive and cooperative relationships, then analyzes the heroines of Wharton's novels in light of these two poles. John Halperin's chapter, "Edith Wharton's Dressing-Room," pp. 161–200 in *Novelists in Their Youth,* traces Wharton's themes of frustration and suppression to her perception of her parents' marriage. Halperin finds in Wharton's early short story collection, *The Greater Inclination,* evidence that from the beginning of her career Wharton questioned conventional values and took a relativistic view of human behavior. Margaret McDowell's revised edition of *Edith Wharton* (TUSAS) incorporates critical and biographical materials that have come to light since 1976 and provides a solid introduction to the novelist.

Janet Goodwyn builds her proficient study *Edith Wharton: Traveller in the Land of Letters* (St. Martin's) around Wharton's use of specific landscapes, tracing the "particular geography" of Wharton's fiction from *The Valley of Decision* to *The Buccaneers,* her last, unfinished novel. Although Wharton set her novels in a variety of countries, these landscapes are complementary, reflecting her "sense of the unity of culture between America and Europe." Penelope Vita-Finzi's *Edith Wharton and the Art of Fiction* (St. Martin's) sets out to "piece together a portrait of Edith Wharton, the writer" by studying *Hudson River Bracketed, The Gods Arrive,* and drafts of her unpublished early novel *Literature.* Unfortunately, Vita-Finzi's discussion of Wharton's transformation of *Literature* into the two later novels, intended to illuminate Wharton's views on the nature of art and the artist, though sound, is somewhat rambling.

There were three contextual studies of note. Mary E. Papke asserts that, while neither can be called a feminist writer, Wharton and Chopin both produced "female moral art in works that focus relentlessly on the dialectics of social relations and the position of women therein" in *Verging on the Abyss: The Social Fiction of Kate Chopin and Edith Wharton* (Greenwood). Wharton depicts the social wars of New York symbolically as she portrays the reality of women's roles during a time of "social transformation and ideological mutation." Papke's provocative and ideological readings of Wharton's canon define her art as nonpolemical, but nevertheless political. Dale M. Bauer's *"Twilight Sleep:* Edith Wharton's Brave New Politics" (*ArQ* 45, i:49–71) places Wharton within the context of contemporary debate over women's rights, eugenics, and anesthesia. Arguing against "the charge of political quietism and collaboration with reactionary politics," Bauer attributes a "feminist politics of writing" to Wharton, demonstrating that the novel, though chaotic, is a brilliant satire of modern life and simple solutions. Monika M. Elbert investigates Wharton's treatment of motherhood in "The Politics of Maternality in *Summer"* (*EdWR* 7, ii:4–9, 24), arguing that the "matriphobic atmosphere" of the novel is closely allied to the wartime destruction and lack of respect for life created by "man-made" governments.

The House of Mirth inspired a number of items. Linda Wagner-Martin's The House of Mirth: *A Novel of Admonition* (Twayne Masterwork Series) is a clear reading of the novel that incorporates current feminist approaches as well as earlier interpretations. Although Wharton's novel was perceived as nonthreatening by her audience, Wagner-Martin points out the gaps in narrative that create a subtext critical of convention. Louise K. Barnett offers a lucid discussion of "the code of verbal restraint that governs utterance" in "Language, Gender, and Society in *The House of Mirth"* (*Connecticut Review* 11 [1989]:54–63). "Within the dominant discourse of society gender specific sub-categories exist that reflect the role and status differences between men and women," and Lily is unable to transcend the external circumstances imposed by discourse restraints, unable to find a "saving language," unable to integrate her social and individual selves. In "The Antimodernist Unconscious: Genre and Ideology in *The House of Mirth"* (*AQ* 44 [1989]:55–79), Catherine Quoyeser's formal analysis concentrates on the novel's opening and closing in a Marxist reading that incorporates the ideas of Fredric Jameson. Quoyeser argues that Wharton combines naturalism, realism, and sentimental melodrama to represent "the crisis of bourgeois individualism." Annette Larson Benert suggests that Wharton wrote about people in relation to their houses, streets, and towns, and her topic is women who "live on the margin between the interior of houses and the exterior of the urban or pastoral landscape" in "The Geography of Gender in *The House of Mirth"* (*SNNTS* 22:26–42). Wharton employs her extensive knowledge of architecture and interior decoration in *The Age of Innocence* in her delineation of character, according to Ada Van Gastel in "The Location and Decoration of Houses in *The Age of Innocence*" (*DQR* 20:138–53). Since the close-knit society of New York in the 1870s "operated as much by signs as by way of words," the location and decoration of the characters' houses in the novel function as "signs" in a "hieroglyphic world."

Two brief articles discuss *Summer*. Wharton's interest in architecture leads Christine Rose to remind us that the term "summer" means "a large horizontal supporting beam or girder." Not only is the title consistent with the doubleness that pervades the novel's structure and imagery, but the paradoxical Lawyer Royall can be seen as the "supporting cross-beam" of the novel. Peter L. Hays suggests that Wharton uses fairy-tale elements to "create a story of harsh reality" and examines Wharton's use of language and metaphor to link themes in "Signs in *Summer*: Words and Metaphors" (*PLL* 25:114–19). In "Clare Van Degen in *The Custom of the Country*" (*SAF* 17 [1989]:107–10), Rosemary Erickson Pierce calls our attention to the easily overlooked Clare Van Degen as Wharton's ironic counterpart to Undine Spragg, who dominates the novel "just as she attempts to dominate the society portrayed within it." On the other hand, Ellen Dupree uses Luce Irigaray's identification of the strategy in which a woman deliberately exaggerates or apes patriarchal discourse for the purpose of escaping its power to defend Undine Spragg's monstrous qualities in "Jamming the Machinery: Mimesis in *The Custom of the Country* (*ALR* 22, ii:5–16). Wharton wrote her novel "against" Robert Grant's *Unleavened Bread*, using mimesis as "a means of unsettling the male discourse, of casting doubt on its ability to define Undine." "Making Room for the Artist in Edith Wharton's *Old New York*" (pp. 66–84), Sharon Shaloo's persuasive essay in *The Modern American Novella*, ed. A. Robert Lee (St. Martin's, 1989), seeks to establish the novella as "not so much the end of Wharton's great beginning as, instead, the beginning of her great end" by considering each discrete fiction within the context of an artistic vision that binds them together in a work portraying not only creative fulfillment, but emotional and sexual fulfillment.

Wharton's war stories provoked comment from three critics. In " 'Behind the Lines' in Edith Wharton's *A Son at the Front*: Rewriting a Masculine Tradition" (*JAmS* 24:187–98), Judith L. Sensibar argues that Wharton anticipated the feminist critics of the late 20th century in her exploration of the effect of the social disruptions of World War I on socially constructed notions of masculinity and femininity. Alan Price appreciates Wharton's formulaic short story "Coming Home" for its biographical and historical dimensions, and argues that her fusion of stereotypical characters and plot with her own war experience produced a story worthy of the "larger canon of World War I literature" in "Edith Wharton's War Story" (*TSWL* 8:95–100).

As of Spring 1990, the *Edith Wharton Newsletter* became the *Edith Wharton Review.* The *Review* is a steady source of information for Wharton scholars; especially useful are Alfred Bendixen's continuing bibliographic essays.

The Wharton chapter in Josephine Donovan's *After the Fall* (pp. 43–83) enlarges the Demeter-Persephone myth to include Hecate, the goddess of death, in the choices Wharton gives her women: "Demeter, non-oedipal, preliterate silence; Persephone, freedom from Demeter but patriarchal captivity and incest; Hecate, death." Wharton adopted the "rebellious but male-identified daughter's point of view"; her self-identification with the masculine narrator demonstrates her intention of becoming a patriarch. Donovan offers readings of some of the lesser-known works, including many of the short stories; her discussions of *Ethan Frome,* in which the central theme is the revenge of Demeter in her dark aspect of Hecate, and *Summer,* a "repetition of the rape of Artemis-Persephone and the death of Demeter," are particularly cogent.

Turning to Glasgow (pp. 129–54), Donovan explores manifestations of the "new woman's" rebellion from a third perspective. Like Wharton, Glasgow often locates the underground captivity of Persephone in New York City, but her women survive because they retain some connection with the world of Demeter. Donovan also pays considerable attention to the rejected mothers, whom she sees as ineffectual, neurasthenic, or self-sacrificial, sometimes demonic and vengeful. *Virginia* is the first clear expression of Glasgow's central thesis: to survive, women must engage in the real world, "a Darwinian jungle governed by a patriarchal ethic." *They Stooped to Folly* explores the mother's consciousness; Donovan compares Glasgow's treatment of Mrs. Littlepage to Virginia Woolf's Mrs. Ramsey. Arguing that *Barren Ground* can be ranked with *O Pioneers!* and *My Ántonia* in its depiction of the Demeter-Persephone resurrection myth, Donovan links the writing of this novel to Glasgow's own passage "from the wilderness of male-supremacist ideology toward the 'promised land' of woman-identification. . . ."

Susan Goodman's comparison of Wharton and Glasgow in "Competing Visions of Freud in the Memoirs of Ellen Glasgow and Edith

Wharton" (*CLQ* 25 [1989]:218–26) shows that, in both form and approach, *The Woman Within* and *A Backward Glance* represent their authors' fiction. Believing that a work's fidelity was tied to its "value as psychology," Glasgow offers herself as a case study, revealing Freud's influence; Wharton resists Freud's construct of self, choosing to emphasize social realism in her autobiography. "Healing the Woman Within: Therapeutic Aspects of Ellen Glasgow's Autobiography," pp. 93–106 in J. Bill Berry, ed., *Located Lives,* is Marilyn R. Chandler's competent discussion of *The Woman Within* as Glasgow's means of "purging her soul of the sorrows that had festered there" to achieve both strength and peace. In "A Knowledge in the Heart: Ellen Glasgow, the Woman's Movement, and *Virginia*" (*ALR* 22, ii:30–43), Dorothy M. Scura suggests that, though Glasgow was in no sense an activist, she transformed her feminism into *Virginia,* a subversively political novel. In *Daughters of Time: Creating Woman's Voice in Southern Story* (Georgia), a study of the strategies used by Southern women to create a unique "voice" in a society that remained solidly patriarchal far longer than other regions of the country, Lucinda H. MacKethan discusses Glasgow and Zora Neale Hurston and Eudora Welty (pp. 35–77). Glasgow began her autobiographical "journey" by confronting the tension between mother and father, then rejected the father, "who for her represented the stifling of sympathy and creativity." Writing *The Woman Within* changed Glasgow's relationship with her family, freeing her to leave her father's house in pursuit of her vocation, and ultimately allowing her to return "home" in her fiction.

Julius Rowen Raper's "Once More to the Mirror: Glasgow's Technique in *The Sheltered Life* and Reader-Response Criticism," pp. 136–55 in Thomas Young, ed., *Modern American Fiction: Form and Function* (LSU, 1989), is a close reading of the novel "in the manner of the New Critics augmented by the incorporation of reader-response theory." Using the image of "a pyramid composed of three mirrors with one face toward the universe of its characters, another toward the author, and a third turned toward the reader," Raper explains how Glasgow's characters use each other to see images of themselves as a model for the reader's response. In "Inventing Modern Southern Fiction: A Postmodern View" (*SLJ* 22:3–18), Raper examines the four major movements—local color, naturalism, realism, modernism—in Glasgow's development that also define the evolution of modern Southern fiction. Beth Harrison puts Glasgow at the head of a female pastoral tradition that emphasizes community, values friendship between women (and between lovers), and questions exploitation of others for the sake of property in "Ellen Glasgow's Revision of the Southern Pastoral" (*SoAR* 55, ii:47–70). Harrison compares Dorinda Oakley to Cather's Alexandra Bergson and Hurston's Janie Crawford in her discussion of *Barren Ground* as Glasgow's "successful agrarian myth," and she takes a provocative look at the Native American captivity narrative in *The Iron Vein* as Glasgow's means of emphasizing female "wildness" or sexuality.

iii Gertrude Stein and Sherwood Anderson

Two major studies offer scholars new ways to read Stein. In *The Public Invited to Dance: Representation, the Body, and Dialogue in Gertrude Stein* (Stanford, 1989), Harriet Scott Chessman argues that Stein's writing invites the reader to consider the act of reading as "one not of mastery or consumption but of an ongoing and open-ended process of dialogue." With lucid and original readings, Chessman shows how Stein's texts not only incorporate referential language, but elicit a bodily response. Chessman illustrates Stein's construction of a modernist and feminist aesthetic by pointing out intersections between Stein's forms of literary doubling and the feminist theories of Nancy Chodorow, Julia Kristeva, and Luce Irigaray. In a splendid final chapter, Chessman advances closely "dialogic" readings of two later novels: *Blood on the Dining-Room Floor,* in which Stein directly invites our presence as "loving readers," and the "profoundly feminist" *Ida,* in which all the aspects of dialogue culminate in an exploration of "twinship." An equally impressive study is Lisa Ruddick's *Reading Gertrude Stein* (Cornell). Ruddick traces the development of Stein's thought and work from *Three Lives* through *Tender Buttons,* identifying the changes that occurred as Stein defined herself first against William James, then in terms of Freud's idea of the unconscious, finally developing the hermetic style that allowed her to espouse feminist themes and to develop "a set of sophisticated ideas about the play of drive in language." Ruddick's brilliant reading of *Tender Buttons* as an expression of Stein's gnostic vision introduces a different theoretical vocabulary from that of post-structuralism (though she incorporates its interpretations), which maintains that "a text can be polysemous and still have themes"; *Tender Buttons* is "far more intellectually cohesive than has been supposed." Ruddick proves that it *is* possible "to integrate some of the insights of poststructuralism with . . . a humanist understanding of the artistic process."

Other discussions of the encounter between reader and text are Ellen Berry's "On Reading Stein" (*Genders* 5 [1989]:1–20) and Stephen Ratcliffe's "Memo/: Re: Reading Stein" (*AmerP* 6 [1989]:22–32). Berry reviews the conventional and feminist approaches to Stein's texts, then suggests productive reading is possible only when we acknowledge the "difference of the other woman with whom we are engaged in our intimate textual dialogue." Ratcliffe argues that Stein relinquished the role of author-as-guide by using repetition, which forces a continual *re-reading* of the text, to become "author-making-world-out-of-words."

Two books for the novice also appeared this year. Bettina L. Knapp's *Gertrude Stein* (Continuum) is a solid biographical-critical introduction to Stein. *Really Reading Gertrude Stein: A Selected Anthology with Essays by Judy Grahn* (Crossing Press, 1989) includes excerpts from a wide range of Stein's works arranged in three sections introduced by Grahn's essays containing practical (and elementary) hints on how to read them. Richard Kostelanetz has edited *Gertrude Stein Advanced: An Anthology of Criticism* (McFarland). The 27 essays reprinted here proceed from the general to the more specific and include an essay extracted from the unpublished papers of Wendall Wilcox.

Steven J. Meyer's essay "Stein and Emerson" (*Raritan* 10:87–119) sheds new light on both. Demonstrating that Stein is more "canonical" and Emerson more daring than we might think, Meyer proves that Stein is a direct literary descendant of Emerson and restores his right to the name rebel. Charles Carmello's discussion of Stein's claim to the Jamesian succession, "Portrait Narration: Generals James and Stein" (pp. 103–20 in Patrick O'Donnell and Robert Con Davis, eds., *Intertextuality and Contemporary American Fiction* [Hopkins, 1989]), advances the view that Stein is to James "what contemporaneity is to modernism." In an intertextual discussion of *Tender Buttons* and *The Waves,* Rachel Blau DuPlessis explores the conjuncture of Stein and Virginia Woolf in "WOOLFENSTEIN," pp. 99–114 in Ellen G. Friedman and Miriam Fuchs's *Breaking the Sequence: Women's Experimental Fiction* (Princeton, 1989).

Several essays focus on autobiography. Joseph Fichtelberg's long and substantive chapter, "Reluctant Modern: Gertrude Stein," pp. 162–208 in *The Complex Image: Faith and Method in American Autobiography*

(Penn., 1989), investigates Stein's four autobiographies as a record of her struggle to accommodate her essentially conservative temper to the radically changing world. Fichtelberg examines Stein in relation to James, Adams, Bergson, and Whitman. Barbara Mossberg points out very real similarities between Stein and Emily Dickinson in "Double Exposures: Emily Dickinson's and Gertrude Stein's Anti-Autobiographies" (*WS* 16 [1989]:239–50); both consciously use the "coquette's etiquette": deliberate and self-conscious practices of deception, a culturally determined coyness. Timothy Dow Adams explores autobiography as a metaphorically authentic attempt to reconcile one's life with one's self in *Telling Lies in Modern American Autobiography* (No. Car.), arguing that lying in literary biography is not simply inevitable, but often a "deliberate and highly strategic decision" on the author's part. In his chapter on Stein (pp. 17–38), Adams reads *The Autobiography of Alice B. Toklas* as a traditional American tall tale or hoax in which Stein simultaneously exaggerates her own importance to the literary world and presents through the book's form Toklas's predilection for disguising herself as another person.

A number of miscellaneous items are worthy of mention. Maria Diedrich examines Stein's four war texts in "'A Book in Translation about Eggs and Butter': Gertrude Stein's World War II," pp. 87–106 in Maria Diedrich and Dorothea Fischer-Hornung, eds., *Woman and War: The Changing Status of American Women from the 1930s to the 1950s* (Berg). Stein defies the conventions of traditional war literature by deconstructing the male-dominated paradigms of war discourse as she attempts to aesthetically redefine the meaning of war from the perspective of a female noncombatant. "Gertrude Stein: Exile, Feminism, Avant-Garde in the American Theater" (pp. 111–29) is Dinnah Pladott's contribution to *Modern American Drama,* ed. June Schlueter. Locating Stein's plays and operas within the context of Julia Kristeva, Jacques Derrida, and Michel Foucault, Pladott argues that Stein's work provides a new model of dramatic discourse "created by an exile (expatriate, woman, Jew, Lesbian) intent on proposing new forms outside the established discourse." Finally, "A Radio Interview" (*ParisR* 32:85–97) makes available for the first time the November 12, 1934, transcript of William Lundell's live interview of Stein.

Sherwood Anderson's three contradictory autobiographies are also the subject of a chapter in Adam's *Telling Lies* (pp. 39–68). The consequence of Anderson's constant admissions of lying is a more accurate image of the author than a straightforward, factual biography could produce, Adams contends. David D. Anderson explores fictional portraits of Anderson's relationships with other writers (Ben Hecht, Faulkner, Hemingway, and Margaret Anderson) in "Sherwood Anderson in Fiction" (*Midamerica* 16 [1989]:80–93). *Sherwood Anderson's Love Letters to Eleanor Copenhaver Anderson* (Georgia, 1989), ed. Charles E. Modlin, gives scholars a first-hand look at 224 of the more than 1,400 letters Anderson wrote to his fourth wife from the first days of their courtship in 1929 until shortly before his death in 1941. Sealed until 1984, the correspondence provides evidence that his pursuit of Eleanor and her interest in labor causes had a powerful impact on his writing. Of tangential interest to Anderson scholars (and of primary interest to film historians) is William Mac-Adams's biography, *Ben Hecht: The Man Behind the Legend* (Scribner's), the first full-length study of Hecht's influence on American cinema. MacAdams investigates the relationship between the literary scene—particularly the Chicago Renaissance—and the developing movie industry in a thoroughly researched book that includes a bibliography and a filmography.

Winesburg, Ohio continues as Anderson's most provocative work. This year's scholarship includes Ray Lewis White's Winesburg Ohio: *An Exploration* (Twayne Masterwork Series), and *New Essays on* Winesburg, Ohio, ed. John W. Crowley (Cambridge), which features Crowley's substantial introduction and essays by David Stouck, Marcia Jacobson, Claire Colquitt, and Thoman Yingling that consider the text in the contexts of the expressionist movement, the American boy book tradition, the work of Sarah Orne Jewett, and the rise of industrial capitalism. In *"Winesburg, Ohio:* An Existential Microcosm" (*CLAJ* 33 [1989]:130–44), Celia Esplugas explains that Anderson anticipated Saul Bellow and Samuel Beckett in his portrayal of the dismal condition of the modern individual. On the other hand, Robert Dunne suggests that Anderson does, in fact, demonstrate that a person can "cure" himself of grotesqueness, though he is never as clear in explaining the cure as in describing the symptoms, in "Beyond Grotesqueness in *Winesburg, Ohio*" (*MQ* 31:180–91). *Sherwood Anderson: Early Writings,* ed. Ray Lewis White (Kent State), collects Anderson's earliest published writings, clearly apprentice work, adding to the Anderson canon several hitherto unknown essays and stories. White provides connecting passages for coherence, as well as helpful notes that establish the historical context and explain allusions. Stephen Enniss makes two contributions to the year's work on

Anderson. His "Alienation and Affirmation: The Divided Self in Sherwood Anderson's *Poor White*" (*SoAR* 55, ii:85–99) demonstrates that, although Anderson was a writer firmly rooted in the tradition of alienation, his characters' actions are a clear indication of their faith in what can be regained and reaffirmed in the present. Enniss ("Sherwood Anderson and Paul Gauguin: A Forgotten Review" [*SAF* 18:118–21]) has also discovered a previously forgotten book review by Anderson of Beril Becker's biography *Paul Gauguin: The Calm Madman,* in which Anderson reveals his own conception of the artist's life.

iv Theodore Dreiser, H. L. Mencken, and Sinclair Lewis

The most significant contribution to Dreiser studies this year is the second volume of Richard Lingeman's two-volume biography, *Theodore Dreiser: An American Journey, 1908–1945* (Putnam), as impressive in its scholarship as the first (*Theodore Dreiser: At the Gates of the City, 1871–1907* (see *ALS 1986,* p. 244). Lingeman follows Dreiser's tumultuous career with a social historian's eye, evaluating the consequences of his friendship with H. L. Mencken, measuring the impact of his marriages, and locating the sources of his political radicalization. Literary criticism is clearly secondary here, but Lingeman does offer some insights into Dreiser's creative life; in particular, his discussion of *An American Tragedy* demonstrates how deeply Dreiser lived in his characters. The book includes 16 pages of photographs.

Conrad E. Ostwalt, Jr.'s chapter on Dreiser in *After Eden* (pp. 75–110) argues that Dreiser's work explores the consequences of the American social dream. Redefining social space in naturalistic terms, Dreiser reappropriates the American worldview, painting a picture of a social world that "no longer provides access to otherness but one that is otherness itself." In a similar vein, Joseph K. Davis notes the similarity of thematic concerns in *An American Tragedy, The Great Gatsby,* and *The Sun Also Rises,* all of which charge that 20th-century attitudes, values, and lifestyles result from an urbanized, secularized worldview in "The Triumph of Secularism: Theodore Dreiser's *An American Tragedy,*" pp. 93–117, Davis's contribution to Thomas Young's *Modern American Fiction: Form and Function* (LSU, 1989). S. D. Trigg sees Dreiser's targets in *An American Tragedy* as the process of trial, the jury, the theatrics of lawyers, and the cruelty and inhumanity of death row in "Theodore Dreiser and the Criminal Justice System in *An American Tragedy* (*SNNTS* 22:429–

40). Lee Clark Mitchell's chapter in *Determined Fictions* (pp. 55–74) is a skillful exploration of Dreiser's use of narrative repetition, relentless foreshadowing, and psychic doubling to deny Clyde Griffiths an autonomous selfhood. Ronald Schleifer's intertextual reading of *An American Tragedy* and Norman Mailer's *The Executioner's Song* advances both as models of *"absolute* difference from the novel of manners in America" in "American Violence: Dreiser, Mailer and the Nature of Intertextuality," pp. 121–43 in Patrick O'Donnell and Robert Con Davis, eds., *Intertextuality and Contemporary American Fiction* (Hopkins, 1989).

In *"The Genius:* Dreiser's Testament to Convention" (*CLAJ* 33:402–14), the single article on Dreiser's "most misread, most misunderstood book," Miriam Gogol suggests that Dreiser is more moral and Puritan than naturalistic. The psychological processes of the characters in *Sister Carrie* interest Bertil C. Nelson, who points out similarities between Dreiser's interpretive psychology and William James's theories of mind in "William James's Concept of Self and the Fictive Psychology of Theodore Dreiser in *Sister Carrie*" (*EAS* 19:45–64). Paul Orlov gleefully announces his discovery of the first issue of Dreiser's *Ev'ry Month.* He details the magazine's contents in "Theodore Dreiser's *Ev'ry Month,* I, 1, Found at Last: Revealing More Roots of a Writer's Thought" (*ALR* 22, i[1989]:69–79). Scholars should check *Dreiser Studies* for bibliographical updates; a special issue (21, ii[Fall 1990]) contains papers presented at the Brockport conference.

The eagerly awaited publication of *The Diary of H. L. Mencken* (Knopf, 1989), ed. Charles A. Fecher, is the most notable event in Mencken scholarship in several years. The book constitutes about one-third of the total diary, selected, as Fecher explains in his introduction, to be representative and interesting. Scholars will find Mencken's comments about his impressive circle of friends (Dreiser, Lewis, particularly Joseph Hergesheimer) valuable. Although the diary does not reveal the isolated, bitter man some had expected, it does expose the extent of Mencken's prejudices—his hatred of Roosevelt, his attitude toward blacks, his anti-Semitism. The controversy over those racial attitudes dominates critical (and popular) discussion. *Menckeniana,* which continues to include even brief mentions of Mencken in Vincent Fitzpatrick's checklists, devoted the Spring 1990 number (113) to an analysis of reaction to the *Diary,* including a transcript of the Mencken Society panel discussion (pp. 7–15).

With the exception of articles debating Mencken's racial attitudes,

Mencken scholarship in journals other than *Menckeniana* is meager, although several books have appeared. *Fante/Mencken: A Personal Corre-spondence, 1930–1952* (Black Sparrow, 1989), ed. Michael Moreau, collects the confessional letters of young, aspiring California writer John Fante and the generous and even-tempered responses of an older, wiser Men-cken. Although Fante and Mencken never met, they corresponded until Mencken's incapacitating illness, after which Fante wrote to Mencken's secretary. Moreau's notes fill in the gaps and explain the context of the letters. In Vincent Fitzpatrick's *H. L. Mencken* (Continuum, 1989), a brief biography precedes the critical discussion of Mencken's work. Fitzpatrick organizes the book by dividing Mencken's career into five major periods. Designed primarily to introduce new readers to Men-cken, the book is authoritative and readable. Mayo DuBasky, whose series on Mencken's use of pseudonyms in the *Smart Set* appeared in *Menckeniana* (109 [1989]:10–11; 111 [1989]:13–15; 116:10–11), has compiled *The Gist of Mencken: Quotations from America's Critic* (Scarecrow), a welcome collection of quotations from newspapers, magazines, books, letters, and manuscripts that also contains caricatures by Mencken's contemporaries and a bibliography. Three main divisions and multiple subdivisions make the book easy to peruse, and it has a comprehensive index.

Sinclair Lewis's wives got as much attention as he did this year. Suggesting that Lewis can be seen as a feminist writer because, energized by assertive women in his life, he writes about women as persons in their own right, Sally E. Parry looks at Lewis's relationships with Grace Hegger and Dorothy Thompson (his wives) and Marcella Powers (his mistress) to find the sources for his memorable female characters in "The Chang-ing Fictional Faces of Sinclair Lewis' Wives" (*SAF* 17 [1989]:65–79). Lewis's fictional portraits of these three women became increasingly critical as his relationships with them soured. Parry speculates that Lewis failed to create fully realized women in his later novels because he never had another long romantic relationship after Powers left him. *American Cassandra: The Life of Dorothy Thompson* (Little, Brown) by Peter Kurth is worth mentioning here. In addition to its equitable treatment of Thompson's career, this biography judiciously explores her relationship with Lewis and the extent of her influence on his career.

Although Thompson probably had some influence on Lewis's treat-ment of fascism in *It Can't Happen Here*, Stephen L. Tanner suggests that Raymond Gram Swing's collection of essays, *Forerunners of American*

Fascism, which appeared a month before Lewis began writing his novel, is a more likely source in "Sinclair Lewis and Fascism" (*SNNTS* 22:57–66). Tanner's second contribution to this year's Lewis scholarship is "Sinclair Lewis and the New Humanism" (*Modern Age* 33:33–41), which defines the philosophical climate of the twenties, identifies Lewis's allegiances, and then lucidly follows the literary quarrel between the two major intellectual camps: the new generation of writers who identified with Mencken's antipuritanism, and the New Humanists, adherents of Irving Babbitt and Elmer More's intellectual conservatism. Elaine Ware's psychological analysis of Martin Arrowsmith, "A Psychological Portrait of Infantile Regression in Sinclair Lewis's *Arrowsmith*" (*JEP* 9 [1989]:166–73), catalogs his psychological problems—insecurity, feelings of inferiority, depression, mania, alcoholism, and neurasthenia—then finds reasons for them in the text.

v John Dos Passos, Jack London, and Upton Sinclair

Dos Passos scholars will benefit from the publication of previously unaccessible material. The first volume of the Archive of Literary Documents, *Afterglow and Other Undergraduate Writings: A Facsimile Edition* (Omnigraphics), ed. Richard Layman, consists of 13 stories, essays, and poems submitted by Dos Passos in his advanced composition classes at Harvard. Two of these works were published in the *Harvard Monthly* while Dos Passos was a student; the rest are previously unpublished, including his first novel *Afterglow.* A handsome, oversized format permits the reproduction of each manuscript page, complemented by a typescript on the facing page; comments by Dos Passos's professors, Charles Townsend Copeland and Le Baron Russell Briggs, are also reproduced. Dos Passos's *Streets of the Night* (Susquehanna), ed. Michael Clark, long out of print, is available again in an edition that provides an authoritative text. Based on the first American printing, it includes the autograph changes Dos Passos made in the novel's typescripts. The book also includes textual notes that identify the novel's allusions, Dos Passos's diary entries concerning the novel, and a list of the substantive variants between the American and British first editions. In *Dos Passos's Early Fiction, 1912–1938* (Susquehanna), Clark undertakes to provide the analysis he outlines in his introduction to *Streets of Night.* Working with unpublished manuscripts and Dos Passos's first several novels, Clark identifies a distinctly American pragmatism (William James) and love of the mythical dimension of nature (Whitman) as the defining ideas that shaped Dos Passos's aesthetics and his four best novels: *Manhattan Transfer* and the *U.S.A.* trilogy. This coherent and cogent study ends with the suggestion that the later, less satisfactory works pose other critical problems; perhaps Clark will address those next.

John Rohrkemper's contribution to *Rewriting the Good Fight: Critical Essays on the Literature of the Spanish Civil War* (Mich. State, 1989), ed. Frieda S. Brown et al., examines Dos Passos's retreat from the stylistically experimental and socially conscious form of *U.S.A.* to the cramped style and repressive pessimism of his next novel, *Adventures of a Young Man.* Disillusioned by the Spanish Civil War, Dos Passos lost faith in the dialogue between philosophy and politics, and in the co-constructive power of language itself. With some help from the poststructuralists, Clara Juncker reads *The Big Money* as a "satiric diagnosis of the American malaise" in which Dos Passos uses a stereotypic radical heroine to dramatize his dual disillusion with capitalism and communism in "Romancing the Revolution: Dos Passos' Radical Heroine" (*Works and Days* 8:57–66). Mark T. Bassett's translation of Indro Montanell's 1949 uncomplimentary narrative portrait of Dos Passos, previously unavailable, appeared in the *Lost Generation Journal* (8, 21[1989]:16–18). A literary portrait is Robert E. Fleming's topic in "The Libel of Dos Passos in *To Have and Have Not*" (*JML* 15 [1989]:597–601). Fleming reports that another libelous portrait of a literary character, who resembled Dos Passos more precisely than Richard Gordon does, was eliminated from the manuscript of *To Have and Have Not.*

Jack London scholars now have a one-volume authorized edition of his short stories. *Short Stories of Jack London* (Macmillan), ed. Earle Labor et al., collects 50 of the 200 stories, including both the 1902 and 1908 versions of "To Build a Fire." The fine, thorough, and evenhanded introduction reviews London's biography, indicates intellectual influences on his work, and situates him in the cultural milieu of his time. A handy new edition of *The Kempton-Wace Letters* (NCUP), ed. Douglas Robillard, is also out this year. Mark E. Zamen's *Standing Room Only: Jack London's Controversial Career as a Public Speaker* (Peter Lang) is the first extensive study to focus on London's speaking career. Like Emerson, London used the platform as a means of disseminating his social and political ideas and relied heavily on his own written essays for his public speeches. Of the eight lectures collected in the book, seven were published as essays. All are reproduced in full, with the exception of three tables and 11 footnotes. Zamen provides informative editorial comments and, in an appendix, includes article synopses from selected newspapers and periodicals. Earle Labor and Robert C. Leitz III discuss London's estrangement from Alexander Berkman and Emma Goldman in light of his unsympathetic remarks about anarchism in "Jack London on Alexander Berkman: An Unpublished Introduction" (*AL* 61 [1989]:447–56). In "Homecoming in the California Visionary Romantic" (*WAL* 24 [1989]:1–19), Charles L. Crow reads London's *The Valley of the Moon* as the first major narrative in the visionary tradition that sees California as a place where things work out and dreams come true and which includes Ernest Callenbach and Ursula Le Guin.

Upton Sinclair: Literature and Social Reform (Peter Lang), ed. Dieter Herms, collects 21 papers presented at the 1988 Upton Sinclair World Conference into five groups: literary technique, education and history, autobiography, approaches to the literary works, and impact and reception. Particularly noteworthy is Alfred Hornung's "Literary Conventions and the Political Unconscious in Upton Sinclair's Work" (pp. 24–38), a deconstructive reading of *Manassas, The Jungle, The Brass Check,* and *American Outpost* that reveals Sinclair's nostalgia for a Southern aristocratic past.

vi African American Authors

Among African American authors, W. E. B. Du Bois attracted the most attention this year. Du Bois always wrote from a political perspective, and his politicization of his own autobiography is the subject of William E. Cain's "W. E. B. Du Bois's *Autobiography* and the Politics of Literature" (*BALF* 24:266–313). Cain's article "Violence, Revolution and the Cost of Freedom: John Brown and W. E. B. Du Bois" (*Boundary 2* 17:305–30) demonstrates that, in Du Bois's hands, the study of John Brown becomes "an inquiry into the souls of blacks" as well as a celebration of revolutionary action. Dianne Johnson's chapter on *The Brownies' Book,* ed. Du Bois and Jesse Fauset, in her *Telling Tales: The Pedagogy of African American Literature for Youth* (Greenwood) discusses Du Bois's efforts to include positive black images in popular culture. In "W. E. B. Du Bois' First Efforts as a Playwright" (*CLAJ* 33:415–27), Walter C. Daniel outlines Du Bois's influence as a forerunner in the establishment of African American drama, and John Hope Franklin relates the parallel histories of his relationship with Du Bois and his struggle in academics in "W. E. B. Du Bois: A Personal Memoir" (*MR* 31:409–28).

Single articles appeared on Jean Toomer, Claude McKay, and Nella Larsen. Robert B. Jones calls attention to Toomer's unpublished collection of short stories (in the Toomer collection at Yale) in "Jean Toomer's *Lost and Dominant:* Landscape of the Modern Waste Land" (*SAF* 18:77–86). Comparing Toomer with T. S. Eliot, Jones argues that Toomer joins other members of the Lost Generation in portraying the character of the era. P. S. Chauhan argues that McKay must be read in the context of a colonial sensibility, if he is to be understood at all, in "Rereading Claude McKay" (*CLAJ* 34:68–80). McKay's ambiguities make more sense in light of the English attitudes and European sensibility he brought to bear on Harlem. Ann E. Hostetler sees Helga's fascination with clothing and color as emblematic of her attempt to construct both a racial and a female identity in "The Aesthetics of Race and Gender in Nella Larsen's *Quicksand*" (*PMLA* 105:35–46). *Quicksand* draws on the materials of urban life to present an alternative strain of African American woman's writing that deals with problems of cultural identity and assimilation. Mary Sisney argues that Nella Larsen and Jesse Fauset have much more in common with Edith Wharton and Jane Austen than they do with Claude McKay and Countee Cullen in "The View from the Outside: Black Novels of Manners," pp. 171–86 in *Reading and Writing Women's Lives,* ed. Bege K. Bowers and Barbara Brothers. Sisney links Fauset's *The Chinaberry Tree* and Larsen's *Quicksand* and *Passing* to the novel of manners in three shared fundamental concerns: the fight for acceptance, the loss of identity, and the sense of oppression.

vii Western Writers

A biography highlights this year's work on Westerners. A major contribution to Native American and women's studies, *Mourning Dove: A Salishan Autobiography* (Nebraska) represents an immense effort on the part of its editor, Jay Miller. From Mourning Dove's unfinished and semiedited drafts, Miller has reconstructed her autobiography around three themes: female activities, seasonal activities, and incidents from recent history. Mourning Dove frequently tells two versions of the same events: "a descriptive ethnography of the Okanogans and Colvilles" and a personal history. Miller places Mourning Dove squarely in the English tradition of autobiography which "celebrates individuality and creativity within a confessional form" (rather than in the Native American communal and collaborative tradition) and the tradition of female autobiography, written as a compensation for loneliness and suffering. The book is annotated, with a bibliography and a glossary of Colville-Okanogan terms. Alanna Kathleen Brown's article "Mourning Dove's Canadian Recovery Years, 1917–1919" (*CanL* 124–25:113–22) contains extensive excerpts from letters between Mourning Dove and her mentor and friend, L. V. McWhorter.

Mary Austin: Song of a Maverick (Yale, 1989), Esther Lanigan Stineman's critical biography, is another solid study that presents Austin as a troubled and often difficult woman, well ahead of her times on issues of class, race, and gender, who made Native American and Hispanic traditions a part of her own stories and essays. Nancy Morrow compares Austin's treatment of the female performing artist to Anne Douglas Sedgwick's in "The Artist as Heroine and Anti-Heroine in Mary Austin's *A Woman of Genius* and Anne Douglas Sedgwick's *Tante*" (*ALR* 22, ii:17–29). Although similar in thematic concerns, the novels are strikingly different from one another. Austin's heroine Olivia chooses her own destiny; Sedgwick's antiheroine Mercedes allows others to suffer for her artistic ambition.

Owen Wister, Zane Grey, and Ole Rölvaag continue to generate interest. "Owen Wister: Wyoming's Influential Realist and Craftsman" (*GPQ* 10:245–59) by Leslie T. Whipp emphasizes Wister's influence on canonical literature by demonstrating the similarities between *The Virginian* and Cather's *My Ántonia*. Max Westbrook argues that *The Virginian* is "a literary and political con game" in which the folk hero is actually an aristocrat, and he uses Wister's comparisons of the Virginian to Shakespeare's Prince Hal and Turgenev's Bazarov to prove his point in "Bazarov, Prince Hal, and the Virginian" (*WAL* 24 [1989]:103–11). William E. H. Meyer, Jr., puts Zane Grey in the American literary tradition of Emerson and Whitman in "Zane Grey and the American Hypervisual Tradition" (*JAC* 12, iv[1989]:59–69). Grey's descriptions of Western panoramas and vistas and his hawk-eyed heroes express the paradoxical problem of American language trying to transcend the verbal for the visual. Ronald Tranquilla explains some fundamental differences between the significance of the West in the mythos of Canada and the United States in "Ranger and Mountie: Myths of National Identity in Zane Grey's *The Lone Star Ranger* and Ralph Connor's *Corporal Cameron*" (*JPC* 24:69–79). Carlton Jackson's chapter updating Zane Grey studies since 1973 is the major addition to his revised edition of *Zane Grey* (TUSAS 218). The most interesting of the Rölvaag pieces, "The Indian Hill in Rölvaag's *Giants in the Earth*" by Priscilla Homola (*SDR* 27, i[1989]:55–61), investigates his handling of "the Indian question." The centrality of the Indian Hill and Beret's and Pers's reactions to the Indian presence on their newly claimed land are indications that Rölvaag is uneasy and ambivalent about the land-taking experience, suggesting its poignancy and tragedy. Einar Haugen competently explicates Rölvaag's unpublished apprentice work "Nils og Astri" in "Rölvaag's Lost Novel" (*NAS* 32 [1989]:209–19). In *George Wharton James* (WWS 93), Peter Wild reminds us that "only a handful of James's many books has enduring literary merit," but credits James for recognizing that the West's "ethnic, geographic and historical diversity" would, in time, produce a distinctive body of work. James was right.

viii   General Studies and Additional Authors

The most important general study this year is Linda Wagner-Martin's *The Modern American Novel, 1914–1945.* Clearly revisionist, exciting in its fresh approach toward modernism, this is a major study that demonstrates just how much literary history benefits from decanonization. Beginning with a detailed chronology that gives a sense of the volume and variety of the literature published during this seminal period, Wagner-Martin provides a stunning series of juxtapositions to "bring the sense of rich innovation back into our concept of modernism." A comprehensive bibliography makes this an invaluable tool for scholars, and Wagner-Martin's admirably clear style makes it a joy to read. In *Vicious Modernism: Black Harlem and the Literary Imagination* (Cambridge), James De Jongh explores the motif of black Harlem in creative literature. "The Legendary Capital: The 1920s and 1930s" (pp. 5–72) is an excellent overview of the period. Also invaluable for scholars are two appendixes containing checklists of black Harlem in poetry and novels. Elaine Sargent Apthorp's long essay, "Sentiment, Naturalism, and the Female Regionalist" (*Legacy* 7, i:3–22), surveys the development of a gendered aesthetics that allowed women writers to develop a technical sophistication that differs from both traditional realism and traditional naturalism and to create an "emphatic style" that roots in the domestic sentimental novel. A useful resource is *Americans in Paris, 1900–1930: A Selected,*

Annotated Bibliography (Greenwood, 1989), compiled by William G. Bailey.

Two formal studies deal with individual authors. James Phelan examines Ring Lardner's "Haircut" in "Narrative Discourse, Literary Character, and Ideology," pp. 132–46 in *Reading Narrative: Form, Ethics, Ideology* (Ohio State, 1989), ed. James Phelan. Suggesting that the story can best be seen as an analogue to the dramatic monologue, Phelan convincingly and clearly explains the effects of narrative shifts between "instabilities" and "tensions" by which Lardner creates an artistically and ideologically complex narrative technique. In "Comprehension, Composition, and Closure in Elizabeth Madox Roberts's *The Time of Man*" (*KRev* 10:21–37), Stephen Bernstein offers a formal analysis of the carefully constructed chapter closures in the novel which, taken together, "dramatize and thematize a process of growth."

Book-length studies helped keep two other reputations alive. Paul Skenazy's *James M. Cain* (Continuum, 1989) traces the development of Cain's terse, vivid style with reference to the writer's own "tormented and restless life." The book includes 10 movie stills, a bibliography, and a filmography. James D. Reimer's *From Satire to Subversion: The Fantasies of James Branch Cabell* (Greenwood, 1989) examines the apparent contradiction in the two strains that run through Cabell's fantasy literature: the medieval, mythological, and folk sources of high fantasy and the dark, satirical vein close to the postmoderns. Cabell's complex fantasies reveal a preoccupation with the search for meaning or truth, a dismantling of our concepts of unique identity and linear time, and the dissolution of the boundaries between the real and the unreal.

The discovery—or rediscovery—of a wide variety of new works and writers illustrates the scope of this chapter. In "The Lost Generation Lives Again" (*WS* 18:129–34), Doris L. Eder calls our attention to two recently republished books about World War I: *We Were That Young: A Novel* (1932) by Irene Rathbone (Feminist, 1989) and *Not So Quiet: Stepdaughters of War* (1930) by Helen Zenna Smith (Feminist, 1989), written in response to Erich Maria Remarque's *All Quiet on the Western Front*. Although written in quite different styles, Rathbone's and Smith's books manifest an alternative vision to the male version of war. Evelyn Scott's star is on the rise again. *The Southern Quarterly's* Summer 1990 issue (28, iv) included five essays selected from a 1985 symposium on Scott and Caroline Gordon. Noteworthy are Mary V. Davidson's " 'De-

fying the Stars and Challenging the Moon': The Early Correspondence
of Evelyn Scott and Jean Stafford" (pp. 25–34) and Steven T. Ryan's
analysis of isolation and negativism, "The Terroristic Universe of *The
Narrow House*" (pp. 35–44). Judith Reick Long's *Gene Stratton-Porter:
Novelist and Naturalist* (Indiana Historical Society) rectifies inaccuracies
in previous accounts of Stratton-Porter's life and offers a fairly balanced
critical reading of her works. One of Long's significant discoveries is
that *The Strike at Shane's,* published anonymously in 1893, was actually
Stratton-Porter's first book. Long's volume includes helpful notes, a
bibliography, a listing of archives where Stratton-Porter papers can be
found, and 38 photographs. *Strange Shadows: The Uncollected Fiction of
Clark Ashton Smith* (Greenwood, 1989), ed. Steve Behrends et al., includes short stories, material associated with short stories (lists of titles
and synopses), prose poems, and plays, as well as several short pieces of
nonfiction prose. Smith's published but uncollected prose is here as well,
and appendixes contain an article on Smith's missing weird fiction, Don
Carter's first draft of a Carter/Smith collaboration, and Sidney-Fryer's
Addenda to his transcription of Smith's *Black Book.* Finally, Eric J.
Sandeen's selection of excerpts from 41 previously unpublished letters
can be found in "Bourne Again: The Correspondence Between Randolph Bourne and Elsie Clews Parsons" (*AmLH* I [1989]:489–509).

Drew University

14   Fiction: The 1930s to the 1960s

Charlotte Hadella

American authors who were publishing from the 1930s to the 1960s appear to be more popular with critics than ever before. The designation of African American writers to their respective chapters in *American Literary Scholarship* expands this section considerably. Though Southerners as a group dominate the current critical arena, John Steinbeck received more critical attention than any single author for this period possibly due to delayed responses to the fiftieth anniversary of *The Grapes of Wrath* in 1989. The Beats were noticed this year; but, with a few exceptions, significant discussion of Iconoclasts and Innovators, Expatriates and Émigrés, and Detectives was scarce.

Since projects of this nature are normally susceptible to sins of omission, I am sure to have overlooked pertinent material. For those inevitable transgressions, I apologize in advance.

i Proletarians

a. John Steinbeck   *The Short Novels of John Steinbeck: Critical Essays with a Checklist to Steinbeck Criticism* (Duke), ed. Jackson J. Benson, is this year's most valuable contribution to Steinbeck scholarship. The collection includes Steinbeck's preface to the 1953 Viking edition of short novels, a checklist of criticism, 10 reprinted essays by notable critics such as Joseph Fontenrose, Tetsumaro Hayashi, John Ditsky, and Peter Lisca, as well as 12 new essays. In *"The Red Pony* as Story Cycle and Film" (pp. 71–84), Warren French revises his own reading of *The Red Pony* using Northrop Frye's schematic analysis of archetype to suggest that "Steinbeck created not just a story of one youth's coming of age but a movingly realistic tale that recapitulates a basic pattern in human experience . . ." (p. 76). French insists that the film version does not attempt to live up to a mythic model and must be examined on its own terms as an autonomous work of art. "A Historical Introduction to *Of Mice and Men*" by Anne Loftis (pp. 39–47), not meant to be an analysis, succeeds as an overview. To place *Of Mice and Men* in its sociohistorical context, Loftis enlists statistics on itinerant workers and details of Steinbeck's personal experiences as a harvester; she also summarizes an early story about migrant workers which was published in the *Stanford Spectator* 12 years before publication of the novella. A thorough historical analysis of a novel appears in "Steinbeck's 'Deep Dissembler': *The Short Reign of Pippin IV*" (pp. 249–57), by Louis Owens, the only critic to contribute two new essays to Benson's collection. Through an impressive compilation of historical details and textual analysis, Owens establishes clearly what earlier critics have merely suggested—that Steinbeck intended *Pippin* to be "a rather black critique not of France and French politics but of America and American politics" (p. 250).

In "Nonteleological Thinking in Steinbeck's *Tortilla Flat*" (pp. 31–38), Robert Gentry highlights evidence of nonteleological thinking in Steinbeck's work even before the original *Log from the Sea of Cortez* (1941). According to Gentry, Steinbeck's Mexican-American characters offer his most consistent view of the nonmaterialism of "is" thinking. Another essay in the collection which analyzes Steinbeck's nonmaterialistic stance is " 'Some Philosophers in the Sun': Steinbeck's *Cannery Row*" (pp. 119–31) by Robert S. Hughes, Jr. Hughes identifies the Christian, Taoist, pantheist, and Transcendentalist blend in *Cannery Row* as denigrating middle-class prudery and materialism and championing simple pleasures and ease. In "Critics and Common Denominators: Steinbeck's *Sweet Thursday*" (pp. 195–203), Louis Owens discusses *Sweet Thursday* as Steinbeck's deconstruction of *Cannery Row*. This essay offers an insightful assessment of Steinbeck's entire career as Owens explains not only how, but why, *Sweet Thursday* represented for its author "a watershed, a shifting of course, a satirical retrospective and attempt to cut himself free of the burden of California and Steinbeck country" (p. 200).

The Short Novels of John Steinbeck features three new essays on *The Pearl*. In "The Shadow and the Pearl: Jungian Patterns in *The Pearl* (pp. 143–61), John Timmerman discusses the book as a parable of self-discovery which "parallels the Jungian confrontation with the shadow of the unconscious, an ultimate act of reading one's own life" (p. 143). Michael J. Meyer in "Precious Bane: Mining the Fool's Gold of *The Pearl*" (pp. 161–72) argues effectively that "through setting, characters, and symbols," Steinbeck unfolds a "complex moral lesson" (p. 162). Roy Simmonds presents a New Historical treatment of *The Pearl* and insists that any discussion of the novella must "bear in mind its genesis and the circumstances in which it was written" (p. 174). In "Steinbeck's *The Pearl:* Legend, Film, Novel" (pp. 173–84), Simmonds traces the history of the story to show that *The Pearl* was an experiment in the form of a "film-novelette" (p. 179) in the same way that *Of Mice and Men* and *The Moon Is Down* were experiments in the play-novelette form.

Two essays on *Burning Bright* and an overview of Steinbeck and the stage round out the lineup of new critical material collected by Benson in this volume. Carroll Britch and Clifford Lewis in *"Burning Bright:* The Shining of Joe Saul" (pp. 217–34) look beyond the abstract theme of good and evil to examine "the human problem of hate and love" (p. 221) as the major focus of the piece. While Britch and Lewis take issue with critical attacks against *Burning Bright,* Mimi Reisel Gladstein looks at the work as an unsuccessful sequel to Steinbeck's previous play-novelettes, *Of Mice and Men* and *The Moon Is Down.* In "Straining for Profundity: Steinbeck's *Burning Bright* and *Sweet Thursday*" (pp. 234–48), Gladstein also considers the comparative weaknesses of *Sweet Thursday* in light of the success of *Cannery Row.* Though Gladstein admits that the blame for the inferiority of these two works is "difficult to assess" (p. 247), her skillful analysis leads to an indictment of Steinbeck's "obvious authorial manipulation" of language and plot devices (p. 248). Robert Morseberger in "Steinbeck and the Stage" (pp. 271–93) also comments on the language of *Burning Bright,* condemning it as "stilted, abstract, self-conscious, and pretentious" (p. 287). On the other hand, Morseberger applauds the vernacular speech which is responsible for the success of *Of Mice and Men* as a play and *The Grapes of Wrath* as a film, and he proclaims *Of Mice and Men* "an enduring classic of the American stage, one of the ten best plays written in America" (p. 293).

Susan Shillinglaw is the guest editor for an issue of *San Jose Studies* (16, i) that collects the papers given March 16–18, 1989, at San Jose State University: *"The Grapes of Wrath,* 1939–1989: An Interdisciplinary Forum." Illustrated throughout with Thomas Hart Benton's work from the 1940 edition of *The Grapes of Wrath,* the issue begins with a discussion of Benton's career as it related to Steinbeck's work. In "Thomas Hart Benton's Illustrations for *The Grapes of Wrath*" (pp. 6–18), Henry Adams compares Steinbeck and Benton as "tough-minded reporters of the American scene" (p. 6) but argues that by the time Benton illustrated

Steinbeck's novel, "the Marxist thrust of his art had been deflected by his deepening distrust of political dogma" (p. 11). Elaine S. Apthorp's essay, "Steinbeck, Guthrie, and Popular Culture" (pp. 19–39), delineates parallels between the careers of Steinbeck and Woody Guthrie. This issue of *SJS* serves as a compendium for varied approaches to Steinbeck criticism. In "The Metaphysics of Style" (pp. 40–45), Marilyn R. Chandler looks at the novel through a metaphysical rather than social lens to show that the romantic devices and conventions in *The Grapes of Wrath* are "qualified and ironized by jarring discontinuities, shocking juxtapositions, and depictions of those things that make for community, cohesiveness, and continuity" (p. 44). Deborah Schneer in "A Psychoanalytic Reading" (pp. 107–16) uses the concept of "splitting," or psychological projection of guilt, to describe "the psychological underpinnings and consequences of [the] crises" in America during the 1930s that Steinbeck dramatizes in *The Grapes of Wrath* (p. 113). Brian Railsback explains the Darwinian methodology, "a holism, and a scientific outlook realized in *The Grapes of Wrath*" (p. 98), in "Selectivity, Sympathy, and Charles Darwin" (pp. 98–106). John H. Timmerman in "Comic Vision in *The Grapes of Wrath*" (pp. 133–41) argues that Steinbeck used humor "to capture the fullest possible portrait of the migrant lives, to mitigate the tragic tenor of their story, and to create a force of dignity for them" (p. 134), while Anne Loftis compares Steinbeck's interpretation of the federal camp program with details about the camps from other sources to try to reconstruct the historical record in "Steinbeck and the Federal Migrant Camps" (pp. 76–90).

In addition to the various critical readings of *The Grapes of Wrath*, this *SJS* volume includes Roy S. Simmonds's assessment of the original manuscript of the novel (pp. 117–29) as well as evaluations by Kiyoshi Nakayama, Warren French, Leslie Fiedler, and John Ditsky of the decades of critical responses. Fiedler, as the only naysayer in the group with his essay, "In Looking Back After 50 Years" (pp. 54–64), claims that "*The Grapes of Wrath* was originally overprized because it seemed to embody so perfectly the mood and sensibility, the anti-puritanical morality, the leftist politics—and especially the apocalyptic vision of the 30s" (p. 55). Ditsky's thorough analysis in "*The Grapes of Wrath* at 50: The Critical Perspective" (pp. 46–53) surveys the various critical approaches that the novel has successfully withstood and concludes that "there is plenty left to be said about *The Grapes of Wrath*" (p. 50).

The Steinbeck Newsletter (Fall 1990), also from San Jose State, published announcements of meetings, reports on acquisitions to the Steinbeck Research Center, and a whimsical piece by Robert DeMott which catalogs Steinbeck's published minutia. In " 'Working Days and Hours': Steinbeck's Writing of *The Grapes of Wrath*" (*SAF* 18:3–15), DeMott documents major stages of the novel's composition with parallel biographical anecdotes. DeMott argues that after *The Grapes of Wrath* "the unique qualities (the angle of vision, the vital signature, the moral indignation) that made [Steinbeck's] art exemplary in the first place could never be repeated with the same integrated force" (p. 12). In "The World of John Steinbeck's Joads" (*WLT* 64:401–40), Robert Murray Davis gives a modern Oklahoman's assessment of Steinbeck's fictional world. Davis points out that Steinbeck "understood and presented extraordinarily well certain kinds of processes, from the way a good mechanic fixes a car to the way a people adapt physically and socially to new situations" (p. 404).

New Essays on The Grapes of Wrath (Cambridge), ed. David Wyatt, contains Wyatt's introduction highlighting the extremities of critical responses to Steinbeck's novel plus four original essays. In "Pilgrim's Politics: Steinbeck's Art of Conversion" (pp. 27–46), Stephen Railton argues that Steinbeck's epic dramatizes the turning away from capitalism and from the promise of individual opportunity toward socialized democracy—a system which Steinbeck considered as "quintessentially American as the individualistic dream it [would] replace" (p. 28). Nellie Y. McKay's " 'Happy[?]-Wife-and-Motherdom': The Portrayal of Ma Joad in John Steinbeck's *The Grapes of Wrath*" (pp. 47–69) begins slowly with an extended discussion of gender roles. McKay finally addresses characterization of females in the novel, applauding Ma Joad's usurpation of leadership whenever the men fail to lead, but regretting that each of these episodes is followed by Ma's return to the domestic sphere as soon as the crisis subsides. In "The Mother of Literature: Journalism and *The Grapes of Wrath*" (pp. 71–99), William Howarth draws on details from Jackson J. Benson's 1983 Steinbeck biography and Demott's *Working Days: The Journals of* The Grapes of Wrath (*ALS* 1989, pp. 225–26) to discuss Steinbeck's interest in documentary and the influence of this form on the novel's final chapters. Howarth contends that after Steinbeck completed several journalistic projects focusing on migrant laborers, he then turned to fiction, not as "a higher, truer form of expression," but "to make his story more artful, not truthful" (p. 83). The story as documentary is Leslie Gossage's concern as well in "The Artful Propaganda of Ford's *The Grapes of Wrath*" (pp. 101–25). Gossage analyzes the film version of *The Grapes of Wrath,* concluding that the power of the film as propaganda centers on "Ford's talent for iconographic tableaux" (p. 119). Tetsumaro Hayashi added to this year's flood of Steinbeck criticism *Steinbeck's* The Grapes of Wrath: *Essays in Criticism* (Steinbeck Society), a monograph collection of Hayashi's choice of the seven finest essays on Steinbeck's masterpiece that have appeared in the *Steinbeck Quarterly* over the past 15 years.

But *The Grapes of Wrath* was not the only Steinbeck work to receive critical attention this year. In one of the few articles ever published about Steinbeck in *American Literature,* "Steinbeck's Anglo-Saxon 'Wonder Words' and the American Paradox" (62:310–17), Hassell A. Simpson uses a translation of Anglo Saxon to explain the nationalistic overtones of Ethan's actions in *The Winter of Our Discontent.* Moreover, the Winter-Spring issue of the *Steinbeck Quarterly,* which could well have been titled "Steinbeck and His Brotherhood," features "Steinbeck's Debt to Dos Passos" by Barry Maine; "Darwin and Steinbeck: The 'Older Method' and *Sea of Cortez*" by Brian Railsback; and "Songs of 'Anger and Survival': John Steinbeck on Woody Guthrie" by H. R. Stoneback. Each piece is engaging in its own way and sheds light on its narrow topic. Also included is John Ditsky's lively keynote lecture at the Steinbeck festival in 1988. Ditsky's speech, "John Steinbeck—Yesterday, Today, and Tomorrow," highlights the major trends in Steinbeck studies over the years, then speculates on the turns they are likely to take in the near future. In the Summer-Fall issue of *StQ,* Hayashi analyzes the writer's "ethical and educational concern for America" (p. 89) in "Steinbeck's America in *Travels with Charley,*" explaining some of the central paradoxes of the text and detailing Charley's role as Steinbeck's alter ego. This same issue features "A Garden of My Land: Landscape and Dreamscape in John Steinbeck's Fiction" by Louis Owens. Focusing on Steinbeck's remarkable ability "to describe a place so exactly and yet evoke in that description a kind of metaphorical dreamscape" (p. 79), Owens creates his own metaphor to describe Steinbeck's fiction—a contour map. Like the complexities of terrain represented by lines on a contour map, the layers of meaning in Steinbeck's best fiction "may indeed seem printed over one another until the whole thing blurs. Careful scrutiny of the text, however, can always reorient us" (p. 81). Yet another essay by Owens, "The Mirror and the Vamp: Invention, Reflection, and Bad, Bad Cathy Trask in *East of Eden*" appears in *Writing the American Classics,* ed. James Barbour and Tom Quirk (No. Car.). Owens's analysis brings the events of the composition of *East of Eden* into focus and provides an enlightening discussion of the novel as a work of self-conscious fiction.

John Timmerman's *The Dramatic Landscape of Steinbeck's Short Stories* (Okla.) is valuable for its extensive treatment of the earliest, and most often ignored, fiction. Using composition chronology as the format, the study deals with the decade beginning at Stanford and ending with the drafting of *The Long Valley* stories in 1934. Showing how the short stories reveal Steinbeck's "experimentation with, and eventual mastery of, narrative points of view, character, plot, setting, and patterns of imagery" (xii–xiv) is Timmerman's goal. Timmerman's interest in analyzing stories clearly within the artistic context of their composition dates gives his study its critical edge.

b. Richard Wright, Ralph Ellison, Langston Hughes, and Others

Wright's novel *Native Son* is the subject of a collection of essays in the American Novel series from Cambridge University Press. Keneth Kinnamon, editor of *New Essays on* Native Son, introduces the collection with a fine historical and textual analysis of Wright's classic work (pp. 1–33). Drawing on Wright's letters, notes, manuscripts, the galley and page proofs of *Native Son* at Yale, and statements made by Wright himself in his essay, "How Bigger Was Born," Kinnamon concludes that "Wright's effort in the novel is to reconcile his sense of black life with the intellectual clarity and the possibility of social action provided by Communism, to interpret each group to the other" (pp. 3–4). (Kinnamon's essay also appears in a slightly altered form as "How *Native Son* Was Born" in *Writing the American Classics*.)

All four contributions to *New Essays on* Native Son measure up to the high standard set by Kinnamon's introduction. John M. Reilly in "Giving Bigger a Voice: The Politics of Narrative in *Native Son*" (pp. 35–62) discusses the accuracy of mimetic detail in the book, but argues that "to take up the challenge presented to him by the political configurations of American discourse on race, Richard Wright had to do more than create a narrative that would be recognizably accurate in its localized detail" (p. 41). According to Reilly, Wright achieves political as well as artistic goals through "signifying"—"a distinctive language practice in Black English whereby an innocuous statement outwardly conforming to conventional expectation carries within it a critical or satiric judgment offered from the perspective of the ostensibly powerless social subordinate" (p. 41). Trudier Harris in "Native Sons and Foreign Daughters" (pp. 63–

84) demonstrates how black female characters in the novel conflict with Bigger only superficially while they remain "true to Wright's notion of what black women are and what they believe: they will use the larger world in quiet, unassuming ways in their efforts to carry out their mundane wills in the black community" (p. 64). Houston A. Baker, Jr., also addresses Wright's conception of black women in "Richard Wright and the Dynamics of Place in Afro-American Literature" (pp. 85–116). Through a complex analysis of Wright's *12 Million Black Voices,* Baker claims that "Wright allowed the astonishing technological power of the West, represented by factories and machines, to blind him to the woman's (and by implication, 'folk') power of a black nation within" (p. 105). Craig Werner's essay, "Bigger's Blues: *Native Son* and the Articulation of Afro-American Modernism" (pp. 117–52), considers Wright's novel "specifically in the matrix of Euro-American modernism" and seeks "to reclaim access to a modernist tradition compatible with the communal, kinetic, and political (though usually not ideological) imperatives of the Afro-American blues tradition" (p. 119).

In "The Blindness Motif in Richard Wright's *Native Son*" (*CLAJ* 34:44–57), Willene P. Taylor details the "limited vision" of all of Wright's major characters which results in metaphorical blindness causing the white characters to suffer from lack of psychological insight, and the black characters to "lack the ability to understand the reality of their predicament." Onita Estes-Hicks in "The Quest for a Place in Two Mississippi Autobiographies: *Black Boy* and *Coming of Age in Mississippi*" (*CLAJ* 34:59–67) looks at the similarities between the lives of Anne Moody and Wright in terms of their "singular preoccupation focussed on escaping the modern-day slavery which their plantation origins had in store for them" (p. 60). George Uba in "Only a Man: The Folkloric Subtext of Richard Wright's 'Down by the Riverside'" (*ELWIU* 17:261–69) offers a convincing argument for African American folklore as a key to appreciating an often neglected story from Wright's collection, *Uncle Tom's Children.* According to Uba, the folktale structure in "Down by the Riverside" "justifies the seeming contortions of the plot while accommodating Mann's actions within a meaningful frame of reference" (p. 262). By identifying African folk types such as the trickster, the "Bad Nigger," and the perverse god, and showing how these characters operate in the text, Uba proves that Wright "successfully compresses an entire history of oppression into the course of a single day, defining the terms under which blacks were doomed to compete, while evoking—without moral condemnation—the means they employed in order to survive" (p. 268).

Several articles address elements of characterization in Ralph Ellison's *Invisible Man*. In "Ellison and the Twentieth-Century American Scholar" (*SAF* 17 [1989]:93–106), Eleanor Lyons presents a persuasive portrait of Ellison's narrator as an "ironic counterpart" to Emerson's ideal scholar (p. 94). However, by the end of the novel (which is really its beginning), when the narrator has gone underground to think things over and to figure out his own life, he has begun to live up to the self-reliant standards of Emerson's hero. Albertha Sistrunk-Krakue's discussion, "The Significance of Female Characters in *Invisible Man*" (*CLAJ* 34:23–31), does little more than state the obvious about "a disparate portrayal of white and black women characters by Ellison in *Invisible Man*" (p. 26).

Langston Hughes scholars will welcome the publication of Thomas A. Mikolyzk's *Langston Hughes: A Bio-Bibliography* (Greenwood) which should be an important resource for courses and discourses in American literature and African American history. The work includes a chronology of events in Hughes's life, as well as a brief biography. The four major divisions of the annotations cover books by Hughes, shorter works by Hughes, books about him, and articles about him. Mikolyzk has cited collectible published works, contemporary reviews, scholarly articles, book-length studies, and dissertations. Two appendixes add to the book's usefulness: the first provides an alphabetical listing of Hughes's works, including place and date of publication, and the second describes special collections in the United States of Hughes's personal material as well as detailing *The Langston Hughes Review*, the official journal of the Langston Hughes Society.

Another important contribution to Hughes studies is R. Baxter Miller's *The Art and Imagination of Langston Hughes* (Kentucky, 1989). Miller characterizes the "deep tropes" of Hughes's literary world as tragicomic because the author's purpose was that of mediator between dreams of freedom and social limitations. In a discussion which cuts across the various genres of Hughes's oeuvre, Miller argues that the writer is present as a "narrative self as well as an ironist and moralist. Though he was a social and political rebel, he was an early deconstructionist as well: he subverted the very conventions of genre through which tradition and modernity have sought to confine the free imagination" (p. 5). Miller's study does not claim to be comprehensive, but it offers clear analysis of the lyricism of Hughes's prose and the historicism of his poetry.

Formal experimentation which subverts the conventions of genre is also the focal point of Shelley Fisher Fishkin's essay, "The Borderlands of Culture: Writing by W. E. B. Du Bois, James Agee, Tillie Olsen, and Gloria Anzaldua," in *Literary Journalism in the Twentieth Century,* ed. Norman Sims (Oxford). Fishkin remarks that Du Bois, Agee, Olsen, and Anzaldua produce "passionate cultural reports" (p. 134) in their nonfiction which not only expand the boundaries of cultural understanding in America, but also establish new standards for journalism in the 20th century. All four of these writers employ distinctive formal techniques to "defamiliarize the familiar, explode conventional expectations, break down the reader's sense of equilibrium, surprise, challenge, and throw the reader off guard" (p. 135). Another essay which examines the journalistic accomplishments of a literary figure is John S. Wright's "Sterling Brown's Folk Odyssey" in *American Literature, Culture, and Ideology* (Peter Lang), ed. Beverly R. Voloshin. An informative discussion briefly outlines the history of African American folklore studies and explains Brown's involvement in the Federal Writer's Project which led to his collection of ex-slave narratives. Wright identifies Brown's approach of "correlating folklore with social and ethnic history" (p. 338) as a major contribution to black folklore studies.

ii Southerners

a. Erskine Caldwell, Thomas Wolfe, and William Styron   *Erskine Caldwell Reconsidered,* ed. Edwin T. Arnold (Miss.), contains six new essays on Caldwell's life and works and interviews with his first and fourth wives. Reprinted here is John Hersey's "Tribute to Erskine Caldwell" (pp. 9–13), a speech delivered at the American Academy of Arts and Letters shortly after Caldwell's death. Harvey L. Klevar in "Caldwell's Women" (pp. 15–35) claims that "the catalyst which first fueled Caldwell's creative surge and later compromised it was his essential dependence on women. More than anything else, he yearned for their love and approval" (p. 15). At times, Klevar seems to blame the women in Caldwell's life for demanding either too much or too little from the enigmatic writer. Also included in this collection are Klevar's "Interview with Helen Caldwell Cushman" (pp. 86–97) and Edwin T. Arnold's "Interview with Virginia Caldwell" (pp. 99–110). Henry Terrie's "Caldwell at

Dartmouth" (pp. 36–41) details Caldwell's association with Dartmouth College, as well as the history and contents of the Caldwell collection there. Fujisato Kitajima in "Caldwell in Japan" (pp. 42–28) explains the writer's popularity in Japan. Kitajima credits translators who promoted Caldwell's work, but he also notes that American GIs of the occupation army after World War II read Caldwell paperbacks and passed them on to the Japanese.

The remaining essays in *Erskine Caldwell Reconsidered* deal critically with Caldwell's fiction. Sylvia J. Cook in "Caldwell's Fiction: Growing Towards Trash?" (pp. 49–58) suggests several reasons for Caldwell's artistic demise in the 1940s and proposes that his frustration with readers' responses evolved into intensified conflict with critics and "an increasing tendency to spell out in bluntly naturalistic terms his meanings and morals, without the complicating contexts of strangeness and unpredictability that marked the earlier work" (p. 55). In "Caldwell Stage and Screen" (pp. 59–72), William Howard argues that dramatic adaptations of Caldwell's work distort the writer's artistic and social vision. Howard analyzes specific scenes from *Tobacco Road* and *God's Little Acre* to argue that playwrights and filmmakers "packaged their versions [of the South] to correspond with popular audiences' preconceptions" (p. 59). In "Canonize Caldwell's *Georgia Boy:* A Case for Resurrection" (pp. 73–85), Ronald Wesley Hoag presents a thorough and convincing case for the literary integrity of *Georgia Boy,* the story cycle which Caldwell himself touted as his best fiction.

In addition to the usual Thomas Wolfe minutia, this year's *TWN* provides a memoir by Margaret Roberts, Wolfe's favorite teacher, " 'An Uncommon Urchin,' Thomas Wolfe: A Memoir" (*TWN* 14, i:8–15). Wolfe critics will more likely be interested in the fine assortment of critical essays in the journal this year. In *"Look Homeward Angel:* An American Masterpiece" (14, i:1–7), John L. Idol, Jr., while admitting to the flaws of Wolfe's first novel, argues for its place among the best works of American literature because "it gives us ways of looking at ourselves and what we have done to ourselves as a nation" (p. 1). Richard S. Kennedy's "Thomas Wolfe, Coleridge, and Supernaturalism" (14, i:27–32) deals with the supernatural elements in a one-act play written by Wolfe during his college years, and the young author's explorations into the spiritual world evident in three college compositions written while Wolfe was studying the Romantic poets under Professor John Livingston Lowes at Harvard. Mary Ann Mannino explores Wolfe's "approach-avoidance attitudes toward women," including an analysis of George Webber's fantasy female in "Thomas Wolfe's Ambivalence Toward Women in *The Web and the Rock*" (14, i:34–43); and Ted Slaughter looks at sources for Wolfe's "dark celestial imagery, and [themes of] the death of a beloved brother, and the search for a father" in "Thomas Wolfe and the *Epic of Gilgamesh*" (14, i:44–52). In "American Motif in 'O Lost': Crucial Material Deleted from *Look Homeward, Angel*" (14, ii:34–39), Margaret Kimpel Bokelman argues that the unpublished material from the original manuscript of *Look Homeward, Angel* establishes that Wolfe "had already begun to envision himself as a representative American" (p. 34) as early as the preliminary compositional stages of his first novel.

Wolfe's second novel, commonly accepted as his first attempt to write a specifically American fiction, is the focus of both John Hagan's "An Approach to Thomas Wolfe's *Of Time and the River*" (*TWN* 14, ii:3–16) and Terry Roberts's "Irreconcilable Talents: Thomas Wolfe's Struggle to Compose *Of Time and the River*" (*MissQ* 43:23–32). Arguing that the novel has been greatly undervalued by critics, Hagan examines Eugene Gant's struggle for transcendence through art and Wolfe's emphasis on the contrasts between the permanence of earth and the transience of earth's inhabitants. Roberts, too, defends Wolfe's second novel as worthy of critical study, proposing, however, that consideration of it requires scholars to "differentiate between Wolfe's evocative, dramatic, often experimental *best* and his verbose, insecure, often hurried *worst*" (p. 23).

Valarie Meliotes Arms highlights the reasons for William Styron's popularity in France in "A French View of William Styron: Topicality vs. Universality" (*SoQ* 29, i:47–70). Meliotes dubs Styron "a moralist who remains free from allegiance to chapels and schools" (p. 47) and argues that Styron's lack of concern for topicality and his search for universal themes appeal to French readers. In " 'a new father, a new home': Styron, Faulkner, and Southern Revisionism" (*SNNTS* 22:308–22), Christopher Metress applies Harold Bloom's notion of "anxiety of influence" to Styron and Faulkner to suggest that Styron's confrontation with *The Sound and the Fury* is more complex than an impulse to complete Faulkner or to fill in imaginative gaps left empty by Faulkner. Metress maintains that in *Lie Down in Darkness* Styron uses repetitions which appear to mimic Faulkner's work, but "the repetitions give way to discontinuities and the stance of *The Sound and the Fury* is undone. Eventually the discontinuities envelop the repetitions and *The Sound and the Fury* is emptied of its priority, its originality" (p. 315).

b. Zora Neale Hurston In *New Essays on* Their Eyes Were Watching God (Cambridge), Michael Awkward, editor of the anthology, gives a thorough account of the novel's critical history (pp. 1–27) and credits the emergence of feminist criticism and Afrocentric criticism in the 1970s with establishing the canonicity of *Their Eyes Were Watching God*. The strength of Awkward's essay is its analysis of specific forces which account for both the obscurity of Hurston's novel and its emergence. Robert Hemenway, Hurston's biographer, questions whether or not white patronage affected Hurston's work. In a fine essay, "The Personal Dimension in *Their Eyes Were Watching God*" (pp. 29–49), Hemenway emphasizes that all of Hurston's major creative work came after her patronage period (1927–32); nevertheless, patronage did shape Hurston's artistic vision in that it gave her a counterforce, "a foil that forces the writer into articulating the *difference* between his or her environment and that of the patron" (p. 36). Nellie McKay's "'Crayon Enlargements of Life': Zora Neale Hurston's *Their Eyes Were Watching God* as Autobiography" (pp. 51–70) reveals how "writer Hurston—the experiencing self—and character Janie—the narrative self—take us on a journey of personal discovery to the place where language, gender, and culture merge to give full voice to the otherwise often-marginalized black female self" (p. 54). In "The Politics of Fiction, Anthropology, and the Folk: Zora Neale Hurston" (pp. 71–93), Hazel V. Carby expresses her interest "in the contemporary cultural process of the inclusion of Hurston into the academy" (p. 72), a process Carby finds as interesting as Hurston's writing. Carby presents a clear analysis of Hurston's involvement with "the cultural struggle among black intellectuals to define exactly what the people were that were going to become the representatives of the folk" (p. 77). Hurston's romanticized depiction of a black rural consciousness, argues Carby, is the reason that *Their Eyes* has become such a privileged text in the 1980s and 1990s, a time of intense urban crisis and conflict. To conclude this excellent anthology of essays, Rachel Blau DuPlessis in "Power, Judgment, and Narrative in a Work of Zora Neale Hurston: Feminist Cultural Studies" (pp. 95–123) discusses the paradoxical nature of Janie's character. DuPlessis argues that "Janie can be seen from the very first moments of the novel to be made of signs," and that "these signs of Janie are constructed by Hurston to be conflictual and heterogeneous in the array of race, gender role, age, class, and sexual markers" (p. 95).

In "Myth and History: Discourse of Origins in Zora Neale Hurston and Maya Angelou" (*BALF* 24:221–34), Elizabeth Fox-Genovese identifies sources of personal myth as well as collective wisdom of the oral culture that appear in *Dust Tracks on a Road*. She warns readers to exercise caution in reference to Hurston's "facts" since Hurston's "Northern education and, in its wake, membership in the literate culture of the nation shaped her expectations of her readers and, in some measure, shaped her representation of herself" (p. 228). Along this same line, Alice A. Deck's reading of *Dust Tracks* may answer questions that critics have about the biographical facts of the book. In "Autoethnography: Zora Neale Hurston, Noni Jabavu, and Cross-Disciplinary Discourse" (*BALF* 24:237–56), Deck identifies Hurston's role as that of a cultural mediator rather than an autobiographer (p. 239). Pointing to the dialogic, polyphonic structure of Hurston's work, Deck argues convincingly that *Dust Tracks* "consists of an intricate interplay of the introspective personal engagement expected of an autobiography and the self-effacement expected of cultural descriptions and explications associated with ethnography" (p. 238).

Discourse analysis is also central to Tejumola Olaniyan's essay "God's Weeping Eyes: Hurston and the Anti-Patriarchal Form" (*Obsidian* 5, ii:30–45). Olaniyan spurns Richard Wright's designation of Hurston's novel (no theme, no message, no thought) to argue for the "grand theme and thoughtful message" of the book. Olaniyan delineates Hurston's antipatriarchal gestures through an analysis of space and subversion of space and a discussion of the double-voiced discourse of Janie's narrative. Werner Sollors also contends with the negative response to Hurston's work by black male writers. In "Of Mules and Mares in a Land of Difference; or, Quadrupeds All?" (*AQ* 42:167–90), Sollors discusses an uncollected essay by Hurston, "Court Order Can't Make Races Mix," which appeared in the *Orlando Sentinel* in 1955 and may have sparked resentment against Hurston for her political conservatism that did not appeal to black male writers of the time. Sandra Pouchet Paquet's essay, "The Ancestor as Foundation in *Their Eyes Were Watching God* and *Tar Baby*" (*Callaloo* 13:499–515), offers another favorable assessment of Hurston's work, explaining that Janie, who is alienated from her culture and sexuality by Nanny, becomes connected to these essential elements of self through her marriage to Tea Cake and her immersion in the "folk" of the Everglades.

c. Eudora Welty   Most useful in this year's numbers of the *Eudora Welty Newsletter* (vol. 14) are a bibliographic checklist as well as lists of textual variants of three short stories: "The Wide Net," "A Visit of Charity," and "Livvie." Welty stories "Death of a Traveling Salesman" and "A Still Moment" were the subjects of brief commentary in *Notes on Mississippi Writers,* which also published three article-length pieces of Welty criticism: Carolyn J. Kates's "Apollo and Dionysos: The Mysterious Duality of Eudora Welty's Fiction" (22:1–13), Ronald H. McKinney's "The Metafictional Art of Eudora Welty's Autobiography" (22:15–27), and Jonathan Bates's "Welty's Improvisation of Powerhouse: Is This the Portrayal Fats Would Have Wanted?" (22:81–94). Of these three essays, Bates's takes the most innovative approach to Welty's work. Enlisting Bakhtin's concept of heteroglossia to distinguish between the author's view, the narrator's view, and the central character's situation in "Powerhouse," Bates argues persuasively that "Welty's narrator changes to show the variety of people that Powerhouse encounters, and to demonstrate the effectiveness of his improvised retorts to their shallow impressions of him. She fashions her blacks to fit her purposes, but they are no more primitive, and in most cases they are more human, tha[n] the whites in 'Powerhouse' " (p. 84). Bates, however, needlessly complicates the issue with references to Fats Waller's biography.

That critics are producing feminist readings of Welty's fiction comes as no surprise; but Price Caldwell's rather subversive application of feminist criticism to two of Welty's short stories is both surprising and interesting. In "Sexual Politics in Welty's 'Moon Lake' and 'Petrified Man' " (*SAF* 18:171–81), Caldwell insists that the evil of patriarchal oppression in Welty's stories has not been imposed on modern culture by the patriarchs but that the perception of evil "is a sign of the paranoia of the culture out of which it comes. For the culture Eudora Welty describes is matriarchal, not patriarchal . . ." (p. 172). Harriet Pollack's complex application of reader-response theory, "On Welty's Use of Allusion: Expectations and Their Revision in 'The Wide Net,' *The Robber Bridegroom* and 'At the Landing' " (*SoQ* 29, i:5–31), contends that mere source hunting is an inadequate response to Welty's fiction: "What needs to be attended instead is the relationship of her sources to her new text: that is, the work performed when two or more narratives are simultaneously brought to a reader's mind" (p. 3).

Perhaps just as useful as Pollack's approach, though tactically less complex, are essays found in *American Literature, Southern Folklore,* and the *Mississippi Quarterly.* Gail L. Mortimer's exercise in good, old-fashioned New Criticism, "Image and Myth in Eudora Welty's *The*

Optimist's Daughter (*AL* 62:617–33), identifies four major "image patterns" in the novel (vision and blindness, rushing water, hands, birds), then discusses their significance in relation to the text's "wider mythic substructure" (p. 633). Loretta Martin Murrey's essay, "From Religious Ritual to Family Ritual: The 'Holiness of Life' in Eudora Welty's *Losing Battles*" (*SFolk* 47:239–47), reveals how Welty depicts holiness in the social ritual of Granny's birthday celebration while ridiculing the lack of holiness in the various religious rituals which are cataloged in *Losing Battles*. In "Modernity and the Literary Plantation: Eudora Welty's *Delta Wedding*" (*MissQ* 43:163–72), Albert J. Devlin points to the sociocultural influences of World War II on the composition of *Delta Wedding* to frame his argument for the book as a "new form." Devlin contends that Welty fuses the ideology of modernity and the conventions of plantation writing in order to address "a civilization beset by wrenching violence to mind and spirit" and to offer that world "the hope of preserving a humane order" (p. 171).

In addition to "Some Talk about Autobiography: An Interview with Eudora Welty" (*SoR* 26:81–88) and a note on *Photographs,* "Welty's Snapshots: Motions in Place" (*MissQ* 43:237–39), Sally Wolff also contributes an essay, "Eudora Welty's Autobiographical Duet: *The Optimist's Daughter* and *One Writer's Beginnings*" (pp. 78–92) to *Located Lives,* ed. J. Bill Berry (Georgia). Wolff argues convincingly that *"The Optimist's Daughter* and *One Writer's Beginnings,* taken together, reveal Welty more fully as autobiographer than either one separately can" (p. 81). Wolff points out the difficulties in discerning fully the autobiographical nature of Welty's art "partly because the writer is an extremely private person who believes that knowing the life is not essential for understanding the fiction" (p. 79), a critical stance for which Ruth Vande Kieft applauds Welty in "Eudora Welty and the Right to Privacy" (*MissQ* 43:475–78). Vande Kieft rails against recent assessments of Welty's work by both Carolyn Heilbrun and Frank Lentricchia, claiming that "the two critics seem ignorant of Welty's own theory and practice, which is often contradictory, paradoxical, above all embracing of double truths" (p. 475).

Welty's novels are the focus of *Serious Daring from Within: Female Narrative Strategies in Eudora Welty's Novels* (Greenwood), wherein Franziska Gygax makes the unspectacular claim that Welty's narrative techniques establish female authority and frequently undermine patriarchal values. The book is useful for an overview of the criticism related to

Welty's novels and an introduction to Weltian narratology. Gygax emphasizes the exclusion of the male point of view in *Delta Wedding* and notes that the re-vision of myths in *The Golden Apples* goes beyond merely placing female characters in the roles of heroes. Gygax argues that Welty questions "the exclusiveness of the relationship between the male creative spirit and the female passive muse" (p. 46) by transforming male-gendered myths. Focusing on Miss Eckhart's role in *The Golden Apples,* Gygax contends that "Welty's theme of the wanderer, the artist, and the foreigner is as complex as it is in *Ulysses,* but it is much more decisively linked with the question of gender and its social implications" (p. 47). The social implications of "unmediated dialogue" (with references to Bakhtinian theory) dominate the analysis of *Losing Battles.* Most useful in this section is the distinction between Jack's and Gloria's speech behavior and the speech acts of the family circle during the reunion. Gygax's repetition of terms such as "locution," "illocution," and "perlocution," however, seems superfluous and gets in the way of an otherwise succinct analysis.

d. Carson McCullers, Flannery O'Connor, and Katherine Anne Porter

In "Cafes and Community in Three Carson McCullers Novels" (*SAF* 18:233–39), Kenneth D. Chamlee makes an intriguing claim that "despite the apparent failure of cafes as places of authentic communion, Carson McCullers does not employ them as symbols of despair" (p. 238). The brief article raises some interesting points but can do little else but generalize with such a broad topic as the café as a characterization device in *The Heart Is a Lonely Hunter, The Member of the Wedding,* and *The Ballad of the Sad Cafe.* Virginia Spencer Carr's fine book, *Understanding Carson McCullers* (So. Car.), supplements a brief overview of McCullers's life with chapters on each book, the plays, and the short fiction. The biographical sketch stresses McCullers's consistent commitment to her art in spite of a very troubled life. Each chapter on the fiction begins with useful information fixing the composition of the piece into a biographical framework by noting significant events in the author's life at the time of composition. Though some of the essays are heavy on plot summary, when Carr analyzes, she does so clearly and concisely, tempering the sensationalism of the author's biography with perceptive critical analysis and a useful summary of important criticism.

Tony Magistrale develops a provocative argument for a nonmodernist view of Flannery O'Connor's fictional world as a cosmos which operates according to Hieronymus Bosch or Dante. In "'I'm Alien to a Great Deal': Flannery O'Connor and the Modernist Ethic" (*JAmS* 24:93–98), Magistrale points out that the characters in O'Connor's stories who are the victims of psychopaths and thieves resemble O'Connor's readers— "'well-adjusted' landowners and college-educated humanists for whom God is either an unapprehended reality or an easily dismissed theoretical abstraction" (p. 94). Thus, the violence inflicted on the characters is also an assault on the reader's "intellectual and political comprehension" (p. 93). Along this same line, Kathleen G. Ochshorn in "A Cloak of Grace: Contradictions in 'A Good Man Is Hard to Find'" (*SAF* 18:113–17) explains that "O'Connor chalked up all the misreadings and confusion [about her stories] to the spiritual shortcomings of the modern reader" (p. 113). Ochshorn details the critical reactions to "A Good Man Is Hard to Find" and O'Connor's claims about the meaning of the story to argue that "the complexity of this story in part explains its broad appeal to audiences who do not see [it] as a parable of grace" (p. 114). In "Flannery O'Connor's World Without Pity" (*NConL* 20, ii:8–9), Diane Vipond notes that the reader of "A Good Man Is Hard to Find" is shocked "into a recognition that pity . . . must replace fear" (p. 9) if contemporary society is to overcome the pettiness and cruelty which pervades it. Joseph Church comments on this same subject in "An Abuse of the Imagination in Flannery O'Connor's 'A Good Man Is Hard to Find'" (*NConL* 20, 3:8–10) by focusing on the limitations of the grandmother's imaginative capabilities and her failure "to establish responsible—not picturesque—connections with a needful world" (p. 10). Steve Perisho looks at another popular O'Connor story in "The Structure of Flannery O'Connor's 'Revelation'" (*NConL* 20, 4:5–7), noting the parallels between descriptions of the doctor's waiting room and the pig parlor—similarities which contribute to the thematic unity and irony of the narrative.

Janis P. Stout's *Strategies of Reticence* (Virginia) includes a fine discussion of "Noon Wine." In "Katherine Anne Porter and the Reticent Style" (pp. 112–46), Stout selects "Noon Wine" as the story most central to the point she is making about the association between Porter's theme and style. Through a close reading of the text and perceptive analysis of characters, Stout demonstrates that Porter values reticence and distrusts talkativeness. Stout links her observations about the fiction to biographical details of Porter's life, specifically the author's sociocultural training.

e. Caroline Gordon, Evelyn Scott, Peter Taylor, Robert Penn Warren, and Others *The Southern Quarterly* devoted issues (28, iii and 28, iv) to Caroline Gordon and Evelyn Scott, respectively. Guest editors Eleanor H. Beiswenger and Steven T. Ryan collected material from the 1985 Gordon/Scott Symposium held at Austin Peay State University in Clarksville, Tennessee. Danforth Ross in "Caroline Gordon, Uncle Rob and My Mother" (28, iii:9–22) describes the ritual of everyday life at Merimont, the home of Gordon's grandmother, which he believes is championed by Gordon in her fiction. The influence of locale on Gordon's work is also the subject of "Benfolly in Fact and Fiction" by Charles M. Waters (28, iii:23–32). Waters relates a history of the estate, "Benfolly," including a catalog of the writers such as Malcolm Cowley, Katherine Anne Porter, Robert Penn Warren, and Ford Madox Ford who visited Tate and Gordon there. Deborah Core in "Caroline Gordon, Ford Madox Ford: A Shared Passion for the Novel" (28, iii:33–42) describes the relationship between Ford and Gordon and identifies what Core calls "Ford's legacies to Caroline Gordon": dedication to one's craft, a careful stewardship of one's gifts, and a "passion for the novel" as a form more worthy of a writer's talent than the short story (pp. 34–35).

Quite appropriate for a publication which focuses so much attention on an author's life is the inclusion of an essay by Gordon's biographer, Veronica Makowsky. In "Caroline Gordon on Women Writing: A Contradiction in Terms?" (28, iii:43–52), Makowsky examines the ways in which Gordon "internalized her culture's attitudes toward women and writing, both in her life and in her work" (p. 43). "Caroline Gordon's 'Old Red'" by Ashley Brown (28, iii:53–62) reports the publication history of the story and its function in the story cycle about a single character, Aleck Maury, the subject of later novels and stories. Brown argues effectively for "Old Red" as a microcosm of the whole cycle and as one of Gordon's best stories. Larry Allums in "From Classical to Christian: Versions of the Hero in the Novels of Caroline Gordon" (28, iii:63–70) builds on a common assessment of Gordon's work that notes a "striking shift of artistic method" around 1947, the time of Gordon's conversion to Roman Catholicism (p. 63). Allums maintains, however, that Gordon's strategy as exemplified in *The Women on the Porch*, published three years before her conversion, and evident in later works as well, is to regard "the Christian God's plan for mankind—the Incarnation—as the lens through which to read the Greek myths anew" (p. 69). Anne Boyle's "The Promise of Polyphony, the Monotony of Monologue:

Voice and Silence in Caroline Gordon's Later Novels" (28, iii:71–87) is an excellent Bakhtinian treatment of Gordon's fiction. Framing the discussion with a biographical incident—a meeting in Paris in 1928 between Gordon and Gertrude Stein—Boyle goes on to show that Stein's female characters bear out Stein's beliefs that an empowering voice is essential, as in *Ida,* where "to be a self-reflective, beautiful and inarticulate woman is really not 'enough'" (p. 72). In Gordon's world, however, "it is particularly difficult and perhaps unnatural for the female to achieve voice" (p. 73). The issue closes with a photographic essay, "Clarksville Women" by Bruce Childs, which is prefaced by Steven T. Ryan's "An Interview with Bruce Childs" (28, iii:89–96).

In the introduction to the *SoQ's* issue on Evelyn Scott, Beiswenger and Ryan describe Scott as "a rebellious, individualistic and experimental personality. Her stance derived from a rejection of America's early-century bravado" (28, iv:5). Robert L. Welker, in "The Love-Death Vision of Evelyn Scott, an Overview" (28, iv:9–23), reviews the psychological, expressionistic, and imagist techniques for which Scott was known in her "hey-day" (p. 10). Welker's analysis is best when dealing with biography, relating specific developments in Scott's artistic technique to particular traumatic personal events which influenced *Escapades into Living*. In "Defying the Stars and Challenging the Moon: The Early Correspondences of Evelyn Scott and Jean Stafford" (28, iv:25–34), Mary V. Davidson highlights the forty years' worth of letters from Scott which Stafford saved, and she credits Scott with nurturing Stafford's artistic growth. Ryan's "The Terroristic Universe of *The Narrow House*" (28, iv:35–44) compares Scott to John Hawkes: "both see human sexuality as inseparable from problems of self-awareness and repression" (p. 35). Scott's early fiction, says Ryan, "creates a terroristic universe and equates the destruction of natural sexuality to the destruction of life," linking individual perversity to puritanism (p. 35). This issue also includes "Selected Letters of Evelyn Scott" (pp. 63–76); an essay by Scott, "Writing for Children" (pp. 55–61), which was originally published in *The Horn Book;* and "Evelyn Scott's Fiction for the Young" (pp. 45–54), in which Peggy Bach reviews several of Scott's books for children.

Both Allen Tate and Peter Taylor were noticed by critics this year. Fred Chappell in a far-ranging article, "A Choice of Romantics: Allen Tate's *The Fathers*" (*Shenandoah* 40, iv:30–42), relates Chappell's reading of *The Fathers* to his childhood in North Carolina, only to arrive, somehow, at a useful discussion of Poe's influence on Tate's novel. David M.

Robinson in "Engaging the Past: Peter Taylor's 'The Old Forest'" (*SLJ* 22:63–77) offers a feminist explication of Taylor's story arguing that the women in the narrator's life show Nat how fragile his world of social power really is. Albert J. Griffith's revised edition of his 1970 study, *Peter Taylor* (Twayne), will satisfy Southern literature enthusiasts who have been waiting for substantial evaluations of Taylor's latest fiction. Griffith has expanded his treatment of Taylor's canon to include discussions of *In the Miro District* (1977), *The Old Forest* (1985), and *A Summons to Memphis* (1986).

Robert Penn Warren's achievements as critic, poet, and fiction writer are the subject of several critical publications. *Talking with Robert Penn Warren*, ed. Floyd C. Watkins, John T. Hiers, and Mary Louise Weaks (Georgia), brings together 24 reprinted interviews which took place from 1950 through 1987. The collection opens with "A Self-Interview" which first appeared in the *New York Herald Tribune Book Review* on October 11, 1953. The chronologically arranged interviews have been edited to highlight Warren's voice—to accentuate his theory of fiction, his philosophy of history, and his particular vision of America. An important addition to Warren scholarship, *Talking with Robert Penn Warren* makes many of the author/critic's insights about literature and history accessible in one volume. Literature and history in Warren's poetry is the central concern of *Robert Penn Warren and the American Imagination* by Hugh Ruppersburg (Georgia). Ruppersburg points to a major paradox in Warren's patterning of American history—the depersonalization of modern man is "the ironic fate of a nation whose Declaration of Independence and Constitution served to *personalize* and empower the individual" (p. 10). Though Ruppersburg devotes most of the book to Warren's poetry, specifically *Brother to Dragons, Audubon,* and *Chief Joseph,* students of Warren's fiction will also be interested in the discussion of "agrarian" as it applies to Warren in particular. Ruppersburg claims that Warren transformed himself "from regional agrarian to agrarian of the Western world" by viewing the South from a "more critical and objective perspective than he might otherwise have managed" (p. 36).

Focusing specifically on Warren's fiction, Randolph Paul Runyon's *The Taciturn Text: The Fiction of Robert Penn Warren* (Ohio State) examines each of the 10 novels, as well as the story collection *The Circus in the Attic,* as self-referential texts. The close readings of the fiction are reasonable and often original, though at times Runyon uses the term "text" rather broadly. For example, the analysis of the relationship between Willie Stark and Jack Burden in *All the King's Men* centers on Willie's mysterious wink as "a text whose only decipherable message is that it may not *be* a text . . ." (p. 64). However, the discussion of how Jack seeks to decipher Willie's "indecipherable sign" (p. 62) leads to insightful conclusions about the "symbolic network of Warren's novels of the father's power to produce an indecipherable text" (p. 67). Runyon also relies heavily on Freud's *Interpretation of Dreams*. Emphasizing the role of the unconscious in creation, Runyon supplies a number of examples from the novels and stories to illustrate his claim that Warren's narratives "are not only sometimes *about* dreams but are possibly constructed *like* dreams" (p. 5).

iii Easterners

a. Saul Bellow Bellow criticism this year ranges from articles which look at single stories to books which assess the writer's entire career. Ellen Pifer's *Saul Bellow: Against the Grain* (Penn.) fits the latter category. Pifer contends that Bellow's fiction goes "against the grain of contemporary culture and its secular pieties" (p. 2) by presenting in novel after novel his belief in the soul, a thesis which is applied to Bellow's work from 1944 through 1989. Taking issue with Charles Newman's (*The Post-Modern Aura*) assessment of Bellow's fiction as harking back to traditional 19th-century realism in search of a dead past or a dead culture, Pifer claims that Bellow challenges "the authority of culture itself," that the "massive accumulation of material fact and concrete detail" in the fiction undermines itself, "subverting the realist's traditional faith in material circumstances and the world of appearance" (p. 3). Pifer notes tendencies toward a transcendent self in Bellow's fiction long before *Seize the Day* when such a vision was recognized by other critics. Using hindsight as a rather interesting critical perspective, Pifer identifies a psychic rift caused by the secular/soul tensions throughout Bellow's career.

Michael K. Glenday's *Saul Bellow and the Decline of Humanism* (Macmillan) also deals comprehensively with Bellow's career. Glenday argues that Bellow uses the novel to expose "the inauthenticity of the everyday, that system of reality which is dominant in American life" (p. 1). In Bellow's fiction, the worlds of business, technology, and entrepreneurial guile cater to scientific rationalism and stifle humanistic sensibility. Glenday seeks to remove Bellow from the "humanist never-never land" (p. 5) where critics such as Daniel Fuchs and Jonathan

Wilson have placed him. According to Glenday, Bellow rejects the humanist ethic: "his heroes are humanists *manque,* rejected and defeated by an American ethos so inimical to their basic human needs that they are forced to adopt various strategies of withdrawal" (p. 11).

Jonathan Wilson in *Herzog: The Limits of Ideas* (Twayne) directs his critical inquiries toward beginning and veteran Bellow scholars alike. From the succinct opening chapters which establish the historical and critical contexts of Bellow's third novel, to the final chapter which addresses the issue of postmodern, self-creating characterization in the book, Wilson's discussion of *Herzog* is informative and interesting. The full treatment of individual female characters challenges a common critical complaint that there are no "real women" in *Herzog* and leads to a thorough analysis of "the female realm" of Herzog's world (pp. 21–37). Wilson also answers complaints about the structure of the novel by drawing parallels between Bellow's plot movements and Hegel's prime triad of thesis, antithesis, and synthesis (p. 79). Wilson effectively examines critical issues raised by readers of the novel since 1964 and poses new questions for today's critics.

The Saul Bellow Journal offers a potpourri of material about Bellow's life, personal responses to his fiction, and some serious critical commentary. Several contributions focus on elements of irony in the fiction. Karl F. Knight in "Saul Bellow's *More Die of Heartbreak:* Point of View and Irony" (9, i:1–20) renders a close reading of Bellow's dark sexual comedy to point out that "the dismal irony dominating the book is that the theorizing of Kenneth does not simply fail to bring order to his world; instead, it is a pair of blinders making him vulnerable to the assaults of reality" (p. 20). Elaine B. Safer's "Degrees of Comic Irony in *A Theft* and *The Bellarosa Connection*" (9, ii:1–17) details Bellow's ironic juxtaposition of romantic ideas and pragmatic behavior, while "Ironies and Insights in *The Bellarosa Connection*" by Coral Fenster (9, ii:20–27) does little more than express a personal enthusiasm for Bellow's work and summarize the plot. In "The Ontic, Epistemic and Semantic Nature of Saul Bellow's *Herzog*" (9, ii:38–53), Suzanne Lundquist identifies Herzog as an ironist in search of a final vocabulary which will define his reality in absolute terms.

Discourse analysis provides the critical framework for other essays in the *Journal*. Marianne Friedrich's "Bellow's Renaissance Courtier: Woody Selbst in 'A Silver Dish'" (9, i:21–35) looks at Bellow's use of different levels of speech to achieve "tension between an intensely imagined personal, individual, framed-in world, and its projection—by way of detail—against another reality that transcends the limitations of time and place" (p. 35). In "Mental Travel in *Henderson the Rain King*" (9, ii:54–67), Faye I. Kuzna asserts that storytelling, which is Henderson's means of mental travel, functions in the novel in two ways to perpetuate dialogue: "to give voice to subconscious, previously unexpressed feelings and attitudes and to show Henderson repositioning himself away from the privileged voice of World War II heroism" (p. 57).

Gregory Johnson in "Jewish Assimilation and Codes of Manners in Saul Bellow's 'The Old System' " (*SAJL* 9:48–60) argues that the themes of this much-neglected short story are more explicitly Jewish than those of Bellow's more famous works. Johnson insists that "The Old System" ranks "as Bellow's most unified and concentrated treatment of the national behavioral problem dramatized by Jewish assimilation" (p. 49).

b. Conrad Aiken   From the Georgia State Literary Studies Series, *Conrad Aiken: A Priest of Consciousness,* ed. Ted R. Spivey and Arthur Waterman (AMS Press, 1989), includes selected essays written earlier for an issue of *Studies in the Literary Imagination,* 10 new essays, and updated bibliographic material. As Spivey explains, this volume looks at the autobiographical threads of Aiken's poetry, fiction, and essays. Included are papers by Lewis Turco ("Corresponding with Conrad Aiken," pp. 265–70), Catharine F. Seigel ("Conrad Aiken: His Hour Come Round At Last?" pp. 271–84), and Kathe Davis (*"Ushant* in John Berryman's *Dream Songs:* Consciousness as Metafiction," pp. 285–97), all from the conference at the 1988 MLA meeting which dealt with connections between Aiken's life and work.

Spivey and Waterman have collected essays that provide a wide view of the writer and his work, but of particular interest are the two articles which deal specifically with Aiken's fiction: "Conrad Aiken's Heroes: Portraits of the Artist as a Middle-Aged Failure" by Mary Martin Rountree (pp. 121–30) and "The Murderous Act of the Mind: A New Reading of *King Coffin*" by Helen Hagenbuchle (pp. 131–54). Rountree outlines the "dialogue of the divided self" motif as it occurs in a number of Aiken's works, identifying William Demarest of *Blue Voyage* as a prototype for Aiken's artist-hero who must "explore his neurotic compulsion to create" (p. 122). Hagenbuchle notes that Aiken's "concern with unbridled egotism, his interest in the irrational and demonic, as well as his preoccupation with literary authenticity" (p. 132) in *King Coffin* represent the author's response to the subjectivity/objectivity question of the modernist movement. From this angle, Hagenbuchle argues cogently that in *King Coffin* Aiken "uses a sensational murder plot to deal with a highly serious philosophical problem" (p. 135).

iv Westerners

This year marks the appearance of the first book-length study of an often neglected Native American writer, *Word Ways: The Novels of D'Arcy McNickle* (Arizona) by John Lloyd Purdy. Perhaps most valuable for the compilation of biographical details which reveal how cultural and social forces influenced McNickle's art, *Word Ways* contains a thorough treatment of McNickle's struggle to produce the final draft of *The Surrounded.* Contending that the early manuscript, "The Hungry Generations," echoed the conventions and perceptions of the times, including the American Dream, Purdy explains that McNickle wanted to avoid romanticizing events as he worked toward his final revision. *Word Ways* presents useful discussions of *The Surrounded, Runners in the Sun,* and *Wind from an Enemy Sky,* but Purdy at times romanticizes his own subject matter. Identifying a vision-quest motif in both the evolution of Archilde's story in *The Surrounded* and the development of McNickle's artistic vision, Purdy strains for an optimistic, though not "happy," interpretation of the final events of *The Surrounded.*

Though Lyman B. Hagen's monograph on Dee Brown for the Western American Writers Series (Boise State) offers no piercing analysis, it does provide an especially good overview of Brown's early works—the historical trilogy of annotated, illustrated historical volumes: *Fighting Indians of the West, Trail Driving Days,* and *The Settlers' West.* Hagen stresses the historical integrity of Brown's work, and also comments on the author's respect for minorities and women before such demeanor was demanded by the American reading public.

The personal history of Wright Morris, specifically how certain childhood incidents influenced his fictional world, is the subject of G. B. Crump's, "Wright Morris, Author in Hiding" (*WAL*, 25:3–14). Crump identifies the image of the hidden child as "an important unifying thread" in Morris's memoirs— *Will's Boy, Solo,* and *A Cloak of Light*—and attaches psychological implications to the image, especially as it reveals the author's feelings about his mother and his father (p. 3).

Two important essays in *WAL*, "Wallace Stegner's Version of Pastoral"

(25:15–25) by Russell Burrows, and " 'Eastering': Wallace Stegner's Love Affair with Vermont in *Crossing to Safety*" (25:27–33) by Jackson J. Benson, comment on the shift in Stegner's ecological stance from conservation to preservation. Analyzing several of Stegner's earlier novels in light of their pastoralism, Burrows notes that in *A Shooting Star* Stegner is "too willing to slight the story at hand in favor of making an appeal to the political allegiances of his readers" (p. 17). In later works, beginning with *All the Little Live Things* and continuing through to *Crossing to Safety*, characters make important distinctions between preservation and conservation, but "the intellectual content of their positions appears as the natural and inevitable outcome of their personalities and their stories" (p. 24). Benson, too, focusing on *Crossing to Safety*, argues convincingly that by setting his last novel in the East, Stegner was making "a declaration of defeat, a statement that the environmental battle is gradually being lost and that whatever we valued most in the West at one time is now irretrievably gone and can be recovered only in history and nostalgia" (p. 27).

Complete with chronological listings and cross-references, Nancy Colberg's *Wallace Stegner: A Descriptive Bibliography* (Confluence) provides descriptions of all the works covering Stegner's more than 50-year career up to October 1988. Colberg had Stegner's support as well as access to his personal records, book collection, and agent's files while compiling this material. James Hepworth, editor of the American Author Series, supplies the introduction to Colberg's volume, an insightful, entertaining essay which identifies Stegner's major themes and highlights some quotable quotes by Stegner about his own work. A revised edition of the 1983 *Conversations with Wallace Stegner on Western History and Literature* by Wallace Stegner and Richard W. Etulain (Utah) contains only one revision, but an important one: a conversation between Etulain and Stegner which took place in Stegner's California home on December 27, 1989. In "After Ten Years: Another Conversation with Wallace Stegner," the author explains how his impulse to fictionalize events led inevitably to his "inventing scenes and suppressing things, and bringing things forward in order to make the story work" as he tried to tell "the utter, unvarnished truth" (pp. xi–xii) in *Crossing to Safety*. From there, the conversation looks back to Stegner's philosophy of the West in *The West as Living Space* and to the writer's thoughts on the literary community of Western authors.

Jean Stafford's life and work are the subject of both a biographical essay, "Jean Stafford: The Wound and the Bow" by William Leary (*SR* 98:333–49), and a literary biography, *Jean Stafford: The Savage Heart,* by Charlotte Margolis Goodman (Texas). To support the claim that all of Stafford's work is autobiographical, Leary discusses two stories: "And Lots of Solid Color," written at the beginning of Stafford's career, and "The Tea Time of Stouthearted Ladies," one of Stafford's last stories. According to Leary, the portrayals of the mother and father as unacceptable parents for a gifted child in these two stories "permit us to see starkly the social crucible in which Stafford created the weapon of irony with which she thereafter confronted the world, both in her life and in her fiction" (p. 349). Leary's thesis, though reasonable, can hardly be proven by looking at just two short stories, but Goodman's biography of Stafford bears out Leary's assessment of Stafford as a tragicomic figure whose disappointing family life became fuel for fiction. *The Savage Heart* presents a thorough, chronological report of the writer's life, accompanied by a running commentary on the various pieces of fiction as they relate to specific experiences and personal relationships. Relying on sheer weight of detail and refraining from playing the literary psychologist, Goodman succeeds in portraying Stafford as a "fascinating though not always likable woman" (p. xi) whose work deserves more attention from literary critics.

v Iconoclasts and Innovators

a. Jack Kerouac, William S. Burroughs, and Others   It was an upbeat year for criticism on the Beat Generation, thanks to Gregory Stephenson's *The Daybreak Boys* (So. Ill.) which brings together a number of essays published since 1983 and includes an extensive selected bibliography. Stephenson concisely summarizes the influences of the Lost Generation, hipsterism, bohemianism, dadaism, surrealism, and American Transcendentalism on the writers whom he christens the Daybreak Boys: Jack Kerouac, William Burroughs, John Clellon Holmes, Allen Ginsberg, Neal Cassady, Michael McClure, Gregory Corso, and Lawrence Ferlinghetti. To justify consideration of these varied writers as a "generation," Stephenson identifies a common denominator of the Beat aesthetic as "the downward quest for identity and vision, the beat-beatific movement, the journey through night to daybreak" (p. 8). The thorough treatment of Kerouac's Duluoz Legend novel cycle clarifies "the pattern of finding, losing, and struggling to find again" as "germane not only to *On the Road* but to *Duluoz Legend* as a whole" (p. 22).

Stephenson's discussion of Burroughs's gnostic vision skillfully argues that "the violence, obsessive sexuality, and nightmare horror that are so often characteristic of Burroughs's work represent an attempt to purge the psyche of these influences by means of their symbolic enactment" (p. 72). In this light, Stephenson reads Burroughs's work as an expression of "human liberation" (p. 73). In his conclusion, Stephenson declares that the Beat movement deserves critical attention because these writers discovered "a new idiom of consciousness" which "served to expand the parameters of American literature" (p. 172).

Also worth a look are two autobiographies by people with strong connections to Kerouac, Cassady, Ginsberg, and others: Herbert Huncke's *Guilty of Everything* (Paragon) and Carolyn Cassady's *Off the Road: My Years with Cassady, Kerouac, and Ginsberg* (Morrow).

b. Nathanael West and Henry Miller   Though West criticism was sparse this year, Beverly Jones makes an admirable contribution to the cause with "Shrike as the Modernist Anti-Hero in Nathanael West's *Miss Lonelyhearts*" (*MFS* 36:218–24). Jones's study focuses on "Shrike's messianic mission . . . to expose the hypocrisy of Lonelyhearts' christianity, with its neurotic fixation on the dark mysteries of blood and martyrdom" (p. 220).

Drawing on primary and secondary materials that have appeared since the 1963 edition of *Henry Miller* (TUSAS), Kingsley Widmer's revised edition delivers on his promise "to put a sensitive but sharp knife to Miller's conglomerate writings, to cut away the fat, and to probe some of the major themes, meanings, and qualities that give those materials significance in our literature and sensibility" (p. viii). Widmer comments on all of Miller's literary productions, but treats *Tropic of Cancer* the most thoroughly, arguing that it is one of the "lively antibooks of American individualism . . ." (p. 18).

Southern Oregon State College

Jerome Klinkowitz

Two trends indicate that fiction of the past three decades has taken on a more stable identity, at least in terms of scholarship and criticism. In general studies, particularly those of book length, "postmodern" is used more frequently than "contemporary" to identify the period. And in a field where general treatments have been far more common, 1990's shelf holds a much greater number of single-author studies. As the innovators of the 1960s die (John Gardner, Donald Barthelme, Richard Brautigan, Jerzy Kosinski) or retire from their regular professorships (John Barth, Grace Paley, John Hawkes), such a summing up of individual careers is to be expected. One must ask, however, in what sense adopting the term "postmodern" is similarly conclusive.

i General Studies

The two most important books of 1990 suggest that using the term "postmodern" favors a new rhetoric. In the past, such a label was embraced as a badge of difference, the prefix indicating that such fiction was virtually post-everything, not the least of which was mimetic. Now in *Contingent Meanings,* Jerry A. Varsava proposes a reader-centered view which recasts the most innovative of contemporary fictive works so that the reader rather than the author establishes the text's reference to the world. Previous critics have argued for the referentiality evident in the works of Barthelme (by means of irony), Barth (myth), and Pynchon (a paradigm of sciences), but Varsava goes further by centering his study on the much more esoteric group of writers who have always proven to be the ultimate fallback for die-hard innovationists: Walter Abish, Gilbert Sorrentino, and the later Robert Coover (supplemented by a look at that most postmodernly Americanized of German-language authors, Peter

Handke). The first half of Varsava's study is limited by the rhetoric of its
thesis. Whereas in fact Ronald Sukenick, Gilbert Sorrentino, and William H. Gass have argued (in *In Form, Something Said,* and *Fiction and
the Figures of Life,* respectively) that conventional realism dictates control
of the reader's imagination, Varsava feels their own contrary strategies do
the same, to the extent that their anti-Aristotelian innovations are nothing more than the familiar formalist domination practiced in a sense of
art for art's sake. There is much more to their theory than this; rather
than an "aestheticism" in the manner of Pater and Wilde, these writers
are deconstructing arbitrary notions long taken as natural or absolute.
This beginning emphasis is unfortunate and unnecessary, because Varsava's true interest is in how readers respond to such texts. As such,
Contingent Meanings' second half is a valuable exercise in discovering
what actually happens in such texts as Abish's *How German Is It* and
Minds Meet, Coover's *Spanking the Maid,* Sorrentino's *Mulligan Stew,*
and (in a work by Peter Handke that all Americanist critics should know
for its affinities with current practice) *A Sorrow Beyond Dreams.* The
secret to understanding Abish is perceiving how he challenges the stability of the world's familiar order by defamiliarizing its surface (and its
surface is the quality by which we know it). The stories of *Minds Meet*
take this approach as a technique, while the novel *How German Is It*
examines such semiotic activity as a theme. As such, Abish deconstructs
our worldview. Coover prefers to amuse himself and us with the problems connected with a worldview's construction, a reminder that human
beings live by fictions. While Coover's earlier novels become elaborate
games generated by such notions, *Spanking the Maid* carries epistemological and even moral weight in the way it reveals "the foibles of classical
pattern making" that relate to gender relations. In Handke's work,
Varsava finds a motive common to many American innovative fictionists: by exploring language's coercion, he opens it up—as an arbitrary
system—to the possibility of a constructive revision. Finally, Sorrentino's
Mulligan Stew establishes intertextuality as the condition of language's
status in society and history, and then by carnivalesque parody subverts it
back into the materials of an artistic act.

Just the opposite conclusion is drawn by Arthur M. Saltzman, whose
Designs of Darkness is predicated on the understanding that a "tradition
of insecurity about the communicative capacities of language" underlies
postmodern fiction. Like Varsava, Saltzman believes there is still work for
the reader to do, but in a manner that "forces a drawing up of revised

contracts" between themselves and the text. The novel no longer intends to totalize one's experience; as a result, the classic epiphany of modernist fiction is discarded as "an anthropomorphic distortion." Thus many of Varsava's exemplary narratives are read by Saltzman in a radically different manner. Coover's *Spanking the Maid* is not a lesson in gender conditioning but is rather a textual exercise in which "Master and maid, locked in mutually dependent identities, are ostensibly striving to perfect their respective offices, which are determined for them by the ambiguous 'manual' " that is, in fact, the generative force behind the story. Sorrentino is less interested in simple parody than in discrediting the usual means for achieving closure, his way of emphasizing how postmodern fiction has defaulted on providing the "finalist determination" of narrative. Abish is less concerned with political struggle than the linguistic ground on which it takes place; as an analog, Saltzman reads E. L. Doctorow's *The Book of Daniel* as a "systematic assault on the very concept of verifiability," based as the narrative is within the deconstructive principles of language (just as Abish finds new German history "rewritten" on a blank surface covering the past). Language itself leads readers away from the epiphanic confrontations Varsava savors because the very guarantee of familiarity that language offers effaces any true discovery of what might be real. Two of Saltzman's most original readings are of Kenneth Gangemi's *Olt* and Steve Katz's *Moving Parts,* in which composition yields to "sheer apprehension of the discrete, atomized materials of contemporary life" and hierarchic order falls to a persistent confession of "the indistinguishability of all the ingredients" the narrative can comprise.

The opposition of Varsava's and Saltzman's books points out the progress that has been made in treating postmodern fiction. As always, there are two camps: the cautiously conservative and the more radically innovative. But whereas in the past traditionalist readings dismissed postmodern fiction altogether and called for a return to moralistically based realism, now the tradition itself has moved so far toward innovation that a schematically left wing/right wing debate takes place well within the boundaries of what was formerly the most radical part of the canon, over works a previous decade's traditionalists would dismiss entirely.

Several books with more specific theses to argue show the same sense of comfort in working with novels formerly pertinent only to critics arguing for a great disruption. *In a Dark Time: The Apocalyptic Temper in the American Novel of the Nuclear Age* (Purdue) serves as Joseph Dewey's argument that such a disposition "has proven a most capable strategy for American writers, who have projected events of the nation's history into a cosmic design that has reassured even during the most uncertain times that America is possessed of a destiny greater than the disturbances of its own history." Such faith in the creative potential of people fits with how innovators privilege the imagination, even though certain contemporaries tend to exhaust such possibilities by noting history's "menacing drift." In recent decades, however, writers have struggled to reconnect with the apocalyptic tradition, rejecting the notion that "to accept history is to abandon hope." Witness Kurt Vonnegut's steadying voice even as his characters "dance off into the darkness that he himself creates," Robert Coover's metafictive challenge to "navigate within the ceaselessly changing universe defined by quantum physics" (after having been denied the straight line of conventional narrative and Newtonian mechanics), Walker Percy's complicated satire maintained against his own narrator in *Love in the Ruins* (a reminder of Vonnegut's steadying voice), Thomas Pynchon's "exhilarating private nativities that forsake the self-destruction of history when promise collapses into grim certainty," and the constructively unsettling fears of William Gaddis and Don DeLillo in an age of administrative plenty whose security sometimes smothers.

Like the apocalyptic, the comic can also generate a worldview that influences the form of fiction, which is what Lance Olsen points out in *Circus of the Mind in Motion: Postmodern and the Comic Vision* (Wayne State). Comedy always subverts the dominant culture; unlike irony, a staple of modernism that assumes the presence of a meaning behind the text, humor accommodates the postmodern view by believing "primarily in surface, in no positive content." Postmodern fiction itself encompasses a broad arc, beginning with Guy Davenport's demonstration that "postmodernism is in a way the failure of the renaissance in our century," continuing through Donald Barthelme's more positively inclined play that rewards our suspicions that the shared language, values, and perceptions that form our culture are in fact fictions constructed from debris, to Walter Abish's yearning for a neoconservatism by which his text "expresses a longing for centrism that its form seems to dismantle." With Saltzman, Olsen is one of the most astute readers of such texts.

Lesser studies still contribute in specific ways. Although Charles Berryman's *Decade of Novel/Fiction of the 1970s: Form and Challenge*

(Whitston) forsakes not only a rhetorical principle of organization but even chapter numbers (in favor of the decade's succeeding years), essaylike insights are found among the author's commentaries on John Updike's *Rabbit Redux* (television as an illusion of history), Kurt Vonnegut's *Breakfast of Champions* (a self-mockery of the author's fears), E. L. Doctorow's *Ragtime* (the matter of editorial focus in creating history as a fiction), John Hawkes's *Travesty* (life in the context of annihilation), and the satiric properties in Gore Vidal's *Kalki* and Joseph Heller's *Good as Gold*. Challenges to traditional ontology inform the novels Marguerite Alexander studies in *Flights from Realism: Themes and Strategies in Postmodern British and American Fiction* (Edward Arnold). Postmodernism introduces "a new distance" between reader and author that is further expanded by concerns about "treachery—enacted between individuals, obscurely at work within society, and, more generally, the treacherous nature of appearance." Such unease is ameliorated by thematic interest in romance and history, a tactic that by its prominence in British novels makes the postmodern textual terrain more realistic than in American fiction. That there need be no gap at all is argued by W. Ross Winterowd in *The Rhetoric of the "Other" Literature* (So. Ill.), where classical rhetoric's understanding of how an aesthetic response is elicited removes the dichotomies between fiction and nonfiction. Appeals to ethos and pathos remain the key, specifically as they create a "presentational" literature that gains more from emotion than from assertion.

In these and other discussions, history is a key term—not as a stable concept but as a relative, constructed term, drawing as much on an interest in humankind's projection of it as in any verifiable record. A major contribution is made by Naomi Jacobs, whose *The Character of Truth: Historical Figures in Contemporary Fiction* (So. Ill.) examines just what happens when William Styron, E. L. Doctorow, and Robert Coover put "real" (historical, that is) characters in their novels. As comic types, such figures are not only less than conventionally real, but often serve to criticize such concepts. The reader's own creative role, something overlooked in Winterowd's classical rhetoric, is used to blur the conventional fact/fiction boundary, whether it be in matters of identity (Michael Ondaatje), corporate being (Ishmael Reed), or the imagination itself (Kathy Acker). Jacobs's study fits the tone of the essays collected by Theo D'haen and Hans Bertens in *History and Post-war Writing* (Rodopi), where my own treatment of Max Apple's ritualizations of history complements Marc Chénetier's study of how America's own national narra-

tive, a highly ritualized affair, invites deconstructive readings and rewrit-
ings.

Then there is the matter of play, which in postmodern fiction comes
full circle to join history in the task of creating a world through the manner of its perception. Central to understanding this task is Christian K.
Messenger's *Sport and the Spirit of Play in Contemporary American Fiction*
(Columbia), a three-part examination of male physical self-definition
(which resists customary ritualization in James Dickey's *Deliverance* but
succeeds in Norman Mailer's work), heroism in play spirit (such as
McMurphy's creation of his own rites in Ken Kesey's *One Flew Over the
Cuckoo's Nest* and Coover's control through the performative ritualizing
of everything in *The Public Burning*), and team sport (where baseball's
sense of history makes it the ideal vehicle of expression). Baseball rivals
allegorical romance in its ability to create a framework, Cordelia Candelaria argues in *Seeking the Perfect Game: Baseball in American Literature*
(Greenwood 1989), with sport itself as a fictive emblem of almost mathematical purity (consider Coover's primal need for the mythic and Philip
Roth's theme of achieving immortality through the game's imagination).
A steady progress toward this ideal in baseball writing itself can be seen
from the selections made by editor George Bowering in *Taking the Field*
(Red Deer College Press).

Insightful work on contemporary American fiction can take place just
about anywhere, and a likely place to look is in scholarship of its Latin
American cousins. Consider chapter eleven, "The Legacy," in Gene H.
Bell-Villada's *García Márquez: The Man and His Work* (No. Car.). Here,
the influence of the great Colombian writer is seen in the magic of Toni
Morrison's *Song of Solomon,* the ghosts populating William Kennedy's
Ironweed, the family history of Alice Walker's *The Color Purple,* the
mystic spectacle of Robert Coover's *The Public Burning,* and most emphatically in Paul Theroux's adventurism and John Barth's interest in
both self-reflexivity and fabulative storytelling. The inescapable conclusion is that Latin American fiction has replaced French as models for
American innovation, a feeling shared by many contributors to editor
Edna Aizenberg's *Borges and His Successors: The Borgesian Impact on Literature and the Arts* (Missouri). "Fiction today proceeds in the projected
shadow of Borges," says Geoffrey Green, who senses the Argentinian's
presence everywhere, even where the modeled works do not resemble
each other. The key, goes Green's argument in "Postmodern Precursor:
The Borgesian Image in Innovative American Fiction" (pp. 200–213), is

in the perspective by which fiction writers "create their precursors." By matching up these various Americans' comments on Borges with elements in their own work, Green finds Barth moving beyond the "used-upness" of literary forms to a new balance of algebraic technique and the fire of passion, Coover reaching past exhaustion to create diverse futures of "forking effects," Updike expressing a huge confidence in "our own country" without fear of repeating himself, Pynchon opposing versions of the self and contradictory perceptions of reality, Hawkes exploring the terrain of dream-become-reality, and DeLillo obsessed with the nightmare of real things.

Then there is the matter of literary politics, always a contentious issue when a field is still being laid out. *Crit* 31, iv, an issue devoted to "Unspeakable Practices: A Celebration of Iconoclastic American Fiction," publishes the proceedings of a conference at Brown University. The tone, however, is less iconoclastic than funeral, dedicated as the occasion was to the retirement of John Hawkes, an effect even more somber in retrospect as the discussions are haunted by the soon-to-die Donald Barthelme. The critics, ranging from Leslie Fiedler and Robert Scholes to Larry McCaffery and Tom LeClair, recall their own iconoclasm of a previous age but for the present and future prefer to tidy up their economic investments in more conservative styles of both fiction and criticism. Reminiscent of how radical New Dealers of the 1930s struggled to rectify their images during the early 1950s, these symposia and question-and-answer sessions (without a paper or fully expressed position among them) tell less about the truly iconoclastic state of creative and scholarly work than do commentaries by the true giants of such innovation, none of whom was in attendance. Consider Ronald Sukenick's series of comments in *LitR* 33:183–84 ("Literature at the End of the Century"), *Black Ice* 5:v–vi ("Not for Everyone"), *AmBR* 12, i:3 ("The NEA: Art and Money"), and *Witness* 3, ii–iii:7–9 ("The Dirty Secret") espousing fiction that "breaks out of the modes of [officially sanctioned] literature into something resembling the freaky uniqueness of individual experience beyond the usual brainwash of official culture," and Gilbert Sorrentino's recollections of launching a literary revolution at Grove Press in "Working at Grove," an interview conducted by S. E. Gontarski for an issue on Grove Press done by *RCF* 10, iii:97–110. The way establishment fiction and scholarship about it are subsidized by the grants industry concerns a symposium published in *Northwest Review* 28, iii; contributions by Robert Hedin (pp. 20–22), myself (pp. 27–29), and

Richard Kostelanetz (pp. 29–30) specify the exclusionary tactics of such conservatively channeled support. That the gathering at Brown University was funded not only locally but by a lavish grant from a foreign government makes it even more apparent how yesterday's iconoclasts can be reemployed as today's makers of reverential altarpieces.

ii Women

Feminist Alternatives: Irony and Fantasy in the Contemporary Novel by Women (Miss.) is Nancy A. Walker's rejoinder to those *"acceptable* fantasies" in pulp romances that "endorse rather than challenge cultural assumptions about women's nature and aspirations." Ironic texts question both writerly and readerly assumptions, yet admit that the overwhelming need for fantasy speaks for a dissatisfaction with elements of real life. Fantasy combined with irony allows just such a critique, based on an understanding of language's ability to both control and subvert the authority of reality. Walker studies how first a voice for such expression must be found, and how multiple narrative perspectives are needed for such continual "starting over." Characters dream of alternative realities, a device that can extend to fantastic time travel. With a focus on feminist concerns, such novels eventually transcend dream to take an ironic stance toward the "absurdity and its sources" underlying the unacceptable real.

The working nature of becoming and being a writer is a recurrent interest in Mickey Pearlman and Katherine Usher Henderson's *Inter/View: Talks with America's Writing Women* (Kentucky), yet most authors also reveal special facets of their works, such as Alison Lurie's war for control of space, Joyce Carol Oates's privileging of memory and place, Susan Fromberg Schaeffer's powerful respect for the forces of memory (which can take the form of daydreams, nightmares, and ghosts), Francine Prose's feeling for existence in a limited space, Laurie Colwin's resistance to fixed ideas, Louise Erdrich's tension between open space and home, and Lynne Sharon Schwartz's understanding of both Brooklyn and the repression that effaces its happy memory. Such elements as compression, a paucity of words, and blank space are key factors in Janis P. Stout's *Strategies of Reticence,* which discusses the works of Jane Austen, Willa Cather, Katherine Anne Porter, and Joan Didion; in Didion's case, "the heart of the narrative is a certain calculated ellipsis" in which absence becomes presence and visual voids provide "an epistemology of limitation." Stout argues that because women can be reluctant to speak or express grief too overtly and are furthermore oppressed by their sexual identity, a form of minimalism becomes their apt mode of expression, a curtailment of the text that withholds through silences an "aggressive reticence" which serves as a sarcastic strategy.

Women and their bodies interest other critics. In *Abortion, Choice, and Contemporary Fiction: The Armageddon of the Maternal Instinct* (Chicago), Judith Witt focuses on how the theme of maternal choice is expressed by Barth (whose *The End of the Road* shows men controlling experience by turning it into speech, a speech that Rennie disrupts by turning it into pregnancy in a try for her own narrative that the men abort), Didion (who in *Play It as It Lays* sees abortion as an encounter with nonbeing, an experience that is "never over when it's over"), and Marge Piercy (whose *Braided Lives* calls for reproductive freedom). A parallel theme is that of "fear of fathers," evident in Thomas Keneally's *Passenger* and John Irving's *The Cider House Rules* where the doctor becomes an outlaw in relation to his female patient, a deep reference to his own sexuality and fatherhood. How a lesbian text engenders a specific literary imagination is detailed by Bonnie Zimmerman in *The Safe Sea of Women: Lesbian Fiction, 1969–1989* (Beacon). In the process of shaping a new sexual consciousness (as opposed to old stereotypes), new boundaries for the world are mapped—boundaries that serve less as reflections of the real than of how completely a new reality might be created. Such matters as "a feminist-vegetarian reading of the vegetarian body" concern Carol J. Adams in *The Sexual Politics of Meat: A Feminist-Vegetarian Critical Theory* (Continuum); the inability to accommodate one's understanding of living animals as consumable meat makes the following of such a diet a case of succumbing to Derrida's "absent referent," a structure obvious in Anne Tyler's *The Clock Winder.*

Subgenres also benefit from womanly interest. *Feminist Utopias* (Nebraska, 1989) is Frances Bartkowski's appraisal of how such a mode employs political concerns, such as Joanna Russ's interruption of the epic narrative with a "godlike prophetic voice" in *The Female Man* and Marge Piercy's use of alternate futures as possible wrong turns in *Woman at the Edge of Time.* How the women's movement itself has contributed more active female characters into fiction, as in novels by Erica Jong and Maxine Hong Kingston, is detailed by Resa L. Dudovitz in *The Myth of*

the Superwoman: Women's Bestsellers in France and the United States
(Routledge). A "superwoman" is one who can accede to greater power
without changing the social order, an order dominated by concerns of
family life and love. The 20th-century romance novel replicates the form
of the previous century's "feminine" novel; even today best-seller conventions dominate, not as formulae but as keys to a general social
melodrama. As such, identities are created by family sagas, while adventure comes through marriage. In the 1980s, movement-oriented writers
eclipse these limits yet satisfy the subgenre's formal demands by positing
the superwoman who can do anything and everything to great success,
yet still love and be loved. To editor Linda Anderson's *Plotting Change:
Contemporary Women's Fiction* (Edward Arnold), Rosemary O'Sullivan
contributes "Listening and Telling in Counterpoint: A Conversation
with Grace Paley" (pp. 99–110), in which it is emphasized that Paley
herself is not her character Faith, the divorced mother of two teenage
boys; Paley had lived with her first husband for 22 years and has not
written stories featuring a daughter so as not to embarrass her own child;
instead, Paley's work emphasizes artistic properties, with real-world cor-
relations coming from larger concerns than those of her own family.

Among individual authors, Leslie Silko and Sylvia Plath receive noteworthy treatment. Silko's *Ceremony* is a key text for Elizabeth A. Meese in
(Ex)tensions. Value from identity within a common heritage reminds us
that such merit should be intrinsic to a work but in reality is relative to
contingent forces, for even noncanonical Third World literature is interpreted according to imperialist First World values. *Ceremony* straddles
such boundaries, remaining "inbetween" racial, social, and economic
divisions, and thereby it "provides an occasion to reexamine the violence
required to construct the continuous narrative of literary (or other forms
of) history and of singular identity." Virginia Woolf as a literary mother,
as a "better parent" than Aurelia Plath, is explored by Steven Gould
Axelrod in *Sylvia Plath: A Wound and the Cure of Words* (Hopkins). Plath
enacts her mentor's desire for female fiction, a tradition which becomes
subverted with hates and grievances. Thus the power of anger is a
compelling force but also an obstacle in Plath's art, to the extent that
"Woolf's exclusion of aggressivity and gender identification from fiction
must have had a negative impact" on the author of *The Bell Jar*. The great
benefit of Axelrod's study is that instead of merely tracing autobiographical or allegorical elements in the fiction, he examines Plath's intertextual

involvement with literary history. "Consciously or unconsciously, Plath substituted Woolf's textual immanence for her mother's empirical reality," he explains, finding a motive for existence in the creative enterprise, "a salve for life's injury."

iii Alice Walker, Gloria Naylor, and Other African Americans

New and forthcoming books suggest that the 1990s will be the decade of women and women writers in African American fiction. Editor Henry Louis Gates's trend-setting collection, *Reading Black, Reading Feminist* (Meridian), gathers important previously published essays and introduces several new ones. Noteworthy are Bell Hooks's "Writing the Subject: Reading *The Color Purple*" (pp. 454–70) and Barbara Christian's "Gloria Naylor's Geography: Community, Class, and Patriarchy in *The Women of Brewster Place* and *Linden Hills*" (pp. 348–73). Alice Walker's novel invites a fresh exploration that locates itself between the text itself and conventional critical points of departure; as a narrative of sexual confession, the novel enfolds many secrets, but for anti-male domination it uses strategies similar to pornography, such as defining characters through their function. For Gloria Naylor, character can become a function of place, inasmuch as displacement is an important part of black history. It is unusual, however, in black American fiction for African American neighborhoods to be contrasted with each other (as opposed to the more familiar comparison with white areas); by doing such, Naylor is able to detail class distinctions within a common race, with the structure of her novels found in the origin and history of communities. Barbara Christian also has the most outstanding essay in editors Joanne M. Braxton and Andrée Nicola McLaughlin's *Wild Women in the Whirlwind: Afra-American Culture and the Contemporary Literary Renaissance* (Rutgers). Her " 'Somebody Forgot to Tell Somebody Something': African-American Women's Historical Novels" (pp. 326–41) reveals how some writers have avoided using history for fear that the knowledge of slavery and discrimination might deter a younger generation's hopes for the future. We must know and use all of the past, Christian argues, lest memory itself become an abstraction—after all, it was slaveowners who strove to efface their slaves' willingness to remember. Re-visions of the past are central to works by Toni Morrison, Alice

Walker, and Sherley Anne Williams, with a focus on historical aspects of motherhood (the locus for Morrison's chaotic space and Williams's double-edged conception of the "mammy" figure).

Central to the study of these ideas is the issue of *BALF* devoted to women writers. Removing the veil of secrecy and the need for revisions and "re-visions" concern several of the general essays, while Toni Morrison's struggles with madness and evil and the challenge to portray the black figure on the white page of "the master's language." The complex of political issues behind such work is given apt delineation by Edward Guerrero in "Tracking 'The Look' in the Novels of Toni Morrison" (*BALF* 24:761–73), in which oppression extends from language to how women are regarded in male vision.

Coincidentally, one of the more insightful treatments of Imamu Amiri Baraka's life is found in *How I Became Hettie Jones* (Dutton) by Hettie Jones. From its title to its narrative strategy, Jones's book is reminiscent of Baraka's own *The Autobiography of LeRoi Jones* (Freundlich Books, 1984), for as the latter's story consists in how LeRoi Jones became Imamu Amiri Baraka, the former's tale is devoted to how Hettie Cohen first became Hettie Jones and then struggled to keep that identity even as her husband and the times deserted her. Despite such desertion, *How I Became Hettie Jones* is wonderfully free of bitterness and recrimination. Instead, the focus is on the joyful struggle of creating such a life in the 1950s and early 1960s. Especially valuable are portraits of colleagues that Baraka has erased from his own published memories: Gilbert Sorrentino, Joel Oppenheimer, and Fielding Dawson.

iv Leslie Silko, James Welch, and Others from the Southwest and West

The many stories and story-poems in Leslie Silko's novel encourage a multidimensional reading, not the least of which involves dealing with invisible characters moving through the text, argues David E. Hailey, Jr., in "The Visual Elegance of Ts'its'tsi'nako and the Other Invisible Characters in *Ceremony*" (*WSRev* 6, ii:1–6). In creating a reality by means of her "actual ceremony," Silko uses the interpolated poems as visual imagery, skeletal structures on which she hangs illustrations of the spirit helpers so central to her ritual.

A similar multidimensionality is found in James Welch's fiction by John Purdy, whose " 'He Was Going Along': Motion in the Novels of

James Welch" (*AIQ* 14:133–45) considers how "the preponderance of minute, detailed descriptions of motion in relation to setting" yields a special form of character development, one of motion defined in relation to place. How time can disappear into space and challenge one's ability to recover it is explored by Louis Owens in "Earthboy's Return—James Welch's Act of Recovery in *Winter in the Blood*" (*WSRev* 6, i:27–37); Native American men who no longer feel secure or know themselves leave vacuums to be filled by women, whose friendship in turn makes balance and self-knowledge possible. Lamentation thus serves as liberation, for sorrows are mixed with complaints that in effect make something out of nothing, a passage from crying for pity to articulating and explaining. In an essay slanted toward the ideas in this novel, " 'Distance,' Desire, and the Ideological Matrix of *Winter in the Blood*" (*ArQ* 46 ii:73–100), Stephen Tatum sees the protagonist's isolation from the social matrix as an indication that a novel's traditional manner of charting meaningful intersections and resolving enigmas cannot be employed for this story. Instead, Welch debates whether any representations can be truly known, given the inherent reductiveness of language. Therefore, other ideologies must be used for establishing a workable epistemology, a process that leads to a unique unveiling of truth in a world where signifiers have slipped away from their referents. " 'The Lost Children' in James Welch's *The Death of Jim Loney*" (*WAL* 25:35–48) finds Nora Barry considering the Gros Ventre and Blackfeet folktales of abandoned children as a device for connecting the characters' predicaments and the novel's narrative structure to the traditional past. Such a "pre-text" lends the story "an elegaic" but "not despairing tone, in that the Indian characters are mourning for lost ancestors and a lost culture."

N. Scott Momaday's centrality to the Native American canon is underscored by editor Kenneth M. Roemer's "Approaches to Teaching Momaday's *The Way to Rainy Mountain*" (MLA, 1988). Significant are essays by Matthias Schubnell on tribal identity and the imagination (how a sense of self is developed within the Kiowa oral tradition), Lawana Trout on the historical record of calendrical writing in this same tribe, William Oandasan's reading of triadic structures within the novel's episodes, and Susan Scarberry-Garcia's understanding of how the natural can be sacred thanks to a continuity of the spiritual with ordinary experience. Momaday himself tells how his writing continues an oral tradition anchored by a sense of place in Laura Coltelli's *Winged Words,* an important volume which also features commentary by Paula Gunn

Allen (on the acculturized shift from a woman-centered culture and the different ways male and female writers develop characters), Louise Erdrich (recalling her storytelling roots in the Chippewa language), Leslie Marmon Silko (whose narratives revolt against historical time in archaic societies), Gerald Vizenor (who inserts details of the self into a historical frame), and James Welch (with thoughts on the surrealism in his fiction).

Overcoming a literary aesthetic of invisibility has been the challenge faced by writers from Mexican-American communities of the Southwest, argues Ramón Saldívar in *Chicano Narrative*. Because such work itself challenges canonical tradition, Saldívar seeks alternative strategies in a wide range of postmodern critical discourses, with the result that a "dialectics of difference" is evolved that demystifies relations between minority and dominant cultures. Far more than just "reading the literature of [Chicano] experience," a true understanding involves establishing the grounds on which the structures of such fictions are built. There is a destruction and reconstruction of reality involved here, a process that creates a "resistance literature" that allows Rudolfo Anaya to be appreciated as a master of multiformed time (with as many as four distinct temporalities marking *Bless Me, Ultima*) and Isabella Ríos to be understood as a master of the novel of pure dialogue (where the characters' voices stand without narrative mediation, a strategy in which the male properties of diegetic narrative stand aside to let "the women speak").

Rudolfo Anaya figures again in an interview with John F. Crawford (pp. 82–93) from editors William Balassi, John F. Crawford, and Annie O. Eysturoy's *This Is About Vision*. A special interest is the author's role for older people in Hispanic culture as they relate to influences, models, metaphors, and borrowings in the fiction at large; subsequent discussions include thoughts on the power of imagination in relation to the power of place and on Anaya's role in the emergence of Chicano literature in the 1960s. Anaya's mastery of structuring systems is described by Paul Beckman Taylor in "The Mythic Matrix of Anaya's *Heart of Aztlan*" (*Swiss Papers in English Language and Literature* 5:201–14); a family's displacement and destabilization reveal the destruction and reconstruction that Ramón Saldívar has mentioned, and by making the strange look not only familiar but at times stranger, Anaya is able to bring structuring principles into high profile. Welcome attention to a newer text is provided by Marta E. Sánchez in "Arturo Islas' *The Rain God:* An Alternative Tradition" (*AL* 62:284–304), a study that shows how by giving voice to the voiceless and using narrative strategies that highlight a minority's mediating role, Islas not only enlarges the canon but "goes further to instruct Anglophonic, monolingual readers to become self-conscious about the fragility of the presumed centrality of their own culture."

v Cynthia Ozick, Philip Roth, and Other Jewish-Americans

A fresh view of familiar fiction is taken by Hans Borchers in "The Difficulty of Imagining Germany: Some Observations on the Work of Cynthia Ozick" from editor Peter Freese's *Germany and German Thought in American Literature and Cultural Criticism* (Essen: Die Blau Eule, pp. 285–304). A complex set of contrasts motivates the short fictions in *The Pagan Rabbi and Other Stories*—not just between Germany and America but between past and present as those time frames contribute to national distinctions, a controversy that throws into even higher relief possible differences between being Jewish-American and American. As such, certain ideas formerly perceived as programmatic in Ozick's work now seem more literary in their rich dimensionality.

Philip Roth's work grows in such dimensionality almost yearly, and thus provides a rich resource for perceptive critics. In *Understanding Philip Roth* (So. Car.), Murray Baumgarten and Barbara Gottfried see one of Roth's favorite subjects as the enormous change our world has experienced in recent decades. The Jewish-American experience, for example, has become in Roth's view so materialized that the surface of everyday life now provides sufficient challenge to character (for both confrontation and subversion). In *The Counterlife,* Roth challenges realistic fiction, yet everything he makes happen remains within the realm of possibility, given who his character Zuckerman is and how he has been created with an eye toward this common reality. Sanford Pinsker's *Bearing the Bad News* includes "Deconstruction as Apology: The Counterfictions of Philip Roth" (pp. 137–52), a brilliant interpretation of the postmodern turn in which self-consciousness about writing and fictionality invites constructions to deconstruct, texts to breed countertexts, and satirical attack to become abject confession. How Roth's autobiography, *The Facts,* contributes to this view is outlined by Charles Berryman in "Philip Roth and Nathan Zuckerman: A Portrait of the Artist as a Young Prometheus" (*ConL* 31:177–90); "a comment on the source and meaning of his art in the form of a rather sentimental autobiography," this book parallels Roth's debate in *The Counterlife* about the nature and purpose of art, a commingling of religion, conscience, and aesthetics that moves well beyond any simple relationship for fiction and fact (in which the artist becomes a combination Stephen Dedalus and Hamlet).

A more homely view of the storyteller's role is presented by John Guzlowski in " 'Freud, Schmeud; Complex, Shmomplex': Isaac Bashevis Singer vs. the Psychologizers" (*Germany and German Thought,* pp. 389–406). Opposition to psychological interpretations runs through Singer's memoirs and interviews, even though he is intensely interested in the dynamics of the human mind. This apparent contradiction is resolved by seeing how Singer feels that modern psychology "not only places an inordinate emphasis on the inner self, it further distorts it by universalizing the workings of the human mind." The key is telling stories about the mind's "desire to know," a perfect premise for narrative since knowing one's self is a classic riddle.

vi Anne Tyler, Mary Lee Settle, and Other Southerners

Two radically different views distinguish the more important essays in editor C. Ralph Stephens's *The Fiction of Anne Tyler* (Miss.). Doris Betts does an able job of establishing Tyler's importance within the critical vocabulary of traditional criticism of Southern writing; her "Tyler's Marriage of Opposites" (pp. 1–15) shows how the author's narratives start and stop in terms of seeing the centrality of home but also acknowledging the urge to get away from it. Death itself can be overcome by love or a new life, a style of Quaker hope Betts appreciates, though she also understands how such quiet persistence and survival beyond crisis prevents Tyler's heroines from being "angry enough to star in the average Women's Studies syllabus." Susan Gilbert takes a different approach in "Private Lives and Public Issues in Anne Tyler's Prize-winning Novels" (pp. 136–45), charging that *The Accidental Tourist* and *Breathing Lessons* suffer rather than benefit from a sense of "quietism." There are political implications to Tyler's subject, the family, especially as it moves from stagnant wealth to "the other side of town" where respectability is exchanged for spontaneity—but with no social imperative for Tyler's readers.

John Crane's interview, "The Art of Fiction CXVI: Mary Lee Settle" (*ParisR* No. 114, pp. 44–77), has the novelist discussing what she has

drawn from Charleston, West Virginia (where she spent her adolescence), and how the Beulah Quintet took form. "Waiting for voices" is
the key to Settle's method, an approach that takes material from reality
and "turns it into what it isn't." How Walker Percy elevates such transformations into the mythic-historical interests J. Donald Crowley and Sue
Mitchell Crowley, whose "Walker Percy's Grail" in editors Valerie M.
Lagorio and Mildred Leake Day's *King Arthur Through the Ages, Volume 2*
(Garland, pp. 257–77) traces sanctions for Percy's attack "on Stoicism
and the chivalric codes of courtly love and the broad sword as they
developed in the 1970s in America," both of which are insufficient
redoubts against the onslaught of sexual abuse and modern violence. The
anxiety of influence, of Faulkner's influence on Southern writing in
particular, makes a compelling subject for Christopher Metress in "'A
New Father, a New Home': Styron, Faulkner, and Southern Revisionism" (*SNNTS* 22:308–22), especially since it lets us see *Lie Down in
Darkness* as an attempt to usurp and rewrite *The Sound and the Fury*.
Indirection and mediation are techniques for expressing the inexpress-
ible, argues Richard G. Law in "The Reach of Fiction: Narrative Technique in Styron's *Sophie's Choice*" (*SLJ* 23, i:45–64); different narrative
perspectives cue alternations between these rhythms of confrontation
and evasion, with the important qualification that through all of this
Stingo is seeing not Auschwitz but its effects on another person.

Two broadly reaching essays by leading critics promise to become classics of Southern literary scholarship. In "From Combray to Ithaca; Or,
the 'Southernness' of Southern Literature" (*VQR* 66:47–63), Louis D.
Rubin, Jr., shows how sensitivity to the delineations of class and community relationships allow a field for fiction action that becomes as rich as
Proust's, especially when a writer has a feel for such roles becoming
outdated (as in Walker Percy's case). How for women writers this same
interest has in recent years become matriarchal is discussed by Linda
Wagner-Martin in "'Just the Doing of It': Southern Women and the
Idea of Community" (*SLJ* 22, ii:19–32), where the right to place and its
relation to means of expression weave a textual bond.

vii Joyce Carol Oates, Norman Mailer, and Others in the Realistic Tradition

The Berlin Wall's function as both fact and metaphor is a small but
telling part of Joyce Carol Oates's work, according to Hanspeter Dörfels's

contribution to *Germany and German Thought*, "Images of Germany and the Germans in Some of Joyce Carol Oates' Short Stories" (pp. 267–84). Violence in her own work pales in comparison to violence wrought by Germany during World War II, around which she builds her own containing wall. Warfare's relation to capital and profit in Norman Mailer's work is treated by Richard Godden in *Fictions of Capital;* here, *Why Are We in Vietnam?* poses war as a permanent economy in which overproduction complements hypercivilization as capital consumes its own forms in a rite of cannibalization, while *Armies of the Night* shows the Pentagon as dedicated primarily to profit. Godden feels this state of affairs is a paradigm for Mailer's literary career, with Mailer himself as the inadequate liberal occupying the dead center of control while the country is left rudderless in a sea of hysteria. In "Romantic Self-Creations: Mailer and Gilmore in *The Executioner's Song*" (*ConL* 31:434–47), Mark Edmundson reminds us that romantic writers are not only prone to exemplifying their own visions of originality but, following Emerson's doctrine of self-reliance, caught in a process of self-destruction as full accumulations are regularly cleared away in order to start anew. As a psychopath, Gary Gilmore "replays the past event in the present so that he can gain back what was lost, score victories where he was, in childhood, forced to make concessions," a reinvention that entails almost total destruction.

A rewarding look at John Knowles's masterwork is provided by Hallman Bell Bryant in A Separate Peace: *The War Within* (Twayne); from the novel's manuscript Bryant draws clues for the nature and motivations of characters, including how their attitudes are shaped, while whole short story and essay sources are combined with historical background to show the book's range. Gore Vidal's *The City and the Pillar* is read as a bildungsroman by Claude J. Summers in *Gay Fictions, Wilde to Stonewall: Studies in a Male Homosexual Literary Tradition* (Continuum), a sympathetic interpretation in which the protagonist's gradual acceptance of homosexual identity is played against the violence that results from derogatory labeling.

E. L. Doctorow (Continuum, 1991) provides John G. Parks with a chance to praise the author of *Ragtime* as the great visionary of an era's end in which protagonists themselves are transitional. The key to Doctorow's method is his grasp of a crisis in not just history but in historiography as it becomes of use to fictionists; the historical romance seeks socio-moral change, while the historical consciousness per se strives to avoid meaningless repetitions as a fate rather than moral challenge. History itself must be wrested from myth, something that demands a Foucaultian understanding of power. Carol Harter and James R. Thompson's *E. L. Doctorow* (TUSAS) agrees that history, politics, and sociology are less important as subjects than as promptings for technique, especially as both allegorical patterning and frank realism can be drawn from connections among history, autobiography, and fiction. In his first novels, Doctorow inverts formulaic subgenres (the Western and science fiction), perhaps as a prologue to his similar inversions of history in *Ragtime*. At this point, however, the study becomes deplorably uncritical, simply taking Doctorow's word that *Big as Life* does not belong in his canon instead of asking why or considering what the novel and then its rejection tells us about his art. Letting their book close with the assurance that Doctorow "will, no doubt, continue" and that he "will, no doubt, continue his firmly established pattern of innovation and discovery" makes the authors seem less like scholar-critics than press agents.

The importance of a novelist's roots, in this case Albany, New York, not only as a resource but as a strategy that makes place critical to fiction is reestablished by Edward C. Reilly in *William Kennedy* (TUSAS). Kennedy's *The Ink Truck* is representative of 1960s fiction in its use of lunacy, oppression, and belief that the individual can be saved (if not the world); *Legs* becomes the author's transitional work, an occasion for experiments with various narrative techniques; but it is *Ironweed* that shows Kennedy's masterful style, unified as the storytelling is by a centrality of place. Voice is also a concern, argues Charles Fanning in *The Irish Voice in America*, for behind Kennedy's lyrical description are important *"written* effects," drawing on an eloquence rendered from the thoughts of inarticulate people. Then there are the doings of politics, an understanding of which Kennedy shares with Joan Didion. The latter's ability to integrate her own political autobiography with the projected experiences of her characters is a key factor in Michael Tager's "The Political Vision of Joan Didion's *Democracy*" (*Crit* 31:173–84), a reading that underscores the antidemocratic forces at work in both the novel and in American society.

The major force in realistic fiction remains, even after his death, the influence of John Gardner. The interviews collected by editor Allan Chavkin in *Conversations with John Gardner* (Miss.) reveal how the debate over *On Moral Fiction* occupied the last half-decade of the author's life. In the reprinted material and in new discussions with

Charlie Reilly and Gregory L. Morris, the autobiographical emerges as
an important element in the fiction, but it is the tragedy not only of
Gardner's death but of how much of his last years was consumed by the
moral fiction controversy that inspires such vivid writing on the critics'
behalf. Dean McWilliams is more harsh in his judgment of the affair, as
expressed in *John Gardner* (TUSAS), complaining that *On Moral Fiction*
remains "misguided in its basic assumption, poorly reasoned in its
argument, and mean-spirited in tone." Even more deeply indicting is
McWilliams's belief that the greatest casualty of Gardner's critical attack
was his own fiction, which came to be read in terms of *On Moral Fiction*'s
overly narrow moralistic definition, whereas in fact a Bakhtinian dialogy
of polyphonous narratives is the key to Gardner's fictive art, the investigation of which makes McWilliams's book one of the finest on this
writer. A worthy addition to Gardner scholarship is Barry Fawcett and
Elizabeth Jones's "The Twelve Traps in John Gardner's *Grendel*" (*AL*
62:634–47), in which the zodiacal cycle is seen as a structure for the
testing of a dozen cultural and historical worldviews.

Literary historians have seen a major movement develop in Gardner's
wake, a basically realistic style known as neorealism or minimalism. The
challenge, of course, is to see just how realistic or nonrealistic such work
is, and that becomes a project for Barbara T. Ryan, whose "Decentered
Authority in Bobbie Ann Mason's *In Country*" (*Crit* 31:199–212) finds a
great deal of poststructuralist activity in the heroine's "changing conception of the authority she seeks," a journey which makes her an audience
for several different types of narrative. A more traditional study of
personal loss and effects on the community is presented by Sandra
Bonilla Durham in "Women and War: Bobbie Ann Mason's *In Country*"
(*SLJ* 22, ii:45–52), a reading addressed to the more customary tragedies
of war. Yet behind much of current neorealism lies a concern with
liminality and marginality, especially as these interests help to shape the
nature of narrative, a matter Catherine Rainwater investigates thoroughly in "Reading between Worlds: Narrativity in the Fiction of Louise
Erdrich" (*AL* 62:405–22); structural features by which a storyteller constructs a tale from whatever materials at hand frustrate conventional
understandings, but by using such techniques Erdrich encodes marginality into the reader's experience of the text. Then there is the more
familiar but no less challenging way adults talk about love, something
Donald J. Greiner finds to be important in "The Absent Friends of
Frederick Busch" (*GettR* 3:746–54), in which "making contact with the

people who matter in one's life" can be problematic indeed. Busch's canon is divided between the narrative voices of dominant males, who wreck women's lives while frustrating their own, and "hesitant males," whose memories and needs "invade the female's life while trying to define" their own. Then there are the two most prominent minimalists, Raymond Carver and Ann Beattie, whose work prompts some of the field's brightest criticism. In "Raymond Carver and Postmodern Humanism" (*Crit* 31:125–36), Arthur A. Brown finds this supposed realist to be validly postmodern in his dedication to surface as true subject, a style of "contour drawing" that finds the real humanism to be not in shared moral views but in the commonality of creating a fiction. Editors Marshall Bruce Gentry and William L. Stull collect interviews that in *Conversations with Raymond Carver* (Miss.) emphasize the topical in his work, yet a certain "precisionism" (rather than just minimalism) as derived from the teachings of Ezra Pound makes the author's work something other than mere social realism. "An Interview with Ann Beattie" (*ConL* 31:404–21) allows Steven R. Centola to draw out Beattie on the topic of minimalism, which she deplores as a pejorative label but appreciates when it is applied to "the specifics of my work and how the particularities establish emotion."

That this new style of realism can polarize critics just as effectively as any innovative fiction is shown by two contrasting essays, John W. Aldridge's "The New American Assembly-Line Fiction: An Empty Blue Center" (*ASch* 59:17–38) and Arthur M. Saltzman's "To See a World in a Grain of Sand: Expanding Literary Minimalism" (*ConL* 31:423–33). Aldridge's argument against such fiction is predicated on criticism's failure to influence the literary marketplace, but even on its own terms minimalism fails to impress as anything other than being an MFA-generated system that presents hundreds of new authors to the culture each year (instead of the dozen or so Aldridge feels critics can capably handle). Such workshop writing exists not to garner merit but to confirm the continuing need for workshops; success is measured not in terms of aesthetic success but in "membership in the fraternity" whose primary interest is in the teaching of writing (rather than in writing itself). The fiction produced reminds Aldridge of "the scenic blips of television" in which experience is too quick and fragmentary to be absorbed and evaluated, making everything forgettable. Nothing coalesces into drama or insight—which is, of course, the antiepiphanic imperative Arthur Saltzman's *Designs of Darkness* (see **i.** above) praises in such work. Saltzman's judgment of minimalism is made most directly in his *ConL* essay, which to his book's argument adds an understanding of this literature's perceived aridity and flatness as less of a stylistic program than a mode of inquiry. Close attention to "the ordinary conceits of our world" does not necessarily lead to satire, for minimalists open fiction to new meaning by taking the world "at its considerable face value." An aural corollary for such visual fascinations is found in the work of Stephen Dixon, whose ear for language, especially the "urban lingoes" of people at work in small-time jobs, creates a fiction rich enough to fascinate any semiotician but one that still offers common narrative interest, an urgency that by percolating "in every corner of contemporary culture" guarantees attention's reward.

viii John Updike, John Cheever, and Other Mannerists

Reinforcing Donald J. Greiner's position as the foremost authority on Updike's work is the critic's "Body and Soul: John Updike and *The Scarlet Letter*" (*JML* 15 [1989]:475–95). Updike transforms rather than reflects Hawthorne's masterpiece by taking Hawthorne's own meditations on sex, sin, and salvation and seeking to unite the otherwise disparate realms of material and purely spiritual. Updike's characters reject *The Scarlet Letter*'s uncertainty of faith and its resultant gloom, and by taking Chillingworth's point of view the novel itself emphasizes the role of close observation. Instead of a "blackness of darkness," *Roger's Version* relies on Karl Barth's belief that while humanity cannot reach God, God can still touch humanity. Just as sex and religion cannot be separated in Updike's canon, so a reading of his re-vision of *The Scarlet Letter* "shows that the contemporary reconstruction of the body requires a reconsideration of faith," a theme and practice that unifies *A Month of Sundays, Roger's Version,* and *S.*

A modern home for the novelists of manners is found by Shaun O'Connell in *Imagining Boston: A Literary Landscape* (Beacon). For John Cheever, Massachusetts roots provide a complex path of beginning, loss, and rediscovery that provides an identity not just of vocation but of spiritual direction. John Updike creates a New England of his own imagination, in which place engenders an attitude which in turn produces a standard of value (O'Connell notes that Updike is being increasingly identified as a New England writer, despite his roots in

Pennsylvania and allegiance to it as a subject). O'Connell's most valuable critique is of novelist Dan Wakefield, who has found in his Boston residency a metaphor for physical and spiritual recovery based on a sense of identity, community, and home.

ix Experimental Realism: Grace Paley

Two ground-breaking studies establish the centrality of Grace Paley's canon to American fiction and demonstrate how her writing takes advantage of innovations within both abstract and mimetic styles of composition. *Grace Paley: Illuminating the Dark* (Texas) by Jacqueline Taylor takes its cue from Paley's politics. Committed as she is to issues of feminism and antimilitarism, Paley finds her initial challenge not just in finding a voice for fiction in postmodern times but in reshaping language so that unheard voices can be given a locus for expression. Such writing serves "a distinctly woman-centered point of view and in so doing validates an experience and a perspective that have been muted in our language and our literature," and such stories cannot be told within the language of male dominance. Risking the charge of being mute or inarticulate, Paley moves beyond male categories and meanings to find a comic impulse for constructing a woman-centered perspective. Most importantly for fiction, Paley "revises and reinvents not only words and definitions but narrative structure as well, a resistance to the beginning-middle-end syndrome that sentences many women's stories to being untold or misunderstood. The ultimate authority to be undermined is that of the narrator, whose power must now be shared via cooperation with her characters. In *Grace Paley: A Study of the Short Fiction* (Twayne), Neil D. Isaacs sees Paley's work as an example of feminist expression but also as a means of bringing social concern back into otherwise innovative, antimimetic fiction. To Taylor's backdrop of feminist literary theory, Isaacs adds considerations drawn from comparison with Paley's friend Donald Barthelme's fiction and from employment of innovator Jonathan Baumbach's commentary. In this view, Paley's individuality is less of a style than a "sound" (in the way distinctive jazz musicians are so readily identified); "voice" constitutes her entire presence not as a person but as a writer, which may be the ultimate metafictive self-reflexivity—one that because of her commitment to social issues need not keep humane concerns banished from fiction. Finding a form for this voice's telling of stories constitutes the critical progress of her work.

x Kurt Vonnegut, Joseph Heller, and Other Early Innovators

After a brief lull, book-length scholarship of Kurt Vonnegut's work is again under way. Chief among these is Leonard Mustazza's *Forever Pursuing Genesis: The Myth of Eden in the Novels of Kurt Vonnegut* (Bucknell). Though some may feel Mustazza overemphasizes the optimistic side of Vonnegut's vision and locates it too traditionally within the romantic, his thesis does a magnificent job of unifying the author's canon, the later additions to which other critics have not always been able to harmonize with the earlier novels. The key is Vonnegut's continuous use of the Genesis myth, particularly its narrative structure of Creation, Innocence, and Fall, especially the fall into nature and imperfection which his protagonists try to restore by either creating new worlds of their own or shrinking the present cosmos to manageable dimensions. Although the process is evident in all of Vonnegut's novels, the "core of his escapist-Edenic vision, his reinvented universes," is *Mother Night, Slaughterhouse-Five, Slapstick,* and *Deadeye Dick,* in which mythic allusions "bridge the gap between familiar reality and his characters' peculiar illusions." My own *Slaughterhouse-Five: Reinventing the Novel and the World* (Twayne) looks not to mythic patterns or other external groundings but to the specific things the author does when conventional forms render his story untellable; Vonnegut's metafictive activity is a part of it, but foremost is his discovery of how intertextual elements, including his own presence in the narrative and its telling, can be used to speak the unspeakable, an impulse that exists as early as 1945 in an RAF prisoner's diary (noting the entry of Vonnegut's unit into Dulag Luft IVb) and in two Vonnegut family letters from that year printed here for the first time.

An important revision of the Vonnegut critical canon is undertaken by editor Robert Merrill in his *Critical Essays on Kurt Vonnegut* (Hall). Merrill's lengthy and detailed introduction (pp. 1–27) describes early responses that sought to establish Vonnegut's seriousness as an author, followed by more critical work in the mid-1970s debating the merits of moralism and nihilism in the fiction. By the decade's end, however, Vonnegut's acceptance into the mainstream was offset by a decline in critical attention made even worse by the misdirections offered by John Gardner (immoralism) and Josephine Hendin (psychosis). In the 1980s, attention to myth in several essays by Kathryn Hume and by Loree

Rackstraw (the best of which are reprinted here) recovered the author's reputation for postmodernist and especially feminist times. Merrill's editorial selections reflect this progress, and the four new essays he commissioned imply a direction for new scholarship. In "Tangled Up in You: A Playful Reading of *Cat's Cradle*"(pp. 94–108), John L. Simons clarifies the novel's complexities and moral implications, in which a philosophy of flow (Bokononism) exceeds the more limited nihilistic views of the book's characters, a strategy that is "Dostoevskian in its riddling contradictions." Recognizing that Vonnegut's recent works have received little sustained attention, Merrill encourages Charles Berryman to contribute "Vonnegut's Comic Persona in *Breakfast of Champions*" (pp. 162–70) and "Vonnegut and Evolution: *Galápagos*" (pp. 188–99) and David Cowart to write "Culture and Anarchy: Vonnegut's Later Career" (pp. 170–88). Berryman begins with Vonnegut's talent for self-parody and sees it leading ultimately to a way in which the materials of *Galápagos,* including setting, characters, and narrative strategy, are related to the central theme of evolution that empowers Leon Trout as an ideal combination of his father's cynicism and his mother's hopefulness. Cowart praises this same balance between "nihilist despair and humanist affirmation." Isolation causes the modern malaise, and Vonnegut counters this loneliness by developing extended families and communities in his later works. As such, he bridges the gap between modernism's fragmentation (with classical standards as an antidote) and postmodernism's polymorphous perversity (where textual parodies mask the absence of subject).

Merrill's own "Kurt Vonnegut as a German American" (*Germany and German Thought,* pp. 230–43) discounts earlier interpretations of Vonnegut's family life as pleasantly happy, seeing it instead as a source of irony in which his parents' German culture seems Eurocentrically escapist of current American realities. The author's childhood roots are known primarily through their absence, a marginality enhanced by his memories of a German-American family whose riches and culture were devastated by the depression and the coming of Nazism. A good reading of *Slaughterhouse-Five* is undertaken by Jonathan Morse in *Word by Word: The Language of Memory* (Cornell); here, history's tragedy is seen in that its significance lies only in irony, which means in Vonnegut's novel the foundational referent can be only the author's self. Words themselves fail to extend beyond virtual meaning, with no reference beyond their own structured language; Billy Pilgrim is thus able to succeed as a protagonist only by living outside the law of human syntax.

Vonnegut and Joseph Heller play important roles in "Mimesis and Digesis in Modern Fiction" (pp. 25–44), a key chapter in David Lodge's *After Bakhtin: Essays on Fiction and Criticism* (Routledge). Vonnegut's sudden identification of "That was I. That was me. That was the author of this book" in *Slaughterhouse-Five* breaks the narrative frame and thus exposes the constructive device behind all fabrication, a postmodern technique in that rather than being smoothed over by realism (and thereby subordinated to mimesis) this digesis is foregrounded against mimesis itself in which "the stream of consciousness has been turned into a stream of narration." Heller's *Good as Gold* similarly violates the realistic code by admitting that Gold is a character in a book with no autonomy beyond what the author wills, thus giving shock effect to the previously suppressed words, "I" and "book."

Richard Brautigan, Richard Fariña, and Jerzy Kosinski are given attention in three worthwhile studies. Mary Jane Hurst takes a new approach to *Trout Fishing in America* by contrasting it with William Peter Blatty's *The Exorcist;* within the framework of her *The Voice of the Child in American Literature* (Kentucky), Brautigan's novel is seen not as a child's view but as a child's experience become significant in terms of adult sensibility and understanding (in which the narrative has a flavor of childhood rather than its essence), while *The Exorcist* features the evil of an outside world striking into childhood's innocence (in which language signifies the demon speaking within). Fariña's minor classic, *Been Down So Long It Looks Like Up to Me,* is the last segment in Gregory Stephenson's fine study of the Beat Generation, *The Daybreak Boys;* here, innocence becomes a strategy of affirmation in which the Beat hipster serves as a new American Adam spreading immunity against disease. Welcome attention to an overlooked later book is provided by Barry Nass in "Androgyny, Transsexuality, and Transgression in Jerzy Kosinski's *Passion Play*" (*ConL* 31:37–57), a defense of the author's interests by allying them with efforts against patriarchy. Transsexuals seek to define their identity "at any cost and in defiance of all norms"; boundaries of the self are thus redrawn surgically, allowing a metamorphosis Kosinski values as the power of will to change one's life.

xi John Barth, John Hawkes, and Thomas Pynchon

Barth and Pynchon inevitably attract the most postmodern scholarship, and this year critics have returned to John Hawkes with similar gusto.

For Barth's work, what many critics regard as a regressive disappearance within the parochial complexities of his own later fiction is for Max F. Schulz the highpoint of a career. *The Muses of John Barth: Tradition and Metafiction from* Lost in the Funhouse *to* The Tidewater Tales (Hopkins) praises the author for his ability to maintain voice and story while pushing self-reflexivity to its ultimate. Fueled by a parallel interest in human sexuality, Barth's concern for the author's role enables him to finally pass beyond the stage of apprenticeship to Joycean modernism and attempt fiction truly pertinent to our aesthetic and philosophic times. Not merely a parodist, Barth produces independent versions of myths "done in late twentieth-century American idiom." Yet Schulz's professed belief that Barth undertakes such works in the service of timeless universal values, combined with the critic's admitted avoidance of postwar literary theory, limits his readings to conventional humanistic interpretations, when in fact Barth has schooled himself in the thought of our age (if only to reject it all the more convincingly). A better feel for Barth's importance (and how he achieves it) is found in *Understanding John Barth* (So. Car.), Stan Fogel and Gordon Slethaug's informed account of how the author revels both in the act of storytelling and in its dislocation. Somewhat of an antipositivist, Barth sees life as secondary to language (a corrective to Schulz's homely humanism), yet in *The Tidewater Tales,* by a balance of sailing lore and social politics, he is able to interrelate writing and the national condition. As opposed to other interests of innovative fiction, it is Barth's love of language and narrative that motivates his work.

LETTERS attracts praise from Kim McMullen in "The Fiction of Correspondence: *LETTERS* and History" (*MFS* 36:405–20) and scorn from Johnny Payne in "Epistolary Fiction and Intellectual Life in a Shattered Culture: Ricardo Piglia and John Barth" (*TriQ* no. 80:171–205). Payne's complaint is that Barth tries to substitute "sheer formalism" for considered social inquiry, making historical claims, yet relying on "repetition, recurrence, and re-enactment" for his substance, the sum of which lacks viable engagement with its times. McMullen is more interested in the textual possibilities that an exchange of letters in history can provide; challenging the traditional historical notion "that assumes a prior object to which the text simply corresponds and referentially constitutes," *LETTERS* invites history and fiction to compete as intertextual forms "of lettered construction." Thus, the set of rules for producing and distributing discourse is reflexively engaged to show how

America is in fact constituted by competing narratives which in turn
order the practices of those who are so articulated.

Barth himself takes a hand in the issue of *RCF* 10, ii devoted to his
work with an in-progress excerpt plus a talk on "The Spanish Connection" (pp. 25–34). The issue's best critical contribution comes from
Creed Greer, whose "Abortion Stories: The Sexual Metaphorics of
Organizing Barth's Texts" (pp. 76–81) looks to *Sabbatical* as an example
in which the act of abortion reflects how an author's attempt to put
stories in order by removing one of them has "an organizational impact
on the remainder of the text or corpus," the issue being Fenn and Susan's
decision of how to dispose of the story of her tears. Charles B. Harris
finds a similar disruption in Barth's supposed attempt to return to
"straight" realism, and in "The Age of the World View: The Critique of
Realism in John Barth's *Sabbatical*" (*Germany and German Thought*,
pp. 407–32) reads the novel as "a self-conscious and ultimately parodic
reorchestration of the conventions of nineteenth-century literary realism
as well as a critique of the epistemological assumptions literary realism
implies." Barth's own appreciation of how long and complex novels are
required for fiction to do its job of "getting out of oneself (in order,
naturally, to return, bringing something back)" is explained in his "It's a
Long Story" (*Harper's* 281, i:71–78), which also pleads for *Don Quixote* as
the first postmodern novel (thanks to its "incremental awareness of itself
as fiction," "its transcendent parody of the genre," and "its half-ironic
amplitude").

The "radical theory of male heterosexuality" expressed in John
Hawkes's novels of the 1970s is summed up in protagonist Konrad Vost's
transformation, says Peter F. Murphy in "Male Heterosexuality in
Hawkes's *The Passion Artist*" (*TCL* 36:403–18), a study of how comfort
with one's sexuality is achieved by acknowledging both "the woman
within" and the capability of women for both seduction and love. The
polar imperatives of cruelty and innocence inform all of Hawkes's novels, according to Rita Ferrari; her "The Innocent Imagination in John
Hawkes' *Whistlejacket* and *Virginie: Her Two Lives*" (*ArQ* 46, i:105–29)
examines the author's reflective treatment of authorial power in its
productive rhythms between these poles, with only the text itself, here
figured as Virginie herself, being able to take a perspective from both
sides.

Like his fiction itself, scholarship on Thomas Pynchon is by its bulk
and complexity calculated to overwhelm. In *The Gnostic Pynchon* (Indi-

ana), Dwight Eddins follows Kathryn Hume's mythic grounding (see *ALS 1987*, p. 303) as he traces Pynchon's religious quest for a principle of organic order, an undertaking that seeks to avoid both the hopelessness of ambiguity and the absolutistic extremes of chaos and control. This desire constitutes "a persistent modernist nostalgia for vanished axiological foundations in the midst of vividly experienced anomie"; postmodern instabilities are thus viewed as corrupt deviations from normalizing structures (the old humanism) instead of as liberating invitations to play. Eddins goes so far as to call Pynchon's project a modernist "home-building" of Eliot and Pound, a testament to "something in humanity that will not let us go." Given such nostalgia for ontologically grounded values, gnosis "opens the way to God for spirit," the key as always being the ability to ground such moments in something beyond the cabalistic (*V.* remains locked within a gnostically reductive system, *The Crying of Lot 49* finds harmony with the present, while *Gravity's Rainbow* surpasses even the previous novels' either/or duality to find a sympathetically Orphic nature). Just the opposite approach is taken by Theodore D. Kharpertian in *A Hand to Turn the Time: The Menippean Satires of Thomas Pynchon* (Fairleigh Dickinson); here, concern with genre rather than theme reveals a fiction of carnivalization in the service of fertility and delight, and iconoclasm that in the wake of realism's loss of trust feels ambivalent even with myth, certainly with myth's pretense at corresponding to anything real. *V.* succeeds as a parody structure of a quest for the fantastic, while the questing in *The Crying of Lot 49* satirizes a monological America; *Gravity's Rainbow* attacks the whole Western sensibility, especially its rationalization of death by synthesis and control, and in the process uses Menippean multiplicities to produce a kaleidoscopic effect.

The most original contribution in years comes from Alex McHoul and David Wills, whose *Writing Pynchon: Strategies in Fictional Analysis* (Illinois) reads the novels as analogs of contemporary literary theory. From such obvious affinities as bricolage-style borrowings, quotation, and play, McHoul and Wills follow the fiction beyond the logocentric tradition in ways that successfully counter the humanist core that Eddins and others believe it affirms. *The Crying of Lot 49* cuts meanings loose, while *Gravity's Rainbow* becomes effectively postrhetorical by expressing itself in indeterminacies, indistinguishable characters, intralinguistic play, and a plethora of themes. When all distinctions fail, nothing comes from reversals, and all dualities are constantly overruled, it becomes clear that all transcendental signifieds, like V herself, are effectively deconstructed.

David Cowart, a leading Pynchon scholar, narrows his focus yet broadens his conclusions in "Germany and German Culture in the Works of Thomas Pynchon" (*Germany and German Thought,* pp. 305–18) to tell how international folly courses along the traditional East-West interface that Germany traditionally provides. Pynchon's early short fiction indicates how trash defines a culture's counterhistory, according to Stuart Barnett's "Refused Readings: Narrative and History in 'The Secret Integration'" (*PNotes* 22–23 [1988]:79–85). This same story details a source for a later geographical setting, Donald F. Larsson indicates in "From the Berkshires to the Brocken: Transformations of a Source in 'The Secret Integration' and *Gravity's Rainbow*" (*PNotes* 22–23 [1988]:87–98). The transformation from modern to postmodern views of art, self, and history are apparent to Maarten Van Delden in "Modernism, the New Criticism, and Thomas Pynchon's *V.*" (*Novel* 23:117–36), where Pynchon's approach involves parodying modern masters. That a writer's use of metaphors saves him and his readers from despairing over the separation of the metaphysical from the physical is an argument advanced by Elizabeth Campbell in "Metaphor and *V.*: Metaphysics in the Mirror" (*PNotes* 22–23 [1988]:57–69). Competing versions of entropy as defined by scientific and literary paradigms lead to cultural contradictions that only myths can mediate, a theme in *The Crying of Lot 49* that is explicated by Frank Palmeri in *Satire in Narrative;* important reminders are that metaphors are tools, not truths, and that in parody one focuses less on the subject than its restraining conditions as a model or genre. *Gravity's Rainbow* draws on both German and American models of science and technology, according to two well-researched essays in *Germany and German Thought:* Robert L. McLaughlin's "I. G. Farben and the War Against Nature in *Gravity's Rainbow*" (pp. 305–18) and Georg Schmundt-Thomas's "America's Germany and the Pseudo-Origins of Manned Spaceflight in *Gravity's Rainbow*" (pp. 337–53). Three substantial essays in *PNotes* nos. 22–23, Strother Purdy's "*Gravity's Rainbow* and the Culture of Childhood" (pp. 7–23), Robert L. McLaughlin's "Pynchon's Angels and Supernatural Systems in *Gravity's Rainbow*" (pp. 25–33), and Yves-Marie Léonet's "Waking from the Apollonian Dream: Correspondences Between *The Birth of Tragedy* and *Gravity's Rainbow*" (pp. 35–45) argue, respectively, that Pynchon's own childhood during the years of World War II prompts him to employ fairy-tale structures and the peculiar horror of anonymous destruction, that mysteriously appearing agents are less Rilke-like creations than agents of the paranoid Other, and that Nietzsche's masterwork influenced Pynchon's use of opera. In *The Culture of Redemption* (Harvard), Leo Bersani suggests that Slothrop follows the course of Oedipus in his astonishment at learning of connections and their causality in the hands of a malevolent fate. In *Gravity's Rainbow*, however, there is no catharsis, just an assumption of fate as the character disappears into the "pop role created for him." As a novel of excess, Pynchon's book fights back against an encyclopedic culture by showing how art can humanize knowledge, in the process absorbing and denying technology's attempt to totalize and control. A similar role is performed by the novel's wide range of discourse, says Christopher Ames in "Power and the Obscene Word: Discourses of Extremity in Thomas Pynchon's *Gravity's Rainbow*" (*ConL* 31:191–207), while John Johnston finds a world deeply enmeshed in its own history (and histories) in "Pynchon's 'Zone': A Postmodern Multiplicity" (*ArQ* 46, iii:91–122). An issue of *Crit* 32 is somewhat prematurely devoted in full to Pynchon's recent novel, *Vineland*, but worthy first readings are provided by David Cowart in "Attenuated Postmodernism: Pynchon's *Vineland*" (pp. 67–76), where the author's use of history and myth in his career are Joycean, and by Joseph W. Slade, whose "Communication, Group Theory, and Perception in *Vineland*" (pp. 126–44) shows how the dangers of an Information Age are as formidable as the older threat of nuclear holocaust.

xii Paul Auster, Robert Coover, William Gaddis, Joseph McElroy, and Don DeLillo

Alison Russell brings a new writer into the innovative fiction fold with "Deconstructing *The New York Trilogy*: Paul Auster's Anti-Detective Fiction" (*Crit* 31:71–84), an analysis of how a semantic journey of neverending arrivals and departures denies any locus for meaning (a deconstructive process worthy of Derrida). *Gerald's Party*, already a key text for general studies (see **i.** above), garners two important essays, "Coover's Comedy of Conflicting Fictional Codes" by Christopher Ames (*Crit* 31:85–99) and Larry McCaffery's "The Recognitions: An Editorial Collaboration with Robert Coover's 'Party Talk'" (*FictI* 18, ii:176–86). Ames appreciates the carnivalesque aspects of this novel, finding its success in a collision of different codes (detective, slapstick, masquerade, dream tale, and ritual sacrifice). McCaffery introduces a previously unpublished section of the book as an enhancement of Coover's recognition that creation "is a compositional *process* comprised of different kinds of texts." Similar interests course through John Johnston's *Carnival of Repetition: Gaddis's* The Recognitions *and Postmodern Theory* (Penn.), anchored as they are by Bakhtin's carnivalization of many contending voices, Deleuze's difference and repetition (in which there is no original but endless copies whose validity is in their repetition), and the unseated authority of broken-down homologies as practiced by Jean-Joseph Goux.

Joseph McElroy and Don DeLillo grow in scholarly prominence, thanks to two excellently edited journal issues on their work. As has become the practice in such *RCF* numbers, McElroy takes a hand in the work via an interview, essay, and work-in-progress; among the 18 critical essays and bibliography that make this issue (10, i) the most important existing repository for McElroy scholarship, even generalists will wish to note Brian McHale's "Women and Men and Angels: On Joseph McElroy's Fiction" (pp. 227–47), Tom LeClair's "Opening Up Joseph McElroy's *The Letter Left to Me*" (pp. 258–67), and Pamela White Hadas's "Green Thoughts on Being in Charge: Discovering Joseph McElroy's *Plus*" (pp. 140–55). As LeClair indicates, it is McElroy's mastery of an age's excesses that puts his fiction in league with Pynchon's and counters the deprecations of those who would condemn an entire era even before its literary artists are given a chance. LeClair himself has been a frequent commentator on mastery in another writer, Don DeLillo (see *ALS: 1987*, pp. 305–06), and his interpretation squares with the excellent commentaries provided by editor Frank Lentricchia in *SAQ:* 89, ii, the most interesting of which is John A. McClure's "Postmodern Romance: Don DeLillo and the Age of Conspiracy" (pp. 337–53), a consideration of how such popular forms as the espionage thriller, imperial adventure novel, western, science fiction, and "even the genre of occult adventure" let the author prove modernism wrong in decertifying romance as a valid form of expression. LeClair's interpretive influence, this time with regard to the need for inclusive systems, is seen in Eric Mottram's "The Real Needs of Man: Don DeLillo's Novels" (pp. 51–98), a contribution to editor Graham Clarke's *The New American Writing: Essays on American Literature Since 1970* (St. Martin's) that also draws on Ilya Prigogine's understanding of pathological communications in power relationships—relationships that accept the "passage from local to global" as an obsessional need. Nietzsche, a common allusion in Pynchon scholarship, pops up in Mark Osteen's "Against the End: Asceticism and Apocalypse in Don DeLillo's *End Zone*" (*PLL* 26:143–63); self-denial seems the key to primal simplicity in all of DeLillo's protagonists, but in *White Noise,* ends as well as origins become an ascetic concern.

xiii The Innovative Extreme: Walter Abish and Ronald Sukenick

Abish, who provides key texts for general study (see **i.** above), is studied in two important and insightful essays, both of which make capital of his writerly interest in politics and history. In "Walter Abish's *How German Is It:* Postmodernism and the Past" (*Salmagundi,* nos. 85–86, pp. 172–94), Maarten Van Delden takes issue with my own belief (see *ALS 1981,* p. 303, and *ALS 1984,* p. 294) that Abish's special brand of realism avoids contentual referentiality. The novelist's purpose is instead to break apart the frames of familiarity "and so to restore to the reader a sense of the actual shape of things," which in terms of recent German history makes for a complex process of dealing with the relative knowability of the past and the force that history exercises in our lives. That the narrator of this novel has a specific interpretation of German history and present-day "Germanness" concerns Anthony Schirato in "The Politics of Writing and Being Written: A Study of Walter Abish's *How German Is It*" (*Novel* 24:69–85). That Nazism is not an aberration but the essence of this country's beliefs is a serious charge; yet even as he makes it, the narrator seeks to impose a new fiction that comically deconstructs itself, resisting closure in the way he would intend and instead revealing itself as a matter of sleight of hand. Any scheme can only be sustained "by emphasizing details that fit," while the genius of fiction is that its significance "can be reversed by a single 'circumstantial' detail," a rhythm that Abish's novel employs to great effect.

Ronald Sukenick continues to distinguish himself as a spokesman on issues relating to fiction itself (see **i.** above), but his full range of activities is covered by David Seed in an important piece, "An Interview with Ronald Sukenick," appearing in *Over Here* [Nottingham] 10, i:1–6. To familiar notions such as the effaced distinction between autobiography and fiction and the phoniness of contrived endings, Sukenick adds new thoughts on the inadequacy of paranoia (in *Blown Away*) and the transitional roles of Henry Miller and Kenneth Patchen in opening the way for innovative fiction.

xiv Fiction of the Vietnam War

An unfortunate misreading of Vietnam War fiction, advanced in the cause of a neoconservative reaction against both the postmodern theory and innovative practice that inform this literature, is undertaken by Philip H. Melling in *Vietnam in American Literature* (Twayne). To make his case, the critic argues that writers of the war were influenced to a much greater degree by Puritan testimonials and the sense of mission behind America's early theocracy than by the philosophies and fictive styles of their own days; in the process he reads these novels flatly with an eye to theme alone, as if history itself (and not even the rendering of it) is more important than any work of art. An interesting corrective can be observed in Carl Freedman's study of a novel that was historically addressed to an entirely different era, that of the Korean War, but whose manner speaks of the newer reality of Vietnam. "History, Fiction, Film, Television, Myth: The Ideology of M*A*S*H" (*SoR* 25:89–106) reminds us how the roles of doctoring and soldiering contradict each other, and that putting them together "enables a certain rebelliousness while finally serving an ideologically neutralizing function" emblematic of a postmodern orientation. A fine survey of American war fiction and how it has changed since the end of World War II is provided by Arne Axelsson in *Restrained Response: American Novels of the Cold War and Korea, 1945–1962* (Greenwood); the military novel after Hiroshima and Nagasaki was "as cut off from its tradition and its past as the military itself" and not until *Catch-22* (1961) is the form straightened out.

Rendering rather than simply reporting is the emphasis Kalí Tal makes in "The Mind at War: Images of Women in Vietnam Novels by Combat Veterans" (*ConL* 31:76–96), a study that realizes a combat veteran has a very personal stake in how the story turns out; the finished product therefore constitutes a "working out" of the event experienced. Given that a loss of empathy is initially a survival device but becomes later an obstacle to retelling, female characters often represent the level of the veteran's alienation in both circumstances. Often the figure of an Asian woman provides the means for reconciliation. That the essence of the war might exist elsewhere is suggested by John Limon's "War and Play: A Theory of the Vietnam Sports Novel" (*ArQ* 46, iii:65–90). In the 1960s there was a "spate of sports novels . . . all written by noncombatants, all alluding to Vietnam by indirection or misdirection," and in these works Limon finds that the border which sports novels share with play and warfare allows a greater field of expression for the war's ambiguity and ungraspability than do other, more direct forms that in seeking to totalize actually restrict our understanding.

xv Popular Subgenres: Science Fiction, Fantasy, Crime, and Nonfiction Novels

A curiosity of contemporary studies is that scholars who make their initial mark as advocational commentators on the newest of mainstream fiction rarely stay with it, almost always turning to arcane and even esoteric interests: witness Ihab Hassan's loss of interest in the contemporary fiction he championed in *Radical Innocence* in favor of the gnosis of pure thought, Leslie Fiedler's turn from the novelists of his own generation to a style of lowbrow entertainments German critics quite accurately call "popwash," and Robert Scholes's abandonment of the writers he introduced in *The Fabulators* for a new concern in the culturally isolated field of science fiction (followed by a current interest in strategies of reading). The latest to follow this path is Larry McCaffery, whose work of the 1970s helped establish the canonical importance of a new generation of now-mainstream writers. To keep the pattern of recent critical history intact, McCaffery insures that no major critics of one decade's mainstream fiction will yet address themselves to the primary fiction of the next by redirecting his interest to a monstrously alienated form of literature written by a few isolated writers and read by initiates far outside the general culture, the "cyberpunk" fiction produced by William Gibson, Bruce Sterling, and others no more likely to have a part in serious American literary history than those long-forgotten authors of the 1930s who churned out pulp thrillers about a future Earth ruled by electronic lizards from the planet Remulac. The merit of McCaffery's *Across the Wounded Galaxies: Interviews with Contemporary American Science Fiction Writers* (Illinois) lies in its mastery of ideas already in the tradition, such as Ursula K. Le Guin's concern with the premises of worlds apart, Thomas M. Disch's ability to "mathematize" literature, the semiotics that inform Samuel Delany's fiction, and the musical forms Joanna Russ uses to structure her novels. Though the headnotes to some of these interviews make gestures toward allying current science fiction with the issues of postmodernism and deconstruction, McCaffery's authors rarely entertain such trends, and the critic's introduction does little to recover such works for larger cultural pertinence. Most revealing is

McCaffery's own motive for reading SF, which he admits was initiated as a form of escape from an unhappy childhood endured with alcoholic parents living in the repressive atmosphere of a military base.

A critic less interested in escape is Elizabeth Cummins, whose *Understanding Ursula K. Le Guin* (So. Car.) traces Le Guin's interest in the anthropology of diverse cultures to her parents' work in that field. Relations between place and person lead to world-building, in which humans find their identities with reference to a changing set of physical worlds. In proposing such structures, Le Guin draws on both fantasy (for different foundations of knowledge) and science fiction (different principles of science). The close connection between love and being prompts an essay by J. R. Wytenbroek, "Taoism in the Fantasies of Ursula K. Le Guin" (pp. 173–80), contributed to editor Olena H. Saciuk's *The Shape of the Fantastic* (Greenwood); when balanced, these forces constitute a fully realized person, a Taoist ideal informing *A Wizard of Earthsea* and *The Farthest Shore*. A pair of "reader's guides" from Garland, *Fantasy Literature* and *Horror Literature*, each ed. Neil J. Barron, do a good job of bringing scholarship on both fields up to date, thanks to (respectively) Maxim Jakubowski's "Modern Fantasy for Adults, 1957–88" (pp. 223–304), in which post-Tolkien fantasy is described as a commercial rather than literary genre now devoted to "the manufacture of yard goods," and Keith Neilson's "Contemporary Horror Fiction, 1950–88" (pp. 160–326), where distinctions among subtypes (pastoral horror, surreal narration, etc.) allow consideration of writers as diverse as Stephen King and Jerzy Kosinski. King's success is ascribed to his borrowings from other genres, while Jakubowski borrows writers from the mainstream (Philip Roth, Robert Coover, Thomas Pynchon, John Barth, and Donald Barthelme) to similarly enrich the world of fantasy.

University press attention to popular subgenres continues to yield insightful work. How the "crime" novel as opposed to the detective novel thrives on antirationality and a deconstructed sense of order fascinates Tony Hilfer, whose *The Crime Novel* builds on such empirical observations that the killer and not the detective is the protagonist to show how such fiction thrives on insecurities of time and space; in the end, an ontological uncertainty motivates an attempt to recover rational grounding, whereby survival is achieved by rejecting emotion and commitment. A key figure in these literary possibilities for negation is novelist Jim Thompson. A lively consideration of "the other part of popular fiction" is found in Thomas J. Roberts's *An Aesthetics of Junk Fiction* (Georgia); here "form-intensive" novels are read as verbal textures that revel in intricacies of narrative design, designs which in the case of science fiction are welcomed as things in themselves by readers who want something "truly awful." Indeed, readers of such junk fiction read by genre rather than by author or subject, becoming enthusiasts for the times and tides of generic reinvention.

Literary nonfiction, which stretches from the marginally reportorial "New Journalism" to the seriousness of the nonfiction novel, is given a thorough and synthesizing treatment by Barbara Lounsberry in *The Art of Fact: Contemporary Artists of Nonfiction* (Greenwood). Such writing is distinguished by its documentable subject, exhaustive research, narrative sense of scene, and fine writing. In the hands of Gay Talese, such practices yield individual psychodramas that "become the national psychodramas of us all"; satire and criticism lead to virtual jeremiads in the works of Tom Wolfe, while John McPhee takes a gentler approach reminiscent of the 19th-century Transcendentalists. In the book's most original chapter, Joan Didion's "look backward to the fall" fits her conservatively constricting vision, as opposed to Norman Mailer's use of individual achievement as a model for social growth.

University of Northern Iowa

Lee Bartlett

i William Carlos Williams

While there is much to be said for Marjorie Perloff's sense that the first half of 20th-century American poetry and poetics divides between readers of Ezra Pound and readers of Wallace Stevens, since at least the late 1950s, probably more significant younger poets have paid homage to William Carlos Williams as a primary source for their understanding of the possibilities for poetry than to Pound and Stevens combined.

I would not describe this year's work on Williams as a bumper crop, but the harvest provided enough for a very decent and varied meal, with one (rather brief) book-length study as a memorable main course. Bryce Conrad's *Refiguring America: A Study of William Carlos Williams'* In the American Grain (Illinois) offers a reading of Williams's seminal prose collection. Conrad's thesis is both provocative and, thanks to his close reading of the text(s), convincing: "Williams' frequent erasures of the semiotic sutures between his text and those he appropriates, the virtual absence of any accompanying bibliographical documentation . . . and the blur of historical fact and verbal creation, makes his text a difficult terrain—yet therein lies much of its richness." Mirroring to a certain extent Williams's own style—"anarchically disruptive," Conrad calls it—this analysis argues that a key to the work is understanding that "Williams was strongly aware of the irremediable gap between the past and its narrative representations. . . . Even though Williams explicitly points to certain sources and origins in American history, he just as emphatically erases and disguises others, making history, ultimately, deceptive ground in *In the American Grain.*" Of particular interest is Conrad's fourth chapter, "The Poetics and Politics of Sexuality," in which he forcefully argues that "though Williams attempts to cultivate the ground of an indigenous American tradition, the book ultimately depicts American history as the destruction of the native female element necessary to that tradition. . . . American history, for Williams, is largely the story of the destruction of the female body—and not just as metaphor, but also as literal fact." I have always regarded *In the American Grain* as probably the most powerful yet quirky, useful yet mysterious, book of prose by a 20th-century American poet; Conrad's well-researched, innovative, and illuminating *Refiguring America* deserves a place on the shelf next to it.

William Chapman Sharpe's *Unreal Cities: Urban Figuration in Wordsworth, Baudelaire, Whitman, Eliot, and Williams* (Hopkins) interestingly focuses on "cities of mind, cities of words—into which the metropolis has been transformed by the power of art," examining the ways "preexisting forms and figures have influenced the poetic art of the modern city." In his final chapter, Sharpe turns his attention to "gender and revelation" in *Paterson,* arguing that Williams's long poem becomes "a quest for an ideal, redemptive marriage that [can] repair the division of man from woman, city from nature, and daily language from the needs of authentic speech" as the poet attempts "to rediscover the pure tongue of his native ground" as the "reunifying" force. And yet, the poem accepts a ground of "doubleness" over against a kind of forced unity, and thus for Williams "the culminating image of the sexualized city, the woman met on the streets of Paterson in Book V, embodies both whore and virgin."

Unlike such contemporary admirers of Williams as Levertov, Ginsberg, and Creeley, Robert Bly is not particularly drawn to him, and Bly's new collection of previously published essays, *American Poetry: Wildness and Domesticity* (Harper), is worth at least a glance as engaged and engaging counterargument. In his influential "A Wrong Turning in American Poetry" (first published in 1963), Bly attacks Pound, Eliot, Moore, and Williams as sources for a contemporary poetry "without spiritual life," "without even a trace of revolutionary feeling," and "essentially without the unconscious." "If American poetry has a center," he concedes, "it would seem to be William Carlos Williams"; Williams was "a noble man, of all the poets in his generation the warmest and most human." His poetry, however, "shows a fundamental absence of spiritual intensity. He is in fact as much caught up in destructive expansion as the others." On a more positive note, in "Leaping Up into Political Poetry" (written five years later), Bly reverses himself a bit, arguing that Williams's "refusal to ignore political lies was passed on to Allen Ginsberg," while by the 1973 "The Wheel of Intelligence" Bly calls Williams's "contagious hospital poem" a "masterpiece."

Certainly the most important Williams text to appear in the 1980s was *The Collected Poems,* published in two volumes by New Directions, ed. A. Walton Litz and Christopher MacGowan. This year the *WCWR* (16, i) offers papers from a Modern Language Association section devoted to the new edition, introduced by Robert Berthoff, with contributions by Patricia C. Willis, Paul Mariani, Terence Diggory, and Christopher MacGowan. Berthoff's opening remarks (pp. 1–3) compare the production of the Williams edition to an almost simultaneous project, Hans Gabler's new edition of Joyce's *Ulysses,* declaring that "unlike the ruckus in the Joyce community over *Ulysses,* the Williams community produced new editions that demonstrated the growth and achievement of Williams as a poet—and with genuine good will." In her "The Text of *The Tempers:* An Examination of the New *Collected Poems*" (pp. 4–7), Willis usefully traces the evolution of what the new *Collected Poems* offers as Williams's first book, *The Tempers,* through its 1913, 1938, and 1951 incarnations, touching the larger question of authorial intention. Mariani in "A White-Hot Man Become a Book" (pp. 8–15) calls the new *Collected Poems,* "texts which I can trust, stripped, cleansed, restored, like the images on the ceiling and walls of the Sistine Chapel." Mariani animatedly argues for comparisons of Williams to Stevens rather than Pound. Diggory's "New Contexts for Reading Williams: The Christmas Series" (pp. 16–21) discusses those poems which are "characterized by iconography associated with Christ's birth, the Holy Family, or the Christmas season" and which also "share a concern for art as a more or less explicit theme." Coeditor MacGowan's "In Response" (pp. 22–25) makes a plea for anthologists making better use of the possibilities afforded them by the new *Collected Poems,* agreeing with Willis's notion that textual editing often involves compromise.

The same issue of *WCWR* offers three further notes of interest. In "A Proletarian Portrait? Williams in Germany" (pp. 26–29), Charlotte Melin provides a good sketch of the publication history of Williams's texts and their reception in the GDR. Debby Rosenthal's " 'Accurate Equivalents': Comparing Williams' 1913 and 1936 'Translations from the Spanish' " (pp. 30–35) argues that the earlier translations draw on the Spanish romance tradition, while the later work reflects Williams's "heightened political awareness" in its translation of "current antiFranco poems to show his support for the Republican cause in Spain." Finally, Richard M. Ratzan, M.D., offers "A Note on How Dr. Williams Probably Did *Not* Deliver Allen Ginsberg in 1926" (pp. 36–37), complete with the reprinting of a copy of Ginsberg's birth certificate. Having spent many sleepless nights meditating on that particular chestnut, I certainly hope this is not a put-on.

Sagetrieb's special "HD/WCW" issue (9, iii) provides three useful essays on Williams as well as an analytic bibliography. Sharon Dolin in "Enjambment as Modernist Metaphor in Williams' Poetry" (pp. 31–35) convincingly argues that Williams's frequent enjambment bodies forth "a new conception of metaphor—where, instead of one object or idea subsuming another, there exists a parity among the terms of the metaphor," an idea the poet derived from "the transposition of positive/negative space or of figure/ground reversals we find in Cubist paintings." A few critics have attempted to chart the influence of Whitehead's thought (especially his poetics of process) on Charles Olson and Robert Duncan. Now, Bruce Holsapple's "Williams, Whitehead and *The Embodiment of Knowledge:* 'A New Order of Knowing'" (pp. 57–96) succeeds in its dual purpose: to show "the importance of [*Embodiment*] as a statement of Williams' poetic" and "the relationship of that poetic to Williams' reading of Whitehead's *Science and the Modern World.*" Both books share a central premise, Holsapple posits. The need to restructure education, with increased attention to "aesthetic experience," as "knowledge, as both the basis of art and the material of thought, is located outside the mind; knowledge is what the mind brings into unity or aesthetic design." John Lowney in "'A Plot of Ground': The Problem of Cultural Identity in the Emergence of Williams' Avant-Garde Stance" (pp. 97–120) sees Williams's "commitment to experimentation and the destruction of traditional forms" in such "collage structures" as *Spring and All* and *Paterson* to "engage readers as active producers, analogous to the more overtly Dadaist, Surrealist and Futurist Texts"; the essay concludes that Williams's "stance" as an innovator often conceals "contradictory politics of cultural identity." Vincent Prestianni's "William Carlos Williams: An Analytic Bibliography of Bibliographies and Selective Checklist of Surveys of Criticism, Special Collections, Previously Unpublished Work, and Miscellanea" (pp. 231–46) completes the issue's Williams material.

WCWR (16, ii) prints a scholarly edition of Williams's previously unpublished "Introduction" to his short stories, the 1961 *The Farmers' Daughters,* edited and introduced by Hugh Witemeyer (pp. 1–25). Like Conrad and Sharpe, Linda Arbaugh Taylor is interested in questions of gender in Williams, as her "Lines of Contact: Mina Loy and William

Carlos Williams" (pp. 26–47) continues this issue of *WCWR* with a discussion of the relationship between Mina Loy and Williams. Taylor sees Loy's influence on Williams's work to include "her example in opening his poetry to sexuality as a way of deromanticizing love conventions"; Williams's "notions of gender are encouraged and mediated by Loy's feminist example." In "Kor(e)a in Hell: Williams' Lyrics of the Late 1940s" (pp. 48–54), Gian Balsamo examines Williams's "configuration of hell" offered in four poems of the late forties, arguing that the poet's "ceaseless modulation of Kora's voice defines the outline of the post-nuclear ruins among which a disconsolate humankind is trying to exorcise the specter of its own sterility." Terry G. Halladay provides "A Descriptive List of Books from the Library of William Carlos Williams Purchased by the William Reese Co., 1987" (pp. 55–63); of particular interest are inscribed presentation copies of early books by a number of younger poets, including Charles Bell, Michael Benedict, Cid Corman, Robert Creeley, James Laughlin, Denise Levertov, and Robert Lowell.

Finally, in " 'A Rose to the End of Time': William Carlos Williams and Marriage" (*TCL* 36:155–172), Ann W. Fisher-Wirth reads poems through Williams's career, finding marriage to be "the deepest and central metaphor, the wellspring of his art," though inner- rather than outer-directed.

ii Wallace Stevens

Barbara M. Fisher's *Wallace Stevens: The Intensest Rendezvous* (Virginia) proposes "the erotic dimension of his poetry"—"diverse expressions of desire" rather than a "collection of ideas"—to be "the key to the dynamics of Stevens' work." Focusing on a number of "aspects of desire" ("Contraries and the Necessary No," "Love of Place," "Native Passion"), Fisher traces "the transformations of eros" which "determine the vital structures and configuration of the entire [Stevens] canon." Closely reading a number of poems, this study examines Stevens's work as "seduction parables," parody, and negation leading to "an 'immaculate beginning' "; further, Fisher looks at some length at Stevens's "mysterious paramour" as "in a line of Wisdom figures beginning with Parmenides," fire imagery (arguing that "the erotic impulse [is] converted to purposes of prophecy"), Stevens's relationship to Dante, and the writer's "poetics of place." My one minor reservation is that given her focus, while making my way through the text I kept hoping that Fisher might ground her discussion more thoroughly in the immediate historical context, most especially drawing on appropriate issues in Stevens's biography. Still, an interesting and illuminating addition.

A second valuable study this year is Tom Quirk's *Bergson and American Culture: The Worlds of Willa Cather and Wallace Stevens* (No. Car.). Quirk finds the "national mood" at the turn of the century—"vitality, optimism, confidence, progress, and hope were accepted bywords"—to have its philosophic equivalent in Henri Bergson's "vitalism." Following chapters discussing the intellectual and cultural history of the period, Quirk examines Cather and Stevens as two writers who "read and responded to Bergson in interesting ways" and who were "deeply affected by the sudden social changes that occurred between 1910 and 1915." Relating Cather and Stevens, Quirk argues that they share "a political conservatism and a feeling for an atavistic past," as well as being Francophiles. Of Stevens in particular, the Bergsonian influence will not come as a surprise to most readers of this essay, though Quirk provides a careful and fluid articulation of the epistemological convergences. Especially good discussions of the poet's sense of the image, "resemblance and identity," and "the irrational intuitions of the real as constant flux" make *Bergson and American Culture* of significant interest.

Three essays take up the issue of relation this year. M. Keith Booker's "'A War Between the Mind and Sky': Bakhtin and Poetry, Stevens and Politics" (*WSJour* 14, i:71–85) suggests that while Bakhtin's theory of "the dialogic imagination" is most usually applied to fiction, it might profitably serve in a discussion of modern poetry: "In his incessant interrogation of varying modes of poetic discourse, in his ability to accept contradiction, and in his fierce and relentless resistance to closure of interpretation," Stevens's stance mirrors Bakhtin's. Glen MacLeod's "Surrealism and the Supreme Fiction: 'It Must Give Pleasure'" (*WSJour* 14, i:33–38) discusses Stevens's interest in Surrealism as an attempt to "reduce the opposition between the imagination and reality." In "A Relativity of Angels: Wallace Stevens and Luce Irigaray" (*WSJour* 14, ii:153–60), Mary Doyle Springer proposes to read Stevens as participating "in a semiotic and feminine view of language, thought, and feeling that anticipates by decades the work" of many French feminists, especially Irigaray.

Stevens's wartime poetry drew two commentators. In "Life Anywhere but on a Battleship: Stevens's Wartime Poetry and the Apolitics of Postwar Criticism" (*Criticism* 32, i:101–27), John Timberman Newcomb deplores that for all the recent critical attention to Stevens, there is still no "comprehensive and intelligent account of the sociopolitical aspects of his work." Newcomb's essay argues that the poet's "ostensible evasion of the political is largely a fabrication of Stevens criticism after 1940." Newcomb discusses the critical history of "Life on a Battleship," the poet's "most explicit examination, demystification, and rejection of absolutist myth." Alan Filreis's "Stevens' Home Front" (*WSJour* 14, ii:99–122) seems to agree, reading in "Repetitions of a Young Captain" and other wartime work Stevens's sensitivity to "the vicissitudes of the home front, but also his knowledge of various military campaigns and even his perception of the danger of life under Nazi occupation."

Other work collected in *WSJour* this year includes Lyall Bush's " 'Satisfactions of Belief': Stevens' Poetry in a Pragmatic World" (14, i:3–20), which examines the poet against the backdrop of pragmatism, arguing that "relation is an illusion that is an only ambiguously useful fiction." "Crispin's Dependent 'Airs': Psychic Crisis in the Early Stevens" (14, i:21–32) by David R. Jarraway offers "a psychoanalytic view" of "the great enigma of Stevens' early career"—the six years of "ominous silence" following the trade publication of *Harmonium.* Using Freud as a base, Jarraway argues that in "The Comedian," "de-familiarization in the poem actually constitutes *de-familialization*" and that Stevens emerges from his period of "mediating sleep" having uncovered "the Idea of Order."

If we accept the general notion that "Peter Quince at the Clavier" is the "point where Stevens first found an authentic poetic voice," as B. J. Leggett suggests in "Apollonian and Dionysian in 'Peter Quince at the Clavier' " (*WSJour* 14, i:39–61), "we must also recognize that it is, in its subject, its apparently disjointed structure, and its undisguised eroticism, truly a bizarre beginning." Starting with a rather detailed history of criticism surrounding the poem—which generally has seen it as a "rather conventional statement on form in art"—Leggett attempts to read "Peter Quince" through Nietzsche as a poem "about the way art leads one to an *affirmation* of the transience of life." Lea Baechler is also interested in Stevensian affirmation in her "Pre-Elegiac Affirmation in 'To an Old Philosopher in Rome' " (*WSJour* 14, ii:141–52). "Philosopher," Baechler notes, is "a distillation of explorations" found in the later poems, "testing once again the integrity" of Stevens's aesthetics when confronting a landscape of old age and death.

In "Doughty's Vesuvius in 'Esthetique du Mal' " (*WSJour* 14, ii:123–39), Alison Rieke provocatively traces the presence of Charles Montagu

Doughty (author of *Travels in Arabia Deserta*) in Stevens's poem about "pain, evil, and psychic disease." Thomas Trzyna also looks at the poem in "'Esthetique du Mal' as Parody of Burke's Sublime" (*WSJour* 14, ii:167–73), finding its source in "the eighteenth-century tradition of the sublime," playing "on the tension between the views characteristic of Santayana and Burke."

Ron Klaren's "Wallace Stevens and the Cummington Press: A Correspondence, 1941–1951" (*WSJour* 14, i:62–70) describes in some detail the 191 letters between the poet and the press, which include Stevens's comments on *Notes Toward a Supreme Fiction*. Finally, Vincent Prestianni provides us with "Wallace Stevens: A Survey of Bibliographies and Related Material, 1940–1990" (*WSJour* 14, ii:174–80), with useful annotations.

iii Gertrude Stein, H.D., Marianne Moore

The longer works on Gertrude Stein and H.D. this year tended to focus on their fiction, though these books on two of our still most vastly undervalued writers are certainly worth mentioning. Lisa Ruddick's *Reading Gertrude Stein: Body, Text, Gnosis* (Cornell) is a volume in the Reading Women Reading series, a project "committed to furthering international feminist debate." Ruddick attempts twin narratives, as "onto the drama of Stein's self-situation within twentieth-century thought is grafted another drama, that of the private emotional crises that her intellectual evolution simultaneously reflected and prompted." Ruddick's approach provides productive discussion of any number of crucial issues—repression of the mother figure, patricide, the balancing of the polysemous and the traditionally thematic. *Tender Buttons*, "a wild mumbling," emerges as "an anti-patriarchal wisdom," as "the meaning to Stein of her rich and playful new style is incest." This is a challenging study drawing on the best elements of traditional and newer critical approaches; highly recommended. Bettina L. Knapp's *Gertrude Stein* (Continuum) follows a "handbook" format as part of Continuum's Literature and Life: American Writers series, but the critical section offers far more than mere plot summary. The chapter on *Tender Buttons* in particular provides a fascinating reading of the work as "the perception of that single moment when the mind comes into contact with the object of its consciousness," a work that is at once "representational" and "increasingly abstract and hermetic."

Like the Stein volumes, Susan Stanford Friedman's *Penelope's Web: Gender, Modernity, H.D.'s Fiction* (Cambridge) should properly be dealt with at some length in one of the fiction chapters, but as most of us know H.D. primarily as a poet I should like to give this book at least a nod. Volumes in Cambridge Studies in American Literature and Culture have been uniformly first-rate, and Friedman's study is no exception. It takes as its task the examination of H.D.'s "modernity" as "patterned by gender, genre, and history," arguing that her "poetic and prose texts exist in symbiotic relationship." Friedman reads the prose as more personal and disruptive than the "impersonal discourse of her early lyrics," more "disturbing in its linguistic excesses, its bisexual desire." Thus, alongside extended and fascinating discussions of the prose, Friedman also offers her sense of the early "lyric impersonalism," H.D.'s relation to Imagism, and an analysis of *Trilogy* (which, as a "paired text" with the prose *The Gift*, she reads as "a poem that bears witness to the Nazi holocaust and celebrates the rebirth of civilization").

In "Two Ways of Spelling It Out: An Archetypal-Feminist Reading of H.D.'s *Trilogy* and Adrienne Rich's *Sources*" (*SR* 266–84), Albert Gelpi (who serves as general editor of the Cambridge series) attempts to reconcile archetypal psychology with feminist theory, focusing on the concept of the anima/animus. For Gelpi, "the impulse informing all H.D.'s writing is the effort to define her own identity as an individual and a woman," an effort "played out, complicated and resolved, through her relation to the masculine." Further, through this process H.D. "sublimates and encodes autobiography into hieroglyphic symbol," with *Trilogy* enacting "autogenesis in archetypal robes." Dana R. Shugar's "Faustine Re-Membered: H.D.'s Use of Swinburne's Poetry in *Hermione*" (*Sagetrieb* 9, i–ii: 79–94) suggests that the poet was drawn to Swinburne because "of all Victorian poets, he alone ventured into stigmatized sexuality," yet she was forced to literally revise his work "to complicate his narrow definitions of lesbian sexuality."

The special issue of *Sagetrieb* (9, iii) devoted to H.D. and William Carlos Williams offers Adalaide Morris's "Signaling: Feminism, Politics, and Mysticism in H.D.'s War *Trilogy*"(pp. 121–34), which argues that the poem is "a warning, a command" which demands that "a poem not only means but does." Morris's essay offers discussion of ritual and "mystical politics" in a poem of "bold engagement with issues of gender and power." In the same issue, Kevin Oderman's "H.D.: The What in a Word" (pp. 135–43) valiantly attempts to deal with "H.D.'s sounding of

the etymological depths," etymologies which for her "are not just historically interesting but also spiritually significant."

Charles Molesworth's *Marianne Moore: A Literary Life* (Atheneum)
gives us the first biography of the poet. Though Moore obviously was
(for a time at least) a poet to reckon with, and though she counted
among her friends any number of significant writers of the day, her life
was not particularly dramatic. Further, while Molesworth was allowed
access to the crucial and extended Moore family correspondence, he was
not allowed to quote from it, thus forcing quite a bit of paraphrase. In
spite of these difficulties, however, Molesworth manages a clearly written
record, not only ranging through the biographical details but reading
many of the major poems, discussing intellectual and aesthetic influences, and attempting to place Moore's achievement in the Modernist
project. The chapter on Moore's work on *The Dial* is of particular
interest.

Jeredith Merrin's *An Enabling Humility: Marianne Moore, Elizabeth
Bishop, and the Uses of Tradition* (Rutgers) devotes two chapters to
Moore. The first discusses her work in terms of 17th-century prose,
sensing that her poetry enacts "a tension or torsion of Renaissance and
modernist forces"; Thomas Browne (who "promulgated, on the whole,
humane and latitudinarian Christian views") is "a sort of spiritual father." Chapter 3 reads Moore's "The Grave" as "a revision of the tradition," a poem in which she "adapts the terms—the dominant figures or
tropes—of her Romantic inheritance in order to come to terms with it."
The final chapter attempts to develop the relationship between Moore
and Elizabeth Bishop, arguing that the older poet was the younger's
"most important connection with the first generation of American mod-
ernists."

In "The Asperities of Survival in Marianne Moore's 'The Jerboa'"
(*Sagetrieb*, 9, i–ii:217–23), Anne Shifrer gives Moore "a postmodernist
hearing," sensing that the poet "dismantles her parables even as they are
being made."

iv Jeffers, Frost, Fletcher

Like Stein and H.D., Robinson Jeffers is a poet whose achievement is
probably at least slightly exaggerated by his few supporters and vastly and
unfairly undervalued (or most probably unread) by most everyone else.
James Karman's *Critical Essays on Robinson Jeffers* (Hall) draws together

61 book reviews focusing on work from *Flagons and Apples* (1912) to *The Beginning and the End and Other Poems* (1963), as well as 13 articles and essays by Kenneth Rexroth, Lawrence Clark Powell, William Everson, Tim Hunt, Robert Zaller, Robert J. Brophey, and others, providing a good map to the poet's problematic position in our literary landscape. Karman's extended introduction provides an articulate context, touching especially such issues as Jeffers's run-ins with Marxist critics and his exclusion from the New Critical canon.

Like Tom Quirk, B. J. Sokol is interested in the influence of Bergson. His "Bergson, Instinct, and Frost's 'The White-Tailed Hornet'" (*AL* 62:44–59) reads the poem as Frost's most direct meditation on issues raised in *Creative Evolution,* a meditation ending not "in convinced belief but complex and ramified doubt." Frank Lentricchia's "The Resentments of Robert Frost" (*AL* 62:175–200) interestingly looks into the history of the modernist presence in poetry anthologies, using Frost as a focus.

Finally, we do not hear much about John Gould Fletcher these days, a situation Lucas Carpenter attempts to begin to rectify in his study, *John Gould Fletcher and Southern Modernism* (Arkansas). Carpenter admits that Fletcher's "place in literary history has been secured because of his association with the Imagist movement and with the Southern Fugitive-Agrarians," but he argues that such an assessment obscures the poet's actual achievement as "the prototype of the Southern modernist writer." His book is an evenhanded effort to resituate Fletcher, dealing with such issues as Symbolist influence, "Imagism and 'Amygism,'" and the "Old" and "New" South.

University of New Mexico

17   Poetry: The 1940s to the Present

Richard J. Calhoun

The inaugural year of another decade of criticism was a year of biographies. Two rather important ones came out in 1990, William H. Pritchard's on Randall Jarrell and Paul Mariani's on John Berryman. Pritchard's may not do much for Jarrell's reputation as a poet, but it should help us see his importance as a man of letters in his own time and his potential value today as a reminder of what the poet-critic used to be. Mariani does for Berryman, in a fitting way for that poet, what Lawrance Thompson did for Frost, Ian Hamilton for Lowell, and feminist studies for Sylvia Plath—reveal the distress from which the poetry often had to come. These may not be the last word, but they are the books of the year. I am again impressed by the quantity and often the quality of studies of women poets. The criticism on Plath and on Adrienne Rich again predominates. After several good years it was not a year for criticism on Anne Sexton. It was for Denise Levertov and Elizabeth Bishop. There are still further discoveries that there was more to confessionalism than personal confessions. The later poetry of Robert Lowell is being reexamined. W. D. Snodgrass reappears in the best interview of the year, or of the last several years. John Ashbery was also interviewed but reveals little. Attempts to distinguish postmodernism and modernism and the former from the latter seem to grow murkier every year. If there is not quite an establishment in the poetry of Ashbery, Merrill, Ammons, there is critical homage paid to these three poets each year. No major broad study appeared. Charles Altieri's *Painterly Abstraction in Modernist American Poetry* (Cambridge) is relevant to this *ALS* chapter for Altieri's brief comment on postmodernism (pp. 359–63), on how "Modernist art shares the Postmodernist dilemma." A significant change to this chapter's coverage is the section "African American Poets Since 1940." For his help, I am indebted to the work of my colleague Abasi Malik, a poet himself and a specialist in this field.

i Overview, Collections

The collection of essays on contemporary poets exacting the longest discussion in 1990 is Leonard M. Trawick's *World, Self, Poem* (Kent State). Part of its value comes from coverage of contemporary American and British poets. The American poets given individual chapters are Gerald Stern, Louise Glück, Gary Snyder, Wendell Berry, Adrienne Rich, Denise Levertov, John Ashbery, William Stafford, and the late Robert Duncan. Among the debits would be that the essays are now slightly dated and have no unifying theme: these were papers delivered at a conference, the Jubilation of Poets festival, celebrating the 25th anniversary of the Cleveland State University Poetry Center. A number of conference topics are discussed, the most interesting of which are the "I" in contemporary poetry, the pastoral vein, use and misuse of history, and, predictably, political involvement and noninvolvement. The three groupings of essays accord with the title: "world," "self," "poem."

What is of special interest? Jeff Gundy reports in "Arrogant Humility and Aristocratic Torpor: Where Have We Been, Where Are We Going?" (pp. 20–27) that American poetry since the early 1970s has been less "politically" and "socially" charged, less concerned with public lives and "more concentrated in the minutiae of private lives." Exemplary in this direction is the poetry of John Ashbery. The response of poets to the materialism of the Reagan years was that their poetry "must avoid moral claims and judgment," concentrate on form, and specialize in irony and wit. Critical works that contributed to a new aesthetic conservatism were Robert Pinsky's *The Situation of Poetry* (1976) and Paul Hoover's essay "Moral Poetry" (1984), with its attack on the moral poet and praise for ironists like Ashbery. Gundy prefers "moral" poets who are not "self-righteous," and David Ignatow is his cardinal example of a poet who maintains this desirable balance. At the other extreme, Louis Simpson is a poet who remembers that "the suffering of others is truly our responsibility." John Gery in "The Sigh of Our Present: Nuclear Annihilation and Contemporary Poetry" (pp. 72–93) shifts the focus from a concentration on form and on the view that art can be timeless to the prevailing view that by focusing on "modest moments of the human spectacle" a poet is somehow implicitly taking a stand "against nuclear negation." He sees this attitude as "desensitization," borrowing the concept from Robert Jay Lifton's *Death in Life: Survivors of Hiroshima.* Gery, nevertheless, attempts to reveal a variety of "concerns with nuclear annihilation" from the protest poetry of Ginsberg and Snyder to the confessional poetry of Plath, which incorporates the imagery of apocalypse into metaphors of personal experience. The most intriguing group of poets are those who feature, not the devastation of a nuclear holocaust, but the psychic condition of annihilation itself as the "way of nothingness" we must learn to articulate if "we wish to survive into some future." Exemplary are Levertov's poems that do not express a direct objection to the threat of nuclear annihilation but rather "embody that experience in the same way that any private experience informs a poet's sensibility" and James Merrill's articulation of "nature's gift to man" in the form of "resistance" to the nuclear attitude toward annihilation, evidenced in *The Changing Light at Sandover.* Peter A. Siedlecki in "Gerald Stern's Mediation of the I and the I" (pp. 110–19) makes a novel distinction between the Eliotian modernist "egocentric I" as persona and the Olsonian postmodernist "proprioceptive I" and finds the salvation of contemporary poetry in an effective mediation between the two perspectives. This equilibrium between the personal and the nearly scientific "I" confronts a "fiercely binary world" in the poetry of Gerald Stern. Lynn Keller, " 'Free/of Blossom and Subterfuge': Louise Glück and the Language of Renunciation" (pp. 120–29), applies the feminist theory of the woman poet's struggle between aspiring to the male status of poet and defining one's own female identity to the poetry of Glück, whose four volumes reflect her "changing responses to the dilemma of being at once poet and woman." Glück has not resolved this conflict, as the use of Achilles in her latest volume discloses. Her inconclusiveness is not a limitation, but a sign of an inner battle that "electrifies her poetry."

Thomas B. Byers in "Adrienne Rich: Vision As Rewriting" (pp. 144–52) examines "re-vision" in two sets of Rich's poems. The early poem "At a Bach Concert" acquiesces to the patriarchy of the time. But in the 1973 poem "The Ninth Symphony of Beethoven Understood at Last as a Sexual Message," Rich asserts herself angrily against assimilation to the culture of a male master. The only thing new here is the extension of the revolt against patriarchy to modernist techniques and New Critical theories of interpretation. Rich is seen as moving from a feminist rebellion against patriarchs to a vision of power in the community of other women poets. Lorrie Smith, "Dialogue and the Political Imagination in

Denise Levertov and Adrienne Rich" (pp. 155–62), cursorily glimpses the political activism of Levertov and Rich as a contribution to "a larger movement among women poets toward the merging of personal lyricism and political engagement." The import here is how for both as political poets, but most tellingly for Rich, dialogue has been the ideal communication, opening a poetic field to test commitments and beliefs.

Thomas E. Benediktsson's "Montana Ecologue: The Pastoral Art of William Stafford" (pp. 196–206) recruits Jonathan Holden's observation that the best poetry in the postmodernist Romantic tradition "is apt to be pastoral" to extoll Stafford's pastoral poetry. He views modern pastoral as a rhetorical strategy that copes with the contradictions between the real world and the world of pastoral fantasy. The purest pastoral poet today is Stafford, whose special quality is to create through surrealist metaphor a dialectic of the sentimental and the demonic. This is one of the more enlightening essays in the collection. Lionel Basney in "Having your Meaning at Hand: Work in Snyder and Berry" (pp. 130–43) compares Snyder and Berry as poets who have created a dialogue between a poetry of work and social definitions of work, even suggesting social programs. Fred E. Maus, "Ashbery and the Condition of Music" (pp. 178–86), attempts to find a common ground between "Ashbery's style and aspects of Western instrumental music" but has time for only a single example, "Whether It Exists," oddly compared to passages from a piano sonata in G Minor by Joseph Haydn, finding in both "enigmas of individuation associated with polyphony." He may convince us that Ashbery sensed his poetry as analogous to music, but he does not make poem and music notably similar. Burton Hatlen's "Robert Duncan's Marriage of Heaven and Hell: Kabbalah and Rime in *Roots and Branches*" (pp. 207–26) makes a case for Duncan as the true successor of Yeats in a belief that "poetry itself has become the true heir of the Judeo-Christian religious tradition." Duncan was not a true believer himself, rather a poet who "cultivated *writing itself* as a magical act."

Two essays deal with types of contemporary poetry. Stephen Matterson, in "Contemporary and Found" (pp. 187–97), borrowing the concept from Louis Simpson, discusses ever so briefly, and inconsequentially, works which may be read as poetry though they were not intended to be. Mary Lewis Shaw, "Concrete and Abstract Poetry: The World as Text and the Text as World" (pp. 163–77), distinguishes concrete poetry from neoformalist poetry, yet finds a "profound and paradoxical relationship" in that both reject the "traditional treatment of language as medium of representation." Formalist and language poetry intends self-sufficient utterance; concrete poetry tends to deconstruct. The concern is much more with French poetry than with American. *World, Self, Poem* suffers from deficit (too many brief essays) and excess (too many diverse essays), both attributable to its conference origins.

Wyatt Prunty's *Fallen from the Symboled World* attempts to demonstrate that "the gap between modern and contemporary poets . . . does not rest along the borders of romanticism and realism. In fact, these two 'isms' still thrive among the diverse offerings of contemporary poetry." Yet it also contends that much recent poetry retains such modernist features as experimentation, discontinuity, alienation, despair, and even questions about the reality of the objective world. Prunty's idea is that the shift that distinguishes contemporary from modern poetry is not an exchange of romanticism for realism or metaphor for metonymy but the replacement of symbol and allegory with "simile-like tropes," figures that "constitute relation through likening." He believes that the concentration by literary historians on mere episodes in the history of poetry, such as the Black Mountain School, Confessionalism, Concrete Poetry, Language Poetry, or New Formalism, overstates the importance of form and fails to ask the important question of what tropes poets believe they can use. Prunty focuses tropes that appear in the work of contemporary poets—the late Howard Nemerov, Mona Van Duyn, Anthony Hecht, Robert Pack, Donald Justice, John Hollander, Richard Wilbur, Elizabeth Bishop, X. J. Kennedy, J. V. Cunningham, Edward Bowers, and Robert Pinsky. Why these poets are included and other contemporaries excluded is never made clear. His title comes from a Nemerov poem, "The Loon's Cry," iterating that many poets believe we are "fallen from / the symboled world." Prunty finds evidence of change in Lowell's tropes in poems even before *Life Studies* and engages in a somewhat questionable effort to show analogies or "likenings" between Lowell's later poetry and Edmund Husserl's method in *Cartesian Meditation: An Introduction to Phenomenology.* His main thrust is to show that among these contemporary poets there is a shift, not to rejection, or to rebellion against tradition, but to a questioning of hierarchy.

James McCorkle believes in the significance of the poet as critic. He has invited most poets of stature to provide essays for his collection *Conversant Essays,* and a good number replied either by contributing new essays or recommending essays previously published. Unfortunately, the reviewer committed to new work in criticism has to depend on memory and a careful reading of the acknowledgment pages to separate the new from the old. The responses to his requests evidence that most poets had on hand previously published prose essays they could recommend. Only 12 out of 52 supplied new prose works. I agree with McCorkle's contention in his introduction, "The Prose of the Poet" (pp. 17–32), that the poet can tell us in prose something about poetry and "its intersections with the world" and teach us to read his or her poetry as well as poetry in general: "a poet's essay belongs to a genealogy that addresses issues of poesis as well as reveals the poet's strongest convictions." Not all of the essays are relevant to poetry since 1940, and James Dickey and Galway Kinnell, poets who are known for their critical statements in prose, are not included. This collection is recommended for what it is, a collection of critical statements in prose by a large number of poets.

In another addition to the usual concerns in feminist studies, Jeredith Merrin in *Enabling Humility* (Rutgers) asks the ongoing question of how a creative woman poet can find her own distinctive voice in response to a male-dominated literary canon in a male-dominated culture. Her thesis is the familiar one, applied to Marianne Moore and Elizabeth Bishop. What these two poets shared was a commitment to "the tradition" and to a friendship, a virtual sisterhood in the arts. But they also shared a willingness (atypical for feminists) to be influenced by male poet models, by George Herbert and by 17th-century poetry and Romantic poetry, and to wear a mask of humility, of self-effacing modesty that sheltered "a complex and often subtly combative attitude." This is a capable comparative influence study which shows that there can be something new and valuable from the often set approaches of feminist studies.

Jonathan Monroe's "Mischling and Metis: Common and Uncommon Languages in Adrienne Rich and Aime Cesaire" (pp. 282–315) is the only relevant item in Gustavo Pérez Firmat's edition *Do the Americas Have a Common Literature?* Monroe establishes that there is common cause among radical poets to expand the ordinarily perceived range of poetry. Rich has moved toward a woman-centered aesthetics challenging "a poetic tradition dominated by white Anglo-American men." Cesaire, from the beginning of his career, rebelled against poetry and was concerned with negritude, particularly in language, conflicting with "the standard French" he felt was suffocating him. Since Rich's political commitment initiated a change in her well-received early poetry, she has had to face criticism that this commitment has driven "the poetry out of her poetry." Cesaire has been criticized for "writing a hermetic poetry that makes his political commitment largely inaccessible to the public on whose behalf he has wanted to speak." Both poets have a political commitment to what Rich has designated the "history of the disposed," but they have developed "different poetic strategies and relationships to audiences." I find what is said about Rich's poetic strategies of interest, though not new, and the comparison between the two poets difficult to maintain. Much more is said about Cesaire than about Rich. There are similarities, but there remain unexplored differences. A comparison between two radical feminists in different lands and with different languages would obviously have been less strained. Cesaire's poetry, as Monroe admits, has played an official political role. Rich's political fate has been to be accepted as the representative voice of a community of women poets.

In *Reading and Writing Nature,* Guy Rotella includes Elizabeth Bishop, Robert Frost, Wallace Stevens, and Marianne Moore in an examination of 20th-century poets who use nature as an appropriate setting to pose epistemological and aesthetic questions. The book is far-ranging, tracking American nature poetry from its 17th-century beginnings in Puritanism, viewing nature as "God's work," to the apex reached in the 19th century by Emerson and Dickinson, who in their respective ways regarded knowledge gleaned from nature as a human artifact. The four 20th-century poets enact in their poetry an ambivalence regarding the poet's ability to know from nature, though nature is a source of their poetry. Elizabeth Bishop always had a fascination with what she observed as "something, I suppose, spiritual," though she scaled down any claims of "visions" to simply "looks." Her secular, rather than religious, concern owes something to the Transcendentalist poetic maneuver from description of a scene in nature to discovered truth, although she questions, denies, or postulates an alternative to the analogies earlier poets claimed. Rotella finds that Bishop develops a "diminished" mode of correspondence which becomes central to her work, and he supports his view through his reading of "Filling Station" as a "deflated and secular" version of Frost's "Design." Rotella believes that Bishop "descends" from the Transcendentalists without any sense of a falling off. For her, the book of nature may be neither a canonical text nor a lucid one, but it is not a blank slate. From *North and South* on, nature poems with epistemological and aesthetic implications become central to her work. "Chemin de Fer" and "Large Bad Picture" are analyzed as poems marking this transition. Some of the finest poems in her last three books are landscape or nature pieces still exploring the relationship of seeing to significance, while others show distrust of human readings of nature. Bishop's poems may deny revelation, but Rotella concludes that they also "keep it living in surmise." He suggests that a comparison of Frost's "The Most of It" and Bishop's "The Moose" reveals nature as a world independent and apart, whereas in the work of more recent poets (John Ashbery, A. R. Ammons, Robert Haas are mentioned) the notion of nature as wholly separate from the human sphere may "itself be dead or dying," seen as just one more human invention.

Regional studies continue to flourish, and the current direction is away from South to Southwest, to explore that region's rich resources of Hispanic and Native American writers. The prime study of 1990 is John F. Crawford, William Balassi, and Annie O. Eysturoy's *This Is About Vision*. Most of the writers included are not primarily poets (e.g., the best-known, N. Scott Momaday, who chooses not to discuss his one volume of poetry). The poets included are not as well-known as novelist John Nichols of *The Milagro Beanfield War* fame or playwright Mark Medoff (*Children of a Lesser God*). Poets interviewed include Margaret Randall, an interviewer herself; Paul Gunn Allen, of Native American descent; Pat Mora; Chickasaw poet Linda Hogan; Joy Harjo (from "Creek and other Oklahoma/Arkansas people"); Chicano writer Jimmy Santiago Baca; and Navajo Luci Tapahonso. This is a politically correct multicultural resource book which manages to map out some regional differences. The sense of "place" celebrated in Southern writers of the Faulkner-Welty generations is for these Southwestern writers of another place and of a later time. Place for them is not something concrete, "out there," as a setting for their works but a feeling internalized as part of their vision. Although "politically correct," it does not exclude "Anglo writers" but rather accepts them as contributors to the literature of the region who helped change the shape of human behavior there and the character of the region itself. Several of the Southwestern writers are of mixed blood but acknowledge this as part of "all me," whether Anglo and Native American or Hispanic. One heritage is not discounted in the name of another.

The objective of Jefferson Humphries's *Southern Literature and Literary Theory* sounds auspicious. Youth will be served. It is designed as a collection of essays on Southern literature by a generation of critics younger than that represented by the Louis Rubin-generated *History of Southern Literature*, reviewed in *ALS 1985*. The younger scholars use critical approaches current for their generation—feminist, African American studies, deconstruction, even Marxism, all in contrast to the literary history and New Critical formalism of the older generation. This new generation reexamination of Southern literature does fairly well with fiction but hardly bothers with contemporary Southern poetry, including only James Applewhite's Derrida-induced glance at the middle earth landscape of his own poetry, "The New Landscape and the Far: Nature and Human Signification" (pp. 22–30); a reprint of "James Dickey: From 'The Other' through 'The Early Motion'" (pp. 31–47) by Harold Bloom, a critic certainly not of their generation; and Kate M. Cooper's brief use of "contemporary language theory" ("Reading Between the Lines" pp. 88–108) for a look at Fred Chappell's allegorical poem, *Castle Tzingal.* I am glad to see attention given James Applewhite and Fred Chappell, and I appreciate Harold Bloom's advocacy of James Dickey. But surely appropriate critics could have been found for a new generation look at poets of the stature of James Dickey and A. R. Ammons.

Ann Massa's *American Declarations of Love* is intended as a correction of the view held by Leslie Fiedler and a band of others that there is "something odd about the way in which American literature has or hasn't approached the subject of love." American literature has been associated with death or violence, and it has portrayed heterosexual love as "alien to the American literary consciousness." American writers as either spokesmen for or Jeremiahs against a society striving to be more democratic and manifestly better than others cannot be satisfied with everyday relationships. One essay is of issue here, John A. Ward's " 'Not Avoiding Injury': Robert Lowell's 'The Dolphin'" (pp. 137–54). Ward reclaims *The Dolphin* from recent critical neglect by focusing on Lowell's statement in the title poem that he has plotted "too freely with my life" and in the process been guilty of "not avoiding injury to others, / not avoiding injury to myself." As a consequence, he cannot "ask compassion" from those he has wronged. Among critics there has been disagreement as to whether Lowell "affirms or denies love's power to regenerate." Axelrod, not surprisingly, finds a tension in the poems between naming and living, describing the poet's experience with exposing those named to the scrutiny of the public. Both the poet and those named are at risk. Ward attempts to describe his own reader response to the acts of naming in *The Dolphin* in the light of the revelations of Ian Hamilton's biography. Ward wonders whether Lowell can make poetry of the often complaining words of others. And he finds that complexity is added to through the dual perspective—the poet's ability to define his own fault and the factualness of the woman's complaints. In previous books, Lowell wrote moving love poems without "naming." Ward contrasts "Man and Wife" and "To Speak of Woe That Is in Marriage" to "Records" and "Heavy Breathing" in *The Dolphin,* where Lowell has decided that "disembowelling" himself and others is unavoidable and acceptable.

ii The Middle Generation and Confessional Poets

a. Jarrell   The first two things to be said about William H. Pritchard's *Randall Jarrell: A Literary Life* (Farrar, Straus & Giroux) are that it is well-written and that it makes a good companion piece to his Frost biography, reviewed in *ALS 1988.* I suppose it is an implied criticism to believe that Pritchard does not make a convincing case for the importance of Jarrell as poet or critic in the 1990s as he had seemed in the 1950s. This book, like the Frost, is not one of those decade-long projects of research or critical pondering. Like its predecessor, it is adequately researched and poem-oriented. If you want to know what was happening to Jarrell when he wrote a major work and what that work became, this is a top-drawer reference work. One has to accept the genre—literary biography.

Pritchard's attention is directed to the "complex interaction" between Jarrell's life and his major works. Based on my own infrequent contacts with Jarrell, I sense that if the portrait of both the man and of the man of letters does not quite satisfy, some of it has to do with the elusiveness of the subject. Like Frost, Jarrell was not easy to decode. There is more of this Jarrell revealed in Mary Jarrell's edition of the letters than in Pritchard's book. Pritchard unquestionably comprehends the current status of Jarrell's reputation. If he is to be considered a major writer, he must be appreciated as a poet as well as a critic, and his criticism must be read now as it was when it was written. I was intrigued with Pritchard's account of Jarrell's friendship with the music critic B. H. Haggin. For some intellectuals in the '50s, Haggin was as much the critic for music as Jarrell was for poetry. There are similarities in their overbearing confidence in their own subjective judgments and in an occasional brutality in criticism. To assess Jarrell as a poet, Pritchard might have used Jarrell's own standard: How often did lightning strike? How many great poems did he write? Pritchard does target a weakness that crippled Jarrell as both critic and poet. He was inflexible. He never changed his mind about a poet, or a poem; he learned almost nothing from his contemporaries. I would suggest that one of the reasons is that except for his *Nation* stint, Jarrell lived apart from the literary scene, remaining a provincial from North Carolina in spite of his brilliance. Pritchard demonstrates convincingly that in his poetry, in his criticism, and in his life, Jarrell suffered from a lack of self-criticism.

One part of Jarrell's story as poet that Pritchard should tell more about is the last book—the criticism of which at the time may have helped kill Randall Jarrell—*The Lost World,* now regarded as likely his best book of poetry. Pritchard quotes Lowell's view on these poems as Jarrell's "last and best book," and he seems to agree; but, unfortunately, Pritchard devotes only a half-dozen pages of commentary and avoids a real assessment. Pritchard is deadly accurate on Jarrell's major weakness, evident even in these last good poems. Jarrell's speakers talk on too long, and he does not spend enough time on rendering situations. In sum, Pritchard's analysis is good as far as it goes, good enough to make me wish he had gone further; but he chooses to end his book rather anticlimactically with comments on one of Jarrell's children's books, *The Animal Family.* The ending disappoints.

Bruce Bawer's "The Enigma of Randall Jarrell" (*NewC* 8, ix:30–40) earns mention as a review of Pritchard's book which becomes a sketch of the book that might have been written. Bawer contends that Jarrell's poetry cannot be known without a better and more focused account of Jarrell's life. He offers his own minibiography of a private man who hid part of himself from others (perhaps even from himself) and who was incapable of expressing important parts of himself outside of a poem. The disappointment is that Bawer does not himself add much of substance to what he accuses Pritchard of not doing. Undoubtedly, something of Jarrell has eluded both Pritchard and Bawer. No Boswell has been found.

In another addition to a remarkable Jarrell year, Richard Flynn in *Randall Jarrell and the Lost World of Childhood* (Georgia) makes a compelling case for the importance of the residual child in Jarrell's personality and of the centrality of this child figure in the poetry. As a consequence of his thoughtful and thorough treatment, Flynn establishes a reason for Jarrell's importance as a poet in the respectable company of Rilke and Wordsworth: it is in his poetic handling of innocence and victimization. Flynn's approach is both biographical and critical, detecting Jarrell's concerns with childhood in his poetry in the unhappiness of his own childhood, particularly as the consequence of his parents' divorce and his own separation from them. Flynn may overplay Jarrell's role as victim, certainly when his case is compared to the hard cases of Lowell and Berryman; but Flynn is undoubtedly correct in tracing from this sense of victimization the influences of Wordsworth and Rilke on Jarrell in developing a Romantic view of the child in his poetry as well as on a personally held view that understanding the child can be a link to the unconscious. I agree, but I would demur that the modern Wordsworthian or Rilkean Jarrell is not the only Jarrell. There is the soldier in the early war poems that originally established Jarrell's reputation; there is also the poet who achieved considerable success with the woman figure in his poetry, perhaps awaiting discovery by feminist critics. Flynn does detect the child in both figures. The crucial thing about Flynn's book is that his reading does Jarrell's reputation the important service of countering the view that the pathos in the poetry signifies his own sentimentality. At its best, Jarrell's poetry, like his criticism, is cultural criticism of no small import.

b. Berryman The considerable style expected of a Paul Mariani study is evidenced in the brief preface to *Dream Song: The Life of John Berryman* (Morrow) and then disappears, replaced by a surprisingly sparse and factual account of Berryman's life. This is probably appropriate, for the facts are sensational enough not to require embellishment. Mariani's is not the kind of literary biography currently in fashion; it is resolutely a biography, an account of the troubled life of a man who became a famous poet but who was never famous enough to satisfy himself, and who lived as an infamous friend for all of those who had to endure him. It is a truthful account of that life, and little extraneous judgment of the man or the poet is offered. Mariani admits that Berryman as a subject has not been "an easy master." He forgoes a critical study. His explanation for eschewing judgment on "Berryman's place in the pantheon of poets" is that he believes it is still too early to determine since "the full impact of Berryman's poetry has yet to be felt." He does not even attempt to guess what this impact may be. Mariani makes it clear that out of a difficult life Berryman somehow left a "body of extraordinary poems." What Mariani communicates vividly are the contradictions in the man. Berryman was an alcoholic who seriously sought help; in his personal relations he was often arrogant, irritating, irascible, but incredibly kind to those who also had severe personal problems. He was a man who was "clearly bent on self-destruction whose original wound from his father's own self-destruction never sufficiently healed." The literary life he lived was a search for fathers—teacher fathers like Mark Van Doren, R. P. Blackmur, and Allen Tate, and poet fathers like Auden, Stevens, Eliot, Yeats. The accounts of his often ambivalent relationship with writers who were his contemporaries, Jarrell, Lowell, William Meredith, make this biography provocative reading. Berryman's relationship with women was problematic and drastic. They were either friend or enemy, to be idolized or savaged. The villain here is the mother he feared and thought responsible for his father's suicide. Mariani's book is an intriguing biography that is never shallow. Perhaps I expected even more, and I am surprised at some minor inaccuracies (such matters as identifying librarian Roy Basler as Bassler); but I read this with great interest, as an account of both Berryman and a literary epoch.

c. Lowell William Doreski, "His Own Country: Robert Lowell in Maine" (*REAL* 6, viii:19–37), opens with a statement that Lowell made to Ian Hamilton: "I found I wrote about only four places, Harvard and Boston, New York and Maine. These were places I lived in and symbols, conscious and unavoidable." Doreski finds that Maine does not represent nature or symbolize an ideal pastoral society but is part of a tension in Lowell's poems between nature and the human failure to devise a society adequate to the challenge presented by the natural order. "Skunk Hour" dramatically evidences the inadequacies of the artifice that is Maine's human society. What I like about this article is that Doreski establishes just how many good poems Lowell gave a Maine setting. Maine's cold sea and windblown lands were functional symbols for making connections between places, to express his feelings about the decline of American society and the torments of self. There are exceptionally good readings of the landscape and self in "Skunk Hour," "To Theodore Roethke," and "Water," and a promising foreshortened reading of the sonnet sequence "Long Summer."

Allan Johnston in "Modes of Return: Memory and Remembering in the Poetry of Robert Lowell" (*TCL* 36, i:58–75) convincingly illustrates how Lowell's "spiraling in and out of self" causes him to doubt the fixity of what poetry of the self always requires—memory. Johnston believes that the altered perspective on the nature of memory is directly connected to a resolution of the Oedipal structures he discloses in the poems. There are shifts in Lowell's psychic models of his parents that seem "to point to an effort to escape fixation on the past by entering a state of present centeredness." Johnston goes even further to contend that "paradoxically, Lowell perceives acceptance of death as ultimately life-affirming." His thesis permits fresh looks at relevant poems in *Life Studies, Notebook 1967–68, History,* and *Day by Day.*

Jeffrey Myers in "The Mosler Safe in Lowell's 'For the Union Dead' " (*ANQ* 3, i:23–25) discovers more meaning in the reference to the survival of the American safe at Hiroshima than meets the eye. The first advertisement appeared in the *American Banker* on July 13, 1946. The insensitivity of this bit of commercialism was highlighted by a publicized letter written to the Mosler Safe Company by a Japanese bank manager who declared the advertisement "a perfect representative of the calculating commercial mentality." The letter suggests Lowell's own reaction to American insensitivity to nuclear devastation and to what was happening in Little Rock and his own criticism of the technology that not only made the indestructible safe but produced the bomb that "led directly to the destruction of 150,000 people."

d. Snodgrass   W. D. Snodgrass reappears in a first-rate interview, "W. D. Snodgrass: An Interview by Elizabeth Spires" (*APR* 19, iv:38–46). The interview proper was conducted on July 14–15, 1986, at the Snodgrass farmhouse, updated by a conversation in Newark, Delaware, on December 9, 1989. Snodgrass confesses his own dislike for the term "confessional poetry," coined by M. L. Rosenthal, especially now that the confessional style is out of favor, and he remains the one who receives blame for its transgressions since he is the only practitioner still alive. He divulges an attempt on his part and on the part of a fellow poet, Robert Shelley, in Lowell's seminar at Iowa to write simple, straightforward poems. This was rebellion, since young poets were taught back then that the times were too complicated for such poetry. Snodgrass also discusses the change in his own style for the poems in *After Experience* out of sheer boredom with doing the same old thing and on the constant urging of his friends to write about social problems. He adds that psychotherapy also helped to get the energy flowing again. He was led to free verse by playing with Whitman's rhythms. He is proudest of these poems, especially of the Van Gogh poems, and bears witness that it is exactly this, playing with the rhythms, that creates the voice of the poem. Snodgrass regards *The Fuehrer Bunker* cycle as his most significant achievement, and he discloses that he has published only half of the poems he has written on the Third Reich. He admits that the poems are actually about him, even more autobiographical than his first poems, but this time disguised. He also discusses his Cock Robin poems as a "comic version of Orpheus, the god of song." Lately, he has been involved in writing two groups of critical prose that will appear in books: autobiographical sketches, some of them published in periodicals, to be called *After Images,* and critical essays he believes he will call *To Sound Like Yourself.* His newest poems are all different from one other, including four villanella, a dance suite, and a sequence called "Autumn Variations." It is appropriate for Snodgrass to bring us up to date on his work in a highly readable interview, even though his memories of Anne Sexton in his seminar do not seem especially insightful in the context of recent re-evaluations of her work. This is but a minor quibble, however, about what is unquestionably the interview of the year.

e. Wilbur Richard Wilbur's poetry remains a good subject for brief explications. Isabella Wai in "Wilbur's 'On the Marginal Way' " (*Exp* 48, iv:286–89) illustrates the poet's ability to converse with the past. In this case, the speaker compares his contemporary surroundings (the time is the Vietnam War) with depictions of violence and human destruction in a past ranging from a 19th-century Gericault painting of a pillaged French town to the "final kill" at Auschwitz. If the juxtaposition of present and past leads to despair, another past-present juxtaposition directs to solace of another artist of the past God, whose "artwork" continues to renew as it has for all of time. Delving into the past is a serious artistic task.

iii Women Poets

Among the five women poets in Joanne Feit Diehl's *Women Poets and the American Sublime* are three contemporary major subjects for the exercise of feminist criticism—Adrienne Rich, Elizabeth Bishop, and Sylvia Plath. The poetic fathers that these women poets are compelled to have a "dialogic relationship" with are the two patriarchs of American literature—Emerson and Whitman. What women poets have had to contend with is the Emersonian and Whitmanesque tradition of the poet as central "man" and the poetic sublime as a "male identified" experience. Each of the women poets has had to make her own individual contribution to the emergence of a woman-authored tradition, which Diehl designates "the counter sublime." This approach is familiar, psychoana-

lytical, and gender-lensed, identifying a feminist tradition of the "counter sublime," calling for a reconstruction of the canon—this time poetry
on the sublime. The result is interesting, instructive, but limited by an
insistence on seeing everything too dogmatically through the lens of
feminist criticism. One might ask for a little eclecticism, a text generated
by the poetry rather than by the thesis. Diehl does add a deft touch of
Wittgenstein in order "to imagine a language means to imagine a form of
life" and to show that through remaking language, women poets "strive
to reinvent themselves." I like the stress on "reinvent."

Adrienne Rich's career is observed once more as a turn from initiation
to "encoded representations of women's experience" and to a radical
poetics seeking to "reimagine the relationship among writing, eros, and
sexual identity." What is provocative here is Diehl's attempt to see Rich's
poetry as enacting Whitmanian power together with the new tradition
of Dickinson's "alternative sublime." The counter sublime of this woman
poet requires renunciation of the power and conversion to "a force of
equal grandeur."

Elizabeth Bishop is a more difficult paradigm because she resisted
classification as a woman poet. Nevertheless, Bishop's poetry can be seen
through the identical lens as revealing the same conflict between American woman poets and the American Romantic tradition. Diehl has the
important advantage of Bishop's own notes and remarks in her personal
edition of *Leaves of Grass* to document her initial response to Walt
Whitman. Especially influential was Whitman's "definition of erotic
pleasure through absence and the unspoken." Through her own kind of
"verbal masking," Bishop's intent is "to preserve the erotic while deconstructing heterosexist categories." Though less admiring of Emily
Dickinson than Rich is, Bishop uses similar poetic encodings. Instead of
assuming the persona of the recluse as Dickinson did, Bishop assumes
the role of traveler, "the voice of the child, the testimonies of grotesque,
liminal creatures" to convey experience "profoundly felt and obliquely
expressed," only apparently evading issues of sexuality and gender. There
is an expert and fairly convincing analysis of a major poem, "Crusoe in
England," and Diehl's examples of Bishop's approach to the sublime
occasion readings of "Waiting Room" and "The Moose" from *Geography
III*. This may be the most persuasive chapter in the book.

In Sylvia Plath's poetry, Diehl finds a conflict between a desire for
access to the powers of the Romantic imagination and a determination
"to bear witness to the alternative situation of the woman poet who

refuses to disengender herself for art." What she sought in her poetry was "to inscribe sexual identity in poems." Her persona of self as aerialist is always at risk and "punished for its ability to please male authority." Plath is in the Whitman tradition of the sublime in her desire to establish a relationship with the world and in her use of the language of sensation. But her moments of sublime (or rather her feminist counter sublime) are moments of "effacement of either self or of world" beyond the pleasure principle in the pursuit of death. For help in her interpretation of Plath as caught in a "double bind" between regendering her language and poetics and inscribing maternal and female experiences in her work, Diehl calls on Freud and Richard Wollheim's concept of the "bodily ego," a body in fantasy, to define Plath's poetic identity. Plath's career is representative as a warning of potential self-victimization for the woman poet who continues to see herself in the American Romantic tradition. Her search for a sustaining poetics ended early with her suicide before her alternative course was ever reached. Diehl, like other feminist critics, is best at describing what fits the feminist "mythos" and less good at explaining deviations. Although this approach helps explain the power that comes from struggle, not all of Plath's good poetry was written according to a feminist script.

a. Levertov Linda Wagner-Martin continues her prolific and valuable contributions to contemporary poetry with *Critical Essays on Denise Levertov* (Hall), largely reprints. In addition to her introduction, Wagner-Martin adds her own new essay, "Levertov: Poetry and the Spiritual" (pp. 196–203), and Jerome Mazzaro's "Denise Levertov's Political Poetry" (pp. 172–86). The collection lacks a concluding interview and includes a surfeit of reviews. The claims for Levertov's importance are the usual, a concern with the techniques and philosophy of poetry over a 40-year period in England and in the United States. What this collection unfortunately reflects is the dearth of extensive, or for that matter, intensive critical comment on Levertov's work. Critics have found her poetry difficult to deal with because they could not classify, categorize, or place her in any neat way and because, when she turned to political poetry, many critics reacted against active political rhetoric. Political poetry in the 1970s was not considered "good poetry." Wagner-Martin considers Ralph J. Mills's *TriQuarterly* essay, "Denise Levertov: Poetry of the Immediate" (pp. 98–110), still the best accounting. She does not find or publish an equivalent account of the political poetry, although Bonnie

Costello's *Parnassus* review, "Flooded with Otherness" (pp. 41–44), identifies the centrality of *Life in the Forest* to Levertov's intentions. Wagner-Martin identifies Sandra M. Gilbert as placing Levertov's work in the context of other women poets, but Gilbert's analysis is not reprinted here. From this collection I would recommend Mazzaro's new essay as an intelligent placing of Levertov's political rhetoric in relation to the meditative lyric. Mazzaro moves in the appropriate direction of seeing her poetry as a whole, as poetry intended to help her readers make sense of outward reality as well as to live fuller lives.

Audrey T. Rogers in " 'Fragments of a Pattern': The Early Poetry of Denise Levertov" (*AmerP* 7, iii:31–48) is concerned with "central consistencies" in Levertov's poetry before she left England that have remained despite inevitable changes that have resulted from her American experiences. The themes of chaos, darkness, and death originate in the poet's experience of war. Early poems examined include "Listening to Distant Guns" (about Dunkirk) and other war poems, "They, Looking Back, the Eastern Side Beheld," "Christmas, 1944," "The Barricades," "The Conquerors," "To the Inviolable Shade," "Fable," "Ominous Morning," and "Childhood's End." There is an extensive and analytical look at a recent poem, "Candles in Babylon," to illustrate continuity between the early and recent poetry. No doubt this continuity is there, but Levertov's poetry has been sensitive to literary changes. Her early poetry also was influenced by the romanticism of those times, and the changes toward use of personal and ordinary experiences are integral to her status today. Wagner-Martin in "Levertov's 'Continuum' " (*Expl* 48, iv:289–92) seeks to direct attention away from the more recent poetry's "political" perspective (influenced by Neruda, Solzhenitsyn, Kim Chi Ha, among others) to a consistent underlying spiritualism which leads the poet to believe strongly in the "good" as inherent in people. It is this firm belief that is the basis for what has been read as political. "Continuum," from Levertov's 1978 collection *Life in the Forest,* is explicated to support a view that the song of the hardworking beetle in the poem is the continuing song of the artist in a search for truth, pressing toward a faith in human goodness. Levertov's political voice is actually the voice of the artist angered from seeing in her travels to Vietnam, Central America, and the American South the failure of human goodness. This article goes beyond mere explication to provide a perspective on much of Levertov's recent poetry.

b. Rich Marianne Novy's feminist *Women's Re-Visions of Shakespeare* requires mention because of Peter Erickson's chapter, "Adrienne Rich's Re-vision of Shakespeare" (pp. 183–95). The question raised hardly seems to have anything to do with Shakespeare: "how does her presentation of the father-daughter relationship change, and what is the significance of these changes for her work as a whole?" The relevance emerges from Rich's poem "After the Dark" and the later repercussions in her poetry of the parallel drawn in this poem between Cordelia and Lear, and between Rich and her father. Erickson finds three phases of development in this pairing: "a troubled fusion with her father in poems" down through "After the Dark"; a drastic "separation from the father" seen as a "precondition for establishing an independent self" in the great middle phase of her poetry in the early 1970s, particularly those portraits of the father in "When We Dead Awaken: Writing as Re-Vision" and *Of Women Born;* a third phase in the 1980s of "the surprising and moving reemergence of the father," suggested first in the 1982 essay, "Slit at the Root," and developed in the poetry that immediately followed, especially in *Sources* in 1983. In these poems, Rich undertakes a reassessment of differences among women, attuning herself to her Jewish identity, reviving the connection with the father, sanctioning a new view of him. Erickson's conclusion is that our "Shakespearean expectations" of "woman's forgiveness" are effectively cheated. Rich rewrites Cordelia's "silence" and effectively qualifies any compassion for the father. She permits a re-vision not of Shakespeare's dramatic greatness, but of his values. Albert Gelpi's "Two Ways of Spelling It Out: An Archetypal-Feminist Reading of H. D.'s Trilogy and Adrienne Rich's Sources" (*SR* 26, ii:266–84) has more on H. D. than on Rich, but it combines Jungian myth criticism and feminist criticism to find for both poets an engagement with animus, "conflicted for Rich," and "metamorphosis: the emergence of the self from the cocoon," the feminine self, of course. *Trilogy* uses "archetypal robes"; *Sources* enacts autogenesis in person.

c. Bishop Jacqueline Vaught Brogan in "Elizabeth Bishop: Perversity as Voice" (*AmerP* 7, ii:31–49) sees Bishop as a social revolutionary whose lyric style is actually a subversion or "perversion" of a patriarchal genre. "Quai d'Orleans" and "In Prison" are analyzed as poems that have been superficially read. Brogan sees both poems as feminist lyrics that seek to dismantle the "largely phallocentric perspective dominating the poetics of the lyric." This is an approach to Bishop as a social revolutionary that limits the concept to feminist literary politics, valuable for what it reveals and limited because of what it leaves out.

d. Plath   With Stephen Gould Axelrod's *Sylvia Plath: The Wound and Cure of Words* (Hopkins) this year we move away from feminist biography and demythologizing back to the primary job of criticism of the poetry. The change is welcome and consequential, focusing on a study of Plath's struggle for voice. Axelrod combines Freud and neo-Freudian psychoanalytic theory with "the rhetoric of literary criticism," and it is the latter emphasis that makes this an interesting critique. Within the limitations of a relatively brief study, Axelrod realizes a great deal. Exploring the boundaries of self and text, he manages to enhance the feminist approach to Plath by stressing tensions in her creative force between her creative drives and the inhibiting biological father and male literary forefathers. He explores her "ambiguous, charged relations" with her mother and with literary women, particularly with Virginia Woolf and Emily Dickinson. In the final chapter, he uses John T. Irvine's concept of "doubling" to consider Plath's "doubling" relationship to husband Ted Hughes, especially in her poems of the mirror and the shadow in which she hides the self's creative double. This is an ambitious and informative study, comprehensive enough for the reader to feel informed about the poetry even if he objects to psychologizing Plath again to attest a link between the narrative of the double and the tragic story of her own life. With a few reservations, I recommend it as one of the most enlightening of the many recent Plath studies.

Brita Lindberg-Seyersted makes one of her valuable contributions to American studies with "Sylvia Plath's 'Poem for a Birthday': Self-analysis with Surrealistic Elements" (*SN* 62:151–62), an attempt to show how surrealism can function in poetry that should be read as part of a poetic self-analysis. Surrealist themes are identified, and the sequence is judged to be "a significant step in Sylvia Plath's growth as a poet" in that she finds subject matter and themes genuinely her own and learns how to use more intrinsically a fairy-tale and nursery rhyme world. Plath "shares the Surrealists' general purpose of uncovering the subconscious and placing it beside the conscious . . . by the sharp juxtaposition of images. . . ." The influence of Roethke's greenhouse poems in a journey from fetus to young adult is plausibly acclaimed. Since Plath's surrealistic poems have not been subjected to extensive image analysis, the value of Lindberg-

Seyersted's study is that she conveys some of the value of that approach. Image patterns she notes include "Alice in Wonderland," the fetus, the father, the Yaddo landscape, the wax doll, the African folktale as a resource—all part of a self-analysis of the poet as young adult. This is a worthy article.

Plath scholarship perpetuates with a new tool, Sheryl L. Meyering's useful *Sylvia Plath: A Reference Guide, 1973–1988* (Hall). A brief introduction traces, without adding any new information, the development of the Plath myth as well as the countermyths climaxing in Anne Stevenson's demythologizing biography. Everything of any importance published on Plath during these 15 years seems meticulously included and concisely summarized. The limitations of a bibliography at this time may be evidenced in the last word recorded here, Linda Wagner-Martin's view that "a full and just assessment of her work is not possible at the present time."

There is only one justification for mentioning Sally Greene's "Fathers and Daughters in Sylvia Plath's 'Blossom Street' " (*SAF* 18:22–31). Greene uses the fiction to show that the gender question raised by a woman who feels oppressed by men makes "it impossible to pay unflinching spiritual allegiance to a religion whose primary symbols are patriarchal."

There are still doubters about the recent high regard of critics, especially women critics, for Plath's poetry, as reported in the last few issues of *ALS*. Harold Fromm in "Sylvia Plath, Hunger Artist" (*HudR* 43:245–56) uses a review of Anne Stevenson's *A Life of Sylvia Plath* to laud the demythologizing of the person and uses this as a springboard to attack the poet on her "feminism" and her "craft." To find "greedy vengeance" in the feminism and "madness" in the craft is to overstress the anger and violence and fail to see the power that Plath's recurring motifs gather as they resonate through different strategies of formal control. As I read Fromm's article, I recalled a remark that David Perkins made in his *History of Modern Poetry:* "Were her poetry less harrowing she might be viewed as witty." There is more truth in this comment than Fromm realizes. He begrudges her craft, but judges her faulty in her responsibilities as a person.

e. Wakoski David M. Brown provides a listing for Diane Wakoski's "The Fear of Fat Children" from her 1986 book, *The Rings of Saturn* (*Expl* 48, iv:292–94). This is a staid New Critical analysis of the symbolism of "a fat child," incorporating her distaste over an obese student, her own fear of the "fat of a wasted life," and subtle implication that her poetry is "protection against a wasted life."

f. Miles   Lisa M. Steinman, "Putting on Knowledge with Power" (*ChiR* 37, i:130–40) revisits a woman poet once greatly admired but rarely appreciated today, Josephine Miles—teacher, critic, and poet. Steinman believes that Miles's poetry should be rediscovered if there is a serious current critical interest in lyrics concerned with other lives and ordinary events without writing narrative or transforming the world into something "too emblematic of the self." Miles raised issues that are ethical and political, and she proposed the question of "how poetry engages the language and cultures of its world." Steinman makes clear that Miles's poetry was learned from the older tradition (Yeats, Stevens, Williams), and she finds her later poems to be more overtly political. Steinman makes a point that Miles may deserve another look, but she does not make a forceful case for it.

iv   Beats, Open Form, Deep Image

a. Rexroth   Kenneth Rexroth's reputation as the finest of the minor San Francisco poets may be enhanced by a double entry into the canon, his cantankerously entertaining correspondence with his publisher, James Laughlin, ed. Lee Bartlett, *Kenneth Rexroth and James Laughlin: Selected Letters* (Norton), and Linda Hamalian's biography, *A Life of Kenneth Rexroth* (Norton). The correspondence is valuable as a resource for the once in a while comic, every so often difficult, relationship between an occasionally devilish poet and often saintlike publisher from the late 1940s to the early 1980s. The biography is handsomely formatted, well-written, and provides an interesting account of the life of a poet, painter, newspaperman, and political activist who had Robert Duncan and Louis Zukofsky among his contemporaries, and Ginsberg, Snyder, and Levertov among his friends. It is a difficult life to fathom, described by Hamalian as "a tissue of contradictions." She does a good job of recounting the contradictions and a less convincing, but interesting, job of seeing Rexroth as "precursor for late-twentieth-century Deconstruction." She convinces that he was a man of talent and imagination who "confronted the dilemmas created by the social and political crises of the thirties and beyond" and tried to resolve his own personal conflicts by writing. What is just as convincing is that his way of life often interfered with the success of the literary life, or, as Hamalian says, "he could not always get his head and his heart to work together." Rexroth could be genuine in his poetry, but not always in his personal life.

b. Olson Paul Christensen's *In Love, In Sorrow: The Complete Correspondence of Charles Olson and Edward Dahlberg* (Paragon) deserves mention as a source for the development of Olson's critical ideas in, first, a mentorship from Edward Dahlberg, then, a critical divergence as he found his own directions. The friendship has been charted before in John Cech's *Charles Olson and Edward Dahlberg: A Portrait of a Friendship* (1982), but Christensen now provides us with much of the primary material as well as a sparkling introduction to a literary friendship that is interesting if not as consequential as those of Pound and Eliot or Hawthorne and Melville, as Christensen seems to claim.

c. Snyder Patrick D. Murphy's *Critical Essays on Gary Snyder* (Hall) follows the format of this series with an introduction, reprinted essays by Thomas Parkinson, Charles Altieri, Sherman Paul, Charles Molesworth, and other luminaries, and four new items: Murphy's own "Alternation and Interpenetration: Gary Snyder's *Myths & Texts*" (pp. 210–29); Katsunori Yamazato's "How to Be in This Crisis: Gary Snyder's Cross-cultural Vision in *Turtle Island*" (pp. 230–47), a definitive account of the Buddhism in this work; Jack Hicks's "Poetic Composting in Gary Snyder's *Left Out in the Rain*" (pp. 247–57); and David Robertson's abbreviated interview, "Practicing the Wild—Present and Future Plans: An Interview with Gary Snyder" (pp. 257–62). In his introduction, Murphy supplies a brief biographical draft and sketches the criticism from Thomas Parkinson's 1968 essay in the *Southern Review* through post-1986 reviews of *Left Out in the Rain*. After 20 years of scholarship, it is surprising there are still no biographies and only two book-length introductory studies. Obviously, there is a need for Snyder's collected essays. Of value in the new items are Murphy's argument for the importance of *Myths & Texts* as both mythopoeic and metamythopoeic, "creating a myth and comment on that process of mythmaking"; and Hicks's case for *Left Out in the Rain* as more than "juvenilia, ephemera, and poetic turnings," but instead a collection that reveals Snyder's development as man and mature poet, even the principle of his "poetic composting." David Robertson's interview reveals Snyder looking ahead to his future writing projects, an excellent way to end.

d. Ferlinghetti S. E. Gontarski's "Lawrence Ferlinghetti on Grove Press" (*RCF* 10, iii:128–31) deserves brief mention for calling to our attention the importance of the second issue of *Evergreen Review,* "The San Francisco Scene," as providing the first national exposure of the poetry of San Francisco. Censorship was still a problem, and the reprints in *Evergreen Review* had omissions. It was the legal battles over "Howl" that set a precedent, particularly Judge Clayton Horn's legal criterion of redeeming social significance that helped clear the way for the publication of Henry Miller and of *Lady Chatterley's Lover.*

v Older Generation: Warren, Oppen

a. Warren Last year I did not sufficiently praise an important addition to Robert Penn Warren criticism as a fine study of Warren's long poems, Hugh Ruppersburg's *Robert Penn Warren and the American Imagination* (Georgia). This year I would focus on Randolph Paul Runyon's *The Braided Dream: Robert Penn Warren's Late Poetry* (Kentucky). Ruppersburg's book was concerned with Warren's vision of American history in his fiction, nonfiction, and three long narrative poems—*Brother to Dragons, Audubon: A Vision,* and *Chief Joseph of the Nez Perce*—a splendid account of the intellectual development of a writer revealed in concerns with deviations in 20th-century America from the ideals of our forefathers. Warren's imagination is an important American creative force, but it is perhaps even more of a Southern imagination in his concern with agrarianism, civil rights, and the threat of science and technology. Runyon's *The Braided Dream* focuses on the poetry that qualifies Warren for this chapter, the poetry of the old man. It is commendably a careful reading of the last four books published from 1976 through 1984, making clear a major phase and a major accomplishment by a poet in his seventies and eighties. This concentration on the poetry of a decade makes the study estimable. Runyon believes that Warren's accomplishment as a poet has not been tangibly recognized in criticism, though the man of letters was acclaimed during his last years, culminating in his designation as our first poet laureate. An assessment of the late poems is needed, as evidenced in the second volume of David Perkins's *A History of Modern Poetry,* which covers Warren's poetry up to 1966, leaving it to readers to judge the poetry of the next decade. Runyon's readings, through a focus on continuity and lineages, reveal a considerable poet and a careful craftsman in individual poems, especially in poetic sequences toward which he naturally tended, and even in the typographical design of his books.

Tributes to Warren as "man of letters" appeared in memorial sections of the *Sewanee Review* (98, ii) and the *Southern Review* (26, i). Neither section was primarily on the poetry. I would single out as an eloquent tribute to the poet in the man, Louis D. Rubin's "R. P. W. 1905–1989" (*SR*, pp. 237–45).

I also would call attention to the special issue, "A Legacy of Robert Penn Warren," of my own *South Carolina Review* (*SCR* 23, i:3–86). Relevant to the poetry are a brief tribute by his friend and colleague Cleanth Brooks ("Robert Penn Warren: A Brief Tribute," pp. 5–8); a final word on the value of his contributions to literature from the unorthodox viewpoint of Leslie Fiedler ("Robert Penn Warren: A Final Word," pp. 9–16); and a reminder of what we should value in his poetry by George Garrett ("Warren's Poetry: Some Things We Ought to be Thinking About," pp. 48–58).

b. Oppen　　Rachel Blau DuPlessis's *The Selected Letters of George Oppen* (Duke) is another addition to what is fast becoming a major resource for biographical material—the correspondence of poets. The particular value of this book is that the letters are the collected prose of Oppen, practically his only comments on his poetry or anyone else's. He wrote only one essay and one essay-review. The introduction provides a useful outline of Oppen's career, including his poetic silence from 1934 to 1958, his political activities that led to an extensive FBI file, the centralness to much of his poetry of his World War II wound, the restoration of his passport in 1958, the submission to psychoanalysis, and a return to the writing of poetry. The correspondence is eccentric and difficult in style and maddening in punctuation, but it contains lively comments on a great many contemporary poets.

vi　Nature: Realism, Surrealism, Metaphysics

a. Berry　　Thomas L. Altherr in " 'The Country We Have Married': Wendell Berry and the Georgic Tradition of Agriculture" (*SoSt* 1, i:105–15) revisits the agrarian country of Wendell Berry's poetry, refashioning it in terms of the Virgilian Georgic tradition which stressed the virtues of work over those of ease. Hardly startling, but it is useful to see Berry as a Southern agrarian and as a current farmer-poet reacting against technology and agribusiness. In short, he may be "Georgic," but he is clearly his own contemporary edition of such poetry. More thoroughly than anyone else, Altherr describes Berry's criticism of modern life in his prose, novels, and criticism as well as in his poetry. Altherr deals effectively with the relationship between the farmer and his land as a metaphor of marriage; he rather convincingly distinguishes the tone of scorn directed toward modern agribusiness as Georgic in its vitriolic intensity; and he has his own metaphors for Berry's commitment to getting Americans back to the land, seeing him as a literary subversive against agribusiness and a modern Virgil "stirring the Georgic longings of the collective consciousness." If distinctiveness, even uniqueness, is an argument for a poet today, Altherr makes a case, even if overstated, for Wendell Berry.

b. Bly   William V. Davis makes brief comment in "Affinity and Judgment: The Private and Public Poems of Robert Bly's Early Career" (*NCL* 20, i:7–9) on the "leap" by Bly from the private, inwardly directed poems in *Silence in the Snowy Fields* to the public political controversies solicited in *The Light Around the Body*. There are useful comments on "The Executive's Death," the first poem of the later volume, as a key transitional poem in a movement from "inwardness to outwardness, from affinity to judgment, from individual circumstance to artistic imagination." No judgments are offered as to why Bly's more traditional and bucolic poems, his inward private poems, are superior to the more public poems.

c. Wright   The "Focus on Poetry" issue of the *Gettysburg Review* (3, i) offers a feature on James Wright. E. L. Doctorow ("James Wright at Kenyon," pp. 11–22) characterizes Wright's eccentric but central role among the student literati there and vividly sketches (as my own experience as a summer student at the Kenyon School of English in 1949 verifies) life at a school that in the 1940s and early 1950s played the New Criticism as "Ohio State played football." But Wright, he makes clear, refused to play that critical game. Peter Stitt ("James Wright's Earliest Poems: A Selection," pp. 23–34) prints with a brief introduction nine early poems, seven of them written while Wright was in high school. He follows this with "An Introduction to James Wright" (pp. 35–48), chronicling how Wright's poetry emerged from an environment of contrasts "between the urban and the natural, between the city and the garden, between society and the wilderness," and succinctly outlining his literary life.

d. Creeley Robert Creeley would get my vote as the most exceptional correspondent among contemporary poets. His extended correspondence with Charles Olson has emerged, and now Ekbert Faer and Sabrina Reed have edited *Irving Layton and Robert Creeley: The Complete Correspondence* (McGill-Queens). The value in this correspondence between a Canadian and an American poet in part comes from a chronicling of the entry of poets in both countries into postmodernism. Of special interest in the early Creeley-Layton correspondence is an account of the Black Mountain experience, including questions about and comments on the defections of Kenneth Rexroth and Paul Blackburn and the publication history of *Black Mountain Review.* It is a transamerican correspondence and, for a time, transoceanic contrast with Layton in Canada asking and Creeley in Majorca answering questions on such subjects as his near neighbor Robert Graves; the response, "one hell of a bore." In his foreword to Gerard Burns's *A Thing About Language* (So. Ill.), Creeley implies that the appeal of this book is that it offers a small degree of the intensity of Lawrence's zealous *Studies in Classic American Literature,* or follows in the tradition of W. C. Williams's *In the American Grain,* Charles Olson's *Call Me Ishmael,* or Edward Dahlberg's *The Leafless America.* I would like to see such a book, but Creeley's critical advocacy to the contrary, this is not it. In a minor way, it reintroduces a comic note, even a touch of wit, to reviews. On John Ashbery, Burns remarks: "I don't like John Ashbery, for the whine under the line, and for pretending to live in clock time and then complaining about how dreary it is. . . ." On critics on Ashbery, he adds "Whatever poetry can no longer do, the presumption is that John Ashbery is no longer doing it." This is actually a slim book of short essays and short reviews from the *Southwest Review.*

e. Dickey It is gratifying to be surprised by articles that do not appear promising. Ernest Suarez's "The Uncollected Dickey: Pound, New Criticism, and the Narrative Images" (*AP* 8, supplement, pp. 128–45) would seem to be about two decidedly unrelated subjects. It is not. Suarez begins with a plea for attention to James Dickey's early uncollected poetry. He reveals how Dickey, after rejections, in order to be published disciplined his Romantic predilections by adjusting his writing to the New Critical tenets favored by most of the literary magazines of the season. Then he touches on something that Dickey never talked about but which was also evident in the early poetry, the influence of Ezra Pound. Suarez provides an interesting account of Dickey's substantial friendship with Pound, including accounts of visits and considerable correspondence. What seemed unpromising turns out to be an interesting early chapter in Dickey's career as a poet subject to critical influences that few poets of his generation could avoid, not even Dickey. Suarez sustains what many critics have failed to see and what Dickey was never disposed for them to see, in spite of the "more life" persona, just how academic he has always been. I need to add my regret that this item appears in the final issue in magazine format of an important source for interesting material on contemporary poetry, *American Poetry*.

The James Dickey Newsletter features Gordon Van Ness's reading (" 'The Thing is there!'—The Briefings of a Writer: James Dickey's Early Notebooks," *JDN* 7, i:2–8) of Dickey's 1950s notebooks, written in three unpublished ledgers, as early examples of a habit of exploring his literary life that led to what he called "journals" in *Sorties* (1971). The notations detail "ideas and sketches for stories, novels, and poems; specific experiments with words and even lines; thought and analyses of other writers and their works; and might be called possible course corrections regarding narrative and poetic methods." Dickey's attention is entirely devoted to literary plans and efforts without the concern for personal and family matters evident in *Sorties* or in *Self-Interviews* (1970). These notes reveal that Dickey was always working simultaneously on poetry and fiction, seeking a new kind of poetry while retaining forms. Marion Hodge in "James Dickey's Natural Heaven and the Tradition" (*JDN* 7, i:15–21) reexamines Dickey's use of the word "heaven," contrasting and comparing his use with the "tradition" in American poetry as represented by Whitman, Thoreau, Emerson, Stevens. The tradition in which Dickey fits dictates that we must accept and love "our world as it is."

Romy Heylen revisits a work which has not often surfaced these days—Dickey's *The Zodiac* ("James Dickey's *The Zodiac*: A Self-Translation?" *JDN* 6, ii:2–17)—identifying Dickey's source for the Dutch poem by Hendrik Marsman as an English translation by Adriaan J. Barnouw, which originally appeared in the *Sewanee Review* in 1947. Heylen contends that Dickey's poem is foremost about interpreting and writing and should be classified as a second "self-translation by and of a poet who cannot escape his self and who delivers a pastiche of his own poetics." *The Zodiac* should be read both as a participation poem in the experiences of another poet and as a performance poem for Dickey's own ideas.

Ken Autrey provides a second account of the early journals ("Working the Notebook to Death, James Dickey's Journals," *JDN* 6, ii:19–24) as revealing Dickey's fascination with journals as a literary form and as "primarily of interest for what they reveal about Dickey's early development and his attempts to define for himself a poetic philosophy." I would add that the journals document not only how carefully Dickey apprenticed himself as a writer in his reading of other writers but also recorded (in surprisingly Jamesian fashion) what he was later to use in his poems and novels.

The Pittsburgh Series in Bibliography admirably achieves its purpose of establishing an author's canon through identifying the first appearance of everything he wrote and enabling a reader to determine whether the copy he is examining is identical to the one described. Matthew J. Bruccoli and Judith S. Baughman have edited *James Dickey: A Descriptive Bibliography* (Pittsburgh). Of value to scholars and critics is the complete listing of all interviews and articles quoting Dickey, the justification for mention here.

f. Kinnell   Daniel Schenker ("Galway Kinnell's 'The Last River': A Civil Rights Odyssey" *MissQ* 43:207–91) reexamines the 400-line poem, "The Last River," which is rooted in Galway Kinnell's experience as a civil rights worker in Louisiana. He is especially concerned with the three versions of the poem and believes that this poem, as it developed, registers changes in Kinnell's political sensibility from the mid-1960s to the early 1980s. Certainly this is the most detailed explication of this important poem. Schenker properly stresses that "The Last River" is "essentially a narrative poem interspersed with lyric and visionary episodes." It is a poem of self-knowledge from which Kinnell learned something about political events and about himself. The later versions are less optimistic about the effects of the civil rights movement, viewed by Schenker as something of an antijeremiad opposed to the earlier version jeremiad, in the sense that values are called into question. As the versions proceed, Thoreau comes to be admired not just for his act of civil disobedience but because he sees the ambiguous values of such acts.

vii **Eastern and New Establishment**

a. Ashbery Paul Munn publishes "An Interview with John Ashbery" recorded at the University of Minnesota in 1987 (*NOR*, 17, ii:59–63). Ashbery confesses that he never really enjoyed writing art criticism; it was simply the only way for a while that he could earn a living. His *Selected Poems* should not be taken as a codex and was simply based on what he liked or no longer cared for. He has little or no desire to have a "complete poems" or to reedit early poems as Auden often disastrously did. He does not believe that readers have to be familiar with poets like Auden or Bishop who might have influenced him to have access to his own poems. He never notably thought of his poetry as difficult until some critics found it so, and he knows readers who have not read such critics and who think the poetry is reasonably accessible. Ultimately, he agrees with Eliot: you do not have to understand poetry to enjoy it. He may have written poems that are not "anti-voice" poems and feature an "I," but it is an "I" that is, as Rimbaud said, "an other," just one of his voices. His interest is in the "movement of the mind, how it goes from one place to the other." He concludes with comments on "At North Farm." The title was suggested by the Finnish epic folk poem the *Kalevala* as a place near hell "but not in it." The first part may have come from a cinematic memory of *Lawrence of Arabia* of someone "galloping across a desert stream" or a memory of the epigraph to John O'Hara's *Appointment in Samarra,* in which a man says he has to go to Samarra to avoid death. "A lot of the imagery comes from fairy tales and things I read when I was young." It was a poem he wrote with great ease. He is able to use clichés when he finds "colloquial, overheard" beauty he would like to steal for his poetry. When asked whether there are literary reminiscences from Yeats and Keats, he agrees only in that some of their poems "are all part of our subconscious, if not our conscious." That is why he does not have footnotes or explanations of where things come from. Munn's brief introduction states that "Eliot's notion of poetry as 'superior amusement' may have found its greatest example in the work of Ashbery." The same may be said of his interview. It is like good conversation, entertaining without in any way seriously getting into the poetry. It could be called "a conversation with John Ashbery," not the kind of interview as criticism spoken by Dickey or Kinnell. Evidence that more than sophisticated amusement, even meaning or symbolic meaning, can be fathomed in Ashbery's poetry is convincingly presented in Kevin

Clark's "John Ashbery's 'A Wave': Privileging the Symbol" (*PLL* 26:271–79). This is the best explicatory item on Ashbery's poetry. For those interested in the prose poem category, Margueritte S. Murphy's "John Ashbery's Three Poems: Heteroglossia in the American Prose Poem" (*AmerP* 7, ii:50–63) is definitely worth a look.

b. Merwin   William V. Davis (" 'The Light Again of Beginnings': W. S. Merwin's Little Apocalypse" (*NCL* 20, iv:8–9) finds in the diminutive seven-line poem "The First Darkness" "the essence of Merwin's contribution to the apocalyptic mode that is so important to the history of recent American poetry. The poem begins with a reversal of the myth of Genesis by positing the possibility of God's existence by his very absence, a twist given, perhaps, to Paul Tillich's argument for God's being by denying his existence. Merwin's version is that a nonexistent God can actually exist in departures and in a "first darkness" before darkness and light. This is a minor poem, but it does identify what Frost called a "nick," a gloss on understanding Merwin's use of the apocalyptic mode.

c. Ammons   James S. Hans in "The Aesthetics of Worldly Hopes in A. R. Ammons's Poetry" (*ELWIU* 17, i:76–93) examines the aesthetic of a poet "who is not greatly at odds with his world," a rare contemporary poet whose outstanding attribute is the overall serenity of his voice. Ammons is a poet "who sees the world aesthetically" and regards life as a "playful activity that affords one a perspective based on the tragic joy that life embodies when it is seen aesthetically." To say that Ammons's stance is aesthetic is not to say that he is at a distance from reality. He is involved in the processes and fully aware of living organisms' "thrust of joy" and risk of death. The way to tragic joy is through a way of life that rejects categorizations, beginnings, and ends for "an ever present middle," even denying the validity of an anthropocentric world. In his poetry, Ammons decenters the self, seeing himself as always part of "a field of action." He is aware of "the freedom of limits," of giving up, of getting lost only to see that one has no chance to get lost, and of recognizing the limits placed on any human measuring of the world. The goal of his poetry is to present specific emotions in the articulation of the part-whole, many-one relationships, a process that begins with one's understanding one's own small place within a particular field. Hans credits Ammons's poetry for accepting the risk of our natural existence, but not of our existence in the social contexts in which we live. His approach is a valid articulation of the

aesthetics behind Ammons's "tragic joy," but it can also be seen as a too
elaborate development of a point made succinctly by Josephine Miles
(which he quotes): "The peopled world and the constructed world are
not [Ammons's] chief substance." Unfortunately, not much of Ammons's
poetry, except for "Corson's Inlet," is involved in Hans's analysis.

d. Merrill   Mutlu Konuk Blasing's "Rethinking Models of Literary
Change: The Case of James Merrill" (*ALH* 2:299–317) raises the significant question of how to associate Merrill's poetry with postmodernism.
The usual assessments of modernism, such as a shift from a rigid
formalism to antiformalist experiments in free verse or even in prose,
allow Merrill to appear to be one of the "new formalists." As a poet he is
comfortable with conventional metrical and stanzaic forms but dismisses
"the very ideology of modernity." Blasing locates Merrill very well, but
then sidesteps a new reading of the poems in a rather laborious attempt
to answer "the larger question of what exactly changes in the process of
literary change." Wyatt Prunty in *Fallen from the Symboled World* contends that it is "tropes." Blasing proposes attention "to functional and
rhetorical discontinuities within formal continuities and to formal discontinuities within functional continuities" as well as to "indifferent
tropological models of figurations—of temporality, precedence, continuity, and change that inform the work of different poets." What this
focus permits us to do with a poet like Merrill is to see that in the
postmodern period, "closure (metaphysical, moral, or political) can
occur within open forms, which have conventional, closed forms." We
are given as exemplar a reading of "An Urban Convalescence" to show
that for "Merrill, change and continuity are not polar opposites: continuity is infected with change and change with continuity." Blasing's
thesis on postmodernism is complex enough to require discussion of
more than one poem and even more than one poet.

viii   Others

a. Stern   Jane Somerville's *Making the Light Come: The Poetry of Gerald
Stern* (Wayne State) is the first book-length study of a contemporary of
Allen Ginsberg and John Hollander who did not begin serious publication until the late sixties and was never identified with any side on the
divergent positions poets have taken on key issues in contemporary
poetry. He is not easily designated "traditional, confessional, deep image,

or language poet." Somerville sees her book as an introduction to and interpretation of a body of poetry "far more intricate and multifaceted than it seems at first reading." The approach she chooses is to analyze the roles played by Stern's "eccentric speaker," both a voice and a character, whom she sees as "the controlling principle in a poetry of performance." What is constant in the poetry examined is "the tragi-comic as a generic position for the speaker and the poetry he controls." She finds an "impulse" activating his poetry, the nostalgia of the return journey, and among the roles enacted by the speaker she discovers the figure of the gardener, a contrasting wanderer and rabbi, and a presiding angel. The goals of the book are admittedly "old-fashioned"—interpretation and appreciation. I do not fault the interpretation. If, as Cleanth Brooks seemed to suggest, explication is evaluation, Somerville's careful readings make Stern's poetry valuable. But her appreciation does not establish his importance face to face with his illustrious contemporaries for the reader of poetry in the 1990s. I miss a final chapter, a summation rather than an anticlimactic discussion of his personae and the figure of the angel.

Stern appears again in Sanford Pinsker's "Weeping and Wailing: The Jewish Songs of Gerald Stern" in Daniel Walden's edition of *SAJL,* "American Jewish Poets: The Roots and the Stems" (*SAJL* 9, 2:186–216). Pinsker's emphasis is on Stern as "the ultimate wanderer," a contemporary manifestation of the Jewish-American sense of having lost Jewishness but not having found an American identity. Pinsker nearly begs the question by asserting that Stern's Jewishness is there even if you cannot put your finger on it. He quotes Louis Armstrong's answer to a question about what is jazz—"Pops, if you have to ask, you'll never know." What is identified in Stern's poetry is a "Romantic temperament" and a "residue of Jewish disposition." Pinsker indicates how these two elements of special interest to Jewish poets coalesce in subjects like the Sabbath, the Holocaust, and becoming "an old Jew." His comparisons with Delmore Schwartz do more for determining Stern's poetic status than does Jane Somerville's book.

b. Strand David Kirby's preface to his A Literary Frontiers Edition, *Mark Strand and the Poet's Place in the Contemporary World* (Missouri), provides a useful, though minute, introduction to a good poet, Mark Strand, whose work has not been rewarded with enough critical scrutiny. The selected bibliography does not even include a major article. Why such disregard? Kirby surmises that Strand has appeared to lack a distinctive voice: his poetry sounds like that of a number of other contemporary poets. He has also been criticized for sounding "distant and disembodied," turning out poems that seem "plain" and "almost without detail." What Kirby contends forcefully is that the distance established by Strand's persona is in reality the strength of his art. He has deliberately stepped away from the self and from contemporary life and re-situated his persona in that tradition of Western thought in which the self is detached in a search for a peace within. As an American poet, Strand is writing in a tradition that includes *Walden, Huckleberry Finn, The Scarlet Letter, Moby-Dick, A Farewell to Arms, Franny and Zooey,* and *Invisible Man.* Kirby's examples are notably from American fiction, not poetry. Strand has described his poetic version of that tradition "the winding course that I have made of love and self." The difference Kirby finds between Strand's persona and other personae in this tradition is that "the Strand persona has figured out a way to save himself. To escape from the cave of the self, the Strand persona, an adventurer suitable for our times, becomes no one." He expresses admiration for Strand's intellectual honesty in not being restricted to any one possibility for salvation, including self-effacement, resolutely refusing to accept an easy answer. Kirby's book is too short for any definitive illustration of how to read Strand's poetry, and he may try too hard to make Strand appear singular among his contemporaries. Still, even if he tends to make Strand's work appear even more of a piece than it is, Kirby does tell us much about Strand's persona and his use of it in a technique crafted to accomplish as a poet exactly what he wants to do, "interrogating and dismantling" the concept of the self. Kirby concludes with a reminder that Strand, like John Ashbery, is an art critic and, like a few of his contemporaries, has turned to children's literature, even though it is fiction not poetry. This is a valuable book, not for its comprehensiveness, but as a first study, though brief, of an underappreciated poet, officially honored in 1990 and 1991 as our poet laureate.

c. Simic The University of Michigan Press Poets on Poetry series happily continues with a collection of the essays and other prose of Charles Simic, *Wonderful Words, Silent Truth: Essays on Poetry and a Memoir.* Simic, a recent Pulitzer Prize winner, writes well; but the essays and fragments are primarily self-referential, providing interesting insights into Simic's autobiography, especially concerning his reading and his childhood in Yugoslavia. He writes on Emerson, Dickinson, and

Frost, but not on his contemporaries, except for brief comments reprinted from *Field,* on William Stafford's poem "At the Bomb Testing Site."

ix African American Poetry

a. Brooks African American poetry at the beginning of the 1990s remains a dynamic and vital entity in contemporary American literature. Young black poets are now benefiting from a critical interest that was denied the older generation of poets at this stage in their careers. The most celebrated poet is Pulitzer Prize winner Gwendolyn Brooks, a living legend and a forceful instigator of new poetic forms. In 1990, she received as much attention as any contemporary American poet. George E. Kent's biography, *A Life of Gwendolyn Brooks* (Kentucky), is remarkably candid and much more informative than the autobiographies the poet has already written. He maintains a delicate balance between the chronology of events in a life that Brooks has described as having "very little drama in it," and the extraordinary poetry that has won her recognition as one of America's greatest living poets. Up to his death in 1983, Kent compiled an enormous number of Brooks's notes and records and conducted extensive interviews with her family, friends, and acquaintances. The biography creates a vivid image of a brilliant, sensitive, and creative poet devoted to her family, her art, her country, and her race. An afterword adds a concise summary of events in Brooks's life from the time of Kent's death to the book's publication. This biography is definitive on the relationship of the poet's life to her work.

Brooke Kenton Horvath focuses on Brooks's early style in "The Satisfactions of What's Difficult in Gwendolyn Brooks's Poetry" (*AL* 62:606–16). He analyzes "Do Not Be Afraid of No" from *Annie Allen* to show how Brooks's "classic style" (vaguely defined) relates to black concerns. Horvath's difficulties come from trying to say too much about Brooks's style and her concern for black people from too little, an analysis of only one poem. More questions are raised than answers given.

Brooks is also discussed in D. H. Melhem's *Heroism in the New Black Poetry* (Kentucky) along with five other black poets: Imamu Amiri Baraka, the most renowned male black poet; Jayne Cortez, the "surrealist" obsessed with "dynamic imagery"; Haki R. Madhubuti, the revolutionist who legitimized new poetic forms for contemporary black poets; Dudley Randall, the inspiring publisher/poet who gave definition to the term "second Black literary renaissance"; and Sonia Sanchez, a brilliant writer who "possesses an extraordinary culmination of spiritual and poetic powers." Melhem finds "humanism and heroism" both in the poetry and in the actions of and examples set by the poets themselves. She analyzes poems by each poet and compares and contrasts them. In addition, she includes interviews with each poet on subjects of importance about black poetry and American poetry. Melhem's book is essential reading for future studies of new black poetry.

Two additional studies further Melhem's emphasis on the humanism of contemporary black poetry. Arlene H. Mitchell and Darwin L. Henderson in "Black Poetry: Versatility of Voices" (*EJ* 79, iv:23–28) specify how significant black poetry embodies "universal ideas." Exemplary of how black poetry shows its own "natural cadence" and is "as varied and as complex" as the poetry of their white peers is the poetry of Gwendolyn Brooks, Langston Hughes, Nikki Giovanni, Paul Laurence Dunbar, Sterling A. Brown, and Lucille Clifton. Mitchell and Henderson use black poetry to illustrate the importance of teaching the literature of all ethnic groups to show the diversity but unifying common concerns of American literature.

b. Tolson   Michael Berube offers a brilliant thesis on Melvin Tolson in "Mask, Margins, and African American Modernism: Melvin Tolson's *Harlem Gallery*" (*PMLA* 105:57–69). He offers persuasive testimony that the often controversial poetry of Tolson's *Harlem Gallery* has something "to say about modernism's relation to African American literature." Tolson's acceptance of modernism ensued from his conscious emulation of Eliot. It is this influence that earned his reputation as "a late modernist writing in the midst of the Black aesthetic of the sixties." In his reading, Berube shows how the narrator (the curator) and the time of narration are the central issues in a work in which in modernist fashion "indeterminacy is inscribed in the poem at every term." But from a modernist context Tolson has written an "odd parable," one that speaks to "the politics of separatism." His purpose was "letting revolutionary discourse sound in the ears of conservative whites" and, consequently, "any account of the fate of African American modernism [would] be inadequate without a thorough reading of Tolson."

Melvin B. Tolson, Jr., reprises his father's place in American literature in "The Poetry of Melvin B. Tolson, 1898–1966" (*WLT* 64:395–400). Tolson writes of his father with compassion and intimacy, colorfully describing him as the "poet, orator, teacher of English and American Literature, grammarian, small-town mayor, theatre founder and director, debate coach" whose poetry, contrary to the beliefs of many critics, was greatly influenced by "the blues" and contemporary black writers as well as "the modernism of the period." This well-articulated account includes a brief biography that highlights the poet's influences in West Africa which caused him to be named poet laureate of the Republic of Liberia. It analyzes how the poet's work, especially *Harlem Gallery,* is able to portray the "whole history of the diaspora of African Americans. . . ." It also describes how Tolson's poetry never lost "its exultant belief in the final triumph of the 'little people.'" The son has paid tribute to the father by writing one of the best accounts of his poetry.

c. Others Doris Davenport is part of "a tradition of Black poets who work with music." She theorizes in her article, "Music in Poetry: If you can't feel it/you can't fake it" (*Mid-AmerR* 10, ii:57–64), that people with "the right ears can hear music in black poetry. . . . Poems can not be a non-tone or delivered in a monotone voice." In her poetry, readers hear the music of black people—rhythm and blues, jazz, gospel, and spirituals—which Davenport contends "ought to 'seduce' the senses." When she recites, Davenport seeks "a kind of spiritual atmosphere" and brings out the music—which she believes "is necessary for the poetry to appear." Davenport has described what she believes to be a characteristic of her own and undoubtedly a characteristic of much black poetry. Her theory is not unique for black poetry or for poetry in general—witness the theories of Edgar Allan Poe and Sidney Lanier.

x Caveats and Apologia

An account of contemporary poetry can never be seen as complete or actually achieve that status. As a magazine editor I never wanted one of my items to be left out, and I do not wish to leave out anything worthy. We are *PMLA* bibliography-oriented, and no library has all of the little magazines in which articles on contemporary poets might appear. My caveat is that what might seem to belong to this section turns out not to. I have already cited Charles Altieri's book, and I would add Albert Gelpi's difficult and brilliant "The Genealogy of Postmodernism: Contemporary American Poetry" (*SoR* 26:517–41). It is the beginning of his work on postmodernism, provocative in theory, using examples, so far, from a few contemporary poets to find in recent American poetry a "complicated dialectic between Neoromanticism and Postmodernism"—a chapter beyond his treatise on modernism in *A Coherent Splendor* (1987). Each year some books are ordered and articles requested that must go unexamined because they do not come, this year, notably, Marjorie Perloff's collected essays, *Poetic License* (Northwestern). I shall always try to make redress next year.

Clemson University

18 Drama

Peter A. Davis

Continuing a trend of recent years, significant scholarly publication in American theater and drama remains generally sparse. Perhaps as a sign of the recent recession, publishers appear locked into one of two predictable patterns, either frivolous commentary on popular works or rehashed doctoral dissertations in hardcover. Journal production fares only slightly better, with the usual swath of entries on the usual subjects. Innovation, insight, and originality are at a premium this year, with few scholars genuinely aware of the fundamental changes occurring around them in criticism or history.

There are, of course, notable exceptions which are highlighted. Among these, feminist, African American, and Hispanic American studies dominate. But as an indication of the trend in drama publication, I estimate that some 20 percent fewer books were published this year than last—a figure that may only be an economic aberration. But if protracted, it could portend an ominous future for theatrical scholarship.

i Reference Works

As usual, there is no shortage of reference books in theater. Author/producer Steven Suskin has edited a lengthy catalog of over 250 musicals between 1943 and 1964 entitled *Opening Night on Broadway* (Schirmer). He has arranged the entries alphabetically and provided vital information on writers, directors, producers, and original casts. The work is distinguished by its inclusion of excerpts from opening night reviews. Suskin provides brief summaries of each production and a "Broadway Scorecard" (presumably for the statistically inclined) that indicates the number of performances, money earned, and the number of reviews that were rave, favorable, mixed, unfavorable, and pans. The book is exhaustive in its coverage, and the collation of critical opinion is both useful and amusing. Several unusual photographs add visual appeal as well as historical curiosity.

The third edition (in paperback) of Stanley Green's *Broadway Musicals: Show by Show* (Hal Leonard) offers a similar source, but is more comprehensive (ranging as far back as the 1866 production of *The Black Crook*) and certainly more affordable. Unlike Suskin's book, this text is strictly informational. Again, each entry contains a list of pertinent personnel, a production photo, and opening night credits. The difference comes in its plot summaries and production histories. Another advantage is the separate indexes for show, composer/lyricist, director, choreographer, major cast members, and theaters. Even the chronological table of contents is a concise historical outline of the American musical, an invaluable list for any student of the American stage. New to the third edition are major shows since 1987, including *Les Miserables, Starlight Express,* and *The Phantom of the Opera.*

One of the more important collections of recent years is *Edwin Booth's Performances: The Mary Isabella Stone Commentaries* (UMI Research Press), ed. Daniel J. Watermeier. Although it may be too limiting to discuss it under only one heading (the book could easily qualify as a historical work and is every bit as important), it is an invaluable source of production history, enlightening the most popular performances of the greatest American actor of the last century. Watermeier has taken the extensive notes of a 19th-century fan who witnessed Booth's work between 1881 and 1884 and juxtaposed them with the promptbooks of Booth's productions of *Hamlet* and *Othello.* Although Watermeier states that his intent is not to produce a performance reconstruction, the result is a remarkable document of historical performance. Given the difficulties of interpretation from a single infatuated audience member, Watermeier guides the reader with expert annotations, noting dates of comments and performances, and citing references to earlier studies. All in all, it is a remarkable work and fascinating reading for anyone with a fondness and talent for promptbook analysis.

Greenwood Press has proven again to be the leading publisher of theatrical reference books. This year it produced two outstanding works on African American theater. Thomas A. Mikolyzk has compiled *Langston Hughes: A Bio-Bibliography,* the second offering in Greenwood's Bio-Bibliographies in Afro-American and African Studies. Apart from the usual chronology and bibliographic lists, the book contains an excellent

biographical summary and separate author, title, and subject indexes. It
is a careful and thorough compilation. No less impressive is Bernard L.
Peterson, Jr.'s *Early Black American Playwrights and Dramatic Writers: A
Biographical Directory and Catalog of Plays, Films, and Broadcasting
Scripts*. This work ranks among the very best this year. It is an extraordinary compendium of African American playwrights that covers almost
130 years of writing from the 1820s to 1950. The biographical directory
contains entries on almost 200 black authors, each entry giving a brief
biography and annotated list of works with plot summaries. Appendixes
include a chronology and a detailed list of information sources. In
addition, the indexes are divided between title, theater organizations,
and general. The work is a refreshing addition to the canon of American
theater books and should serve as a vital reference for many years.

ii Anthologies

Despite the perception that anthologies are becoming rare (and indeed
the common complaint that there is a paucity of adequate anthologies is
still prevalent among academics), there were several notable collections
published this year. Following the recent trend of celebrating regional-
ism, William B. Martin has edited a collection aptly entitled *Texas Plays*
(SMU Press). Among the plays are Preston Jones's *Lu Ann Hampton
Laverty Oberlander*, Horton Foote's haunting memory play, *The Trip to
Bountiful*, and James McLure's popular twosome, *Lone Star* and *Laundry
and Bourbon*. Six additional pieces complete the volume.

   Out from Under: Texts by Women Performance Artists (TCG), ed.
Lenora Champagne, is the first anthology of texts by women performance artists in the United States. Among its contents are some of the
most pivotal works of the last two decades: Holly Hughes's *World
Without End*, excerpts from Laurie Anderson's seven-hour performance
United States, *The Constant State of Desire* by Karen Finley, and Champagne's *Getting Over Tom*. In her brief introduction, Champagne defines
her choices as "provocative, ambitious and full of [the] body. Beneath the
powerful writing is the under-the-skin experience of oppression. . . ."
This collection will certainly become a standard source for a vital albeit
controversial movement. One hopes it will not be a single contribution.

   A wonderful complement to last year's *Black Female Playwrights*, ed.
Kathy A. Perkins, is Elizabeth Brown-Guillory's *Wines in the Wilderness:
Plays by African American Women from the Harlem Renaissance to the*

Present (Greenwood). Meant in part to be an adjunct to her 1988 study of African American women playwrights, *Their Place on the Stage* (Greenwood), the collection brings together 15 plays by nine authors. Notable contributions include Marita Bonner's *The Pot Maker* (1927), Gloria Douglas Johnson's *Blue Blood* (1926), Eualie Spence's *Hot Stuff* (1927), Shirley Graham's *It's Mornin'* (1940), Alice Childress's *Florence* (1950) and *Wines in the Wilderness* (1969), and Sybil Kein's *Get Together* (1970). Brown-Guillory has included her own piece *Mam Phyllis* (1985) and provided succinct introductions and synopses. An extensive bibliography with sections on "Published Plays by African American Women," "Produced Plays by African American Women," "Anthology Sources including Plays by African American Women," and "Biographical and Critical Sources for Further Reading," is an added bonus. Its use as a required text in any course on American theater is assured.

Another fine addition to the growing collection of African American anthologies is *The Roots of African American Drama: An Anthology of Early Plays, 1856–1938* (Wayne State), ed. Leo Hamalian and James V. Hatch. Seeking to remedy a terrible omission in the American canon of dramatic art, the editors have focused on African American playwrights before 1938. What they have assembled is a rare group of 13 plays and dramatic scenes, some never before published, that illustrates the intensity and diversity of early black theatrical expression. William Wells Brown's *The Escape* (1858) and Pauline Elizabeth Hopkins's *Peculiar Sam* (1879) are indicative of the extraordinary power and resonance of these plays. These works carry the message of 19th-century black experience far beyond the simplistic white perspective and spectacular melodrama of Aiken and Stowe. George A. Towns's *The Sharecropper* (1932) and Abram Hill's *On Strivers Row* (1938) vividly advance this black aesthetic into the 20th century. In between are plays by Katherine D. Chapman Tillman, Mary Burrill, Jodie and Susie Edwards, Willis Richardson, Zora Neale Hurston, Joseph S. Mitchell, Shirley Graham, May Miller, and Owen Vincent Dodson. Like the Perkins and Brown-Guillory anthologies, this one should become an essential addition to any scholar's library.

iii History of Theater and Drama

Echoing my concerns of last year, contributions in this area continue to be weak. The need for a comprehensive, thoughtful, and methodologically current history of American theater increases every year. Yet the likelihood of such a volume appearing any time soon will remain nil as long as academics persist in confusing New Historicism (i.e., dramatic criticism in a time frame) with genuine theater history. The situation will only resolve itself once it is acknowledged that theater history is not the history of dramatic literature. Nonetheless, there have been some noteworthy publications this year.

Despite her reputation as one of the greatest actresses on the American stage in the 19th century, despite her position as the first woman to lead a professional theater company in the United States, and despite her notoriety for being on stage at Ford's Theatre on that fateful night in 1865, Laura Keene has never received the scholarly attention she deserves. Ben Graf Henneke has attempted to remedy this situation in his biography, *Laura Keene: Actress, Innovator, and Impresario* (Council Oak Books). The last published account of her life was a 19th-century paean without much value or authority. A 1966 dissertation by Dorothy Jean Taylor briefly revived Keene's credibility as a scholarly subject, but was never published. Thus Henneke's book comes as a welcome addition to the historical canon of 19th-century American theater. Henneke, who wrote the book after his retirement as president of the University of Tulsa, claims a lifelong interest in Keene, and much of his affection for the actress is apparent in his writing. He takes a traditional biographical approach, pursuing a chronological development in a popular style that borders on the juvenile. The volume includes several fine photographs (some from the University of Tulsa's theater collection) and primary tidbits, but the overall effect is one of blandness—of an author too close to his subject to pursue genuine controversy.

When the Shubert Archive was finally created in 1976, theater historians celebrated what they thought would be a flood of new research based on the wealth of material contained in the production and management records of the monopoly that transformed American entertainment in the 20th century. Such was not to be. Apart from occasional articles in the archive's semiannual newsletter, "The Passing Show," substantive research on the Shubert organization has been rare. Finally, Brooks McNamara, founding director of the Shubert Archive, in an effort to remedy the situation has put together a popular history of the organization culled from the collections, entitled simply *The Shuberts of Broadway* (Oxford). As one would expect, the book is richly decorated with photographs and documents. In between, McNamara has sketched a tidy history of the brothers and their corporation. Oddly, there is nothing surprising in the book. McNamara tells the story, as most of us know it, from the Shuberts' humble beginnings in upstate New York to the U.S. Supreme Court ruling of 1955. The book is written for a popular audience and is therefore lacking in scholarly annotation. The many photographs, designs, and posters only hint at the extent of the collection's holdings. Although the book is fun reading and a useful historical summary, it is not the scholarly monograph I had anticipated. Nonetheless, it should keep the archive in the public's eye, and perhaps a more thorough treatment may yet be forthcoming.

Orson Welles on Shakespeare: The WPA and Mercury Theatre Playscripts (Greenwood), ed. with an introduction by Richard France, might well be placed in the reference section of this chapter. But the introduction and annotations make this a valuable examination of performance history as well as a research document. France, who wrote the noted 1978 study, *The Theatre of Orson Welles,* has included the three Shakespearean productions that helped thrust the Mercury Theatre and Welles into national prominence, *Macbeth, Julius Caesar,* and *Five Kings* (the monumental adaptation of the history plays). France's introduction gives a suitable background of social and political influences, while his annotations demonstrate Welles's adaptive genius.

As little as 10 years ago, David Glassberg's *American Historical Pageantry: The Uses of Tradition in the Early Twentieth Century* (No. Car.) might have been overlooked for such a review essay. There may still be some who consider such a study to fall under popular culture or social theory rather than theater history. Fortunately, the field has broadened somewhat in the last decade, and popular amusements which were once on the periphery of theater studies now constitute a major current in the theater history mainstream. Glassberg presents an impressive examination of pageants in America as a cultural expression of community and popular sentiment, a form of American volksbühne. The book places these extraordinary displays within the context of the American psyche. While celebrating this peculiar form of civic amusement, Glassberg spends much of his energies refuting the stated intentions of such displays—to inspire community pride and civic identity. It is a fascinating and revealing history of a most unusual form of American entertainment. Along similar lines, Karen J. Blair writes about the use of pageantry in support of women's suffrage in "Pageantry for Women's Rights: The Career of Hazel MacKaye, 1913–1923" (*TS* 31, i:23–46). Although largely a chronological description, its subject matter makes it well worth reading.

Collections of historical essays are not as common as they should be in American theater. So it is always of some interest when one appears. This year, three of the most respected American theater scholars have jointly edited a volume in the DQR Studies in Literature Series, entitled *Theatre West: Image and Impact* (Rodopi). The stated purpose is to "find manifestations of the western American experience in the live theatre." As a result, the editors attempt to take a truly historical approach by consciously avoiding articles which "concentrate on dramatic texts to the exclusion of their production and performance." It is a noble statement and one that would sound utterly ludicrous to any "true" historian. But such is the fickle nature of theater history. The text contains 19 articles by a number of renowned historians that cover a range of Western topics. Staying true to the editors' stated purpose for the most part, the book has surprisingly little substance. Most pieces are brief sketches of events or people, some of questionable value. Some have the aura of poorly conceived and hastily executed conference papers. Nonetheless, there are a few that deserve attention and would be of value to probing graduate students, including Joanne Lafler's "Seeded in the Grove Itself: Theatrical Evolution at the Bohemian Club Encampment" (pp. 18–42), Margaret B. Wilkerson's "The Black Theatre Experience: PASLA (Performing Arts Society of Los Angeles)" (pp. 69–83), "Frontier Melodrama" (pp. 151–60) by Rosemarie Bank, and Albert Wertheim's *"Polly:* John Gay's Image of the West" (pp. 195–208).

In light of the NEA controversy, a renewed interest in censorship and its history has apparently surfaced. Perhaps the most important decade in this century for the development of obscenity laws was the 1920s in which a number of crucial events led to some of the most restrictive legislation ever passed against the freedom of expression. Ronald H. Wainscott describes this era and one of the more pivotal productions in "Attracting Censorship to the Popular Theatre: Al Woods Produces Avery Hopwood's *The Demi-Virgin*" (*THStud* 10:127–40). The article is an excellent production history of a minor sex farce that would eventually lead to the passage of the repressive Wales Padlock Law of 1927 in New York. Typical of Wainscott's work, it is well-written and expertly researched. Another piece by Wainscott worth reading is "American Theatre Versus the Congress of the United States: The Theatre Tax Controversy and Public Rebellion of 1919" (*TS* 31, i:5–22). Here, Wainscott examines the unsuccessful attempt by Congress to levy a 20 percent tax on theater tickets to offset the cost of World War I. Revealed in the article is the surprising power theatrical managers wielded at that time and the effectiveness of public protest and petition.

Another fine history of a little-known phenomenon is Iska Alter's study of the Yiddish theater, "When the Audience Called 'Author! Author!': Shakespeare on New York's Yiddish Stage" (*THStud* 10:141–61). In addition to presenting a detailed description of Shakespeare's production history in the Yiddish theater between 1890 and 1930, Alter has uncovered several rare photographs and a unique synopsis of "The Jewish King Lear." Christina M. Pages offers a detailed description of "The Decline of a Shakespearean Tradition in Charleston, South Carolina, 1869–1900" (*TS* 31, i:85–106). Kathleen L. Carroll compares Henry Irving's 1882 production of *Much Ado About Nothing* with Augustin Daly's 1896 version in "The Americanization of Beatrice: Nineteenth-Century Style" (*TS* 31, i:67–84).

The Journal of American Drama and Theatre, in only its second year, continues to produce the most consistent writing in American theater history. In its three 1990 editions, the journal published a number of notable studies. Amelia Howe Kritzer, in her article "Feminism and Theatre in Eighteenth-Century Boston" (2, iii:22–34), has written an excellent short history of one of America's first female playwrights, Judith Sargent Murray. Apart from short entries in occasional encyclopedias, there has been little work on this important writer. Kritzer's piece, though succinct, sheds much-needed light on Murray, her plays, and the position of women at the turn of the 19th century. Another fine but brief study of women on the early American stage can be found in Vera Mowry Roberts's "Olive Logan and 'The Leg Business'" (2, i:5–10). The article illustrates how Logan, a popular actress and writer, became a respected member of the suffrage movement from her published attack on the exploitation on stage of women and nudity—as defined by that age. Lewis E. Shelton resurrects the curious story of America's first full-time professional stage director in "Mr. Ben Teal: America's Abusive Director" (2, ii:55–80). Often overlooked by historians, Teal is best remembered for his 1899 staging of *Ben Hur* and his volatile temperament. Apart from summarizing Teal's work, Shelton has provided a chronological list of plays he staged. An overview of the origins and growth of French theater in New Orleans during the early 19th century is the subject of Charles S. Watson's informative study, "Early Drama in

New Orleans: The French Tradition" (2, i:11–26). Alice Kae Koger looks at the unexpected professional demise of one of America's leading 19th-century playwrights in *"Under Cover:* Edward Harrigan's Final Act" (2, iii:70–87), while Mary Maddock reexamines feminist social satire of the 1930s in "Social Darwinism in the Powder Room: Clare Boothe's *The Women"* (2, ii:81–97).

iv Criticism and Theory

New publication in criticism and theory was most disappointing this year. Apart from the usual plethora of articles, there was a decided lack of substantial monographs. Natalie Crohn Schmitt produced an unusual volume on performance theory entitled *Actors and Onlookers: Theater and Twentieth-Century Scientific Views of Nature* (Northwestern). Schmitt begins her study by noting the similarities between current aesthetic principles and modern scientific perceptions of nature. With this as her basis, she extrapolates the aesthetics of John Cage and the current avant-garde by comparing this new worldview to that of Aristotle and the traditional view. Her argument is well thought out and articulated. Using this new perspective, she compares the Wooster Group's *Rumstick Road* to O'Neill's *Long Day's Journey into Night*—Cage versus Aristotle in performance. There is even room to recognize how the postmodern has crept onto Broadway in an evaluation of *A Chorus Line.* As a final display of the pervasiveness of the new worldview, Schmitt deconstructs the acting theories of Stanislavsky in light of contemporary theorists. It is a tidy analysis of postmodern dramatic theory and quite convincing.

Shakespeare has been a cultural icon in America since colonial times. His plays, poetry, characters, and themes are germane to American cultural values. Michael D. Bristol, in examining this phenomenon in impressive detail in *Shakespeare's America, America's Shakespeare* (Routledge), produces a cultural and intellectual history of Shakespeare in American aesthetics. From Charlie the Tuna to Northrop Frye, the work masterfully exposes how we have shaped our cultural values and defined our cultural worth through our interpretations of Shakespeare—and how in turn Shakespeare serves as a model for many of our American values. It is well worth the read and a valuable contribution to American cultural history.

One of the oddest and yet most exciting anthologies in recent years is

By Means of Performance: Intercultural Studies of Theatre and Ritual (Cambridge), ed. Richard Schechner and Willa Appel. Presented as a festschrift for the late anthropologist Victor Turner, the text contains 16 essays on what must be the most diverse collection of topics ever seen in theater. Many are fascinating studies that follow Schechner's well-known bridge between theater and anthropology. The editors use Turner's classic piece, "Are There Universals of Performance in Myth, Ritual, and Drama?" (pp. 8–18), to open the collection, followed by Schechner's "Magnitudes of Performance" (pp. 19–49). By the third essay, Colin Turnbull's "Liminality: A Synthesis of Subjective and Objective Experience" (pp. 50–81), one gets the sense that the book is really a communal explication of the NYU Performance Studies Program. Indeed it may well be. There are pieces on Yaqui ceremonies and dances, Hasidic celebrations of Purim, Sri Lankan rituals, and role-playing by Korean shamans, as well as a critique of circus clowning, among other essays. It is a rare collection and not for everyone. But it provides a useful casebook for anthropological study of theater and certainly brings together some of the most respected scholars in the field.

v Feminist Studies

It is encouraging to see that feminist theory remains at the cutting edge of dramatic criticism, as it has for the last several years. I feel it appropriate, therefore, to continue to highlight these ground-breaking contributions in a separate section, despite some political arguments to the contrary. One reason for the continued vitality of feminist writing may be that, like most new and innovative scholarship, there is an inevitable period of self-definition, of theoretical exploration—not simply clarification or intellectual positioning, but a vigorous debate in which all sides and extremes are often presented, refined, absorbed, or rejected. Such active articulation produces much to be celebrated and much to be ignored. Anthologies are the common result, while substantive applications of theory are often lacking. Happily, this year has produced important contributions in both venues.

Gayle Austin's *Feminist Theories for Dramatic Criticism* (Michigan) is the best book-length distillation of recent feminist theory to date. In six concise chapters, Austin has written a valuable overview of the history and current state of feminist criticism. In contrast to some of the leading feminist writers, like Sue-Ellen Case and Jill Dolan, who articulate a theory of past and present political orientation, Austin examines feminist theory in an entirely new way—through its various disciplinary origins. In successive chapters, she evaluates "Feminist Literary Criticism," "Feminist Anthropology," "Feminist Psychology," and "Feminist Film Theory," infusing some of the major canonical works with refreshing insight, including O'Neill's *The Iceman Cometh,* Miller's *Death of a Salesman,* Hellman's *Another Part of the Forest,* Jane Bowles's *In the Summer House,* Shepard's *The Tooth of Crime,* and Childress's *Wine in the Wilderness.* It is remarkable in both content and clarity, offering new perspectives for incorporating different disciplines into feminist dramatic criticism. Theater students and those professionals new to the field of feminist dramatic criticism will find this book an invaluable introduction.

June Schlueter has edited a collection of short critical essays, *Modern American Drama: The Female Canon* (Fairleigh Dickinson). The text—awkwardly divided into two sections—contains 22 entries, most of them quite readable, on a wide range of topics. The first part, subtitled "Eighteenth- and Nineteenth-Century Backgrounds," has two brief articles and appears to be an unincorporated homage to historical background. Part two, on the other hand, simply titled "Twentieth-Century Playwrights," constitutes the bulk of the work. The articles are too numerous to discuss individually, but rest assured the editor has made every effort to include essays on most of the major names in women's playwriting of this century—Rachel Crothers, Susan Glaspell, Djuna Barnes, Zoë Atkins, Sophie Treadwell, Gertrude Stein, Lillian Hellman, Carson McCullers, Lorraine Hansberry, Megan Terry, Adrienne Kennedy, Alice Childress, Ntozake Shange, Clare Boothe, Wendy Wasserstein, Maria Irene Fornes, Beth Henley, Wendy Kesselman, Marsha Norman, and Meredith Monk. Among the most interesting entries is the final essay by Lynda Hart, "Canonizing Lesbians?" (pp. 275–92), which adroitly challenges the assumptions posed by Schlueter in her introduction. It is much to Schlueter's credit that she included this as a concluding chapter. Nevertheless, in an effort to incorporate the most inclusive definition of the female canon, a task Schlueter herself acknowledges as being inherently problematical, the book loses some focus. Though the majority of the contributions are valuable, the collection is a bit too facile. As a quick overview of major women writers, it serves its purpose.

One anthology sure to attract attention is *Performing Feminisms: Feminist Critical Theory and Theatre* (Hopkins), ed. Sue-Ellen Case. In her introduction, Case implies that the book represents the culmination of her effort "to publish the feminist critique in theatre studies and even more broadly, to publish critical theory in theatre studies" during her years as editor of *Theatre Journal*. Indeed, all but two of the collection's 20 articles were previously published under Case's editorship. As if to emphasize the connection, the book even uses the same font and format as *Theatre Journal*. Case points out the controversy that arose during her editorial tenure which kept her from undertaking such a project; this collection seems to be an answer to her critics. Notable contributions include Jill Dolan's " 'Lesbian' Subjectivity in Realism: Dragging at the Margins of Structure and Ideology" (pp. 40–53), Elin Diamond's "Refusing the Romanticism of Identity: Narrative Interventions in Churchill, Benmussa, Duras" (pp. 92–105), Phyllis Rankin's "Anti-Historians: Women's Roles in Shakespeare's Histories" (pp. 207–22), and Judith Butler's "Performative Acts and Gender Constitution: An Essay in Phenomenology and Feminist Theory" (pp. 270–82).

vi African American Theater

Several excellent contributions in this area have been covered above. I refer to Mikolzyk's bio-bibliography of Langston Hughes, Peterson's bibliographic dictionary of early black writers, and the anthologies by Brown-Guillory and Hamalian and Hatch. Paragon has reissued *Arna Bontemps-Langston Hughes Letters, 1925–1967,* ed. Charles H. Nichols. Some may recall that the volume was originally published in 1980 by Dodd, Mead. Apart from the cover, I can find no substantive changes.

Indicative of a new criticism evolving within a black feminist perspective is Serena Andrelini's unusual assessment of Ntozake Shange's famous play, " 'colored girls': A Reaction to Black Machismo, or Hues of Erotic Tension in New Feminist Solidarity?" (*JADT* 2, ii:33–54). Andrelini evaluates the play as a feminist/homoerotic celebration while redefining the nature of black feminism. Equally interesting is Judith L. Stephens's "The Anti-Lynch Play: Toward an Interracial Feminist Dialogue in Theatre" (*JADT* 2, iii:59–69). Stephens, who is white, states her "intention to discuss the anti-lynch play as feminist drama is not intended as an exclusive appeal to white women." Instead, she maintains "it is . . . an offering of a common meeting ground for interracial woman-centered dialogue on the dramatic text as argument for social change." For this reason, I have included it here. To make her point, she evaluates three works by black women playwrights—*Rachael* (1916) by Angelina Weld Grimke, *A Sunday Morning in the South* (1925) by Georgia Douglas Johnson, and Alice Childress's *Trouble in Mind* (1952). It is a thoughtful study and convincingly presented.

vii Hispanic Drama and Theater

Hispanic theater remains a vital and productive field for scholarship. Last year saw several outstanding contributions, and this year two more fine texts have been added to the canon. *A History of Hispanic Theatre in the United States: Origins to 1940* (Texas), by Nicolas Kanellos, is one of those long-overdue texts that will define the subject for many years to come. As Kanellos acknowledges, the work is incomplete and contains inevitable "gaps left by too many missing documents." The body of the study focuses on four principal cities—Los Angeles, San Antonio, New York, and Tampa—with a chapter on touring companies. On the whole, it is an excellent survey, though the first chapter on origins seems truncated and the emphasis through the rest of the book on the 1920s and 30s gives an unbalanced feeling. Nonetheless, Kanellos's research is detailed and his examination of Hispanic theater within the context of American culture makes this book an essential addition to American theater history.

Another scholar of note is Elizabeth C. Ramírez, who has recently emerged as one of the country's leading authorities on Hispanic theater. Her book, *Footlights Across the Border: A History of Spanish-Language Professional Theatre on the Texas Stage* (Peter Lang), brings to light a more specific history than Kanellos's study—the development of Hispanic theater in Texas up to 1935. While the text is brief and reads like a dissertation, it is an interesting study containing some important documents. As a serious historical monograph, its contribution to this field is significant. One hopes more detailed studies of this sort will soon be forthcoming.

viii American Musical Theater

Given the nonstop fascination with the American musical, it is somewhat surprising that this year produced so few published paeans to this national obsession. Although I am certain this dearth represents only a statistical aberration which will be amply remedied in 1991, it is a welcome relief not having to comb through the usual drivel that this area normally generates. In fact, the three offerings to be discussed were quite palatable and should satisfy the cravings of most musical fanatics.

Joanne Gordon has written a 10-chapter study of Stephen Sondheim, *Art Isn't Easy: The Achievement of Stephen Sondheim* (So. Ill.). Its intention is to provide a scholarly evaluation of Sondheim's productions from *A Funny Thing Happened on the Way to the Forum* to *Into the Woods*. Each chapter is devoted to one of Sondheim's many hits, including *Company, Follies, A Little Night Music, Pacific Overtures, Sweeney Todd,* and *Sunday in the Park with George.* There is an attempt at comprehensiveness, and the analysis is in places reasonably thorough. Overall, however, there are too many quotations from playscripts and there is too little genuine criticism. The chapters often become a retelling of each play's plot line, concluded with a moralistic summary. For those not familiar with this prolific producer, Gordon's book offers a convenient study of Sondheim's major works. As a detailed scholarly monograph which places Sondheim and his work within the greater context of American art, culture, and history, this study comes up a bit short.

True fanatics should get a thrill from *On the Line: The Creation of "A Chorus Line"* (Morrow). Written by theater critic Robert Viagas, with ample assistance from original cast members Baayork Lee and Thommie Walsh, the work is a blow-by-blow account of the original production, from its conception in 1974 through its lengthy run and the dispersal of the original cast in 1977. The last chapter carries the story up to 1990 including Michael Bennett's untimely death in 1987 and the deaths of lyricist Ed Kleban (1987) and co-librettist James Kirkwood (1989). There is even an appendix that details the lives of the major cast members up to the minute of publication. For true *Chorus Line* fans, this book is not to be missed; but as a scholarly study, it is much too chatty and anecdotal to be of much value.

As rare as genuine scholarly studies on the musical may be, some occasionally make it into print. This year's collection is salvaged by Joseph P. Swain's *The Broadway Musical: A Critical and Musical Survey* (Oxford). This book is clearly not intended for the typical musical fan. It is a thoroughly researched and detailed study, richly illustrated with musical notation. Indeed, one needs a firm command of music to get its full benefit. Swain begins his analysis by examining the foundations of the form in the 20th century. He narrows his research in chapter 2 to

Show Boat but includes pertinent comparisons to contemporaneous productions. The remaining chapters follow a similar pattern, with each focusing on one or two primary examples to support his conceptual outline. Swain has neatly placed the major musicals into one of 11 categories: folk opera, *Porgy and Bess;* morality play, *Carousel;* Shakespearean, *Kiss Me, Kate;* pure love story, *The Most Happy Fella;* myth, *My Fair Lady;* tragedy, *West Side Story;* ethnic, *Fiddler on the Roof;* religious experience, *Godspell;* history, *Evita* and *Jesus Christ Superstar;* frame story, *A Chorus Line;* and thriller, *Sweeney Todd.* Even the venerated *Oklahoma!* is discussed in an early chapter defining the second maturing of the musical. Of course, one could quibble endlessly over the nature of the outline and the selections—how about the musical's origins in the 19th century? its debt to minstrelsy and vaudeville? the film musical? where do such odd hits as *The Fantastiks, Hair,* or *Cats* fit in? But such peripheral niggling would be pointless. Although the organization may tend toward reductivism, the book is a fine example of music history and as such provides the most complete musical analysis of the form to date.

ix O'Neill

With the celebration last year of the O'Neill centennial, an overflow of publications in 1990 might be expected. But such was not the case. Like most other areas in drama, even O'Neill suffered from the publication drought. As if to prove the point, the normally abundant *Eugene O'Neill Review* was reduced this year to one combined edition. Apart from the usual collection of performance and book reviews, volume 14, nos. 1 and 2 produced only seven substantive articles. *The Great God Brown* received the most attention in this year's *Review* with two critical essays devoted to dissecting the play within the context of current analytical theories—Michael Manheim's "*The Great God Brown* in the Light of O'Neill's Last Plays" (pp. 5–15) and "*The Great God Brown* and the Theory of Character" (pp. 16–24) by Brian Richardson. Shyamal Bagchee tackles an interesting comparison entitled "On Blake and O'Neill" (pp. 25–38). Kurt Eisen's essay "Novelization and the Drama of Consciousness in *Strange Interlude*" (pp. 39–51) is noteworthy, as is Frederick C. Wilkins's study "O'Neill's Secular Saints" (pp. 67–77). Sheila Hickey Garvey writes an unusual production history in "*Anna Christie* in New Haven: A Theatrical Odyssey" (pp. 53–66), while Michael Hinden adds a most peculiar yet fascinating study on "The Pharmacology of *Long Day's Journey into Night*" (pp. 47–52). Although the volume may not be up to the journal's usual standards, there are some pieces worth reading. The hope remains that next year will see a return of the quality and quantity normally expected from this series.

Conversations with Eugene O'Neill, ed. Mark W. Estrin, is a long overdue addition to the Literary Conversation Series by the University Press of Mississippi. Like the other entries in this series, most of the text is composed of published interviews spanning much of the author's career. Beginning in 1920 with a short piece from the *New York Tribune,* by Philip Mindil, which serves as a curious introduction to the upstart playwright, the book traverses a vast warehouse of interviews and articles concluding with the playwright's last interview in 1948. Notable entries include the 1922 interview with Malcolm Mollan in which O'Neill defines and defends his version of tragedy and his 1946 press conference, written up by John S. Wilson, in which he declares the United States to be "the greatest failure." In addition, the book includes the usual chronology and introduction, plus a short but helpful index. Much can be gleaned from this collection, not only reference material for critical studies, but insight into the personality and professional development of America's foremost playwright.

O'Neill is the subject of another popular series this year. Twayne's Masterwork Studies has produced a concise critical history entitled *"Long Day's Journey into Night": Native Eloquence* by Michael Hinden. Following the format of previous editions, the book is a succinct compendium of history and analysis directed toward the devout O'Neill lover and undergraduates. With such chapter headings as "Historical Context," "The Importance of the Work," "Composition and Critical Reception," the inevitable sense of being spoon-fed cannot be avoided. But such is the nature of the series. Again, a chronology and brief bibliography complete the text and help make it both a useful tool for quick reference and an introduction for the uninitiated.

Two other articles on O'Neill should be noted, Nicholas F. Radel's "Provincetown Plays: Women Writers and O'Neill's American Intertext" (*EiT* 9, i:31–43), which does a nice job comparing O'Neill's *Great God Brown* and *Welded* to Joyce's *Exiles,* and Ralf Erik Remshardt's "Masks and Permutations: The Construction of Character in O'Neill's Earlier Plays" (*EiT,* 8, ii:127–36), which examines O'Neill's plays up to *Strange Interlude* (1928) for patterns of character treatment.

x Recent Dramatists (Odets, Williams, etc.)

Also in short supply this year were substantive studies of modern playwrights. Among those overlooked in 1990 are William Inge, Lillian Hellman, Elmer Rice, and William Saroyan.

Tennessee Williams remains a favorite topic, and of all the 20th-century playwrights (O'Neill excepted) he still generates the greatest productivity among scholars. Twayne's Masterwork Studies Series produced two volumes on Williams in 1990, The Glass Menagerie: *An American Memory,* by Delma E. Presley, and A Streetcar Named Desire: *The Moth and the Lantern,* by Thomas P. Adler. Both conform to the format and content of the series, offering a summary of critical thought and analysis on each play and including brief chronologies and bibliographies. Presley's appears to offer the more complete overview of the two, but both nicely fit into the rigid confines of the Twayne requirements, while providing some original criticism amid the summary of recent analyses. A more personal record of Williams is found in *Five O'Clock Angel: Letters of Tennessee Williams to Maria St. Just, 1948–1982* (Knopf), with commentary by Maria St. Just. As the title indicates, the book is a collection of correspondence between the two and shows just how dependent Williams was on St. Just's advice and opinion. It is a remarkably revealing collection that is sure to have traditional critics scattering to reevaluate the playwright's work.

Another entry into the field of personal memoirs by close friends is Bruce Smith's ragged vision of Williams's last few years, *Costly Performances, Tennessee Williams: The Last Stage* (Paragon). The text offers yet one more perspective on the playwright's tortured final years. Smith, who served as Williams's publicity manager from 1979 to 1981, describes his personal endeavors to ease Williams's life as the playwright struggled to regain the acceptance and validity he felt had been lost. There are several retellings of popular events that marked the final years, and the author does provide some new insights. But on the whole the work is a private story told from a single perspective. I imagine there will be several more books of this nature published on Mr. Williams in the near future before the genre has run its course.

Clifford Odets: An Annotated Bibliography, 1935–1989 (Meckler), by Robert Cooperman, offers the first comprehensive bibliography of the playwright and his work. It should prove to be a useful resource for the serious theater student.

xi Current Dramatists (Albee, Miller, Shepard, etc.)

Only three texts of note were published in this area in 1990. While it may be a further sign of a dismal year in drama publications, the relatively poor showing over the last several years may indicate a broader trend among scholars to avoid the most contemporary artists in preference for the more established writers. Even those occasional authors who venture into this area typically write conventional studies, attempting perhaps to place their subjects into more palatable contexts. It is a sad trend that I hope will be short-lived.

Rounding out Twayne's Masterwork Series for 1990 is Matthew C. Roudane's Who's Afraid of Virginia Woolf? *Necessary Fictions, Terrifying Realities*. Although much of this work resembles the other volumes in the series—the formatted first section, the short chronology, and brief bibliography—Roudane has taken his study a step further and inserted a modicum of originality in his critical assessment. Certainly there is the usual rehash of established ideas and interpretations, but unlike most of the others, Roudane includes novel comparisons and unusual insights. His use of Artaud and Girard as a basis for his critical evaluation serves the play well, and his juxtaposition of Albee and Virginia Woolf provides some of the most insightful criticism of this work in years. Unlike many offerings in the Twayne series, Roudane's study is one to be read by any theater scholar. Much of it may not surprise or enlighten, but taken in the context of the entire series, it is a valuable addition that should be used as a model for future volumes.

An interesting adjunct to the text is Susan Spector's "Telling the Story of Albee's *Who's Afraid of Virginia Woolf?*: Theatre History and Myth-making" (*TS* 31, ii:177–88). Spector recounts the development of the production in 1963, from artistic concept through rehearsals and the final performance a year later. It is a competent study drawn largely from an interview with Uta Hagen and from Alan Schneider's autobiography. Another article which may not get the attention it deserves is "Albee's Lost Decade" (*JADT* 2, i:55–65), by Andrew B. Harris. Sifting through the archives of the Billy Rose Theatre Collection in New York, Harris has assembled some wonderful material on Albee's so-called "lost decade"— the shadowy years immediately prior to the publishing of his first play, *The Zoo Story*, in 1958. Speculating that Albee's reluctance to admit his homosexuality may have caused him to suppress his early work, Harris reveals that the playwright was far more productive in these years than previously known, writing several unpublished plays, poems, and novels. Evaluating the collection, Harris discovers numerous sources and sketches for Albee's later and more successful plays. Although short, it is a most informative piece and a genuine contribution to Albee scholarship.

A text-by-text analysis of five David Mamet plays is the focus of Anne Dean's dissertation-turned-monograph, *David Mamet: Language as Dramatic Action* (Fairleigh Dickinson). With the expected complement of quoted passages as illustrations, Dean examines Mamet's plays from a strong linguistic approach and succeeds in placing his works within her distinct framework. Less successful are the use of actors' reminiscences and the author's attempt to contextualize the plays within their social and historical elements. Nonetheless, Dean does provide some new insights into the five plays she has chosen—*Sexual Perversity in Chicago, American Buffalo, A Life in the Theatre, Edmond,* and *Glengarry Glen Ross.* Despite its pedantic style, it is a worthwhile linguistic assessment and critical evaluation of Mamet's plays.

Christopher Bigsby is the editor of a celebratory collection honoring Arthur Miller's 75th birthday, *Arthur Miller and Company* (Methuen). As Bigsby acknowledges at the start, the book is not intended to be a critical collection. Instead, the editor assembled more than 80 actors, designers, directors, reviewers, and writers to express their thoughts on Miller and his work. The result is a pleasant anthology of complimentary statements and observations that have little scholarly importance but are amusing and enlightening just the same. Clearly Bigsby made a great effort to include a wide variety of commentators—among those cited are Richard Dreyfuss, Dustin Hoffman, John Malkovich, Vanessa Redgrave, Michael Holt, Arvin Brown, Dan Sullivan, Edward Albee, Carlos Fuentes, Vaclav Havel, Harold Pinter, and Arnold Wesker, to name a few. It is an entertaining, readable volume. Also of interest is James A. Robinson's *"All My Sons* and Paternal Authority" (*JADT* 2, i:38–54). The author assesses Miller's father/son relationships and the resulting conflict inherent in his Jewish ethnicity.

Finally, this year, Erik MacDonald examines the metaphysical mechanisms in the plays of Richard Foreman through a comparative analysis with Derrida's textual system in "Richard Foreman and 'The Closure of Representation'" (*EiT* 9, i:19–30). Robert Baker-White has written an entertaining assessment of Sam Shepard's *The Tooth of Crime* from a pop/rock perspective entitled "Rock/Poetry: Popular Theatricality in *The Tooth of Crime*" (*JADT* 2, i:66–87). Although such an approach may seem obvious with Shepard's work, Baker-White's point is well-argued, drawing on a diverse base of authority from the Rolling Stones to Rene Girard and Arnold van Geenep.

University of Illinois, Urbana-Champaign

19   Themes, Topics, Criticism

Michael Fischer

In *Doing What Comes Naturally* (Duke, 1989), Stanley Fish predicts that "theory's day is dying; the hour is late": there will come a time "when the announcement of still another survey of critical method is received not as a promise but as a threat, and when the calling of still another conference on the function of theory in our time will elicit only a groan." The impressive books under review here make Fish's tongue-in-cheek prophecy seem premature. Theory remains a burgeoning field, the source of crucial questions about the scope and purpose of contemporary literary study.

i   Literary Theory

Several collections of essays highlight the political and educational questions that occupy many contemporary theorists. Among the best of these volumes I would place *Reorientations: Critical Theories and Pedagogies,* ed. Bruce Henricksen and Thaïs E. Morgan (Illinois), which explores how theory can influence educational practice. Solid essays by Reed Way Dasenbrock, Robert Scholes, Brook Thomas, and Gregory L. Ulmer assess the importance of theory to the canon, classroom teaching, reading strategies, and composition studies. Barbara C. Ewell's contribution, "Empowering Otherness: Feminist Criticism and the Academy," does an especially good job raising (without finally resolving) key questions for the feminist teacher: "Feminist classrooms often struggle against diffusion, degeneration into rap sessions, and the loss of critical thought. Evaluation becomes tangled in the mire of subjectivity: how can 'standards' be applied when their distorted perspective has been deliberately exposed? How can the teacher exert authority when its deconstruction is in process?" (p. 55).

Literary Theory Today, ed. Peter Collier and Helga Geyer-Ryan (Cornell), also features important critics dealing with timely questions, among them the wartime writings of Paul de Man (Barbara Johnson); undecidability in interpretative theory (Michael Riffaterre); feminism and literature (Elaine Showalter); psychoanalytic theory (Julia Kristeva); and poststructuralism, marginality, postcoloniality, and value (Gayatri Chakravorty Spivak). Stephen Greenblatt's "Resonance and Wonder" is a characteristically lucid discussion of some basic New Historicist tenets.

Less successful collections of essays include *Theory Between the Disciplines,* ed. Martin Kreiswirth and Mark A. Cheetham (Michigan). A rather turgid introduction sets the tone for many of the essays that follow, which touch on such topics as Paul de Man's critique of aesthetic ideology (Gary Wihl) and the feminine look (Carole-Anne Tyler). Martin Jay's "Name-Dropping or Dropping Names?: Modes of Legitimation in the Humanities" is a refreshing exception to the theory-speak that mars many of the other essays.

The States of "Theory," ed. David Carroll (Columbia), originated in lectures and colloquia organized by the Critical Theory Institute at the University of California, Irvine. The volume exhibits the theoretical sophistication—and often convoluted writing—that characterizes the Continental theorizing Irvine continues to champion. As if responding to the common charge that this theorizing neglects history, several of the contributors reflect on how theory can be historical, in particular Carolyn Porter ("Are We Being Historical Yet?"), Lynn Hunt ("History Beyond Social Theory"), and, above all, Jacques Derrida, who wants to claim that a concern with history "was already active, present and fundamental . . . in the very poststructuralism which the supporters and promoters of new historicism think it is absolutely crucial to oppose" (p. 68). Derrida has many sharp things to say about (sometimes against) the New Historicism, but readers must struggle to find them in his labyrinthian prose. The title of his essay—"Some Statements and Truisms about Neologisms, Newisms, Postisms, Parasitisms, and other Small Seismisms"—may indicate what I mean.

Finally, *Why the Novel Matters,* ed. Mark Spilka and Caroline Mc-Cracken-Flesher (Indiana), is a mishmash of articles previously published in *Novel,* conference papers, and transcripts of conference discussion sessions. Many of the contributors have important points to make: for example, Nancy Armstrong and Nancy K. Miller on feminist criticism and the novel; Daniel Schwartz on the case for a humanist poetics;

Don H. Bialostosky on Wayne Booth, Mikhail Bakhtin, and the future of novel criticism; and David Lodge speaking from his vantage point as a practicing novelist. The volume, however, could have been trimmed. (One quibble: thanks to the diminutive type, the footnotes are almost illegible.)

Two more specialized collections also deserve to be mentioned: *Victor Turner and the Construction of Cultural Criticism,* ed. Kathleen M. Ashley (Indiana), and *Reading Material Culture,* ed. Christopher Tilley (Blackwell). Both volumes advance the increasingly important dialogue between anthropology and literary theory.

Several collections of previously published essays by individual critics have appeared this past year. Sanford Pinsker's *Bearing the Bad News* is a clear, wide-ranging, but often disappointing gathering of essays. The best take up topics, writers, and critics often overlooked by literary theorists: for instance, the cultural criticism of Irving Howe and the apparent disappearance of formative books like *Catcher in the Rye.* The weakest essays, especially the superficial look at the controversy surrounding Paul de Man's wartime journalism, promise more than they deliver.

Charles Altieri's *Canons and Consequences* (Northwestern) is much better. Particularly in essays like "An Idea and Ideal of Literary Canon," "Canons and Differences," and "Going On and Going Nowhere: Wittgenstein and the Question of Criteria in Literary Criticism," Altieri takes on the quixotic task of defending a basically humanist position on the canon, selfhood, and ethics. Unlike many other critics of deconstruction and New Historicism, Altieri has done his homework. He appreciates the force of demystifying forms of criticism while underscoring and trying to overcome their limitations. Sometimes Altieri's heavy prose resembles the worst passages in the philosophers who have influenced him. But his book as a whole should be mandatory reading for anyone interested in the ethical value of literary works.

Hazard Adams's *Antithetical Essays in Literary Criticism and Liberal Education* (Florida State) is another impressive volume. Adams, too, thoughtfully considers the canon (in "Canons: Literary Criteria/Power Criteria") and the organization of university education (*"Humanitas* and Academic Politics" and "Neo-Blakean Prolegomena to an Unlikely Academic Structure"). I like how imaginative writers (most prominently William Blake) as well as literary theorists and philosophers enter into Adams's thinking. Whereas novelists and poets are often the objects (some would say victims) of theoretical inquiry, in Adams they are full-fledged participants.

I can only briefly cite four other collections by eminent scholars: G. Thomas Tanselle's *Textual Criticism and Scholarly Editing* (Virginia) brings together eight of his important essays on textual criticism (among them "The Editorial Problem of Final Authorial Intention" and "Textual Study and Literary Judgment"); Roman Jakobson's *On Language,* ed. Linda R. Waugh and Monique Monville-Burston (Harvard), includes numerous essays providing an overall view of Jakobson's linguistic theory; Northrop Frye's *Myth and Metaphor,* ed. Robert D. Denham (Virginia), features lively, humane essays on diverse subjects by one of the most important critics of our time; and Umberto Eco's *The Limits of Interpretation* (Indiana) adds to his distinguished work in semiotics.

Books devoted to literary theory continue to take many forms, among them studies of individual critics, genres, and issues. There apparently still is a demand for explications of Michel Foucault and Jacques Derrida, despite the many commentaries already available. Roy Boyne's *Foucault and Derrida* (Unwin Hyman) is a helpful exposition but breaks little new ground. Gary Saul Morson and Caryl Emerson's *Mikhail Bakhtin* (Stanford), on the other hand, is a major new work, a magisterial overview of Bakhtin's oeuvre and ideas.

The ethics and politics of literary study preoccupy several books. Philip Goldstein's *The Politics of Literary Theory* (Florida State) argues for a poststructuralist Marxism that taps the strengths, while avoiding the shortcomings, of New Criticism, liberal humanism, phenomenological criticism, reader-response theory, structuralism, and some versions of feminism. That list should suggest the daunting scope of Goldstein's book: virtually everyone who is anyone in contemporary Anglo-American literary theory gets analyzed. Although Goldstein is generally fair and careful, he sometimes sacrifices depth for breadth. He moves too quickly through the critics he criticizes—again, a rather long list.

Much as Derrida wants to vindicate his concern for history, J. Hillis Miller tries to redeem the ethical seriousness of deconstruction in *Versions of Pygmalion* (Harvard), a fitting sequel to his *The Ethics of Reading* (Columbia, 1987). Chapters devoted to various literary works (among them *What Maisie Knew* and "Bartleby the Scrivener") raise these excellent questions: "Is there an ethical dimension to the act of reading as such (as opposed to the expression of ethical themes in the text read)? Does some moral good come to me out of the solitary act of reading? How would one measure that good accurately, and what kind of good, exactly, would it be? Reinforcement and creation of my values, my further incorporation into the values of my society?" (p. 13). The book exemplifies Miller's strengths as a critic, in particular his erudition, clarity, and attentiveness to detail and figurative language. I think Miller goes too far when he claims that prosopopoeia is central to the ethics of narration and reading, but I sympathize with his wish to make the literary work "effective here and now, to reactivate its performative power" (p. viii).

Leo Bersani goes off in an apparently different direction in *The Culture of Redemption* (Harvard), "a frankly polemical study of claims made in the modern period for the authoritative, even redemptive virtues of literature" (p. 1). Provocative, lucid readings of several texts, including *Moby-Dick* and *Gravity's Rainbow,* help Bersani make such controversial claims as "the self is a practical convenience; promoted to the status of an ethical ideal, it is a sanction for violence" (p. 4). For better or for worse, this is not a cautious book.

Other books dealing with the social and ethical ramifications of literary study include Carey Kaplan and Ellen Cronan Rose's *The Canon and the Common Reader* (Tennessee), an interesting but uneven response to the current controversy surrounding the canon. Johnson's canonization of Shakespeare (the subject of chapter 2) provides a useful point of departure and the writers do a good job contesting what they call "the paranoid approach to canon formation" (p. 86), which holds that the dominant ideology neutralizes any potential opposition. Although "canon formation is inescapably ideological," the "values of the 'dominant social order' are constantly challenged by subversive elements within it . . ." (p. 86). Unfortunately, Kaplan and Rose leave us with the very questions I had hoped they would answer: for instance, "What are we going to do with the literary manifestations of gender differences while we wait for [as opposed to work for?] social change?" (p. 164). James S. Hans's *The Value(s) of Literature* contends that "all literature is fundamentally ethical in nature" (p. ix), a point he supports with readings of Walt Whitman, Wallace Stevens, and A. R. Ammons. Unsubstantiated gibes aimed at "critics" (i.e., theorists) and "academic criticism" weaken Hans's otherwise thoughtful case. Robert Hodge's *Literature as Discourse* takes a more moderate tack, aiming to forge alliances between the old and the new, traditional criticism and theory. Drawing on social semiotics, Hodge analyzes how literary works take part in the social construction of meaning.

Long-standing problems in hermeneutics concern two significant new books. In *The Resistance of Reference* (Hopkins), Ora Avni carefully examines what she sees as the ineluctable referentiality of literary works. Philosophy of language (Gottlob Frege, Bertrand Russell, J. L. Austin), linguistic theory (Ferdinand de Saussure), and literary texts ("Report to an Academy" and *Three Musketeers,* among others) creatively interact in Avni's argument: each contributes something to the other two. In *Conflicting Readings,* Paul B. Armstrong speaks to the many issues raised by disagreement and conflict among critical interpretations. Armstrong steers between absolutism and relativism, concluding that "irreconcilable conflict is possible in interpretation, but understanding is still subject to various constraints and tests, even if these cannot conclusively settle all disagreements about how best to construe a text" (p. ix). I occasionally tire of Armstrong's middle-of-the-road circumspection and long for a little political fervor (he does make the good point that "interpretive conflict requires democratic institutions and practices, and effective democracy requires facility in interpretive conflict" [p. 150]). But, in general, I found this well-argued book to be a major contribution to interpretive theory.

I briefly mention several other books that will be of interest to literary theorists. The much-discussed relationship between literature and history is scrupulously analyzed in Lionel Gossman's *Between History and Literature* (Harvard), which shows how history and literature inform one another, without, however, either discipline offering a "terra firma from which the other can be securely surveyed" (p. 3). Jonathan Morse also underscores the importance of history to literature and language in his rather disjointed *Word by Word* (Cornell). Richard A. Posner's *The Problems of Jurisprudence* (Harvard) will be mandatory reading for the growing number of literary theorists rightly interested in such questions as "Are there right answers to legal questions?" and "How are judges' visions changed?" Seymour Chatman's *Coming to Terms: The Rhetoric of Narrative in Fiction and Film* (Cornell) builds on his influential *Story and Discourse* by taking a much closer look at film and by reconsidering the terminology of narratology.

Finally, three hard-to-pigeonhole texts merit attention. *The State of the Language,* ed. Christopher Ricks and Leonard Michaels (Calif.), offers essays and poems on language use today. Many of the essays will be interesting to literary theorists, among them Henry Louis Gates's "Talking Black," Alison Lurie's "Notes on the Language of Poststructuralism," and Sandra M. Gilbert's "Reflections on a (Feminist) Discourse of Discourse, or, Look, Ma, I'm Talking!" Gilbert asks a question that properly concerns many feminist critics: "As those of us who are women, feminists, and academics begin increasingly to 'deploy' an exclusionary 'discourse of theory,' what happens to our 'status' in a political movement that has long celebrated sisterhood—and motherhood and daughterhood—as both powerful and empowering? . . . [To] whom do we speak, for whom do we speak, and in what words do we say our say?" (p. 130).

Anatomy of Racism, ed. David Theo Goldberg (Minnesota), is a timely collection of sophisticated essays, some by authors familiar to literary critics (Edward Said, Julia Kristeva, Roland Barthes, Barbara Christian), others by scholars in law, social theory, and philosophy. I especially liked Nancy Leys Stepan's "Race and Gender: The Role of Analogy in Science" (on how metaphors and analogies can shape "empirical" research and ratify the "discovery" of invidious differences and similarities among people) and Henry Louis Gates's "Critical Remarks" (*"only* the master's tools," he insists, "will ever dismantle the master's house" [p. 326]).

Critical Terms for Literary Study, ed. Frank Lentricchia and Thomas McLaughlin (Chicago), is a valuable introduction to contemporary criticism. Instead of characterizing different contemporary "critical schools" or "approaches," the book presents some prominent theorists at work "doing theory." These theorists work at defining important terms in contemporary critical discourse, in each case examining the term's history, "the controversies it generates, the questions it raises, the reading strategies it permits" (p. 3). We get W. J. T. Mitchell on representation, Barbara Johnson on writing, J. Hillis Miller on narrative, Barbara Herrnstein Smith on value/evaluation, Stanley Fish on rhetoric, and Myra Jehlen on gender—among many other excellent contributions.

ii American Literature

Critics interested in furthering the dialogue between contemporary literary theory and American literature must read Gregory S. Jay's *America the Scrivener* (Cornell). The book's subtitle—*Deconstruction and the Subject of Literary History*—registers Jay's wish to show how deconstruction has reshaped our sense of literature, history, politics, and subjectivity. In part one of the book Jay defends deconstruction against charges of nihilism and political inconsequence; part two initiates a dialogue between recent theory and classic American writers (Poe, Emerson, Henry Adams, Frederick Douglass), critics (Parrington and Trilling), and the teaching of literature. Jay's own position, presumably underwritten by deconstruction, is that "the subject of Western humanism has been modeled on the historical class of Euro-American heterosexual males of the middle and upper classes" (pp. 313–14). Even though I disagree with many of Jay's conclusions, I endorse his ultimate aim—"the theorization of a practice of multicultural social existence" (p. x).

Ramón Saldívar's *Chicano Narrative* takes a similar approach, drawing on current literary theory to analyze Chicano literature, in particular works by Américo Paredes, Tomás Rivera, Rudolfo Anaya, Rolando Hinojosa, Isabella Ríos, and several others. Saldívar aims at fashioning "an authentically reconstructed American literary history" (p. 8), one that includes the thus far muted voices of Hispanic men and women. Some of Saldívar's mimetic-sounding claims for Chicano narrative—for instance, that it helps readers uncover "their real conditions of existence in postindustrial twentieth-century America" (p. 5)—seem at odds with the textualist theories on which he relies. Even so, this is a consistently challenging, pioneering book. Theorists as well as Americanists can learn from it.

Also committed to revising the canon of American literature, *Redefining American Literary History*, ed. A. LaVonne Brown Ruoff and Jerry W. Ward, includes essays on African American, Native American, Hispanic, and Asian-American literature by such noteworthy critics as Houston A. Baker, Juan Bruce-Novoa, Amy Ling, and many others. In light of more recent work like *Chicano Narrative*, some of these essays (especially the previously published ones) feel out-of-date. But the volume as a whole is a good introduction to multicultural literary study. The bibliographies are very useful, and scholars will appreciate the concluding directory of journals and small presses (with addresses) publishing work in this area. Ruoff's *American Indian Literatures* (MLA) also features an exhaustive bibliography of literary and critical work in Native American literature as well as an informative introduction to the subject.

Another collection of essays involving theory and American literature is the Autumn 1990 issue of *New Literary History, Papers from the Commonwealth Center for Literary and Cultural Change*. The most interesting contributions have a pedagogical slant: Gayatri Chakravorty Spivak's "The Making of Americans, the Teaching of English, and the Future of Culture Studies"; Mary R. Lefkowitz, "Should Women Receive a Separate Education?"; Gerald Graff, "Other Voices, Other Rooms: Organizing and Teaching the Humanities Conflict"; and Carol Camp Yeakey, "Social Change Through the Humanities: An Essay on the Politics of Literacy and Culture in American Society."

Stanley Cavell's *Conditions Handsome and Unhandsome,* like his work in general, is difficult to categorize. For at least two decades Cavell has been claiming that Emerson and Thoreau underwrite ordinary-language philosophy as practiced by J. L. Austin, Ludwig Wittgenstein, and Cavell himself. Literary critics and philosophers have not known what to make of this claim, but in Cavell's own writing it has led to provocative, difficult books like this one. The first chapter in particular tries again to recommend Emerson "to the closer attention of the American philosophical community" (p. 33). Literary critics as well as philosophers can benefit from Cavell's painstaking, original commentary.

Crucial figures in American literary and cultural criticism appear in three books. *American Literature, Culture, and Ideology,* ed. Beverly R. Voloshin, is a collection of essays dedicated to Henry Nash Smith by such critics as Leo Marx, Larzer Ziff, and Eric Sundquist. Several of these essays have been previously published and will be familiar to many readers (for instance, Annette Kolodny's "A Map for Rereading: Or, Gender and the Interpretation of Literary Texts"). The volume would be better if the essays were more explicitly related to Nash's work. *The Portable Malcolm Cowley* (Penguin), ed. Donald W. Faulkner, presents excerpts from Cowley's correspondence, memoirs, essays, books, and poetry and provides a detailed introduction and chronology. Casey Nelson Blake's *Beloved Community* (No. Car.) takes a sympathetic but critical look at the cultural criticism of Randolph Bourne, Van Wyck Brooks, Waldo Frank, and Lewis Mumford. This is a clearly written, thoroughly researched book that draws attention to the often overlooked strengths of these writers while conceding their weaknesses.

Finally, Susan Coultrap-McQuin's *Doing Literary Business* (No. Car.) is a consistently informative study of how several 19th-century American women writers (Harriet Beecher Stowe, E. D. E. N. Southworth, Mary Abigail Dodge, and others) made their way through the literary marketplace; Kenneth Cmiel's *Democratic Eloquence* is a lucid, detailed investigation of 19th-century American debates over linguistic usage; and

The Making of the American Landscape, ed. Michael P. Conzen (Unwin Hyman), features fascinating essays by some eminent historical geographers on such topics as landscapes of wealth and power, the Americanization of the city, and landscapes redesigned for the automobile.

iii Gender Studies

Some of the best work in literary theory continues to go on in gender studies. Many of the texts discussed above take into account the importance of gender; these books make it their overriding concern.

The best of the books that I was able to survey is Thomas Laqueur's *Making Sex,* a remarkable study of "body and gender from the Greeks to Freud" (to quote the book's subtitle). Although most critics today pay lip service to "difference," we are only beginning to appreciate the difficulty of determining difference. When considering what results in difference, most critics today opt for some mix of race, gender, class, sexual orientation, nationality, and maybe age. Each of these terms requires further explanation, not to mention the emphasis we may want to give one or two (or three or four) of them. Laqueur shows that "no set of facts ever entails any particular account of difference" (p. 19). More specifically, biological data do not fix gender, but they do legitimize its social construction. To paraphrase the title of his second chapter, social destiny is anatomy—not the other way around. Chapters drawing on a dazzling range of writings—from medicine and anatomy to philosophy, psychology, and literature—reveal that "two sexes are not the necessary, natural consequence of corporeal difference. Nor, for that matter, is one sex. The ways in which sexual difference have been imagined in the past are largely unconstrained by what was actually known about this or that bit of anatomy, this or that physiological process, and derive instead from the rhetorical exigencies of the moment" (p. 243). Laqueur acknowledges the reality of the body, but I see him regarding the body as a Kantian thing-in-itself—really there but off-limits, or visible only through cultural lenses that shape what we see. As he remarks, "almost everything one wants to *say* about sex—however sex is understood—already has in it a claim about gender" (p. 11). I am not sure how Laqueur can hold onto "almost" in this statement, but I will not press the point. *Making Sex* is a crucial contribution to the debate on difference and gender.

At the opposite end of the theoretical spectrum is Camille Paglia's *Sexual Personae,* a massive (718-page) study of art and decadence from

Nefertiti to Emily Dickinson (to be followed by a second volume on how movies, television, sports, and rock music incorporate pagan themes of classical antiquity). Paglia underscores what she sees as "the truth in sexual stereotypes" and "the biologic basis of sex differences" (p. xiii). From her point of view, menstruation and childbirth are "spectacles of frightful squalor" (p. 17) and are "too barbaric for comedy" (p. 17). The female genitals are "lurid in color, vagrant in contour, and architecturally incoherent" (p. 17). Convinced that "there is no escape from the biologic chains that bind us" (p. 19), she despises what she sees as the sentimental optimism of feminism, modern emancipation movements, liberalism, and humanism, all of which mistakenly feel that "if we keep tinkering with the social mechanism long enough, every difficulty will disappear" (p. 14). This is a vituperative book, bent on rubbing our noses in nature, for Paglia an "inhuman round of waste, rot, and carnage" (p. 28) that sabotages dreams of equality and progress. When Paglia descends from ranting to reading an extraordinary range of literary texts, she can be brilliant. But even her best arguments get bogged down in overstatement and invective. Among my many reservations about this book, I question her timing. Social hope seems much more fragile—modern emancipation movements much less powerful—than she supposes. Instead of tempering our hope for social progress at this time, we need to shore it up.

Here I agree with Toril Moi, who, commenting on "the reactionary backlash of the eighties" (p. 102), finds the present situation "to be pretty gloomy," a time of "retreat for the left, including feminism" (p. 100). I quote from the insightful interview with Laura Payne that concludes Moi's *Feminist Theory and Simone de Beauvoir* (Blackwell), the third volume in the Bucknell Lectures in Literary Theory series. This brief book also includes a helpful introduction to Moi's work by Michael Payne and two essays by Moi on Simone de Beauvoir. The essays are chiefly valuable as a preview of a coming attraction—Moi's much-anticipated book on de Beauvoir, for Moi "the most important feminist intellectual of the twentieth century" (p. 108).

An earlier moment in the history of feminism also concerns Elaine Showalter in *Sexual Anarchy* (Viking), a readable, lively study of gender and culture at the end of two centuries—the 19th and the 20th. Showalter claims that "from urban homelessness to imperial decline, from sexual revolution to sexual epidemics, the last decades of the twentieth century seem to be repeating the problems, themes, and metaphors of the *fin de siècle*" (p. 1). "Seems to be" signals caution that Showalter does not always show, as she readily posits many similarities between then and now. I applaud Showalter for apparently trying to reach a general audience and for addressing such timely issues as AIDS, the debate on pornography, and the sexual abuse of children. Some of her parallels between the 1890s and 1990s are questionable, however, and I am not sure that the past enforces the sanguine lesson she wants to teach: "Yet if we can learn something from the fears and myths of the past, it is that they are so often exaggerated and unreal, that what looks like sexual anarchy in the context of *fin-de-siècle* anxieties may be the embryonic stirrings of a new order" (p. 18). More specifically, "what seems today like the apocalyptic warnings of a frightening sexual anarchy may be really the birth throes of a new sexual equality" (p. 208). I hope she is right, but I am not certain that she has justified her admittedly tentative optimism.

Elizabeth A. Meese's *(Ex)Tensions* (Illinois) is a much more theoretically ambitious, stylistically tortuous book. Picking up where her first book *Crossing the Double-Cross* (No. Car., 1986) left off, Meese aims a self-described deconstructive ideological critique at "the construction of knowledge within Feminist Literary Criticism, exposing its own 'dark sides,' the repression of which permits mono- and ethnocentric assertions of authority and domination, read in the marginalization of African-American and Native-American literatures and the continued deferral of lesbian feminism" (p. 27). Chapters devoted to Leslie Silko's *Ceremony,* Nadine Gordimer's *Burger's Daughter,* Sherley Anne Williams's *Dessa Rose* (among other works) help Meese turn feminism into "a space from which difference can speak and be spoken with respect, a space where we can write and/or speak *with* one another rather than for or against each other" (p. 28). This is a laudable aim but, despite Meese's thoughtful work, I still wonder whether a critic needs deconstruction to accomplish it.

Some excellent collections of essays also deal with the questions raised by Meese and the other critics I have been discussing. One of the best is *Gender in the Classroom,* ed. Susan L. Gabriel and Isaiah Smithson (Illinois). I admire the ways in which several of the contributors, working from a feminist vantage point, grapple with such everyday pedagogical problems as getting (or allowing) students to talk in class, marking and grading papers, and making assignments. Penny L. Burge and Steven M. Culver's "Sexism, Legislative Power, and Vocational Education" is an especially noteworthy piece. Although race, gender, and class make up a familiar trinity in contemporary theory, class often gets shortchanged.

We still hear very little from (or about) working-class people. Burge and Culver try to ally feminism with vocational education, which in their view "has always had a commitment to the less powerful members of society, whether they be women, the poor, or skilled laborers" (p. 161). Nina Baym's challenging essay "The Feminist Teacher of Literature: Feminist or Teacher?" is also very much worth reading. She is concerned about the silencing of women students, inside as well as outside feminist classrooms, and she urges the teacher "to encourage her women students to say what she does not expect them to say and perhaps would rather not hear. Otherwise, the only real reader in the class will be the teacher, whether she is a feminist or not" (p. 75).

Four other collections of essays take gender studies in other directions. *Performing Feminisms,* ed. Sue-Ellen Case, is mostly made up of articles previously published in *Theatre Journal.* This ground-breaking book looks at diverse kinds of drama, always "raising the theoretical issue of the codes and meanings of the female body on stage—as a performance site and as a social determinant" (p. 5). *Lesbian and Gay Writing,* ed. Mark Lilly (Temple), is a theoretically tame collection of essays on Ivy Compton-Burnett, Sylvia Townsend Warner, Ronald Firbank, and other writers. *Lesbian Texts and Contexts,* ed. Karla Jay and Joanne Glasgow (*NYU*), is a much better indication of the important work being done in this area. Difficult questions—defining lesbianism, decoding it, and relating it to heterosexual culture—are dealt with by such critics as Valerie Miner, Elizabeth Meese, Jane Marcus, Judith Fetterly, and Catharine R. Stimpson.

Three other books deserve mentioning: Elizabeth Kamarck Minnich's *Transforming Knowledge* (Temple), a philosophical attempt (greatly influenced by feminism) to change not just what but how we think, with emphasis on the still dominant liberal arts curriculum; Madelon Sprengnether's *The Spectral Mother* (Cornell), which strives for a rapprochement between feminism and psychoanalysis that rectifies Freud's avoidance of the pre-Oedipal mother; and Jean Wyatt's *Reconstructing Desire,* which also turns to the pre-Oedipal in exploring how several literary texts by women help us imagine alternative family relations.

iv Modernism and Postmodernism

Feminism/Postmodernism, ed. Linda J. Nicholson (Routledge), is a good collection of essays on the possible value of postmodernism to feminism.

I say "possible" because, as Nicholson points out in her insightful introduction, while postmodernism seems in many ways "a natural ally" (p. 5) of feminism, it is at least questionable whether postmodernism provides the "stopping points" (p. 8) (such as gender) that feminist political theorizing may need. Commenting on the contributions to the volume by Nancy Hartsock and Susan Bordo, Nicholson warns that "to invoke the ideal of endless difference is for feminism either to self-destruct or to finally accept an ontology of abstract individualism" (p. 8). Nicholson and another key contributor to the volume, Nancy Fraser, hold out the hope that "a carefully constructed postmodernism" (p. 11) can reinforce feminism, but they appreciate the fear that postmodernism undermines political action. This is a thought-provoking volume, with important implications not just for feminists but for all critics concerned with the theoretical underpinnings of political practice.

Also indebted to feminist criticism, *The Gender of Modernism,* ed. Bonnie Kime Scott, is a useful anthology dedicated "to the forgotten and silenced makers of modernism"—such writers as Mina Loy, Katherine Mansfield, Charlotte Mew, Zora Neale Hurston, and Djuna Barnes, among others. Selections from these writers' work, introduced by such critics as Susan M. Squier and Carolyn Burke, provide the materials for a gendered reading of modernism. Familiar figures like T. S. Eliot and Ezra Pound also appear, but instead of *The Waste Land* or the *Cantos,* we get Eliot's introduction to *Nightwood* and Pound's letter to Marianne Moore. This volume is useful as an introduction to the subject.

Another book concerned with gender, Susan Robin Suleiman's *Subversive Intent* (Harvard), studies the relationship between feminism and various European, largely male avant-garde, movements and figures, among them the Surrealists and Alain Robbe-Grillet. Suleiman's concluding chapter on feminism and postmodernism is a lively, personal look at feminist appropriations of postmodernism. Benefiting from her analysis of previous avant-garde movements, she asks, "What hope is there for postmodernism, and specifically for feminist postmodernism, as an oppositional avant-garde practice?" (p. 198). Her answer is cautiously optimistic.

Astradur Eysteinsson's *The Concept of Modernism* (Cornell) is a more conventional scholarly treatment of the subject. Eysteinsson treats the many questions raised by the attempt to define modernism: the apparent tension between modernism and realism; the relation of modernism to the avant-garde; reading modernism through postmodernism; modernism and feminism; and modernist attitudes toward literary history. This is a thorough, clearly written study.

Less comprehensive but still useful studies of modernism include Ernst Behler's *Irony and the Discourse of Modernity* and Anthony Giddens's *The Consequences of Modernity.* An eminent sociologist, Giddens writes on various social theorists whom literary critics often overlook (Talcott Parsons, Daniel Bell, Graham Allen, among others). Frank Lentricchia also broadens the discussion of modernism in "Philosophers of Modernism at Harvard, circa 1900," his contribution to the Fall 1990 *SAQ* (devoted to "American Issues"). From Lentricchia's point of view, George Santayana, William James, and Josiah Royce are not just background figures but contributors to "the original metapoetic idiom of the youth of Eliot, Frost, and Stevens" (p. 790). This is an important article for critics interested in stretching "modernism" to include developments outside the arts and architecture.

Finally, brief mention goes to three books. Nevill Wakefield's *Postmodernism* (Pluto), taking off from Jean Baudrillard's *Simulations,* sketches a by now familiar postmodern world "where clarity and obscurity, failure and success constantly exchange" (p. 4). Jon Stratton's *Writing Sites* (Michigan) offers a genealogy of much the same postmodern world. Synthesizing work by Karl Marx, Foucault, Baudrillard, and Derrida, Stratton links (too schematically) three *epistemes*—classical, modern, and postmodern—to three forms of capitalism—mercantile, production, and consumption. Also influenced by Marxism, Neil Larsen's *Modernism and Hegemony* (Minnesota) characterizes modernist ideology as a displaced politics. Larsen deserves credit for bringing Brazilian and Mexican literature into the discussion, but his prose is turgid, often pretentious. Literary theorists would do well to keep in mind the questions raised by Sandra Gilbert in her contribution to *The State of Language:* to whom do we speak when we write like this? Does such writing "cut us off from many of the readers we need to reach" (p. 132)?

University of New Mexico

i French Contributions: Michel Gresset

a. General Last year I began my report with two general remarks, one on translation and one on current trends in the French reception of American writers. This year I would like to begin with four comments. The first again has to do with translation. Although perhaps this is not apparent to everybody, because of the very strong transparency myth, good translation is still the only key to the success of foreign writers in any country. What we know now, however, is that there is no end to the process. One of the finest (although generally unnoticed) renderings of a piece of American literature in 1990 was a choice of tales by Edgar Allan Poe newly translated (as well as carefully annotated, since the series was devised for students) by Henri Justin under the title *The Black Cat* (Le Livre de poche). Included are "A Decided Loss," "The Conversation of Eiros and Charmion," and "The Colloquy of Monos and Una"—titles not often anthologized, nor so well translated as here (rendering "The Imp of the Perverse" as "Le Mauvais esprit" is far more Poesque than Baudelaire's "Le démon de la perversité"; it lifts the curse of gothic romanticism from the tale). The Coindreau Prize for the best American book in translation, however, went to a contemporary work, Pierre Gault's skillful rendering of Annie Dillard's *Pilgrim at Tinker Creek*.

My second remark is on the growing number of guides, handbooks, and manuals overtly designed to "help" the French reader/student with the practice of American literature or culture or history (in fact, publishers are quite simply after the academic public). This may well be the motivation behind the publication by Presses universitaires du Mirail (Toulouse) of two small volumes—*Études textuelles: littérature moderne de langue anglaise* and a slimmer companion, *Langages littéraires: textes d'anglais*—but the result is far more valuable than just one more such handbook. The first volume, signed by G. Cordesse, E. Epstein, G. Lebas, and Y. Le Pellec, is described as a "pedagogical experiment": it is thus placed deliberately in the wake of the "revolutionary" phase that followed May 1968 in the groves of academe. It consists of 25 passages taken from English (12) and American (13) literature, all modern or contemporary (with the sole exception of Emily Dickinson). Each extract is followed by several pages of analysis, in English, along lines described as a sort of "zero degree" of textual analysis. "The main ideological approaches of our times, be they Marxist, psychoanalytic, or feminist, have generally been avoided, not out of systematic disapproval, but because their application becomes fully valid only after a careful elucidation of enunciative modes and/or narrative techniques has been carried out." Not surprisingly, the book is therefore placed under the aegis of Gérard Genette. The companion volume, by the same authors minus E. Epstein, is the reverse: it is theoretical, in French, and it draws only a few examples from the texts. It is meant as an attempt at "refocusing certain notions, too often hidden under the nebula of literary genres." Yes, these two little books are wholly recommendable.

My third preliminary comment concerns two big books published after (probably) being defended as doctoral dissertations. It is only through its chapter 15 ("Is There a Culture in the United States?") that Jacques Portes's *Une Fascination réticente: les États-Unis devant l'opinion française, 1870–1914* [A Reluctant Fascination: The United States and French Opinion] (PUN) bears on our subject. The answer, as may be expected from the dates, is negative. It was generally admitted at the time that whatever culture there was in the United States must still be dependent on Europe. The other book (published jointly in 1988 by Centre national de la recherche scientifique and Presses universitaires du Mirail) is Daniel Baylon's *L'Amérique mythifiée* [The Myth of America]: *le Reader's Digest de 1945 à 1970* (1988); a thorough study, from "Anatomy of a Magazine" to "The Reasons for Success," it is a token of a growing interest in what I might call the paraliterary aspects of literature in the United States—including the book industry, as shown by Claire Bruyère's "Le best-Seller" in no. 280 of *Magazine littéraire*.

The fourth remark must simply be a warning against the idea that this review might include articles dealing either with "paraliterature," such as cartoons and comics, or with a comparison between literature and art, or yet specifically with art—generally the visual arts. If it cannot be a surprise to our U.S. colleagues to read that there has always been a deep interest in the American cinema in France, it may be news to them to hear that American painting now seems to be the trend—so much so that one can no longer count the reproductions of paintings by Edward Hopper on front covers of French translations of American books.

b. Colonial The first of two items came out in a festschrift, *Confluences américaines: Mélanges en l'honneur de Maurice Gonnaud* (PUN), a miscellany in honor of a retired Americanist of the University of Lyon, composed of contributions by his local colleagues and by his close collaborators at Association française d'Études américaines, of which he succeeded Roger Asselineau as president in 1976. These two items were Bernard Vincent's "La lecture des auteurs français, et leur influence, dans l'Amérique coloniale du 18ᵉ siècle: constat bibliographique" and Sim Copans's "Tocqueville and American Literature." The first is a review of books published years ago and now almost forgotten; it reaches the somewhat unexpected conclusion that the impact of such French authors as Voltaire and Montesquieu on colonial, even on revolutionary, America was only "an epiphenomenon" in the formation of American culture. In a wistful postscript, Vincent even remarks that things do not seem to have changed: "whether it be books or films, French culture remains a third-type culture in the U.S." The second article, by American-born Copans, is also a well-documented review of books and articles, from Ernest Renan (1854) to Cushing Strout (1986), found to have a bearing on Tocqueville and American writing.

c. 19th-Century Literature Under an ambitious title, Marcienne Rocard's "Le pélerinage en Europe," in *Confluences américaines* (pp. 79–89), is a review of a few works from *The Innocents Abroad* (1869) to Alison Lurie's *Foreign Affairs* (1986) via Henry James on the new "grand tour," or the (often fallacious) traditional American trip to the culture of Europe.

Poe's tales continue to excite the critical imagination of French academics, who have always tended to find in them paradigms of later literary or even cultural phenomena, the extraordinary success of "The Purloined Letter" in French postmodern culture being only the best example. Another is given by Daniel Ferrer, who introduces the thick volume *Transformation, Métamorphose, Anamorphose* (GRAAT no. 7, Tours) by taking Poe's "Gold Bug" as a pretext in his "Métamorphoses du scarabée" (pp. 7–17). Ann Lecercle used her former article (see *ALS 1989*:484), in which she drew on the possibility that Poe resorted to Ann

Radcliffe's *The Mysteries of Udolpho* to frame his tale, in order to set "The Oval Portrait" within the larger question of the function of the gaze in (fantastic) literature. Her new contribution is "L'Inscription du regard" (*Du Fantastique en littérature: Figures et Figurations* [Publications de l'Université de Provence]: 77–93). The same publication has Jean-Louis Grillou's " 'The Fall of the House of Usher': Un cryptogramme alchimique?" which, much like what Viola Sachs does with the texts of Melville, interprets the tale strictly as an illustration of the alchemist's quest for the philosopher's truth (pp. 111–26). In " 'The Pit and the Pendulum': Inconscient et Intertextualité," (*RFEA* 45:119–36), without raising the question as to who is being psychoanalyzed, Denis Gauer surprisingly (i.e., even after Claude Richard) finds it necessary to start from Marie Bonaparte once more, only to show that her criticism is somewhat outré and oversimplified, and that history plays a part in the tale after all. In *JSSE* 14:25–40, Mary Lucas rightly stresses the importance of the dramatic in two tales: "Poe's Theatre: 'King Pest' and 'Hop Frog.' "

Along with Poe comes Hawthorne, whose tales were on the syllabus of the *agrégation* in 1990–91, and to whom therefore the first number of a new review published in Montpellier after the demise of both Claude Richard and *Delta* was devoted. The first issue of *Profils américains* contains two general articles and four articles on particular tales. In "Cris et chuchotements: Les modulations de la voix dans les contes de Nathaniel Hawthorne" (*PA*:1–34), Yves Carlet takes his clue from a passage in *Mosses from an Old Manse* in which Hawthorne confesses to aural voyeurism in order to explore the rewarding subject of voice in the tales; and in "Hawthorne, 1825–1851: des contes au roman" (*PA*:97–122), Philippe Jaworski traces the part played by tale writing in the writer's development from the time of a letter he wrote to his mother in 1821 to authorship of *The Scarlet Letter*. Françoise Charras surprisingly submits irony to the test of gothicism in "Alice Doane's Appeal" (*PA*:35–45); Paul Carmignani offers a symbolic reading of "The May-Pole of Merry Mount" (*PA*:46–57); Michel Granger rehabilitates the eponymous hero in "Exil intérieur et aveuglements dans 'Wakefield' " (*PA*:58–74); and Claude Fleurdorge in "Narration et point de vue dans 'The Minister's Black Veil' " examines that tale in great, almost finicky detail.

Perhaps because of the centenary of his death, there is a decided renewal of interest in Melville. Because they were published in 1991, the larger number of publications devoted to his works (sometimes newly translated) must wait for next year's review, but a few were published in

1990, and one, overlooked in my last review, in 1989. It is a new commercial volume, *Les Iles enchantées* (Flammarion), containing "Bartleby," "The Encantadas," and "The Belltower" in a new translation by Michèle Causse, followed by a 30-page, original postface, "Bartleby ou la formule," in which philosopher Gilles Deleuze penetratingly analyzes the implications of Bartleby's famous "formula" and concludes that Bartleby is "not at all the sick man, but the doctor of a sick America, the medicine-man, the new Christ or the brother of us all." This interesting excursion should be translated and published in the United States. In a special number (*RFEA* 44) devoted to "The Body in American Culture and Literature," Agnès Derail-Imbert writes about *"Moby-Dick; or, The Whale:* la fable du ventre [the Fable of the Belly]" (*RFEA* 44:11–22). Finding support in Jaworski, Richard, Durand, Pétillon, Viola Sachs, Deleuze, and Derrida, she traces the rather obvious food/digestion/dyspepsia motif throughout the book, discovering that, much as with Carlyle, with Melville "bodies are congenitally dyspeptic." In the course of *Moby-Dick,* "Ishmael and the universe finally fall prey to the temptation of cannibalism," and because of the words "the button-like black bubble," the ending is seen as a symmetrical cosmic spewing up of the reason given for taking to the sea in chapter 1: "growing grim about the mouth." The most dire conclusion must be drawn if one admits with Derail-Imbert that the mouth is less Melville's medium of the word than the outlet of upheaval, and that the last word must be left to Pip, or the ventriloquist. I for one would have thought there was more than this to *Moby-Dick* in the end.

In "De Harvard à *Walden:* romantiques, unitariens et transcendantalistes," *Confluences américaines,* pp. 41–52, Yves Carlet studies "the strange process" by which (Perry Miller's enthusiastic statement to the contrary) the Transcendentalists welcomed the Romantic revolution in Great Britain, particularly the ideas of Coleridge and Carlyle. This, Carlet argues, occurred in spite of the Unitarians of Harvard and Cambridge who stuck to the classic ideal: "the notion of the sublime was the Trojan horse by which disorder, irregularity and extravagance were introduced in New England." In "Les Saintes Ecritures [The Holy Writ] de la Nouvelle-Angleterre selon Henry D. Thoreau," Michel Granger (pp. 53–64) also reveals the contradiction between the writer's claims and his achievement. Granger writes, "Rather than those of a Holy Writ [for New England], Thoreau has drawn the lines of an individualistic 'economy' based on self-awareness, yet endowed with a representative value which cannot be denied." In the same volume, Agnieszka Salska goes "From Fact to Vision" and writes in English on "Versions of the Emersonian Paradigm in Some Poems by Emily Dickinson" (pp. 187–201). There is also a vindication, by Etienne de Planchard of "L'oeuvre 'créole' de G. W. Cable au Carrefour de l'Ancien Monde et du Nouveau" (pp. 153–61), in which both *Old Creole Days* and *The Grandissimes* are examined, and the conclusion is that it was clear to Cable that chief among what the United States ought to forswear in order to let progress settle in was the very order on which the Old South rested.

d. Late 19th- and 20th-Century Fiction to the Fifties Chief among publications on Henry James was the book drawn by Evelyne Labbé from her doctoral dissertation and published by Presses universitaires de Lyon, *Ecrits sur l'abîme: les derniers romans de Henry James* [Written Over the Abyss: Henry James's Last Novels]. (The metaphor in the title is borrowed from "The Turn of the Screw.") Labbé's study is divided into three parts, each devoted to one later novel, *The Ambassadors, The Wings of the Dove,* and *The Golden Bowl.* With a remarkable mixture of modesty and subtlety, and with the support of a number of modern literary critics, what is analyzed over 250 pages is the "double articulation between theme and structure which constitutes the main characteristic of the last novels." In "The Dual Outsider in Henry James's *Princess Casamissima*" (*L'Etranger dans la littérature et la pensée anglaises,* CARA [Centre Aixois de recherches anglaises] 7:205–18), Margaret Goscilo shows how James "chose to merge his protagonist's double nationality with the figurative foreignness of bastardy"; Goscilo concludes that Hyacinth Robinson is "a typical dispossessed outsider-son of the XIXth century novel." In "Turning the Tables: The Stories of Henry James," Bruce Bassoff, guest contributor to *EA* 3 (pp. 284–93), asserts after examining a few of James's major stories that "if they renounce life and love," James's protagonists or "ghosts" "do so in order to make a virtue out of necessity—in order to re-gain indirectly what they could not gain directly."

The whole number 13 of *Annales de l'Université de Savoie* was devoted to Henry James's friend Henry Adams's main work, under the title "L'Envers de l'écriture [The Other Side of *écriture*] dans *L'Education de Henry Adams*," no doubt because the book was on the *agrégation* syllabus in 1990. After a useful introduction in which Alain Bonora justifies the general title, this number includes eight contributions, the last four closely devoted to study of the text, while the first four are more general. In "Sur deux villes et sur un lieu commun [On Two Cities and One Commonplace]" (pp. 15–25), Roland Tissot manages to keep his tendency to Lacanian puns at bay in discussing Adams's perception of "two women-cities, Rome and Paris, both tropes of the unconscious desire whose expression he tries to implement." In "Henry Adams et la guerre de sécession [Henry Adams and the Civil War]" (pp. 27–33), Paul Carmignani finds that Adams, who always felt guilty for standing aloof, had correctly foreseen the war's impact. Pierre Lagayette's title, "Voyage au bout de l'ennui: Henry Adams dans les Mers du Sud [Journey to the End of Ennui: Henry Adams in the South Seas]" (pp. 35–44), is self-explanatory. At the end of his brief "Henry Adams et les dangers de l'historicisme" (pp. 45–52), Jean Rouberol asks whether Adams, rather than being born too late as he claimed more than once, was not lucky enough to be born "fifty years too soon." The other articles in the journal number look at the book proper. François Pitavy's "L'Autobiographie à la troisième personne" (pp. 53–62) accurately reflects its title. In "The Structure of *The Education of Henry Adams*," Marie-Claude Perrin-Chenour argues rather convincingly that the book is structured like an hourglass (pp. 63–76). Quite different is Bleuette Pion's plan, which compares several articles on the question of irony in the book. Her "La 'Voie oblique': aspects et rôle de l'ironie dans *The Education of Henry Adams*" (pp. 77–99) develops the idea that irony is "the oblique way through which could be conveyed a discourse in open contradiction with the new, official discourse of the Gilded Age." Last is a long article in English by Alain Bonora, "The Tricks of a Blind Man's Dog in *The Education of Henry Adams*," which explores the autobiography's system of metaphors and uncovers a network of private associations that reveal the book to be everything but a literal statement (pp. 101–26).

In "Willa Cather's Love Affair with France," James Woodress dutifully reviews the five trips to France of a writer whose "French interests never flagged" and whose "love affair" with France resulted in a significant use of French culture in her work (*CA* 91–102). The title of Patricia Bleu-Schwenninger's *"Manhattan Transfer:* le manifeste cubiste de Dos Passos" (*CA* 163–75) suggests the article's subject, although the essay does not mention the important influence on Dos Passos of Blaise Cendrars (nor does it mention James Joyce). Bleu-Schwenninger's interesting conclusion is that whereas the book's content (and later *USA*) was typically American, its technique was the product of "European thinking"—

which may be the reason why, apart from Gide, everybody in France (Sartre in particular) greeted Dos Passos as a great writer.

Americana 5 devotes four articles to *Tender is the Night*. This magazine, published (and rather poorly proofread) by University Paris IV, devotes one number every year to writers whose books have been set on the *agrégation* syllabus. As a result, the articles are often geared to students rather than to experts or scholars. In "Le 'Moi' divisé dans *Tender Is the Night* de F. Scott Fitzgerald" (pp. 57–69), Michèle Bonnet develops the thesis that Dick Diver is the idealist, the man of imagination, whose dreams cannot come true unless they are isolated from reality—unless they take place in a sort of theatrical space. The novel's outcome is even more cruel than just a disillusion, since Diver has been betrayed by his own people. In the end, only nostalgia prevails. Marc Saporta contributes "Scott Fitzgerald en son temps" (pp. 71–79), and Colette Gerbaud announces her program in her title: "Amérique et féminité, ou le rêve, l'or et la nuit dans *Tender Is the Night* [America and Femininity, or Dream, Gold, and Night in *Tender is the Night*]" (pp. 81–96). More original is Patrick Hubner's "Le Génie du lieu dans *Tendre est la nuit*" (pp. 97–107): the thesis being that "the autobiographical fiction of the novel bears the mark of the writer's obsession with dizzy[ing] places." In *JSSE* (14:87–110), Elizabeth M. Varet-Ali writes at length (in English) on "The Unfortunate Fate of Seventeen Fitzgerald 'Originals': Towards a Reading of the *Pat Hobby Stories* 'on their own Merits Completely.'" She argues that these stories are about "the destructive aspects of the 'innate conditions of the industry' when based on waste of talent, negation of art, culture and integrity." Fitzgerald speaks (in inverted terms) for professionalism and quality in art. The stories genuinely belong to the Fitzgerald corpus.

Prior to 1990, no one, to my knowledge, had written on the sense of smell in Faulkner's fiction. The article devoted by Paul Carmignani to "William Faulkner: à vue de nez" in *RFEA* 45:137–48 is therefore a welcome beginning. However, it was published simultaneously in an English version entitled "Olfaction in Faulkner's Fiction" (*MissQ* 43:305–15). This is not to point out the author as an exception, but to protest against what is fast becoming a rule. It may be that there is a penalty being paid by the English-speaking world as more and more articles published by French writers in French magazines are translated and published overseas for no reason except that they may reach a wider public in America. It is urgent that magazines insist on publishing only

unpublished manuscripts. Guillaume Fauconnier's "Le livre que Faulkner n'a pas écrit" in *Etudes américaines* 7:99–109 is a pure speculation on
what might have been The American Dream that Faulkner was planning
in the middle 1960s. Another article on Faulkner was Nicole Mou-
linoux's self-descriptive *"Sanctuary, Absalom:* variantes gothiques" in *Du
Fantastique en littérature* (pp. 141–51), which goes by the worn-out and
yet still apparently unquestioned cliché that the Gothic literary tradition
has found a "land of election" in the South. (The two novels have in
common a colonial house which is the modern form of the feudal castle,
etc.)

It is perhaps fitter to place Saul Bellow at the end of the moderns
rather than at the beginning of the postmoderns. In "Bellow's Hero and
the 'Reality Instructors': Just a Punch and Judy Show?" (*SBN* 9, 2:29–
37), Marie-Christine Pauwels de la Roncière asks a relevant question
about the novelist's evolution as evinced in the teacher figures/questing
protagonists' contacts. The (sad) conclusion is simply that "there is
definitely no reconciliation with the world in [the] later novels."

e. 20th-Century Fiction: Contemporary   One figure, looming large
behind contemporary fiction (not only American), imposes itself at the
outset: that of Vladimir Nabokov. To him, apparently a favorite with
French readers, all kinds of late tributes were paid when a French
translation of the 1939 Russian original was published under the title
L'Enchanteur in 1986 (even before the 1987 English publication) with a
fair amount of success. Nabokov's works will soon enter the French
pantheon of Gallimard's Pléiade Library under the direction of Gilles
Barbedette. Danièle Roth-Souton has given an explicit title to her "Language Deficiency as Luzhin's Defense and Vladimir Nabokov's Metaphor
for Exile" (*RFEA* 45:149–60), while Suzanne Fraysse concludes her study
of "Miroirs dans *The Eye* de Vladimir Nabokov" (*Polysèmes* [Université
Paris III] 2:69–89) with the idea that Nabokov's fascination with echo,
deviation, and reflection not only confirms the absence of origin and
transcendence, but insofar as the "I" has only the multiple images of
Smurov as the means of access to utterance also confirms the impossibility of uttering the literal by any means other than metaphorical ones.
Fraysse has also contributed a brief article on the writer's special relationship with the English language as it is spoken in America in "Nabokov et
la langue américaine," which was part of a special number of the
magazine *Europe,* no. 733:25–28. This number, "Ecrivains des États-

Unis," was edited by Marc Chénetier in the wake of his book (see *ALS*
89:394–96). Chénetier has translated two-thirds of the 12 extracts offered
(sometimes without a hint as to their origin) as illustrations of and
complements of to this issue's 12 short articles devoted to individual
writers. I will refer to these articles as I proceed, just as I do with some of
the articles in no. 281 of *MagL,* ed. the same Chénetier with a view to the
public at large under the misleading title (probably not Chénetier's):
"États-Unis, 1960–1990: 30 ans de littérature [Thirty Years of American
Literature, 1960–1990]." Not only are all poets, essayists, or nonfiction
writers tacitly excluded, but the "Dictionnaire des romanciers" (pp. 79–
126) omits many fiction writers. Because of the abundance of material, I
limit myself to those articles contributed by French writers, and will not
discuss the 90 vignettes that make up about half of the whole. If a
bibliographical check is needed, however, neither of these two commercial publications replaces the descriptions on almost 400 writers in
Chénetier's 1989 book—so that consultation of the three books may well
prove necessary, although in a number of cases not even this is enough. It
would be a great help if a bibliography of French translations of and
publications on contemporary American literature, with periodic additions, could be made available.

In spite (or because) of his having produced only three books, William
Gaddis also appears as a formidable figure behind the contemporary
scene—although his name is only for the happy few. A three-page
"Gaddictionnaire" subtitled "Introduction à l'oeuvre de William Gaddis" was offered by Brigitte Félix as a preamble to her translation of an
extract of *JR* (still unpublished in French, even after the publication of
Carpenter's Gothic in 1988) in *Europe* 733:109–11. An American, John
Johnston, has written about "*JR* and the Flux of Capital" in *RFEA*
45:161–71. Johnston's argument is that "by simply recording the speech
acts of the characters . . . , the novel has no difficulty showing that
capitalism as an informational and communicational system has ceased
to be either 'economic' or 'social.' . . . Seen from this perspective, *JR*
intends neither compensation nor redemption; it is simply a demonstration, in the most rigorous terms imaginable, of the conditions under
which we now live."

A third heavyweight (with only five books published) in contemporary fiction is Thomas Pynchon, about whose work Bénédicte Chorier,
who has already published lavishly on him, asks the question: "Thomas
Pynchon: la fin de l'histoire?" in *RFEA* 43:9–17. Quoting Pointsman

who, in *Gravity's Rainbow*, sees Slothrop as "historically a monster," Chorier asks how one can be a historical monster when history itself is denounced as "a serpent hypnotic and undulant" (*V*). The answer lies in "the narrower your sense of Now, the more tenuous you get." *Gravity's Rainbow*, she suggests, is in fact an enormous hiatus, an 800-page gap gaping in the imminence of the fall of the rocket, a story set in history without a historical determination. The same critic and Anne Battesti have joined forces in offering the duet of their reading impressions in "Lire Thomas Pynchon" (*Europe* 733:34–36).

The reviewing mood must have seized Chénetier when he wrote his long and vastly encompassing "History in Contemporary Fiction, or the 'Constrained Nightmare' " (the latter part of the title is a take-off from historian Georges Duby's "History Is a Constrained Dream") in Theo D'haen and Hans Bertens, eds., *History and Post-war Writing* (Rodopi), pp. 147–69. I shall be content with quoting the section titles and some of the books or writers briefly examined: "Derision" (*Catch-22, The Sot-Weed Factor*, etc.), "Protest" (Ishmael Reed), "Debunking" (Jerome Charyn's *The Franklin Scare*), "Ironical Visions" (Russell Banks, John Barth), "History/Fiction/Politics" (Robert Coover), and finally no less than "History and Writing" (*How German Is It*).

With the contemporary novel, one name looming almost as large as Pynchon and Gaddis is John Barth, who Françoise Sammarcelli equates with "la séduction du double" in *Europe* 733:29–33. A recent favorite of academic readers is Raymond Carver, whose fine essay "On Writing" was translated by Pierre-Emmanuel Dauzat in *MagL* 281:31–34. What must have been one of Carver's last interviews, in April 1987, was translated by Claude Grimal in *Europe* 733:72–79. Claudine Verley devotes an article (in English) to one of his later stories in "The Window and the Eye in Raymond Carver's 'Boxes' " (*JSSE* 15:95–106). She finds that "the window-topos which has been defined as a simple, even minimal pattern, proves to be the organizing and unifying principle of the story on the narrative, semantic and textual levels." Less well-known is William Gass, to whom Claire Maniez devotes a brief introduction, "Le Champ de la voix [The Field of Voice]." In the sixth publication of Groupes de recherches anglo-américaines de l'Université François-Rabelais de Tours (GRAAT), *Exil de l'auteur, exil des genres*, Maniez focuses on "William Gass et l'essai-fiction" (pp. 25–33), a number closed by Brigitte Félix's analysis of one of the three stories published under the title "The Sentient Lens" in *Pricksongs and Descants* in her "Robert Coover: 'Scene for Winter,' ou la fiction fait son cinéma [Fiction's Theatrics]" (pp. 79–89). With Chénetier on Stanley Elkin ("L'écriture et la voix," *Europe* 733:37–40), and even more so, perhaps, with Laurence Zachar on Guy Davenport ("L'originalité d'un traditionnaliste," *Europe* 733:41–43), one finds writers whose works, to all practical purposes, remain unknown in France in spite of a couple of translations. Donald Barthelme's work has become a little better known since *Snow White* met with some success in 1969. In *Europe* 733:48–51, Maurice Couturier admires this "tight-rope writer," as he calls him rightly, to the point of losing a sense of proportion in finding him "apart in literature, like Sterne, Joyce, and Nabokov in their days."

Next in *Europe* 733 is an article on Walter Abish by Florence Césari ("Absence, Forgetting and Metamorphosis," pp. 52–54), another on Don DeLillo by François Happe ("The Empire of Signs," pp. 55–58), one by Pascale Guilpain on Joseph McElroy ("The Poet of the Neuronic," pp. 59–63), and one by Claude Grimal on Paul Auster, perhaps the only contemporary American writer who is really well-known in France these days, at least partly due to the untiring publicity by his French publisher, Actes-Sud ("In the Heart of the Labyrinth," pp. 64–66). It remained for Noelle Batt to sum up "The Eighties" (*Europe* 733:67–71) by asking the question of their specificity and answering that by far the most operative concept is probably that of "generic hybridation," e.g., in Auster's books. Claude Grimal has written precisely on "The 'New York Trilogy' and the Tradition of the Detective Novel" (a tradition which is not pure ornament in Auster, as could have been expected) in GRAAT 6:66–77. In the same number, Claudine Raynaud has written (in English) a well-documented study of "Hybridization and Marginality: Autobiographical Writings by African-American Women Writers" (pp. 49–65).

In *MagL* 281:55–58, Paul Carmignani asks "What Remains of the South of Yore?" One is not surprised to find him at a loss for an answer, divided as he is between "there is no South any longer" and "the South is America's distorting mirror." But one is surprised to find that he has overlooked the rather obvious fact that the South has produced a number of remarkable *women* writers, from Kate Chopin to Anne Tyler and Eve Shelnutt, and including Caroline Gordon, Katherine Ann Porter, Eudora Welty, Carson McCullers, Flannery O'Connor, Elizabeth Spencer, Sylvia Wilkinson, Doris Betts, etc.

"Tinkering Extravagance: H. D. Thoreau, H. Melville and A. Dillard" is a long essay in English, apparently also published in *Critique*

31:157–72, in which Chénetier lavishly builds thematic and verbal parallels between *Walden*, Melville's tales, and *Pilgrim at Tinker Creek*. In "Métamorphoses des *Métamorphoses:* Patricia Eakins, Wendy Walker, Don Webb," Chénetier (at equal length, though in French this time) compares three small publications of 1988 with Ovid's original, *Uncle Ovid's Exercise Book, The Hungry Girls,* and *The Sea-Rabbit, Or, the Artist of Life* (*Transformation, métamorphose, anamorphose,* GRAAT 7:223–42). To GRAAT 6:35–47, Chénetier has also given an article already published twice in slightly different forms, in English, including one under the same title, in 1989 (see *ALS 1989,* p. 397): "Why William S. Wilson Doesn't Write Like Franz Kafka: The Story as Operation."

Also focusing on a younger writer—one of the most puzzling and, in my opinion, difficult novelists writing in America today—was Catherine Vieilledent, who chose a classic approach in "Mythe et récit dans *Passion,* or 'The Inessential Art of Robert Steiner'" (*RFEA* 43:47–57). As for Maurice Couturier, he seems, as it were, to have specialized in generality, as he contributes a perfectly explicit essay on "La banalisation de la sexualité à l'époque postmoderne" in which, after reading Robert Coover's *Gerald's Party* as the ultimate outcome of a tendency, he clearly regrets that "sexual desire is no longer the foundation if not even the model of all other desires" (*RFEA* 44:49–63). Even more bravely general is "Le réel et la postmodernité" in which, after briefly reviewing Pynchon's *The Crying of Lot 49* and Coover's *Gerald's Party* again, Couturier concludes that the novel now explores the gaps in the real or the lapses in a common discourse still founded on a common representation which, for lack of a better phrase, we call reality.

f. Ethnic Literature With 16 contributions under the generic title *Multilinguisme et multiculturalisme en Amérique du Nord,* and the specific subtitle "Espace: seuils et limites [Space: Thresholds, Limits]," number 15 of the publications of *Annales du C.R.A.A.* is even more lavish than the preceding ones. The contributions are by the same 14 members of the group as in 1988 and 1989, to whom have been added two specialists on Canada. Pierre Spriet contributes the only study which, even though it bears on the question of the frontier as the whole number is supposed to, is applied to a nonliterary subject: "L'Espace américain dans le *Rapport de Lord Durham sur l'Amérique du Nord britannique (1839)*" (pp. 179–92)—a title which might be paraphrased: "The Question of the Proximity of the United States in Lord Durham's 1839 *Report.*" The conclusion is that while Lord Durham was badly mistaken on the future of French Canada, he was right (as history has shown) in recommending a separate entity from both the United States and the British Crown. And Marie-Line Piccione writes briefly about the latest novel by Yves Beauchemin, Québec's other popular writer besides Michel Tremblay ("A la recherche du passé perdu: une lecture de *Juliette Pomerleau* [In Quest of the Lost Past: A Reading of *Juliette Pomerleau*]," pp. 209–15).

As was the case last year, the larger number of contributions (six) covered by this section are devoted to Chicano literature, to which Elyette Andouard-Labarthe contributes an introductory essay, "La frontière: essai de typologie d'un espace littéraire chicano" (pp. 7–21). Andouard-Labarthe has provided a useful rationale in distinguishing between three types of literary works, from the less to the most recurrent: (a) crossing the frontier is impossible; (b) it is possible but it is extremely grievous; (c) cultural fusion is achieved. The four articles that follow are devoted to writers "who mourn interminably for those who die from finding out that the country of their dreams no longer exists." Regardless of ethnic origins, this is the case with Miguel Méndez's *Steelio* (article by Christian Lerat, pp. 23–33), with Reinaldo Arenas's *The Ill-fated Peregrinations of Fray Servando* (Jean Cazemajou, pp. 35–50), with Garibaldi Lapolla's *The Grand Gennaro* (Robert Rougé, pp. 51–61), and with what may well be called a classic of ethnic literature, Scott Momaday's *House Made of Dawn* (Bernadette Rigal-Cellard, pp. 63–78). (It seems relevant to mention here Diane Cousineau's article in English, "Leslie Silko's *Ceremony:* The Spiderweb as Text," in *RFEA* 43:19–31.) Next is the category of those who cross the frontier, but at the cost of extreme grief; such is the case in Rachel Guido de Vries's *Tender Warriors* (Nicole Bensoussan, pp. 91–98), and in Louise Erdrich's *Tracks*, the subject of Elizabeth Béranger's article on pp. 79–90. Béranger's wistful conclusion on Native Americans is that their last refuge lies in writing, because only in writing can the "tracks" of the lost earth be read. Among the many writers whose works illustrate integration, even though this is far from turning America into the promised land, is *Red Ribbon on a White Horse*, by Anzia Yezierska (Ginette Castro, pp. 99–111). The next six articles are clearly meant to avoid the identification of an attitude with an ethnic origin. Jimmy Santiago Baca's collection of poems *Immigrants in Our Own Land* is examined by Yves-Charles Grandjeat (pp. 113–24); Corinne Demass Bliss's novel *The Same River Twice* by Nicole Ollier (pp. 125–42); Nash Candelaria's *Memories of the Alhambra* by Suzanne Durruty (pp. 143–52); and Jean Béranger has chosen to study Helen Barolini's 1974 novel, *Umbertina* (pp. 153–67). Serge Ricard, who had already published two articles on Rolando Hinojosa, writes on *Partners in Crime: A Rafe Buenrostro Mystery* (1985) and concludes wistfully on the necessity of "separating geography from writing." Jean Cazemajou also published a thorough study of "The Search for a Center: The Shamanic Journey of Mediators in Anaya's Trilogy, *Bless Me, Ultima; Heart of Aztlán,* and *Tortuga*" in César A. González-T., *Rudolfo A. Anaya: Focus on Criticism* (La Jolla, Calif.: Lalo Press), pp. 254–73.

An entire 250-page book written by four of the people involved in the CRAA proceedings—Yves-Charles Grandjeat, Elyette Andouard-Labarthe, Christian Lerat, Serge Ricard—*Ecritures hispaniques aux États-Unis: mémoire et mutations* (Publications de l'Université de Provence) was also devoted to Hispanic-American literature. The project consisted of manipulating (rewriting and summarizing, in some cases) the product of several conferences organized by research centers, most of which have published their papers elsewhere. This is the case particularly with the main provider, Jean Béranger's CRAA at the University of Bordeaux III, but also with Geneviève Fabre and CIRNA at the University of Paris VII, with Jean-Pierre Martin and GRENA at the University of Provence, and with Jean-Robert Rougé and CEDRIC at the University of Paris IV. In a general introduction, Grandjeat weaves together as many threads as he can, often quoting the four of them as the square deific of Chicano studies in France. The book is then divided into nine chapters, respectively devoted to "Thousand-Faced Aztlán" (Andouard-Labarthe and Grandjeat), "The Border and National Identity in the Space of Chicano Literature" (Andouard-Labarthe), and then to six writers and their work: Sabine Ulibarrí's *Tierra Amarilla* (Lerat), Ron Arias's *The Road to Tamazunchale* (Lerat), José Antonio Villareal (Ricard), Rolando Hinojosa (Ricard), Alurista's poetry (Andouard-Labarthe), and "Ricardo Sanchéz and Chicano Poetry" (Grandjeat). A last chapter consists of an introduction to *nuyorican* poetry (Grandjeat); it is followed by a 70-title bibliography of works in both English and French.

In *ALS 1989* I overlooked an article written in English by two French colleagues at New Mexico State University, Jacques M. Laroche and Claude J. Fouillade, explicitly entitled "A Socio-Cultural Reading of *Lake Wobegon Days* or Can You Go Home Again to Mid-America?" (*RFEA* 42:427–38). There is now an interest, in the French world of academe as well as in America, in the kind of national success illustrated by Garrison Keillor's hymn to provincial life—were it only because it is unthinkable as a product for export. One might even suggest "The Americanness of *Lake Wobegon*" as a paper topic! However, the trend is to popular literature in general, as shown by a conference organized by Centre de Recherches sur les littératures populaires of the University of Limoges in March 1989. In the proceedings, published as *Le Roman sentimental,* Claire Bruyère contributes "La Place du roman sentimental dans les pratiques culturelles de ses lectrices dans les États-Unis d'aujourdhui" (pp. 303–15). The title is a little heavy because the (serious) author, who has read abundantly and interviewed intensively before launching into this relatively new field (for France), has relied on two kinds of sources: primary—mainly interviews with female readers of these novels, and secondary—Janice Radway's *Reading the Romance,* Carol Thurston's *The Romance Revolution,* and Margaret Ann Jensen's *Love's Sweet Return: The Harlequin Story,* among others. Her conclusion is that "sentimental" fiction has made possible "a quiet progress of feminism."

g. Poetry   The first part of *Americana* 5 was devoted to Walt Whitman, whose *Leaves of Grass* were on the *agrégation* syllabus in 1990. This year's crop on Whitman was reaped by Jeanne-Marie Santraud, who wrote a none-too-new "Introduction to *Leaves of Grass*" (pp. 9–18, in English); by Marc Saporta, who based a thin "Walt Whitman et son temps" (pp. 19–27) on quotations offered in the most traditional translations, when a new and superb (even when it is obviously debatable) translation was given, along with a 20-page introduction, in 1989 by Jacques Darras; by Roger Asselineau, the well-known specialist on the American poet, on "Poetry and Politics" in *Democratic Vistas* (pp. 29–37, in English); and by James E. Miller on "Whitman's Camerados in *Leaves of Grass* (pp. 39–53, in English). Also devoted to Whitman was an article by Claudette Fillard, "Quand l'herbe a des feuilles [When Grass Grows Leaves]," *EA* 43:14–28. With a good deal of sense and insight, the author concentrates on the meaning of the poet's "indefectible attachment to an immutable title." Annalisa Goldoni of the University of Rome also starts from Whitman and moves on to Rich, Plath, Duncan, Olson, and Creely in her "The Poetics of Physicality" (*RFEA* 44:37–48). In the same number, under a telltale title, Gayle Wurst of the University of Fribourg has contributed " 'I've boarded the train there's no getting off': The Body as Metaphor in the Poetry of Sylvia Plath" (pp. 23–35). Jean-Louis

Chevalier, an anglicist, has written "Sur la beauté: étude d'un sonnet de [Edna] St. Vincent Millay" ("La Beauté: Convergences no. 6," *Cahiers de l'Université* [Paul], no. 16, pp. 37–50). The well-known sonnet examined begins, "Euclid alone has looked on Beauty bare." Last in this section, though by no means least since it is extremely rare when a whole book is devoted to an American poet in French (the occasion was perhaps once more the *agrégation* syllabus), comes Marie-Christine Lemardeley-Cunci's 200-page *Adrienne Rich: Cartographies du silence* (Presses universitaires de Lyon). In a note appended to her brief introduction, the author explains why she has translated all the quotations into French. Unfortunately, her normal (if not her only) reader is one who can read English; it is therefore a great pity that nowhere in this book can a quotation in English be found. While a summary of its seven chapters is impossible, this is a study about what it means to be a woman poet. However, one cannot but agree in principle with the statement at the end of her introduction: "To read Adrienne Rich is to be willing to explore unmarked territories run over with contrary movements. A woman invested with a mission, she is after the breaking of reluctances, the filling of gaps, the naming of absences. The way is to make the poem into a place where meaning occurs. And yet what her secret maps offer us is a journey toward silence." To these studies of American poetry should of course be added the final three chapters of *Ecritures hispaniques aux États-Unis: mémoire et mutations* (on Alurista, Ricardo Sanchéz, and *nuyorican* poetry) that were quoted in section f.

h. Valedictory For several reasons which need not be expatiated upon here, this is the last of my three consecutive contributions to *American Literary Scholarship*. Maurice Couturier also served for three years before Marc Chénetier took over for seven: there must be a magic of numbers working in us French Americanists. As I bid farewell to my conjectural American readers, and wish good luck to my equally conjectural successor, I would simply like to repeat two of my chief concerns. The first is that an end should be brought to the process of double publication, which is fast encroaching upon the candidness (or indifference?) of directors and editors on both sides of the Atlantic; they apparently never think of demanding that whatever is contributed to their magazine be unpublished, preferably in *any* language. The second consists in insisting that, especially as the use of an international language (English) tends to make its way into national publications, there is no justification what-

soever in not quoting the original text in a foreign medium for American
literary scholarship.

Université Paris VII

ii Italian Contributions: Massimo Bacigalupo

This is a busy period for American studies in Italy. AISNA, the national
association, has inaugurated a new journal, *RSAJ,* and has been very
active in promoting conferences ("The City as Text" in 1989, "Melville"
in 1990, "Gender" and "William Carlos Williams" in 1991). Three new
or revised histories of American literature have appeared within a few
months. Many books have been devoted to authors and themes, especially by young scholars, whereas their seniors have been usually content
with forewords and afterwords, or collections of essays. So, though
American literature is no longer the myth it was to Europeans until the
1960s, and though openings at the university level are as always scarce,
there is no lack of activity—and talent and scholarship—in the field. In
fact, so many books and articles have been accumulating on my shelves
that parts of what follows will look more like a catalog than a survey.

a. Literary History and Theory   Two histories of American literature
were published in Turin, both of them translations with additions.
Einaudi brought out a new two-volume edition of *Storia della letteratura
americana* by the late Marcus Cunliffe (1922–90), based on the 1986
revision of his *The Literature of the United States* (Penguin). I did the
necessary editorial work and added a few titles to the bibliography. In the
process, I again appreciated Cunliffe's sensible and sympathetic approach, which, though sometimes a little bland, is surely a pleasant
contrast to much doctrinaire criticism. Cunliffe was not out to prove
anything. At the end of his new introduction he did list some of the
claims most often made about American literature. It is only right that
the student should know about the kind of statements that D. H.
Lawrence and many others have produced. Whether there is any but a
subjective truth to them is another matter. Cunliffe also suggested in one
of his additions (chap. 15) that the whole question of the "canon" is
something of a red herring, since authors regarded as canonical in our
century (the "American Renaissance") were largely ignored in their day.
So the debate on the canon is really a debate between two or three

generations of academics, not between the postmodern age and the much-maligned 19th century.

It will be interesting for Italian readers and students to compare Cunliffe's commonsensical approach to the ambitious teamwork of Emory Elliott's *CLHUS,* now available in a handsome three-volume Italian version, *Storia della civiltà letteraria degli Stati Uniti* (Turin: UTET), Volumes 1 and 2 correspond to *CLHUS,* with the addition of a preface by Claudio Gorlier, a very ample bibliography by Gorlier and Stefano Rosso (pp. 1049–1150), and many excellent photographs; volume 3 is a 480-page companion to American literature and civilization, ed. Romano Carlo Cerrone, with alphabetic entries on authors, historical figures, periodicals, cities, states, etc., and a final chronology. The entries are compact but not meager, with ample lists of works of such lesser-known authors as Zona Gale or Christopher Morley. Incidentally, Morley's novel *The Trojan Horse* (1937), translated in 1940 by Cesare Pavese, has been reissued by the original publisher: *Il cavallo di Troia* (Turin: Einaudi, 1991). Thus, despite some blemishes in the translations of the original *CLHUS* essays (and, I suppose, in the essays themselves), one can only be thankful for an excellent publishing and editorial job. Rosso discusses some of the literary-historical background of the *CLHUS* in "Quaderni del Dipartimento di Linguistica" (Bergamo) 6:135–46; I reviewed the enterprise in "Viva le minoranze," *Secolo XIX,* December 27.

Theoretical concerns figure largely in Alessandro Portelli's "Oralità, letteratura e democrazia in America," *Asino d'oro* (2:111–26), an intriguing account of the oral versus the literal in such texts as Irving's "The Legend of Sleepy Hollow," Cable's *The Grandissimes,* and Thoreau's *Walden.* A gathering of structuralist readings of, among others, *The Rise of Silas Lapham* (by Donatella Izzo), *The Wings of the Dove* (by Lida Incollingo), and *The Woman Warrior* (by Carla Mucci) is *Il racconto allo specchio: mise en abyme e tradizione narrativa,* ed. Donatella Izzo (Rome: Nuova Arnica Editrice). Autobiographical writing is the concern of another group of scholars, who have collected their findings in *Identità e scrittura: studi sull'autobiografia nord-americana,* ed. Anna Lucia Accardo et al. (Rome: Bulzoni, 1988). This rich volume includes seven essays in Italian (Igina Tattoni on Thomas Wolfe, Ugo Rubeo on "The Crack-Up," Accardo on slave narratives, Stefania Piccinato on Frederick Douglass, Roberta Mazzanti on Charlotte Perkins Gilman, Paola Zaccaria on

Audre Lorde's *Zami,* Sara Poli on interviewing women writers) and seven essays in English (Paul John Eakin on "veracity" in Mary McCarthy and Lillian Hellman, Maria Ornella Marotti on Mark Twain and "A Typology of Women's Autobiography," Tattoni and Accardo on Sherwood Anderson's *A Story-Teller's Story,* Laura Ferrarotti on anthropologist Oscar Lewis, Accardo on Franklin, Alessandro Portelli on *Coal Miner's Daughter* by Loretta Lynn). Marotti also provides an ample bibliography on American and English autobiography (pp. 235–60).

b. Urban Themes Thirty-four papers given at the 1989 AISNA conference on "The City as Text" (which took place in the beautiful and quite unurban setting of Capo Caccia, Sardinia) are collected in *RSA* 8, a 440-page volume, carefully edited by Angela Vistarchi. There are a few general essays, like "The Modern City as Text and Context" by Thomas Bender, "Case americane" (i.e., American Houses) by Francesca Bisutti, and "City Maps and City Alphabets" by Mario Maffi and Franco Minganti (with a response by William Sharpe), which discusses among others Galway Kinnell, Fay Chiang's poem "Chinatown," Tato Laviera and Nuyorican Poetry, Miguel Piñero, Jerome Charyn, Paul Morissey, Catherine Texier, and Mark Helprin. Other papers provide a capsule literary history of a given city (Morris Dickstein on "New York as a Literary Idea," Lothar Hönnighausen on "Washington, D.C., and the National Myth"). Most articles discuss the conjunction of a given writer or group of writers and one city: chiefly New York (Cristina Giorcelli on *Maggie,* Alberta Fabris on Edith Wharton, Sylvia Notini on *The Tenants,* Gianfranca Balestra on "Poetry of the Subway," Francesco Mulas on the New York Italian-American Novel, Cristina Scatamacchia on the New York Intellectuals), but also Los Angeles (Franco Meli on N. Scott Momaday, Mario Corona on "Slouching Towards L.A."—this last paper published in *Nuovi Annali* (Messina: Facoltà di Magistero) 7 (1989):635–44). There is a good sampling of European cities: the London of Henry James's *In the Cage* (Paola Cabibbo), the "Barcelona, 1936" of Muriel Rukeyser (Gigliola Sacerdoti Mariani), the Venice of Irving, Poe, and Cooper (Rosella Mamoli Zorzi), the Rome of Leslie Fiedler's *The Second Stone* (Guido Fink) and of F. Marion Crawford (Alessandra Contenti), the Naples of Jerre Mangione's *Reunion in Sicily* (Maria Anita Stefanelli). John Winthrop's "City upon a hill" is discussed by editor Vistarchi, Djuna Barnes's "translinguistic city" by Paola Zaccaria, H.D.'s "city as palimpsest" by Marina Camboni, while no less than three scholars confront Thomas Pynchon's nightmare streets: Maria Vittoria D'Amico (the labyrinth theme), Daniela Daniele (*The Crying of Lot 49*), and Alessandra Calanchi (*Gravity's Rainbow*).

Calanchi is also the author of a lively study on the theme of neighbors and neighborhood in American culture, *Vicini e lontani: solitudine e comunicazione nel romanzo americano* (Ravenna: Longo), which, as Guido Fink notes in his foreword, freely moves from John Dos Passos to Alfred Hitchcock, from Marcel Roncayolo's 1978 article "città" (*Enciclopedia Einaudi*) to the ghettos of Henry Roth and Mike Gold, from *Walden* to *Peyton Place* (in fact, given the multifarious contents, an index would have been helpful). After wondering if Calanchi is a literary critic or a sociologist, Fink finally decides that she is working on the "negotiations" of Stephen Greenblatt and his fellow New Historicists. I find this short book serious, accurate, intelligent, and readable.

A few other city-oriented articles should be mentioned, such as the four American contributions to *QDLLSM* 4 (Alessandra Fantoni Costa on Walt Whitman, Luisa Villa on "the metropolis and its subject" in Henry James, Bonalda Stringher on Hart Crane, myself on "modern city and symbolic landscape" in Eliot and Pound); also, Andrea Mariani's "Roma fra surrealismo ed espressionismo" (*Comparatistica* 2:77–97), which touches on Horace Gregory, John Ciardi, and Richard Wilbur, and closes with an account of James Merrill's "Walks in Rome" (which, however, I would not call a "surrealist" poem).

Chicago receives its share of attention in Bruno Cartosio's informative and perceptive reading, *"Chicago: City on the Make* di Nelson Algren: esperienza e memoria della città," *Contesti* 2–3:203–34. The Chicago of Algren's 1951 prose poem is closer, Cartosio tells us, to Baudelaire's Paris, "corrupt but magic," than to T. S. Eliot's "desolate and haunted" London. While Richard Wright's poor lead a life of unrelieved emotional deprivation, Algren, an admirer of Sandburg and Lindsay, feels that "the narrow streets of the tenements seem to breathe more easily, as though closer to actual earth, than do these sinless avenues. Where *Reader's Digest* is a faith and nothing but Sunday morning services can dissuade the hunter one moment from the prey." Cartosio praises Algren's "sardonic humor" (p. 217) and finds it at its best and most economical not in his novels but in the short stories and in *Chicago*. He shows Algren as picking up where the proletarian writers of the 1930s left off, while also "anticipating the Beats by introducing subproletarians and drug addicts" (p. 222). Algren's attitude to Chicago is summed up in a passage of *City on the Make* quoted by Studs Terkel to Cartosio in a 1986 interview: "Once you've come to be part of this particular patch, you'll never love another. Like loving a woman with a broken nose, you may well find lovelier lovelies. But never a lover so real" (p. 214).

c. Other Collections   Several scholars examined D'Annunzio's American and English connections, 50 years after the poet-warrior's death, in conference proceedings gathered in *Gabriele D'Annunzio e la cultura inglese e americana,* ed. Patrizia Nerozzi Bellman (Chieti: Solfanelli). Andrea Mariani, who is always drawing parallels between literature and art, contributes a piece on the painter Romaine Brooks and the lesbian writer and celebrated Paris hostess Natalie C. Barney, who were both friends of D'Annunzio; Sergio Perosa retraces (in English) Henry James's pronounced interest in, and critical pronouncements on, the author of *Il fuoco,* a 1900 novel which shares its central symbol with *The Golden Bowl;* Caterina Ricciardi knowledgeably considers D'Annunzio's reading of Whitman; John Paul Russo and I devote two papers to D'Annunzio's influence on those former fellow-writers and fellow-boxers in Paris, Ernest Hemingway and Ezra Pound. Russo shows that Hemingway had little sympathy for the "hyphen-headed old vulture" (p. 188) he saw getting out of his plane in Venice, whereas Pound thought D'Annunzio a hero, "the only living author who has ever taken a city or held up the diplomatic crapule at the point of machine-guns" (p. 181). But Russo also believes that *Il fuoco* "is a key to *Across the River and Into the Trees*" (p. 193) and devotes several pages to proving it. *Notturno,* another D'Annunzio novel, was much admired by Pound (who quoted it in Canto 2) and was praised by Hemingway in *Across the River* (p. 198). So the disagreement between Ez and Hem does not seem to run very deep—and both in turn follow the lesson of the Master, H.J.

"The Fine Arts as a Guideline in Henry James' Major Phase" is one of 13 articles (three in English) collected by Marilla Battilana in her book *Civiltà di frontiera: saggi e studi sulla letteratura americana, 1789–1989* (Udine: Campanotto). Other subjects are Gothic fiction in England and America, Poe as our contemporary, "America versus Europe: Fenimore Cooper's divided mind," recent American humor, 20th-century poetry of social concern, and Gouverneur Morris, author of the magnificent *Diary of the French Revolution,* from which Battilana quotes some gruesome and bawdy episodes. These quotations from Morris satisfactorily prove her point that it is a scandal that he should be neglected (for example in the *CLHUS*) and out of print. Battilana's approach is always personal, lively, and nonacademic in the sense that she really cares for the writers she discusses. I may disagree with some of her conclusions, but I am never bored, and usually instructed.

Battilana's article on Cooper is also included in *L'esilio romantico: forme di un conflitto,* ed. Joseph Cheyne and Lilla Maria Crisafulli Jones (Adriatica: Bari), a collection of papers on exile and Romanticism, most of them in English, three on American subjects. Alessandra Pinto Surdi discusses early American travelers in Rome, from John Morgan (1764) and Joseph Sansom (1801) to Washington Irving and Peter Irving (1805–07) and James Sloane (1816). John Paul Russo offers a subtle critique of some later literary travelers, "The Harvard Italophiles: Longfellow, Lowell, and Norton" (pp. 303–24), and of the preconceptions they brought with them to Italy as those emerge from their occasionally outraged accounts. Parallels with Ezra Pound and Wallace Stevens are glanced at in my paper on "Wordsworth and the 'Absolute Perspective of Exile'" (pp. 129–46).

d. 17th and 18th Centuries Tommaso Pisanti's *Il Ragno e l'Aquila: Sei/Settecento americano* (Naples: Liguori) offers a condensed and informative literary history of "Puritan origins," Puritan poetry (with a bilingual anthology), and some 18th-century figures. Maria Giulia Fabi inaugurates the first issue of *RSAJ* (1:7–26) with *"The Coquette* or the Ambiguities," which claims that Hannah Foster's 1797 epistolary novel "creates the first female individualist in American literature, Eliza Wharton, but places her within the restrictive and punitive confines of a conventional seduction narrative."

e. 19th Century John Neal, another writer who failed to make it into the *CLHUS* (but who, like Gouverneur Morris, has an entry in the third volume of the Italian edition), is the subject of Francesca Orestano's informative and well-documented book, *Dal neoclassico al classico: John Neal e la coscienza letteraria americana* (Palermo: Istituto di Lingue e Letterature Straniere), which has chapters on Neal's disputed place in the canon, on the poetry (especially "The Battle of Niagara"), the novels (from *Keep Cool,* 1817, to *Rachel Dyer,* 1828), and the criticism—Neal being, according to H. L. Mencken, "the best critic of his time." Tommaso Pisanti stays on safer ground (his title notwithstanding) in *Dalla zattera di Huck: Ottocento letterario americano* (Naples: Liguori), a companion volume to *Il Ragno e l'Aquila,* which collects 11 well-balanced essays on Irving ("between Europe and America"), Cooper, Thoreau, Hawthorne, Poe, Melville ("from the Typees to the Whale"), Whitman, Twain, Norris, Crane, Dickinson, and Emerson. The latter is a reprint of Pisanti's introduction to his selection from *Essays,* First and Second Series ("Nature," "History," "Self-Reliance," "Love," "The Poet," "Experience," "Gifts," "Politics"), *Natura e altri saggi* (Milan: Rizzoli)—a title which may be just a little misleading, for the volume does not contain the 1836 *Nature,* but the later essay of that name.

Edgar Allan Poe's 181st birthday signaled a notable flurry of activity. Besides the revised reprint of Carlo Izzo's collected edition (see *ALS* 1989, p. 425), there was a new annotated translation of *Pym* by Roberto Cagliero, *Il racconto di Arthur Gordon Pym* (Milan: Garzanti), with a 50-page introduction by Francesco Binni. The latter is a booklet in itself, offering a critical biography of Poe and many notable and sophisticated insights under such headings as (I translate) "the concentrated universe of the tale," "typological differentiation," "the politics of the subjects," "a discourse on the world," "mystification and illegibility," "a theory against itself," "the slavery of writing," "publish or perish," "underwriting the I," "Poe and Pym: how to write one's own name." It is noteworthy that an inexpensive paperback edition should contain some of the most advanced critical work that has been done on Poe in this country. (Another foreword that should receive mention, even if belatedly, is by Nadia Fusini to a Poe collection called *Stravaganze* [Rome: Lucarini, 1987].) Gianfranca Balestra provides in her compact study *Geometrie visionarie: composizione e decomposizione in Edgar Allan Poe* (Milan: Unicopli) a balanced survey of Poe's reputation, informative chapters on several themes (voices, "the enigma of the face and the absence of the body," the fantastic in "The Black Cat" and "Metzergentein"), and a bibliography. Paola Zaccaria analyzes the concept of repetition (with reference to Kierkegaard, Nietzsche, Freud, Lacan, Deleuze, Derrida, Jakobson, Genette, Poulet, Blanchot, etc.) in "Silence—A Fable" (*RSAJ* 1:27–43): "Here one is told of the unsayability of the sayable, here one is told of the tragic and comic impossibility to awaken the superficial, to give voice to the profound" (p. 41). By the way, I was able to lay my hands on Giorgio Ghidetti's mysterious *Poe, l'eresia di un americano maledetto* (see *ALS* 1989, p. 428), which turned out to be a layman's passionate reading of the author who, Ghidetti says, "chose him" as his reader, and also includes (the jacket claims) "the most complete bibliography on E. A. Poe," running to no less than 60 pages.

As there are neglected authors, so there are neglected works. Daniela and Guido Fink rescue from relative oblivion Nathaniel Hawthorne's "Legends of the Province House" in a compact and attractive bilingual booklet, *Leggende del Palazzo del Governatore* (Venice: Marsilio). In his exhaustive and voluble preface, Guido confesses that he himself in his 1978 study of narrative techniques, *I testimoni dell'immaginario,* has been culpably silent about these four minor Hawthorne gems. He is in good company, with F. O. Matthiessen, Yvor Winters, F. C. Crews, and Leslie Fiedler. However, the "Legends" did not escape the eagle eye of the best reader Hawthorne ever had, Henry James, who gives an admiring and detailed account of them in his *Hawthorne.* This study has been translated at long last with much care by Luisa Villa (Genoa: Marietti), and one reviewer went so far as to call it "perhaps the best book ever written about American literature" ("Uniti dalle streghe," *Unità,* December 28). Angela Giannitrapani, *Martha's Vineyard e i suoi cimiteri* (Viterbo: Università della Tuscia), offers a careful and passionate defense of an even more obscure Hawthorne sketch, "Martha's Vineyard" (1836, reprint in Arlin Turner's *Hawthorne as Editor,* 1941), investigating its ties to "Chippings with a Chisel" as well as to the opening scene of *The Scarlet Letter.* The pamphlet is to be reprinted in a forthcoming second edition of Giannitrapani's *Pantheon dell'Ottocento americano* (1979).

Ruggero Bianchi's uniform edition of Herman Melville's fiction has reached volume 5, *Pierre o le ambiguità, Israel Potter* (Milan: Mursia), skipping volume 4 (*Moby-Dick*) for the interim. Bianchi provides as usual an extensive introduction, in which he first reconstructs the novels' genesis and critical reception (pp. xi–xxvii) and then offers two critical essays, "Exit Romeo, Enter Hamlet" (pp. xxviii–liv)—a title referring to the heavy change in Pierre's fortunes, and "Ancora una volta, con sentimento" (i.e., "Once More with Feeling," pp. ll–lxvi), about Israel in Egypt and Potter's Fields. The new and welcome translations are by Bianchi (*Pierre*) and Floria Conta (*Israel Potter*). Both novels had been translated only once before, in the 1940s, unlike that other tale of a Potter's Field, "The Encantadas," which has always attracted European readers because of its dark humor and elaborate pictorial effects, and has had no less than three Italian translations (1946, 1952, 1954). To these I added a new one, *Encantadas* (Florence: Casa Usher), with ampler notes than heretofore, a discussion of previous criticism (pp. 112–17), and an interpretation in the guise of an afterword (pp. 81–111). I have heard that this translation was serialized by a newspaper in Sardinia—perhaps the story's first periodical appearance since *Putnam's*. I also provided a new translation (the sixth, if my count is correct) of "Bartleby" (Milan: Mondadori) as part of a series of fantastic tales supposedly edited by Jorge Luis Borges, with prefaces by the phantom editor. That Borges really wrote these prefaces is doubtful, though he signed them. They contain certain very curious statements, such as this one in the preface to *Bartleby lo scrivano:* "[Melville] finished his college education at Harvard and Yale" (p. 7). With which compare *Moby-Dick,* chap. 24, "A whaleship was my Yale College and my Harvard." Was Borges, author of "The Aleph," pulling our leg, or just nodding? Another sensitive reading of "The Encantadas" is Vito Amoruso, "Verso il silenzio," *Contesti* 2–3:185–201.

Walt Whitman has become something of a popular success with young people since the furor over Peter Weir's slick tearjerker, *The Dead Poets Society,* where "O Captain, My Captain" was featured prominently. A new selection of the poems, shrewdly titled *O capitano mio capitano,* translated with some felicity by Antonio Troiano (Milan: Crocetti), and including "When Lilacs Last," was in its third printing by spring 1991; other translations appeared here and there, such as one (*Poesia* 29:22) in which I noticed with amusement that "old maid" ("Song of Myself," 7) was rendered as "anziana vergine" (i.e., "aged virgin"). On the critical front, Marina Camboni contributed an introductory pamphlet, *Il corpo dell'America:* Leaves of Grass *1855* (Palermo: Istituto di Lingue e Letterature Straniere), which also stressed Whitman's contemporaneity and relevance to the struggle of "excluded subjects (ex-colonial people, women, ethnics)" (p. 11).

A new translation of *The Adventures of Tom Sawyer,* by Vincenzo Mantovani, was published by Garzanti of Milan, with a foreword on "memory and idyll" and a note on sources (pp. xxv–xxxiii) by Marisa Bulgheroni. The same praiseworthy Garzanti paperback series, which is called Grandi Libri, offered a new translation, also by Mantovani, of Henry James's somewhat bitter idyll, *Washington Square,* with a rich preface by Franco Cordelli. In *The Better Sort* (1903), James published a story, "The Papers," which is perhaps even less known than "Legends of the Province House," and which Donatella Izzo, a subtle exegete, has retrieved and translated for a small publisher: *I giornali* (Macerata:

Liberilibri); she also wrote the illuminating preface, where she says: "The 'loss of the aura,' the deconsecration of the role of the intellectual and the artist in modern civilization, is the common condition in which the characters of the story move" (p. xv). Another out-of-the-way James story is found by Izzo to say much more than meets the eye in her interesting article " 'Rose-Agathe': Henry James e la donna-oggetto," *Merope* (Chieti) 1 (1989):101–20. Izzo makes good use of Griselda Pollock's *Vision and Difference* (1988) and W. J. T. Mitchell's *Iconology* (1986), and she shows the story to touch on fetishism and the view of woman as object, not "she" but "it"—which is "ce dont ['Rose-Agathe'] parle sans le dire" (Izzo quoting Pierre Machery, *Pour une théorie de la production littéraire* [1980]). I appreciate the fact that Izzo does not drop names but uses her theoretical background to come up with observations of great relevance to the text under consideration. In another well-argued paper, "*Daisy Miller* e il discorso dell'ideologia" (*RSAJ* 1:45–68), Izzo points to a similar moral in the Master's one best-seller: a resistance to encroachment and reification. Graziella Pagliano, a literary sociologist, surveys the long gallery of portraits in James's fiction in "Il gioco pericoloso: Henry James e il ritratto" (*LAmer* 33–34 [1986]:71–91), a motif which she finds "indicates the autonomy of the work of art." Vittoria Intonti also uses painting as a key to James's method and style in "Rappresentazione e crisi della rappresentazione: *The Sacred Fount*," in Clotilde de Stasio et al., eds., *La rappresentazione verbale e iconica: valori estetici e funzionali* (Milan: Guerini), pp. 139–51.

Another neglected figure will provide a suitable tail to this section. Gordon Poole edited *Il magnifico Crawford* (Naples: I.U.O.), a collection of papers in Italian and English "distributed exclusively in the U.S.A. by The F. Marion Crawford Society" of Nashville, Tenn. Some of the contributions are of high quality, like Carlo Pagetti on Crawford's theory of the novel and *In the Palace of the Kings* (1903), Alessandra Contenti on "Crawford and Magic," Gianfranco Corsini on the novelist's popularity, Barbara Arnett Melchiori on *The Princess Casamassima* and *Marzio's Crucifix* (1887). Gore Vidal comments wittily and suggestively on "The Political Novel from Darius the Great to President Chester Arthur" (pp. 37–42), noting that he and Crawford, besides having both chosen to live in the same part of Italy, and having some common New York society background, "are often drawn to the same themes. In *Creation* I deal with Zoroaster and the court of the Great King Darius. In *Zoroaster* Crawford does the same. I will not make Plutarchan comparisons, as graduate students must not be deprived of their discoveries" (p. 38). He goes on with some astute observations on Crawford and James: "By and large, the great writers, though they may themselves enjoy a vast reader-ship like George Eliot, do not pay much attention to their humble confreres, the professional story-tellers." But James's early rage at Craw-ford's success (he later became a friend and visited him in Sorrento) offers a rare opportunity to see James "losing, for an instant, his nerve. If no one wants the novel to be high art, why is he wasting his life?" (p. 41). *Il magnifico Crawford* has several misprints, but these are amply compen-sated by a magnificent set of rare photographs, collected by Antonino De Angelis and exhibited in 1988 in Crawford's splendid Sorrento villa, with the gracious permission of the nuns who now live there.

f. 20th-Century Prose   Gordon Poole turns his attention from Sorrento to a tougher scene in "The Drunken Scheherazade: Self-Reflection in Jack London's *The Road, Martin Eden* and *John Barleycorn*" (*RSAJ* 1:69–80), an informative paper about the connection of drinking and writing in London's life and work. London said that "Realism constitutes the only goods one can exchange at the kitchen door for grub"—or booze—but there his allegiance to such "figments" as "Love, socialism, the PEOPLE" appears to end, and Poole shows how he worked out an opposition between life-writing-illusion and death-drinking-truth. For, as London wrote, "The so-called truths of life aren't true. They are the vital lies by which life lives, and John Barleycorn gives them the lie." Social concern is also one of the themes of a 1907 novel by Edith Wharton that has found few admirers. Maria Novella Mercuri devotes herself to its rescue, The Fruit of the Tree *e la narrativa di Edith Wharton* (Salerno: Edisud), a scrupulous study which applies with thesislike thoroughness Gérard Genette's theories to Wharton's "narrative rhet-oric," "complex and subtle thematic structure," and "convincing por-trayal of character" (to quote the titles of some chapters). There is a final bibliography, from which we learn that 17 translations of Wharton have appeared in Italy, five of *Ethan Frome*.

Gertrude Stein has fared even better than Wharton, though probably reaching a more specialized public, with 15 translations between 1938 and 1990. These are listed in the bibliography of *Conferenze americane,* ed. Caterina Ricciardi and Grazia Trabattoni (Rome: Lucarini), a translation of "Composition as Explanation" (1926) and of five of the six original *Lectures in America* (1935). In their prefaces the editors comment in detail on the playful and misleading syntax of Stein's "explanations" and on the difficult choices a translator must face. Ricciardi also unearthed, translated, and annotated an apparently forgotten Djuna Barnes story, "The Diary of a Dangerous Child," which appeared in *Vanity Fair*, July 1922: "Il diario di una bambina pericolosa," *Malavoglia* (Viterbo) 5:1–3.

During a 1948 visit to Cortina, Ernest Hemingway told his translator, Fernanda Pivano, that the main effort of his generation had been to escape from the influence of Sherwood Anderson and Gertrude Stein. He never really freed himself from Stein's parataxis and repetitions, says Pivano in the biographical introduction to her handsome edition of the complete short stories, *Tutti i racconti* (Milan: Mondadori), tr. Vincenzo Mantovani, Ettore Capriolo, Bruno Oddera, with a careful bibliography by Rosella Mamoli Zorzi. The Hemingway-Steinbeck relationship is one of the subjects touched on in Giuseppe Lombardo's *Ombre sui pascoli del cielo: utopia e realtà nei romanzi di John Steinbeck* (Rome: Herder), a persuasive and admiring study of *East of Eden, To a God Unknown, In Dubious Battle, Of Mice and Men,* and *The Grapes of Wrath*—in that order, because Lombardo sees *East of Eden* as "the goal of Steinbeck's artistic engagement in the '30s and '40s." Lombardo also takes a look at the "old polemics" on Steinbeck's status and provides a mine of bibliographical information, largely in the footnotes, without allowing his thorough documentation to encroach on his well-developed argument. Franco Meli's "Letteratura e/o biologia? *The Log from the Sea of Cortez* di John Steinbeck," *Lingua e letteratura* 14–15:25–40, agrees with Guido Fink (in the introduction to the 1983 Italian translation) that Steinbeck's book of travel and natural observation is "a true key-text to his poetics," and goes on to some detailed commentary.

Donatella Breschi in *Ultime voci dal silenzio: J. D. Salinger dopo il giovane Holden,* with a preface by Gaetano Prampolini (Florence: Atheneum), applies Genette's narratology to account for what is going on in Salinger's stories of the Glass family and reads them as progressing toward a self-conscious (postmodern) narration ending in silence. Breschi's study is commendable for clarity, elegance, and concision. In "I giochi del giovane Holden" (*LAmer* 33–34 [1986]:123–46), Maria Anita Stefanelli offers a suggestive account of *The Catcher in the Rye* in the light of game theory and finds that at the end of the novel "the condition of Holden . . . is similar to the condition of Christ who disappears from the world. The Word incarnate dies on the Cross and ceases to speak."

Mario Materassi thoughtfully reviews a number of recent books of short stories in "Racconto d'annata, D.O.C." (*Lingua e letteratura* 12 [1989]:130–38). (By the way, this handsome biannual literary journal, sponsored by I.U.L.M., Milan 20143, is sent free on request to scholars and libraries.) Materassi writes appreciatively of Hemingway's 21 later stories, dismisses Alice Walker for her "profound dishonesty of representation," provides admiring critical notes on Grace Paley and her "sense of joyous participation," and finds Raymond Carver good in small quantities. "His limit is never to dare more than a little, never to come out of the narrative world he has invented. . . . His limit is writing to a formula. As the great Ernest knew only too well." Michele Balice is far less cautious, to the point of being uncritical ("Carver is often considered the best heir of the great authors of American literature"), in his otherwise careful note, "Realtà e scrittura in Raymond Carver" (*Paragone* 486: 103–07). Roberto Cagliero, "Robert Coover e il Watergate del romanzo storico" (*Paragone* 482:110–12), comments perceptively on Coover's *Whatever Happened to Gloomy Gus,* which appeared in Italy as *Un campione in tutte le arti* (Parma: Guanda). In a longer article, "The Bonfire of the Vanities di Tom Wolfe. Il grande romanzo realista?" (*Culture* [Univ. Milano] 4:161–74), Maria Cristina Paganoni shows convincingly that Wolfe is not a realist but a satirist, and that his novel is a "merciless caricature . . . of the ridiculous weaknesses of the individual as social animal and of the limits of so-called civilized society." Franco La Polla forcefully puts the case for Richard Brautigan, more poet than satirist, in a review article (*Lingua e letteratura* 14–15: 262–65).

David Mamet, *Teatro II: Perversioni sessuali a Chicago, Lakeboat,* tr. Rossella Bernascone (Genoa: Costa & Nolan, 1989), has a polemic preface by Guido Almansi, who defends Mamet from Jonathan Lieverson's strictures (*NYRB,* July 21, 1988), and even finds an important religious component in Mamet's plays. The writer, singer, and performer Laurie Anderson is the subject of a perceptive and innovative analysis by Daniela Daniele, " 'Il corpo umano diventa paesaggio': corpi elettronici e paesaggi artificiali nella performance multimediale di Laurie Anderson" (*Nuova Corrente* 105:75–99), which draws parallels with Thomas Pynchon, John Barth, James Graham Ballard, William S. Burroughs, and Walter Benjamin. The latter is quoted by Anderson in her album *Strange Angels* (1989): "History is a pile of debris / And the angel wants to go back and fix things. . . . But there is a storm blowing from Paradise / And the storm keeps blowing the angel / Backwards into the future."

g. Ethnic Literature   The debris of history weighs heavily on the black poets discussed in Ugo Rubeo's major study, *L'uomo visibile: La poesia afroamericana del Novecento* (Rome: Bulzoni). Rubeo takes "visibility" as his guiding theme. In his first chapter, he outlines the emergence of black culture "out of the shadow," and he goes on to devote a chapter each to Gwendolyn Brooks ("Feminine visibility"), Jones-Baraka ("Do I contradict myself?"), and Etheridge Knight ("An escape in full day"). Chapter 5 considers the "new models of visibility" of the 1970s (Don L. Lee, Mari Evans, Nikki Giovanni, Sonia Sanchez, Audre Lorde, Ishmael Reed, and others) and closes with Michael Harper's "ripeness": "The dark interior / of this book I write of the Shadow." Rubeo's well-balanced study also includes an ample bibliography (pp. 251–85).

Franca Bacchiega provides generous samplings of 20 Chicano poets, from Alurista to Bernice Zamora, in *Sotto il Quinto Sole: antologia di poeti chicani* (Florence: Passigli), and suggests that one of their attractions is the sense of community they evoke. Franco Meli mounts a general argument for and about American Indian poetry in his article " 'We are the land': la poesia indiana americana contemporanea" (*Lingua e letteratura* 13 [1989]:68–80). Meli uses quotations from N. Scott Momaday, Simon J. Ortiz, James Welch, and Leslie Silko to indicate main themes (orality, space, commitment, home, organism, "coyote" as symbol of pan-Indianism) and concludes that "the Indian voice is indispensable." This is very much the theme of Laura Coltelli's excellent collection of 10 interviews, *Winged Words: American Indian Writers Speak* (Nebraska), which allows us to hear the thoughtful voices of 11 notable artists, from Paula Gunn Allen and Louise Erdrich to Gerald Vizenor and James Welch. "I write," says Simon Ortiz, "about universal things. What else could I write about? I am a human being. I write about the same things that Robert Browning or Shelley or Shakespeare did, maybe not in the same way. Everything changes all the time" (p. 116). Gerald Vizenor, the subject of the longest of these interviews, writes in the postmodern mode about tricksters, whom he sees as both disruptive and compassionate: "I'd like to imagine myself moving through certain contradictions and conflicts with good humor and maybe a lesson here and there and slipping past it without being damaged by it" (p. 164). Fedora Giordano offers a competent summary of his writings in "Gerald Vizenor, trickster postmoderno" (*Merope* 1 [1989]:159–71). Giordano also edited an issue (4, ii) of *ERNAS* devoted to Italian contributions, including careful readings of Vizenor's *Wordarrows* (1978) by Maria Vittoria D'Amico (pp. 9–14) and of Paula Gunn Allen's *The Woman Who Owned the Shadows* (1983) by Giordano (pp. 15–20). The issue offers a remarkable thematic survey by Elémire Zolla, "American Indian Literature from 1970 to 1990: The Redemptive Mountain" (pp. 3–8).

The Jewish-American literary event of the year was surely the publication of Henry Roth's *Alla mercé di una brutale corrente* (Milan: Garzanti), a translation by Mario Materassi of the first 100 pages of Roth's unpublished work-in-progress, *Mercy of a Rude Stream,* of which more than 3,000 pages are known to be extant. It is highly unusual for a work to appear in translation when the original has not been published. In this way, Henry Roth wants to keep his hands free for revision; in fact, he intends *Mercy* for posthumous publication so as not to worry about coincidences and departures between fact and fiction. Rules often have exceptions, and Roth has authorized publication of pages 138–49 of his manuscript in the first issue of *RSAJ* (1:113–19), with a foreword (pp. 109–12) in which his friend and editor Materassi explains the facts of this literary thriller. In the fragment, as in *Alla mercè,* we meet an immigrant family, the Stigmans, reminiscent of the Schearls of *Call It Sleep,* but the mythical method and Joycean technique of the novel have been replaced by a more direct and nuanced description, possibly closer to its autobiographical sources. So, for example, Chaim Stigman, though a menacing father like Albert Schearl, is much frailer (as a trolley car conductor, he suffers from diarrhea), and it is his wife who protects him. In Italy, Roth is better-known than at home, chiefly because of Materassi's efforts, and *Alla mercè* was widely and respectfully reviewed, among others by Irene Bignardi (*Repubblica,* March 10), Guido Fink (*Messaggero,* March 25), Benedetta Bini and Alessandro Portelli (*Manifesto,* March 30), and Giordano De Biasio (*Indice,* June); some reviewers noticed a lack of intensity in comparison to Roth's novel. Another moving fragment, "La prima candela per Muriel," related to the death of Roth's wife, appeared in *Panorama* for July 15 ("Threnody of the Prose Writer" is the original title).

Memory and tradition in Jewish-American culture is the subject of a handy collection of 21 essays ed. Guido Fink and Gabriella Morisco, *Memoria e tradizione nella cultura ebraico-americana* (Bologna: CLUEB). There are contributions on Harold Bloom's gnosticism (Giovanna Franci) and Geoffrey Hartman's deconstruction (Vita Fortunati), on Abraham Cahan's American beginnings (Elena Ginzburg Migliorino) and *The Imported Bridegroom* (Marina Orsini), on Ludwig Lewisohn and Harvey Swados (Roberto Birindelli), on *Herzog* (Gigliola Sacerdoti Mariani) and *More Die of Heartbreak* (Alessandra Calanchi), on *The Fixer* with a 1974 interview with Bernard Malamud (Gabriella Morisco), on the genre of the memoir as deployed by Mary McCarthy and Isaac Bashevis Singer (Alessandra Contenti), on "Jewish identity in American and German novels" (Regine Rosenthal), on "memory and desire in Philip Roth" (Giordano De Biasio), on Raymond Federman's *The Voice in the Closet* (Maria Vittoria D'Amico), on Martin Sherman (Mario Calimani), and on Art Spiegelman's *Maud* comics (Franco Minganti). After so much enlightening talk of memory, Fink reminds us in his afterword of the uses and abuses of oblivion: "The more recent and significant literary voices, not only Jewish nor only American, express, so far as I can see, a great and insatiable desire for oblivion" (p. 388). As examples of this process, Fink cites Vonnegut's *Galápagos,* Malamud's *God's Grace,* and Henry Roth's *Mercy.*

"The book of laughter and oblivion" is Luciana Pirè's caption for *The Day of the Locust* in her fine study *Le favole infrante di Nathanael West* (Bari: Adriatica). She writes that West's Hollywood story is "a great modern novel, because it closes in a cemetery of idleness and barbarism the adventure of looking and all possible escapes of imagination and salvation" (p. 181). Pirè devotes a chapter to each of West's "inverted fables" (his own term), discussing them with notable penetration, much seriousness, and an extraordinary richness of reference to literal and cultural sources. For example, the notes to chap. 1 refer us to Lillian Hellman, Malcolm Cowley, Jean-Paul Sartre, Edmund Wilson, Alfred Kazin, Giacomo Debenedetti, Paul Valéry, Theodor W. Adorno, Marc Shell, Max Weber, James Russell Lowell (why is *A Fable for Critics* called "a poem in prose"?), Joris-Karl Huysmans, Emile Cioran, and many others. This apparatus is far from cumbersome, for Pirè writes with consistent elegance and even clarity, though her somewhat oracular historicism will be of use only to those who are already familiar with West's writings. Pirè brings out West's pessimism, a pessimism which she clearly shares. His Hollywood is "a total theatre where the will of the subject has been dismissed neither secretly nor discretely" (p. 199). Homer Simpson, "true and legitimate hero" of *The Day of the Locust,* "awaits, in the absence of words and desires, the dissolution of the last residues of the human"; he is "like a little man out of Chagall blundering into a Buster Keaton movie" (p. 213). Pirè's compact volume (the first of a

new series from Bari called Perspectives) is one of the most impressive I
have read this year.

A somewhat different encounter between a Jewish-American writer
and an Italian bluestocking is divertingly narrated by Letizia Ciotti
Miller, translator of *Herzog*, in "My Name Is Saul Bellow" (*Paragone*
486:50–60). On February 18, 1970, a gray morning in Rome, as she was
trying to recover from all kinds of personal and historical hangovers,
Miller received a call from someone who announced, "My name is Saul
Bellow." For a while she disbelieved the assertion, but finally had to
accept that this was her author calling to invite her to meet him at the
Caffè Greco and even offering to pay her taxi fare. In their conversation,
Miller told Bellow that "American Jews, unlike WASPS, have a feeling
for death, as we have in Italy, though unconsciously" (p. 56), and that
this accounts for humor and expansiveness in Chicago as well as in
Naples. "Who gives a damn for self-control!" She also detailed the bad
life of a translator: "It is all a market of haste and small money—not a lira
in advance, late payments, killing deadlines—and arbitrary unpardon-
able rewriting by the editors. He was speechless" (p. 58).

Twenty years later things have not changed much. Masolino d'Amico
explained good-humoredly in *La Stampa*, April 1, 1989, that in translating *A Theft* he had to work on Bellow's rough draft, for the book was still
unpublished in the United States, and this did not make things any
easier. Daniela Fink's fine translation of selected stories of Eudora Welty,
Non è posto per te, amore mio (Milan: Leonardo), was nearly spoiled by an
officious editor's wrongheaded emendations, which were not communicated to the translator until it was too late to correct any but the most
glaring misreadings. In such cases, a phone call from Saul Bellow can go
a long way in consoling us, the much-suffering laborers of the scholarly
and publishing industry.

h. 20th-Century Poetry Francesco Rognoni uses Henderson's reflection that "The world is a mind. Travel is mental travel" as a starting point
for his excellent essay "Immagini della realtà e sacrificio nella poesia di
Wallace Stevens e T. S. Eliot" (*Confronto letterario* 14:365–89), which is
more about Stevens than Eliot ("If Eliot is the Donne, Stevens is the
Spenser of our time"), and offers persuasive readings of "The Plain Sense
of Things" (compared with *Burnt Norton* I), "Mrs. Alfred Uruguay," and
especially "An Ordinary Evening in New Haven" (pp. 377–87). Rognoni

suggests that in canto 6 of this poem "infant A" is Stevens and "other free romantic spirits," while "twisted, stooping, polymatic Z" is somebody like Eliot and R. P. Blackmur, who, "as the clock strikes midnight . . . step into their nightshirts and kneel down to say their prayers" (*Letters,* p. 624). Rognoni has a fruitful imagination: he imagines Stevens reading *Henderson the Rain King,* or even composing *The Cocktail Party*—in which case, he assures us, Lavinia's final line would be not "Oh, I'm glad. It's begun," but, "It's beginning." He wonders in the end if "the absence of pain (or anyhow the resistance to its representation) is the severest limit or the major triumph of Stevens's art," and he suggests that the answer depends on "the kind of reader, and the circumstances of reading" (p. 384). So, impalpable Stevens gets an impalpable response. In *Ritmica* (Univ. Rome) 2–3:132–43, Salvatore Marrano writes somewhat more laboriously but nevertheless helpfully of "Stevens o dell'armonia. Ragioni poetiche e procedure formali in *Harmonium,*" analyzing "The Curtains in the House of the Metaphysician" (the first line of which is not, as Marrano has it, a hexameter), "The Wind Shifts," "Bantams in Pine-Woods," and "The Death of a Soldier," "one of the most beautiful war poems (or rather peace poems) ever written in English" (p. 141). The article is followed by translations of seven short texts. Some Stevens translations, by Vittorio Lingiardi, also appear in *Poesia* 36 (1991):2–11, with an interview about Stevens, conducted by Lingiardi, with depth psychologist James Hillman.

A gallant attempt to salvage from neglect Amy Lowell is *Poesie* (Turin: Einaudi), a collection of 57 poems ed. and tr. Barbara Lanati. In her introduction (pp. v–xxxviii), Lanati places Lowell in the context of the avant-garde. But (as I pointed out in my review in *Unità,* October 26) when we turn to poems like "After Hearing a Waltz by Bartok" (1914), we may wonder if this is justified ("But why did I kill him? Why? Why? / In the small gilded room near the stair? / My ears rack and throb with his cry, / And his eyes goggle under his hair"). Lanati's anthology is unusual because, as Francesco Rognoni noted in a careful review (*Indice,* February 1991), it is arranged not chronologically but in four thematic sections. This makes it difficult to follow the poet's development, if any. Lanati approaches Lowell as some feminist critics have approached Dickinson, i.e., as a practitioner of light, womanist writing, to be understood quite differently from the male product. But whereas Dickinson stands up under nearly any treatment, Lowell's weaknesses are all too easily appar-

ent. Hence, the comment of a poet I know: "Ezra Pound was right."
Another poet, Franco Loi, was notably more generous in his review in
Sole-24 Ore, May 26, 1991.

Ezra Pound's version of the avant-garde, and its connection with
Continental precedents, is studied in illuminating detail by Roberto
Baronti Marchiò, *Il futurismo in Inghilterra: tra avanguardia e classicismo*
(Rome: Bulzoni). The Vorticists usually denied any debt to Marinetti
and his circle, while taking over many ideas and methods, and Marchiò's
well-documented study redresses the balance, while providing excellent
analyses of the poetics and poems of Pound's Vorticist period (and of
Wyndham Lewis and T. E. Hulme).

When Pound came to Italy in the 1920s, he spent much time in
Romagna researching his Malatesta Cantos. Luca Cesari, a young poet
from Pesaro, has followed in his footsteps and gathered some of the
results in *"Passava per Rimini in giugni . . . ": Ezra Pound e il Montefeltro*
(Urbino: Editrice Montefeltro). The quoted phrase ("I passed through
Rimini in June") is from a 1922 letter to a Rimini librarian, asking for
Malatesta materials (p. 103). Cesari also organized a Poundian event in
Rimini, Cesena, and Pennabilli—where "the road lead[s] under the cliff"
(Canto 8). A postcard of the Valmarecchia (with "the mud-stretch full of
cobbles") was printed for the occasion. The magnificent Biblioteca
Malatestiana of Cesena is the only library that received a complimentary
copy of *Cantos I–XVI* (1925), and the library is planning to reprint it. So
Cesari's gathering of documents is the first of a series that will help us
read the early *Cantos.*

The proceedings of a 1985 symposium held at the Queen's University,
Belfast, are collected in *Ezra Pound Centenary,* ed. Ghanshyam Singh
(Udine: Campanotto), a thoroughly bilingual volume with notable contributions by critics such as Singh and Walter Baumann ("Ezra Pound
and Ireland"), and by poet-critics C. H. Sisson, Mario Luzi, and Giovanni Raboni. Singh is professor of Italian at Belfast, so the volume is
quite Poundian in being an Irish-Italian-English-American-Indian venture. Poundians will also be interested in Giovanni Giudici's dramatization of Dante, *Il Paradiso: Perché mi vinse il lume d'esta stella* (Genoa:
Costa & Nolan, 1991), produced in Bari on March 27, 1991, which in
scene 3 introduces Pound on stage as an expert on Cunizza da Romano's
peccadillos: "One moment! Here is an important witness: the poet Ezra
Pound! Do you have something to say?" (p. 31). And Pound, "a tall

character, very much the *artiste* in dress," obliges with a passage from Canto 29.

The genesis of some later Cantos, and of H.D.'s *End to Torment,* is scrutinized in my article "Ezra Pound e H.D. nel 1956–59: un romanzo epistolare tardomoderno" (*Nuova Corrente* 106:185–216). I review the materials that went into H.D.'s fine memoir and quote (in Italian) passages omitted from the printed version. An extremely interesting correspondence (also quoted) followed when late in 1959 a nearly broken Pound read *Torment* and attempted in some of his last and most revealing letters to defend himself from H.D.'s implicit criticisms ("I did not put anyone into Buchenwald"). The letters are in turn a workshop for *Drafts & Fragments:* "Marvelous, marvelous evocation—That you should have remembered them in such detail—The beauty of your mind thru it all, permeating, the marvelous retention of visual detail—& abundance—& innocence, blessed innocence" (p. 215). The article attempts to show late-modernist writing at its best as it is made, in the inescapable confusion (or vortex) of poetry and life.

Marina Camboni continues her studies of H.D. in two articles. "Il tempo in una stanza. *Bid Me to Live* di H.D." (*RSAJ* 1:81–98), a discussion of the 1960 autobiographical novel, begins with the following assertion: "Time ticks as a clock in *Bid Me to Live (A Madrigal),* a novel on time, like *Mrs. Dalloway* and *The Magic Mountain,* like *A la recherche du temps perdu.* A novel on time because it narrates a time, an epoch is made. A novel on time because time in its pure state is the object of narration." "Le parole sono farfalle: mitopoiesi verbale nella poesia di H.D." (*Galleria* 40:530–46) discusses word-play in *Hermetic Definition* and *Trilogy,* making good use of unpublished papers: "For H.D. the divine is the word and harbors in the least letter of the language. To the letter she returns, making of it the germinating nucleus of her rewriting of names and myths."

Laura Barile devotes chapter 2 of *Adorate mie larve: Montale e la poesia anglosassone* (Bologna: Il Mulino) to the sense of uncanny guardianship in some of Eugenio Montale's later poems and in *The Cocktail Party* (which the Italian Nobel laureate greatly admired: "The second act is the greatest poetry that modern theater has offered since the times of Chekhov"). Chapter 3 relates the autobiographical verse of Montale's old age to Robert Lowell's final volumes—a less productive comparison, though Barile is always a careful writer and is well worth reading. The

Eliot article also appears in an issue (103) of *Nuova Corrente* devoted to
"T. S. Eliot and Italy," ed. Stefano Verdino. Most of the articles discuss
Eliot's influence on several major Italian poets such as Attilio Bertolucci,
Mario Luzi, and the experimental Novissimi. Ghanshyam Singh contributes an account of Eliot's reading of Dante (pp. 157–74), I write
(pp. 141–56) about Eliot's bad luck with his official Italian translators
who have yet discovered that "Think now" in "Gerontion" is an imperative and that the "dingy shades" of "Preludes" are screens and not
shadows, while Andrea Carosso studies rather intricately the "crisis of
theory in T. S. Eliot's philosophical writings" (pp. 175–99), having had
access to unpublished papers.

Gianfranca Balestra dedicates an article, "Macchine per la comunicazione, macchine per la guerra," in Clotilde de Stasio et al., eds., *La
rappresentazione verbale e iconica* (Milan: Guerini), pp. 223–31, to Archibald MacLeish's radio dramas in verse *The Fall of the City* and *Air Raid*.
In "Un'altra 'imitation' di Robert Lowell" (*RSAJ* 1:99–106), Francesco
Mulas reminds us that the sonnet "Will Not Come Back (Volveràn)" of
Notebook and *History* is an imitation of Gustavo Adolfo Bécquer's famous "Volveràn las oscuras golondrinas," a fact characteristically unrecorded in the *Norton Anthology of American Literature,* and goes on to a
comparison of the two poems. Lowell's friend and peer Elizabeth Bishop
is the subject of an attractive study by Gabriella Morisco, *La reticenza e lo
sguardo* (Bologna: Pàtron), which reprints some earlier articles in revised
form with a few new chapters. Despite a slight degree of repetition
among the essays, the cumulative effect is illuminating. Bishop has
found a careful and modest commentator of the kind she would have
liked, who does not try to hypnotize her readers or make extravagant
claims, but leaves us quite sure of Bishop's unique status. Morisco quotes
from a typical letter written when Bishop contributed "Visits to St.
Elizabeths" to the 1956 Pound issue of *Nuova Corrente* and was told there
would also be articles by Montale and Eliot: "I am somewhat intimi-
dated by appearing between two such prominent and magnificent poets,
and I am very much afraid my simple (in English, at least) poem will not
stand the weight—it will be like a busybody's finger caught between two
mill-stones" (p. 39). Of course, "Visits" was to remain by far the most
memorable contribution to that symposium, without which it would
perhaps never have come into being. Morisco's chapters take up in turn
"poetic narrative" ("The Fish"), "geography as central motif," "landscape
as verbal icon" (on Bishop and painting), "In the Village" and voluntary

memory, and finally a comparative study of moon and mirror images in Bishop and other poets (Plath, Rich, Levertov, Sexton, Swenson).

Rita Di Giuseppe offers a cogent survey of contemporary American poetry, "Have a Good Gestalt!" (*Lingua e letteratura* 14–15:141–61), with quotations from, and notes on, Emmett Williams, Paul Blackburn, James Dickey's "The Surround" ("one of the most original of American elegies"), Chad Walsh, Denise Levertov, Adrienne Rich, Diane Wakoski, Louise Glück, Joanne Kyger, David Antin, Anne Waldman, Charles Simic, and many others, concluding with Albert Goldbarth ("most prolific and versatile"). Di Giuseppe finds that the tendency is to "move away from formalism" (p. 160), apparently unaware of all the recent talk of New Formalism, e.g., *Expansive Poetry,* ed. Frederick Feirstein (Santa Cruz, Calif.: Story Line Press, 1989). Interestingly, there is practically no overlap between her poets and the ones who appear in the fine issue of *Poetry Review* (81, i [1991]) on "The American Brag."

Two senior American poets also receive attention. John Paul Russo, honorary Italian-Americanist, writes admiringly of "An Opportune Game: The Ouija Board in James Merrill's *The Changing Light at Sandover*" (*LAmer* 33–34 (1986):147–71), noting the poet's humanism ("Merrill says it is time for man to build paradise—on earth"). Mary de Rachewiltz collects old and new translations of James Laughlin in *In un altro paese* (Venice: Edizioni del Leone). In my review (*Unità,* June 14, 1991), I note of "Song" ("O lovely lovely so lovely / just fresh from a night of / it") that Laughlin's poetry "is immersed in the social situation, does not aspire to be anything more than a sketch, but in this way reaches the important goal of objectification and of the reader's interest." The Italian love story told in the title sequence "In Another Country" is also particularly endearing in the light of Laughlin's "studies" with Pound in Rapallo ("I was / 18 she was 15 and her name / was Leontina"). It is good to know that while Ezra was instructing Laughlin in the arduous tasks of literature and economics, little Leontina was seeing to his sentimental education.

Università di Genova

iii Japanese Contributions: Hiroko Sato

I have been doing this review every other year for the past 10 years or so, and every time I sit down to write it I am overcome by a sense of futility. Most of the books and articles that I review are written in Japanese and are therefore inaccessible to most scholars of American literature throughout the world. But this year I can proudly point to brilliant achievements by three young scholars, all written in English, although by doing so my usual chronological pattern will be disrupted.

The first of these studies is Hiroko Uno's *Emily Dickinson Visits Boston* (Kyoto: Yamaguchi-shoten). Noticing that biographers of Dickinson such as Richard Sewall and Cynthia Wolff pay little attention to her visits to Boston and other major Eastern cities several times in her youth, Uno tries to show how this urban exposure affected the young poet. During her visits, Dickinson closely observed the realities of the growing Boston, with its thousands of Irish immigrants and its new scientific innovations, and Uno points out that she made these visits via railroad, a product of new technology. Using maps in libraries, municipal offices, and historical societies in the Boston area, Uno determines the places where the poet stayed and visited. Her juxtaposition of old pictures and present-day photographs of the same locations is helpful in detailing the kind of urban culture to which Dickinson was exposed. Uno's contention that these experiences were of major importance in forming Dickinson's imaginary world is effectively presented.

The second study is Naoki Onishi's "Increase Mather and the Reforming Synod of 1679" (*AmerR* 24:23–40). This article deals with one of the major intellectual, moral, and physical crises that the early New England colonies had to face—King Philip's War. Using Increase Mather's diary, his autobiography, and writings such as "A Brief History of the Warr with the Indians in New England" and "The Day of Trouble is Near," Onishi examines how this crisis was linked to "the current social and religious conditions of the colonies." King Philip's War, which was regarded by some as God's Judgment on New England, raised in colonists' minds the question of "what is to be done so that those evils may be reformed." This study illustrates how, through his controversy with William Hubbard, Increase Mather, a staunch believer in the renewal of the covenant, gained influence and power and moved to a central position in the New England theocratic system.

The importance of women writers in the 19th century has been gradually recognized in Japan. After publication of my own *Amerika no Katei Shosetsu* [Domestic Fiction in America] in 1987, interest in the field has produced several noteworthy studies. This year sees the appearance of an outstanding article by Nobuo Kamioka, "Catherine Maria Sedgwick and James Fenimore Cooper: Indians, Landscapes, and History"

(*SELit* English number: 91–108). Comparing Sedgwick's *Hope Leslie* with Cooper's *The Last of the Mohicans,* Kamioka tries to prove the importance of the former on the basis of Sedgwick's vivid descriptions of the heroine, her humanistic reinterpretation of American colonial history, and her fine picture of ways of life of colonial society and the physical environment in which it existed. This essay is an ambitious attempt to combine cultural materialism and aesthetics in literary criticism and an appropriate undertaking when the canonical works of American literature are in question.

Before reviewing 1990's other achievements, I would like to note that the articles examined here will be restricted to the major Japanese periodicals *EigoS, SALit, SELit,* and the *American Review.* Unless otherwise indicated, all books mentioned have been published in Tokyo.

a. 18th- and 19th-Century Prose   Critical works on the period's literature were far fewer this year than in 1989. In "Modern Japan and Franklin" (*EigoS* 136:181–83), Shigenobu Sadoya examines Benjamin Franklin's influence on Japan during the Meiji era. In this interesting article, Sadoya points out how Franklin's philosophy was used in the education of the royal family and of intellectuals of the period and how it thereby affected the formation and growth of modern Japan.

Two articles on Henry David Thoreau are worth mentioning. Shoko Ito's "*On the Origin of Species* and 'The Dispersion of Seeds'—Darwin and Thoreau" (*EigoS* 136:222–26) is a suggestive study of Darwin's influence on Thoreau. Thoreau demystified his conception of nature after he read *Origin of Species.* Through observing the natural world, especially the mechanism for the evolution of pine and oak woods, Thoreau came to accept Darwin's theory of natural selection as true and to develop his own idea of the dispersion of seeds. However, according to Ito, Thoreau could not wholly escape the Transcendental mystification of nature; hence, his idea of the natural world continued as the promise of fertility, which Americans had dreamed of since the colonial period. The other article on Thoreau is Philip Jay Lewitt's "Thoreau as the First American Dharma Bum" (*SELit* English No.: 109–21). It can be included among the articles on contemporary literature as it examines the similarity between Thoreau's philosophy and that of Gary Snyder and Jack Kerouac. Through an examination of Thoreau's *Walden* and his journal, Lewitt asserts that Thoreau was able to achieve his belief in the Transcendental eternal now, an equivalent to "the heightened state of awareness of deep meditators and Zen masters" to which Snyder and Kerouac aspired.

Edgar Allan Poe is said to have criticized illustrations for literary works. However, *Graham's Magazine* carried two engravings to illustrate two of his own short stories, "The Island of the Fay" and "The Gold Bug." In "E. A. Poe and Illustrations—In the Cases of 'The Island of the Fay' and 'Spectacles' " (*EigoS* 135:538–40), Ichigoro Uchida shows how the illustrations provide later readers with the story's contextual background.

Nathaniel Hawthorne and Henry James are two masters to whom Japanese scholars of American literature often pay homage. Hideo Masuda's book-length study, *Hawthorne to James—Sakuhin Kenkyu* [Hawthorne and James—A Study of Their Works] (Kyoto: Yamaguchi-shoten), is typical of this tendency. The book is divided into three parts, "Search and Revelation," "Isolation and Egotism," and "Sin and Evil." Though full of interesting analyses of such stories as "My Kinsman, Major Molineaux," "The Wives of the Dead," "The Pupil," and "The Liar," Masuda fails to convince his readers that the juxtaposition of these two writers is useful for understanding their works. Masuda's only rationale is that James wrote *Hawthorne* and frequently referred to his predecessor in his writings.

Brief mention should be made of several articles on Hawthorne and Melville. Suzuko Shindo's "The Black Man in *The Scarlet Letter*" (*SALit* 27:1–16) attempts to read the novel as depicting the growth of Dimmesdale. In "A Book of Sacred Rites—Herman Melville's *Typee*" (*SALit* 27:17–31), Harumi Hirano tries to prove that *Typee's* structure is itself the sacred rite of initiation. Two articles of interest on James appeared in *SELit:* "The Significance of Fiction in Henry James's 'The Birthplace' " by Yoshio Nakamura (66:255–69) and Kuniko Izumi's "Governing the Governess: The Social and Historical Context in *The Turn of the Screw*" (67:63–77). Nakamura thinks it important that James wrote "The Birthplace" after the traumatic experience of the failure of *Guy Domville*. Through this experience, James came to realize the existence of an audience (his readers) which observed the world of literary works from the outside; this led to his understanding of the importance of fabricating an imaginary world. Izumi's article is more on the side of cultural materialism. She asserts that *The Turn of the Screw* reflects the distressing conditions that women employed as governesses had to face in mid-Victorian England. When we pay more attention to the circumstances in which governesses lived at that time, the significance of the inhuman relationship in the novel between the governess and the unnamed employer becomes clearer, Izumi contends.

Biographical information on Brett Harte is supplied in "The Tradition of the Western Novel—Brett Harte" (*EigoS* 136:136–37) by Ichiro Ishi. Ishi contends that Harte was completely forgotten after an explosive popularity in the early 1870s because he was essentially an Easterner who stereotyped the West. Masao Tsunematsu's "Materials for Stephen Crane Studies" (*EigoS* 135:590–92) supplies information on the 1988 edition of *The Correspondence of Stephen Crane*. Comparing this two-volume collection with *Stephen Crane: Letters* (1960), Tsunematsu indicates what editorial work has been done and what insights can be obtained from the new collection. An informative article for Crane scholars. Masashi Orishima's "Frank Norris and the Killing of Clocks" (*SALit* 27:33–47) is an ambitious attempt to read Norris's novels in the context of the 19th-century discourse of industrialism—the translation of time into money.

b. 20th-Century Fiction   Two books on Ernest Hemingway can be regarded as proof that he is still our favorite American writer. In *Hemingway to Neko to Onnatachi* [Hemingway, Cats, and Women] (Shinchosha), Tateo Imamura begins with Hemingway addressing a letter to his first wife, Hadley, in which he called her "Dear Kat." The felinity of Hemingway women is then discussed, which leads to the general question of sexuality in his novels. Using references from such early stories as "Cat in the Rain" to such posthumous works as *The Garden of Eden*, Imamura clearly explains the world of the novelist by following the catwoman theme. The book shows the usual limitations of a single-minded approach, but it provides an enjoyable trip into the novelist's world for general readers. Nobuyoshi Miki's *Hemingway no Kenkyu* [A Study of Hemingway] (Kaibunsha) is more a record of Miki's personal reading of Hemingway's novels than an analysis of his work, so the title is a bit misleading. In "3 and 5 in Hemingway—Mysterious Numbers in His Works" (*EigoS* 135:488–90), Iwao Nishio points out the novelist's use of these two numbers in *A Farewell to Arms, For Whom the Bell Tolls,* and *The Old Man and the Sea,* and then suggests the possibility of an allegorical reading of these works.

Two articles on Southern women writers are worth mentioning. One is Naoko F. Thornton's "Eudora Welty and Civil Rights Movements" (*EigoS* 136:231–33), and the other is Ichiro Inoue's "Flannery O'Connor's

Own Landscape" (*SELit* 67:79–90). Thornton's article is a kind of apologia for Eudora Welty: Welty is not the type of person who would openly protest against the social injustice which was addressed with passage of the Civil Rights Bill of 1964. Using "The Demonstrators" as an example, Thornton explains that Welty believes that only in silence can one really absorb the deep sadness occasioned by such political violence. Inoue notices that almost all of Flannery O'Connor's stories present "rural landscapes . . . the sky and the earth, with a black line of woods . . . all very similar to one another." He defines this as "an original landscape," from which the "fragmentary descriptions in each story derive" or which serve to "build" that landscape. Inoue also pays attention to the apocalyptic meaning of the sunset when sun and woods appear to be greatly enlarged; against this background the significance of the crucifixion emerges.

Hajime Sasaki's "Malamud's Unpublished Work" (*EigoS* 135:582–83) reports on his visit with Bernard Malamud's widow and of their talk on the now-published *"The People" and Uncollected Stories*. The April issue of *EigoS* features "The Vietnam War and American Literature" (136:8–21) in which five articles from various viewpoints are collected. Kenji Inoue's "The Style of Vietnam War Novels" sets the tone. Inoue points out a great difference between the writings of previous wars and those of Vietnam. No great "classical" works such as *A Farewell to Arms* or *The Naked and the Dead* have been written on the Vietnam War, he claims. Inoue keenly observes that one reason for this absence of masterpieces was the nature of the war itself: the war's movement was not linear but circular. Therefore, it occasioned the rise of a new genre, "journalism fiction." Akio Oura's "The Conceptualization of Vietnam War Experiences—The Case of Tim O'Brien," Kenji Kobayashi's "Vietnam in Reminiscence—Philip Caputo and Michael Herr," and Konomi Ara's " 'Born in the U.S.A.'—Bobbie Ann Mason and Country Boys," all deal with individual writers' war experiences and so supplement Inoue's article. Eiko Ikui's article, "The Future of Apocalypse—American Movies and the Vietnam War," uses Francis Coppola's *Apocalypse Now* to illustrate how the traumatic Vietnam experience has changed the self-image of the American people.

Quite unlike recent years, little work has been done on African American writers in 1990. Only one book has been published on an African American writer, *Watashitachi no Alice Walker* [Our Alice Walker], subtitled *For All the Women on the Earth* (Ochanomizu Shobo), ed.

Kazuko Kawachi. This work is a potpourri, very strongly scented, including translations of Alice Walker's writings, articles on Walker, and essays by five women members of minority groups in Japan on their experiences with discrimination. For all its diversity, this is a highly stimulating book which tells readers that gender and race are truly hot political issues.

The Japanese reading public retains a strong liking for contemporary American novels. Works by Mary Morris, Tess Gallagher, and Jayne Anne Phillips, for example, have been translated and enthusiastically received.

c. 20th-Century Poetry However brilliant a method of literary analysis may be, the basis of any literary criticism is close reading of the text and personal experience of the world of literature. Aiko Chujo's *Robert Frost no Sekai* [The World of Robert Frost] (Fukuoka: Univ. Kyushu Press) is an excellent example. The reader finds no superficial brilliance, but Chujo's reading of Robert Frost's poetry based on her Christianity leads to a solid understanding of the poet's world.

William Faulkner's poems rarely come to our attention, despite his reputation as a great novelist. Takeshi Morita's "Faulkner's Poetry—The World of New and Old, Old and New" (*EigoS* 136:446–47) invites us to experience the poems. By analyzing the poetry of Faulkner's twenties, Morita points out its rampant archaism in terms of themes, forms, and techniques. Morita tries to prove how these old-fashioned elements, which seem too loud in his poetry, turn into merits in his fiction.

Yozo Tokunaga's *Amerika Gendaishi to Mu* [Nothingness and Contemporary American Poetry] (Eichosha) is mainly a protest against Harold Bloom's *Wallace Stevens: The Poems of Our Climate.* In Tokunaga's book, essays on Wallace Stevens, William Carlos Williams, W. S. Merwin, and other contemporary poets are collected. Tokunaga's reading is based on his own Oriental conception of "nothingness": hence, his resistance to revisionist and semiotic approaches. Although Tokunaga insists on a subjective reading of poetry, the intertextuality of the Oriental and the Occidental is interestingly exhibited.

Two other short essays on contemporary poetry should be mentioned: Tomoyuki Iino's "Odes of the Graveyard—Karl Shapiro's Occasional Poems" (*EigoS* 136:234–36) and Katsumi Yamasato's "Gary Snyder and the Nature of the West" (*EigoS* 136:129–31). Iino traces the influence of W. H. Auden on Shapiro and characterizes Shapiro's poetry as satire and cultural criticism as well as a record of American scenes. Yamasato tries to prove how the nature of the West is the perpetual source of poetic imagination for Snyder. A highly informative survey of American poetry in the 1980s is Hisao Kanaseki, Momoko Watanabe, and Shunichi Niikura's round-table talk (*EigoS* 135:470–79), which supplies extensive information on American poetry of the period, providing historical perspective in terms of past and future.

d. 20th-Century Drama   Only one book on drama appeared in 1990, Hiromasa Takamura's *Steinbeck to Engeki* [Steinbeck and Drama] (Kyoto: Aporonsha). Steinbeck tried the form of a play-novelette four times in his career, and Takamura points out the writer's strong inclination toward drama and emphasizes the importance of this inclination in forming his novels. He uses Steinbeck's letters and essays as supporting evidence.

In conclusion, I would like to mention a book which will be of great help to Japanese students of American literature. *American Poetry and Prose* (Kenkyusha), ed. the late Masami Nishikawa and his younger colleague at the University of Tokyo, Kenzaburo Ohashi, is a substantial anthology of the canonical works of American literature, beginning with John Smith and ending with John Updike. Publication of this kind of solid collection has long been awaited by Japanese college teachers. Some Americans might think it anachronistic to have this kind of book appear now, but I think it is what we need at a time of questioning. Unless we have a certain idea of the canon, there can be no discussion of its authenticity.

Tokyo Woman's Christian University

iv Scandinavian Contributions: Jan Nordby Gretlund, Elisabeth Herion-Sarafidis, Hans Skei

The Scandinavian harvest of scholarly work in American literature for 1990 is varied and interesting, although one could wish for greater activity. Most work is devoted to 20th-century literature, with a clear emphasis on fiction. Works by John Dos Passos, Flannery O'Connor, Walker Percy, Gail Godwin, Stephen King, and Tom Wolfe are discussed in articles, and Willa Cather's use of classical themes is investigated in a book-length study. Hemingway and Faulkner are not the subject of any work this year, and even T. S. Eliot is missing when we turn to poetry.

Three articles by the same scholar discuss poems by Sylvia Plath, and Anne Sexton is treated in a chapter in a Danish festschrift. Women's literature of this century is also surveyed in an article in which different feminist trends are investigated. Some studies of 19th-century authors and works reveal a particular Swedish bias, as in the case of the book-length investigation of Emerson's influence on the Swedish poet Vilhelm Ekelund and an article tracing differences between the numerous Swedish translations of Mark Twain's *Huckleberry Finn* and the original. Another study of influence concerns certain Swedenborgian echoes in the poetry of Walt Whitman. In a brief article, Twain's *A Connecticut Yankee in King Arthur's Court* is compared to Edward Bellamy's *Looking Backward,* and a Danish article discusses Edgar Allan Poe's use of intuition in "The Murders in the Rue Morgue." Finally, the Swedish immigrant writer Gustav Nathaniel Malm's literary achievement is discussed in a chapter of a book about this immigrant's varied career.

No work on American drama has been published, and the scattered articles and essays that can be found on American literary theory and criticism are not written in English and hardly deserve mention here.

a. 19th-Century Fiction Henning Goldbaek's "Mordene i Rue Morgue som historieskrivning" [The Murders in Rue Morgue as Writing of History] (*TID SKRIFT: Moderne kultur—og tekstanalyse* 12:26–39) has little to do with the writing of history. Instead, it attempts to show that an essential part of Poe's genius was his ability to use his intuition to the exclusion of the traditional thought patterns of deduction and induction. Poe's deliberate choice of the intuitive as method, Goldbaek argues, is illustrated in the creation of Auguste Dupin, and the superiority of intuition over traditional deductive science is demonstrated in "The Murders of the Rue Morgue," "Marie Roget," and "The Purloined Letter." The world and the city in particular, Goldbaek continues, are perceived by Dupin through intuitive reasoning. The most interesting part of the argument is that Dupin—and Poe—are supposed to have used intuition as a gigantic bulwark against a shocking and dangerous reality, which finally defies all reason, anyway. In the stories, Dupin is seen in an exalted position of control of his world, which he rules by means of language, and he is able to remain untouched by the worldly conflicts about him. The built-up bastion is particularly effective against the influence of all would-be authorities, the power of money, and women. As Goldbaek sees it, Poe wrote of the gray area between the known and

the unknown, which he invoked by means of his intuitive reasoning, and
it is this constant presence of the unknown in his work that saves him
from being a mere writer for effect. This essay suggests interesting ideas,
but none of them are developed fully.

The changes a literary text may undergo in translation is the subject of
Erik Löfroth's "Huck, for Short; or One Hundred Years of Solicitude (*SN*
62:61–77). In a careful study, Löfroth has conducted a sentence-by-
sentence comparison between the 15 different translations and adaptations of *Huckleberry Finn* that have appeared in Swedish between 1885
and 1984 and a Norton reprint of the first American edition from 1885 as
his American version of the text. He has perused the translations—
including versions aimed at an adult audience, at children, and for easy
reading—looking for possible patterns in the replacements, omissions,
and additions, believing that the alterations to Twain's text have not been
haphazard, but have occurred because the text "has been considered hard
to read, calling for cultural context adaptations, or unsuitable, calling for
purification." He also assumes that the various translators have adhered
to what has been considered suitable for children at the time of publication, thereby reflecting the cultural and ideological climate of the time.

In earlier editions, there is a marked desire to clean up the text and
tone down or eliminate undesirable material, such as Huck's disrespect-
ful remarks about education and his and pap's cursing. When it comes to
violence, the opposite trend seems to be true; the earlier translations stay
fairly close to Twain's text, whereas several recent translators have omitted the entire Grangerford feud and the scene with pap's d.t.'s. Another
sign of the times is that the issue of racism has become important in later
translations. As it is essential to appear to be politically correct when it
comes to race these days, the text must be cleaned up so as not to give any
hints of Jim being superstitious, foolish, or generally inferior.

One major trend is the increasing brevity of the Swedish texts, this
being the case also with reissues. None of the texts is "complete and
unabridged." The final section has been most often reworked, Löfroth
suggests, because of its elaborateness. The changes are often so drastic
that they amount to a rewriting more than a translation. A second trend
appears to be that recent translators feel less free to delete, and even add
material, than was the case. Abridgements, however, are common, and a
few editions seem actually not to be based on Twain's text but on a
shorter version prepared somewhere else and intended for an international audience.

Most significant, and disturbing, is the fact that with all the cuts and alterations, the moral dimension of Twain's story has disappeared, the novel being turned into a story of adventure pure and simple. Löfroth points to a general trend toward simplification of matters of morality, revealed for instance in leaving out Huck's pangs of conscience about the fate of the king and the duke. In the adaptations, one of the book's key scenes in which Huck struggles with his conscience over whether or not to betray Jim is either eliminated or drastically cut, thereby reducing the moral dilemma, eliminating Huck's spiritual growth, and actually leaving Swedish readers with quite a different, much less complex text than Twain's *Huckleberry Finn*.

Ronald M. Johnson's "Future as Past, Past as Future: Edward Bellamy, Mark Twain, and the Crisis of the 1880s" (*AmerSS* 22:73–80) considers the obviously different visions of American society in *Looking Backward* and *A Connecticut Yankee in King Arthur's Court*. Both novels are from the late 1880s, and both are time-travel narratives. Both books are concerned with economic, social, and political reforms; and under the influence of the cultural disintegration they believed was affecting Victorian America, both authors speculate about the nature of an ideal society. Johnson demonstrates that in spite of the common background and aim, the two works represent widely different expressions of the utopian novel. Bellamy's work is "largely *utopian*," Johnson argues, whereas Twain's novel is considered "primarily *dystopian*." The focus is Twain. Bellamy is interesting mainly because he shared Twain's concern for the plight of the nation and like Twain spoke out on economic and social problems; yet he suggested entirely different solutions. Johnson shows that Twain for a while was influenced by the optimistic vision of the future in *Looking Backward* and became an active supporter of Bellamy's ideas during this brief period. Twain's final evaluation of Bellamy's future world of hope is expressed through Hank Morgan, the Yankee who returns from Camelot with one hard-earned lesson: when taken to its extreme, modernity will undermine the stability and balance of any society. Twain was never fully convinced, Johnson writes, that social change was really possible. This well-written essay makes clear that it was the publication of Bellamy's untroubled vision that compelled Twain to consider the future in the light of his own time and technological development. In this dystopic fable of a time-traveling Yankee, his final assessment of the future is troubled and pessimistic.

The focus in *Möte: Vilhelm Ekelunds Emersontolkningar* med inledning och kommentar av Claes Schaar [*Living Encounter: Vilhelm Ekelund's Interpretations of Emerson,* with Introduction and Comments by Claes Schaar] (Ellerströms) is the importance of Emerson's writings, in particular *The Journals,* for the Swedish poet and essayist Vilhelm Ekelund (1880–1949). In 1932, Ekelund was asked to undertake a selection of translations from Emerson's works for a philosophical anthology to be published in Sweden. The 54 entries he settled on, the result of a somewhat distracted effort, were all in the nature of aphorisms and all taken from Bliss Perry's *The Heart of Emerson's Journals* (1926). But the work on these translations, or interpretations, never saw completion, and they were not included in the anthology. It is Schaar's impression after having read the manuscripts that most of the texts were translated during the 1930s and that rather than being a finished product they have the appearance of a first draft.

Schaar traces Ekelund's longtime interest in Emerson, dating it back to 1912, and outlines aspects of the American's thinking that might have appealed to Ekelund, such as the obligation of a "scholar" to win the hearts of men, to lead and teach them. Then follow the translated entries, each with a rather loosely associative comment by Schaar dealing, first, with the translation itself, then with speculations as to the choice of the particular quotation. The comments primarily attempt to throw light on the text in question and show its significance for Ekelund and often also for Emerson. The focus of these comments and speculations shifts as Schaar makes use of literary as well as biographical material, and he frequently includes a detailed discussion of the existing body of Ekelund scholarship. The portrait Claes Schaar paints of the Swedish poet is very personal. Schaar certainly lives up to his declared intention of taking his reader on a subjective, at times even a somewhat meandering, journey. In part, this can also be attributed to the diverse nature of the selected texts themselves, which comment on the writer and his audience, the importance of good health and of having "a room of one's own," the nature of power, the status of Jews and Negroes, and observations on politics, as well as Carlyle, Wordsworth, and other of Emerson's contemporaries.

It is clear that Ekelund felt a strong sense of spiritual affinity with Emerson, dating from the time of a serious illness when his reading of the *Journals* had a profound and healing effect. Ekelund was a man of passionately held likes and dislikes and a sensuous relationship to words, endowing language with curative faculties. Well-known for his ability to use language innovatively—in all probability the foremost writer of aphorisms in his own language—he lived according to the motto "accept no word which does not speak." Such a man would be more attracted to Emerson the aphorist than Emerson the lecturer; more interested in the intensity of personal experience than in the vastness of accumulated knowledge. It has been said about Ekelund that as a poet he bestowed the same passionate love on nature that others bestow on a woman. Like Emerson, he had an ongoing conversation with the writings of authors that he admired; echoes and voices of other writers and poets are a resounding presence in his essays. As for the act of translation, he saw it as a manner of dialogue between translator and translated, the result to a large extent a product of the translator's personality. As a stylist, Ekelund was considerably more epigrammatic than Emerson; adverse to discursive speculative writing, he sought instead to base his thinking in experience, opting in his essays for concentration and brevity. Schaar finds that Ekelund often has actually improved on Emerson's original, condensing, pruning, and sharpening the focus of an observation, living up to his own ideal of a superior translator.

b. 19th-Century Poetry   Emerson appears again (see above), this time as intermediary, in another work, a short article dealing with the influence of Swedenborg's ideas on Walt Whitman. In "Naturtingens hermeneutik: Whitman och Swedenborg [Hermeneutics of the Natural World: Whitman and Swedenborg] (*Tidskrift för Litteraturvetenskap* 19:50–58), Anders Hallengren discusses the Swedenborgian notion that "the world is a hieroglyphic grammar," that it is possible to recognize the essence, the true meaning, of each and every creature from the shape God has given it. Man himself is the divinity in hieroglyphics, a belief found in Emerson's essays as well as in Whitman's poetry. Using Swedenborg's notions of correspondences, that grass represents "what is alive in man," the spiritual life force, while leaves represent "truths," Hallengren intriguingly suggests that the title *Leaves of Grass* could be rephrased, "Truths about what is alive in man."

c. 20th-Century Fiction   Erik Ingvar Thurin has set himself several tasks in *The Humanization of Willa Cather: Classicism in an American Classic* (Lund). Cather's fascination with classical themes and myths has often been noted, but it has never been the subject of a comprehensive study that takes her complete works into account. Embracing Cather's articles and reviews, as well as stories, novels, and unpublished letters, Thurin aims to redress this situation as he identifies the classical sources in her texts and traces the importance of the classics for the development of her prose style. His inquiry has an essentially evolutionary perspective, wanting to establish changes over time in Cather's preoccupation with the classics and how these are tied to the emergence of a poetic-symbolic prose style. The journalism, poetry, and short fiction are treated in the first three chapters, but most attention is devoted to the novels, which are dealt with one at a time.

Thurin feels that Cather had a long apprenticeship before achieving mastery in her use of classical themes, but that in the novels, the work of her artistic prime, she has turned away from an explicit, rather superficial use of the classics to an implicit, more thematically integrated one. He suggests that the spacious format of the novel offered room "both for concealment and revelation" and freed her to work with "hidden references" in an allusive, intricate manner which served to underline her message. He also believes that the "autobiographical impulse" was a significant factor "in the development of the allusive, poetic-symbolic prose style" of the novels, instead of, as has often been claimed, a function of her finding "her Midwestern material."

Thurin has what he terms "a psychosexual focus" in his readings of Cather's texts, claiming that her work strongly suggests that an identity problem is part of the tension behind it. "She is a troubled woman in the process of 'straightening herself out,' " he states, discussing a confessional streak in her writing. Her sexual orientation may help explain her interest in same-sex liaisons, in classical and mythological same-sex friendships. Finding her in this respect wanting in adherence to the values of classical humanism, he writes: "Cather's male-spirited classicism is by no means to be viewed as a studied gesture of outward conformism; it is genuine enough. But deftly handled it does have the double advantage of providing an aid to lesbian self-expression and a stamp of respectability and conservatism."

Thurin establishes the values of classical humanism as something of a norm and, somewhat strangely, proceeds to determine whether Cather measures up to the standard. At times surprisingly uncritical toward its subject, *The Humanization of Willa Cather* is marred by unnecessary value judgments. The study is, however, a learned endeavor to comprehensively assess Cather's production and to outline how her early interest in classical paganism, her "un-platonic zest for life," gave way to a calmer, less passionate view. Her use of the classics changed over the years, reflecting changes in her own life and outlook that evolved to bring her "more in line with the classicist/humanist respect for human reason."

Clara Juncker's "Dos Passos' Movie Star: Hollywood Success and American Failure" (*AmerSS* 22:1–14) shows that the movie star emerged as a postwar symbol of American alienation and disillusion in John Dos Passos's *U.S.A.* trilogy. Juncker writes, "The vitriol of satire flows richly over most pages . . . and secretes a series of two-dimensional, cliché-ridden characters, who themselves constitute an accusation of the society responsible for their existence." It was to highlight the shortcomings of his contemporaries, Juncker continues, that Dos Passos created Margo Dowling, a mercenary Hollywood star, so they might see their pitifulness as in a distorted mirror image. Dos Passos regretted the universal lack of consciousness in the face of the materialism of the 1920s, and he knew that in the "eyeminded" culture around him a movie star would get attention. The cinema queen had already appeared in Dos Passos's work in 1922 in a poem from *A Pushcart at the Curb*. This preview of Dos Passos's later star portraits begins: "Says the man from Weehawken," and Juncker quotes the entire poem in her essay. She makes it clear that in spite of his moral and political condemnation of Hollywood, Dos Passos was always intrigued by his golden-headed Margo Dowling. For him, she was not only the synthetic screen star, a symbol of a commercialized American Dream, but also a symbol of American energy and enterprise. In a surprising twist at the end of her essay, Juncker sees Margo as "a pioneer woman of a New America." She argues that as America's newest sweetheart, Margo is "an ideal revolutionary form" because she mirrors the negativity of a nation's dreams. It is possible that Margo in *The Big Money* can be seen as a creation "subversively on the side of social change," but this is not what the essay has been leading up to. Juncker's interesting final argument cries out for further substantiation.

Erik Nielsen's "Flannery O'Connor og Thomas Aquinas" (*Edda* 90:313–28) argues that O'Connor's reading of the *Summa Theologica* helped accentuate her respect for the world of the senses and brought her to see the importance of the concrete. She learned that faith in the mysteries of life can be strengthened, almost verified, through the observation of man in nature. Nielsen shows how O'Connor changed St. Thomas's theory of reading (the Bible) into her own theory of writing fiction. St. Thomas found a relation between *sensus litteralis* and *sensus anagogicus* that Nielsen sums up as signs, which indicate signs, that signify "the eternal Glory." O'Connor's anagogical vision implies that we (her readers) in the concrete world of her fiction may find signs, which indicate signs, that signify the realities of the holiness of life. The literal and the spiritual are in O'Connor interdependent; she seems to have followed a rule in her writing that observes a balance between the spiritual and the sensual presence, and her image of ultimate reality is always embedded in her image of the concrete world. Nielsen is successful in showing that O'Connor's faith is organically integrated in her art and that there is finally no point in trying to distinguish between her view of her faith and her view of her art. Faith is the prerequisite of her art, and her art an expression of faith. Much more can and will be said of O'Connor's Thomism, but Nielsen offers rewarding illustrations of O'Connor's "religious existentialism," arguing that "in *The Violent Bear It Away* the sacrament of baptism has the impact and physical presence of a gun in a good realistic crime novel. It is perhaps hard to accept but the sacrament . . . is a basic means of creating suspense."

Walker Percy had an abiding interest in the Danish philosopher Søren Kierkegaard, whose influence on his work is considerable. Perhaps this is one of the reasons why Scandinavian scholars seem to have taken a particular interest in Percy. A seminar on Percy was held in Denmark in 1989, and Hans Skei's essay, "The Banality of the Past: Time and Narrative in Walker Percy's *Lancelot*" (NMW 22, ii:49–59), was originally a paper at this conference. (A volume of other essays from the conference will be published later.) Skei's main focus is on the peculiar narrative handling of the monologue in *Lancelot,* which leads to a text that repeats itself, contradicts itself, and perhaps even deconstructs itself. The text is basically dialogic, but the novel is also marked by its many borrowings and allusions. The *intertextuality* of *Lancelot,* especially with reference to time and temporality, is Skei's other main concern. He discovers in the novel an opposition between what the text insists on through the philosophy of its protagonist and what the language and style imply. The investigation of Percy's narrative method thus leads to thematic interpretations, so that in the end *Lancelot* shows how difficult it is to find a viable balance that would enable its protagonist simply to endure being alive on the planet. *Lancelot* is perhaps the strongest and most successful of Percy's novels, and Skei's essay indicates some of the ways in which it may be approached in future studies.

Gail Godwin is a writer with a didactic streak, a desire to depict and explore the life of contemporary women, to clarify patterns of behavior and structures inherent in the patriarchal society they inhabit. But she also wants to create role models, "fully human heroines," courageous and questioning women who search for awareness. In her feminist reading of Godwin's novels from the 1970s and 1980s, Kerstin Westerlund focuses on the five that deal specifically with female development and male-female relationships, as a character's development in Westerlund's view is intimately tied to her relationship to men. The title, *Escaping the Castle of Patriarchy: Patterns of Development in the Novels of Gail Godwin* (Almqvist & Wiksell), reveals Westerlund's basic contention that Godwin's treatment of the spiritual growth of her female characters, as well as male-female dynamics, changes over time. Three phases are outlined: a move from female subordination and passivity in the first two novels, *The Perfectionists* and *The Glass People*, to awareness and rebellion in *The Odd Woman* and *Violet Clay*, toward "a vision of transformation—male and female—in *A Mother and Two Daughters*." *The Finishing School* and *A Southern Family* are dealt with less extensively in the third category.

That Westerlund is well-read on the subject of American women and feminism in the seventies and eighties is clear, but her chapter with that title seems superfluous, little more than a recounting of commonly known historical and sociological data from the period, and never integrated into the whole work. The next task she has set herself is to identify Godwin as a feminist writer, albeit a rather apolitical one, who is interested in portraying women in a male world and probing the roles traditionally prescribed, and who rejects the notion that women can find fulfillment in such a compartmentalized world. As Westerlund shows in sensitive readings of the novels, Godwin is more interested in depicting the struggle "within" a character than with overt political action; in her fictional world, men and women seem to live in opposing, incompatible universes; men are generally depicted as rigid and static, pure mind, whereas the women are spiritually mobile, searching and open and aware that life has much more to offer them. The title of the chapter dealing with *The Perfectionists* and *The Glass People* suggests the female protagonists' states of mind: "Woman Contained: Marriage as Enclosure." But the two heroines are too much a part of the patriarchal order to be able to break out and change their situations. Moving on to the second "phase," Westerlund argues convincingly that the female characters in *The Odd Woman* and *Violet Clay* are stronger; able to take charge of their own destinies, they act instead of being passively acted upon, rejecting marriage "to maintain their integrity and creative freedom." Men still do not encourage a dialogue and seem unable to imagine a male-female relationship along lines other than the traditional. As a result, women cannot have both "a life of their own," in the sense of a career, and a marriage based on equality. Women must still make a choice. Westerlund shows that *A Mother and Two Daughters* is more open-ended, that the three central female characters by the end of the novel have come a long way toward self-awareness, learned how to set boundaries and take responsibility for their own lives. They live more harmoniously; and in their interactions and relations with men, there is a sense of new openings that herald an interesting and possibly hopeful future.

Kathleen J. Weatherford calls attention to the absence of John Dos Passos's name from the list of writers that Tom Wolfe claims he wants to emulate as a social novelist; yet, she argues, in terms of his overall scheme for *The Bonfire of the Vanities,* he resembles Dos Passos more than the writers spoken for in his manifesto for a new social novel. The novel's popular success has not been ignored in Scandinavia. In her essay, "Tom Wolfe's Billion-Footed Beast" (*AmerSS* 22:81–93), Weatherford sets out to show how far Wolfe is from writing the kind of novel he claims he wants to write. She criticizes him for the lack of depth of his characterizations: his characters lack selfhood and personality, and possibly all inner life. But she praises the ironic exposé of affectation in American society as "savage satire." Wolfe is seen as a master of irony and sarcasm in the tradition of Swift, but for Weatherford, he remains a satirist and does not qualify as the realist and "true social novelist" that he pretends to be. In the end, according to this essay, "Wolfe's ironic humor does not lead to a productive political or social vision and sometimes seems to have little purpose but scintillating verbal abuse for its own sake." Weatherford suggests that Saul Bellow's vision of American society in *Mr. Sammlar's Planet* and *The Dean's December* provides a sustaining alternative to Wolfe's cynical view of the billion-footed beast.

"In the Age of Lawspeak: Tom Wolfe's *The Bonfire of the Vanities* and the Litigiousness of American Society" (*P.E.O.* Odense [June] 43–68), Helle Porsdam sees Wolfe as a critical commentator of American litigiousness. She argues that American society is now so thoroughly legalized that "legal vernacular shapes people's attitudes towards political, social and moral issues." For this phenomenon she coins the word "lawspeak." Wolfe's novel is used as an example of how Americans live in an age of lawspeak in which there is no difference between law and politics. The novel shows that law *is* politics, and that the litigation and adversary system has run wild. "Not much is left," Porsdam writes, "of the old common-law ideal of the jury as a safeguard for the accused by the time Tom Wolfe is done with it." The essay praises Wolfe's portrait of a world in which all is selfishness and vanity, but Porsdam claims that Wolfe's description of war between ethnic groups obscures what should have been the real issue: the idea of equal justice for all. She detects racist undertones in the novel and claims that the author shares his white characters' fear of losing power. As Porsdam sees it, Wolfe calls for a return to white justice only, so that his successful novel finally becomes a symptom rather than a cure for the malady it describes so convincingly. But was *The Bonfire of the Vanities* written by a scared white man afraid of losing his political power? Is the novel really marred by white suprema-cist ideas? This aspect of Porsdam's argument deserves an in-depth study with more documentation than her essay presents.

In "Contemporary Horror Fiction: The Case of Stephen King" (*P.E.O.* Odense, 55:1–20), Christen Kold Thomsen points out that contemporary horror fiction reflects ambivalence about traditional fam-ily life. Thomsen argues that Stephen King's fiction in *The Shining, Salem's Lot,* and *It* has roots in Hawthorne's New England Gothicism and in the 19th-century case-stories from the science of medicine. The stories seem to plead for a return to an accepted normality, especially in their unbelievable happy endings, but, as Thomsen shows, King does not offer any examples of what this "normality" could be, and the idea exists *apart* from his narrative plots. But the Gothic mode in which he writes presupposes a normal and moral world, and in this way supports rather than undermines realism. King and other writers of contemporary horror fiction appear titillated, if somewhat disturbed, by the destruction of "normality" and their inability to recover "normal" family-centered lives. The superimposed happy endings do not really convince us that the monsters can be dealt with according to traditional rules of the fairy tale. Thomsen suggests that King's fiction "expresses the realization of a wish: if only the world was a horror story!" And he argues convincingly that criticism written about the genre reveals a similar fascination with the failure of moral perception and King's supernatural explanations, a fact Thomsen ascribes to a dominant cultural pessimism about "modern-ization" and the recovery of traditional moral virtue.

In a lengthy article, "American Women's Literature in the Twentieth Century: A Survey of Some Feminist Trends" (*Amst* 22, i:25–37), Helge

Normann Nilsen attempts to show that the history of women's literature in the 20th century really began in the 1880s—or even earlier—with Charlotte Perkins Gilman, Sarah Orne Jewett, Mary Wilkins Freeman, and Kate Chopin. Although Chopin is treated at some length, Nilsen can do little but cover well-known ground. Edith Wharton's place in this tradition is perhaps less obvious, but Nilsen's discussion of *The Custom of the Country* proves beyond doubt that Wharton belongs here. Turning to the modernist movement, Nilsen's arguments become more general, and his article becomes more of a catalog of different names, titles, and trends. Nevertheless, the similarities he points to between Gertrude Stein and Willa Cather are interesting, as is his observation that Ellen Glasgow's fiction "reflects a growing feminist awareness." Katherine Anne Porter, Tillie Olsen, and Zora Neale Hurston are then briefly mentioned before a discussion of the postwar generation of such writers as Mary McCarthy, Carson McCullers, Flannery O'Connor, and Eudora Welty. Unfortunately, the material Nilsen presents must by necessity be brief (e.g., only the short story "Livvie" in the case of Welty!).

Sylvia Plath becomes Nilsen's starting point for a list of feminist poets, followed by the *real* feminist movement in the '60s and '70s, for which Nilsen takes Betty Friedan's *The Feminine Mystique* as his point of departure. Erica Jong's *Fear of Flying* is mentioned before Marilyn French is said to be "the most consistently feminist novelist of today." Among the many writers listed, Alice Walker and Toni Morrison are singled out for brief comment, but they hardly get the praise they deserve. In general, the article falls short when it comes to *evaluation* and *tendencies,* and is thus less useful than it might have been.

Dorothy Burton Skårdal's chapter, "The Literary Achievement of G. N. Malm," in Emory Lindquist, ed., *G. N. Malm: A Swedish Immigrant's Varied Career* (Lindsborg, Kansas), gives a detailed and precise portrait of the literary career of G. N. Malm: "a man of many talents and considerable achievement in several different fields." Skårdal makes the claim that Malm was "one of the three or four most important writers in Swedish-American literature," which, of course, is no strong claim. Skårdal then discusses at considerable length Malm's only novel, his unpublished collection of short stories, and his play and two additional short pieces. The novel, *Charlie Johnson, Swedish-American,* appeared in 1909 and is praised for the remarkable novelistic techniques it demonstrates. In Skårdal's opinion, this is "the best novel written in Swedish by an immigrant to the United States." Skårdal proves her points about the novel in a fine and detailed analysis of character and plot, although she feels that the author has thrown away the suspense he otherwise might have achieved by writing a preface. The novel is clearly intended for Swedish-Americans of his day, although it functions well today as a record of a vanished time.

This detailed study of Malm's novel is followed by an equally close investigation of an *unpublished* short story collection, *Among Prairie Folks,* which Malm planned on the basis of 23 texts published in newspapers and magazines from 1912 through 1921. Skårdal's discussion of the play *Out Here* and two other short works (one the only short story Malm wrote in English, "Peace and Good Will") makes up the rest of the survey. Seen from today's point of view, Skårdal's evaluation of Malm's total work is aptly concluded: "As many of his characters look back to pioneer days as a kind of golden age, so we today can look back to Malm's work as bathed in the same golden light of rural peace and rural values, but with dark undertones reflecting loss and foreshadowing a darker future."

d. 20th-Century Poetry   In "Sylvia Plath's 'Poem for a Birthday': Self-analysis with Surrealistic Elements" (*SN* 62:151–62), Brita Lindberg-Seyersted attempts to clarify the extent to which Sylvia Plath may be called a surrealist poet, a term occasionally used to describe her writing. Lindberg-Seyersted offers a reading of the seven poems which make up "Poem for a Birthday," identifying "devices which can be labelled surrealistic," examining their "function in the individual poems seen as parts of a poetic persona's self-analysis." She finds Plath's overall purpose to be a portrayal of a woman's spiritual quest, a mnemonic autobiographical journey into the past in an attempt at exploring and coming to terms with her relations to her earliest influences, her parents. And in the overall idea of allegorical self-analysis, Lindberg-Seyersted finds a link to Surrealism, the opening of doors to the unconscious and the bringing forth of a hidden self being significant Surrealist themes. Another link, she suggests, is the use of imagery from African folktales, as well as Plath's more frequent reliance on elements from fairy tales and nursery rhymes. The Surrealists valued "primitive art and folk culture as revealing more of authentic life than civilized art and elitist culture." Surrealistic distortions of scale and sharp juxtapositions of images as an aid in uncovering the subconscious are other features of "Poem for a Birthday" that show an influence, though Lindberg-Seyersted concludes by stating that despite such affinities, Plath cannot be termed a surrealist poet.

Lindberg-Seyersted has published two more articles dealing with Plath's poetry. Both may be less interesting than the one just discussed, although "Dream Elements in Sylvia Plath's Bee Cycle Poems" (*Amst* 22, i:15–24) also touches on surrealistic elements. In this essay, Lindberg-Seyersted points to dreamlike elements as one aspect of Plath's surrealism and identifies a number of devices the poet employs to "create a semblance of the dream." She concentrates on "The Bee Meeting" and mentions the other "Bee" poems only in passing. Using biographical facts and realistic details, she shows how Plath's poems disguise and transform ordinary experience so that uncertainty and elusiveness, typical of a dream, are the result. Thus, the poems also serve to uncover hidden fears and desires on the speaker's part. Some specific details in these poems are convincingly interpretated, although it might have been interesting to include a discussion of the cycle's place in *Ariel*.

In "Sylvia Plath's Psychic Landscapes" (*ES* 71:509–22), Lindberg-Seyersted places particular emphasis on Plath's transformation of actual, "realistic" landscapes into psychic ones throughout her career. Lindberg-Seyersted uses biographical facts to study the poetic process and is able to establish a development in Plath's career from the concrete or realistic through to "psychic" landscapes, which in the end become fragmented. The interpretations of individual poems are interesting enough, but most important is Lindberg-Seyersted's attempt to establish a useful approach to Plath's poetry which links earlier material with the later, more famous poems. In short, the article offers a way of dealing with Plath's total oeuvre which should enable future scholars to understand her poetry more fully and offer more convincing interpretations. There can be no doubt as to the development in Plath's creation of landscapes, and it may well be that to follow this approach to Plath's poetry will "clear the ground for entering deeper into her poetic world."

Bodil Hedeboe's "Kvinder foedes to gange: Om poesien som livline i Anne Sextons digtning" [Women Are Born Twice: Art as Lifeline in Anne Sexton's Poetry], ed. Hans Hyllested et al. (*SPOR, Til billedet og poesien: Festskrift til Niels Egebak* [Viborg], pp. 87–107), shows how Sexton poured into her poems the experience of being different, strange, witch, mad, woman, poet, and a being on the margin in a marginalized body. Hedeboe makes it clear that poetry was more than a therapeutic occupation for Sexton: first, because she achieved the control of reality she sought only in the *good* poems; but also because her confessional poems, more than a selection of daring topics, are expressions of true craftsmanship. Most of Sexton's poetry that looks like prose poems or free verse is on examination found to be traditional forms in classic meter. In her attempt to show this, Hedeboe focuses on *Transformations*, a collection of poems in which Sexton transforms some of the fairy tales collected by the brothers Grimm. She closely reads Sexton's version of "Little Red Riding Hood" and sees it as a poem about deception and self-deception. It is the moment of realization of the deception that functions as a kind of rebirth into a continued life in spite of the now somewhat mutilated image of the self; in this sense, it is argued, the writing of poetry was a lifeline for Sexton. Hedeboe sees Sexton's poems as expressions of a longing for continuity, a longing for the time before the first realization of deceit. It is also argued that the lifeline finally snapped because Sexton in her material from all of Western culture failed to find a permanently sustaining element for the woman as poet.

Odense, Uppsala, Oslo Universities

21 General Reference Works

Louis Owens

As is customary, I will for the most part leave to individual *ALS* chapters those bibliographies, concordances, and reference guides relating to specific authors, periods, or genres. However, reference resources proliferate apace, led as ever by the indefatigable Gale Research *Dictionary of Literary Biography* program, with its assorted permutations.

Gale's *Twentieth-Century Literary Criticism* for 1990, ed. Paula Kepps, includes three volumes: *TCLC* 34, devoted to such topics as "The Muckraking Movement in American Journalism," "New Criticism," and "World War I Literature"; and *TCLC* 35 and 36, with critical excerpts covering a wide swath of American writers, from S. Weir Mitchell and Mark Twain to John Gould Fletcher and the obscure Native American novelist John Milton Oskison. Volumes 57 and 58 in Gale's *Contemporary Literary Criticism* this year, a series ed. Roger Matuz, together cover in excellent fashion 22 American writers of both established and incipient reputations, including such figures as T. S. Eliot, Josephine Humphreys, Truman Capote, Kay Boyle, Alice Walker, and Maxine Hong Kingston. Even the relatively little-known western gothicist Cormac McCarthy gets satisfying coverage. *CLC* 59, the *Yearbook* for 1989, offers "The Year in Review," "New Authors," and so forth, including a sound critical summing-up in "The Fiftieth Anniversary of John Steinbeck's *The Grapes of Wrath*." *CLC* volumes 60 and 61 provide critical samplings for another 26 American authors ranging across the decades from the turn of the century to the present, from Hemingway to Ishmael Reed.

Volume 11 of Gale's *Literature Criticism from 1400 to 1800*, ed. James E. Person, Jr., provides a 60-page overview of Edward Taylor, while volumes 25 and 26 of Gale's *Nineteenth-Century Literature Criticism*, ed. Janet Mullane and Robert Thomas Wilson, feature a pair of American writers between them, Henry Timrod in 25 and E. D. E. N. Southworth (plus songwriter Stephen Foster) in 26. Volume 27 of this series, ed. Mullane and Laurie Sherman, includes James Fenimore Cooper among an assortment of non-Americans, while volume 28, this year's *NCLC* "Topics Volume," ed. Sherman, focuses on "The American Frontier in Literature." The frontier survey gathers representative work by major writers such as Henry Nash Smith, Richard Slotkin, and Roy Harvey Pearce in an efficient and useful overview. I wonder, however, when a publication of this stature is going to recognize the importance of inviting a Native American, such as Vine Deloria, Jr., perhaps, to write on "Portrayals of Native Americans." It is time for publishers of such works to recognize that there are experts in this subject who also happen to be Native Americans.

Volumes 28–30, ed. James G. Lesniak, of Gale's *Contemporary Authors* series for 1990, continue to provide an essential resource. Gale's companion *Contemporary Authors: Autobiography Series,* volume 11, ed. Mark Zadrozny, and volume 12, ed. Joyce Nakamura, between them offer often fascinating and helpful autobiographical essays by 32 American writers, among whom, however, only four are women. Ethnic minority writers are also poorly represented. While Chicano novelist Rudolfo Anaya has previously been included in this autobiography series, one searches in vain for such respected contemporary figures as the late Arturo Islas, or James Welch, Leslie Silko, Gerald Vizenor, Luci Tapahonso, and so forth.

Gale's *DLB Yearbook* for 1990, ed. James W. Hipp, offers the expected assortment of somewhat idiosyncratic overviews: "The Year in the Novel," by David R. Slavitt; "The Year in the Short Story," by George Garrett; "The Year in Poetry," by R. S. Gwynn; and "The Year in Drama," by Howard Kissel. All in all, despite the above caveat, Gale continues to fulfill admirably the goal announced in the foreword to the *Yearbook:* "to make literary achievement better understood and more accessible to students and the literate public, while serving the needs of scholars." That sums up the project nicely, though one of Gale's 1990 ventures, *Characters in 20th-Century Literature,* by Laurie Lanzen Harris, is a somewhat unfocused listing of mostly American "characters" from both 19th- and 20th-century works. This volume is clearly accessible to students but of only marginal interest to scholars.

Most notable among the large assortment of bibliographic undertakings for 1990 is the *Bibliography of American Literature, Volume Eight: Charles Warren Stoddard to Susan Bogert Warner,* compiled by the late

Jacob Blanck and ed. Michael Winship (Yale). Nearly half a century after the monumental *Bibliography of American Literature* project began, this latest volume covers 29 authors from Stoddard to Warner and continues the tradition of high quality expected in this set. Of practical use for scholars is James K. Bracken's *Reference Works in British and American Literature, Volume I: English and American Literature* (Libraries Unlimited). This volume is annotated (with Bracken's critical evaluations of resources) and thorough. A true labor of love this year is *The Feminist Companion to Literature in English,* by Virginia Blain, Patricia Clements, and Isobel Grundy (Yale). Proclaiming that "Literary history has long required an account of women's writing in English," the authors proceed to provide that account, "from the beginning to the present." A truly impressive achievement, the 1,231-page volume groups authors by date (from pre-1400 to 1985), with indexes by topic and author names (chronologically), as well as a useful cross-reference index. It is rare that such a ponderous volume is so accessible and readable.

Also broad in its sweep is Norman Kiell's *Psychoanalysis, Psychology, and Literature: A Bibliography* (Scarecrow). Marred only by the vast, gray expanse of Scarecrow's faint typeface, this supplement to the second edition of Kiell's two-volume 1982 edition is well designed to continue leading us to everything we ever wanted to discover on this subject. Two additional 1990 volumes merit attention. Barbara A. White's *American Women's Fiction, 1790–1870: A Reference Guide* (Garland) is an invaluable bibliographic resource for a heretofore neglected area of American literature. *Harlem Renaissance and Beyond: Literary Biographies of 100 Black Women Writers, 1900–1945* (Hall), by Lorraine Elena Roses and Ruth Elizabeth Randolph, is a splendid new resource with biographical essays as well as extensive bibliographic references.

The annual array of general bibliographies of somewhat narrower scope also continues, including Deborah A. Butler's *American Women Writers on Vietnam: Unheard Voices: A Selected Annotated Bibliography* (Garland), with nearly 800 entries. More arcane yet is Jefferson D. Caskey's *Appalachian Authors: A Selective Bibliography* (Locust Hill Press), which covers in sometimes less-than-satisfactory detail 17 authors, including such familiar figures as Wendell Berry and Harriette Arnow. Frederick S. Frank's *Through the Pale Door: A Guide to and Through the American Gothic* (Greenwood) should serve scholars of the American Gothic well, with more than 500 annotated bibliographic entries from Brockden Brown to Stephen King. Critical sources are cited and the

American Gothic is defined in a sound introduction. A more unusual bibliographic endeavor is *Sequels: An Annotated Guide to Novels in Series* (ALA), by Janet Husband and Jonathan F. Husband. An updating of the first 1982 edition, this bibliography is governed by the authors' subjective determination of a writer's significance. For example, Louise Erdrich's works are included, but those of Gerald Vizenor and Ivan Doig, who have also published separate works that show "development of plot or character from book to book," are not.

The distant reaches of bibliographic scholarship continued to generate publications in 1990. Testifying to current interests in critical research, and the expanding canon, is this year's second edition of *Uranian Worlds: A Guide to Alternative Sexuality in Science Fiction, Fantasy, and Horror,* by Eric Garber and Lyn Paleo (Hall). The authors have considerably enlarged the previous edition's bibliography of gay and lesbian science fiction and fantasy. Neil Barron has contributed two more volumes to Garland's Reference Library of the Humanities: *Fantasy Literature: A Reader's Guide,* and *Horror Literature: A Reader's Guide.* Barron overlaps material between the two works (a questionable habit given the $49.95 price tag of each), but the entries are exhaustive and useful. In the same Garland series is prolific bibliographer Albert J. Menendez's *The Subject Is Murder: A Selective Subject Guide to Mystery Fiction, Volume 2.* The title tells the story. Everett F. Bleiler continues his inexorable outpouring of reference volumes with *Science Fiction: The Early Years* (Kent State), an exhaustive bibliography up to 1930, with five excellent indexes, marred, however, by blindingly difficult type. Also worthy of mention for 1990 are Michael Paris's *The Novels of World War Two: An Annotated Bibliography of World War Two Fiction* (Library Association); Jacques Barzun and Wendell Hertig Taylor's *A Catalogue of Crime* (Harper), a revised edition of the 1971 book with an additional 2,000 or so entries for novels in English (including translations) from September 1939 to 1988; John Conquest's *Trouble Is Their Business: Private Eyes in Fiction, Film and Television, 1927–1988* (Garland); *Spy Fiction: A Connoisseur's Guide* (Facts on File), by Donald McCormick and Katy Fletcher; Bernard A. Drew's latest Garland volume, *Heroines: A Bibliography of Women Series Characters in Mystery, Espionage, Action, Science Fiction, Fantasy, Horror, Western, Romance and Juvenile Novels;* and Laura Sue Fuderer's *The Female Bildungsroman in English: An Annotated Bibliography of Criticism* (MLA).

Volume 12 of *Review* (Virginia) for 1990, ed. James O. Hoge and James L. W. West III, evaluates work on Thoreau, Dickinson, Twain, Pound,

Dreiser, Wharton, and James, as well as such ambitious critical endeavors as Cathy N. Davidson's *Revolution and the World: The Rise of the Novel in America,* Michael T. Gilmore's *American Romanticism and the Marketplace,* and other monographs. With the real and present danger of reviews becoming deadeningly circumambient, however, the reader is encouraged to review this year's *Review* for him/herself.

As a final note, among the year's indispensable office-shelf volumes is *The Concise Oxford Dictionary of Literary Terms* (Oxford), by Chris Baldick, with a thousand definitions, including handy illustrations of usage. Next to Baldick's dictionary, one might want to lean *The Writers Directory, 1990–92,* 9th ed. (St. James), with its (well-indexed) list of 17,000 living authors publishing in English, and perhaps even *Nobel Laureates in Literature: A Biographical Dictionary,* ed. Rado Pribic (Garland). Frank N. Magill's *Cyclopedia of Literary Characters II* (Salem Press), a costly set designed to mesh neatly with *Masterplots,* may best be left to a well-heeled university library.

University of California, Santa Cruz

Author Index

Subject Index

DATE DUE

GAYLORD			PRINTED IN U.S.A